A Companion to Ame

WILEY BLACKWELL COMPANIONS TO AMERICAN HISTORY

This series provides essential and authoritative overviews of the scholarship that has shaped our present understanding of the American past. Edited by eminent historians, each volume tackles one of the major periods or themes of American history, with individual topics authored by key scholars who have spent considerable time in research on the questions and controversies that have sparked debate in their field of interest. The volumes are accessible for the non-specialist, while also engaging scholars seeking a reference to the historiography or future concerns.

WILEY BLACKWELL COMPANIONS TO AMERICAN HISTORY

A Companion to the American Revolution
Edited by Jack P. Greene and J. R. Pole

A Companion to 19th-Century America
Edited by William L. Barney

A Companion to the American South
Edited by John B. Boles

A Companion to American Women's History
Edited by Nancy Hewitt

A Companion to American Indian History
Edited by Philip J. Deloria and Neal Salisbury

A Companion to Post-1945 America
Edited by Jean-Christophe Agnew and Roy Rosenzweig

A Companion to the Vietnam War
Edited by Marilyn Young and Robert Buzzanco

A Companion to Colonial America
Edited by Daniel Vickers

A Companion to American Foreign Relations
Edited by Robert Schulzinger

A Companion to 20th-Century America
Edited by Stephen J. Whitfield

A Companion to the American West
Edited by William Deverell

A Companion to the Civil War and Reconstruction
Edited by Lacy K. Ford

A Companion to American Technology
Edited by Carroll Pursell

A Companion to African American History
Edited by Alton Hornsby

A Companion to American Immigration
Edited by Reed Ueda

A Companion to American Cultural History
Edited by Karen Halttunen

A Companion to California History
Edited by William Deverell and David Igler

A Companion to American Military History
Edited by James Bradford

A Companion to Los Angeles
Edited by William Deverell and Greg Hise

A Companion to American Environmental History
Edited by Douglas Cazaux Sackman

A Companion to Benjamin Franklin
Edited by David Waldstreicher

A Companion to World War II (2 volumes)
Edited by Thomas W. Zeiler with Daniel M. DuBois

A Companion to American Legal History
Edited by Sally E. Hadden and Alfred L. Brophy

A Companion to American Sports History
Edited by Steven Riess

A Companion to the U.S. Civil War (2 volumes)
Edited by Aaron Sheehan-Dean

A Companion to the Meuse-Argonne Campaign, 1918
Edited by Edward G. Lengel

A Companion to Custer and the Little Big Horn Campaign
Edited by Brad D. Lookingbill

A Companion to the History of American Science
Edited by Georgina M. Montgomery and Mark A. Largent

A Companion to the Gilded Age and Progressive Era
Edited by Christopher M. Nichols and Nancy C. Unger

A Companion to U.S. Foreign Relations: Colonial Era to the Present
Edited by Christopher R. Dietrich

WILEY BLACKWELL PRESIDENTIAL COMPANIONS

A Companion to Franklin D. Roosevelt
Edited by William Pederson

A Companion to Richard M. Nixon
Edited by Melvin Small

A Companion to Theodore Roosevelt
Edited by Serge Ricard

A Companion to Thomas Jefferson
Edited by Francis D. Cogliano

A Companion to Lyndon B. Johnson
Edited by Mitchell Lerner

A Companion to George Washington
Edited by Edward G. Lengel

A Companion to Andrew Jackson
Edited by Sean Patrick Adams

A Companion to Woodrow Wilson
Edited by Ross A. Kennedy

A Companion to John Adams and John Quincy Adams
Edited by David Waldstreicher

A Companion to James Madison and James Monroe
Edited by Stuart Leibiger

A Companion to Harry S. Truman
Edited by Daniel S. Margolies

A Companion to the Antebellum Presidents, 1837–1861
Edited by Joel Silbey

A Companion to the Reconstruction Presidents, 1865–1881
Edited by Edward O. Frantz

A Companion to John F. Kennedy
Edited by Marc J. Selverstone

A Companion to Warren G. Harding, Calvin Coolidge, and Herbert Hoover
Edited by Katherine A. S. Sibley

A Companion to Ronald Reagan
Edited by Andrew L. Johns

A Companion to Gerald R. Ford and Jimmy Carter
Edited by Scott Kaufman

A Companion to First Ladies
Edited by Katherine A. Sibley

A Companion to Dwight D. Eisenhower
Edited by Chester J. Pach

A COMPANION TO AMERICAN LEGAL HISTORY

Edited by

Sally E. Hadden and Alfred L. Brophy

WILEY Blackwell

This paperback edition first published 2021
© 2013 John Wiley & Sons Ltd

Edition History: John Wiley & Sons Ltd (hardback, 2013)

All rights reserved. No part of this publication may be reproduced, stored in a retrieval system, or transmitted, in any form or by any means, electronic, mechanical, photocopying, recording or otherwise, except as permitted by law. Advice on how to obtain permission to reuse material from this title is available at http://www.wiley.com/go/permissions.

The right of Sally E. Hadden and Alfred L. Brophy to be identified as the authors of the editorial material in this work has been asserted in accordance with law.

Registered Offices
John Wiley & Sons, Inc., 111 River Street, Hoboken, NJ 07030, USA
John Wiley & Sons Ltd, The Atrium, Southern Gate, Chichester, West Sussex, PO19 8SQ, UK

Editorial Office
111 River Street, Hoboken, NJ 07030, USA

For details of our global editorial offices, customer services, and more information about Wiley products visit us at www.wiley.com.

Wiley also publishes its books in a variety of electronic formats and by print-on-demand. Some content that appears in standard print versions of this book may not be available in other formats.

Limit of Liability/Disclaimer of Warranty
While the publisher and authors have used their best efforts in preparing this work, they make no representations or warranties with respect to the accuracy or completeness of the contents of this work and specifically disclaim all warranties, including without limitation any implied warranties of merchantability or fitness for a particular purpose. No warranty may be created or extended by sales representatives, written sales materials or promotional statements for this work. The fact that an organization, website, or product is referred to in this work as a citation and/or potential source of further information does not mean that the publisher and authors endorse the information or services the organization, website, or product may provide or recommendations it may make. This work is sold with the understanding that the publisher is not engaged in rendering professional services. The advice and strategies contained herein may not be suitable for your situation. You should consult with a specialist where appropriate. Further, readers should be aware that websites listed in this work may have changed or disappeared between when this work was written and when it is read. Neither the publisher nor authors shall be liable for any loss of profit or any other commercial damages, including but not limited to special, incidental, consequential, or other damages.

Library of Congress Cataloging-in-Publication Data

A companion to American legal history / edited by Sally E. Hadden and Alfred L. Brophy.
   pages cm. – (Wiley-Blackwell companions to American History)
Includes bibliographical references and index.
ISBN 978-1-4443-3142-4 (hardback) – ISBN 978-1-1197-1165-0 (Paperback) –
   ISBN 978-1-118-53372-7 (Wiley online library)
   (print) – ISBN 978-1-118-53374-1 (bro) (print) – ISBN 978-1-118-53375-8 (emobi) (print) –
   ISBN 978-1-118-53376-5 (epdf) (print) – ISBN 978-1-118-53377-2 (epub) (print) 1. Law–
United States–History. I. Hadden, Sally E., editor of compilation. II. Brophy, Alfred L.,
   editor of compilation.
KF352.C66 2013
349.7309–dc23
2012042385
A catalogue record for this book is available from the British Library.

Cover Design: Wiley
Cover Image: © izzet ugutmen/Shutterstock

Set in 11/13pt Galliard by SPi Global, Pondicherry, India
Printed and bound by CPI Group (UK) Ltd, Croydon, CR0 4YY

10 9 8 7 6 5 4 3 2 1

For our mentors
Bernard Bailyn, Charles Donahue,
William Gienapp, and Morton Horwitz

Contents

Notes on Contributors   x

Introduction   1
Sally E. Hadden and Alfred L. Brophy

Part I   Chronological Overviews   5

1   Reconsidering the Seventeenth Century: Legal History in the Americas   7
Elizabeth Dale

2   What's Done and Undone: Colonial American Legal History, 1700–1775   26
Sally E. Hadden

3   1775–1815   46
Ellen Holmes Pearson

4   The Antebellum Era Through Civil War   67
Alfred L. Brophy

5   Beyond Classical Legal Thought: Law and Governance in Postbellum America, 1865–1920   86
Roman J. Hoyos

6   American Legal History, 1920–1970   105
Christopher W. Schmidt

Part II   Individuals and Groups   125

7   Native Americans   127
Christian McMillen

8	African Americans in Slavery *Thomas J. Davis*	152
9	African Americans in Freedom *James Campbell*	171
10	Women's Legal History *Felice Batlan*	190
11	Families *David S. Tanenhaus*	209
12	Who Belongs? Immigrants and the Law in American History *Allison Brownell Tirres*	228
13	The Legal Profession *Mark E. Steiner*	247

Part III Subject Areas — 267

14	Law and the Economy of Early America: Markets, Institutions of Exchange, and Labor *Christine Desan*	269
15	Law and the Economy in the United States, 1820–2000 *Harwell Wells*	289
16	Law and Labor in the Nineteenth and Twentieth Centuries *Deborah Dinner*	308
17	Siting the Legal History of Poverty: Below, Above, and Amidst *Felicia Kornbluh and Karen Tani*	329
18	Taxes *Robin L. Einhorn*	349
19	Law and the Administrative State *Joanna L. Grisinger*	367
20	Law and Religion *Steven K. Green*	387
21	Legal History and the Military *Elizabeth L. Hillman*	406
22	Criminal Law and Justice in America *Elizabeth Dale*	422
23	Intellectual Property *Steven Wilf*	441

Part IV Legal Thought — 461

24	Law and Literature *Jeannine Marie DeLombard*	463

25	Legal Thought from Blackstone to Kent and Story *Steven J. Macias*	484
26	American Jurisprudence in the Nineteenth and Early Twentieth Centuries *James D. Schmidt*	506
27	Critical Legal Studies *John Henry Schlegel*	524
28	The International Context: An Imperial Perspective on American Legal History *Clara Altman*	543
Index		562

Notes on Contributors

Clara Altman is a doctoral candidate in American history at Brandeis University and a National Fellow at the Miller Center of Public Affairs at the University of Virginia. Her research focuses on law, imperialism, and international affairs in the twentieth century.

Felice Batlan is Associate Professor of Law at IIT/Chicago-Kent College of Law. She is a leading scholar on legal history and gender and is the author of the forthcoming book *Engendering Legal Aid: Lawyers, Social Workers, and the Poor, 1863–1960*.

Alfred L. Brophy is the Judge John J. Parker Distinguished Professor of Law at the University of North Carolina at Chapel Hill. He is the author of *Reconstructing the Dreamland: The Tulsa Riot of 1921* (Oxford University Press, 2002) and *Reparations Pro and Con* (Oxford University Press, 2006), the lead co-author of *Integrating Spaces: Property Law and Race* (Aspen, 2011), and co-editor with Daniel Hamilton of *Transformations in American Legal History: Essays in Honor of Morton J. Horwitz* (Harvard, 2009 and 2010).

James Campbell is Lecturer in American History at the University of Leicester. He is the author of *Slavery on Trial: Race, Class, and Criminal Justice in Antebellum Richmond, Virginia* (University Press of Florida, 2007) and *Crime and Punishment in African American History* (Palgrave, 2012).

Elizabeth Dale is Professor of History at the University of Florida, where she is also an affiliate at Levin College of Law. She is the author of several works of legal history, including *A History of Criminal Justice In America, 1789–1939* (Cambridge, 2011) and *Debating–and Creating–Authority: The Failure of a Constitutional Ideal, Massachusetts Bay 1629–1649* (Ashgate, 2001).

Thomas J. Davis is Professor of History at Arizona State University,

Tempe. A historian and lawyer, he teaches U.S. constitutional and legal history, focusing particularly on issues of race and law. He is the author of *Plessy v. Ferguson* (Greenwood Press, 2012), *Race Relations in America* (Greenwood Press, 2006), and *Africans in the Americas: A History of the Black Diaspora* (with Michael L. Conniff; Blackburn Press, 2002).

Jeannine Marie DeLombard is Associate Professor of English at the University of Toronto. She is the author of *In the Shadow of the Gallows: Race, Crime, and American Civic Identity* (University of Pennsylvania Press, 2012) and *Slavery on Trial: Law, Print, and Abolitionism* (University of North Carolina Press, 2007) and a contributor to *Early African American Print Culture* (University of Pennsylvania Press, 2012), as well as the forthcoming Oxford History of the Novel in English (Vol. 6: American Novels, 1870–1940), the *New Cambridge Companion to Herman Melville*, and the *Oxford Handbook of the African American Slave Narrative*.

Christine Desan is a Professor of Law at Harvard Law School. She is the co-director of Harvard University's Program on Capitalism, and the author of a forthcoming book on money as a legal institution called *Making Money: Coin, Credit, and the Coming of Capitalism*.

Deborah Dinner is Associate Professor of Law at Washington University in St. Louis. She is the author of articles examining the legal history of second-wave feminism and its opponents and is working on a book manuscript based on her dissertation, *Pregnancy at Work: Sex Equality, Reproductive Liberty, and the Workplace, 1964–1993*.

Robin L. Einhorn is Professor of History at the University of California Berkeley. She is the author of *Property Rules: Political Economy in Chicago, 1833–1872* (Chicago, 1991), and *American Taxation, American Slavery* (Chicago, 2006), and also a contributor to *The New Fiscal Sociology: Taxation in Comparative and Historical Perspective* (Cambridge, 2009).

Steven K. Green is the Fred H. Paulus Professor of Law and Adjunct Professor of History at Willamette University, where he serves as the director of the interdisciplinary Center for Religion, Law and Democracy. He is the author of *The Second Disestablishment: Church and State in Nineteenth-Century America* (Oxford University Press, 2010) and *The Bible, the School, and the Constitution: The Clash that Shaped Modern Church-State Doctrine* (Oxford University Press, 2012).

Joanna L. Grisinger is Senior Continuing Lecturer at the Center for Legal Studies at Northwestern University. She is the author of *The Unwieldy American State: Administrative Politics since the New Deal* (Cambridge University Press, 2012).

Sally E. Hadden is Associate Professor of History at Western Michigan University. She is the author of *Slave Patrols: Law and Violence in Virginia and the Carolinas* (Harvard University Press, 2001), a contributor to the *Cambridge History of Law in America* (Cambridge University Press, 2008), as well as co-editor with Patricia Minter of *Signposts: New Directions in Southern Legal History* (University of Georgia Press, 2013).

Elizabeth L. Hillman is Professor of Law at the University of California Hastings College of the Law. She is the author of two books, *Military Justice Cases and Materials* (with Eugene R. Fidell and Dwight H. Sullivan; LexisNexis, 2012, 2nd Edition) and *Defending America: Military Culture and the Cold War Court-Martial* (Princeton University Press, 2005) and many essays, including a chapter in *Prosecuting International Sex Crimes* (Forum for International Criminal and Humanitarian Law, 2012).

Roman J. Hoyos is Associate Professor of Law at Southwestern Law School in Los Angeles, California. He is currently completing a book on popular sovereignty entitled *The Rise and Fall of Popular Sovereignty: Constitutional Conventions, Law, and Democracy in Nineteenth Century America*.

Felicia Kornbluh is an Associate Professor of History and Director of the Women's and Gender Studies Program at the University of Vermont. She is the author of *The Battle for Welfare Rights* (University of Pennsylvania Press, 2007) and of articles on law, poverty, disability, gender, and sexuality, and is writing on the blind constitutional theorist Jacobus tenBroek and on the place of claims for economic justice in twentieth-century U.S. social movements.

Steven J. Macias is Assistant Professor of Law at Southern Illinois University, Carbondale. His history dissertation, "The Creation of Legal Science in the Early Republic" (UC Berkeley, 2012), examined the intellectual motivations behind the movement to formalize legal studies in the early American republic.

Christian McMillen is Associate Professor of History at the University of Virginia. He is the author of *Making Indian Law: The Hualapai Land Case and the Birth of Ethnohistory* (Yale, 2007). He is the author of several articles on the history of medicine.

Ellen Holmes Pearson is Associate Professor of History at the University of North Carolina at Asheville. She is the author of *Remaking Custom: Law and Identity in the Early American Republic* (University of Virginia Press, 2011).

John Henry Schlegel has been a Professor of Law at the SUNY/Buffalo Law School for going on forty years. A participant in the Critical Legal Studies movement, of late he has been researching and writing about law and economy in the twentieth century.

Christopher W. Schmidt is an Assistant Professor at Chicago-Kent College of Law and a Faculty Fellow at the American Bar Foundation. He has published articles on various topics relating to the intersection of social mobilization and legal change in recent American history, and he is currently writing a book on the use of *Brown v. Board of Education* in debates over the Constitution and the courts.

James D. Schmidt, Professor of History at Northern Illinois University, is the author of *Free to Work: Labor Law, Emancipation and Reconstruction, 1815–1880* (University of Georgia Press, 1998) and *Industrial Violence and the Legal Origins of Child Labor* (Cambridge University Press, 2010). He is currently working on the legal history of corporal punishment and school authority.

Mark E. Steiner is Professor of Law at South Texas College of Law. He is the author of *An Honest Calling: The Law Practice of Abraham Lincoln* (Northern Illinois University Press, 2006).

David S. Tanenhaus is Professor of History and Chair of the UNLV History Department and the James E. Rogers Professor of History and Law at the William S. Boyd School of Law. He is the author of *Juvenile Justice in the Making* (Oxford University Press, 2004) and *The Constitutional Rights of Children: In re Gault and Juvenile Justice* (University Press of Kansas, 2011).

Karen Tani is Assistant Professor of Law at the University of California, Berkeley. She has published articles in the *Law and History Review* and the *Yale Law Journal* (forthcoming), and is currently working on a socio-legal history of public welfare administration between the New Deal and the Welfare Rights Movement.

Allison Brownell Tirres is an Assistant Professor at DePaul University College of Law. Her work has appeared in the *American Journal of Legal History*, the *Georgetown Immigration Law Journal*, and various edited collections.

Harwell Wells is Associate Professor of Law at the Temple University Beasley School of Law. A scholar of business associations and legal history, he holds a JD from the Vanderbilt University School of Law and a PhD in American history from the University of Virginia.

Steven Wilf is the Joel Barlow Professor of Law and Associate Dean for Research & Faculty Development at the University of Connecticut. He is the author of *The Law Before the Law* (Rowman & Littlefield, 2008) and *Law's Imagined Republic: Popular Politics and Criminal Justice in Revolutionary America* (Cambridge University Press, 2010), as well as numerous articles in legal history and intellectual property.

Introduction

Sally E. Hadden and Alfred L. Brophy

As early as the eighteenth century writers from Montesquieu to Joseph Priestley linked law to its intellectual, cultural, and economic context. This was followed in the nineteenth century by Oliver Wendell Holmes' *The Common Law*, which famously averred that "The life of the law has not been logic; it has been experience." Yet, those insights were too rarely utilized by historians for much of the twentieth century. The centrality of law to historical analysis – and vice versa – was submerged, with law only playing a supporting role in the development of more traditional historical fields; legal history languished while political, diplomatic, and intellectual history flourished. In the past several decades, however, few if any fields of historical study have seen as much growth as the history of law. Dominated in the 1950s and 1960s by works of hagiography that privileged biography or celebrated the Supreme Court, the history of law now spans an extraordinary range of topics from the early seventeenth century to the recent past.

Changes in the field have been great and reflect the broadening sense of people involved in the legal system, the subject matter studied, and the methods employed. The subjects of study have increased greatly. Where legal history was once mostly discussions about the opinions of great white judges, especially Supreme Court justices, the field now spans the complete spectrum of people involved in law – from traditional actors like judges, legislators, and lawyers, to humble litigants, defendants, even those protesting and seeking to reform law. Similarly, the subject matter has expanded far beyond judicial biography and doctrine as announced in appellate court opinions. For a time, historians of the law wrote only from an "internalist"

A Companion to American Legal History, First Edition.
Edited by Sally E. Hadden and Alfred L. Brophy.
© 2013 John Wiley & Sons Ltd. Published 2021 by John Wiley & Sons Ltd.

perspective; they studied how legal doctrine evolved without much regard for exogenous factors. Now legal history is dominated by studies of how legal institutions respond to, are influenced by, and influence surrounding society. The subjects are not just appellate judicial opinions and statutes, as they once were. Now legal historians study everything from the decisions of police and trial courts to administrative agencies' adjudications, local ordinances, and social norms that have the effect of law. Economics and demography, as well as politics and ideology, are key variables that are correlated with law.

The methods have expanded, too. In the realm of cultural and intellectual history, legal historians are concerned with the ideas of people in the streets, with reformers, workers, the enslaved, and people in poverty as well as the more familiar judges, legislators, and lawyers. Social history also looms large. Such studies look to the effects of law on people, as well as how the common person's ideas and motivations provided the impetus to change law.

Following broader trends in history and scholarship generally, legal history has recently expanded further, looking beyond the United States' borders, to see how transnational politics, culture, and economics relate to domestic law and legal practices. This new perspective reduces the privilege often accorded to the United States as nation-state, while encouraging broader, more comparative scholarship (hence our title is a *Companion to American Legal History* rather than a *Companion to United States Legal History*). So now American legal history crosses borders; it encompasses intellectual, cultural, and social history; it studies institutions, like courts, prisons, and states, as well as flamboyant judges, legislators, lawyers, litigants. Sometimes the subjects are famous; at other times they are humble and almost completely forgotten. In all cases, the field of legal history appears to be expanding as rapidly as scholars can publish their findings.

Given how widely legal historians now cast their nets, one may begin to wonder whether there is still a distinct field of legal history. For when "law" is construed broadly, when the subjects used to explain "law" include such expansive categories as economics, politics, religious thought, and literature, when questions span social, cultural, and international history, and when virtually everyone is a subject of study, it is reasonable to think that legal history is becoming synonymous with American history. In fact, some recent literature, such as G. Edward White's *Law in American History* (2012) treats law as embedded in larger American history and, thus, uses law to tell the story of American development from the settlement of transplanted European cultures in the seventeenth century through the epic struggles of the Civil War.

Within law schools, especially, history is increasingly seen as a method of legal analysis, much as economics is a method of legal analysis. The historical method looks to understand how legal structures are dependent on their context and how statutes and cases need to be interpreted based on their context, as well as frame legal institutions to solve problems that have deep roots in our culture. Legal history is not merely studied as an artifact of the past, but to reveal choices made (or yet to be made) in public policy that have implications well beyond the court house or capitol. This "applied" aspect of historical studies in law gives it added relevance for jurists, legislators, or agency administrators contemplating decisions that can affect virtually every realm of human endeavor. Historical analysis demonstrates the complexity of legal institutions. How far that will go remains to be seen, but legal history is certainly going in many different directions simultaneously.

In large part, the prospect of an ever increasing empire of legal history is positive, because it is expanding in geography and demography at the same time it is expanding in subject matter and method. Quantitative historians, those who truck in thick description, and close readers of texts all find ample room for work in this field. But there are downsides to a field growing so rapidly and in so many different directions, for that fragments the efforts of scholars into many different subfields. Likewise, the separation of legal historians into history departments and law schools (and other locales) is reflected in choices made about where to publish findings: history professors tend to publish monographs, while law professors gravitate toward law journals. It can be difficult to keep up with the assorted places where legal history appears. Many people are speaking, but often in different venues, on different themes and with different purposes. Where once there were common themes and a small array of publications to know in the field, now there are many. New areas of research seem to sprout into existence every year: legal history now collides with the history of the book, while the Internet seemingly rewrites legal concepts such as property and privacy almost daily. These developments create a problem for editors who cannot include essays on every topic in a rapidly expanding discipline. The field of legal history, grand and growing, is in search of unifying themes and questions for analysis. The *Companion to American Legal History* offers guidance on where to start, what not to miss, and in many instances, indicates fruitful avenues for future research.

This volume surveys the extraordinarily rich work that has appeared since the 1950s, when J. Willard Hurst first envisioned a field apart from constitutional history that he called legal history. It emphasizes the diverse literature of the last several decades and infuses its analysis with up-to-the-minute information – new studies like David Rabban's *Law's History: American Legal Thought and the Transatlantic Turn to History* (2013) that offer fresh insights about legal historians working in earlier generations. Whether a reader is looking for a subject specific guide, or one arranged by time period or school of thought, this *Companion* should be able to provide a point of entry. Our first six chapters are organized chronologically. Our contributors cover developments from the seventeenth century up through the 1960s. We then have seven chapters that look to groups in American legal history – from Native Americans, to African Americans in slavery and then in freedom, to women, families, and lawyers. Our third section has ten chapters on topics, including the economy, poverty, religion, taxes, the administrative state, and the military. Our fourth and final section looks to jurisprudential explorations, ranging across law and literature, legal thought from the eighteenth through early twentieth century, critical legal studies, and the international context of American law. Like a scout looking down from a mountain top, the *Companion to American Legal History* provides expert guidance to the terrain of our vast scholarly enterprise. We hope it inspires, as well as guides, the next generation of American legal historians.

References

Rabban, David (2013). *Law's History: American Legal Thought and the Transatlantic Turn to History*. Cambridge University Press, New York.

White, G. Edward (2012). *Law in American History: From the Colonial Years Through the Civil War*. Oxford University Press, New York.

Part I

Chronological Overviews

Chapter One

RECONSIDERING THE SEVENTEENTH CENTURY: LEGAL HISTORY IN THE AMERICAS

Elizabeth Dale

Introduction

Commenting in a forum on law in British India, the legal anthropologist Sally Engle Merry noted that colonialism, and colonial law, was always uncertain (2010). Her point applies as well to histories of the seventeenth-century Americas where the uncertainties that Merry identified as arising from law's contradictory roles as source of order and space of contention are complicated by the fact that seventeenth-century America has always been a disputed space. In the seventeenth century, the boundaries of the Americas were subject to disputes between sovereigns, settlers and native peoples, and settlers from different colonies. Today, those boundaries continue to confound: for many legal histories seventeenth-century America is North America, or the closer confines of British North America. But the Americas extended beyond those boundaries, and studies of law and justice in the seventeenth century need to consider New Spain, New France, the New Netherlands, and Native Americans, as well.

To try to capture the complexity of that territory, this chapter tacks between the general and the particular. It begins at the most general level, considering the seventeenth-century Americas as part of a global story of imperialism and sovereignty. The next section tightens the focus to look at regional studies of law and justice in the Americas, while in the third section the perspective shifts out once again, to consider how the various regional studies might be brought into conversation with one another. The final section brings the particular and the general together, suggesting how studies of specific trials might help connect the global to the local.

A Companion to American Legal History, First Edition.
Edited by Sally E. Hadden and Alfred L. Brophy.
© 2013 John Wiley & Sons Ltd. Published 2021 by John Wiley & Sons Ltd.

The Realms of Legal History

Law and Justice

In a recent review, Stuart Banner observed that one "message of this book is that law is almost everywhere, and thus that just about any aspect of the past can be viewed as a facet of legal history" (Banner, 2009: 685). That expansive view has long been a characteristic of the legal histories of British North America (Tomlins and Mann, 2001), and recently has influenced the legal histories of New Spain and New France as well (Owensby, 2008: 5–11; Moogk, 2000). The realm of law in the seventeenth century was blurred for several reasons. Law changed in the Americas, as native people were forced to adapt their systems of law and justice to European settlement (Hermes, 2008), but it also evolved in the early modern European world of which the Americas were a part (Williams, 2010).

Despite the ambiguities at the heart of the law, disputes in the Americas often were cast as legal claims. But even when they were set out in the language of law, disagreements were not exclusively settled through formal litigation. In addition to the courts, disputants could and did appeal to other institutions – imperial governments (Middleton, 2010), a native process (Kawashima, 2001), church congregations (Oberholzer, 1956), or the household (Herzog, 2004) – to resolve their differences. Seventeenth-century actors might frame their claims in the precise terms of law (Offutt, 1995) or the vague language of justice (Herzog, 2004); they could rest their legal claims on custom and practice (Tomlins, 2010), deeds (Baker, 1989), local rules or imperial statutes (Owensby, 2008), scripture or natural law (Dale, 2001), or treaties and charters (Tomlins, 2001).

Studies of law in the seventeenth-century Americas typically share a desire to uncover general principles about law, its place in society and its role in history, precisely because the very nature of law in this period was unsettled. Many concern themselves with law's function, asking whether the aims of a legal system are to achieve order (Konig, 1979), ensure the rule of law (Offutt, 1995), or enforce shared understandings of justice (Herzog, 2004). Still others tease out the relationship between formal systems of law and illegal or extralegal practices (Godbeer, 2004), or consider whether law is best understood as a site of power and dominance (Pagan, 2002), a place of contestation (McKinney, 2010), a space for negotiation and resolution (Baker, 1989), or an uneasy mix of all of the above (Kawashima, 2001). Another group of studies look at how legal and constitutional systems changed over time, exploring whether legal concepts were borrowed and adapted from earlier traditions (Reinsch, 1899) or how the legal developments of the seventeenth century laid the groundwork for subsequent legal practices and assumptions (Morgan, 1975).

Imperial Agents, Colonial Subjects, or Founding Fathers?

Because the seventeenth century was marked by extensive European efforts to colonize and assert legal control (MacMillan, 2011; Pagden, 1995), seventeenth-century legal actors were rarely people playing out their lives on a local stage, but were characters in larger, transatlantic (Amussen, 2007) and imperial dramas (Herzog, 2004). Broadly speaking, studies of law in the seventeenth-century Americas approach that dynamic from one of three perspectives, though there is sometimes considerable overlap. The first considers whether seventeenth-century legal actors were creators of distinctive American legal regimes. This is the oldest tradition, stretching back to Paul Reinsch's work at the end of the nineteenth century (Reinsch, 1899), but it has its share of recent practitioners whose studies look to the seventeenth century to find the roots of modern legal orders (Moogk, 2000).

A second approach considers the legal actors as colonial subjects. This perspective is often taken by studies that consider the impact of European settlement on Native Americans (Pulsipher, 2005), but it also is found in scholarship that looks at the legal impact of negotiations between settlers from different countries (Middleton, 2010), explores the influence of colonial slave regimes on European law and society (McKinney, 2010), or traces out imperial efforts to create distinctive, colonial legal systems (Herzog, 2004). A third approach looks at seventeenth-century legal actors as imperial agents, tracing how their decisions implemented (Moogk, 2000), undermined (Koots, 2011), or adapted (Bernhard, 2010) the imperial projects of their sovereigns. In one study of law in New Spain, Brian Owensby offered a variation on this approach, examining how imperial laws were developed to try to control colonial agents and how Native Americans used the imperial laws to check the local officials (2008: 11).

Read as a whole, these studies confirm John Comaroff's observation that "far from being a crushingly overdetermined monolithic historical force, colonialism was often an underdetermined, chaotic business, less a matter of the sure hand of oppression ... than of the disarticulated, semicoherent, inefficient strivings for modes of rule that might work in unfamiliar, intermittently hostile places a long way from home" (Comaroff, 2001: 311). In such a world, the lines between colonizer and colonized are often blurred and that was particularly true in the seventeenth century, notwithstanding the fact that colonial laws often were enacted in order to mark the divisions between colonized and colonizer, or ruler and ruled (Moogk, 2002). Ultimately, those distinctions did take hold, particularly where racial slavery entered into the mix. But as that process unfolded colonial agents undermined imperial authority and command (McKinney, 2010), colonial subjects thwarted efforts to contain them (Daughters, 2009) and settlers constructed their own legal orders (Pagan, 2002).

Constitutional and International Law

As that suggests, international and constitutional law was in flux across the seventeenth century. Although this was the century of the Treaty of Westphalia, with its effort to define national sovereignty and give sovereign nations legal status (Middleton, 2010: 33–34), the scope and shape of international law was unsettled (MacMillan, 2011) and key concepts, from the meaning of imperial authority (Armitage, 2000) to the nature of sovereignty (Benton, 2010) remained unclear. In the colonies, theoretical disputes over sovereign power were complicated by the everyday as claims of sovereignty were ignored by colonial officials (Herzog, 2004) and local disputes escalated into international problems (Middleton, 2010).

These problems were as much issues of constitutional order as they were questions of international law or sovereignty and they were exacerbated because the seventeenth century was a period of considerable constitutional change. In England the Civil War and related internal constitutional debates significantly altered the old order (Nemmer, 1977) while France was "not yet a nation and scarcely a unified kingdom" (Moogk, 2000: 55) in the seventeenth century and experienced its own constitutional tensions as a result. Constitutional weakness at the center was reinforced by conflict in the colonies. There were constitutional disputes within the colonies over who governed (Breen, 1970), an issue that could be complicated by theological differences (Chu, 1987) or social pressures (Morgan, 1975). There were also questions about who was governed and how: Were Native Americans entitled to the rights and protections of subjects of an imperial power, or the privileges typically accorded the subjects of another sovereign, or neither (MacMillan, 2011)? Were women or children part of the political order, and if so, to what extent (Brewer, 2005)? What was the status of Dutch settlers after the New Netherlands became New York (Merwick, 1999), or German settlers in the English colonies of the Chesapeake (Roeber, 1993)? What about settlers who were not Quakers in Pennsylvania (Offutt, 1995) or not Puritans in Massachusetts (Pestana, 2004)? Constitutional ferment in the periphery helped prompt changes in constitutional ideas and practices in Europe (Norton, 1996) just as much as constitutional changes in the center played a role in shaping the rules of colonial governance (Kettner, 1978).

The wealth of recent work on sovereignty and imperialism (Pagden, 2008) invites further work in these areas of law in the seventeenth-century Americas, but more could be done to explore the connections between local problems and imperial designs or to dig down into the sources to tease out support for Benton's suggestion that "even in the most paradigmatic cases, an empire's spaces were politically targeted; legally differentiated; and encased in irregular, porous and sometimes undefined borders" (Benton, 2010: 2). So too, we could go beyond our recognition that colonial charters were important (Bilder, 2004) to discover how they were understood and what constitutional roles they played in both the center and the periphery.

Regional Interpretations of Law

In contrast to recent studies of colonialism and imperialism, which look at more than one country (Benton, 2002), legal histories of the seventeenth-century Americas usually follow the flag, focusing on the legal orders established by particular imperial powers. Many of these studies examine law in the British colonies (Hoffer, 1992), and while recent studies by Christopher Tomlins (2010), Richard Godbeer (2004), and Bradley Chapin (1983) survey specific areas of law across British North America, most look at only a specific part of Britain's American holdings. The largest share explores the legal history of New England (Ross, 2008), but there are studies of northern colonies that look at law in New York (Goebel, 1944) and Pennsylvania (Offutt, 1995). In similar fashion, histories that study seventeenth-century law in the southern colonies are mostly about Virginia or the Chesapeake (Brown, 1996; Konig, 1982; Roeber, 1981), though some studies of the law or legal institutions of the South discuss law in other parts of the region in the seventeenth century (Hadden, 2001; Wyatt-Brown, 1982). A few recent works have pushed the boundaries of the English Atlantic world to include the law and legal cultures of the Caribbean (Bernhard, 2010; Amussen, 2007) and British Canada (Johnston, 2003). While there are not as many legal histories of the other colonies, there are several important works on law in New Spain. Some cover northern New Spain (Brooks, 2001); others consider Spanish legal regimes in the south (Herzog, 2004). In addition, Peter Moogk has written extensively about law and legal culture in his work on New France (2000), and a handful of studies touch on law and legal regimes in the New Netherlands (Middleton, 2010; Merwick, 1999).

The legal histories that consider law and Native Americans are simultaneously sparse and complex. The best overview of this area of legal history is an article by Katherine Hermes (2008). In it, she described two approaches to Native Americans and law in the Americas. One tries to uncover what she calls the "jurispractice" of Native Americans, the "mixture of thought and action taken by ordinary people to construct the law without elaborate legal theories but with definite understanding about the law and its purposes" (Hermes, 2001: 127 n.9). Thus, in his study of land deeds in seventeenth-century Maine, Emerson Baker reconstructed Native American understandings of land and boundaries (1989); Yasuhide Kawashima offered a view of legal practices and culture among the Native Americans in New England in his study of the Sassamon murder trial (2001). Often those studies look at native treatment of property or crime and punishment, but some touch on native constitutional principles. Owensby, for example, sketched Aztec institutions and distributions of power in his recent study (2008) and Kawashima offered a similar glimpse at constitutional order in his study of the Sassamon murder. Because of the debates over the extent to which ideas from the Iroquois constitution influenced the U.S. Constitution, there is a more extensive literature on Iroquois constitutional practices (Levy *et al.*, 1996).

Most of the studies of Native Americans and the law consider the treatment of Native Americans within the legal systems of the various European colonies (Hermes, 2008). Some specifically look at the impact of colonial laws on native populations (Kawashima, 1986), others consider laws and legal practices as part of a larger history (McManus, 1993). Many of these studies focus on the English colonies (Kawashima, 2004), but Native Americans play a significant role in legal histories of New Spain (Kellog, 1995; Borah, 1983) and New France (Moogk, 2000). Read together, those works demonstrate that legal relations between the native peoples and European settlers could range from the lofty realm of international law, with its claims of sovereignty and negotiated treaties (Brooks, 2001), to local disputes about injury and harm (Herzog, 2004), rights to property (Baker, 1989), or marriage and inheritance (O'Brien, 2003). Often these studies described how law was deployed to subdue native peoples and societies (Hermes, 2008), though some treat law as a space of interaction between settlers and native people (Plane, 2002), or explore the how Native Americans understood, worked within, and sometimes resisted or manipulated colonial laws (Owensby, 2008; Kawashima, 2004).

Connections or Comparisons?

Taken as a whole, these different works make it possible to begin to actually speak of the legal histories of the Americas in the seventeenth century, but most do little to tell us whether those worlds were as separate and their legal trajectories as discrete as their histories suggest. A few studies have tried to push past the limits imposed by political boundaries; some by looking at various American borderlands and considering how law was used to try to control those fluid spaces on land (Demers, 2009) and sea (Benton, 2010), others by considering the colonies themselves as hybrid spaces where people with different legal practices and expectations met (Hermes, 2008). One example of this approach is Gregory Roeber's study of the impact German immigrants had on the laws and legal cultures of the Chesapeake region (1993), another is William Offutt's consideration of cultural clashes and legal differences among English settlers in Pennsylvania (1995). Sometimes, as in Offutt's study or in my own work on Massachusetts Bay (Dale, 2001), legal disagreements arose from different belief systems. But other studies (Allen, 1981) have demonstrated that geography, as much as belief, gave rise to distinctive legal cultures when immigrants from one part of England brought with them legal traditions that were foreign to those from other parts of the country. Given that, more could be done to consider these interactions of legal cultures and the effect they had on the institutions and practices of law in the seventeenth century.

There are other ways that historians might try to connect the separate legal histories of the Americas. One approach, suggested by studies of slave law (Watson, 1989), is a comparative analysis. Scholars have taken that approach within the British colonial world: P.G. McHugh looked at how aboriginal societies in a number of British colonies fared under the common law (2004), Philip Stern compared British colonies in Asia and the Atlantic World (2006), while David Konig compared the legal regimes established in British North America to those set up at roughly the same time in Ireland (1991). But while Richard Ross compared methods of legal communication in the Spanish and English empires (Ross, 2008), little has been done to try to make comparisons across imperial legal regimes. Such an approach is possible and a quick review of some of the themes of seventeenth-century legal history suggests there are a number of points of comparison.

Law and Justice

One recurring theme in the literature that invites comparison is the issue of the relation between justice and law in colonial legal systems. Although the legal system established in the Delaware Valley was marked by a strong commitment to the rule of law from the first (Offutt, 1995), for much of the seventeenth century legal appeals and outcomes were cast in terms of justice, not legal rules (Henretta, 2008). While discretionary justice with its emphasis on community notions of fairness is an established part of the literature, there is little consensus about why that was the case. In his study of law in Virginia, Gregory Roeber argued that for much of the seventeenth century the absence of a significant body of people trained in law encouraged magistrates and other legal actors to appeal to community norms (1981). He found that dynamic ended with the rise of a generation of trained lawyers at the end of the seventeenth century. Recently James Henretta offered another institutional explanation, arguing that because most court systems in British North America lacked separate courts of equity equitable principles often influenced legal outcomes, helping drive the preference for justice (2008). In contrast, Tamar Herzog concluded that the reason appeals to justice and community were more powerful than law in seventeenth-century Quito was ideological, not institutional (2004); Catholic teachings, with their emphasis on the importance of community and fairness, prompted the focus on justice in that outpost of New Spain.

Even studies that look at the shift from justice to law within a particular colony offer a variety of explanations for the phenomenon. In his study of law in Connecticut, Bruce Mann suggested that the shift to a more formal and legal system occurred as the colony's population became larger, more diverse, and more mobile. When strangers replaced neighbors, people looked to law to provide the sorts of protections and sanctions that the community had been able to guarantee before (Mann, 1987). In contrast, Cornelia Dayton concluded that Connecticut's early, informal legal system reflected religious precepts, which were weakened as part of a larger effort to use law to strengthen the power of the patriarchy (1995). A similar disagreement underlies discussions of the shift to a more formal legal system in Virginia. Kathleen Brown and Edmund Morgan both agree that social shifts, particularly the rise of African slavery, prompted the embrace of legal control in colonial Virginia (Brown, 1996; Morgan, 1975), but differ in their understanding of the causes of that shift. Brown argued that racial issues that arose because of the presence of Native Americans and then the arrival of African slaves intersected with gender norms in a way that forced the colony to enact laws that distinguished between wives and female servants; servants and slaves; and whites and blacks. For Morgan the colony's shift from the older, less formal approach to a more legalistic order was shaped by several factors: the environmental elements that led so many English settlers to die in the first decades; the pressures on land that arose when white settler health improved, and the social tensions that arose because the colony had a skewed sex ratio with far more men than women.

In those studies historians rely on several different causal forces, some ideological, some institutional, to explain the shift from justice to law. Comparative study across colonies and imperial regimes might help scholars piece together whether these influences were truly distinctive, or whether there were factors in play that connected some or all of those forces together and might also provide support for another explanation: Most studies that consider the shift from justice to law emphasize local circumstances, but in their studies of law in New Spain Herzog and Owensby argue that the shift was a reflection of a larger, transatlantic transformation (Herzog, 2004; Owensby, 2008). Comparative study might make it possible to determine whether the shift from justice to law in the Americas was part of a larger, transatlantic process, and, if so, whether that process occurred as a result of the pressures of colonization itself or because of changes in the idea of law.

Religion

The intersection of law and religion is another point that invites comparative or transnational study. Several books explore the place of religion in the legal systems of the English colonies (Dale, 2001; Offutt, 1995; Roeber, 1993); others have looked at the relation between law and religion in New Spain or New France (Owensby, 2008; Moogk, 2000). In addition, some studies of Native American law suggest that native religious practices influenced tribal jurispractice (Kawashima, 2001), while other studies suggest the extent to which religious differences influenced constitutional and legal decisions within that colony (Middleton, 2010). Many of these studies explored the ways in which religious doctrine shaped substantive law, and often they assert that religion, particularly the strict Protestantism associated with the Puritans, led to the legal subordination of women and oppressive laws (Norton, 1996; Hoffer and Hull, 1984). But several recent works offer alternative perspectives on the intersection of law and religion. One point of view is offered by Richard Godbeer's *Sexual Revolution in Early America* (2004), which found that the Puritan colonies of New England had complex, not always repressive, attitudes towards women, sex, and sexuality. Godbeer's study reveals legal systems that reflected lay religiosity as much as formal religious doctrine. Several other studies have demonstrated that even established religious teachings sometimes shaped popular attitudes towards law. Cornelia Dayton's study of Connecticut found that the dominant Protestant religion empowered women by offering them avenues in which to bring claims and press charges (1995). Similarly, in her study of the criminal justice system in Quito, Tamar Herzog (2004) argued that religious doctrine in New Spain influenced popular and official attitudes towards the role of law in society.

Yet another approach to the intersection of law and religion is suggested by Owensby's recent study of law in northern New Spain, which looked at the relation between religion and law across the Spanish empire (2008: 45–48). That work suggests possibilities for transatlantic or comparative study; the former might trace the influence of religion on law within transatlantic imperial orders, looking to see if religion influenced law in the same way in London and Boston; the latter might compare the extent to which religion shaped law in New France and New Spain.

Substantive Law

Substantive law also provides a foundation for comparative study, either within a single empire's legal regimes or across them. Criminal law offers the greatest riches, since so many works focus specifically on criminal law

(Chapin, 1983) or consider crime and punishment as part of their more general study of law and society (Moogk, 2000). Given that wealth of material, systems of criminal justice in British North America could easily be compared to systems established in New Spain or New France to see what sorts of actions were criminalized (or were not) (Koots, 2011) and what punishment entailed (Meranze, 2008). The apparently close connections between criminal law and religious teachings suggest that comparative study might be a useful way to piece together the nature and extent of religious influence on law. Did a shared Catholic faith make criminal justice and punishment similar in New Spain and New France, or was the influence of national legal culture more significant than religious teachings? Were the different legal orders of New England and Virginia the product of social and demographic forces, or did they reflect the differences between Anglican and Puritan forms of Protestantism?

There are also a number of works on various subfields of criminal law that offer opportunities for comparative or transnational focus. One subfield of criminal justice that has received considerable attention in seventeenth-century studies looks at witchcraft prosecutions. The prosecutions in Salem at the end of the seventeenth century have been much studied (Kamensky, 2008); Richard Godbeer's study (1994) of law and magic makes it possible to put those trials into their larger transatlantic legal context, while studies that look at witchcraft prosecutions in New France (Moogk, 2000), New Spain (Lewis, 2003), and the Caribbean (Bernhard, 2010), invite a comparative approach. Another possibility is to compare witchcraft prosecutions, which often targeted women, with prosecutions of other, highly gendered crimes like infanticide (Miracle, 2008) or slander (Snyder, 2003). One of the earliest studies of infanticide (Hoffer and Hull, 1984), took a transatlantic perspective on the law, an approach that might be revisited in light of more recent work on women and crime in early modern England (Kermode, 1995).

Comparative and transnational study of substantive law need not be limited to crimes, of course, for a number of works touching on the law of property (Owensby, 2008; Dayton, 1995), households (Brewer, 2005; Moogk, 2000), or slavery (Green, 2007; Brooks, 2002; Gaspar, 2001) invite comparison in those areas of law as well. And it is important to remember that a comparative study of one aspect of substantive law may involve comparison on several levels. In an article, Mark Valeri argued that the laws regulating usury in Puritan New England debunked Max Weber's famous theory that market capitalism was closely tied to Protestantism (Valeri, 1997). Economic regulations designed to protect local merchants and manufacturers at the expense of those in other colonies were fairly common in the seventeenth century and there are several other studies that look at economic regulations (Priest, 2008), but at least one study (Koots, 2011) suggests that efforts to use law to regulate commerce and trade were not particularly successful. A comparative study of commercial regulations would not only expand our understanding of how different colonial systems viewed commercial regulation, but could also permit us to test Valeri's thesis in these other settings, looking at both the law on the books and the law in practice. Similarly, a number of studies discuss laws that regulated all aspects of labor, from wages to terms and conditions of employment (Tomlins, 2010). These laws played several roles, for in addition to controlling transactions they were often used to establish status by defining the rights and privileges of wage and bound laborers (slaves and indentured servants) (Morris, 1946) and establishing special categories for women and children (Brewer, 2005; Pagan, 2002). Similar attempts to regulate status arose in New Spain (Owensby, 2008) and a comparative analysis of these sorts of laws across empires would not only help us understand the differences and similarities across labor regimes, but might add to our understanding of the relationship between sovereign and subject (Kettner, 1978) in the seventeenth century.

Blurring Boundaries, Unsettling Law

Studies of law in the seventeenth century often emphasize how fluid the categories of law were and comparative and transnational studies could also be based on that aspect of colonial legal history. The literature suggests that the interplay of legal categories often was a product of the difficulties of capturing legal subjects, particularly human subjects, in neat legal boxes. Children could be inheritors, raising questions of property and political power (Brewer, 2005), laborers (Tomlins, 2010), or criminals (Steenburg, 2005) and shifts in theories of their legal competence in one area, often affected the way they were treated in another. Likewise, women could be criminals (Kamensky, 1997), wives (Brown, 1996), mothers (Pagan, 2002), or bound servants (McKinney, 2010), and were often several of those things at once (Greene, 2007). Native Americans were both outsiders to be controlled (Moogk, 2002) and holders of desired property (Baker, 1989), slaves (Brooks, 2002) and independent actors (Owensby, 2008). So too, legal categories may be filled by different people at different times, prompting changes in the way law is used and enforced: When deals were made with strangers, rather than neighbors, more law may be necessary (Mann, 1987); when Africans replaced native people and whites as bound labor, new rules needed to be put in place (Morgan, 1975). This problem of fluid categories invites comparisons across colonial systems, to see how different legal regimes tried to capture and contain their human subjects.

At the same time, seventeenth-century legal actors blurred laws in other ways by bringing foreign assumptions into a legal system. Settlers from another country might do so (Merwick, 1999), but foreign legal ideas could follow people from one colony coming into contact with those from another through trade (Koots, 2011) or by virtue of moving from one colony to another (James, 1999). So too, sojourners, like the young Virginia men who traveled to England for an education, could bring about legal change by carrying new ideas and practices with them on their return (Roeber, 1981). A study, transatlantic or trans-regional, that looked at mobility within empires or across imperial boundaries would deepen our understanding of this sort of legal blurring and its impact on seventeenth-century legal systems.

Finally, there are possibilities for comparison and connection outside of the realm of formal law. While legal history seems, by definition, to need to focus on the workings of formal law and legal institutions, Herzog's observation that in the seventeenth-century Quito law "extralegal arrangements were very frequent" (2004: 10), applies to many colonies. In some (though not all, see Brown, 1996), churches could and did judge, reprimand and punish, or assert jurisdiction to hear claims relating to breach of contract to types of crimes (Oberholzer, 1956). Less formally organized groups also played a role in adjudication in several colonies. In Quito, Herzog found that members of local communities could be relied on to investigate charges of misconduct or wrongdoing, define the boundaries of behavior, and punish outliers. Other studies suggest those practices were not limited to New Spain; in an article on the Atlantic slave trade, David Richardson (2001) set out a number of examples of shipboard revolts that were both acts of resistance and attempts to use extralegal means. Studies of slander in English colonies often suggest that it was a type of social control used by women, and others who were outside the structures of power (Kamensky, 1997), while Simon Middleton traced the way that bakers in seventeenth-century New Amsterdam engaged in self help to press for a recalculation of the price of bread (Middleton, 2010). Here again, there is a possibility for further, comparative study that looked at the types of extralegal practices found in different legal regimes and examined how and to what extent colonial governments tried to control them.

Trials and Legal Processes

The comparative and transatlantic (or trans-regional) approaches suggested above are one way to move from the study of many, separate local legalities to studies that look at law across the Americas and try to reconnect the particular and the general. Another way to try to relate the general to the particular is through the use of case studies. Although histories of trials are often microhistories that unpack a trial to try to learn about a local community, several studies of seventeenth-century trials connect the local to the transnational, by considering the various sources of law and their interplay in that particular case. For example, Godbeer's study (2005) of a witch trial in late seventeenth-century Connecticut revealed how English legal principles and rules of evidence collided with local context. Kawashima's study of the John Sassamon murder treated the trial as a clash of competing legal regimes, exploring how and why Plymouth's laws were able to trump Wampanoag systems of punishment (2001). In his study of a series of related trials that arose from an illegitimate birth in Virginia, John Pagan traced how and why English laws changed in response to colonial necessity (2002) while in another study Nan Goodman used Roger Williams's forced exile from Massachusetts Bay to uncover a common law framework for law in seventeenth-century New England. Her study, like Pagan's, explored the ways in which the English common law was adapted to the particular circumstances of the colonies (Goodman, 2009). Each of these case studies brings the general principles of law into the everyday, to show how and why those general principles were adjusted in response to particular problems.

Of course, while trial studies can help us connect the general to the particular, they also provide an opportunity for a closer understanding of local law and can tell us about the role courts played in helping resolve, or exacerbate, local problems (Winship, 2005; Chu, 1987; Boyer and Nissenbaum, 1974). For legal historians, trial studies can fulfill a more basic role. There are only a few studies of actual legal practice in the seventeenth-century Americas (Black, 1965), though some studies address process as part of their larger engagement with law (Owensby, 2008). Histories of trials often provide a close look at legal processes (Kawashima, 2001), principles of evidence (Godbeer, 2005), or legal records (Burns *et al.*, 2008).

Conclusion

In the seventeenth century, the Americas were a site of legal orders established by native peoples, imperial powers, and local communities. Within those orders, law and legal practices covered a multitude of subjects, from domestic relations to labor, from crime and punishment to trade. Histories of law trace out these various legal orders, explaining both their impact and their failures or weaknesses, within the different legal regimes. The result is a literature of both depth and breadth, but it is also a literature that is almost exclusively regional, looking at the legal history of particular colonies in isolation. As I suggest above, the wide range of studies on seventeenth-century legal history invites a shift in focus from the particular to the general.

References

Allen, David Grayson (1981). *In English Ways: The Movement of Societies and the Transferral of English Local Law and Custom to Massachusetts Bay in the 17th Century.* University of North Carolina Press, Chapel Hill.

Amussen, Susan Dwyer (2007). *Caribbean Exchanges: Slavery and the Transformation of English Society, 1640–1700.* University of North Carolina Press, Chapel Hill.

Armitage, David (2000). *The Ideological Origins of the British Empire.* Cambridge University Press, New York.

Baker, Emerson (1989). "'Scratch with a Bear's Paw': Anglo-Indian Land Deeds in Early Maine." *Ethnohistory* 26: 235–357.

Banner, Stuart (2009). "Review: Grossberg and Tomlins, *The Cambridge History of Law in America: The Twentieth Century and After.*" *Law & History Review* 27: 684–685.

Benton, Lauren (2002). *Law and Colonial Cultures: Legal Regimes in World History, 1400–1900.* Cambridge University Press, New York.

Benton, Lauren (2010). *A Search for Sovereignty: Law and Geography in European Empires, 1400–1900.* Cambridge University Press, New York.

Bernhard, Virginia (2010). "Religion, Politics and Witchcraft in Bermuda, 1651–1655." *William & Mary Quarterly* 67: 677–708.

Bilder, Mary Sarah (2004). *The Transatlantic Constitution: Colonial Legal Culture and the Empire.* Harvard University Press, Cambridge, MA.

Black, Barbara Aronstein (1965). "The Judicial Power and the General Court in Early Massachusetts, 1634–1686." Ph.D. diss., Yale University, New Haven.

Borah, Woodrow (1983). *Justice by Insurance: The General Indian Court of Colonial Mexico and the Legal Aides of the Half-Real.* University of California Press, Berkeley.

Boyer, Paul and Nissenbaum, Stephen, eds (1974). *Salem Possessed: The Social Origins of Witchcraft.* Harvard University Press, Cambridge, MA.

Breen, T.H. (1970). *The Character of a Good Ruler: A Study of Puritan Political Ideas in New England, 1630–1730.* Yale University Press, New Haven.

Brewer, Holly (2005). *By Birth or Consent: Children, Law and the Anglo-American Revolution in Authority.* University of North Carolina Press, Chapel Hill.

Brooks, James F. (2001). "'Lest We Go in Search of Relief to Our Lands and Our Nation:' Customary Justice and Colonial Law in the New Mexican Borderlands, 1680–1821." In Tomlins and Mann, eds, *The Many Legalities of Early America*, 150–180. University of North Carolina Press, Chapel Hill.

Brooks, James F. (2002). *Captives and Cousins: Slavery, Kinship and Community in the Southwest Borderlands.* University of North Carolina Press, Chapel Hill.

Brown, Kathleen M. (1996). *Good Wives, Nasty Wenches, and Anxious Patriarchs: Gender, Race, and Power in Colonial Virginia.* University of North Carolina Press, Chapel Hill.

Burns, Margo and Rosenthal, Bernard (2008). "Examination of the Records of the Salem Witch Trials." *William & Mary Quarterly* 65: 401–422.

Chapin, Bradley (1983). *Criminal Justice in Colonial America, 1606–1660.* University of Georgia Press, Athens.

Chu, Jonathan M. (1987). "Nursing a Poisonous Tree – Litigation and Property Law in Seventeenth-Century Essex County, Massachusetts: The Case of Bishop's Farm." *American Journal of Legal History.* 31: 221–252.

Comaroff, John (2001). "Colonialism, Culture, and the Law: A Foreword." *Law & Social Inquiry* 26: 305–314.

Dale, Elizabeth (2001). *Debating – and Creating – Authority: The Failure of a Constitutional Idea in Massachusetts Bay, 1629–1649.* Ashgate, Aldershot.

Daughters, Anton (2009). "A Seventeenth-Century Instance of Hopi Clowning?: The Trial of Juan Suñi, 1659." *Kiva* 74: 447–463.

Dayton, Cornelia Hughes (1995). *Women Before the Bar: Gender, Law and Society in Connecticut, 1639–1789.* University of North Carolina Press, Chapel Hill.

Demers, Paul A. (2009). "The French Colonial Legacy of the Canada-United States Border in Eastern North America, 1650–1783." *French Colonial History.* 10: 35–54.

Gaspar, David Barry (2001). "'Rigid and Inclement': Origins of the Jamaica Slave Laws of the Seventeenth Century." In Tomlins and Mann, eds, *The Many Legalities of Early America*, 78–96.

Godbeer, Richard (1994). *Devil's Dominion: Magic and Religion in Early New England.* Cambridge University Press, New York.

Godbeer, Richard (2004). *Sexual Revolution in Early America.* Johns Hopkins University Press, Baltimore.

Godbeer, Richard (2005). *Escaping Salem: The Other Witchcraft Horror of 1692.* Oxford University Press, New York.

Goebel, Julius (1944). *Law Enforcement in Colonial New York: A Study in Criminal Procedure.* Patterson Smith, Montclair, NJ.

Goodman, Nan (2009). "Banishment, Jurisdiction, and Identity in Seventeenth-Century New England: The Case of Roger Williams." *Early American Studies* 7: 109–139.

Green, Cecelia A. (2007). "'A Civil Inconvenience?' The Vexed Question of Slave Marriages in the British West Indies." *Law & History Review* 25: 1–61.

Greene, Jack P. (2007). "Roundtable, Colonial History and National History: Reflections on a Continuing Problem," *William & Mary Quarterly.* 64: 235–286.

Hadden, Sally (2001). *Law and Violence in Virginia and the Carolinas.* Harvard University Press, Cambridge.

Henretta, James (2008). "Magistrates, Common Law-Lawyers, Legislators: The Three Legal Systems of British America." In Grossberg and Tomlins, eds, *Cambridge History of Law in America: Early America.* 1: 555–592. Cambridge University Press, New York.

Hermes, Katherine (2001). "'Justice Will Be Done Us:' Algonquian Demands for Reciprocity in the Courts of European Settlers." In Tomlins and Mann, eds, *The Many Legalities of Early America*, 123–149. University of North Carolina Press, Chapel Hill.

Hermes, Katherine (2008). "The Law of Native Americans, to 1805." In Grossberg and Tomlins, eds, *Cambridge History of Law in America*, 1: 32–62. Cambridge University Press, New York.

Herzog, Tamar (2004). *Upholding Justice: Society, State and the Penal System in Quito (1650–1750)*. University of Michigan Press, Ann Arbor.
Hoffer, Peter Charles (1992). *Law and People in Colonial America*. Johns Hopkins University Press, Baltimore.
Hoffer, Peter Charles and Hull, N.E.H. (1984). *Murdering Mothers: Infanticide in England and New England, 1558–1803*. New York University Press, New York.
James, Sydney V. (1999). *John Clarke and His Legacies: Religion and Law in Colonial Rhode Island, 1638–1750*. Pennsylvania State University Press, University Park, PA.
Johnston, A.J.B. (2003). "Borderland Worries: Loyalty Oaths in *Acadie*/Nova Scotia, 1654–1755." *French Colonial History* 4: 3–48.
Kamensky, Jane (1997). *Governing the Tongue: The Politics of Speech in Early New England*. Oxford University Press, New York.
Kamensky, Jane (2008). "Forum: Salem Repossessed," *William & Mary Quarterly* 65: 391–534.
Kawashima, Yasuhide (1986). *Puritan Justice and the Indian: White Man's Law in Massachusetts, 1630–1763*. Wesleyan University Press, Middletown, CT.
Kawashima, Yasuhide (2001). *Igniting King Philip's War: The John Sassamon Murder Trial*. University of Kansas Press, Lawrence, KS.
Kawashima, Yasuhide (2004). "Uncas's Struggle for Survival: The Mohegans and Connecticut Law in the Seventeenth Century." *Connecticut History* 43: 119–131.
Kellog, Susan (1995). *Law and the Transformation of Aztec Culture, 1500–1700*. University of Oklahoma Press, Norman.
Kermode, Jenny, ed. (1995). *Women, Crime and the Courts in Early Modern England*. University of North Carolina Press, Chapel Hill.
Kettner, James H. (1978). *The Development of American Citizenship, 1608–1870*. University of North Carolina Press, Chapel Hill.
Konig, David (1979). *Law and Society in Puritan Massachusetts: Essex County, 1628–1692*. University of North Carolina Press, Chapel Hill.
Konig, David (1982). "Dale's Law and the Non-Common Law Origins of Criminal Justice in Virginia." *American Journal of Legal History*. 26: 354–375.
Konig, David (1991). "Colonization and the Common Law in Ireland and Virginia, 1596–1637." In Henretta, Kammen and Katz, eds, *The Transformation of Early American History*, 70–92. Knopf, New York.
Koots, Christian J. (2011). *Empire at the Periphery: British Colonies, Anglo-Dutch Trade, and the Development of the British Atlantic*. New York University Press, New York.
Levy, Philip A., Payne, Jr., Samuel B., Grinde, Jr., David A. and Johnson, Bruce E., eds (1996). "Forum: The 'Iroqois Influence' Thesis – Con and Pro." *William & Mary Quarterly* 53: 587–636.
Lewis, Laura (2003). *Hall of Mirrors: Power, Witchcraft and Caste in Colonial Mexico*. Duke University Press, Durham.
MacMillan, Ken (2011). "Benign and Benevolent Conquest?: The Ideology of Elizabethan Atlantic Expansion Revisited." *Early American Studies* 9: 32–72.
Mann, Bruce H. (1987). *Neighbors and Strangers: Law and Community in Early Connecticut*. University of North Carolina Press, Chapel Hill.

McHugh, P.G. (2004). *Aboriginal Societies and the Common Law: A History of Sovereignty, Status and Self Determination.* Oxford University Press, Oxford.

McKinney, Michelle (2010). "Fractional Freedom: Slavery, Legal Activism, and Ecclesiastical Courts in Colonial Lima, 1593–1689." *Law and History Review* 28: 749–790.

McManus, Edgar J. (1993). *Law and Liberty in Early New England: Criminal Justice and Due Process, 1620–1692.* University of Massachusetts Press, Amherst.

Meranze, Michael (2008). "Penality and the Colonial Project: Crime, Punishment, and the Regulation of Morals in Early America," In Grossberg and Tomlins, eds, *Cambridge History of Law in America*, 1: 178–210. Cambridge University Press, New York.

Merry, Sally Engle (2010). "Colonial Law and Its Uncertainties." *Law & History Review* 28: 1067–1071.

Merwick, Donna (1999). *Death of a Notary: Conquest and Change in Colonial New York.* Cornell University Press, Ithaca.

Middleton, Simon (2010). "Order and Authority in New Netherland: The 1653 Remonstrance and Early Settlement Politics." *William & Mary Quarterly* 67: 31–68.

Miracle, Amanda Lea (2008). "Rape and Infanticide in Maryland, 1634–1689: Gender and Class in the Courtroom Contestation of Patriarchy on the Edge of the English Atlantic." Ph.D. diss. Bowling Green University, Bowling Green, OH.

Moogk, Peter (2000). *La Nouvelle France: The Making of French Canada – A Cultural History.* Michigan State University Press, East Lansing.

Moogk, Peter (2002). "The 'Others' Who Never Were: Eastern Woodlands Amerindian and Europeans in the Seventeenth Century." *French Colonial History* 1: 77–100.

Morgan, Edmund S. (1975). *American Slavery, American Freedom: The Ordeal of Colonial Virginia.* W.W. Norton, New York.

Morris, Richard B. (1946). *Government and Labor in Early America.* Columbia University Press, New York.

Nemmer, Howard (1977). *By Colour of Law: Legal Culture and Constitutional Politics in England, 1660–1689.* University of Chicago Press, Chicago.

Norton, Mary Beth (1996). *Founding Mothers and Fathers: Gendered Power and the Forming of American Society.* A.A. Knopf, New York.

O'Brien, Jean (2003). *Dispossession by Degrees: Indian Land and Identity in Natick, Massachusetts, 1650–1790.* Cambridge University Press, New York.

Oberholzer, Emil (1956). *Delinquent Saints: Disciplinary Action in the Early Congregational Churches of Massachusetts.* Columbia University Press, New York.

Offutt, Jr., William M (1995). *Of "Good Laws" & "Good Men:" Law and Society in the Delaware Valley, 1680–1710.* University of Illinois, Urbana.

Owensby, Brian P. (2008). *Empire of Law and Indian Justice in Colonial New Mexico.* Stanford University Press, Stanford.

Pagan, John Ruston (2002). *Anne Orthwood's Bastard: Sex and Law in Early Virginia.* Oxford University Press, New York.

Pagden, Anthony (1995). *Lords of All the World: Ideologies of Empire in Spain, Britain and France, c.1500–c.1800.* Yale University Press, New Haven.

Pagden, Anthony (2008). "Law, Colonization, Legitimation, and the European Background." In Grossberg and Tomlins, eds, *Cambridge History of Law in America: Early America*, 1: 1–31. Cambridge University Press, New York.

Pestana, Carla Gardina (2004). *Quakers and Baptists in Colonial Massachusetts*. Cambridge University Press, New York.

Plane, Ann Marie (2002). *Colonial Intimacies: Indian Marriage in Early New England*. Cornell University Press, Ithaca, NY.

Priest, Claire (2008). "Law and Commerce, 1580–1815." In Grossberg and Tomlins, eds, *Cambridge History of Law in America: Early America*, 1: 400–446. Cambridge University Press, New York.

Pulsipher, Jenny Hale (2005). *Subjects Unto the Same King: Indians, English and the Contest for Authority in Colonial New England*. University of Pennsylvania Press, Philadelphia.

Reinsch, Paul (1899). "The English Common Law in the Early American Colonies." In Jackson Turner, ed., *Bulletin of the University of Wisconsin Economic, Political Science and History Series*. University of Wisconsin Press, Madison.

Richardson, David (2001). "Shipboard Revolts, African Authority, and the Atlantic Slave Trade." *William and Mary Quarterly* 58: 69–92.

Roeber, A.G. (1981). *Faithful Magistrates and Republican Lawyers: Creators of Virginia Legal Culture, 1680–1810*. University of North Carolina Press, Chapel Hill.

Roeber, A.G. (1993). *Palatines, Liberty and Property: German Lutherans in Colonial America*. Johns Hopkins University Press, Baltimore.

Ross, Richard (2008). "The Career of Puritan Jurisprudence." *Law & History Review* 26: 227–258.

Snyder, Terri L. (2003). *Brabbling Women: Disorderly Speech and Law in Early Virginia*. Cornell University Press, Ithaca.

Steenburg, Nancy H. (2005). *Children and the Criminal Law in Connecticut 1635–1855: Changing Perceptions of Childhood*. Routledge Press, New York.

Stern, Philip J. (2006). "British Asia and British Atlantic: Comparisons and Connections." *William and Mary Quarterly* 63: 693–712.

Tomlins, Christopher (2001). "The Legal Cartography of Colonization, the Legal Polyphony of Settlement: English Intrusions on the American Mainland in the Seventeenth Century." *Law & Social Inquiry* 26: 315–372.

Tomlins, Christopher (2010). *Freedom Bound: Law, Labor and Civic Identity in Colonizing English America, 1580–1865*. Cambridge University Press, New York.

Tomlins, Christopher L. and Mann, Bruce H., eds (2001). *The Many Legalities of Early America*. University of North Carolina Press, Chapel Hill.

Valeri, Mark (1997). "Religious Discipline and the Market: Puritans and the Issue of Usury." *William & Mary Quarterly* 54: 747–765.

Watson, Alan (1989). *Slave Laws in the Americas*. University of Georgia Press, Athens.

Williams, Ian (2010). "'He Creditted More the Printed Book': Common Lawyers' Receptivity to Print, c. 1550–1640." *Law & History Review* 28: 39–70.

Winship, Michael P. (2005). *The Times and Trials of Anne Hutchinson: Puritans Divided*. University Press of Kansas, Lawrence, KS.

Wyatt-Brown, Bertram (1982). *Southern Honor: Ethics & Behavior in the Old South*. Oxford University Press, New York.

Further Reading

Cronon, William (1983). *Strangers in the Land: Indians, Colonists, and the Ecology of New England*. Hill and Wang, New York.

Fernandez, Angela (2005). "Record-Keeping and Other Troublemaking: Thomas Lechford and Law Reform in Colonial Massachusetts." *Law & History Review* 23: 235–277.

Goodwin, Everett (1981). *The Magistracy Reconsidered: Connecticut 1636–1815*. UMI Research Press, Ann Arbor.

Hadden, Sally (2008). "The Fragmentary Laws of Slavery in the Colonial and Revolutionary Eras." *Cambridge History of Law in America: Early America*. In Grossberg and Tomlins, eds, *Cambridge History of Law in America*, 1: 253–287. Cambridge University Press, New York.

Haskins, George Lee (1960). *Law and Authority in Early Massachusetts: A Study in Tradition and Design*. The MacMillan Co, New York.

Henretta, James, Kammen, Michael, and Katz, Stanley, eds (1991). *The Transformation of Early American History: Society, Authority and Ideology*. Knopf, New York.

Herrup, Cynthia B. (1987). *The Common Peace: Participation and the Criminal Law in Seventeenth-Century England*. Cambridge University Press, New York.

Jopp, Jennifer (1992). "'Kingly Government': English Law in Seventeenth-Century New York." Ph.D. diss. SUNY-Binghamton.

Katz, Stanley N., ed. (1993). "Symposium: Explaining the Law in Early American History." *William & Mary Quarterly* 50: 3–122.

McGarvie, Mark and Mensch, Elizabeth (2008). "Law and Religion in Colonial America." In Grossberg and Tomlins, eds, *Cambridge History of Law in America: Early America*, 1: 324–364. Cambridge University Press, New York.

Morris, Thomas D. (1996). *Southern Slavery and the Law, 1619–1860*. University of North Carolina Press, Chapel Hill.

Nelson, William E. (2008). *The Common Law in Colonial America, Volume I: The Chesapeake and New England, 1607–1660*. Oxford University Press, New York.

Parent, Anthony (2006). *Foul Means: The Formation of a Slave Society in Virginia*. University of North Carolina Press, Chapel Hill.

Schmidt, Benjamin (2001). *Innocence Abroad: The Dutch Imagination and the New World, 1570–1679*. Cambridge University Press, New York.

Seay, Scott D. (2009). *Hanging Between Heaven and Earth: Capital Crimes, Execution Preaching and Theology in Early New England*. Northern Illinois University Press, DeKalb, IL.

Tomlins, Christopher (1994). *Law, Labor and Ideology in the Early Republic*. Cambridge University Press, New York.

Walroth, Joanne Ruth (1987). "Beyond Legal Remedy: Divorce in Seventeenth Century Woodbridge, New Jersey." *New Jersey History* 105: 1–35.

Chapter Two

What's Done and Undone: Colonial American Legal History, 1700–1775

Sally E. Hadden

Introduction

Legal history written about the period between 1700 and 1775 seems to fall into a valley between two mountains that rise on either side of it. The 1600s intrigue researchers with their fresh beginnings in the New World and climax with the horrifying 1690s witchcraft trials, while the magical date 1775 signals the start of regime change – the building of a new nation, crafted by masterful Founding Fathers. Both "origins" have generated shelves of legal histories. However, the time between these two beginnings has not attracted the same level of attention, and no dominant narrative has emerged to shape the period's scholarship, though recent suggestive syntheses may push legal history in new directions (Tomlins and Mann, 2001; Grossberg and Tomlins, 2008). Two competing narrative possibilities drove most scholarship up through 2000, and historians tended to follow one or the other: the early eighteenth century was described as a period when the maturing *American* system took root (Nelson, 1975; LaCroix, 2010), or the legal system began to *Anglicize* and move closer to an English model already extant and thought to be better and therefore worthy of closer emulation (Murrin, 1966 White, 2012). A developmental mindset dominated both theories: if law in colonial America seemed like shoots of grass that emerged in the seventeenth century, then the blades began to sway in an eighteenth-century wind, as doctrines, courts, and their personnel moved toward one destiny (American) or another (English).

A Companion to American Legal History, First Edition.
Edited by Sally E. Hadden and Alfred L. Brophy.
© 2013 John Wiley & Sons Ltd. Published 2021 by John Wiley & Sons Ltd.

Nearly lost to these models is the incredible amount of change and increasing diversity being introduced in the American colonies during the early eighteenth century, principally through new arrivals, that might derail either linear narrative (both of which assumed a relatively static background upon which to operate). Immigration paired with natural increase meant that colonial America's population was doubling every twenty-five years, with large new groups joining the throng. Immigrants came in bursts, and tended to settle in clumps: the French Huguenots who migrated to New York and South Carolina starting in the 1690s, the flood of German-speaking immigrants who sailed for America in increasing numbers, and then a massive mid-century relocation of Scots and English settlers (Bailyn, 1986: 26). Nearly two hundred thousand immigrants arrived in the 1760s and 1770s alone, swelling the colonial population by almost a fifth (which grew from 1.2 million in 1750 to 2.5 million in 1775 from immigration and natural increase). Yet we know little about the regulations these multilingual immigrants encountered, the legal barriers they had to overcome (or evaded), and the choices they made about law once they were in America. Legal pluralism, with overlapping and sometimes contradictory systems of law for church, community, and colony, was their reality, yet the developmental models posited about this period generally overlook the variation connected with new arrivals, and often presume that these immigrants had little impact on the world of law – presumptively common law, presumptively English-based. With few exceptions, like David Narrett's study of inheritance in New York (1992), most recent work on colonial law in this period sees it as, at most, the result of negotiations between periphery and center, rather than adopting a pluralist approach that might accommodate immigrants from varied cultural backgrounds (Yirush, 2011).

A closer inspection of the literature about this period also reveals that, while Virginia and Massachusetts still dominate as the locations studied, over the past twenty years more geographically diverse studies have begun to appear (though more are needed). This trend is beginning to move the period 1700–1775 farther away from seventeenth-century studies, where legal histories have clumped together around the two commonwealths for decades. Similarly, recent scholarship covers a greater range of subjects using an increasing number of scholarly methods to study the period from 1700 to 1775, creating a smorgasbord effect that has simultaneously derailed the creation of an overarching narrative or theme to unite these diverse works. In this respect, early eighteenth-century legal history differs little from eighteenth-century history more generally: the fragmentation of historical studies has only accelerated since the 1960s. These somewhat promising signs of increased scholarship, however, remain overshadowed by the mountains of scholarship from before and after this period. Origins still attract; in-between periods still languish.

A survey of extant literature by region and then selected subjects will reveal these contours more precisely. Regional and even local variation was the rule, not the exception, for this period as it was for the seventeenth century (Nelson, 2008), but sweeping generalizations are often still proffered about all colonial legal history as if it were cut from a single bolt of cloth. Many topics still lack even a first investigator, leaving open many possibilities for future, fruitful research.

New England

Although New England from 1700 to 1775 has attracted the lion's share of attention from legal scholars in the past, that attention has not been evenly spread among colonies by any means. Massachusetts has had nearly three times the amount of scholarship devoted to its courts, defendants, judges, and attorneys than Rhode Island and Connecticut combined. Of course, Massachusetts had a larger population than the rest of New England and was home to Boston, a vital colonial seaport and the largest city in 1700. This partiality for scholars working in Massachusetts records can also be accounted for in other ways: Boston's multiple colonial newspapers provide the means to track newsworthy events that affected legal proceedings, like fire, epidemics, and economic dislocations. In addition, the Commonwealth of Massachusetts commenced a records preservation project in the 1970s that organized, catalogued, and made available at the archives in searchable form its legal records much sooner than other states did. The records deposited and cared for by the Commonwealth have several extremely easy research entry points, like Plymouth County's court records, partially transcribed from 1686 to 1859 (Konig, 1979–1981). Massachusetts legal history has added enticements that draw legal scholars to work in its records. It stood at the forefront of legal developments for the periods before and after 1700–1775: first, with its *Laws and Libertyes* in the seventeenth century, welding law to theology, then with its collection of Revolutionary leaders who helped propel the independence movement. The colony seemed to be a hive of legal activity after 1700: in the decades prior to the Revolution, men in the region seeking a legal education went to Boston before returning to their hometowns. Small wonder, then, that many scholars are drawn to Massachusetts to complete eighteenth-century projects.

Slowly, this unbalanced state of affairs in New England's legal history is changing. Online collections and new reference tools, like Chiorazzi and Most's survey of pre-statehood legal materials, make locating source material much easier (2005). Connecticut's early public records, including many statutes and special cases that required intervention by the legislature or governor, have been digitized and put online by the University of Connecticut (2000–present [1850–1890]). Detailed finding aids for

Litchfield and New London county courts have been posted by the Connecticut State Archives, and these supplement the work done by genealogists who have been slowly transcribing segments of legal records in virtually every colony, particularly vital records and probate (Connecticut [State], 2008). Maine's York county court records have been analyzed at the level of plaintiff, defendant, and type of case, with the results likewise uploaded for public access (Maine [State], 2007). These projects, though scattered, are harbingers of even more accessibility for archival legal materials via the Internet.

New England's legal history also benefits from several published comparative histories that transcend the boundaries of one colony. Daniel Cohen's *Pillars of Salt, Monuments of Grace* (1993) on the literature of crime is only one of the most recent to take New England as a whole for its field of study. Likewise, Martha McNamara's pioneering study, *From Tavern to Courthouse* (2004), on the physical structures of courthouses and courtrooms, is firmly rooted in the region. One of the strongest works that tackles the vexed issue of women's property in an age when *feme covert* appeared to triumph over all is Marylynn Salmon's *Women and the Law of Property in Early America* (1986), which remains a standard reference work not just for New England, but for all the colonies. The study of infanticide by Peter Hoffer and N.E.H. Hull, *Murdering Mothers* (1981), casts its net not just over all infanticide in New England, but those occurring in England as well.

However, if one subtracts legal scholarship about the single colony of Massachusetts, then legal history about the region fares badly. A single example reveals the scholarly gap. Consider studies about legal professionals, the lawyers and judges – not doctrine, not social or economic analysis of legal proceedings, but strictly personnel. In the past fifty years, monographs and articles on the subject abound for Massachusetts, from David Flaherty's insightful essay "Chief Justice Samuel Sewall, 1692–1728" (1989) to Peter Russell's much longer study of *His Majesty's Judges: Provincial Society and the Superior Court in Massachusetts, 1692–1774* (1990) and Russell Osgood's essay collection, *The History of Law in Massachusetts: The Supreme Judicial Court, 1692–1992* (1992), occasioned by the tricentennial of that bench. *Massachusetts Legal History* (an entire journal devoted to one state's legal history) published brief biographies of many of the chief justices who served on the high court prior to the Revolution. Multiple studies have been made of Boston-based lawyers: Gerard Gawalt (1979), John Murrin (1966), and Charles McKirdy (1969) have all examined eighteenth-century attorneys in the colony, though only Gawalt's work was ever published in full. Thorough considerations on the nature of the criminal practitioners' bar, and of specific justices of the peace, appeared as chapters in the titanic *Law in Colonial Massachusetts, 1630–1800* (Coquillette, Brink, and Menand, 1984), a collection that ran to nearly six hundred pages on the colony's legal history. All of this omits the publication of primary source materials about the

Massachusetts legal practices of John Adams, Robert Treat Paine, and Josiah Quincy (Wroth and Zobel, 1965; Riley and Hanson, 1992–present; Coquillette and Longley, 2005–2009). By contrast, consider the scholarship about nearby Connecticut and Rhode Island's legal professionals for the eighteenth century. Patrick T. Conley's 1998 volume on the bench and bar of Rhode Island aside, there has been little output on the subject, aside from scattered articles about individual men like Henry Marchant (Hadden and Minter, 2011). The best research on Rhode Island or Connecticut lawyers appeared in the larger, though long outdated, works by Anton-Hermann Chroust (1965) or Charles Warren (1911) on the American bar as a whole. A fine piece of scholarship on nearby early Maine's lawyers is Neal Allen's "Law and Authority to the Eastward: Maine Courts, Magistrates and Lawyers, 1690–1730," (1984) but it has not been followed by many in the same vein. Clearly, colonial Massachusetts has been the subject of the most in-depth studies on the topic of legal professionals (as well as many other legal topics); it will be a long time before the other mainland British colonies, much less the rest of New England, can compare.

The Mid-Atlantic

Second only to New England as a region, the Mid-Atlantic colonies have garnered considerable scholarship about their legal history. New York and Pennsylvania have roughly equivalent numbers of works published about their legal past, with Delaware and New Jersey bringing up the rear. The convoluted connections between lawyers, residents, and courts all sharing the Delaware Valley (comprised of Philadelphia's environs, Delaware's fertile valleys, and nearby Camden, New Jersey) may have contributed to the tendency to put Pennsylvania in the spotlight, while scholarship on the other two colonies is scanty – by describing activities in Philadelphia's courtrooms, scholars may have felt that their work contributed to the overall quantum of knowledge created about neighboring Delaware and New Jersey.

Philadelphia and New York's predominance in scholarship tracks along similar lines to that of Massachusetts, in that both were thriving eighteenth-century ports with a bustling trade to the interior and across the Atlantic. The early history of New York as a Dutch outpost may have stunted legal history scholarship on the colony in the seventeenth century (leaving aside Merwick, 1999 and Narrett, 1992), due to language difficulties for modern-day scholars. In the eighteenth century, however, New York's courts, crime, plaintiffs, and lawyers have all received thorough attention (Hershkowitz and Klein, 1978). Sung Bok Kim's study of property relations in New York thoroughly explains the somewhat unusual manor landholding system that thrived for a time in that colony (1978). Deborah Rosen has considered courts high and low, exploring the Supreme Court of

Judicature in the colony as well the Mayor's Court of New York City (1987, 1997). More recently, Simon Middleton utilized the archives of the Mayor's Court, analyzing legal documents that reveal artisan mentalities about work and demonstrate convincingly the many ties that bound even unskilled labourers to the transatlantic economy (2006). Douglas Greenberg (1976) updated and expanded the Goebel and McNaughton 1944 criminal justice study, giving us the biggest, most complete inquiry into crime and criminal procedure of any colony until the appearance of Marietta and Rowe (2006). The specifics of a particular criminal trial as it relates to the largest colonial slave insurrection have been explored in *The Great New York Conspiracy of 1741* (Hoffer, 2003). The law papers of Alexander Hamilton are published (Goebel and Smith, 1964–1981), though in comparison to Boston, New York's attorneys still seem to run a distant second for primary sources in print. And Daniel Hulsebosch's (2005) sweeping work comparing the intellectual worlds of empire builders and theorizers, with New York as its base, demonstrates convincingly that legal and real conceptions of empire differed remarkably in England, New York City, and New York's hinterland. Property, courts, crime, labor, conspiracies, lawyers – New York's riches have been sounded on a wide variety of legal history topics for the first three-quarters of the eighteenth century.

By contrast, New Jersey and Delaware have not attracted the sort of sustained attention from legal history scholars that their histories might warrant. Aside from William Offutt's excellent *Of Good Laws and Good Men* on the nimbus of courts surrounding Philadelphia proper (1995), legal history about smaller colonies in the region has positively languished. However, an excellent study of property disputes in the 1740s and 1750s in New Jersey, written by Brendan McConville (1999), indicates that New Jersey has much to reveal to the proper investigation. McConville attacked the claims that Anglicization was a process firmly in place by 1776 by demonstrating how ideas of property were contested, in and out of the courtroom, depending upon one's status and wealth in New Jersey society.

Pennsylvania's courts and plaintiffs have been the subject of numerous works – again, in part driven by the principal importance of its major sea port, Philadelphia – yet when compared with New York, legal histories on Pennsylvania are simply not as numerous. This may have something to do with the dreadful state of legal records in the Philadelphia city archives, but it may also be connected to the relative paucity of lawyers' papers to flesh out tribunal proceedings. Papers of major figures, such as John Dickinson and Benjamin Chew, are scattered and unpublished (a newly commenced project at the University of Kentucky promises to rectify this situation for Dickinson); links between Dickinson's legal mentality and predominant Quaker ideals in the period have only recently been explored (Calvert, 2009). The settlement of large numbers of German-speaking settlers into the colony during the eighteenth century, who mainly opted out of the

English-run legal system, may have created some linguistic barriers to research, although A.G. Roeber's masterful *Palatines, Liberty, and Property* (1998) offers an exceptional example of how one scholar has tracked changes in language and meaning about legal concepts on both sides of the Atlantic. Roeber demonstrates the connections between pre-existing European ideas about liberty and property with views held by recently-arrived German speakers in Pennsylvania during this period (1998). Al Brophy's careful work on indentured servants in Pennsylvania helps us consider the legal dilemmas facing individuals who were only temporarily unfree (1991) and deserves to be emulated in other colonies, considering the prevalence of indentures in the period (Daniels, 2001; Snyder, 2011). A top-down study of the colony's Supreme Court (Rowe, 1994) suggests that it played an instrumental role in building democratic sentiment in Pennsylvania, although that claim may be overly broad. Rowe joined forces with Jack Marietta to publish the magisterial *Troubled Experiment*, a full and detailed examination of crime in Pennsylvania that builds upon the Ohio State University Historical Violence Database (2006). Marietta's interest in the colony is a long-standing one; twenty years earlier he published *The Reformation of American Quakerism, 1748–1783* (1984), which demonstrated that Quakers privately adjudicated disputes among themselves rather than resort to public courts where such conflicts could bring the Society of Friends into disrepute. Studies such as this indicate the continuing need to examine regional and local variations during this period, particularly for tightly-knit religious communities.

Upper and Lower South

Works about the Upper South in this period outnumber those on the Lower South by nearly four to one. In part, this fascination can be explained by the excellent record-keeping practices of Virginians and Marylanders, where the archives have worked to transcribe (with the Works Progress Administration's (WPA) assistance) or to upload to the Internet their earliest legal records, as Maryland has largely done (Maryland [State], 2009). One would surmise that Virginia and South Carolina would have roughly equivalent numbers of legal histories written about them, having been long settled by the year 1700 and both economically important within the region. However, the huge gaps in criminal and civil court records for Charleston through the eighteenth century have caused legal scholars to shy away from conducting research there. Other southern colonies, like North Carolina and Georgia, were not densely settled in the early eighteenth century, and thus generated fewer records of all types. Exceptions stick out: a key study on Georgia land law and surveying in the period is essential reading for those who would understand basic property practices of the period (Cadle, 1991). Nonetheless, the ease of accessing many early Virginia records in WPA transcript form, or online from Maryland's State Archives, is likely to foster this continued imbalance in scholarly output, although North Carolina's early court records were also partially transcribed by the WPA – historians simply have not delved into its records as often as Virginia's or Maryland's. Probate inventories in Georgia and dower renunciations in South Carolina have also been partially transcribed by the WPA, which may encourage future legal historians to examine those records for buried treasure.

The story is somewhat different for Florida and Louisiana, long-time colonies of the Spanish and French empires for much of the eighteenth century. Language barriers and difficulty working with records not generated by a common law system have kept many scholars away from these rich and diverse colonies. Jane Landers (1999) and Susan Richbourg Parker (1999, 2013) lead the few who have explored Florida archives' Spanish legal records. Likewise, only a handful of scholars have worked with Louisiana's legal records, and they have tended to work thematically (Haas, 1983). Thomas Ingersoll (1999, 2013) and Jennifer Spear (2009, 2013) have examined the law of status, particularly for slavery and gender, in their multiple works. Areas west of Louisiana, considered part of Northern New Spain in the eighteenth century, have been the subject of several studies by Charles Cutter (1986, 1995) and James Brooks (2001). All of these scholars have emphasized the contingent, negotiated quality of law as a force in colonial societies where little was certain.

Specific courts and the attorneys who worked in them have been the focus of many scholars working on the South. A fine study of the Maryland admiralty court in this period appeared in 1995 (Owen and Tolley), while older work permits direct access to records of the South Carolina Court of Chancery and the General Court of Virginia (Gregorie, 1950; Barton, 1909). The American Historical Association sponsored the publication of such source volumes for a time, like the one pairing records of criminal trials in Richmond with an explanatory essay; one only wishes more had been published (Hoffer and Scott, 1984; Bond, 1933; Morris, 1935; Towle, 1936). Interpreting the raw data produced by courts is essential, but weaving together the cases with their cultural meaning at large, in terms of what court day meant to colonial society as a whole, is at the center of Rhys Isaac's prize-winning study *The Transformation of Virginia* (1988). The largely administrative burdens taken on at the county court level have been admirably explained by Gwenda Morgan (1989). Attorneys have likewise attracted significant attention in southern colonies (Roeber, 1981; Canady, 1987). Even the law books that were available to lawyers and judges in the colonial period have been examined and listed (Bryson, 1978; Johnson, 1978), though we have less information about the acquisition and circulation of those texts. In Maryland, Douglass has examined the diverse legal practitioners who made up Maryland's early bar (1995).

The overwhelming impression one is left with, however, after examining the published works of legal history for this period, is that the South has far fewer legal history studies on any topic than either New England or the Mid-Atlantic regions. If one omitted studies published about Virginia, the ranks would be thin indeed. Yet we know that southern lawyers often had access to equity courts, when those institutions were much rarer in the North (Katz, 1971; Hoffer, 1990). Many legal practices set the South apart from other regions, but awareness of regional variation seems to draw legal historians to one topic repeatedly, rather than to many. In one area only does southern legal history have a generous number of interpreters: colonial slavery.

Special Topics: Slavery, Women, Crime and Violence, Comparisons

Some specific subject areas have attracted repeated attention from legal historians working on the period 1700–1775, driven in part by concerns for individuals disempowered by the law. In particular, the intersection between slavery and the law has had a sizeable group of scholars interested since the 1960s. A seminal study is Philip Schwarz's *Twice Condemned* (1988), analyzing the criminal laws enforced in Virginia before and after transportation provided an alternative to execution. Although it devotes greater attention to the period after the American Revolution than the era before it, Thomas Morris' encyclopedic approach to *Southern Slavery and the Law* should also be consulted (1996). Recently, work by Glenn McNair (2009), Sue Peabody and Keila Grinberg (2007, 2008) has explored how laws and courts restricted the freedoms of slaves and free blacks in a variety of southern and Caribbean settings (Watson, 1989). More scholars seem drawn to the origins of slave laws in the colonies rather than their changing application through the eighteenth century, assuming that enforcement follows enactment (Hadden, 2008). A greater focus upon the role played by custom might correct this assumption (Giusto, forthcoming).

Another area that shows no sign of a slow-down in scholarly production is the subject of women and the law. Among the numerous works that have appeared in the last twenty-five years, studies of unusual women – the never married, the divorced, the widowed – have been published in the largest numbers (Shammas, 1995; Smith, 1995; Conger, 2009; Narrett, 1992; Biemer, 1983). The independence of women with property in Virginia and Philadelphia – women who managed to avoid *feme covert* or found ways around it – has been the subject of thorough investigations by Linda Sturtz (2002), John Kolp and Terri Snyder (2001), and Karin Wulf (2000). Many authors have tackled aspects of dower, women's crime, and domestic relations but much remains to be done (Ditz, 1986; Rowe, 1985; Gunderson and Gampel, 1982). Two of the most interesting works in this area have considered women's appearances in court for all reasons: Cornelia Dayton's *Women before the Bar*, focusing upon New Haven, Connecticut (1995), and Ruth Bloch's exploration of laws relating to courtship (2003).

Studies of crime likewise continue to appear with regularity, driven perhaps in part by the much smaller numbers of criminal cases available for analysis in the period, as well as the potential for linking social deviancy or moral objections to flouted but dominant societal norms. N.E.H. Hull's work on women and serious crime in colonial Massachusetts remains a starting point for much of this literature (1987). Donna Spindel's survey of crime in North Carolina does not push the envelope very much, simply cataloguing which crimes were committed in what numbers during particular decades, but this sort of groundwork is needed for every colony before synthetic studies become possible (1989). Richard Gaskins' early publication on changes in the criminal law in eighteenth-century Connecticut remains one of the few to consider how the criminal law altered during the century, rather than remaining static (1981). Linda Kealey, adopting a more fixed approach, described the patterns of punishment that were meted out in Massachusetts (1986). Elaine Crane's study of criminal deviants (murderers, whores, and abusers), though not comparative, considers specific trials in multiple colonies to illustrate more general themes (2011). How violence intertwined with authority, law, race, and gender was the subject of a special conference in 2001 that resulted in a volume devoted to unrest in multiple colonial settings (Smolenski and Humphrey, 2005).

Another area that should attract greater attention is the comparative context, putting colonial America's legal history into the setting of the Atlantic world, or at least considering it in more than one imperial framework. Early work by John P. Reid comparing the law in mainland North American colonies with the legal regime in Ireland took a long time to inspire later scholars to consider the comparative case (1977). Although the best comparative work in this period is by Lauren Benton and Sue Peabody, much remains to be done because few scholars work comparatively (Benton, 2002 Peabody, 2008). Each of the colonies, regardless of the legal history topic, still largely stands on its own, in relative isolation from the others. A very few works have attempted to span the gaps between colonies: noteworthy exceptions include studies by Michael Hindus (1980), Carol Karlsen (1987), and Hugh Amory and David Hall on crime, witchcraft persecution, and the spread of legal texts in early America (Amory and Hall, 2007). Any work done on legal texts printed in the colonies now must begin by consulting the magisterial work of Morris Cohen, *Bibliography of Early American Laws* (1998), which promises to support much comparative scholarship in the future.

Trends

There are many relatively untouched areas in the eighteenth century still waiting for the attention of some willing legal historian. Foremost among them are environmental law, the legal cultures of non-English-speaking immigrants in colonial America (German, Dutch, French, and others), arbitration and commercial law (particularly in the comparative context), church-based dispute settlement, and Native Americans outside of New England. Even basic work on contracts, property, and crime in many of the colonies remains to be written: New Hampshire, Vermont, Delaware, and Georgia are practically untouched for virtually every legal history topic.

Two recent collections and one new monograph have become essential starting points for legal historians of the eighteenth century looking for innovative project designs and cutting edge research. *The Many Legalities of Early America*, edited by Tomlins and Mann (2001), and a broad synthetic work, the *Cambridge History of Law in America*, edited by Grossberg and Tomlins (2008), offer the reader topical treatments of colonial American legal history that cover much ground. In 2010, Tomlins' *Freedom Bound* offered a stirring integration of immigration, labor, and legal history, while setting out an agenda for future research (see Desan chapter in this volume for more on Tomlins 2010). Together, these collections should spur future research in the period across a wide range of topics.

Among its many fine chapters, the *Many Legalities* volume had three in particular that touch upon Native American law, written by Ann Marie Plane, Katherine Hermes, and James Brooks. While differing in approach and conclusions, the overall connective tissue between them makes them stand together as a group. Brooks wrote about customary justice as a restraining device in relations between Native peoples and the Spanish authorities of the Southwest. Plane focused upon marriage laws and legal pluralism among the Narragansett in eighteenth-century Rhode Island (aligned with her work in *Colonial Intimacies*, 2000). Katherine Hermes described the expectations of reciprocity held by the Algonquian and, in particular, their beliefs about justice and European judges. All three essays relied to a greater or lesser extent upon ethnographic methods. Their emphasis upon custom and legal pluralism provides important models for scholars yet to come, and reinforces the need to peer beyond statutes to discover more about customary practices on the ground.

These three essays exemplify the largely shared qualities to be found in legalities, as Tomlins described them, rather than just law. Where law might seem universal, timeless, and self-legitimating, legalities were plastic rather than static. Colonial legalities seemed "fragile and contingent," giving way with regularity rather than enduring as unchanging monoliths. And "multiple cultures mean[t] multiple legalities." This nod in the direction of legal pluralism, with its overlapping and sometimes conflicting systems, is nonetheless a broader concept, for legalities could be found not just in official legal practice but in "any repetitive practice of wide acceptance within a specific locale, call the result rule, custom, tradition, folkway or pastime, popular belief or protest" (2001: 2–3, 9). In the ebb and flow of the eighteenth century, with its rapidly changing populace, such an interpretive stance seems persuasive, more so than the polestars of Anglicization or Americanization. It was a time less given to linear progressive qualities than some might wish.

A further observation by Tomlins in *Many Legalities* is instructive. In the introduction, he stressed that "as a field of study, early American legal history has remained wedded more to detail than to worldview" (2001: 9). It has not managed to force a reconception of early American history (although Tomlins himself strove to create that more sweeping narrative with *Freedom Bound* (2010)), nor has it overcome its valley-like status as a poor relation in the story of American law writ large. This focus upon detail is, in part, a reflection of how many essential studies for the period have yet to be written: the ones that are complete have dug into the detail, giving their work solidity if not transcendent meaning.

Even essayists who contributed to the one synthetic work that has appeared, the 2008 *Cambridge History of Law in America*, readily admit that there are portions of the law where enough is simply not known to say anything conclusive. Katherine Hermes' excellent essay on Native Americans and legal history for the seventeenth and eighteenth centuries states that "No historian has ever attempted a narrative of indigenous American jurisprudence" (2008: 32). Michael Meranze notes that while many studies have been made about colonial crime, "no overall synthesis or framework for continuing research exists" and the field is "in need of new efforts of analytical and comparative synthesis" (2008: 630). These and other plaintive cries are not the usual chorus of "we don't know enough" often heard from historians regardless of topic or period – for legal history in the eighteenth century, these folks are telling the truth. There are simply not enough colony- or region-level studies completed to permit synthesis to move forward except on the most basic level, because so many colonies have yet to have their legal records tapped. And our willingness to rely upon Blackstone's 1765 *Commentaries* to act as a substitute for local investigation has blinded us to the fact that there was regional variation, that sometimes "Blackstone hides change", which gives some historians the misguided sense that the colonial legal world was more unified than it actually was (Brewer, 2008).

The best overview of colonial legal development in this period is David Konig's essay, "Regionalism in Early American Law" (2008), which emphasizes the distinctive variations in colonial America's legal historical reality. No longer enraptured by New England or Virginia, legal historians of the eighteenth century are beginning to see the need to move beyond those areas into fertile ground that has remained largely untilled, following earlier suggestions in this vein made by John Phillip Reid (1977), Hendrik Hartog (1981), and Stanley Katz (1984). Konig's essay provides a roadmap to the future of legal history for this period: we need to forget about creating a unified legal history that applies in all regions, regardless of fit. Likewise, we need to stop seeing slavery as the great North-South divide and the only regional difference worth investigating, particularly since slavery in this era was more universally accepted than scorned (Hadden, 2008). As one pair of authors have phrased it, "the cultural change experienced by the peoples of the Atlantic basin – whether called creolization, ethnogenesis, Anglicization, or the growth of nationalism – requires that scholars step back from typologies based on generalizations about various national-imperial Atlantic experiences." The cultural transformations individuals experienced from 1700 to 1775 were "fundamentally driven by local variables" (Sidbury and Cañizares-Esguerra, 2011: 184) and that regional or local focus must inform scholarship about their relationship with and use of law. Investigating regional variation and legal pluralism or legalities is how legal histories for this period will move forward in decades to come.

References

Allen, Neal W. (1984). "Law and Authority to the Eastward: Maine Courts, Magistrates and Lawyers, 1690–1830." In Coquillette, Brink, and Menand, eds, *Law in Colonial Massachusetts, 1630–1800*, 273–312. Colonial Society of Massachusetts, Boston.

Amory, Hugh and Hall, David D., eds (2007). *The Colonial Book in the Atlantic World*. University of North Carolina Press in association with the American Antiquarian Society, Chapel Hill.

Bailyn, Bernard (1986). *Voyagers to the West: A Passage in the Peopling of America on the Eve of the Revolution*. Knopf, New York.

Barton, R.T., ed. (1909). *Virginia Colonial Decisions: The Reports by Sir John Randolph and by Edward Barradall of Decisions of the General Court of Virginia, 1727–1741*. 2 volumes. Boston Book Company, Boston.

Benton, Lauren (2002). *Law and Colonial Cultures: Legal Regimes in World History, 1400–1900*. Cambridge University Press, Cambridge, UK.

Biemer, Linda (1983). *Women and Property in Colonial New York*. UMI Research Press, Ann Arbor.

Bloch, Ruth (2003). "Regulating courtship: women and the law of courtship in eighteenth century America." In Ruth Bloch, *Gender and Morality in Anglo-American Culture, 1650–1800*. University of California Press, Berkeley.

Bond, Carroll, ed. (1933). *Proceedings of the Maryland Court of Appeals: 1695–1729*. American Historical Association, Washington.

Brewer, Holly (2008). "The Transformation of Domestic Law." In Grossberg and Tomlins, eds, *The Cambridge History of Law in America. Volume I Early America (1580–1815)*, 288–323. Cambridge University Press, New York.

Brooks, James F. (2001). "'Lest We Go in Search of Relief to Our Lands and Our Nation': Customary Justice and Colonial Law in the New Mexico Borderlands, 1680–1821." In Tomlins and Mann, eds, *The Many Legalities of Early America*, 150–180. University of North Carolina Press, Chapel Hill.

Brophy, Alfred (1991). "Law and Indentured Servitude in Mid-Eighteenth Century Pennsylvania." *Willamette Law Review* 28: 69–126.

Bryson, W. Hamilton (1978). *Census of Law Books in Colonial Virginia*. University Press of Virginia, Charlottesville.

Cadle, Farris (1991). *Georgia Land Surveying History and Law*. University of Georgia Press, Athens.

Calvert, Jane (2009). *Quaker Constitutionalism and the Political Thought of John Dickinson*. Cambridge University Press, Cambridge, UK.

Canady, Hoyt P. (1987). *Gentlemen of the Bar: Lawyers in Colonial South Carolina*. Garland, New York.

Chiorazzi, Michael and Most, Marguerite, eds (2005). *Pre-Statehood Legal Materials: A Fifty-State Research Guide, Including New York City and the District of Columbia*. 2 volumes. Haworth Information Press, New York.

Chroust, Anton-Hermann (1965). *The Rise of the Legal Profession in America*. 2 volumes. University of Oklahoma Press, Norman.

Cohen, Daniel A. (1993). *Pillars of Salt, Monuments of Grace: New England Crime Literature and the Origins of American Popular Culture, 1674–1860*. Oxford University Press, New York.

Cohen, Morris (1998). *Bibliography of Early American Laws*. 6 volumes. William S. Hein, Buffalo.

Conger, Vivian (2009). *The Widows' Might: Widowhood and Gender in Early British America*. New York University Press, New York.

Conley, Patrick T. (1998). *Liberty and Justice: A History of Law and Lawyers in Rhode Island, 1636–1998*. Rhode Island Publications Society, East Providence.

Connecticut (Colony) (2000–present [1850–1890]). *The Public Records of the Colony of Connecticut, from April 1636 to October 1776 ... transcribed and published, (in accordance with a resolution of the General assembly)*. 15 volumes. Brown & Parsons, Hartford. (last accessed October 5, 2012).

Connecticut (State) (2008 [1751–1855]). RG 003, Litchfield County, County Court Files Inventory of Records (finding aid prepared by Debra Pond) and RG 003, New London, County Court Files Inventory of Records (finding aid prepared by Bruce Stark). Connecticut State Library, Connecticut. http://www.cslib.org (last accessed October 5, 2012).

Coquillette, Daniel, Brink, Robert, and Menand, Catherine, eds (1984). *Law in Colonial Massachusetts, 1630–1800*. Colonial Society of Massachusetts, Boston.

Coquillette, Daniel and Longley, Neil, eds (2005–2009). *Portrait of a Patriot: The Major Political and Legal Papers of Josiah Quincy*. 5 volumes. Colonial Society of Massachusetts, Boston.

Crane, Elaine Forman (2011). *Witches, Wife Beaters, and Whores: Common Law and Common Folk in Early America*. Cornell University Press, Ithaca.

Cutter, Charles (1986). *The Protector de los Indios in Colonial New Mexico, 1659–1821*. University of New Mexico Press, Albuquerque.

Cutter, Charles (1995). *The Legal Culture of Northern New Spain, 1700–1810.* University of New Mexico Press, Albuquerque.

Daniels, Christine (2001). "'Liberty to Complaine': Servant Petitions in Maryland, 1652–1797." In Tomlins and Mann, eds, *The Many Legalities of Early America,* 219–249. University of North Carolina Press, Chapel Hill.

Dayton, Cornelia (1995). *Women Before the Bar: Gender, Law, and Society in Colonial Connecticut, 1639–1789.* University of North Carolina Press, Chapel Hill.

Ditz, Toby (1986). *Property and Kinship: Inheritance in Early Connecticut, 1750–1820.* Princeton University Press, Princeton.

Douglass, John E. (1995). "Between Pettifoggers and Professionals: Pleaders and Practitioners and the Beginning of the Legal Profession in Colonial Maryland, 1634–1731." *American Journal of Legal History* 39: 359–384.

Flaherty, David (1989). "Chief Justice Samuel Sewall, 1692–1728." In Pencak and Holt, eds, *The Law in America, 1607–1861,* 114–54. New York Historical Society, New York.

Gaskins, Richard (1981). "Changes in the Criminal Law in Eighteenth-Century Connecticut." *American Journal of Legal History* 25: 309–342.

Gawalt, Gerard (1979). *The Promise of Power: The Emergence of the Legal Profession in Massachusetts, 1760–1840.* Greenwood Press, Westport.

Giusto, Heidi (forthcoming). "'Enemies Foreign and Domestic': War, Slavery, and the Legal Culture of Atlantic South Carolina." Ph.D. diss., Duke University.

Goebel, Julius G. and Naughton, T. Raymond (1970 [1944]). *Law Enforcement in Colonial New York: A Study in Criminal Procedure (1664–1776).* Patterson Smith, Montclair, NJ.

Goebel, Julius G. and Smith, Joseph H., eds (1964–1981). *The Law Practice of Alexander Hamilton: Documents and Commentary.* 5 volumes. Columbia University Press, New York.

Greenberg, Douglas (1976). *Crime and Law Enforcement in the Colony of New York, 1691–1776.* Cornell University Press, Ithaca.

Gregorie, Anne King, ed. (1950). *Records of the Court of Chancery of South Carolina, 1671–1779.* American Historical Association, Washington.

Grossberg, Michael, and Tomlins, Christopher, eds (2008). *The Cambridge History of Law in America.* 3 volumes. Cambridge University Press, Cambridge, UK.

Gunderson, Joan and Gampel, Gwen (1982). "Married Women's Legal Status in Eighteenth Century New York and Virginia." *William and Mary Quarterly* 3rd series 39: 114–133.

Haas, Edward F., ed. (1983). *Louisiana's Legal Heritage.* Perdido Bay Press for the Louisiana State Museum, Pensacola.

Hadden, Sally (2008). "The Fragmented Laws of Slavery in the Colonial and Revolutionary Eras." In Grossberg and Tomlins, eds, *The Cambridge History of Law in America. Volume I Early America (1580–1815),* 253–287. Cambridge University Press, New York.

Hadden, Sally and Minter, Patricia H. (2011). "A Legal Tourist Visits Eighteenth-Century Britain: Henry Marchant's Observations on British Courts, 1771–1772." *Law and History Review* 29: 133–179.

Hadden, Sally and Minter, Patricia H., eds (2013). *Signposts: New Directions in Southern Legal History.* University of Georgia Press, Athens.

Hartog, Hendrik (1981). "Losing the World of the Massachusetts Whig." In Hartog, ed., *Law in the American Revolution and the Revolution in the Law: A Collection of Review Essays on American Legal History*, 143–166. New York University Press, New York.

Hermes, Katherine A. (2001). "'Justice Will Be Done Us': Algonquian Demands for Reciprocity in the Courts of European Settlers." In Tomlins and Mann, eds, *The Many Legalities of Early America*, 123–149. University of North Carolina Press, Chapel Hill.

Hermes, Katherine A. (2008). "The Law of Native Americans, to 1815." In Grossberg and Tomlins, eds, *The Cambridge History of Law in America. Volume I Early America (1580–1815)*, 32–62. Cambridge University Press, New York.

Hershkowitz, Leo and Klein, Milton M., eds (1978). *Courts and Law in Early New York*. Kennikat Press, Port Washington, NY.

Hindus, Michael (1980). *Prison and Plantation: Crime, Justice, and Authority in Massachusetts and South Carolina, 1767–1878*. University of North Carolina Press, Chapel Hill.

Hoffer, Peter C. (1990). *The Law's Conscience: Equitable Constitutionalism in America*. University of North Carolina Press, Chapel Hill.

Hoffer, Peter C. (2003). *The Great New York Conspiracy of 1741: Slavery, Crime and Colonial Law*. University Press of Kansas, Lawrence.

Hoffer, Peter C. and Hull, N.E.H. (1981). *Murdering Mothers: Infanticide in England and New England, 1558–1803*. New York University Press, New York.

Hoffer, Peter C. and Scott, William B., eds (1984). *Criminal Proceedings in Colonial Virginia*. University of Georgia Press, American Historical Association, Athens.

Hull, N.E.H. (1987). *Female Felons: Women and Serious Crime in Colonial Massachusetts*. University of Illinois Press, Urbana.

Hulsebosch, Daniel (2005). *Constituting Empire: New York and the Transformation of Constitutionalism in the Atlantic World, 1664–1830*. University of North Carolina Press, Chapel Hill.

Ingersoll, Thomas (1999). *Mammon and Manon in Early New Orleans: The First Slave Society in the Deep South, 1719–1819*. University of Tennessee Press, Knoxville.

Ingersoll, Thomas (2013). "The Law and Order Campaign in New Orleans in 1763–65: A Comparative View." In Hadden and Minter, eds, *Signposts: New Directions in Southern Legal History*, 45–64.

Isaac, Rhys (1988). *The Transformation of Virginia, 1740–1790*. W.W. Norton, New York.

Johnson, Herbert (1978). *Imported Eighteenth-Century Law Treatises in American Libraries, 1700–1799*. University of Tennessee Press, Knoxville.

Karlsen, Carol (1987). *The Devil in the Shape of a Woman: Witchcraft in Colonial New England*. W.W. Norton, New York.

Katz, Stanley (1971). "The Politics of Law in Colonial America: Controversies over Chancery Courts and Equity Law in the Eighteenth Century." *Perspectives in American History* 5: 257–286.

Katz, Stanley (1984). "The Problem of a Colonial Legal History." In Greene and Pole, eds, *Colonial British America: Essays in the New History of the Early Modern Era*, 457–489. Johns Hopkins University Press, Baltimore.

Kealey, Linda (1986). "Patterns of Punishment: Massachusetts in the Eighteenth Century." *American Journal of Legal History* 30: 163–186.

Kim, Sung Bok (1978). *Landlord and Tenant in Colonial New York: Manorial Society, 1664–1775*. University of North Carolina Press, Chapel Hill.

Kolp, John G. and Snyder, Terri L. (2001). "Women and the Political Culture of Eighteenth-Century Virginia: Gender, Property Law, and Voting Rights." In Tomlins and Mann, eds, *The Many Legalities of Early America*, 272–292. University of North Carolina Press, Chapel Hill.

Konig, David T., ed. (1979–1981). *The Plymouth Court Records, 1686–1859*. 16 volumes. M. Glazier, Wilmington, DE.

Konig, David T. (2008). "Regionalism in Early American Law." In Grossberg and Tomlins, eds, *The Cambridge History of Law in America. Volume I Early America (1580–1815)*, 144–177. Cambridge University Press, New York.

LaCroix, Alison (2010). *The Ideological Origins of American Federalism*. Harvard University Press, Cambridge, MA.

Landers, Jane (1999). *Black Society in Spanish Florida*. University of Illinois Press, Urbana.

Maine (State) (2007). *Courts, 1696–1854*. (MS-Excel 97 format). http://www.maine.gov/sos/arc/databases/index.html#CTS (last accessed September 25, 2012)

Marietta, Jack (1984). *The Reformation of American Quakerism, 1748–1783*. University of Pennsylvania Press, Philadelphia.

Marietta, Jack and Rowe, G.S. (2006). *Troubled Experiment: Crime and Justice in Pennsylvania, 1682–1800*. University of Pennsylvania Press, Philadelphia.

Maryland State Archives (2009 [1883–1972]) *Archives of Maryland*. 72 volumes. Baltimore: Maryland Historical Society. http://www.aomol.net/html/index.html (last accessed September 25, 2012)

Massachusetts Legal History (successor to *Supreme Judicial Court Historical Society Journal*) (1997–present). Boston: Supreme Judicial Court Historical Society.

McConville, Brendan (1999). *These Daring Disturbers of the Public Peace: The Struggle for Property and Power in Early New Jersey*. Cornell University Press, Ithaca.

McKirdy, Charles (1969). "Lawyers in crisis: the Massachusetts legal profession, 1760–1790." Ph.D. diss., Northwestern University.

McNair, Glenn (2009). *Criminal Injustice: Slaves and Free blacks in Georgia's Criminal Justice System*. University of Virginia Press, Charlottesville.

McNamara, Martha J. (2004). *From Tavern to Courthouse: Architecture and Ritual in American Law, 1658–1860*. Johns Hopkins University Press, Baltimore.

Meranze, Michael (2008). "Penality and the Colonial Project: Crime, Punishment, and the Regulation of Morals in Early America." In Grossberg and Tomlins, eds, *The Cambridge History of Law in America. Volume I Early America (1580–1815)*, 178–210. Cambridge University Press, New York.

Merwick, Donna (1999). *Death of a Notary: Conquest and Change in Colonial New York*. Cornell University Press, Ithaca.

Middleton, Simon (2006). *From Privileges to Rights: Work and Politics in Colonial New York City*. University of Pennsylvania Press, Philadelphia.

Morgan, Gwenda (1989). *The Hegemony of the Law: Richmond County, Virginia, 1692–1776*. Garland, New York.

Morris, Richard B. (1935). *Selected Cases of the Mayor's Court of New York City, 1674–1784*. American Historical Association, Washington.

Morris, Thomas D. (1996). *Southern Slavery and the Law: 1619–1860*. University of North Carolina Press, Chapel Hill.

Murrin, John (1966). "Anglicizing an American colony: the transformation of provincial Massachusetts." Ph.D. diss., Yale University.

Narrett, David (1992). *Inheritance and Family Life in Colonial New York City*. Cornell University Press, Ithaca.

Nelson, William E. (1975). *The Americanization of the Common Law: The Impact of Legal Change on Massachusetts Society, 1760–1830*. Harvard University Press, Cambridge.

Nelson, William E. (2008). *The Common Law in Colonial America: Volume I: The Chesapeake and New England 1607–1660*. Oxford University Press, 2008, New York.

Offutt, William (1995). *"Of Good Laws and Good Men": Law and Society in the Delaware Valley, 1680–1710*. University of Illinois Press, Urbana.

Osgood, Russell, ed. (1992). *The History of Law in Massachusetts: The Supreme Judicial Court, 1692–1992*. Supreme Judicial Court Historical Society, Boston.

Owen, David R. and Trolley, Michael C. (1995). *Courts of Admiralty in Colonial America: The Maryland Experience, 1634–1775*. Carolina Academic Press, Durham.

Parker, Susan Richbourg (1999). "The Second Century of Settlement in Spanish St. Augustine, 1670–1763." Ph.D. diss., University of Florida.

Parker, Susan Richbourg (2013). "In My Mother's House: Dowry Property and Female Inheritance Patterns in Spanish Florida." In Hadden and Minter, eds, *Signposts: New Directions in Southern Legal History*, 19–44.

Peabody, Sue (2008). "Slave Law in the Atlantic World, 1420–1807." In David Eltis and Stanley Engerman, eds, *Cambridge World History of Slavery, Volume 3 AD 1420– AD 1804*, 594–630. Cambridge University Press. Cambridge, UK.

Peabody, Sue and Grinberg, Keila (2007). *Slavery, Freedom and the Law in the Atlantic World: A Brief History with Documents*. Palgrave, Macmillan, New York.

Plane, Ann Marie (2000). *Colonial Intimacies: Indian Marriage in Early New England*. Cornell University Press, Ithaca.

Plane, Ann Marie (2001). "Customary Laws of Marriage: Legal Pluralism, Colonialism, and Narragansett Indian Identity in Eighteenth-Century Rhode Island." In Tomlins and Mann, eds, *The Many Legalities of Early America*, 181–213. University of North Carolina Press, Chapel Hill.

Reid, John P. (1977). *In a Defiant Stance: The Conditions of Law in Massachusetts Bay, the Irish comparison, and the Coming of the American Revolution*. Pennsylvania State University Press, University Park.

Riley, Stephen T. and Hanson, Edward W., eds (1992–present). *The Papers of Robert Treat Paine*. 3 volumes to date. Massachusetts Historical Society, Boston.

Roeber, A.G. (1981). *Faithful Magistrates and Republican Lawyers: Creators of Virginia's Legal Culture, 1680–1810*. University of North Carolina Press, Chapel Hill.

Roeber, A.G. (1998). *Palatines, Liberty, and Property: German Lutherans in colonial British America*. Johns Hopkins University Press, Baltimore.

Rosen, Deborah (1987). "The Supreme Court of Judicature of Colonial New York: Civil Practice in Transition, 1691–1776." *Law and History Review* 5: 213–247.

Rosen, Deborah (1997). *Courts and Commerce: Gender, Law, and the Market Economy in Colonial New York*. Ohio State University Press, Columbus, OH.

Rowe, G.S. (1985). "Women's Crime and Criminal Administration in Pennsylvania, 1763–1790." *Pennsylvania Magazine of History and Biography* 109: 335–368.

Rowe, G.S. (1994). *Embattled Bench: The Pennsylvania Supreme Court and the Forging of a Democratic Society, 1684–1809*. University of Delaware Press, Newark.

Russell, Peter (1990). *His Majesty's Judges: Provincial Society and the Superior Court in Massachusetts, 1692–1774*. Garland, New York.

Salmon, Marylynn (1986). *Women and the Law of Property in Early America*. University of North Carolina Press, Chapel Hill.

Schwarz, Philip (1988). *Twice Condemned: Slaves and the Criminal Laws of Virginia, 1705–1865*. Louisiana State University Press, Baton Rouge.

Shammas, Carole (1995). "Anglo-American Household Government in Comparative Perspective." *William and Mary Quarterly* 3rd series 34: 258–280.

Sidbury, James and Cañizares-Esguerra, Jorge (2011). "Mapping Ethnogenesis in the Early Modern Atlantic." *William and Mary Quarterly* 3rd series 68(2): 181–208.

Smith, Merril (1991). *Breaking the Bonds: Marital Discord in Pennsylvania, 1730–1830*. New York University Press, New York.

Smolenski, John and Humphrey, Thomas J., eds (2005). *New World Orders: Violence, Sanction, and Authority in Colonial America*. University of Pennsylvania Press, Philadelphia.

Snyder, Terri L. (2011). "'To Seeke for Justice': Gender, Servitude, and Household Governance in the Early Modern Chesapeake." In Bradburn and Coombs, eds, *Early Modern Virginia: Reconsidering the Old Dominion*, 128–157. University of Virginia Press, Charlottesville.

Spear, Jennifer (2009). *Race, Sex, and Social Order in Early New Orleans*. Johns Hopkins University Press, Baltimore.

Spear, Jennifer (2013). "'Using the faculties conceded to her by law': Slavery, Law, & Agency in Colonial Louisiana." In Hadden and Minter, eds, *Signposts: New Directions in Southern Legal History*, 65–88.

Spindel, Donna (1989). *Crime and Society in North Carolina, 1663–1776*. Louisiana State University Press, Baton Rouge.

Sturtz, Linda (2002). *Within Her Power: Propertied Women in Colonial Virginia*. Routledge, New York.

Tomlins, Christopher (2001). "Introduction: The Many Legalities of Colonization: A Manifesto of Destiny for Early American Legal History." In Tomlins and Mann, eds, *The Many Legalities of Early America*, 1–24. University of North Carolina Press, Chapel Hill.

Tomlins, Christopher (2010). *Freedom Bound: Law, Labor, and Civil Identity in Colonizing English America, 1580–1865*. Cambridge University Press, Cambridge, UK.

Tomlins, Christopher and Mann, Bruce, eds (2001). *The Many Legalities of Early America*. University of North Carolina Press, Chapel Hill.

Towle, Dorothy, ed. (1936). *Records of the Vice-Admiralty Court of Rhode Island, 1716–1752*. American Historical Association, Washington.

Warren, Charles (1911). *The History of the American Bar*. Little, Brown, Boston.

White, G. Edward (2012). *Law in American History, Volume I: From the Colonial Years Through the Civil War*. Oxford University Press, New York.

Wroth, L. Kinvin and Zobel, Hiller, eds (1965). *The Legal Papers of John Adams*. 3 volumes. Harvard University Press, Boston.

Wulf, Karin (2000). *Not All Wives: Women of Colonial Philadelphia*. Cornell University Press, Ithaca.

Yirush, Craig (2011). *Settlers, Liberty, and Empire: The Roots of Early American Political Theory, 1675–1775*. Cambridge University Press, Cambridge, UK.

Further Reading

Johnson, Herbert, ed. (1980). *South Carolina Legal History*. The Reprint Company, Spartanburg.

Kawashima, Yasuhide (1986). *Puritan Justice and the Indian: White Man's Law in Massachusetts, 1630–1863*. Wesleyan University Press, Middletown, CT.

Mann, Bruce (1987). *Neighbors and Strangers: Law and Community in Early Connecticut*. University of North Carolina Press, Chapel Hill.

Nelson, William E. (1981). *Dispute and Conflict Resolution in Plymouth County, Massachusetts, 1725–1825*. University of North Carolina Press, Chapel Hill.

O'Brien, Jean (1997). *Dispossession by Degrees: Indian Land and Identity in Natick Massachusetts, 1650–1790*. Cambridge University Press, Cambridge, UK.

Chapter Three

1775–1815

Ellen Holmes Pearson

Lawyers of the Revolutionary and early-national era had a vested interest in making sure the new nation succeeded. A significant percentage of delegates to the Continental Congress and the Constitutional Convention had been trained in the law, and lawyers also helped to draft and implement the state constitutions. They made decisions about what English legal and constitutional forms to retain and what to scrap in favor of institutions and laws that fit their ideal American republics. But these men were not just interested in crafting laws and modifying legal institutions for the new nation. They participated in local, state and national politics, farmed and pursued commercial interests, dabbled in land speculation, owned slaves, authored fiction and nonfiction works, and had families, among many other ventures. They understood that American law was woven into a larger tapestry that included economic exigencies, race and labor dynamics, religion, language, and relationships with indigenous peoples, among many other social and cultural circumstances.

It took a while for historians to catch on to the idea that if early American lawyers were interested in how their laws fit with all other aspects of their newly-independent societies, then scholars of American law should share that interest. Legal historians treated their field in isolation until the 1950s when James Willard Hurst's (1956) Wisconsin School of legal historians linked law and society. Since then, scholars have continued to expand the reach of law into other corners of history. Not only have legal historians reached outward from their own field, but social, cultural, economic and political historians now engage the law in their work. Because they have been mining sources previously untouched by their colleagues, legal historians have built a more

A Companion to American Legal History, First Edition.
Edited by Sally E. Hadden and Alfred L. Brophy.
© 2013 John Wiley & Sons Ltd. Published 2021 by John Wiley & Sons Ltd.

complete portrayal of legislators' and legal practitioners' influence on the growth of American politics, society and culture.

But elite men trained in the law were not the only ones who helped to shape American culture and identity through their use of the law. Historians have mined legal records to uncover information about those on the lower rungs of the socio-economic ladder and how they exploited the law and legal institutions for their own purposes. The emergence of a field that straddles legal and social history – a field that Stanley N. Katz labeled "socio-legal" history – has produced histories that make the field more representative of all participants. By the last decade of the twentieth century, Katz states, "the techniques of socio-legal history [were] part of the well-trained young social historian's toolkit" (Katz, 1993: 5). Those "young social historians" of the 1990s are now senior members of their field, and although they may not consider themselves "pure" legal historians, they are certainly part of the extended family. Moreover, in the past few decades, cultural, intellectual, economic, and political historians have used legal records to place the law within the context of Americans' lived experiences. Recent scholarship incorporating the law into other aspects of American history shows that this blending of disciplines produces richer, more textured interpretations of life and work in Revolutionary and early national America.

Political Theory, Law, and "Constitution"

One cannot discuss the Revolutionary and early national period without addressing the intersections between law, political theory, and constitution building. As they broke with Britain, America's leaders confronted questions about who should govern, and under what authority. While interpreting these debates, scholars have combined law and political-constitutional theory. They have engaged in a central debate over the ideological origins of the Revolution, producing a confounding variety of interpretations about American concepts of fundamental law and "constitution." At the center of the debates over ideological origins is a group of historians who examine how the ideas behind the Revolution influenced the actions of the Revolutionaries. This group, which includes Quentin Skinner (1978), J.G.A. Pocock (1975), Bernard Bailyn (1967), and Gordon Wood (1969), practices what Alan Gibson labels "linguistic contextualism" (Gibson, 2007: 91–92). These works remain the foundation of any reading list on political theories of the Founding. Bailyn traces republican theory to its numerous sources, including Enlightenment, common-law, and classical-era concepts, among others. Wood adds that Anglo-Americans' conception of "constitution" diverged from that of England to form a firm set of constraints on government power. Colonists contended that England's king and Parliament had violated fundamental rights of Englishmen living in the colonies. Americans fixed these problems by creating written frames of government, drafted by bodies specifically convened for that purpose, that placed sovereignty in the hands of the people.

Bailyn, Wood and Pocock are only the tip of the iceberg when it comes to political theories behind the Founding. With his two volumes on the historiography of the Founding, Alan Gibson (2007; 2010) has cut through these complicated scholarly debates to provide an accessible guide that is particularly useful to graduate students. Beginning with Charles Beard and the Progressive historians' economic interpretations, Gibson provides concise summaries of scholarship through the Liberal historians' "Lockean" interpretation of founding political theories, republicanism and the language of civic humanism, the Scottish Enlightenment approach, and the "multiple-traditions" approach, which combines one or more of the other approaches into a synthesis. Although one might think that there is nothing more to be said about the Founding, Gibson finds avenues yet to be explored, such as the Founders' conception of civil society and what institutions could best foster citizens' commitment to "public spirit;" a comparison of Founders' political thought to ancient and modern political thought, "to more fully appreciate its peculiarity;" and an exploration of the Founders' ideas about liberalism and republicanism and how they related to the "inegalitarian ideologies" that the Founders followed (Gibson, 2007: 156–161).

Empire and Constitution

While "linguistic contextualists" set the terms of debate over the ideologies behind the Founding, scholars such as John Phillip Reid, Barbara Black, and Jack Greene developed the concept of an imperial constitution. They define this constitution as a set of understandings between the colonies and the parent country that laid out rights and limitations of central power. The colonies broke away when their leaders perceived that Britain violated these constitutional commitments (Black, 1976; Greene, 1986; Reid, 1987). Mary Bilder applies these ideas to colonial Rhode Island, where legislators and litigants cleverly manipulated the common law and the transatlantic constitution to preserve the colony's autonomy. The transatlantic constitution's central principle was that "a colony's laws could not be repugnant to the laws of England but could differ according to the people and place" (Bilder, 2004: 1). But over time, British administration of the transatlantic constitution tightened, creating economic and political uniformity throughout the empire. This shift in dynamic between center and periphery follows a familiar trajectory of increased control on the part of the center, discontent among citizens of the periphery, and eventual rebellion in 1776. Although Bilder's research ends at the Revolution, her findings provide important ideas on which historians of the early republic can build.

America retained certain principles from the imperial constitution and applied these principles to their newly-independent governments. Greene and Daniel Hulsebosch show how the imperial constitution took on new forms and kept moving forward after the Revolution. In his conceptual essay "Colonial History and National History," (2007) Greene encourages scholars to consider post-Revolutionary expansion as a continuation of empire. In the colonial period, English settlers "engaged in state building." Each colony established its own unique form of common-law culture until the British Empire had become a loose association of largely self-governing empires (Greene, 2007: 245). This process continued in generally the same manner as the U.S. expanded westward. Hulsebosch reaches the same conclusions in his case study of New York. After 1783, Americans began their own empire with constitutions and laws that retained certain British characteristics, but that recast the meaning of "empire" in important ways. Instead of accepting new territories as inferior polities, for example, the Northwest Ordinance of 1787 ensured that all new states would be brought into the union at an equal status (Hulsebosch, 2005: 220). After the Revolution, as Anglo-American common law migrated further westward with Americans, the Constitution gave settlers "a common legal identity" on the frontier (Hulsebosch, 2005: 205). But they also cherished their local traditions, and although settlers had to negotiate their local authority with the U.S. government, every state continued to operate under its own constitution and laws.

With his fresh interpretation of New Yorkers' concepts of constitution, law and empire, Hulsebosch has opened new avenues of inquiry into state history for other scholars to follow. Greene also suggests that explorations of local history could shed light on the ways in which expansion affected American legal and constitutional thought through the kinds of legal structures that settlers erected and the layers of legal authority that frontier magistrates navigated (Greene, 2007: 249). More work also needs to be done on the negotiations between frontier officials and the Native Americans who inhabited these territories.

Building and Testing the Constitutions

The first bodies charged with applying political theories to frames of government were the conventions and legislatures that created state constitutions. Because the common law was locally variable, framers of state governments could apply Revolutionary ideology to each polity's peculiar situation. The framers' visions of governance originated in town meetings, provincial conventions and state assemblies and were formalized in writing, in order to legitimize newly-independent states' authority. According to Willi Paul Adams, who produced what remains the only systematic study of the first state constitutions, framers drew from a variety of political theories. But the ideas behind these constitutions also emerged out of the experience Americans acquired resisting British political measures in the 1770s. State leaders did not lean on ideological rigidity, but rather they followed "traditional practice" (Adams, 1980: 234). Adams' study illustrates the diversity of state constitutions and the many forms that republican ideas, colonial experience, and political compromise could take. While Adams' work reveals the local character of the common law, it also illustrates the imperial nature of the law, as England's former colonists looked to their colonial roots to find structures and functions that worked well for them in the past.

When framers of the U.S. Constitution decided to craft a "more perfect union," they drew on the models of government already established in the states. But they also added a more centralized layer on the national level, thus constructing America's federal system of government. Jack Rakove's *Original Meanings* (1997) shows how Founders' ideas blended with political compromise to create a multilayered set of governing bodies that rested on the consent of the people. Like Adams, Rakove emphasizes the pragmatism and spirit of compromise between principle and state or local interest. While ideology was important, Rakove points out that "lessons derived from recent experience were arguably as likely to influence their thinking as the maxims and axioms they found in Locke or Montesquieu or Blackstone" (Rakove, 1997: 13). Alison LaCroix (2010) provides fresh perspectives on the ideological origins of federalism. Lacroix locates the earlier English roots of political theories espoused during the Stamp and Townshend Act debates of the 1760s. These theories evolved into visions of a multilevel governmental structure that became the federal system as outlined in the Constitution. Like Rakove, LaCroix considers the Constitutional Convention a "vital moment in which British imperial precedents, colonial practices, postwar exigency, and political theory came together … to form both a new idea of government and an actual new government" (LaCroix, 2010: 132).

The Constitution was a hard sell in certain parts of the nation, and Rakove suggests that the federal and state ratification debates, along with the pamphlets and other published materials that laid out arguments for and against the new frame of government, provide rich resources for interpreting the Constitution's meanings. Those who have followed Rakove's advice have produced valuable studies. Eran Shalev explores the meaning of classical history and its symbols within the ratification debates. Founders wanted their new republics' national identity and political institutions to reflect the best characteristics of classical Rome. Therefore, they often "stretched and blurred" their understandings of classical history as they tried to strengthen their cases for or against the Constitution through their use of classical pseudonyms and political references (Shalev, 2009: 6). While Shalev produces a valuable intellectual history of one element of the debates,

Pauline Maier takes a broader approach. She plumbs the state ratification documents to tell a "grass-roots story" of how Americans received the proposed Constitution (Maier, 2010: xiii). Like Rakove, Maier emphasizes intersections between practical experience and ideas in the ratification debates. She argues that, although delegates paid attention to other state conventions' deliberations, local exigencies shaped each state's debates and decisions. Instead of providing one monolithic original meaning to the components of the Constitution, the discussions produced a variety of arguments both for and against ratification.

Maier's ground-up treatment of the ratification debates illustrates the role that "the people" played in the approval and implementation of the Constitution. Of course, popular sovereignty was at the center of the Constitution. But as Christian Fritz (2008) points out, there was no consensus on how popular sovereignty should operate in the new republics. Competing definitions of popular sovereignty changed over time, as Americans dealt with situations that pointed up their political differences. Two of Fritz's more effective examples of shifting notions of popular sovereignty involve Shays' Rebellion of 1786 and the Whiskey Rebellion of 1794, two popular protests that also reveal how political and social history can merge with legal history. Participants in these protests saw themselves as heirs to a long-standing tradition of taking back the law when their leaders failed to provide order. In 1786, when the Massachusetts Assembly imposed burdensome taxation on backcountry citizens and then ordered the confiscation of property for nonpayment, these frontiersmen sought justice. Calling themselves Regulators after similar movements against inequitable taxation and land laws and lax law enforcement in the pre-Revolutionary Carolinas, they stormed courthouses to disrupt legal processes that they considered inequitable. The resulting disorder convinced some political leaders that a stronger national government was necessary. When a similar insurrection over taxation, the Whiskey Rebellion, occurred in Western Pennsylvania after the Constitution's ratification, federal officials led by President George Washington used force to quell the insurrection.

These conflicts carried legal and constitutional, as well as political and social significance. Fritz argues that the rebels and their opponents articulated two competing ideas about how popular sovereignty should function in the new nation. Those sympathetic to the government believed that citizens' rights to oversee their government officials ended at the point of election. The protestors believed that they should exercise their right "as citizens to scrutinize, petition, and advise government," even after they had elected their government officials (Fritz, 2008: 82). The rebels engaged in what they considered to be a necessary exercise of their popular sovereignty; of course, their opponents considered these acts of rebellion treasonous.

Institutions: The Federal Courts

Constitutional, political, and legal history intersect in the United States' innovative, multilevel judiciary. The framers left the details of the federal courts' construction to the first Congress. Legislative debates circulated around practical matters, such as the economics of establishing an extensive federal court system, when some believed much of the case load could be handled on the state level. Richard Ellis (1971) argues that the debates over the structure of the courts did not cut across Federalist and Republican-Democratic factional lines. Instead, tensions between radicals and moderates within each political faction shaped the conflicts. Moderates, whom Ellis describes as commercial-minded people who wanted a stable, orderly system of laws and courts, won important compromises, such as appointments of judges for life and other measures that ensured a strong and independent judiciary (Ellis, 1971: 233–234). Once Congress approved the Judiciary Act of 1789, inventions such as the Supreme Court justices' circuit riding system gave citizens a glimpse of their federal government at work (Marcus and Perry, 1992: 28–29). This outreach program also gave the justices the opportunity to instruct Americans on issues of national interest through charges to the grand jury (Lerner, 1967).

Many legislators expected to revise or replace the experimental Judiciary Act of 1789 rather quickly. Instead, the Act remained intact for twelve years before Congress replaced it with the short-lived Judiciary Act of 1801, and the structure of the courts still remains essentially the same (Marcus and Perry, 1992: 34). Settling into the new federal court system was not a smooth process, however. Tensions arose between state and local governments as judges and legislators tried to define the boundaries of their power. Absence of federal criminal statutes, for example, caused confusion over criminal jurisdiction. In a 1986 essay that was recently republished in a collection honoring her work, Kathryn Preyer argues that there was no consensus over the existence of a federal common law of crimes until the Supreme Court denied it in 1812. Even after that decision the subject remained hotly contested (Preyer, 2009: 185–232). Linda Kerber joins Preyer in examining the common law's reach in state and federal courts. Kerber locates two opposing definitions of common law. Republicans defined "common law" as those features of English law that the colonies had not adopted. Federalists characterized the common law as a broad metaphor for an extensive and reliable system of national justice that they wanted to establish in the United States (Kerber, 1970: 170).

Although scholars have paid some attention to Congressional debates over the federal judiciary, they have virtually ignored the evolution of inferior federal courts. Constitutional and legal history meet in the intersections between these levels of the judiciary. In their studies of Kentucky and Rhode Island lower federal courts, Mary Bonsteel Tachau (1978) and Kurt

Graham (2010) find institutions that were far more professional and efficient than many historians have acknowledged. Kentucky's lower federal courts provided access to justice for non-elite citizens, handling a large volume of cases that dealt with laws of internal revenue, civil suits, and other matters of local concern. Graham argues that Rhode Islanders chose the federal courts over state courts, because the judges were better trained, thus raising expectations for all members of the state's bar. Moreover, this national presence in a place that initially resisted the Constitution's ratification allowed national authority to take hold. These two studies on states of such different political, economic, and social character should not stand alone. What local variations and similarities might scholars find should they explore other states' inferior federal courts?

Legal History and Merging Disciplines

Like constitutional historians, legal historians have redefined their field by broadening the scope of evidence that they employ to investigate questions about the law and by asking different kinds of questions about that evidence. Conversely, social, cultural and political historians, among others, have used the law as a tool in their investigations, thus becoming members of the legal history family. These new approaches have energized the field, not so much blurring the lines between disciplines as providing a more complete picture of individuals' lived experiences. Moreover, using law as a tool of social, cultural, and economic history has allowed glimpses into the lives of those who possessed little or no political clout.

Out of Hurst's Wisconsin school came a group of legal historians who interpreted the law as a tool of economic power. Morton Horwitz's pathbreaking *Transformation of American Law* (1977) uses this instrumentalist interpretation of American legal development to argue that judges and lawyers conspired with business interests to shape the law in the early republic, and lawyers and jurists used law as an instrument of policy to encourage social change. Like Horwitz, William Nelson (1975) applied the instrumentalist argument to an investigation of state law in his study of early national Massachusetts. Nelson was among the first to venture into county courthouses and municipal repositories, exploring previously unexamined local court and magistrates' records to address the "Americanization" of the law from the municipal and state perspectives. He argues that Massachusetts law became a tool through which commercial interest groups operated to consolidate their wealth and economic power. At the same time, judges began to consolidate power in their own hands at the expense of the jury, signaling a move toward the professionalization of the courts and away from the democratic, common-sense impulses of jury members.

Despite the instrumentalists' important contributions to scholarship on American law's evolution, the image of law as a passive tool in the hands of business interest gave many scholars pause. Most historians agreed that the law was affected by economic exigencies and political circumstances, among other factors, but they did not find compelling evidence that a conspiracy existed. Instead, they found other forces at work in the Americanization of the law. Gregory Alexander (1997), for example, takes on the notion that property ownership was a purely commercial enterprise. He argues that, while some Founders looked on property as a commodity and therefore tried to regulate its exchange more closely, others envisioned property ownership as a way to broaden civic engagement in the new nation. If more men owned property, then more men would participate in the political process, thus fulfilling the republican vision of America as an egalitarian republic.

Property's role in shaping political culture was only one component of the law's Americanization. Other scholars have drawn on intersections between law, society, and culture to explain how early national law contributed to American identities. In Robert A. Ferguson's words, early American lawyers were "professionally dependent on a fusion of law and literature" (Ferguson, 1984: 6). Through lectures, speeches, treatises, pamphlets, charges to the grand jury, and even poetry and fiction, lawyers and judges led in promoting the republican cause. The first generation of American lawyers had to rely on English legal treatises to guide them in practice and procedure. Gradually, American law experts added to or replaced this English literature with works suited to American law, and they deployed their works to debate the major social and cultural issues of their new nation, such as slavery, territorial expansion, and relations with America's First Peoples. As they discussed American law, they also shared their visions for the new nation's emerging societies, while contributing to the making of American identities (Pearson, 2011). Lawyers also wrote literature not related to the law, and often these works, even works of fiction, promoted republican culture. Their legal training influenced the authors' subjects and writing style. Moreover, their literary interests contributed to the ways in which they framed their legal and political opinions (Ferguson, 1984).

State and Local Legal History

Scholars also expressed dissatisfaction with instrumentalists' broad-brush treatment of *American* legal history. Both Horwitz and Nelson, for example, drew their evidence from northern – and primarily New England – courts and legislatures, and their regional bias drew skepticism over depictions of an homogeneous national experience. Historians responded with a flurry of research on state and local law, which illuminate regional differences and offer important corrections to the instrumentalists' interpretation. In studies of Virginia's legal growth, A.G. Roeber (1981) and F. Thornton Miller (1994) also detect trends toward professionalization of legal institutions, but they note other forces of change at work in the Old Dominion. Roeber argues that the power of local courts diminished in 1789 when a new layer of district courts was created between the counties and Virginia's General Court. However, Miller maintains that Virginia's planter gentry retained considerable control over legal matters, and Virginian legal institutions did not see the same centralizing efforts over commercial interests that Nelson and Horwitz discovered in New England.

Recent scholarship on other states has pointed up even more diversity in the Americanization process. Like Nelson, John Philip Reid (2004) finds efforts to professionalize New Hampshire's legal institutions in the early nineteenth century. However, Reid also examines the opposition to reforms, finding that well into the first decades of the nineteenth century, members of the state's Republican party successfully resisted attempts to implement professional requirements for legal practitioners and to formalize legal procedures. Warren M. Billings and Mark F. Fernandez have taken analysis of early national legal development to Louisiana, a place whose colonial legal culture bore a distinctive French and Spanish lineage. One would assume that the new territory's legal culture would have matured differently from those places with common-law roots. Spanish and French legal literature remained influential long after the territory was acquired by the U.S. in 1803. But as members of Louisiana's bench and bar reshaped their laws, they also drew on English treatise writers like Coke and Blackstone, as well as American territorial legislation (Billings, 2001). Common-law trained lawyers assumed key positions on Louisiana's bench, and after achieving statehood, Louisiana's judiciary developed in ways very similar to other southern states' judicial institutions (Fernandez, 2001).

Another group of scholars has taken legal history beyond the state level and into municipal and county records. This unglamorous research involves mining poorly-catalogued archives, often located in moldy courthouse and town hall basements. But historians who are willing to get a little dirty have reaped rich rewards. One early advocate of localized legal history was Hendrik Hartog who, in his classic 1985 essay "Pigs and Positivism," dug into New York's municipal records to break "the relative silence of American legal doctrine on questions of customary law" (Hartog, 1985: 900). By the early nineteenth century, New York custom had evolved into residents' insistence over their legal right to run their pigs on the streets of the city. Hartog's unconventional choice of subject and his localized approach blazed a trail that others continue to follow.

In the following decades, William Novak (1996) and Laura Edwards (2009) used municipal, county, and state records to argue that the local laws of the nineteenth century privileged the well-regulated society even over individual rights. Their conclusions contradict the instrumentalist argument that law was a tool of the business-oriented judges and legislators. Novak's findings point to two layers of regulation with two different, and sometimes conflicting, goals. State laws were designed to protect individual rights – and some individuals' rights more than others' – whereas town, district and county magistrates tended to be more concerned with maintaining a well-regulated society and ensuring the well-being of their citizens.

Edwards found similar concerns for maintaining the "peace," or community order, in towns and counties of North and South Carolina. While state governments assumed control over such matters as property law, other law remained "localized," handled at the county, district, or town level. This localization changed the character of certain kinds of law. An individual's authority depended to some extent on gender, social status, and race, but magistrates and jurors also valued "credit," or a person's reliability based on their reputation. Those women, for example, who fulfilled community expectations of good wifely conduct had a better chance of achieving their goals, up to and including divorce, than a woman who had not built a proper reputation. The institutionalized state regulations may have prescribed certain actions, but flexible local custom sometimes trumped stringent state law.

These local studies offer provocative conclusions that should be tested in other parts of the United States. How might these state and local dynamics play out in other parts of the early republic? And, did relationships between state and local governments differ as American law moved westward with settlers? Legislation and legal treatises prescribed expected societal behaviors, and state and federal court cases allow scholars to compare the intersections between regulation and behavior. But the intimacy of town and county legal proceedings offers snippets of the lives, voices, and personalities of individuals who navigated the law every day. The trend toward localized research adds depth to our understanding of social dynamics in early national America and allows glimpses into the legal, economic, and social activities of women, poor whites, and enslaved and free people of color. In some cases, these records, which include census data, tax roles, and probate documents, as well as municipal, county and state court proceedings, are the only evidence historians can use to get to the actions of marginalized peoples. As social history has gained momentum, legal records have become crucial to scholars' quests for information about non-elite Americans.

Women and Law

Although the Revolution did not seem to affect women's legal status significantly, some scholars have identified post-Revolutionary shifts in family dynamics and domestic law. Mary Lynn Salmon's *Women and the Law of Property in Early America* (1986) compares probate records, court records, and other legal documentation in seven states. Although she finds that the Revolution had minimal immediate effect on women's property rights, she detects a slow improvement in women's legal status in the first decades after independence. Salmon uncovers regional and local variations as well. For example, she finds that New England officials opposed the idea of separate estates for women, in the same period when other parts of the nation adopted this practice (Salmon, 1986: 120–140). In addition to the Revolution, factors such as economic diversification and instability, legal professionalism, improvement in women's education, shifting attitudes toward marriage that emerged with liberal divorce laws, republican concepts of consent, and "republican-motherhood" roles of women in the family contributed to the moderate changes in women's status. She also asserts that although the egalitarian ideals of the Revolution did not produce immediate results for women, they "represented a powerful weapon for future use" by nineteenth-century women's rights activists (Salmon, 1986: xvii).

Suzanne Lebsock (1984) used more localized tactics, mining early nineteenth-century Petersburg, Virginia's marriage contracts, property deeds, court minute books, wills, and other local sources to explore early national transitions in women's legal agency. Like Salmon, Lebsock's study reveals mixed results with regard to improvement in women's status. But her local focus allows Lebsock to explore individual women's choices in ways that Salmon's comparative analysis cannot. In early national Petersburg, although men carried more economic and legal authority, women enjoyed a moderate improvement in economic status, as well as a decreasing dependence on individual men. Petersburg's women tended to draft wills more readily than men, and she speculates that this difference stemmed from women's pragmatic attitudes about death, because they faced their mortality with every pregnancy. She also concludes that women tended to use wills to "play favorites" among their heirs. They privileged personal relationships over financial gain, therefore women more frequently chose heirs according to their level of merit. Women also tended to make special arrangements for slaves in their wills, not out of any aversion to the institution, but rather out of their emotional attachment to certain slaves.

Other historians have followed Lebsock into local records to help uncover important regional similarities and differences in women's experiences. Linda Sturtz's property-owning women in Virginia seemed to maintain some visibility and could potentially break away from the norms as defined in law and prescriptive literature. By the Revolution, "propertied women faced conflicting expectations" about their places in society, but a few women "figured out ways to navigate them" (Sturtz, 2002: 11). During and after the Revolution, Virginia reaffirmed most of the colonial restrictions on married women's property, and propertied women faced more obstacles. Virginia courts upheld married women's property rights through separate estates, but only to protect family assets from creditors (Sturtz, 2002: 181). Cornelia Hughes Dayton's study of New Haven, Connecticut reveals a system in which women became invisible by the 1780s. In the early years of settlement, women used courts "with unparalleled frequency" (Dayton, 1995: 4). The kinds of cases brought to seventeenth-century Connecticut courts, such as neighbor relations, local trade disputes, and violations of sexual and moral conduct, included activities in which women naturally participated, but they still had to depend on the "legal fraternity" of judges, lawyers, and jurors. As colonial society became more sophisticated, women's participation in legal matters faded further into the background, while propertied men took the lead in debt litigation and the legal problems that accompanied the expansion of farming and trade. Dayton sees this change as part of the divergence between men's and women's spheres, which gradually gave the public realm of commerce, law and politics to men and moral dominion over the private household to women.

Children and Household Law

The potential – and the failure of that potential – for the Revolution to make a difference in equality under the law extended into the rest of the family. In *By Birth or Consent*, Holly Brewer argues that changes in the meanings of consent led to shifts in the laws protecting children's rights in England and America. Children in sixteenth-century England could legally consent to marriage or apprenticeships, could make wills, or be hanged for arson or other felonies. But, through the seventeenth and eighteenth centuries, the issue of consent became central to political theories, hinging on contested authority. While Enlightenment theorists argued that all humans possessed the capacity to reason, they also asserted that children lacked reason, and therefore could not give their consent. By the nineteenth century, custody law no longer allowed children to make decisions about their own destinies, because theory held that they did not have full use of their reason. In the question of consent and authority, the paradigm moved from authority based on birthright to authority based on reasoned consent, what Brewer calls a shift from status to contract. She cites passages in Coke and Blackstone to trace the transition in the nature of power and custody from the power of the lord to the "empire of the father" (Brewer, 2007: 341). With this transfer of power, children lost more ground than did women, slaves and free laborers.

Michael Grossberg (1985) and Peter Bardaglio (1995) also address these tensions between republican and patriarchal forces in their works about America's domestic law, but they reach slightly different conclusions from those of Brewer, and from one another. Their works uncover important regional variations on the extent to which domestic relations were "republicanized." Grossberg looks to changes in family relations and the law through appellate decisions, legislation and professional commentaries. But unlike Brewer, he identifies a post-Revolutionary shift away from the father's authority and toward the authority of the courts. He describes a patriarchal colonial household in which government and legal institutions tended to rely on the heads of household to control its members. In the early national period, however, legislators and judges rearranged the balance of power within the home and diminished paternal authority, placing responsibility for domestic affairs in the state. Grossberg's "judicial patriarchy" regulated marriage, parenthood, legitimacy and custody, intruding on what had previously been private family affairs (Grossberg, 1985: 70–71).

Grossberg's republican family, in which household members were bound by egalitarianism and affection, does not hold up in Bardaglio's South. As the North moved toward an increasingly contractual view of domestic relations that challenged the patriarchal ideal of the family, white southerners saw themselves as defenders of traditional patriarchy. Much of Bardaglio's book concentrates on the antebellum period, but his discussion of a distinct kind of republicanism in the South – one that clung to patriarchal elements of culture – applies to the early republic. Slavery complicated the southern picture by extending the household beyond white inhabitants. The household provided the key source of order and stability in southern society, and slavery, honor and localism combined with what Bardaglio calls "agrarian republicanism" to shape southern attitudes that did not welcome state intervention in the household.

Labor Law

Child labor, at the intersection of domestic law and social and economic history, offers another challenging avenue of research that is ripe for further exploration. Ruth Wallis Herndon and John E. Murray's essay in their edited collection, *Children Bound to Labor* (2009), combines aspects of social, legal, and economic history by using official records of children's apprenticeship and indenture contracts. Contract terms varied widely over place and time and depended on the child's family situation and the nature of the labor expected from the child. Magistrates bound out orphans and children of indigent families for servitude in order to relieve the community of the financial burden of taking care of the poor. But, even wealthier families bound out their children, preferably with family members and for a shorter period of time, in order to prepare them for a vocation.

Herndon and Murray detect the same patriarchal trend in local governments that Grossberg and Bardaglio identify in state courts. Servitude was an effective way for local magistrates to shape households under their jurisdiction. If children did not come from an "ideal family" that contained an adult male head of household, then they could resolve that social problem by moving minors to households that fit their vision of a proper upbringing. Masters were expected to raise these children to be productive members of their community, teaching the child a skill as well as the value of work. Although parents often found their children suitable apprenticeships, magistrates frequently stepped in to make sure children of poorer families were educated properly. By the end of the eighteenth century, masters often committed to teaching their charges to read, and perhaps to write and "cipher," in addition to a vocational skill. In the late eighteenth and early nineteenth centuries, manufacturing growth changed the shape of labor, and with the opening of carding and cloth-making mills on a large scale, preference shifted from male craftsmen to female and child labor (Herndon and Murray, 2009: 3-18).

Other scholarship has shed some light on adult servants' legal agency as well. Christine Daniels' work on servant claims in Maryland courts shows that servants could, and did, use the courts to affirm their rights. While statute law has "exaggerated the powerlessness of servants and their duties to their masters" (Daniels, 2001: 220), case law and customary servant law shows that servants had recourse for their complaints, and that judges and juries often found in favor of servants in their claims against their masters. County courts mediated the relationship between master and servant, and in doing so, they created local customs and standards for the treatment of servants. Evidence from county and provincial courts in colonial and early national Maryland demonstrates that many servants understood their legal rights and successfully sought redress for their grievances in county and provincial courts. While they often complained of physical abuse in the seventeenth century, by the late eighteenth century, most servant complaints dealt with neglect, primarily in the form of inadequate food or clothing. Although masters retained legal control over their servants, "courts, pushed by servants," required masters to observe "their duties and obligations to dependents" (Daniels, 2001: 248).

Daniels' servants worked in a heavily-agricultural economy, whereas Christopher Tomlins' laborers operated in an industrializing society. In *Law, Labor, and Ideology* (1993), Tomlins seeks to clarify the contribution of legal discourse to the construction of the new nineteenth-century world of production and employment. Tomlins argues that the Revolution gave workers an opening to insist on egalitarian treatment. On the other hand, law in the early republic privileged protection of property and "judicial ascendancy" over other interests. In the end, judges' decisions generally gave employers the advantage. Most of the significant labor cases took place after 1815, but earlier decisions laid the groundwork for antebellum cases in which journeymen won certain rights to collective bargaining, but lost some of their ability to interfere with already-established contracts in order to negotiate their own agreements with employers. Early in the nineteenth century, courts began to use English common law precedent to limit the actions of journeyman's associations. Tomlins notes that American judges' refusal to break the ties between their law and that of England with regard to labor issues limited the egalitarian impulse of the Revolution.

Slavery

The other form of labor in the early republic, slavery, has probably received more attention than any other historical genre, but with just a few exceptions, scholars have only lightly treated early national slave law as a discrete subject. Paul Finkelman's *Slavery and the Founders* (2001), a collection of revised and republished essays, is one of the few works devoted to early national slave law. In his most original chapters, Finkelman argues that, because Congress' ban on slavery in the Northwest Ordinance of 1787 did not include any enforcement mechanism, the future states of Indiana and Illinois continued to encourage the institution into the nineteenth century (Finkelman, 2001: 37–80).

Two works that cover slavery over longer time periods deserve mention. Thomas Morris' *Southern Slavery and the Law* (1996) synthesizes over three hundred years of slave law in North America and identifies general trends from the colonial period to the Civil War. His analysis is concentrated in the antebellum period, where a critical mass of legal treatises and court cases about slavery can be found. However, Morris identifies a few early-national trends such as the transition from "paternalist notions" of slavery to a "liberal-capitalist" perspective more oriented toward the market (Morris, 1996: 433–434). Part of the story of this liberal-capitalist shift involves the tension between the law's treatment of slaves as persons and as property. States resolved this issue in a variety of ways, but Morris argues that at the center was the notion of a person as a thing. He provides a particularly clear interpretation of legislative debates over whether slaves ought to be designated real or personal property (Morris, 1996: 61–80). Christopher Tomlins' recent contribution to this subject bridges labor and slave law in new ways. *Freedom Bound* (2010) places legal control over labor at the center of Anglo-America's institution of slavery. Tomlins also enters into Greene and Hulsebosch's scholarly conversation about the law's role in migration and colonization. Athough Tomlins concentrates on the colonial foundations of labor regulation and slave law, the final chapters move through the Revolution and early republic and offer fresh perspectives on the law of slavery, labor, and territorial expansion.

While scholars have not paid much attention to the law of slavery as a discrete topic, social historians have embraced legal records as important tools with which to explore the history of slavery and persons of color. Scholars have blended social and legal history to produce so many fine works that a few examples will have to suffice. Laura Edwards, for instance, integrates legal records dealing with slaves' navigations of local governments and laws in her study. Her evidence points to slaves of good reputation gaining some leverage under the right circumstances. For example, slaves legally could not own property, however, a slave who had proven himself trustworthy might be able to get away with extralegal trade activities (Edwards, 2009: 186–198). While Edwards locates some latitude for slaves in one part of the South, Joanne Melish uncovers a tightening of newly-freed blacks' movements in New England. Melish examines court cases and town records among other manuscripts and publications to trace the origins and effects of that region's gradual emancipation laws. She argues that whites often ignored and abused these laws and, even as they freed their slaves, New Englanders established a series of legal and social limitations on the newly-freed people of color that were designed to push them out of New England (Melish, 1998). Melish's conclusions contradict previous assumptions that New England slavery was milder than that of the South and died out in the face of abolitionist sentiment.

Other scholars have used legal records to learn more about those slaves who tried to gain freedom through violence. For instance, James Sidbury and Douglas Egerton took court records and other documentation and produced two very different interpretations of Gabriel's Conspiracy of 1800 in Virginia. Sidbury places the conspiracy trial records in a cultural context, offering close readings of the symbols and rituals of white planter culture and slaves' use of these symbols during the revolt and the ensuing trials. Moreover, the behavior of some blacks who were implicated in the rebellion reveals a far more complicated slave community than scholars previously acknowledged. In the course of the trial, some of Gabriel's co-conspirators turned state's evidence against him, revealing hierarchies and fault lines in a slave community that had previously been depicted as homogenous (Sidbury, 1997). Egerton uses the trial records to illustrate the conspirators' investment in Revolutionary rhetoric and the figures of the Revolution, including George Washington (Egerton, 1993: 102). He also provides a more nuanced sketch of Gabriel himself. An earlier pig-stealing and assault incident in which he was involved indicates that Gabriel's literacy gave him a certain measure of what Laura Edwards would call "credit." Because he was literate and able to recite a Bible passage, the magistrate granted him benefit of clergy and reduced the penalty for his offense. However, Gabriel's owner had to post a steep bond for a year to ensure that his charge would not disturb the peace again (Egerton, 1993: 32–33). This earlier incident confirms Edwards' findings that, when local relationships were involved, magistrates could be flexible, and could even extend "credit" when they believed a slave and his master deserved it. However, in the aftermath of Gabriel's Conspiracy, the state legislature, which privileged group action over individual integrity, wielded its power by passing laws that further restricted slaves' movements.

Conclusion: More Areas for Further Exploration

Blending law with other historical fields is not a new concept, and while historians have recently taken the idea in new directions, there are many facets of Revolutionary and early national legal history left to explore. For example, the legal interactions between First Peoples and white Americans have been only lightly treated for this period. Much of the extant work falls into the colonial period and deals with military, diplomatic, or cultural interactions. Negotiations between First Peoples and Anglo-Americans and local magistrates await scholarly inquiry, especially in the context of westward migrations of the late eighteenth and early nineteenth centuries. The ease of property acquisition in early national America was a point of pride among the Founders, yet few scholars besides Mary Lynn Salmon and Gregory Alexander have addressed the law of property as a discrete subject. Claire Priest has recently taken the history of property law in new directions by providing analysis of a 1732 Debt Recovery Act that had important implications for America long after the Revolution (Priest, 2006). Her study of the colonial roots of American property law through one pivotal piece of legislation serves as a model for future work. Moreover, because property law is created and administered at the state level, these studies could also address regional variations. Finally, the intersections between religion and legal development in the early republic beg for scholarly attention. How did the advent of evangelical strains of Protestantism interact with other aspects of culture and society to reshape the law? This subject would benefit from local studies on the Hartog/Edwards model.

The newly-independent United States boasted cultures and identities that included much more than laws, and historians are engaged in the task of uncovering these connections. New models for study have carried legal history far from its insular origins, and the field now covers a wide range of perspectives and genres, from biographies and institutional histories, to important court cases and specific aspects of the law such as torts, criminal law, and contracts. But, we are also beyond the point where social history, legal history, cultural or political history can exist in a vacuum, and the prospect of even more interdisciplinary work has taken the field in exciting new directions. Set firmly in context, the law comes alive in ways it cannot when it stands alone.

References

Adams, Willi Paul (1980). *The First American Constitutions: Republican Ideology and the Making of the State Constitutions in the Revolutionary Era*. Rita and Robert Kimber, tr. University of North Carolina Press, Chapel Hill.

Alexander, Gregory S. (1997). *Commodity and Propriety: Competing Visions of Property in American Legal Thought, 1776–1970*. University of Chicago Press, Chicago.

Bailyn, Bernard (1992 [1967]). *The Ideological Origins of the American Revolution*. Belknap Press, Cambridge, MA.

Bardaglio, Peter (1995). *Reconstructing the Household: Families, Sex and Law in the Nineteenth-Century South*. University of North Carolina Press, Chapel Hill.

Bilder, Mary Sarah (2004). *The Transatlantic Constitution: Colonial Legal Culture and the Empire*. Harvard University Press, Cambridge, MA.

Billings, Warren M. (2001). "Mixed Jurisdictions and Convergence: The Louisiana Example." *International Journal of Legal Information* 29(2): 272–309.

Black, Barbara (1976). "The Constitution of Empire: The Case for the Colonists." *University of Pennsylvania Law Review* 124(5): 1157–1211.

Brewer, Holly (2007). *By Birth or Consent: Children, Law, and the Anglo-American Revolution in Authority*. University of North Carolina Press, Chapel Hill.

Daniels, Christine (2001). "'Liberty to Complain:' Servant Petitions in Maryland, 1652–1797." In Tomlins and Mann, eds, *The Many Legalities of Early America*, 219–249. University of North Carolina Press, Chapel Hill.

Dayton, Cornelia Hughes (1995). *Women Before the Bar: Gender, Law, and Society in Connecticut, 1639–1789*. University of North Carolina Press, Chapel Hill.

Edwards, Laura F. (2009). *The People and Their Peace: Legal Culture and the Transformation of Inequality in the Post-Revolutionary South*. University of North Carolina Press, Chapel Hill.

Egerton, Douglas R. (1993). *Gabriel's Rebellion: The Virginia Slave Conspiracies of 1800 and 1802*. University of North Carolina Press, Chapel Hill.

Ellis, Richard E. (1971). *The Jeffersonian Crisis: Courts and Politics in the Young Republic*. Oxford University Press, New York.

Ferguson, Robert A. (1984). *Law and Letters in American Culture*. Harvard University Press, Cambridge, MA.

Fernandez, Mark F. (2001). *From Chaos to Continuity: Evolution of Louisiana's Judicial System, 1712–1862*. Louisiana State University Press, Baton Rouge.

Finkelman, Paul (2001). *Slavery and the Founders: Race and Liberty in the Age of Jefferson*. M.E. Sharpe, New York.

Fritz, Christian G. (2008). *American Sovereigns: The People and America's Constitutional Tradition Before the Civil War*. Cambridge University Press, Cambridge, UK.

Gibson, Alan (2007). *Understanding the Founding: The Crucial Questions*. University Press of Kansas, Lawrence.

Gibson, Alan (2010). *Interpreting the Founding: Guide to the Enduring Debates Over the Origins and Foundations of the American Republic*. 2nd Edition. University Press of Kansas, Lawrence.

Graham, D. Kurt (2010). *To Bring Law Home: The Federal Judiciary in Early National Rhode Island*. Northern Illinois University Press, DeKalb, IL.

Greene, Jack P. (2007). "Colonial History and National History: Reflections on a Continuing Problem." *William and Mary Quarterly* 64(2): 235–250.

Greene, Jack P. (1986). *Peripheries and Center: Constitutional Development in the Extended Polities of the British Empire and the United States, 1607–1788*. University of Georgia Press, Athens.

Grossberg, Michael (1985). *Governing the Hearth: Law and the Family in Nineteenth-Century America*. University of North Carolina Press, Chapel Hill.

Hartog, Hendrik (1985). "Pigs and Positivism." *Wisconsin Law Review* 4: 899–935.

Herndon, Ruth Wallis and Murray, John E. (2009). "'A Proper and Instructive Education:' Raising Children in Pauper Apprenticeship." In Herndon and Murray, eds, *Children Bound to Labor: The Pauper Apprentice System in Early America*, 3–18. Cornell University Press, Ithaca.

Horwitz, Morton (1977). *Transformation of American Law: 1780–1860*. Harvard University Press, Cambridge, MA.

Hulsebosch, Daniel (2005). *Constituting Empire: New York and the Transformation of Constitutionalism in the Atlantic World, 1664–1830*. University of North Carolina Press, Chapel Hill.

Hurst, J. Willard (1956). *Law and the Conditions of Freedom in the Nineteenth-Century United States*. University of Wisconsin Press, Madison.

Katz, Stanley N. (1993). "Forum, Explaining the Law in Early American History: Introduction." *William and Mary Quarterly* 50(1): 3–6.

Kerber, Linda (1970). *Federalists in Dissent: Imagery and Ideology in Jeffersonian America*. Cornell University Press, Ithaca, NY.

LaCroix, Alison L. (2010). *The Ideological Origins of American Federalism*. Harvard University Press, Cambridge, MA.

Lebsock, Suzanne (1984). *The Free Women of Petersburg: Status and Culture in a Southern Town, 1784–1860*. W.W. Norton, New York.

Lerner, Ralph (1967). "The Supreme Court as Republican Schoolmaster." *Supreme Court Review* 127: 127–180.

Maier, Pauline (2010). *Ratification: The People Debate the Constitution*. Simon and Schuster, New York.

Marcus, Maeva and Perry, James R., eds (1992). *The Documentary History of the Supreme Court of the United States, 1789–1800. Volume Four, Organizing the Federal Judiciary: Legislation and Commentaries*. Columbia University Press, New York.

Melish, Joanne Pope (1998). *Disowning Slavery: Gradual Emancipation and "Race" in New England, 1780–1860*. Cornell University Press, Ithaca.

Miller, F. Thornton (1994). *Juries and Judges Versus the Law: Virginia's Provincial Legal Perspective, 1783–1828*. The University Press of Virginia, Charlottesville.

Morris, Thomas (1996). *Southern Slavery and the Law, 1619–1860*. University of North Carolina Press, Chapel Hill.

Nelson, William (1975). *The Americanization of the Common Law: The Impact of Legal Change on Massachusetts Society, 1760–1830*. Harvard University Press, Cambridge, MA.

Novak, William (1996). *The People's Welfare: Law and Regulation in Nineteenth-Century America*. University of North Carolina Press, Chapel Hill.

Pearson, Ellen Holmes (2011). *Remaking Custom: Law and Identity in the Early American Republic*. University of Virginia Press, Charlottesville.

Pocock, J.G.A. (2003 [1975]). *The Machiavellian Moment: Florentine Political Thought and the Atlantic Republican Tradition*. 2nd Edition. Princeton University Press, Princeton.

Preyer, Kathryn (2009). *Blackstone in America: Selected Essays of Kathryn Preyer*. Bilder, Maeva, and Newmyer, eds. Cambridge University Press, Cambridge.

Priest, Claire (2006). "Creating an American Property Law: Alienability and its Limits in American History." *Harvard Law Review* 120(2): 385–459.

Rakove, Jack N. (1997). *Original Meanings: Politics and Ideas in the Making of the Constitution*. Alfred A. Knopf, New York.

Reid, John Philip (1987). *Constitutional History of the American Revolution*. University of Wisconsin Press, Madison, WI.

Reid, John Philip (2004). *Controlling the Law: Legal Politics in Early National New Hampshire*. University of Northern Illinois Press, DeKalb, IL.

Roeber, A.G. (1981). *Faithful Magistrates and Republican Lawyers: Creators of Virginia's Legal Culture, 1680–1810*. University of North Carolina Press, Chapel Hill.

Salmon, Marylynn (1986). *Women and the Law of Property in Early America*. University of North Carolina Press, Chapel Hill.

Shalev, Eran (2009). *Rome Reborn on Western Shores: Historical Imagination and the Creation of the American Republic*. University of Virginia Press, Charlottesville.

Sidbury, James (1997). *Ploughshares into Swords: Race, Rebellion, and Identity in Gabriel's Virginia, 1730–1810*. Cambridge University Press, Cambridge, UK.

Skinner, Quentin (1978). *The Foundations of Modern Political Thought*. 2 volumes. Cambridge University Press, Cambridge, UK.

Sturtz, Linda L. (2002). *Within Her Power: Propertied Women in Colonial Virginia*. Routledge Publishing, New York.

Tachau, Mary K. Bonsteel (1978). *Federal Courts in the Early Republic: Kentucky, 1789–1816*. Princeton University Press, Princeton, NJ.

Tomlins, Christopher L. (1993). *Law, Labor and Ideology in the Early American Republic*. Cambridge University Press, Cambridge, UK.

Tomlins, Christopher L. (2010). *Freedom Bound: Law, Labor and Civic Identity in Colonizing English America, 1580–1865*. Cambridge University Press, New York.

Wood, Gordon S. (1998 [1969]). *Creation of the American Republic, 1776–1787*. University of North Carolina Press, Chapel Hill.

Chapter Four

THE ANTEBELLUM ERA THROUGH CIVIL WAR

Alfred L. Brophy

In 1837 Ralph Waldo Emerson delivered the "American Scholar" address to the Harvard Phi Beta Kappa Society. Emerson spoke about Americans' desire to know the reason of things. It captured the spirit of the age, in which irrational precedent was rejected in favor of reason. That spirit of rejection of irrational precedent spread across American culture. For judges, like ministers and intellectuals more generally, were rejecting precedent in favor of reason as they remade the law. Not everyone, however, embraced the remaking of the law; by 1850, when Timothy Walker, a professor at Cincinnati Law School, delivered another Phi Beta Kappa address at Harvard, he opposed the idea that all things were to be made new. Walker was not so happy with the love of the new. He feared the upheaval that came from uprooting old ideas, which was changing such venerable institutions as the family, the church, and even slavery (Walker, 1850: 5-6). That sense that American law, as well as culture, was remade in the antebellum era had been a mainstay of legal history scholarship on the antebellum era for generations now (Klafter, 1993). But as happened at the time, there are questions about which direction the law moved, who benefited, and who was left behind. The questions relate to what kind of changes took place and how to study them, from sources as diverse as local court, family, and business records, newspapers, statutes, appellate decisions, and even fictional literature and oratory.

A Companion to American Legal History, First Edition.
Edited by Sally E. Hadden and Alfred L. Brophy.
© 2013 John Wiley & Sons Ltd. Published 2021 by John Wiley & Sons Ltd.

A Transformation? And If So, What Kind?

In the prosperous and perhaps complacent 1950s, J. Willard Hurst mapped the multiple ways that the antebellum law promoted economic growth. In *Law and the Conditions of Freedom,* published in 1956, Hurst interpreted the nineteenth-century law's role as releasing energy and thus facilitating growth. Hurst portrayed the law of the era positively and in 1960 Karl Llewellyn went a step further. He labeled judicial opinions of this era as "the grand style" – grand because the expansive opinions rejected irrational precedent in favor of reason, often based on considerations of economy and history (Llewellyn, 1960: 64).

Nearly two decades later, in 1977, Morton Horwitz portrayed the changes in less positive terms. Like the others, he saw the antebellum era as one of change. Horwitz labeled it "transformation," though it was not a positive one. He saw the transformation as a shift from a communal law, where things like fair price were key factors of decision, to an impersonal and objective law. Judges enforced contracts, no matter the terms; corporations received a "subsidy" through the law, which shifted the costs of accidents from the corporations to their workers. Horwitz wrote about how tort law restricted recovery by workers injured by "fellow servants." (Horwitz, 1977: 63–108) Similarly, tort law restricted the liability of railroads for damages to neighbors' property (Horwitz, 1977: 75); property law allowed those who had a use of the property that was economically useful to purchase the property of neighbors – through the mill acts and through denial of injunctions and the limitation of plaintiffs to money damages (Horwitz, 1977: 47–53). This has become known in property scholarship as a "liability rule" instead of a "property rule." What separated Horwitz from earlier writers was not the sense that law was changing, but whether the changes were positive or negative. This approach has come in for substantial criticism. One reviewer titled his review, "A Plot Too Doctrinaire" (Reid, 1977).

More recently, Peter Karsten (1998) has challenged the nature of the "transformation." Instead of finding changes that assisted businesses, Karsten found a move in the other direction, towards concern for the poor. He locates this as part of the culture of sympathy and sentimentalism so prominent at the time. Karsten's bold thesis extends other, more narrow articles by legal scholars that questioned how much there was a change. Some asked whether there had ever been a "golden age" of communal law (Simpson, 1979); others asked whether tort law had in fact changed in the direction Horwitz suggested (Kaczorowski, 1990; Schwartz, 1981). To a great extent, this debate turns on ideological issues of how one views United States history more generally – as a place of opportunity where some people are left behind, or as a place where corporations and other powerful interests are able to gain and wield power at the expense of workers, racial minorities, and women. The shift in ideology from Hurst to Horwitz is illustrated by what Eben Moglen referred to as the shift from Hurst's reference to judges as "we" to Horwitz' reference to judges as "they" (Moglen, 1993: 1044). There continue to be substantive disagreements about common law doctrine; perhaps those will attract attention again.

The most recent assessment of the changes that took place from the eighteenth century through the antebellum period comes in Laura Edwards' *The People and Their Peace* (2009). Edwards looks in a different place from the others, who have focused on appellate courts. She looks to the records of local courts, to see who testified and what the law was that the courts applied. In a parallel to Horwitz, Edwards finds a shift from an informal law, where, for instance, local practices permitted enslaved people to testify and where women's property rights were frequently respected. By the 1830s, courts were less open. The process of formalization of law, where the rules were set by appellate judges and legislators in a state capital, displaced the more informal law. The later courts were more concerned with property rights, though at all times the peace (in the form of social stability and behavior according to the "rule of law") was central. Steinberg's 1989 study of criminal prosecutions from 1800 to 1880 finds many parallel transformations, especially in the shift from private prosecutions to state prosecutions and in the development of professionalism in police and prison.

While the interpretations, sources, and methods are dramatically different, legal historians continue to focus on the ways that law shifted. Legal historians have identified shifts, such as from emphasis on community to emphasis on individualism, across a broad spectrum, including economics, property, jurisprudence, legal education and the legal profession. Moreover, race has been a constant and central component of analysis in recent work in this era.

Regulation and the Market: An Economic Interpretation of the Antebellum Era

Running parallel to the thesis that the law became more concerned with individual property rights and freedom of contract in the antebellum era (or that at the least it maintained that concern, which it had inherited from the eighteenth century), is another set of scholarship that emphasizes a theme that is in some ways orthogonal to the liberalism thesis. This second body of work argues that the state regulated property heavily and that it intervened directly to promote economic growth. Around the time of World War II, some legal historians – doubtless influenced by the expansive role of the federal government during the New Deal – focused on the multiple ways that judges and legislators intervened in the economy. A series of studies identified changes in individual states. Louis Hartz' *Economic*

Thought and Democratic Policy (1948) was among the first of these studies. It pointed out how the Pennsylvania legislature and courts were concerned with economics and worked alongside one another to promote growth through direct subsidies to businesses, like railroads, through creating a favorable legal environment, and through constitutional law that permitted, for instance, the purchase of property for railroads. The study of Massachusetts by Oscar and Mary Handlin (1947) is even better known. Like Hartz, the Handlins focused on similar attitudes between legislators and jurists. A few years later Harry Scheiber focused on the Ohio canal era to show that the Ohio legislature directly funded the development of canals and courts worked alongside them (Scheiber, 1969).

William Novak (1996) has revived the theme of government intervention in the economy with a study that shows governments and courts heavily regulated property. While some dispute Novak's story of the extent of regulation (Scheiber, 1997), others have found similar regulation even earlier in American history (Hart, 1996: 1260–1263, 1265–1267). These questions of the extent of regulation are of particular importance to contemporary property lawyers, because it puts into context some of the "original intent" of the Fifth Amendment's prohibition against takings. James Ely has argued consistently and persuasively that an ethos of respect for property rights pervades United States history, especially in the nineteenth century (Ely, 1997). And while at certain moments, particularly during the Civil War, our nation has contemplated confiscation of property, the main ethos is one of respect for property rights (Hamilton, 2007). Hendrik Hartog's charming writing on the corporation of New York City uses pigs as an example of the government's role in regulation (Hartog, 1983: 139–142). Hartog's example has become a cult classic. Among the other important scholarship that touches on these issues, Herbert Hovenkamp (1991) has focused more globally on the federal government's role in promotion of economic growth – partly through government grants of land, and partly by financing "internal improvements." Judges in this era frequently dealt with claims that the legislature was infringing on the rights of corporations (Siegel, 1986). Political historians focus on the national analog to this, Henry Clay's system of "internal improvements," which used direct subsidies to promote transportation and thus spur economic growth (Eyal, 2007).

One place where the rights of property owners most clearly clashed with the state's regulatory power was in the Southern states' restrictions on people freeing their enslaved property (who were also, often, their family members). Bernie Jones has studied this across the South (Jones, 2009). Unsurprisingly, courts were reluctant – or perhaps unable is the better term – to protect property rights of owners to free their slaves (and family members).

There is ample literature on the ways that economic considerations bent the law of slavery (a topic considered below), there is also a robust literature on the ways that American courts and legislatures responded to Native

Americans' claims to land in this period. This is one place where those who see law as mostly heartless have focused their attention. Lindsay Robertson (2005) explores the background to Justice John Marshall's opinion in *Johnson v. McIntosh* that deprived Native Americans of the right to property they inhabited, and Tim Garrison (2009) deals with Southern courts' treatment of Native people.

Property scholars have been particularly active in expanding the debate from regulation (or not) into specific ways that judge-made and statutory law facilitated growth and even how law categorized people. Claire Priest argues in an ambitiously titled essay, "The Rise of Alienability," (2006) that property law increasingly allowed mortgaging of property and, thus, promoted the development of land as a financing tool. Similarly, Jenny Bourne Wahl (1998) demonstrated that Southern judicial opinions on slavery consistently shaped the law towards an efficient outcome. For instance, courts often refused to make masters liable for the torts committed by their slaves. Other studies that link economic thought to law in this period include Edward Balleisen (2001), who details the development of a national bankruptcy law, and Andrew Schocket (2007), who details the development of corporations in Philadelphia.

These legal arguments have made it into mainstream historical literature through a synthesis that appeared in Charles Sellers' *Market Revolution* (1994). Sellers' thesis, that American society was obsessed with the market and transformed by its growth in the pre-Civil War era, provoked substantial criticism among historians (Gienapp, 1994), though the legal thought that Sellers wrote about had little to do with this controversy. And the continuing focus on economic growth that appears in other important recent synthetic works of the era, especially Daniel Walker Howe's Pulitzer Prize-winning *What Hath God Wrought* (2007), confirm the understanding that law was about bringing order and promoting growth. What has received less attention are the ways that the Democratic and Whig parties split over law. Whigs were more protective of property rights than Democrats and also more supportive of imposing restraints through law in general (Kohl, 1989). Those distinctions appear relatively infrequently in the literature on economic development. And that may help explain some of the reasons that there are so many competing versions of the main thrust of American law in this period, because it was pointing in different directions and those directions changed depending on which political ideology was in control in a legislature or (to a lesser extent) a court. Thus, those looking for hierarchy and control, like Horwitz, find it, while those looking for the influence of "little" people to shape litigation and bring down the mighty can sometimes find it as well.

This is one place where legal history may help inform larger debates about the nature of thought and the multiple transformations of pre-Civil War America. For as historians debate the nature of capitalism, the growth of support for classical liberalism, the market, and slavery in the nineteenth century there are ample developments to study in law. Legal historians from Horwitz to Karsten to White (2003) to Hoeflich (2010) have been addressing for many years how American law responded to the revolution in transportation, printing, sentiment, and markets. To take one example, David Brion Davis has hypothesized that as the power of the market grew in the eighteenth and nineteenth centuries there was a corresponding growth in humanitarian sentiments (Davis, 1998). Tort and contract law offer registers for gauging changing attitudes towards sentiment in the wake of expanding markets. They point in the direction sometimes of increased concern for the vulnerable, but at other moments to remove the state from protection of the vulnerable and to leave each person on their own. The extreme individualism of the pre-Civil War period expressed in literature and in the market played out in courts and legislatures.

Jurisprudence and The Perspective of Literature: A Sentimental Interpretation of the Law

The role of law in promotion of the economy was one question of jurisprudence. Pre-Civil War Americans were deeply concerned about the role that law played in the community and the state more generally. Many – often members of the Whig party – emphasized the role of law in establishing and maintaining a stable and ordered community. The Whigs (and Federalists before them) expressed concern over the decline of traditional bonds of community and as Democratic ideas gained strength over the course of the pre-war period, a common theme among many lawyers was the problems that the breakdown of the rule of law posed. This was particularly acute during President Andrew Jackson's presidency. Political historians like Lawrence Kohl and Daniel Walker Howe have provided a framework for understanding the response of Whigs like Abraham Lincoln to Jacksonian Democracy. How one views the rule of law, the Whig search for order, and the countervailing Democratic desires for restrictions on corporate charters and lack of deference to the law, are central issues in the competing interpretations of the age, such as Howe's *What Hath God Wrought* (2007) and David Reynolds' *Waking Giant: America in the Age of Jackson* (2009). Were the Whigs the party of the rule of law and the Democrats the party of violation of law, such as through Indian Removal? This debate shows no signs of being settled soon and there is ample opportunity to look to the judicial opinions of Democrats and Whigs to see those competing visions, particularly on constitutional issues, as well as Democrat and Whig legislators at the state and national level. As with the controversy between Morton Horwitz and those who see different transformations in the antebellum era, much of the controversy seems to turn on how one views American history more generally.

Within the legal profession, there were substantial questions about jurisprudence – about the sources of law, the extent to which judges could depart from precedent, the importance of considerations of economy (also sometimes called utility), the role of sentiment, and the binding authority of the Constitution and statutes in opposition to conscience. Perry Miller's *The Life of the Mind in America: From the Revolution to the Civil War* (1965) was one of the first books to open up the study of pre-war legal thought to serious scrutiny. He turned to a variety of sources, sometimes novels, often oratory and articles, less frequently cases, to understand the shift from the Revolutionary era's Enlightenment to Romanticism, which was dominant in the years leading into Civil War. This shift saw the decline of natural law and the growth of a law calibrated to specific situations, which tried to take account of considerations of economy. It also saw the shift from a sense of natural justice – a sense that rights were greatest in a state of nature – to a sense that humans lived in a community and that each person's rights had to be circumscribed so as to not interfere with others' rights. Miller portrayed this particularly well through the use of James Fenimore Cooper's Leatherstocking Tales, which traced the hero Natty Bumppo as civilization encroached on his domain.

Others have followed Miller's lead in turning to literature to identify key conflicts in American legal thought. Robert Cover's *Justice Accused: Anti-Slavery Judges and the Judicial Process* (1975) examines why judges who were antislavery enforced proslavery laws. Those timeless questions of duty to statutory or constitutional law or internal conscience occupied the minds of antebellum Americans North and South. And while one should be cautious about interpretations of the origins of the Civil War in "law," abolitionists' persistent efforts to thwart a proslavery law they deemed immoral and Southern demands that the law be upheld certainly exacerbated tensions (Finkelman, 1981). Cover details that judges were bound by their duty to law and that duty was often linked in their minds with larger issues like the importance of the Constitution's guarantee of slavery. Cover turned to Herman Melville's *Billy Budd* (1924) to understand the conflicts judges faced when their own moral compass pointed in a different direction from the law. Cover saw in that story, dedicated to Melville's father-in-law, Massachusetts Justice Lemuel Shaw, the problem of a ship captain who knew Billy Budd had only killed a shipmate after being falsely accused of a crime. Yet that captain sentenced Billy to death. Cover's book, which was inspired by the criticism of federal judges who sentenced draft protesters to jail in the Vietnam era, is a penetrating analysis of problems that antebellum Americans resolved finally through war.

But in an attempt to stave off war, politicians and religious leaders frequently made the argument that judges and everyone else had to uphold the proslavery Constitution. This testifies to just how much proslavery law constrained actors. In fact, the argument was so common that abolitionists like Harriet Beecher Stowe wrote about how judges could not be looked to for help against slavery. In her novel *Dred: A Tale of the Great Dismal Swamp* Stowe created a judge who was antislavery in private but issued a proslavery opinion (Stowe, 1856). He did so because the law demanded the result. The conclusion was obvious to her readers: judges' cold, calculating legal reasoning would not free slaves (Brophy, 1998). Where Stowe advanced what one might term a "jurisprudence of sentiment," she, of course, was largely correct; however, sometimes judges broke free from the constraints of law, especially towards the end of the 1850s (Baker, 2010).

At the same time that proslavery writers were promulgating the idea that natural law did not protect against slavery – that in fact, sometimes slavery was even consistent with natural law – they also promoted the idea that rights should be judged in their social context. In place of the Enlightenment idea that there was a universal right to freedom, proslavery legal thinkers advanced the idea that rights should be calibrated to the social conditions of a society. Some people – the enslaved, for instance – were not fit for freedom. They supported this with empirical evidence about what happened in the wake of emancipation. Some abolitionists compiled their own empirical evidence about the horrors of slavery. If proslavery forces wanted to judge slavery based on a weighing of costs and benefits, the antislavery advocates were happy to put the debate on those grounds. In fact, as Jeannine DeLombard (2006) shows, abolitionists put "slavery on trial" in the court of public opinion. That abolitionists turned to legal analogies to combat slavery testifies to the power of legal analogies in the pre-Civil War era, even as they realized that law so frequently abandoned enslaved people. DeLombard's subjects, mostly Northern antislavery writers, were contemporaries of the proslavery advocates and thus had a particularly good vantage for evaluating how Southern law operated. This perspective, coming from Harriet Beecher Stowe, Frederick Douglas, and sometimes a Southern proslavery fiction author, critiques the rigid and strictly logical world of Southern law; it also points out the harshness of the institution of slavery. Perhaps most importantly it shows how pervasive the image of trials was in antebellum America, that when people attacked slavery they turned to law to provide a framework for the attack.

Enslaved people – or formerly enslaved people – advanced important ideas about jurisprudence and legal interpretation as well and increasingly their writings on law are being studied. So far, Frederick Douglas' legal thought has received the most attention (Brandon, 1998: 74–75). One of the great growth areas in legal history of this era will likely be in work that recovers the ideas advanced by those outside seats of power – such as slaves, women, and workers, and reformers. Already there is substantial work along these lines (VanderVelde, 2009).

Robert Ferguson's *Law and Letters in American Culture* (1984) follows Perry Miller's method in reading the fictional literature that judges and lawyers produced in the years leading into Civil War. Lawyers produced a disproportionately high share of the fictional literature and Ferguson uses it to show that law was closely linked to literary culture before the Civil War, with figures from William Wirt to Daniel Webster to Abraham Lincoln. But the "configuration" seems to end with Lincoln, as law became both more professional and less humanist. The shift is from Romanticism to empiricism, it seems. Gregg Crane (2002) offers a parallel account that deals with literature's treatment of citizenship. And other studies link popular literature and trials. Thus, Karen Halttunen (1998) shows that murder and gothic literature were linked and Hendrik Hartog (1997) shows the popular imagination's stereotypes about cheating wives, remorseless philanderers, and vengeful husbands and their relationship to murder prosecutions.

Many of these issues are dealt with best in a specific context, such as through biographies of judges. Leonard Levy's biography of Chief Justice Lemuel Shaw of Massachusetts (1957) brings a lot of these themes together and shows how they operate within a single person – how his conservative Whig ideas correlated with decisions like the development of the fellow servant rule, which allowed a corporation to limit its liability for injured workers. Particularly with law, where context and precedent are so important, biographical studies can detail how many moving parts – economic and religious considerations, facts, precedent, and statutes – fit together. Kent Newmyer's studies of Story and Marshall are examples of this (1985, 2001). Several books have offered a series of jurisprudential studies. (Huebner, 1999; White, 1988; White, 1976). Jurisprudential studies often extend beyond judges' economic reasoning. The construct of "honor," for instance, looms large in Huebner (1999). Often, of course, what was economically efficient also fit with judges' conceptions of morality. That which is useful is moral was not just an idea from utilitarian thought; it was also a fact of much of Southern thought. To take one example, the proslavery religious literature spoke of the duties of masters towards servants and urged humane treatment of slaves. While phrased in terms of morality, humane treatment was also consistent with the economic interests of the owners. Though it is difficult to know the power of judicial ideas of morality, Huebner has revived interest in them. We can say at a minimum that the ideas were important to the judges' opinions. This is one area that invites substantially more work to determine the instances in which considerations of morality (or honor as historians frequently phrase it) distinct from economic interests influenced judges and in what ways.

Legal Education and the Legal Profession

Increasingly the values of jurisprudence and the rising standards of the profession were conveyed in law schools, which grew dramatically in the nineteenth century. There are a series of studies of individual law schools, which detail the schools' students, their effect on the growth of the profession and the content of the courses. There are important studies of the Litchfield Law School, which was later Yale's law school (Kronman, 2004); the Harvard Law School (LaPiana, 1995; Kimball, 2009); and the Cumberland Law School (Langum and Walthall, 1997), among others. One particularly helpful way of studying legal education – and legal thought – is through the writings (and books) of leading educators (Langbein, 1993; Hulsebosch, 2008). There is ample room for more studies along these lines, that link the sources educators, treatise writers, and judges read and what they drew from those readings. There remains substantial work to be done in tracing the social origins of students and their subsequent careers and the role that the curriculum and networking played in the dissemination of key legal ideas. Finally, there remain many questions about the nature of education and the effect on students' professional lives as lawyers, politicians, and jurists.

While some of the work on the history of the bar is hagiography, other studies, like Maxwell Bloomfield's *American Lawyers in a Changing Society* (1976), use lawyers as a gauge of larger trends in American culture. Bloomfield details the move to professionalism and a stratified bar. Much of the work on the development of the profession proceeds through biographies, such as Mark Steiner's *Lincoln as Lawyer* (2005). Steiner looks broadly to Lincoln's practice, which emphasized railroads, though – surprisingly – also he represented a slaveholder. Steiner's intense focus on legal practice allows him to provide a new perspective on Morton Horwitz' question of whether the legal profession tilted towards corporate clients. Steiner sees lawyers on both sides of issues in alternate cases, so he questions whether there is a systematic bias in favor of corporate interests.

Steiner's volume draws on the Lincoln Legal Papers Project, which published on CD the extensive Lincoln Papers (2000). Others have also used those sources extensively, including Billings and Williams (2010). Another substantial documentary publication is the *Daniel Webster Legal Papers* (Konefsky and King, 1982–1989).

There are other important questions about the role of lawyers in regulating society. Despite the optimistic assessments of some that law was about civic republicanism, more recent literature calls into question how frequently lawyers represented abstract issues of justice (Spaulding, 2003). This is especially true – as in slavery cases – where there was such disagreement over what the moral position was, or even the obligations of the law (Schiller, 1992). A key issue for the pre-Civil War profession was the conflict between law and democracy, which appeared in Whig fears that Democrats were ignoring the Constitution and rule of law in areas from Indian Removal, to riots, to the charter rights of private corporations (Howe, 2007: 412–414, 443–445). Another fault line appeared in the movement to elect judges rather than have them appointed (Shugerman, 2012).

Race and Trial

Race and gender are central to the recent literature in legal history, as many of the chapters in this volume demonstrate. It is all the more astonishing, then, how rarely issues of race and gender appeared in legal historical literature of the pre-Civil War period until the 1970s or in some cases the 1980s. Even a work as iconoclastic as Horwitz' *Transformation of American Law* rarely dealt with slavery and Native Americans. It dealt in some more detail with women's property rights. In large part that is because the secondary literature that would have allowed more serious investigation of those areas did not yet exist. This means that studies of race and gender have been particularly rich in the last twenty-five years; they also hold out the promise for many more insights.

Often insights in those fields come from studies of trials. In race in particular, there have been a series of monographs on trials of slaves, many following on the success of a short and powerful volume by Melton McLaurin, *Celia, A Slave* (1991), which details the life of an enslaved woman, Celia, who murdered her "owner" and was then tried for the crime. The rich trial records allow McLaurin to reconstruct Celia's life and the crime in detail. Winthrop Jordan's *Tumult and Silence at Second Creek* (1993) is another very successful book around a single event – a supposed slave uprising about the beginning of the Civil War. There are periodic studies of the Nat Turner Rebellion in 1831, which set in motion a vigorous debate about slavery in the Virginia legislature (Wolf, 2006). John Brown's trial is a perpetual favorite (McGinty, 2009). Such trials frequently reveal efforts to police the boundaries separating free and slave, though often the line blurred when interests of high status white people lined up against each other, for instance when a white man had children with an enslaved woman (Gillmer, 2004). And while not quite trials, studies of interrogations of slaves may yield insight into the nature of slavery, how slaveowners viewed slave personhood and autonomy, and how slaves negotiated their lives under the sometimes control of owners (Auslander, 2011).

Another strand of scholarship uses quantitative analysis of many trials, such as Philip Schwarz' *Twice Condemned* (1988), a study of trials of slaves in Virginia, and James Campbell's *Slavery on Trial* (2007), about trials in the Richmond criminal courts. Campbell's social history of the criminal prosecution from 1830 to 1860 is based on a database of seven thousand prosecutions, of enslaved, free black, and white people. Historians' theorizing about the functions of law meet the cold reality of data, which reveal that many people, including elite white men, were subject to criminal prosecution. Everyone was subject to control, though the law focused on slaves, free blacks, poor whites, and affluent whites with varying degrees of intensity. While simplistic accounts of slavery might predict that the law was only a tool of hegemony, Campbell shows this is not law's only function. For law provided a framework that supported slavery and other forms of order. Those who broke the norms of order were subject to prosecution and often the prosecutions brought people of varying status together in one place for confrontations. The work in Southern legal history invites comparative work on other regions, to see how much the institution of slavery affected the law, for it remains unclear beyond the area of slavery just how different law was in the North, South, and West. Scholars seem to be in agreement that the Deep South was more violent (and more lawless) than other parts of the United States societies (Ayers, 1984).

Ariela Gross' *Double Character* (2001) joins a quantitative study of litigation over contracts for the sale of slaves with an intellectual history of appellate cases, particularly as they focus on honor. This sits at the convergence of social, intellectual, and legal history. For it is the social history of sales of slaves, of who was sold, and for how much. This is measured by a quantitative assessment of conflicts (lawsuits) over sales and how law positioned the rights of sellers and buyers. It also measures the dispositions of judges to know what makes a good slave and what is actionable in terms of fraud against a seller who represents someone as a "good" slave. Some of the cases turned on whether slaves were "defective" – did they behave as a slave could be expected to behave? Other cases put masters' (or renters' or overseers') character on trial. They asked questions like, did masters either mistreat or mismanage slaves? Some suits contained chilling accounts of abuse of slaves, as the court tried to figure out who was at fault for injuries to slaves. *Double Character* details how law took the proslavery ideas of Southern society and made the system work – simply how law supported slavery. Gross looks at civil suits between owners for breach of warranty regarding slaves to learn what the legal system expected of slaves: how they were expected to be docile and deferential. Those who ran away or were otherwise rebellious might subject their seller to a suit for breach of warranty. Gross' methods, which look to the trial courts as well as appellate courts, promise to tell us about the legal system and the expectations of white slave-holding society. This is what one might refer to as the "slaves' image in the judges' minds" (Fisher, 1993).

Double Character turns to the construct of honor to explain much of Southern legal culture. Honor is used to analyze everything from civil suits over fraud (53–54), sitting on juries, silencing slaves during trials (54), and slave sales, where the enslaved endured intrusive examinations, to the old stand-by: dueling (53). Is honor bearing too much interpretive weight? For instance, slave sales included a lot more than loss of honor – it was extraordinary dehumanization and often came with wrenching loss of family and friends. Moreover, the relationship between honor and economic interests is worth more exploration; how, for instance, is litigation over slaves related to a desire by buyers to protect their investments rather than to punish those who violated promises regarding the slaves? Is honor useful in explaining why slaves were not permitted to testify? Could those rules be more closely related to an economic analysis that worried about putting too much power in the hands of slaves to undo their owners?

Though books about trials often involve race, they also deal with other issues. For instance D. Graham Burnett's *Trying Leviathan* (2007) uses a trial about whether a whale was a fish (and thus whale oil subject to state tax) to understand the shifting ideas about science in New York in 1818. At other times trials and the surrounding culture reveal morality. Thus, Donna Dennis' *Licentious Gotham* (2009) turns to the regulation of pornography in the New York legislature and courts to reveal the often-forgotten history of morals regulation.

Civil War

The Constitution and ideas about constitutional culture provided a framework for Southern and Northern thinking about Union, secession and the coming of war. Those are issues addressed extensively in the vast literature on constitutional law in the antebellum era, including Fehrenbacher's *The Dred Scott Case* (1979), though recently historians have rethought the South's case and have often concluded that the Constitution was more proslavery (and hence the South's case was better) than had been acknowledged throughout much of the twentieth century (Graber, 2006). While constitutional thought is one of the largest areas for legal historical literature in the period 1820 through 1865, constitutionalism is beyond the scope of this essay. Nevertheless, the Civil War brought substantial change in the private and public law, as discussed in works from Mark Neely's *Civil Liberties Under Lincoln* (1991) to Stephen C. Neff's *Justice in Blue and Gray: A Legal History of the Civil War* (2010) and Neely's *Lincoln and the Triumph of the Nation* (2011). The growth of the state during the Civil War is one of the war's major impacts, as William Nelson's *The Roots of American Bureaucracy, 1830–1900* (1982) and Richard Bensel's *Yankee Leviathan: The Origins of Central State Authority in America, 1859–1877* (1991) have demonstrated. The most recent literature links the growth of the state to pre-war developments (Balogh, 2009).

Needs and Opportunities

There remain important – really fundamental – questions about how state and federal statutory law changed over this time. While a few areas (like the married women's property acts, state and federal bankruptcy laws, and general incorporation acts) have received attention, we need to know what the changes in law were and why. Were these responses to movements from below – like reform of women's rights, divorce, and landlord tenant law? For instance, how did the sentimental literature and the gothic literature on cities influence, if at all, the development of statutory law and police and court practices? As codification took place, how much did the codifiers respond to movements from reform of court procedure and commercial, social, and criminal laws?

Beyond statutory changes, there remains room for more work on the jurisprudence of the era and how it related to larger cultural ideas and economic reality. This research may include jurisprudential biographies of judges and lawyers; study of the growing sophistication of doctrine, often in response to the burgeoning market; and studies of how treatises fostered the development of law. The latter may be measured in part by how often judges cited treatises. Citation studies can also reveal how judges talked to one another through their opinions. This should be subjected to rigorous quantitative examination. There remain difficult questions about the salience of Whig ideology and Democrat ideology for judicial decision-making. Legal history is so much broader than just the writings of judges – important as that area is. It includes local practices, how people respond to the system of law; how law shapes larger cultural ideas, how it conditions people to think about their rights. There is plenty of opportunity for empirical study of law at local level, similar to Gross (2001) and Edwards (2009), which use litigation and other public records (like probate and mortgage records) to tell us about society. Similarly, there are questions about how sentiment and law interacted and how women, slaves, free black people, Native Americans, foreigners, even other countries influenced the development of law.

We once had a unifying thesis that spoke to people in the 1970s. Horwitz' *Transformation* was about how economically-based jurisprudence emerged that benefited corporations and entrepreneurs. A new paradigm may be emerging that speaks to groups today. That paradigm includes the role of law in oppression, the role of literature in creating new meanings for outsiders, the pluralistic origins of the law, and the ways that ideas emanated from the leaders downward to everyone else and sometimes up from the people to their leaders. Maybe other pieces of this story will speak to those who see law as politics and who ask whether a judge with one background views the law differently from a judge with another background. Of course economic reality remains central to those interpretations.

We have some reasonable prospect of understanding the ways that "law" shaped the surrounding society – economically and socially; and also how those considerations shaped legal institutions. The next generation of scholarship may bring legal doctrine and economics together with legal practice as seen at the local level. Law helps us understand how the system functioned and how well it functioned to meet the needs of culture. This may help relocate law closer to the center of American history in the antebellum era. As our nation continues to struggle with the proper role of the judge in deciding cases and interpreting the common law and statutes, with the proper place of economic thought in the common law, with the preservation of the market and other values as well through government action, and with the role of race in the development of American law, antebellum law – which had such rich debates about all these issues – may contribute to the debate once again.

References

Auslander, Mark (2011). *The Accidental Slaveholder: Revisiting a Myth of Race and Finding and American Family.* University of Georgia Press, Athens.

Ayers, Edward (1984). *Vengeance and Justice: Crime and Punishment in the Nineteenth-Century American South.* Oxford University Press, New York.

Baker, H. Robert (2010). *The Rescue of Joshua Glover: A Fugitive Slave, the Constitution, and the Coming of the Civil War.* Ohio University Press, Athens.

Balleisen, Edward (2001). *Navigating Failure: Bankruptcy and Commercial Society in Antebellum America.* University of North Carolina Press, Chapel Hill.

Balogh, Brian (2009). *Government Out of Sight: The Mystery of National Authority in Nineteenth-Century America.* Cambridge University Press, New York.

Bensel, Richard (1991). *Yankee Leviathan: The Origins of Central State Authority in America, 1859–1877.* Cambridge University Press, New York.

Billings, Roger and Williams, Frank J. (2010). *Abraham Lincoln, Esq.: The Legal Career of America's Greatest President.* University Press of Kentucky, Lexington.

Bloomfield, Maxwell (1976). *American Lawyers in a Changing Society, 1776–1876.* Harvard University Press, Cambridge.

Brandon, Mark E. (1998). *Free in the World: American Slavery and Constitutional Failure.* Princeton University Press, Princeton.

Brophy, Alfred L. (1998). "Humanity, Utility, and Logic in Southern Legal Thought: Harriet Beecher Stowe's Vision in *Dred: A Tale of the Great Dismal Swamp.*" *Boston University Law Review* 78: 1113–1161.

Burnett, D. Graham (2007). *Trying Leviathan: The Nineteenth-Century New York Court Case That Put the Whale on Trial and Challenged the Order of Nature.* Princeton University Press, Princeton.

Campbell, James (2007). *Slavery on Trial: Race, Class, and Criminal Justice in Antebellum Richmond, Virginia.* University Press of Florida, Gainesville.

Cover, Robert (1975). *Justice Accused: Anti-Slavery and the Judicial Process.* Yale University Press, New Haven.

Crane, Gregg (2002). *Race, Class, and Citizenship in American Literature.* Cambridge University Press, Cambridge, UK.

Davis, David Brion (1998). "The Problem of Slavery in the Age of Revolution, 1770–1823." In Bender, ed., *The Antislavery Debate: Capitalism and Abolitionism as a Problem in Historical Interpretation.* University of California Press, Berkeley.

DeLombard, Jeannine (2006). *Slavery on Trial.* University of North Carolina Press, Chapel Hill.

Dennis, Donna (2009). *Licentious Gotham*. Harvard University Press, Cambridge.

Edwards, Laura (2009). *The People and Their Peace*. University of North Carolina Press, Chapel Hill.

Ely, James W. (1997). *The Guardian of Every Other Right: A Constitutional History of Property Rights*. 2nd Edition. Oxford University Press, New York.

Eyal, Yonatan (2007). *The Young America Movement and the Transformation of the Democratic Party*. Cambridge University Press, New York.

Fehrenbacher, Don E. (1979). *The Dred Scott Case: Its Significance in American Law and Politics*. Oxford University Press, New York.

Ferguson, Robert (1984). *Law and Letters in American Culture, 1780–1860*. Harvard University Press, Cambridge.

Finkelman, Paul (1981). *An Imperfect Union: Slavery, Federalism, and Comity*. University of North Carolina Press, Chapel Hill.

Fisher, William W. (1993). "Ideology and Imagery in the Law of Slavery." *Chicago-Kent Law Review* 68: 1051–1427.

Garrison, Tim (2009). *The Legal Ideology of Removal: The Southern Judiciary and the Sovereignty of Native American Nations*. University of Georgia Press, Athens.

Gienapp, William E. (1994). "The Myth of Class in Jacksonian America." *Journal of Policy History* 6: 232–259.

Gillmer, Jason (2004). "Suing for Freedom: Interracial Sex, Slave Law, and Racial Identity in the Post-Revolutionary and Antebellum South." *North Carolina Law Review* 82: 535–620.

Graber, Mark (2006). *Dred Scott and the Problem of Constitutional Evil*. Cambridge University Press, New York.

Gross, Ariela (2001). *Double Character: Slavery and Mastery in the Antebellum Southern Courtroom*. Princeton University Press, Princeton.

Halttunen, Karen (1998). *Murder Most Foul: The Killer and the Gothic Imagination*. Harvard University Press, Cambridge.

Hamilton, Daniel W. (2007). *The Limits of Sovereignty: Property Confiscation in the Union and the Confederacy During the Civil War*. University of Chicago Press, Chicago.

Handlin, Oscar and Handlin, Mary F. (1947). *Commonwealth: A Study of the Role of Government in the American Economy: Massachusetts, 1774–1861*. Harvard University Press, Cambridge.

Hart, John F. (1996). "Colonial Land Use Law and Its Significance for Modern Takings Doctrine." *Harvard Law Review* 109: 1252–1300.

Hartog, Hendrik (1983). *Public Property and Private Power: The Corporation of the City of New York in American Law, 1730–1870*. University of North Carolina, Chapel Hill.

Hartog, Hendrik (1997). "Lawyering, Husbands' Rights, and 'the Unwritten Law' in Nineteenth- Century America." *Journal of American History* 84: 67–96.

Hartz, Louis (1948). *Economic Policy and Democratic Thought: Pennsylvania 1776–1860*. Harvard University Press, Cambridge.

Hoeflich, Michael (2010). *Legal Publishing in Antebellum America*. Cambridge University Press, New York.

Horwitz, Morton J. (1977). *The Transformation of American Law, 1780–1860*. Harvard University Press, Cambridge.

Hovenkamp, Herbert (1991). *Enterprise and American Law, 1836–1937*. Harvard University Press, Cambridge.

Howe, Daniel Walker (2007). *What Hath God Wrought: The Transformation of America, 1815–1848*. Oxford University Press, New York.

Huebner, Timothy (1999). *The Southern Judicial Tradition: Sectional Distinctiveness and State Courts, 1790–1890*. University of Georgia Press, Athens.

Hulsebosch, Daniel J. (2008). "An Empire of Law: James Kent and the Revolution in Books in the Early Republic." *Alabama Law Review* 60: 377–424.

Hurst, J. Willard (1956). *Law and the Conditions of Freedom in the Nineteenth-Century United States*. The University of Wisconsin Press, Madison.

Jones, Bernie (2009). *Fathers of Conscience: Mixed-Race Inheritance in the Antebellum South*. University of Georgia Press, Athens.

Jordan, Winthrop (1993). *Tumult and Silence at Second Creek: An Inquiry into a Civil War Slave Conspiracy*. Louisiana State University Press, Baton Rouge.

Kaczorowski, Robert J. (1990). "The Common Law, Background of Nineteenth Century Tort Law." *Ohio State Law Review* 51: 1127–1200.

Karsten, Peter (1998). *Heart versus Head: Judge-Made Law in Nineteenth-Century America*. University of North Carolina Press, Chapel Hill.

Kimball, Bruce A. (2009). *The Inception of Modern Professional Education: C.C. Langdell, 1826–1906*. University of North Carolina Press, Chapel Hill.

Klafter, Craig A. (1993). *Reason Over Precedents: Origins of American Legal Thought*. Greenwood Press, Westport, CT.

Kohl, Lawrence (1989). *The Politics of Individualism: Parties and the American Character in the Jacksonian Era*. Oxford University Press, New York.

Konefsky, Alfred S. and King, Andrew, eds (1982–1989). *Legal Papers of Daniel Webster*. 3 volumes. University Press of New England, Dartmouth.

Kronman, Anthony, ed. (2004). *History of Yale Law School*. Yale University Press, New Haven.

Langbein, John H. (1993). "Chancellor Kent and the History of Legal Literature." *Columbia Law Review* 93: 547–594.

Langum, David J. and Walthall, Howard P. (1997). *From Maverick to Mainstream: Cumberland School of Law, 1847–1997*. University of Georgia Press, Athens.

LaPiana, William (1995). *Logic and Experience: The Origin of Modern American Legal Education*. Oxford University Press, New York.

Levy, Leonard (1957). *The Law of the Commonwealth and Chief Justice Shaw*. Harvard University Press, Cambridge.

Lincoln, Abraham (2000). *The Law Practice of Abraham Lincoln: Complete Documentary Edition*. University of Illinois Press, Urbana, http://www.lawpracticeofabrahamlincoln.org/Search.aspx (last accessed September 25, 2012).

Llewellyn, Karl (1960). *The Common Law Tradition-Deciding Appeals*. Little, Brown and Company, Boston.

McGinty, Brian (2009). *John Brown's Trial*. Harvard University Press, Cambridge.

McLaurin, Melton (1991). *Celia, A Slave*. University of Georgia Press, Athens.

Melville, Herman ([1924] 1998). *Billy Budd and Other Tales*. Signet Classic, New York.

Miller, Perry (1965). *The Life of the Mind in America: From the Revolution to the Civil War*. Harcourt, Brace & World, Boston.

Moglen, Eben (1993). "The Transformation of Morton Horwitz." *Columbia Law Review* 93: 1042–1060.
Neely, Mark (1991). *The Fate of Liberty: Abraham Lincoln and Civil Liberties.* Oxford University Press, New York.
Neely, Mark (2011). *Lincoln and the Triumph of the Nation.* University of North Carolina Press, Chapel Hill.
Neff, Stephen C. (2010). *Justice in Blue and Gray: A Legal History of the Civil War.* Harvard University Press, Cambridge.
Nelson, William E. (1982). *The Roots of American Bureaucracy.* Harvard University Press, Cambridge.
Newmyer, Kent (1985). *Supreme Court Justice Joseph Story: Statesman of the Old Republic.* University of North Carolina Press, Chapel Hill.
Newmyer, Kent (2001). *John Marshall and the Heroic Age of the Supreme Court.* Louisiana State University Press, Baton Rouge.
Novak, William (1996). *The People's Welfare.* University of North Carolina Press, Chapel Hill.
Priest, Claire (2006). "Creating an American Property Law: Alienability and Its Limits in American History." *Harvard Law Review* 120: 385–459.
Reid, John Phillip (1977). "A Plot Too Doctrinaire." *Texas Law Review* 55: 1307–1322.
Reynolds, David (2009). *Waking Giant: America in the Age of Jackson.* HarperCollins, New York.
Robertson, Lindsay G. (2005). *Conquest by Law: How the Discovery of America Dispossessed Indigenous Peoples of Their Lands.* Oxford University Press, New York.
Scheiber, Harry (1969). *Ohio Canal Era: A Case Study of Government and the Economy, 1820–1861.* Ohio University Press, Athens.
Scheiber, Harry (1997). "Private Rights and Public Power: American Law, Capitalism, and the Republican Polity in Nineteenth-Century America." *Yale Law Journal* 107: 823–861.
Schiller, Reuel E. (1992). "Conflicting Obligations: Slave Law and the Late Antebellum North Carolina Supreme Court." *Virginia Law Review* 78: 1207–1251.
Schocket, Andrew M. (2007). *Founding Corporate Power in Early National Philadelphia.* Northern Illinois University Press, DeKalb.
Schwartz, Gary T. (1981). "Tort Law and the Economy in Nineteenth-Century America: A Reinterpretation." *Yale Law Journal* 90: 1717–1775.
Schwarz, Philip J. (1988). *Twice Condemned: Slaves and the Criminal Laws of Virginia, 1705–1865.* Louisiana State University Press, Baton Rouge.
Sellers, Charles (1994). *The Market Revolution: Jacksonian America, 1815–1846.* Oxford University Press, New York.
Shugerman, Jed Handelsman (2012). *The People's Courts.* Harvard University Press, Cambridge.
Siegel, Stephen A. (1986). "Understanding the Nineteenth Century Contracts Clause: The Role of the Property-Privilege Distinction and 'Takings' Clause Jurisprudence." *Southern California Law Review* 60: 1–119.
Simpson, A.W. Brian (1979). "The Horwitz Thesis and the History of Contracts." *University of Chicago Law Review* 46: 533–601.

Spaulding, Norman (2003). "The Myth of Civil Republicanism: Interrogating the Ideology of Antebellum Legal Ethics." *Fordham Law Review* 71: 1397–2863.

Steinberg, Allen (1989). *The Transformation of Criminal Justice, Philadelphia, 1800–1880*. University of North Carolina Press, Chapel Hill.

Steiner, Mark (2005). *Lincoln as Lawyer*. Northern Illinois University Press, DeKalb.

Stowe, Harriet Beecher (1856). *Dred: A Tale of the Great Dismal Swamp*. Phillips, Sampson, and Company, Boston.

VanderVelde, Lea (2009). *Mrs. Dred Scott*. Oxford University Press, New York.

Wahl, Jenny Bourne (1998). *The Bondsman's Burden: An Economic Analysis of the Common Law of Southern Slavery*. Cambridge University Press, Cambridge, UK.

Walker, Timothy (1850). *The Reform Spirit of the Day: An Oration before the Phi Beta Kappa Society of Harvard University, July 18, 1850*. James Munro, Cambridge.

White, G. Edward (1976). *American Judicial Tradition*. Oxford University Press, New York.

White, G. Edward (1988). *The Marshall Court and Cultural Change, 1815–1835*. Oxford University Press, New York.

White, G. Edward (2003). *Tort Law in America: An Intellectual History*. Oxford University Press, New York.

Wolf, Eva Sheppard (2006). *Race and Liberty in the New Nation: Emancipation in Virginia from the Revolution to Nat Turner's Rebellion*. Louisiana State University Press, Baton Rouge.

Chapter Five

Beyond Classical Legal Thought: Law and Governance in Postbellum America, 1865–1920

Roman J. Hoyos

The story about law in postbellum America is typically portrayed in dialectical (and often didactical) terms. Although the reasons for constructing the dialectic have changed over time, the general story goes something like this: Around the Civil War, jurists built an analytically rigorous legal science that sought to systematize and categorize law. They developed a formalistic mode of legal analysis that separated law from morals and public from private action, creating in the process a "nightwatchman" state concerned merely with protecting the rights of autonomous, formally equal individuals. This mode of legal thought has been variously termed "mechanical jurisprudence," "legal formalism," "legal orthodoxy," and "Classical Legal Thought." "By the turn of the twentieth century," one historian has written, "classicism had become the authentic expression of American law" (Wiecek, 1998: 64), culminating in the rise of the so-called "*Lochner* era," a period in which courts routinely struck down legislation, and narrowed the police power. *Lochner*, the story goes, spurred the development of "Progressive legal thought," classicism's chief competitor, which focused on social or group rights, and social conceptions of justice, science, and law (Kennedy, 2003: 632). While not triumphant, Progressive legal thought laid the foundations for Legal Realism and the New Deal, which ultimately brought classicism to an end (e.g., Wiecek, 1998; Fisher, *et al.*, 1993; Horwitz, 1992; Grey, 1983; Kennedy, 1980; Gilmore, 1977).

Recent scholarship has uncovered a more complex, three-dimensional history of law in postbellum America. Occasionally, the dialectic has been challenged head-on, but the critiques have rarely stuck, or have simply

A Companion to American Legal History, First Edition.
Edited by Sally E. Hadden and Alfred L. Brophy.
© 2013 John Wiley & Sons Ltd. Published 2021 by John Wiley & Sons Ltd.

modified it. Some critics have pointed out causal problems associated with classicism, and the incompleteness of the progressive anti-thesis (e.g., White, 2003). Others have suggested that historians have been overly concerned with economic regulation (e.g. Willrich, 2003: xvii). But there are other reasons to doubt the explanatory reach of classical legal thought. For instance, the rise of accidents, a perceived need for planning, and new assertions of authority seemed to outrun the common law's ability to govern; governments at both the state and federal levels began experimenting with administrative agencies; new areas of law emerged or exploded well beyond their earlier boundaries; state and local governments penetrated ever more deeply into the social, cultural, and economic lives of their inhabitants; and new ideas about the meaning of liberty and freedom emerged. "These were not so much years of governmental lethargy and subservience to vested interests," Morton Keller has explained, "as a time of intense conflict between old values and new pressures generated by massive change" (Keller, 1977: vii). Law was being put to a great many uses (and abuses) that cannot easily be captured by neat conceptual schematics of legal thought.

While a new synthesis is beyond the scope of this chapter, I want to explore the ways recent historiography undermines this classical-progressive dialectic, in particular the idea that classical legal thought dominated the years between 1865 and 1920. First, though, I want to outline the classical-progressive legal thought dialectic, and then explore the frontal challenges to it. After that, I turn to just a few areas in both private and public law in which the actual practice of law confounds the dialectic.

Classical Legal Thought

Classical legal thought is typically characterized by its formalism, conceptualism, categorical thinking, and largely deductive reasoning, as well as its separation of public and private realms of action. Its practitioners conceived of law as a "science," and attempted to impose order and geometric symmetry on the law through the application of a few general principles to particular cases (Grey, 1983). Its aim was to reduce the judge to a neutral arbiter of the law, limiting his discretion to make new law. In fact, judges did not make law at all, they merely "discovered" and applied it (Wiecek, 1998: 7). Discovery was typically the work of treatise writers, who used induced general legal principles from cases, and then deduced specific legal rules to be applied to future cases (Grey, 1983: 19). Principles helped to make law more coherent by reducing "a very large number of actual processes and events … to a much smaller number with a definite pattern" (Kennedy, 1980: 8). Classicists looked for bright-line tests and categorical approaches rather than balancing tests, so that once a judge identified the correct category, he could simply classify the case and put it in the correct box (White, 2003). "Considerations of justice and convenience were relevant, but only insofar as they were embodied in *principles* ..." (Grey, 1983: 150). There was nothing inherently conservative about classicism. Yet it was deployed to largely conservative ends, as it "integrated society, economy, and law [, and] sanctioned the status quo of the American social order. Classicism subordinated state to society and governmental powers to individual liberty. It selectively constrained state authority, yet blessed the application of state power for certain purposes, justifying the subordination of some groups of Americans and their domination by others" (Wiecek, 1998: 64).

Classical legal thought distinguished itself from two other jurisprudential traditions, natural law and historical jurisprudence. Like natural law, classical jurisprudence emphasized reason and universal principles as the main source of law. The two parted company in how they derived those principles. Natural law theorists reasoned abstractly, whereas classical theorists derived their principles from actual cases, giving classical legal thought a certain degree of positivism. This reliance on cases pushed classical thought towards the historical school. But classical thinkers did not equate custom with legal principle. Rather, later-derived principles were considered immanent in the existing body of cases, and that immanence gave it the authority of law. The "discovery" of this immanent principle was understood to be the science of law (Grey, 1983: 30–31).

The rise and fall of legal classicism has been somewhat difficult to periodize. Generally, it is said to have emerged sometime around the mid-nineteenth century, forming the dominant mode of legal thinking until the New Deal (Wiecek, 1998: 64–122; Kennedy, 1980). The "foundations" of classicism have nonetheless been traced to the American Revolution, with its emphasis on limited government, individual liberty, the common law, and judicial review (Wiecek, 1998: 20). Rapid social and economic change, as well as the centrifugal forces of the industrialization and urbanization, placed powerful pressures on law. Classical legal thought thus attempted to adjust an older legal worldview that privileged decentralization, politically and economically, with a new socio-economic order through "a neutral, impartial, and decentralized 'night-watchman' state" (Horwitz, 1992: 4). The two most pernicious legal doctrines growing out of this approach to law were liberty of contract and substantive due process, which formed the basis of classicism's public law manifestation, "laissez-faire constitutionalism" (but see Grey, 1983: 34, n. 134). Judges used these doctrines repeatedly to strike down social legislation, especially in the area of labor relations (Forbath, 1991). This was the "*Lochner* era."

Jurisprudential Pluralism

One of the chief critiques of classical legal thought has been its excessive formalism. Christopher Columbus Langdell, the (in)famous dean of Harvard Law School, has long been identified as the primary agent in formalism's rise to prominence. Through his reforms in legal education, his scholarship, and the work of his disciples, Langdell, it is said, made logic the life of the law. Langdell, who became dean in 1870, has been the bogeyman of anti-formalists since Oliver Wendell Holmes' review of Langdell's work on contract law. The Langdellian thesis, it is said, generated the anti-thesis that became the basis for modern legal thought: "The life of the law has not been logic; it has been experience" (Grey, 1983: 3).

Scholars have not been kind to Langdell. Grant Gilmore, for instance, described Langdell as "an essentially stupid man" (Gilmore, 1977: 42). Yet Langdell's stature as the godfather of classicism has been challenged recently. Bruce Kimball's biography of Langdell has levied a powerful challenge to the idea that Langdell was fundamentally a formalist (Kimball, 2009; see also LaPiana, 1994). Kimball points out that most studies of Langdell have focused on a narrow selection of his work (Kimball, 2004: 280–282). Broadening that selection alone reveals that "Langdell's characteristic mode of reasoning in the field of contracts and, more broadly, in jurisprudence is actually three-dimensional, exhibiting a comprehensive yet contradictory integration of induction from authority, deduction from principle, and analysis of justice and policy." Langdell's jurisprudence and pedagogy, in fact, "reflected the approach of a practicing lawyer who handled technical questions in separate cases for fifteen years," and was mostly concerned with improving the practice of law (Kimball, 2009: 5–6, 111). The caricature of Langdell as simplistic formalist that persists among modern scholars is due less to Langdell's actual jurisprudence than to the needs of realist scholars of the 1920s and 1930s who did not appreciate "the value of analytical logic as a solvent for legal problems" (Kimball, 2004: 303 (inner quotations omitted)). Kimball comes close to destroying the idea that Langdell was a classical theorist. At the very least, his work calls into question classicism's prominence in the late nineteenth century.

Of course, Langdell was not the only classical thinker. Studies of others jurists demonstrate that they employed a range of jurisprudential approaches. Perhaps this is why it has been difficult for scholars to determine exactly who was and was not a classicist. For instance, a study of John Chipman Gray, who was both a colleague and critic of Langdell, categorizes Gray as a classicist while simultaneously undermining the characterization. "To Gray," Stephen Siegel writes, "the 'welfare of the persons subject to a system of law' was more important than 'the logical coherency of the system itself'" (Siegel, 2000: 1548). Public policy and moral concerns similarly animated Francis Wharton's approach to law (Siegel, 2004). Meanwhile, natural law played an important role in the thinking of John Norton Pomeroy, though he believed that eternal principles could be discovered through history rather than reason (Siegel, 1990). In fact, historical jurisprudence, in various guises, characterized the thought of a great number of ostensibly classical thinkers (Rabban, 2003; Parker, 2011, ch. 6). "Far from conservative apologists for the status quo," David Rabban has concluded, late nineteenth century jurisprudes "viewed legal evolution as a response to the changing customs of society and maintained that constitutional as well as common law must reflect these changes" (Rabban, 2003: 547).

It appears, then, that jurisprudence in postbellum America was pluralistic. Neither formalism nor analytic positivism was its singular focus, though the generation or "discovery" of general legal principles may have remained an important goal. The focus on general principles was less about formalism than it was about attempting to bring some coherence to the chaotic explosion of legislation and reported cases in the nineteenth century (Tamanaha, 2010, ch. 3). Postbellum legal thinkers appear to have used a variety of means to uncover broader principles. And while they may have lacked a "sociological jurisprudence" in the sense that progressives used it, the inductive process of generating legal rules would not allow them to escape the social (Welke, 2001: 213). Yet to the extent that classical legal thought was an operative mode of thought in postbellum America, we still have to ask whether courts and other legal actors were of the same mind as the theorists.

"Private" Law in Postbellum America

So-called "private" law (e.g. contracts, torts, property) was once thought to be the singular domain of legal classicism (Grey, 1983). In fact, the definition of these fields as discrete areas of law was largely the work of nineteenth-century legal scientists. One of the primary goals of this definition was to demarcate more precisely the proper spheres of public and private action. But it has never been clear that courts and judges followed the lead of the treatise writers. Courts and judges typically had their own, independent concerns. Treatise writers gave them new categories of law to work with, but judges could never escape the particular facts and parties before them.

The Law of Contracts

Contracts was a relatively new area of law in the nineteenth century, formerly having been mostly subsumed within property law. This newness made it ripe for innovation. Contract's doctrinal origins lay in the common law writ of assumpsit, which provided the recovery of damages for breach of contract (Simpson, 1975). As it emerged from assumpsit, early contracts treatises focused on the specific duties and obligations that arose from a variety of status relationships, for example, master-servant, husband-wife. After the Civil War, securing the enforcement of promises became contract's central concern. This was done through the invention of a new requirement for enforceability: consideration. Enforceable promises were now those promises supported by consideration (Kreitner, 2007: 9). It was through this enforceability of promises that contract came to symbolize the free market. Consideration enforced only those promises made at the cash nexus, excluding gifts, for example, which promised "something for nothing" (Kreitner, 2007: ch. 1; Keren, 2010: 174–177). Thus, "The model of contract theory which implicitly underlay the classical law of contract [was] the model of the market" (Atiyah, 1985: 402).

The free market exchange was based on impersonal rather than status relationships, which was also reflected in the classical law of contract. While early contract law was based on duties owed in hierarchical relationships like master-servant, contracting in the late nineteenth century was understood as an impersonal transaction, between autonomous, freely acting, self-interested individuals, who owed no duties to the other party (*caveat emptor*). Thus, parties were not required to disclose information to each other, nor were there any implied warranties outside of fraud. The role of the courts was simply to enforce the will of the contracting parties, ensuring procedural fairness only (Atiyah, 1985: 398–408). Otherwise, the state was to refrain from interference with "the sphere associated with economic rationality" (Kreitner, 2007: 17).

This construction of classical contract law raises the question whether the kinds of contracts cases that were actually litigated were central to the market economy. Lawrence Friedman, in a detailed study of Wisconsin cases, found that contract cases in three different periods from the mid-nineteenth to the mid-twentieth century rarely dealt with questions central to industrialization. Moreover, he found that the "purity" of contract law often came through expurgation. Major areas dealing with contracts were dealt with statutorily, for example, labor relations, insurance, debtor laws, business regulation (Friedman, 2011: 17). Other areas were not dealt with at all, such as promises given in the family setting, which failed the new consideration requirement (Keren, 2010). To the common law of contracts, Friedman has concluded, was left the "residue" of market transactions not regulated by the state (Friedman, 2011: 17).

Nonetheless, there was something "revolutionary" about contracts in the late nineteenth century (Kreitner, 2007: 3). Its importance, though, was less doctrinal than ideological, as "contract transcended the boundaries of law," becoming "a dominant metaphor for social relations and the very symbol of freedom" (Stanley, 1998: x). Prior to emancipation, contract provided the dividing line between slavery and freedom (Kreitner, 2007; Stanley, 1998). With slavery's demise and the triumph of free labor, contract became the very symbol of freedom, and a site for debates over freedom in a post-emancipation, rapidly-industrializing society. Central to these debates was "whether commodity exchange was a morally defensible model of rights and duties among free persons" (Stanley, 1998: 70). Ultimately, "contract law as an ideology" would help to naturalize the power relations behind impersonal market relationships (Gabel and Feinman, 1998: 500–503).

Classicism's Keystone

If contract was classical law's synonym for a free market economy, classical tort law was the free market's remedial system for the inevitable collisions between autonomous individuals in an industrializing society. This is what made tort law the "keystone" to the architecture of classical legal thought (Witt, 2001: 46). Its cynosure was negligence, which displaced an earlier law of torts centered around the non-contractual duties that individuals, usually within particular status relationships, owed one another, and which (purportedly) held the injurer strictly liable. In contrast to these particular duties, "Negligence was a universal rule, satisfying conceptualist tendencies in legal thought; it was an all-purpose cause of action, supplanting both trespass and case; and it was an evaluative standard for decision-making in cases involving unintentional injuries to strangers" (White, 2003: 688). Fault thus became the basis for liability for accidents rather than injury. Liability for fault was further narrowed by doctrines like contributory negligence, the fellow servant rule, proximate cause, and assumption of risk, which led earlier scholars to argue that tort law was an effort to subsidize industrial development by minimizing the liability of industrial entrepreneurs (Friedman, 2005: 350–358; Horwitz, 1992).

But if tort law was the keystone for classical legal thought, it was precariously placed as it stood at the boundary of public and private law itself (White, 2003: xx). Tort law is fundamentally about the allocation of the risks and burdens of economic development. This is inherently a policy question. And courts appear to have backed off relatively quickly from the harsher operation of liability-limiting doctrines of classical tort law. Courts developed a number of exceptions and counter-doctrines to those enumerated above, like comparative negligence, *res ipsa loquitur*, the vice-principal rule, and relaxed privity doctrines (Friedman, 2005: 357–364). One study has found that contributory negligence was a high standard, and that the burden of proof was placed on the defendant, resulting in few cases where liability was denied on that basis (Schwartz, 1981: 1743). In fact, courts were more likely to find that the nature of the accident spoke for itself (*res ipsa loquitur*). While it is not clear that victims of accidents were made better off, or received compensation for their injuries (Friedman, 2005: 357), it does undermine the subsidization thesis.

Institutional concerns also undermined the reception of classical tort law as well: the massive rise in tort cases, lawyers' use of the contingent fee that compromised their professional obligations, the increasing number of faultless plaintiffs, and the increasing number of women plaintiffs, who challenged judges' assumptions about the responsibility for and consequences of accidents (Witt, 2001: 59–65; Welke, 2001). Highly-publicized industrial accidents could also change "common sense" ideas about causation (McEvoy, 1995). Subsidization also had problems penetrating courtrooms at the ground level; the closer to the ground law lay the more likely a "sporting theory of justice" prevailed. Moreover, classical tort law hardly stood in the way of the "socialization" of accidents in the form of statutory liability at both state and federal levels, mandatory technological and operational safety standards, workmen's compensation, insurance and administrative regulation of accidents (Welke, 2001; Witt, 2001). If it ever existed, the end of the nineteenth century was the beginning of the end for classical torts, as it was displaced doctrinally, statutorily, and administratively.

There was a certain irony involved in the classical effort to use tort law to define "a zone of uninfringed [individual] autonomy" (Witt, 2001: 44), as it involved individuals at their most vulnerable (Welke, 2001). Tragedy, fright, accidents, and suffering of new sorts became defining features of late-nineteenth century America. The Civil War had put suffering on display on a massive scale (Faust, 2008), and "Wars have a way of staying in the mind. Scenes of unimaginable carnage cannot be casually shrugged off" (Lears, 2009: 12). Industrial and rail accidents ensured that injury and suffering would remain common facts of postbellum America, leading one historian to conclude that "Dependence rather than autonomy was a hallmark of modern life" (Welke, 2001: xi). This made tort law's primary concern with defining an autonomous sphere of individual action, as well as narrow conceptions of liability for accidents, deeply problematic. Autonomy required physical and mental integrity. As the industrialization process compromised autonomy, the state stepped in to protect it.

Rather than adumbrating a sphere of private action, tort law appears to have been a vehicle for bringing the facts and conditions of modern life into the courtroom. "Negligence was a question of fact" (LaPiana, 1994: 114), and courts often left this question to be determined by juries (Schwartz, 1981: 1763). Expert witnesses facilitated this process. According to Barbara Welke, "Women's testimony, supported by the expert medical opinions of their doctors, confirmed what jurors already knew: fright and shock could cause a pregnant woman to suffer a miscarriage. Legal scholars and lawyers alike unhesitatingly incorporated this truism into their legal reasoning" (Welke, 2001: 213). This enabled judges and juries to ignore or subvert subsidization doctrines, and impose their own assumptions about causation and liability on law.

The "Ambiguity" of Classical Legal Thought

Property law occupied an "ambiguous" place within classical legal thought (Wiecek, 1998: 105). Property had the longest pedigree of the areas of "private" law. Like tort law, property appeared to mark the boundary between public and private, the state and the individual, where the protections of property rights defined individual rights and delimited state power. The role of the courts was simply to protect "vested interests" in property (Corwin, 1914). This conception can be traced to Blackstone, who held that property was the "sole and despotic dominion" over things. In other words, it was both physicalist and absolutist. Over the course of the nineteenth century, though, property was de-physicalized, becoming understood, as Wesley Hohfeld characterized it, as a "bundle of rights." Yet as the concept of property expanded from physical things to intangible interests over the course of the nineteenth century every act potentially infringed someone's property interest. This expansive concept of property ultimately undermined classical ideas of property by exposing the tension between competing rights, forcing courts to invoke "policy" to decide cases (VandeVelde, 1980; Alexander, 1999; but see Banner, 2012, ch. 3).

Moreover, property remained subject to regulation. Property had long been subject to the police power, which Blackstone referred to as the "'due regulation and domestic order' in the state, whereby 'the individuals of the state, like members of a well-governed family, are bound to conform their general behaviour to the rules of propriety, good neighborhood, and good manners; and to be decent, industrious and inoffensive in their respective stations'" (quoted in Tomlins, 2005: 1218). Massachusetts Chief Justice Lemuel Shaw explained exactly why and how property was subject to the regulation by the state. "All property in this commonwealth," he wrote

> is derived directly or indirectly from the government, and held subject to those general regulations, which are necessary to the common good and general welfare. Rights of property, like all other social and conventional rights, are subject to such reasonable limitations in their enjoyment, as shall prevent them from being injurious, and to such reasonable restraints and regulations established by law, as the legislature, under the governing and controlling power vested in them by the constitution, may think necessary and expedient (*Commonwealth v. Alger*, 1851: 85).

Vermont Chief Justice Isaac Redfield declared this to be "a general principle applicable to all free states" (*Thorpe v. Rutland and Burlington R.R. Co.*, 1855: 149). These courts were not alone in their subordination of private to public rights (Novak, 1996). This regulation did not ease in postbellum America. In fact, as "property" expanded, so too did its regulation. The emergence of so-called "regulatory takings" around the turn of the century was evidence of just how extensive the regulation of property was, not of a laissez-faire state.

One particularly important area of property regulation was land use. Urbanization and industrialization hit cities hard when it came to spatial arrangements. To meet these pressures many municipalities undertook infrastructural development, which "rested on eminent domain to marshal physical resources and on taxation to mobilize capital development. With power to take land and pay for it by special assessments, the city opened, widened, and paved its streets, and built sewer and drainage systems." In other words, cities destroyed existing property rights to provide the basic means by which more people could live in tighter spaces, exercise their rights of locomotion, and enable commerce to move more rapidly through the city. City governments were aided in their efforts by the courts, which "helped by their interpretation of the law. Efforts to restrict the powers of condemnation and taxation met only partial success" (King, 1986: 2).

Courts also played a more active role in the spatial arrangement of cities in their approach to covenants, private agreements restricting the use of land. Cities in this period were marked by rapid change in the character of their neighborhoods. Within a few years a residential neighborhood could be dominated by commercial or industrial enterprises. This led to a spike in the use of covenants. While courts tended to favor the free alienability of land, they tended to uphold covenants if they were part of the bargain for the conveyance of property. Covenants, though, restricted the ways in which subsequent owners could use their property. Thus courts would also invalidate or modify covenants under the changed conditions doctrine, which held that when a neighborhood had changed substantially a covenant limiting property to uses inconsistent with the new conditions would not be enforced. This enabled courts to balance vested rights with creative destruction (Lamoreaux, 2011; King, 1986: 50–51; Selvin, 1980).

Other areas of property highlight the more policy-oriented concerns of courts as well. Nuisance law was driven by market calculations, with liability often determined by the market valuation of the physical injury. Injunctions for nuisances emerged as a common remedy in the late nineteenth century, giving courts more discretion and forcing them to balance various interests, such as the plaintiff's loss, defendant's cost, and public's benefit, even when they appeared to be using formalist doctrines (King, 1986: 83–84, 87). The refusal of American courts to recognize the English common law's ancient lights doctrine, which allowed prescriptive negative easements for light and air, reflected the concern with creative destruction almost demanded by rapidly growing urban communities (King, 1986: 96). The creation of an attractive nuisance doctrine sought to protect children from property owners' careless use of industrial technology (Karsten, 1992).

And the public trust doctrine facilitated municipal ownership of public utilities and ensured an adequate water supply (Selvin, 1980: 1422–1434).

* * *

While classical legal scientists appear to have succeeded in reorganizing doctrine and creating new categories and areas of law (e.g. torts, contracts), it is not clear that their methods penetrated deeply into the actual practice of law. Unlike treatise writers, courts could not ignore the facts and parties before them. The attempt to cordon off an area of private action free of governmental regulation was a chimera. Policy concerns governed a great deal of the judicial decision-making process, and statutory and administrative regulation narrowed the range and effect of core areas of private law.

Public Law in Postbellum America

The classical law thesis on the public law side – in the form of laissez-faire constitutionalism – has been challenged more systematically, though more work remains to be done. The harsher edges of laissez-faire constitutionalism have been softened in recent years. It no longer appears as the midwife to corporate capitalism, but instead as a juristic concern about monopolistic privilege rooted in a combination of Jacksonian equal rights and Republican free labor ideologies (e.g., Benedict, 1985; Jones, 1967; McCurdy, 1975). But even this revision is being revised (Siegel, 2002). In fact, recent studies on the police power and urban governance have identified law as a driving force in the expansion, not the limitation, of state power.

Police Powers Jurisprudence

One of the earliest challenges to the laissez-faire thesis came at the time it was being forged. Charles Warren, writing in the 1910s and 1920s, looked at hundreds of cases considered by the U.S. Supreme Court concerning due process and equal protection challenges to so-called "social legislation." Of those, he identified only three that were struck down. In addition, of 158 liberty of contract cases between 1873 and 1912 related to the police power, he found eleven concerning social legislation held unconstitutional; of the 144 challenged on commerce clause grounds, thirty-eight were held unconstitutional, twenty-five of which related to social legislation. "The actual record of the Court," Warren concluded, "shows how little chance a litigant has of inducing the Court to restrict the police power of a State, or to overthrow State laws under the 'Due Process' clause; in other words, *it shows the Court to be a bulwark of the police power, not a destroyer*" (Warren, 1913a: 310 (emphasis added); see also Warren, 1913b).

Warren also found that the Supreme Court was instrumental in the creation of a federal police power (Warren, 1923: III, 457–460). In contrast to Progressive portrayals of the Court, he continued, the police power cases provided evidence that the Court had adopted "the theory of modern sociological jurists that the law must recognize the priority of social interests" (Warren, 1923: III, 466).

While Warren's approach was perhaps methodologically crude, recent scholarship is confirming his central thesis. In the 1980s, Melvin Urofsky did for the state courts what Warren did for the U.S. Supreme Court. While he found that state courts were more willing than the U.S. Supreme Court to strike down social legislation, Urofsky found that most state judiciaries were sympathetic to such legislation. This sympathy was often due to the work of women reformers, like Florence Kelley (Batlan, 2010). By the end of the postbellum period, state courts gave "wide latitude [to] legislative discretion in applying the police power" (Urofsky, 1985: 80). Thus, Urofsky concludes, reformers were at most delayed by courts, not blocked. In fact, he suggests that the era of a conservative judiciary emerged only in the 1920s (Urofsky, 1985: 89; see also Chomsky, 1993).

William Novak has gone a step further, identifying in the postbellum period "a hidden revolution in American government – a fundamental shift in the scale, scope, techniques, and legitimating rationales of governance" that "forged a distinctly modern state in the United States" (Novak, 2008: 54). Novak, whose earlier work unearthed a rich regulatory tradition in antebellum America rooted in common law conceptions and practices of police (Novak, 1996), has begun to turn earlier interpretations of postbellum governance on their head. Building on Warren's insight, he invites us to focus on the typical rather than the exceptional cases, which allows us to see a transformation in law and liberalism that included new conceptions of the individual, the public good, and the scale of governance. That there were over 18,000 pieces of legislation in 1899 and 1900 alone suggest that constitutional doctrines like due process and liberty of contract had little effect in corralling legislative power. "Beneath the public formalities of constitutional law and the public pieties of democratic theory," Novak writes, "the more concealed, subterranean world of police exposes the exceptional coercive power of this supposedly limited government." In contrast to those who hold that law and police are distinct, usually opposing, modalities of governance, in which law acts as a limit on police, Novak sees the two as intimately connected. The police *power*, in fact, is a legal concept; it "originated and was legitimated in law" (Novak, 2008: 60, 55, 56). This work is exposing the *Lochner* era as more myth than reality (e.g. Lindsay, 2010; Mayer, 2009).

Writing in a similar vein, Christopher Tomlins has found a rapidly increasing federal police power in the nineteenth century (both nationally and internationally), underwritten by the U.S. Supreme Court. Looking specifically at the U.S. Supreme Court's police jurisprudence in the areas of relations with American Indians, immigration, and territorial acquisition, he concludes, that "insofar as the Constitution was even relevant to those powers, [the Court] facilitated their exercise by staying out of the way." In contrast to Novak, Tomlins treats police as a modality of rule independent of, and largely immune from, law, arguing that "in state and federal juridical discourse police expresses unrestricted and undefined powers of governance rooted in a discourse of sovereign inheritance and state necessity ...." In light of this longer genealogy of police, *Lochner* appears not as a myth, but as a "clumsy" attempt "to change the trajectory of police powers jurisprudence." The Court's attempt in that case to use law to limit police by enumerating powers and attempting to set a standard for the evaluation of its exercise, Tomlins argues, ultimately "led nowhere [–] *Lochner* had no 'era'" (Tomlins, 2008: 54, 47, 57, 59).

Law and Governance in Urban America

This attention to state and federal police power jurisprudence should not deflect attention from developments at the local level. As Michael Willrich has pointed out, "at the local level, American courts were the true laboratories of public welfare and social governance" (Willrich, 2003: xxvi). Urban governments (and that includes courts), faced numerous difficulties as cities grew at outrageous rates in the late nineteenth and early twentieth centuries. The influx of new people from around the globe, squeezing into ever tighter spaces, raised novel issues for local governments. New questions about public health, morals, economy, and property put enormous pressure on local governments to act.

Perhaps the most interesting and innovative development involving the judiciary was the reorganization of court systems in major cities across the nation. Leading the way was Chicago, whose city courts provided the model for the rest of the nation. Importantly, the spur to reorganization had nothing to do with classical legal thought or laissez-faire constitutionalism. Rather, it was the justice of the peace system that was unable to meet the needs of the rapidly expanding city. The pejoratively-dubbed "justice shops" were ruled by justices of the peace, laymen who made their money on fees for everything, including guilty verdicts. Reformers across the nation sought to reorganize judicial power, with both trained judges and a corps of university-trained social workers who would regulate the lives of the urban working class. In contrast to the idea that courts were fearful of state power, municipal courts combined social justice with social control to reach "deep into the everyday life of the modern metropolis." Chicago created several city courts – morals, domestic relations, and boys, as well as the Psychopathic Laboratory – that addressed the growing problems of urban life. Rather than separating state from society, "the court *reached into* society. Combining therapeutic ideologies of social intervention and individual treatment with eugenic techniques for population management and racial betterment, the Municipal Court governed everyday life in Chicago" (Willrich, 2003: 4, xxxiii, 98, 115). The creation of the municipal court system was fundamentally about improving the governance of urban society. This aim was typical of urban law.

Of all matters of local governance, public health is the least susceptible to strict legal and jurisdictional boundaries, and the most susceptible to new techniques and technologies of power. "Individual liberty and property rights melt[] away before the state's power – indeed its inherent legal duty – to protect the population from peril" (Willrich, 2008: 76). Concern over public health has long been an agent in the transformation of governmental authority and the redefining of the public interest (Novak, 1996: 191–234; Einhorn, 1991: 204–215). After the Civil War, the triple forces of urbanization, immigration, and industrialization combined to make public health one of the most pressing areas of legal and governmental intervention. A healthy populace was foundational for both economic and moral prosperity. As University of Chicago law professor Ernst Freund put it, "In order that social life may exist, that human faculties may be developed, and the progress of civilisation be made possible, a certain minimum of physical well-being is necessary" (Freund, 1904: 7). Securing the public's health was in an important sense one of the "conditions of freedom" (Novak, 1996: 191–234). Thus, "courts accorded health-related ordinances greater status than welfare ones" (King, 1986: 145).

The most important change in matters of public health after the Civil War had nothing to do with legal thought. The rise of the "germ theory" of disease in the late nineteenth century fundamentally transformed the approach to public health. The prior theory held that general filth was responsible for disease, and focused attention on places and their cleanliness. Sanitary reform was thus the main focus of disease prevention. "Clean streets, airy apartments, a pure supply of water, were certain safeguards against epidemic disease" (Rosenberg, 1987: 6). The germ theory enabled public health and law enforcement officials, as well as judges, to shift the focus of public health from places to people. Health officials thus "worked to replace city-wide clean-up programs with ones focusing on living human germ carriers ... and encouraging personal habits that would protect individuals from the people around them" (Leavitt, 1996: 24). In this new context public health regulation became highly coercive. By the 1890s, courts not only insulated public health officials from liability for wrongful arrests of those suspected of infection, as well as for injuries caused by vaccination, but also allowed them to force individuals to submit to medical procedures (Willrich, 2008: 83).

Although quarantine had long been a tool of public health, the germ theory enabled the quarantine of even healthy carriers of disease, a "new worry" of public health officials (Leavitt, 1996: 25). Facilitating the identification of healthy carriers was state laboratory testing. The first municipal laboratory was established in 1888 (Leavitt, 1996: 37). Now, otherwise seemingly healthy people could, through laboratory analysis of bodily excretions or extractions, be identified as threats to the public. Lab reports were also used as evidence in court trials and hearings to deprive healthy carriers of their liberty. The case of "Typhoid Mary" is the most (in)famous of such cases. An Irish immigrant cook, Mary Mallon was a carrier of typhoid fever and essentially imprisoned for twenty-six years (until she died) because of the threat she posed to public health, despite never having suffered from the disease herself (Leavitt, 1996: 2).

This new threat of healthy carriers of disease meant new techniques of isolation and prevention, as well as new forms of discipline to ensure individual cleanliness, which ultimately formed a "new gospel of individualized public health" (Leavitt, 1996: 25; see also Leavitt, 1982). Forced vaccination, upheld by the U.S. Supreme Court in *Jacobson v. Massachusetts* (1905), was one of the more controversial of the new public health measures, as it entailed the physical invasion of the body itself by the state (Willrich, 2008: 87–90). At a time when the public did not fully understand, if at all, the germ theory of disease, and individuals like Mary Mallon could deny ever having been sick with a disease, the coercive power of the state must have appeared enormous. Michael Willrich's rich descriptions of the popular resistance to the invasions of health officials, often accompanied by police officers, in typically poor neighborhoods during disease epidemics attests both to the power of the state and the fear that it engendered, in matters of public health (Willrich, 2011).

Conclusion

It would seem to go without saying, but bears reminding, that law is a great deal more than jurisprudence. But this is not to repeat the separation between law on the books and law in action; law in the books can be law in action (Fernandez and Dubber, 2012). None of this, then, is to suggest that there was not a way of thinking about law that had the characteristics of what has been termed "classical legal thought." But it is perhaps better described as a jurisprudential movement, which sought greater analytical and conceptual clarity and sophistication, rather than the central theme of postbellum law. Beyond that, it appears to be a construct of progressive and neo-progressive thinkers, a straw man in which to develop and prioritize their own ideas (Tamanaha, 2010). Although there was a debate over formalism and its influence at the turn of the century, no one ever claimed to be a formalist. In fact, the term "formalist" was pejorative (Tamanaha,

2010: ch. 3). And as Gary Rowe has pointed out, the historiography of classical legal thought seems to be more about rescuing *Brown v. Board of Education* and the Founding period, than about explaining postbellum legal history on its own terms. *Lochner* thus becomes the foil by which we can explain (perhaps Whiggishly) the rest of American legal and constitutional history (Rowe, 1999). If we can abandon this master narrative, we can free ourselves to develop new stories, as many historians have already begun to do. We must ask ourselves, then, if the emergence of classical legal thought and the rise of a "*Lochner* era" is not the major theme of postbellum legal history, then what is?

References

Alexander, G. (1999). *Commodity and Propriety: Competing Visions of Property in American Legal Thought, 1776–1970*. University of Chicago Press, Chicago.

Atiyah, P.S. (1985). *The Rise and Fall of Freedom of Contract*. Oxford University Press, New York.

Banner, S. (2012). *American Property: A History of How, Why, and What We Own*. Harvard University Press, Cambridge.

Batlan, F. (2010). "Notes From the Margin: Florence Kelley and the Making of Sociological Jurisprudence." In Hamilton and Brophy, eds, *Transformations in American Legal History: Law, Ideology, and Methods: Essays in Honor of Morton J. Horwitz*. Harvard University Press, Cambridge.

Benedict, M.L. (1985). "Laissez-Faire and Liberty: A Re-Evaluation of the Meaning and Origins of Laissez-Faire Constitutionalism." *Law and History Review* 3(2): 293–331.

Chomsky, C. (1993). "Progressive Judges in a Progressive Age: Regulatory Legislation in the Minnesota Supreme Court, 1880–1925." *Law and History Review* 11: 383–440.

Commonwealth v. Alger, 61 Mass. 53 (1851).

Corwin, E.S. (1914). "The Basic Doctrine of American Constitutional Law." *Michigan Law Review* 12: 247–276.

Einhorn, R.L. (1991). *Property Rules: Political Economy in Chicago, 1833–1872*. University of Chicago Press, Chicago.

Faust, D.G. (2008). *This Republic of Suffering: Death and the American Civil War*. Alfred A. Knopf, New York.

Fernandez, A. and Dubber, M. (2012) *Law Books in Action: Essays on the Anglo-American Treatise*. Hart Publishing, Oxford.

Fisher, W.W., III, Horwitz, M.J. and Reed, T.A. (1993). *American Legal Realism*. Oxford University Press, New York.

Forbath, W.E. (1991). *Law and the Shaping of the Labor Movement*. Harvard University Press, Cambridge, MA.

Freund, E. (1904). *The Police Power, Public Policy, and Constitutional Rights*. Callaghan, Chicago.

Friedman, L.M. (2005). *A History of American Law*. 3rd Edition. Simon and Shuster, New York.

Friedman, L.M. (2011). *Contract Law in America: A Social and Economic Case Study.* Quid Pro Quo Books, New York.

Gabel, P. and Feinman, J. (1998). "Contract Law as Ideology." In Kairys, ed. *The Politics of Law: A Progressive Critique,* 497–510. 3rd Edition. Basic Books, New York.

Gilmore, G. (1977). *The Ages of American Law.* Yale University Press, New Haven.

Grey, T.C. (1983). "Langdell's Orthodoxy." *University of Pittsburgh Law Review* 45: 1–53.

Horwitz, M.J. (1992). *The Transformation of American Law, 1870–1960: The Crisis of Legal Orthodoxy.* Oxford University Press, New York.

Jones, A. (1967). "Thomas M. Cooley and 'Laissez-Faire Constitutionalism': A Reconsideration." *The Journal of American History* 53(4): 751–771.

Karsten, P. (1992). "Explaining the Fight over the Attractive Nuisance Doctrine: A Kinder, Gentler Instrumentalism in the 'Age of Formalism.'" *Law and History Review* 10: 45–92.

Keller, M. (1977). *Affairs of State: Public Life in Late Nineteenth Century America.* Belknap Press of Harvard University Press, Cambridge, MA.

Kennedy, D. (1980). "Toward an Historical Understanding of Legal Consciousness: The Case of Classical Legal Thought in America, 1850–1940." *Research in Law and Sociology,* 3(3): 3–24.

Kennedy, D. (2003). "Two Globalizations of Law and Legal Thought, 1850–1968." *Suffolk University Law Review* 36: 631–680.

Keren, H. (2010). "Considering Affective Consideration." *Golden Gate University Law Review* 40: 165–234.

Kimball, B.A. (2004). "The Langdell Problem: Historicizing the Century of Historiography, 1906–2000s." *Law and History Review* 22: 277–338.

Kimball, B.A. (2009). *The Inception of Modern Professional Education: C.C. Langdell, 1826–1906.* University of North Carolina Press, Chapel Hill.

King, A.J. (1986). *Law and Land Use in Chicago: A Prehistory of Modern Zoning.* Garland Publishing, New York.

Kreitner, R. (2007). *Calculating Promises: The Emergence of Modern Contract Doctrine.* Stanford University Press, Stanford.

Lamoreaux, N. (2011). "The Mystery of Property Rights: A U.S. Perspective." *The Journal of Economic History* 71: 275–306.

LaPiana, W.P. (1994). *Logic and Experience: The Origin of Modern American Legal Education.* Oxford University Press, New York.

Lears, T.J.J. (2009). *Rebirth of a Nation: The Making of a Modern America, 1877–1920.* Harper Collins, New York.

Leavitt, J.W. (1982). *The Healthiest City: Milwaukee and the Politics of Health Reform.* Princeton University Press, Princeton, N.J.

Leavitt, J.W. (1996). *Typhoid Mary: Captive to the Public's Health.* Beacon Press, Boston.

Lindsay, M.J. (2010). "In Search of 'Laissez-Faire Constitutionalism.'" *Harvard Law Review Forum* 123: 55–78.

Mayer, D.N. (2009). "The 'Myth' of Laissez-Faire Constitutionalism: Liberty of Contract During the Lochner Era." *Hastings Constitutional Law Quarterly* 36: 217–284.

McCurdy, C.W. (1975). "Justice Field and the Jurisprudence of Government-Business Relations: Some Parameters of Laissez-Faire Constitutionalism, 1863–1897." *The Journal of American History* 61: 970–1005.

McEvoy, A.F. (1995). "The Triangle Shirtwaist Factory Fire of 1911: Social Change, Industrial Accidents, and the Evolution of Common Sense Causality." *Law & Social Inquiry* 20: 621–651.

Novak, W.J. (1996). *The People's Welfare: Law and Regulation in Nineteenth-Century America*. University of North Carolina Press, Chapel Hill.

Novak, W.J. (2008). "Police Power and the Hidden Transformation of the American State." In Dubber and Valverde, eds, *Police and the Liberal State*, 54–74. Stanford University Press, Stanford.

Parker, K.M. (2011). *Common Law, History, and Democracy in America: Legal Thought before Modernism*. Cambridge University Press, New York.

Rabban, D.M. (2003). "The Historiography of Late Nineteenth Century American Legal History." *Theoretical Inquiries in the Law* 4: 541–578.

Rosenberg, C.E. (1987). *The Cholera Years: The United States in 1832, 1849, and 1866*. University of Chicago Press, Chicago.

Rowe, G.D. (1999). "Review: Lochner Revisionism Revisited." *Law & Social Inquiry* 24: 221–252.

Schwartz, G.T. (1981). "Tort Law and the Economy in Nineteenth-Century America: A Reinterpretation." *Yale Law Journal* 90: 1717–1775.

Selvin, M. (1980). "The Public Trust Doctrine in American Law and Economic Policy, 1789–1920." *Wisconsin Law Review* 1980: 1403–1442.

Siegel, S.A. (1990). "Historism in Late Nineteenth-Century Constitutional Thought." *Wisconsin Law Review* 1990: 1431–1548.

Siegel, S.A. (2000). "John Chipman Gray and the Moral Basis of Classical Legal Thought." *Iowa Law Review* 86: 1513–1599.

Siegel, S.A. (2002). "The Revision Thickens." *Law and History Review* 20(3): 631–637.

Siegel, S.A. (2004). "Francis Wharton's Orthodoxy: God, Historical Jurisprudence, and Classical Legal Thought." *The American Journal of Legal History* 46: 422–446.

Simpson, A.W.B. (1975). *A History of the Common Law of Contract: The Rise of the Action of Assumpsit*. Clarendon Press, Oxford.

Stanley, A.D. (1998). *From Bondage to Contract: Wage Labor, Marriage, and the Market in the Age of Slave Emancipation*. Cambridge University Press, New York.

Tamanaha, B.Z. (2010). *Beyond the Formalist-Realist Divide: The Role of Politics in Judging*. Princeton University Press, Princeton.

Thorpe v. Rutland and Burlington R.R. Co., 27 Vt. 149 (1855).

Tomlins, C.L. (2005). "'To Improve the State and Condition of Man': The Power to Police and the History of American Governance." *Buffalo Law Review* 53: 1215–1272.

Tomlins, C.L. (2008). "Necessities of State: Police, Sovereignty and the Constitution." *Journal of Policy History* 20: 47–63.

Urofsky, M.I. (1985). "State Courts and Protective Legislation during the Progressive Era: A Reevaluation." *The Journal of American History* 72: 63–91.

VandeVelde, K.J. (1980). "The New Property of the Nineteenth Century: The Development of the Modern Concept of Property." *Buffalo Law Review* 29: 325–386.

Warren, C. (1913a). "The Progressiveness of the United States Supreme Court." *Columbia Law Review* 13(4): 294–313.

Warren, C. (1913b). "A Bulwark to the State Police Power – The United States Supreme Court." *Columbia Law Review* 13(8): 667–695.

Warren, C. (1923). *The Supreme Court in United States History*. Little, Brown, and Company, Boston.

Welke, B.Y. (2001). *Recasting American Liberty: Gender, Race, Law, and the Railroad Revolution, 1865–1920*. Cambridge University Press, New York.

White, G.E. (2003). *Tort Law in America: An Intellectual History*. Oxford University Press, New York.

Wiecek, W.M. (1998). *The Lost World of Classical Legal Thought: Law and Ideology in America, 1886–1937*. Oxford University Press, New York.

Willrich, M. (2003). *City of Courts: Socializing Justice in Progressive Era Chicago*. Cambridge University Press, Cambridge.

Willrich, M. (2008). "'The Least Vaccinated of Any Civilized Country': Personal Liberty and Public Health in the Progressive Era." *Journal of Policy History* 20: 76–93.

Willrich, M. (2011). *Pox: An American History*. Penguin Press, New York.

Witt, J. (2001). *The Accidental Republic: Crippled Workingmen, Destitute Widows, and the Remaking of American Law*. Harvard University Press, Cambridge.

Further Reading

Dubber, M.D. (2005). *The Police Power: Patriarchy and the Foundations of American Government*. Columbia University Press, New York.

Forbath, W.E. (2008). "Politics, State-Building, and the Courts, 1870–1920." In Grossberg and Tomlins, eds, *The Cambridge History of Law in America: The Long Nineteenth Century (1789–1920)*, 643–696. Cambridge University Press, New York.

Gillman, H. (1993). *The Constitution Besieged: The Rise and Demise of Lochner Era Police Powers Jurisprudence*. Duke University Press, Durham.

Hurst, J.W. (1956). *Law and the Conditions of Freedom in the Nineteenth-Century*. University of Wisconsin Press, Madison.

Menand, L. (2001). *The Metaphysical Club*. Farrar, Straus, Giroux, New York.

Molina, N. (2006). *Fit to be Citizens? Public Health and Race in Los Angeles, 1879–1939*. University of California Press, Berkeley.

Revell, K.D. (1999). "The Road to *Euclid v. Ambler*: City Planning, State-Building, and the Changing Scope of the Police Power." *Studies in American Political Development* 13: 50–145.

Shah, N. (2001). *Contagious Divides: Epidemics and Race in San Francisco's Chinatown*. University of California Press, Berkeley.

Chapter Six

AMERICAN LEGAL HISTORY, 1920–1970

Christopher W. Schmidt

Historical scholarship on the United States between 1920 and 1970 has traditionally centered on the rise and dominance of liberal thought and policy. The liberal project in twentieth-century America was dedicated to the application of governmental power and expertise to address society's most glaring vulnerabilities and inequities. Between 1920 and 1970 the nation faced a series of fundamental challenges – the Great Depression, World War II and then the Cold War, a succession of social movements by African Americans, women, and other disempowered groups demanding full benefits of citizenship. Each destabilized traditional (often localized or non-governmental) bases of authority; each made new demands on government. The result was an "age of reform" (Hofstadter, 1955), characterized by a steady, seemingly ineluctable expansion of the reach of the formal legal authority, particularly at the federal level. Coming to terms with what appeared to be a durable consensus around modern liberalism as political ideology and practice was the central goal of historical scholarship from the 1940s through at least the 1980s. As law was the primary tool of liberal reform, and lawyers and judges leading figures, the work of legal historians generally fit comfortably within this story (e.g., Murphy, 1972).

Over the past twenty years or so historians have challenged this story of liberalism's ascent and entrenchment. With the emergence of a powerful conservative social, political, and legal movement in the post-1970 period, liberalism's triumph in the middle decades of the twentieth century appears more qualified, more tenuous. Legal historians have highlighted forgotten or under-appreciated voices of dissent to liberalism – those on the political

A Companion to American Legal History, First Edition.
Edited by Sally E. Hadden and Alfred L. Brophy.
© 2013 John Wiley & Sons Ltd. Published 2021 by John Wiley & Sons Ltd.

left as well as the right (and those who resist easy ideological categorization) who questioned the drive toward top-down, centralized approaches to social regulation, the commitment to litigation and rights as tools of social reform. They have given more attention to legal work (broadly defined) taking place outside the courts – in legislatures, administrative agencies, and various informal settings far from the world of elite lawyers and constitutional doctrine. While the Supreme Court still looms large, the best legal history situates the Court within its social, political, and legal context, generally locating the wellsprings of social change in these extrajudicial settings. This chapter focuses on the work of legal historians who have challenged liberalism-centered paradigm that has long dominated twentieth-century historiography. While this is a necessarily selective approach to a wide-ranging collection of scholarship, skewed toward public law and national-scale legal developments, it serves to highlight many of the most significant trends in legal historical scholarship on the 1920–1970 period.

Law in the 1920s

The 1920s, long treated as a relatively quiet prelude to more dramatic upheavals of the following decades, has emerged in recent scholarship as a period of innovative and consequential developments for modern American law.

The Growth of Federal Power

In tracing developments generally associated with the New Deal to the 1920s (and before), legal historians contribute to a well developed trend in historical interpretation. Lizabeth Cohen (1990) has shown the ways in which popular culture and labor activism in the 1920s laid the groundwork for a powerful Democratic coalition, the New Deal's backbone constituency. Daniel Rodgers (1998) has identified a transatlantic reformist intellectual tradition on which the New Deal was built. Political historians and political scientists have traced continuities in American state building from the late nineteenth century through the New Deal (e.g., Karl, 1983; Keller, 1994; Skowronek, 1982). Whether viewed through the lens of culture, ideas, politics, or law, Richard Hofstadter's description of the New Deal as "a drastic new departure ... in the history of American reform" (1955: 303) has come to appear, at best, overstated.

In some ways, the 1920s witnessed what might be considered a retreat of the law: wartime regulations expired and the regulatory fervor of the Progressive Era dissipated. Yet a growing body of legal scholarship demonstrates that much federal regulatory authority not only survived but even expanded in this period. World War I and the 1920s marked a new era in immigration control as the government sharply restricted entrance into the country, thereby creating the new legal category of "illegal immigrant," which was accompanied by expanded regulatory mechanisms (Ngai, 2004). The late nineteenth and early twentieth century saw Americans increasingly call upon criminal law to deal with contentious moral issues – gambling, narcotics, prostitution, alcohol. Those demanding regulation of such disfavored behavior, traditionally the jurisdiction of states and localities, increasingly turned to the federal government. Federal criminal law evolved from a narrow field aimed at protecting distinctly federal enterprises toward a national code of conduct (see generally Friedman, 1993; Stuntz, 2011).

Novel applications of federal power went beyond controlling immigration and vice, as Americans generally faced more legal constraints dictated from Washington, D.C., in the 1920s. Ajay Mehrotra (2010) explores how wartime tax policy ushered in a distinctly modern "fiscal polity," complete with a new administrative capacity and new obligations of "fiscal citizenship." Christopher Capozzola (2008) shows the war to be a watershed moment in transforming the sense of obligation felt by American citizens, from one based in local, private commitments – to clubs, churches, unions, political groups – toward more national and government-oriented commitments. Failure to meet these new obligations brought the potential for legal consequences, made all the more serious by a newly muscular federal surveillance state – another artifact of the war that survived into peacetime. Interventionist government was certainly not an innovation of the twentieth century, a point William Novak (1996, 2008) has been particularly influential in demonstrating. Yet the opening decades of the twentieth century brought an expansion of government authority that was both more distant and more capable of intruding more deeply into individual lives.

Civil Liberties

The U.S. government's newfound capacity for and interest in controlling people's words and actions – expressed most conspicuously through crackdowns on political radicals and enforcement of Prohibition – fueled efforts to protect civil liberties. The late 1910s and 1920s was the foundational period in the development of First Amendment doctrine (e.g., Kalven, 1988; Stone, 2004). Yet, as recent scholarship has shown, the idea of civil liberties that emerged in the twentieth century was less a judicial "discovery" of some dormant American civil libertarian commitment than a series of historically specific efforts, by diverse actors in varied settings, to reassess the line between state authority and individual liberty. Numerous civil libertarian traditions existed in the early twentieth century, some focused on expressive freedom and sexual autonomy (Rabban, 1997), others on the connection between expression and material inequalities (Graber, 1991). In her recent work on the early decades of the American Civil Liberties Union, Laura Weinrib (2012) has emphasized the commitment of early civil libertarians to advancing a class-based concern for economic equality. By working with progressives (who believed tolerance for dissent served the public good) as well as conservatives (who favored individual autonomy), they gradually made a persuasive case for judicial enforcement of expressive freedom. For all these scholars, modern civil liberties emerged from struggles against both defenders of state power and those who advocated alternative conceptions of civil liberties.

Civil libertarianism in the interwar period thus defied easy ideological categorization. Although some progressives embraced civil liberties as a tool for advancing the interests of workers, they tended to be skeptical toward individual rights. Progressive belief that the public good was best pursued through unfettered state authority could lead to notoriously illiberal policy, such as the eugenics campaign, in which law did more to rationalize and streamline the process than it did to protect its victims (Willrich, 1998). It was, as David Bernstein (2011) emphasizes, conservatives of the period who most readily embraced the state-skepticism and commitment to judicial review that was at the heart of modern civil libertarianism. The ultra-conservative Justice James McReynolds wrote the Supreme Court's opinions in the landmark civil liberties cases of *Meyer v. Nebraska* (1923) and *Pierce v. Society of Sisters* (1925), relying upon an expansive, substantive reading of the Fourteenth Amendment's "liberty" clause to strike down nativist-inspired regulations that interfered with parental control over their children's education (Ross, 1994; Kersch, 2004). For liberals to fully embrace this new conception of civil liberties – individualistic in orientation and reliant primarily on judicial remedies – they would need to come to terms with judicial review. They would need to find a way to accept the necessity of judicial oversight for certain purposes while still rejecting the judicial obstructionism they associated with *Lochner v. New York* (1905) and its liberty of contract ideology. This was the dilemma that gave rise to the idea of "preferred" freedoms, or what G. Edward White (2000) terms the "bifurcated review project" – a commitment to judicial scrutiny when fundamental noneconomic rights, such as free speech, were at stake, but judicial restraint otherwise.

Lochnerism in the 1920s

Scholarship on the emergence of civil liberties builds off a revisionist project on *Lochner*-era jurisprudence that has been underway for some time. Revisionists have extracted *Lochnerism* from the political battles of the Progressive and New Deal era, from which emerged a classic winner's history portraying *Lochnerism* as little more than a legalistic cover for protecting business and advancing a conservative laissez-faire agenda (e.g., Corwin, 1941; Twiss, 1942; McCloskey, 1960). As illuminated in a collection of revisionist work (e.g., McCurdy, 1975; Benedict, 1985; Horwitz, 1992; Gillman, 1993; Wiecek, 1998), "classical legal thought" (also labeled "laissez-faire constitutionalism," "orthodoxy," "formalism," "conceptualism") was in fact more thoroughly grounded in longstanding legal traditions than its earlier critics allowed.

Building off this intellectual excavation of classical legal thought, historians have located in classicism's most perceptive critics a substantive and innovative modernist legal vision (e.g., Gillman, 1997; Purcell, 2000) – much more than the blanket calls for judicial deference that many progressive jurists felt was the lesson of *Lochner*'s demise. Revisionist scholarship on classical legal thought has provided a platform for reassessing Legal Realism, classicism's challenger in the 1920s. At their most ambitious, Realists sought to reconceptualize the process of judicial decision-making, the role of social science in legal analysis, the ways in which law was taught, even the nature of law and its place in American society (e.g., Kalman, 1986; Schlegel, 1995). In Morton Horwitz's influential assessment, Legal Realism was a strand of progressivism dedicated to replacing formalist conceptions of law as "neutral, natural, and apolitical" with an acceptance of the inevitability of moral and political commitments in legal reasoning (1992: 170).

A second generation of *Lochner*-era revisionism has sought to break down the stark dichotomies that dominated much of this first round of revisionist work. Scholars have found that constitutional conservatives of the *Lochner* era, particularly in the 1920s and 1930s, were not quite so rigid and categorical in their approach to legal analysis. Robert Post's scholarship on the Supreme Court under Chief Justice Taft offers a notably subtle and probing account of the conservative justices' struggle to reconcile their faith in the market as a site for the "creation of the autonomous self required by democratic citizenship" with the realities of the modern industrial economy (1998: 1542). The lines that separated conservatives from liberals were often fluid, the labels themselves misleading – supposed adherents to classical legal thought regularly seemed to step out of character. *Lochner*-era courts often facilitated expanded regulatory authority (Novak, 2008; Willrich, 2003); and even the Supreme Court upheld far more progressive reform legislation than it struck down (Whittington, 2005; Bernstein, 2011). In his effort to "rehabilitate" *Lochner*, Bernstein (2011) urges that decisions such as *Meyer, Pierce,* and *Buchanan v. Warley* (1917) (striking down a residential racial segregation law) no longer be marginalized as aberrant offshoots of Lochnerism. They too, he insists, belong in our assessment of a constitutional jurisprudence predicated on defending liberty and property against state encroachment. Even *Adkins v. Children's Hospital* (1923), the controversial apogee of the Court's use of substantive due process to strike down economic regulation, includes forward-looking language on matters of sex equality, a point that Reva Siegel (2002) has drawn out in her study of the constitutional potentialities of the Nineteenth Amendment. Brian Tamanaha (2010) has gone so far as to describe the entire concept of "formalist" jurisprudence as a straw man, created by progressive critics in order to justify their attacks on Court. Supposed formalists were not formal in a doctrinaire sense, he argues, just as supposed Realists regularly accepted "formalist" assumptions.

Prohibition

A notable aspect of legal historical writing on the 1920s has been its relative inattention to Prohibition, arguably the most significant legal development of the decade. Yet scholars are beginning to recognize this was a critical event in the history of American law, affecting the reach of government regulatory authority and expectations Americans brought to the law. Prohibition offers a powerful case study of the complexities of legal authority in modern life.

Prohibition demonstrated a remarkable faith in law. The culminating achievement of a century-long temperance movement, the Eighteenth Amendment (ratified in 1919) converted a largely localized moral reform movement into a national mandate, codified into fundamental law and enforced concurrently by state and federal criminal justice systems (Hamm, 1995). The result was "the greatest expansion of federal administrative responsibility since the days of Reconstruction" (Post, 2006: 4). Prohibition, as Robert Post details, posed considerable difficulties for the Supreme Court as the justices struggled to reconcile enforcement with traditions of federalism and skepticism toward legal mandates that cut against entrenched social mores. Prohibition was also notable, argues William Stuntz, because unlike other efforts to enforce cultural norms through criminal law, this "culture war" was "fought by democratic means with reasonably fair and open legal rules" (2011: 185).

Yet Prohibition also put on conspicuous display law's limitations. Pervasive, often flagrant defiance caused many to reassess the capacity of the law to uproot entrenched social norms. Subsequent generations of reformers, particularly civil rights proponents, had to remake the case for law's capacity in the face of charges that Prohibition demonstrated that government was powerless to "legislate morality" (Schmidt, 2008). Prohibition's failure was also a blow to the use of constitutional amendments as a tool for social reform (Kyvig, 1996, 2000). While the Progressive Era produced four amendments, neither the New Deal nor the civil rights movement resulted in significant changes to the Constitution – a point whose implications for American constitutionalism Bruce Ackerman (1991) has explored.

As the teleological narrative of liberalism ascendant further weakens, Prohibition will likely receive a more prominent place in the legal history of the twentieth century. It puts on sharp display the often paradoxical elements of legal reform in modern America – moralism and legalism, social control and antistatism, nationalism and localism. Hardly an aberrant burst of symbolic politics, as scholars long characterized it, this failed experiment was both representative and consequential.

The New Deal Constitutional Revolution

The story of the New Deal constitutional revolution has traditionally relied upon a stark rendering of the sides of the contest. President Franklin Roosevelt, backed by a powerful New Deal coalition, demanded bold government action in response to the Depression. The Supreme Court, dominated by the "Four Horsemen," staunch conservatives who were willing to strike down progressive regulation that failed to align with their increasingly outdated vision of the Constitution, stood in the way. In 1937, after Roosevelt threatened to "pack" the Court with additional justices to secure favorable rulings, the Court shifted direction – the famous "switch in time that saved nine" – abandoning its efforts to enforce constitutional limitations on social and economic policy and thereby bringing the *Lochner* era to a close. This account of the New Deal constitutional revolution as a sharp break with the past, forced by political pressure, emerged in the immediate aftermath of the "switch" (e.g., Corwin, 1941; Wright, 1942), and historians ever since have referenced 1937 as the fulcrum of legal development in the twentieth century (e.g., McCloskey, 1960; Friedman, 2009).

Recent scholarship has challenged this long-prevailing interpretation of the constitutional revolution, questioning whether in fact 1937 was the critical turning point and, more generally, the extent to which the New Deal constituted a new legal order.

1937 Reconsidered

Questioning the significance of the 1937 "switch" has been a generative topic for scholarly revisionism (see generally Kalman, 2005). The standard account places the Court's acceptance of the New Deal in the spring of 1937 as the central event of the constitutional revolution. It also offers a clear causal explanation: political pressures on the Court, most proximately the Court-packing plan, led Justice Owen Roberts to switch sides. William

Leuchtenburg has been a leading defender of this "externalist" or political account (1995). Critics of this interpretation have identified factual discrepancies, such as that Roberts apparently switched before Roosevelt announced the Court-packing plan (e.g., Friedman, 1994). They also insist that the externalist account misses unfolding legal developments within the Court. Barry Cushman (1998) argues that prior to 1937 a majority of the justices had already abandoned core premises of classical legal thought, while the doctrinal transformation was still playing out into the 1940s. The New Deal revolution, according to this interpretation, was not a single dramatic moment but a decade-long process of doctrinal evolution (see also Friedman, 1994). G. Edward White writes that the constitutional revolution is best understood as a "jurisprudential crisis," arising when an emergent twentieth-century "modernist" sensibility undermined a belief in neutral judicial decision-making. This was a transformation "whose revolutionary character was far deeper and wider than any 'switch in time'" (2000: 234–235).

Liberalism Limited

Much of the most innovative recent scholarship on the legal history of the New Deal has ventured beyond the realm of constitutionalism in the High Court. The labor movement, for instance, put forth constitutional arguments that do not readily fit into the established "constitutional revolution" framework. William Forbath (1998) identifies among labor activists a "forgotten egalitarian constitutional tradition," pushed through representative institutions rather than courts and "centered on decent work and livelihoods, social provision, and a measure of economic independence and democracy" (Forbath, 1998: 1; see also Goluboff, 2007; Pope, 1997).

One of the outgrowths of efforts to find alternative constitutional visions outside the courts has been a reconsideration of the limitations of New Deal liberalism. When compared to more ambitious social democratic visions – as found in segments of the labor movement, or as pursued in other industrial democracies – New Deal liberalism looks more like a grudging accommodation than a liberal victory. Attention to the limits of New Deal liberalism goes back to the work of New Left historians of the late 1960s (e.g., Bernstein, 1968) and can also be found in the writings of many political historians (e.g., Karl, 1983). Subsequent scholarship has located additional factors that confined the liberal reform agenda. Alan Brinkley (1995) focuses on conservative opposition to the most ambitious New Deal reforms and the resulting compromises of the late New Deal, while Meg Jacobs (2005) traces the weakness of the New Deal coalition to its reliance on the fragile terrain of consumption politics. Others have highlighted race and sex inegalitarianism as limitations on the social welfare state, its safety net failing those most in need (e.g., Katznelson, 2005; Lieberman, 1998; Kessler-Harris, 2001). Also notable was government reliance on private actors, resulting in a distinctive "public-private welfare state" (Klein, 2003).

Among legal scholars, notions of the New Deal as a fundamental break with what came before has proven more resilient, in large part because the changes in legal doctrine (regardless of the causes and the timeframe of change) were undoubtedly striking. "The New Deal constitutional revolution of 1937 represented a fundamental shift in the constitutional relationship of the states to the federal government as well as of government to economy," explains Morton Horwitz. It was "a genuine paradigm shift" in legal thought (1992: 3). For Horwitz, this was to be celebrated. Others see this as a problematic development. The "increasingly massive, paternalist, neo-mercantilist, bureaucratic state" of the New Deal, argues James Henretta, was a "sharp and important break" not only from laissez-faire ideology and *Lochner*-style jurisprudence but also from alternative approaches to reform, such as Progressive-Era liberalism (2006: 115). Ackerman (1991) has famously drawn on the New Deal to demonstrate the possibility of "constitutional moments" in which the Constitution changes absent the formal amendment process. The common thread of these disparate projects is an assumption that the law in the New Deal experienced a fundamental shift.

Yet other legal historians have questioned this assumption, identifying ways in which legalism served to limit reform. As Forbath explains: "The modern American welfare and regulatory state was not one that any single group intended or envisioned; but it bore the deep imprint of *Lochner's* diverse defenders and the court- and common law-dominated institutional order they fought to preserve" (2006: 180). The New Deal attracted a new, more diverse generation of reform-minded lawyers to federal government, dedicated to using government power to further the liberal agenda. But they were also lawyers, educated in certain modes of analysis and dedicated to administrative expertise, which introduced new limits on the scope of reform (Irons, 1982). The labor movement's shift from government antagonist to ally proved a double-edged sword, for, as Christopher Tomlins shows, with participation came new constraints (1985).

In this way, legal and political historians have questioned the distinctiveness of the legal changes of the New Deal years and insisted on giving more attention to skeptics of New Deal liberalism and their quite different ideas about the lessons of the Depression and New Deal. The legacy of the New Deal can be seen as running along two tracks: persistent ideological contestation over the role of law and government in American society, obfuscated for several decades under a perceived "consensus" around New Deal liberalism; and a clear trend in government practice, most notably the entrenchment of federal power, particularly as exercised through its administrative agencies. What emerged from the 1930s, as Joanna Grisinger nicely puts it, was "less a 'New Deal state' than a state that had survived the New Deal" (2012: 3–4).

The Rights Revolution

The next great transformation of American law was the post-World War II "rights revolution." Beginning in the 1940s and accelerating in the following decades, legal institutions on all levels became increasingly responsive to a variety of individual rights claims. These included protection against various forms of discrimination, stronger rights for criminal defendants, and speech, associational, and privacy rights. Whereas in the *Lochner* era successful rights claimants tended to be those who challenged economic regulation as violating property and contract rights, in the postwar period racial, ethnic, and religious minorities, women, political dissidents, criminal defendants and other disempowered groups demanded, and often received, government recognition of their rights. This new generation of rights claimants demanded not only limits on government authority, but also affirmative government protection against rights violations by nongovernmental actors. The bifurcation of rights into the economic and the noneconomic or "personal" was at the core of Justice Harlan Fiske Stone's famous fourth footnote of *United States v. Carolene Products Co.* (1938), in which he affirmed judicial deference to majoritarian decision-making when regulating economic activity but noted the same deference might not apply when legislation undermined the political process or targeted "discrete and insular minorities." The rights revolution thus provided the other half of modern liberalism, placing the protection of personal liberties and minority rights alongside government responsibility for basic social welfare needs.

The Warren Court and Legal Liberalism

Rights claims in the postwar era resonated across legal institutions, yet it was the judiciary, and particularly the Supreme Court, that became the preeminent symbol of the rights revolution. Much of this had to do with *Brown v. Board of Education* (1954), when, after a decades-long litigation campaign by the National Association for the Advancement of Colored People (NAACP), a unanimous Court, led by Chief Justice Earl Warren, struck down racial segregation in schools. The Warren Court went on to remake numerous areas of legal doctrine. To protect racial minorities and other groups who were unable to effectively defend themselves through the democratic process, such as political dissidents and criminal defendants, the justices extended federal constitutional standards over more and more of

American life and law. The justices became, in Paul Murphy's words, "a broker for have-nots of all stripes" (1972: xvii). Although even in its most contentious rulings the Warren Court rarely ventured beyond the boundaries of national public opinion (Friedman, 2009; Klarman, 1996; Powe, 2000), the image of the Court as a forum of principle and justice prodding a laggard nation became powerfully engrained in the popular imagination (e.g., Lewis, 1964) as well as among legal academics (Kalman, 1996). The rights revolution forged a liberal faith in litigation as an essential weapon in the cause of social justice.

Historical scholarship on the rights revolution long tended toward the celebratory, with a standard narrative portraying heroic lawyers and humane judges using the law to trump prejudiced, inegalitarian, self-serving political decision-making. Richard Kluger's history of *Brown, Simple Justice* (1976), offers a classic example. It revolves around two basic assumptions. One is that there is a direct, unproblematic connection between the needs of subjugated minorities and judicial remedies. The social experience of local African Americans led to litigation, which civil rights lawyers pursued through the judicial system, and, eventually, the Supreme Court responded. *Brown* was, in Kluger's estimation, "nothing short of a reconsecration of American ideals"; it was "simple justice" (710). Little to nothing was lost as the issue moved from social protest to litigation to judicial ruling. The second assumption operates in the other direction: rights victories advance social justice on the ground; the courts can change American society. When just decisions fail to produce just results (as with *Brown*'s limited implementation in its first decade), it is due to insufficient empathy and will on the part of judges and lawmakers more than the limitations of legal doctrine and institutions. These assumptions regarding the responsiveness and influence of the courts – core tenets of what has been labeled "legal liberalism" (Kalman, 1996; Mack, 2005) – operate in countless judicial biographies and histories of notable cases.

Yet alongside the narrative of legal liberalism has always existed a more skeptical assessment of the rights revolution. Alexander Bickel worried that the Warren Court misled liberals into "surrender[ing] to the Court the necessary work of politics" (1965: x); and Raoul Berger chided liberal lawyers for "floating on a cloud of post-Warren Court euphoria" (1977: 4). Meanwhile, critical race scholars argued that white-dominated institutions (including courts) addressed racial inequality only when it served white interests (Bell, 1980); and critical legal scholars dismissed legal rights as a distraction to the achievement of social justice (Freeman, 1978; Tushnet, 1983). A recent generation of legal historians has built on this earlier scholarship (while often paring away its polemical tone and strong normative claims), injecting into mainstream scholarship a more skeptical and chastened attitude toward courts and litigation.

One of the most notable recent trends has been the portrayal of the Supreme Court as generally reflecting majority opinion (see generally

Friedman, 2009; Powe, 2009). This critique of the premise underlying what Bickel (1962) termed the "counter-majoritarian difficulty" draws on a long line of political science scholarship (e.g., Dahl, 1957; McCloskey, 1960). Even the iconic minority and criminal rights decisions of the Warren Court, argue "majoritarian" scholars, reflected dominant public opinion (Klarman, 1996, 2004; Powe, 2000; Lain 2004). Court decisions, Michael Klarman writes, have generally "reflected social attitudes and practices more than they created them" (2004: 443). The historical context in which the rights revolution in the courts took place has taken on increased importance, with World War II and the Cold War receiving particular attention as critical influences in pushing rights onto the national agenda (Dudziak, 2000; Klarman, 2004; Klinkner, 1999; Skrentny, 2002). The end result of this scholarship is a chastened portrait of the Supreme Court, deeply situated into a broader social and political context and limited in its ability (or willingness) to buck public opinion.

The impact of Supreme Court decisions on society has also been the subject of revisionist scholarship. Particularly noteworthy has been scholarship on *Brown*: in *The Hollow Hope*, Gerald Rosenberg (1991) claims that *Brown* had no practical impact on civil rights, while Klarman (2004) argues, in his "backlash" thesis, that *Brown*'s most significant effect was to embolden white segregationists, whose extremism eventually led to increased national support for desegregation. One of the outgrowths of the debate that this scholarship has sparked has been increased attention to the intricacies of judicial impact across varied social and institutional settings (e.g., Brown-Nagin, 2011) – an approach that draws on recent sociolegal scholarship on "legal mobilization" (McCann, 1994).

Rights Outside the Courts

The historical development of rights outside the courts has been of increasing interest in the legal academy as critics of judicial supremacy have gained in numbers and influence. For the study of extrajudicial constitutionalism during the rights revolution, an essential work is Hugh Davis Graham's (1990) study of the interplay between courts, Congress, and the President. Joanna Grisinger's (2012) study of the administrative state in the 1940s identifies an extrajudicial rights story of a quite different kind, in which administrative agencies' defenders embraced procedural due process as a bulwark against accusations of an unaccountable, lawless federal bureaucracy.

Increased attention to those rights claims that courts rejected or never even considered also brings to light a set of themes that differ from those that dominated the judicial agenda. Most obviously, the further one moves from the world of post-New Deal constitutional doctrine, the more prominent issues of economic justice become. The linkages between racial and economic justice activism, prominent in historical scholarship on the labor and radical activism in the 1930s and 1940s (Hall, 2005; Gilmore, 2008), has received increased attention from legal historians focused on rights claims in non-judicial settings. An outstanding recent work is Risa Goluboff's (2007) examination of efforts of Justice Department and NAACP lawyers to forge legal remedies for the economic exploitation of black workers in the 1940s, in which she identifies a "lost" vision of civil rights that was centered on the intersection of race and labor interests and focused on remedies against private as well as state actors.

Whether, in fact, economic concerns were abandoned in the shadow of *Brown* and the civil rights politics of the 1950s and 1960s has been a point of dispute. Turning to state-level fair employment practices commissions, scholars have identified considerable activity at the intersection of race and economics, including some underappreciated achievements, from the late 1940s onward (Brilliant, 2010; Chen, 2009; Engstrom, 2011). In her exploration of workplace discrimination claims in federal administrative agencies in the 1940s through the 1960s, Sophia Lee finds that the NAACP's work in this arena reflected a strand of the civil rights activism squarely based on "class-based collective action" (2008: 376).

Other themes have emerged from studies of legal struggles outside the world of constitution litigation. Tomiko Brown-Nagin's (2011) study of the civil rights movement in Atlanta identifies black lawyers who placed political voice and black empowerment ahead of a frontal attack on segregation. In the legal practice of black lawyers in the interwar period Kenneth Mack (2012) finds strands of voluntarism and Marxism alongside a commitment to fighting discrimination. Brown-Nagin and others also emphasize the central role of women in various grassroots rights struggles (see also, e.g., Kornbluh, 2007).

Rights Multiplied

The rights revolution reverberated in all corners of American legal culture. Public interest law groups grew in numbers and influence, and legal representation for the poor became, for a time, a pressing issue. Law students were encouraged to take legal clinics alongside their doctrinal classes, which were taught by a professoriate that had taken a decided left turn, embracing law and courts as tools for social justice (Kalman, 1996). This "liberal legal network" (Teles, 2008) was a product of the rights revolution as well as a "support structure" for further legal mobilization (Epp, 1998).

Recent scholarship has pushed the legal history of the civil rights era beyond the black-white paradigm. Mark Brilliant's (2010) recent study of racial politics in postwar California urges a view of the civil rights movement as not only chronologically "long" but also multiracially "wide" (see also Perea, 2004). While Brilliant emphasizes the oftentimes divergent agendas of different racial and ethnic groups, others have explored the ways in which the black freedom struggle spurred rights victories for other groups. John Skrentny (2002) examines policymaking in the late 1960s and early 1970s when officials (whose ranks now included former activists) expanded government protection for a growing mosaic of disadvantaged groups – not only African Americans, but Latinos, Asian Americans, American Indians, immigrants, women, and the disabled. Martha Minow (2010) considers *Brown*'s legacy beyond race, examining debates over separate schooling for immigrants, girls, and the disabled, among others. In *Reasoning From Race* (2011), Serena Mayeri analyzes "second-wave" feminists' use of race analogies as a legal strategy in challenging sex inequality.

Scholars have also given more attention to rights claims pursued by actors who do not fit comfortably into the liberal reform paradigm. Historians have sought to portray modern conservatism as something more than a response to liberalism's ascent (Phillips-Fein, 2011). Just as antistatism persisted even during the heyday of New Deal liberalism, libertarianism and various forms of inegalitarianism persisted throughout the rights revolution era (Smith, 1997). There has been increased attention to how white southerners mobilized the law in their stand against the civil rights movement (Walker, 2009; Schmidt, 2013); linkages between southern resisters and modern conservatism (Kruse, 2005; Lassiter, 2006); and cracks in the façade of racial liberalism in the North (Chen, 2009; MacLean, 2006; Sugrue, 2008). An organizing theme of much recent scholarship on the rights revolution is less about the triumph of liberal principles than about persistent, evolving contestation (Siegel, 2004). In this contest, all sides – not just those who claimed the mantle of liberal reform – require careful, empathetic historical consideration. Sarah Barringer Gordon's (2010) history of a diverse array of "religious voices" who called upon the courts to protect their faith commitments illuminates the potential of such an approach.

Conclusion

The general trend of the law in the middle decades of the twentieth century was unmistakable. Government was doing more – regulating more, taxing more, providing more. This was a period of particularly explosive growth of federal authority, with the national government assuming unprecedented levels of responsibility over the lives of the American people. After largely abandoning oversight of economic regulation, judges located new grounds from which to assert their authority, transforming the courts into a critical player in protecting individual rights.

Yet beneath this apparent institutionalization and entrenchment of a liberal consensus, there were also crosscurrents and resilient counter-narratives. Antistatism and localism remained potent factors in American legal culture. So did skepticism toward the courts, led by those who were critical not only of the substance of judicial reforms but also of the idea that courts should try to resolve contentious social issues. By the late 1960s liberalism's critics, from the left as well as the right, were proving persuasive to growing numbers of Americans.

If one were to identify a single overarching trend in how a recent generation of legal historians has written about the 1920–1970 period, it would be the increased recognition of the significance of these crosscurrents and counter-narratives. Historians today see the liberalism's supposed triumph as, at best, a qualified victory. It was qualified in that liberalism's professed goals – reducing racial inequality, making a fairer criminal justice system, creating a social safety net – remained far from realized. It was qualified in that liberalism's dominance marginalized potentially valuable alternative voices. And it was qualified in that one of its most lasting legacies was the resurgence of a conservatism that was dedicated to undoing much of what liberals had accomplished.

The revised portrait of the legal history of the twentieth century lacks some of the dramatic narrative arc of the liberalism triumphant storyline. The turning points are no longer so sharp, the antagonists no longer so clearly defined. The current generation of scholarship has more centrifugal tendencies than its predecessor. It has traded a measure of coherence and clarity for a somewhat messier, pluralist reality, in which the project of legal development is diversified, bringing in more actors – elite and non-elite, formally trained in the law and lay persons – acting in more variegated settings. The challenge going forward will be for legal historians to locate analytical frameworks and narratives that are sufficiently robust to draw together disparate scholarly projects, while minimizing the constraints that invariably accompany these frameworks and narratives.

References

Ackerman, Bruce (1991). *We the People, Volume 1: Foundations.* Harvard University Press, Cambridge, MA.

Bell, Jr., Derrick A. (1980). "*Brown* and the Interest-Convergence Dilemma." *Harvard Law Review* 93: 518–533.

Benedict, Michael Les (1985). "Laissez-Faire and Liberty: A Re-Evaluation of the Meaning and Origins of Laissez-Faire Constitutionalism." *Law and History Review* 3: 293–331.

Berger, Raoul (1977). *Government by Judiciary: The Transformation of the Fourteenth Amendment.* Harvard University Press, Cambridge MA.

Bernstein, Barton J. (1968). "The New Deal: The Conservative Achievements of Liberal Reform." In Bernstein ed., *Toward a New Past: Dissenting Essays in American History*, 163–288. Pantheon, New York.

Bernstein, David E. (2011). *Rehabilitating Lochner: Defending Individual Rights against Progressive Reform*. University of Chicago Press, Chicago.

Bickel, Alexander M. (1962). *The Least Dangerous Branch: The Supreme Court at the Bar of Politics*. Bobbs-Merrill, Indianapolis.

Bickel, Alexander M. (1965). *Politics and the Warren Court*. Harper & Row, New York.

Brilliant, Mark (2010). *The Color of America Has Changed: How Racial Diversity Shaped Civil Rights Reform in California, 1941–1978*. Oxford University Press, New York.

Brinkley, Alan (1995). *The End of Reform: New Deal Liberalism in Recession and War*. Knopf, New York.

Brown-Nagin, Tomiko (2011). *Courage to Dissent: Atlanta and the Long History of the Civil Rights Movement*. Oxford University Press, New York.

Capozzola, Christopher (2008). *Uncle Sam Wants You: World War I and the Making of the Modern American Citizen*. Oxford University Press, New York.

Chen, Anthony S. (2009). *The Fifth Freedom: Jobs, Politics, and Civil Rights in the United States, 1941–1972*. Princeton University Press, Princeton, NJ.

Cohen, Lizabeth (1990). *Making A New Deal: Industrial Workers in Chicago, 1919–1939*. Cambridge University Press, New York.

Corwin, Edward S. (1941). *Constitutional Revolution, Ltd*. Claremont Colleges, Claremont, CA.

Cushman, Barry (1998). *Rethinking the New Deal Court*. Oxford University Press, New York.

Dahl, Robert A. (1957). "Decision-Making in a Democracy: The Supreme Court as National Policy-Maker." *Journal of Public Law* 6: 279–295.

Dudziak, Mary L. (2000). *Cold War Civil Rights: Race and the Image of American Democracy*. Princeton University Press, Princeton, NJ.

Engstrom, David Freeman (2011). "The Lost Origins of American Fair Employment Law: Regulatory Choice and the Making of Modern Civil Rights, 1943–1972." *Stanford Law Review* 63: 1071–1143.

Epp, Charles R. (1998). *The Rights Revolution: Lawyers, Activists, and Supreme Courts in Comparative Perspective*. University of Chicago Press, Chicago.

Forbath, William E. (1998). "Caste, Class, and Equal Citizenship." *Michigan Law Review* 98: 1–91.

Forbath, William E. (2006). "The Long Life of Liberal America: Law and State-Building in the U.S. and England." *Law and History Review* 24: 179–192.

Freeman, Alan (1978). "Legitimizing Racial Discrimination through Antidiscrimination Law: A Critical Review of Supreme Court Doctrine." *Minnesota Law Review* 62: 1049–1120.

Friedman, Barry (2009). *The Will of the People: How Public Opinion Has Influenced the Supreme Court and Shaped the Meaning of the Constitution*. Farrar, Straus and Giroux, New York.

Friedman, Lawrence M. (1993). *Crime and Criminal Punishment in American History*. BasicBooks, New York.

Friedman, Richard D. (1994). "Switching Time and Other Thought Experiments: The Hughes Court and Constitutional Transformation." *University of Pennsylvania Law Review* 142: 1891–1984.
Gillman, Howard (1993). *The Constitution Besieged: The Rise and Demise of Lochner Era Police Powers.* Duke University Press, Durham, NC.
Gillman, Howard (1997). "The Collapse of Constitutional Originalism and the Rise of the Notion of the 'Living Constitution' in the Course of American State-Building." *Studies in American Political Development* 11: 191–247.
Gilmore, Glenda (2008). *Defying Dixie: The Radical Roots of Civil Rights, 1919–1950.* W.W. Norton, New York.
Goluboff, Risa L. (2007). *The Lost Promise of Civil Rights.* Harvard University Press, Cambridge, MA.
Gordon, Sarah Barringer (2010). *The Spirit of the Law: Religious Voices and the Constitution in Modern America.* Harvard University Press, Cambridge, MA.
Graber, Mark A. (1991). *Transforming Free Speech: The Ambiguous Legacy of Civil Libertarianism.* University of California Press, Berkeley, CA.
Graham, Hugh Davis (1990). *The Civil Rights Era: Origins and Development of National Policy.* Oxford University Press, New York.
Grisinger, Joanna (2012). *The Unwieldy American State: Administrative Politics since the New Deal.* Cambridge University Press, New York.
Hall, Jacquelyn Dowd (2005). "The Long Civil Rights Movement and the Political Uses of the Past." *Journal of American History* 91 (March 2005): 1233–1263.
Hamm, Richard F. (1995). *Shaping the Eighteenth Amendment: Temperance Reform, Legal Culture, and the Polity, 1880–1920.* University of North Carolina Press, Chapel Hill.
Henretta, James A. (2006). "Charles Evans Hughes and the Strange Death of Liberal America." *Law and History Review* 24: 115–171.
Hofstadter, Richard (1955). *The Age of Reform.* Knopf, New York.
Horwitz, Morton J. (1992). *The Transformation of American Law, 1870–1960: The Crisis of Legal Orthodoxy.* Oxford University Press, New York.
Irons, Peter H. (1982). *The New Deal Lawyers.* Princeton University Press, Princeton, NJ.
Jacobs, Meg (2005). *Pocketbook Politics: Economic Citizenship in Twentieth-Century America.* Princeton University Press, Princeton, NJ.
Kalman, Laura (1986). *Legal Realism at Yale, 1927–1960.* University of North Carolina Press, Chapel Hill.
Kalman, Laura (1996). *The Strange Career of Legal Liberalism.* Yale University Press, New Haven.
Kalman, Laura (2005). "The Constitution, the Supreme Court, and the New Deal." *American Historical Review* 110: 1052–1080.
Kalven, Jr., Harry (1988). *A Worthy Tradition: Freedom of Speech in America.* Harper and Row, New York.
Karl, Barry D. (1983). *The Uneasy State: The United States from 1915 to 1945.* University of Chicago Press, Chicago.
Katznelson, Ira (2005). *When Affirmative Action Was White: An Untold Story of Racial Inequality in Twentieth-Century America.* W.W. Norton, New York.

Keller, Morton (1994). *Regulating a New Society: Public Policy and Social Change in America, 1900–1933.* Harvard University Press, Cambridge, MA.

Kersch, Ken I. (2004). *Constructing Civil Liberties: Discontinuities in the Development of American Constitutional Law.* Cambridge University Press, New York.

Kessler-Harris, Alice (2001). *In Pursuit of Equity: Women, Men, and the Quest for Economic Citizenship in 20th Century America.* Oxford University Press, New York.

Klarman, Michael J. (1996). "Rethinking the Civil Rights and Civil Liberties Revolutions." *Virginia Law Review* 82: 1–67.

Klarman, Michael J. (2004). *From Jim Crow to Civil Rights: The Supreme Court and the Struggle for Racial Equality.* Oxford University Press, New York.

Klein, Jennifer (2003). *For All These Rights: Business, Labor, and the Shaping of America's Public-Private Welfare State.* Princeton University Press, Princeton, NJ.

Klinkner, Philip A. with Smith, Rogers M., eds (1999). *The Unsteady March: The Rise and Decline of Racial Equality in America.* University of Chicago Press, Chicago.

Kluger, Richard (1976). *Simple Justice: The History of Brown v. Board of Education and Black America's Struggle for Equality.* Knopf, New York.

Kornbluh, Felicia (2007). *The Battle for Welfare Rights: Politics and Poverty in Modern America.* University of Pennsylvania Press, Philadelphia.

Kruse, Kevin (2005). *White Flight: Atlanta and the Making of Modern Conservatism.* Princeton University Press, Princeton, NJ.

Kyvig, David E. (1996). *Explicit and Authentic Acts: Amending the U.S. Constitution: 1776–1995.* University Press of Kansas, Lawrence.

Kyvig, David E. (2000). *Repealing National Prohibition.* 2nd Edition. Kent State University Press, Kent, OH.

Lain, Corinna Barrett (2004). "Countermajoritarain Hero or Zero? Rethinking the Warren Court's Role in the Criminal Procedure Revolution." *University of Pennsylvania Law Review* 152: 1361–1452.

Lassiter, Matthew (2006). *The Silent Majority: Suburban Politics in the Sunbelt South.* Princeton University Press, Princeton, NJ.

Lee, Sophia Z. (2008). "Hotspots in a Cold War: The NAACP's Postwar Workplace Constitutionalism, 1948–1964." *Law and History Review* 26: 327–378.

Lewis, Anthony (1964). *Gideon's Trumpet.* Random House, New York.

Leuchtenburg, William E. (1995). *The Supreme Court Reborn.* Oxford University Press, New York.

Lieberman, Robert C. (1998). *Shifting the Color Line: Race and the American Welfare State.* Harvard University Press, Cambridge, MA.

Mayeri, Serena (2011). *Reasoning from Race: Feminism, Law, and the Civil Rights Movement.* Harvard University Press, Cambridge, MA.

Mack, Kenneth W. (2005). "Rethinking Civil Rights Lawyering and Politics in the Era Before *Brown.*" *Yale Law Journal* 115: 256–354.

Mack, Kenneth W. (2012). *Representing the Race: The Creation of the Civil Rights Lawyer.* Harvard University Press, Cambridge, MA.

MacLean, Nancy (2006). *Freedom Is Not Enough: The Opening of the American Workplace.* Russell Sage Foundation; Cambridge, MA and Harvard University Press, New York.

McCann, Michael W. (1994). *Rights at Work: Pay Equity Reform and the Politics of Legal Mobilizations.* University of Chicago Press, Chicago.

McCloskey, Robert (1960). *The American Supreme Court*. University of Chicago Press, Chicago.

McCurdy, Charles (1975). "Justice Field and the Jurisprudence of Government-Business Relations: Some Parameters of Laissez-Faire Constitutionalism, 1863–1897." *Journal of American History* 61: 970–1005.

Mehrotra, Ajay K. (2010). "Lawyers, Guns, and Public Moneys: The U.S. Treasury, World War I, and the Administration of the Modern Fiscal State." *Law and History Review* 28: 173–225.

Minow, Martha (2010). *In Brown's Wake: Legacies of America's Educational Landmark*. Oxford University Press, New York.

Murphy, Paul L. (1972). *The Constitution in Crisis Times, 1918–1969*. Harper & Row, New York.

Ngai, Mae M. (2004). *Impossible Subjects: Illegal Aliens and the Making of Modern America*. Princeton University Press, Princeton, NJ.

Novak, William J. (1996). *The People's Welfare: Law and Regulation in Nineteenth-Century America*. University of North Carolina Press, Chapel Hill.

Novak, William J. (2008). "The Myth of the 'Weak' American State." *American Historical Review* 113: 752–772.

Perea, Juan F. (2004). "Buscando America: Why Integration and Equal Protection Fail to Protect Latinos." *Harvard Law Review* 117: 1420–1469.

Phillips-Fein, Kim (2011). "Conservatism: A State of the Field." *Journal of American History* 98: 723–743.

Pope, James Gray (1997). "Labor's Constitution of Freedom." *Yale Law Journal* 106: 941–1031.

Post, Robert C. (1998). "Defending the Lifeworld: Substantive Due Process in the Taft Court Era." *Boston University Law Review* 78: 1489–1545.

Post, Robert C. (2006). "Federalism, Positive Law, and the Emergence of the Administrative State: Prohibition in the Taft Court Era." *William and Mary Law Review* 48: 1–183.

Powe, Jr., Lucas A. (2000). *The Warren Court and American Politics*. Harvard University Press, Cambridge, MA.

Powe, Jr., Lucas A. (2009). *The Supreme Court and the American Elite, 1789–2008*. Harvard University Press, Cambridge, MA.

Purcell, Edward (2000). *Brandeis and the Progressive Constitution:* Erie, *the Judicial Powers, and the Politics of the Federal Courts in Twentieth Century America*. Yale University Press, New Haven.

Rabban, David M. (1997). *Free Speech in its Forgotten Years, 1870–1920*. Cambridge University Press, New York.

Rodgers, Daniel (1998). *Atlantic Crossings: Social Politics in a Progressive Age*. Harvard University Press, Cambridge, MA.

Rosenberg, Gerald N. (1991). *The Hollow Hope: Can Courts Bring About Social Change?* University of Chicago Press, Chicago.

Ross, William G. (1994). *Forging New Freedoms: Nativism, Education, and the Constitution, 1917–1927*. University of Nebraska Press, Lincoln.

Schlegel, John Henry (1995). *American Legal Realism and Empirical Social Science*. University of North Carolina Press, Chapel Hill.

Schmidt, Christopher W. (2008). "'Freedom Comes Only from the Law': The Debate over Law's Capacity and the Making of *Brown v. Board of Education*." *Utah Law Review* 2008: 1493–1559.

Schmidt, Christopher W. (2013). "Defending the Right to Discriminate: The Libertarian Challenge to the Civil Rights Movement." In Hadden and Minter, eds, *Signposts: New Directions in Southern Legal History*, 417–446. University of Georgia Press, Athens.

Siegel, Reva B. (2002). "She the People: The Nineteenth Amendment, Sex Equality, Federalism, and the Family." *Harvard Law Review* 115: 947–1046.

Siegel, Reva B. (2004). "Equality Talk: Antisubordination and Anticlassification Values in Constitutional Struggles Over *Brown*." *Harvard Law Review* 117: 1470–1547.

Skowronek, Stephen (1982). *Building a New American State: The Expansion of National Administrative Capacities, 1877–1920*. Cambridge University Press, New York.

Skrentny, John D. (2002). *The Minority Rights Revolution*. Harvard University Press, Cambridge, MA.

Smith, Rogers M. (1997). *Civic Ideals: Conflicting Visions of Citizenship in U.S. History*. Yale University Press, New Haven.

Stone, Geoffrey R. (2004). *Perilous Times: Free Speech in Wartime from the Sedition Act of 1798 to the War on Terrorism*. W.W. Norton, New York.

Stuntz, William J. (2011). *The Collapse of American Criminal Justice*. Belknap Press/Harvard University, Cambridge, MA.

Sugrue, Thomas J. (2008). *Sweet Land of Liberty: The Forgotten Struggle for Civil Rights in the North*. Random House, New York.

Tamanaha, Brian Z. (2010). *Beyond the Formalist-Realist Divide: The Role of Politics in Judging*. Princeton University Press, Princeton, NJ.

Teles, Steven M. (2008). *The Rise of the Conservative Legal Movement: The Battle for Control of the Law*. Princeton University Press, Princeton, NJ.

Tomlins, Christopher L. (1985). *The State and the Unions: Labor Relations, Law, and the Organized Labor Movement in America, 1880–1960*. Cambridge University Press, New York.

Tushnet, Mark (1983). "An Essay on Rights." *Texas Law Review* 62: 1363–1404.

Twiss, Benjamin R. (1942). *The Lawyers and the Constitution: How Laissez Faire Came to the Supreme Court*. Princeton University Press, Princeton, NJ.

Walker, Anders (2009). *The Ghost of Jim Crow: How Southern Moderates Used* Brown v. Board of Education *to Stall Civil Rights*. Oxford University Press, New York.

Weinrib, Laura M. (2012). "The Sex Side of Civil Liberties: *United States v. Dennett* and the Changing Face of Free Speech." *Law and History Review* 30: 325–286.

Wiecek, William M. (1998). *The Lost World of Classical Legal Thought: Law and Ideology in America, 1886–1937*. Oxford University Press, New York.

White, G. Edward (2000). *The Constitution and the New Deal*. Harvard University Press, Cambridge, MA.

Whittington, Keith E. (2005). "Congress Before the *Lochner* Court." *Boston University Law Review* 85: 821–858.

Willrich, Michael (1998). "The Two Percent Solution: Eugenic Jurisprudence and the Socialization of American Law, 1900–1930." *Law and History Review* 16: 63–111.

Willrich, Michael (2003). *City of Courts: Socializing Justice in Progressive Era Chicago*. Cambridge University Press, New York.

Part II

Individuals and Groups

Chapter Seven

NATIVE AMERICANS

Christian McMillen

Felix Cohen – the founder of modern federal Indian law and arguably the single most influential figure in all of Indian law – wrote in 1948 that "Indians have suffered for decades under complexities of law so involved that most … are inextricably entangled in red tape from birth to the grave." The tangle of laws and regulations governing almost every aspect of Indian life was bewildering and stultifying. Cohen's comment illustrates a larger point about American Indian history more generally: it cannot be disentangled from legal history. The law is everywhere. Of course, other subfields of American Indian history need not be looked at through the lens of legal history. Literary history or cultural history do just fine on their own without looking to the law.

But the law almost always lurks just outside the frame. And even in work that is distinctly *not* legal history the law enters the picture. Take a look at Margaret D. Jacobs's *Engendered Encounters: Feminism and Pueblo Cultures, 1879–1934* (1999). Largely about the encounter between Pueblo Indians and anti-modern feminists in New Mexico as they shifted from being assimilationists to becoming cultural relativists, *Engendered Encounters* is concerned with such things as the construction of the primitive Indian as Anglo women (and men) became fascinated by what they perceived to be a group of people living a simple and pure way of life. And yet a centerpiece of the book is about the law; or, more accurately, social control. In 1922 and 1923 the Bureau of Indian Affairs (BIA) – the government body that at the time maintained, or tried to maintain, total control over Indian lives – issued a series of circulars to all reservation

---

A Companion to American Legal History, First Edition.
Edited by Sally E. Hadden and Alfred L. Brophy.
© 2013 John Wiley & Sons Ltd. Published 2021 by John Wiley & Sons Ltd.

superintendents banning a number of cultural practices, among them Pueblo dances the BIA, and its missionary allies, found to be morally offensive. The ban on dancing became a *cause célèbre* among reformers and anti-modernists who were variously concerned with protecting Indian religious freedom, assimilating Indians into the Anglo world, and celebrating Indian "primitivism," and, in Jacobs' view, the ban also became a forum for working out changing sexual mores.

Jacobs's book is not legal history but it illustrates a simple point: The law is everywhere in American Indian history. Among many other things, it has played a role in religious and cultural life; it of course dictated property rights. Because so much of American Indian historiography has been rightly concerned with social control and the regulation of everyday Indian life, land, and resources, so much American Indian history has been concerned with the law. And thus it is that many American Indian historians have written legal history without even knowing it.

American Indians' unique place in the American polity – their government to government treaty relationship, their status as "domestic dependent nations" – has insured that American Indian lives are, as Cohen said, "inextricably tied up in red tape." Further, Indians' status as colonized peoples has meant that they have been ruled by laws not of their choosing, surveilled by legal institutions, and generally subject to a degree of regulation unknown among other American people. For who else has their land owned in trust for them by the U.S. government? Who else has had the proceeds from revenues generated on their land managed in trust by the federal government – money found to have been so mismanaged that Congress recently agreed to pay more than 4 billion dollars compensation for that mismanagement. Who else's dances have been banned? The answer of course to all is no one.

The consequences of all this regulation, surveillance, and management has been the focus of much historical work on American Indians. But two things dominate the history of Indian law: land and sovereignty. The transfer of Indian land to non-Indians and the wresting of control over Indian lives from Indian hands have been the *modus vivendi* of American law as it relates to Indian people. Almost all other legal matters flow from struggles over land and sovereignty: religious freedom, for example, is at base a question of sovereignty. The interpretation of treaties is both a matter of property and very often sovereignty.

So much legal history scholarship, especially the law reviews, tells us much more about courts and the law than it does about Indians. Perhaps that is to be expected; legal history is, after all, about the law. But the imbalance is striking. It is rare to learn much about Indians when reading Indian legal history. Several influential works from the legal literature are prominent examples. Nell Newton's "At the Whim of the Sovereign: Aboriginal Title Reconsidered" (1980) and Joseph Singer's "Well Settled? The

Increasing Weight of History in Indian Land Claims," (1994) consider the entire body of cases dealing with aboriginal title. Among other things they focus their sights on the Supreme Court's conclusion in *U.S. v. Santa Fe Pacific Railroad* (better known as the Hualapai case) that to extinguish aboriginal title, Congress must do so explicitly. They both level a searing critique of what they consider the Court's baseless assault on Indian sovereignty. Their work is rigorous, provocative, and informative. But, of course, it tells one more about the Court than it does about Indians. And it gives no sense of the Hualapai's more than twenty-year struggle – a struggle led by Indians such as Fred Mahone – to get the case to the Supreme Court in the first place. Why, at that particular moment, did the Hualapai case come to trial? What forces were at work? Neither Newton nor Singer note that once the case went back to the District Court the Hualapai regained control of more than 500,000 acres of their original territory largely based on their own oral testimony. Neither author, of course, had any intention of exploring these issues. However, if historians do not pick up where legal scholars such as Newton and Singer drop off, we will never understand the rich and complex history that lies in the stories outside the official discourse of the courts. And we'll learn nothing about Indians.

Perhaps the book on American Indian law most well-known to historians is Charles Wilkinson's excellent *American Indians, Time, and the Law: Native Societies in a Modern Constitutional Democracy* (1987). It effectively tracks change over time in Supreme Court decisions and sets up a very useful way to think about the whole of Indian law as it operated to at once hold up and take down American Indian sovereignty. Wilkinson described two lines of cases: the first – *Worcester v. Georgia* (1823), *Ex Parte Crow Dog* (1883), and *Talton v. Mayes* (1896) – tended to protect Indian sovereignty in legal matters; the second – *United States v. Kagama* (1886), *McBratney v. United States* 1882), and *Lone Wolf v. Hitchcock* (1903) – tended to declare federal power over Indians affairs supreme. Wilkinson discusses these historical cases to argue that since 1959, with the landmark *Williams v. Lee* – which decided the state of Arizona does not have the power to tax on the Navajo reservation – Indians have made crucial legal gains in asserting sovereignty and that the modern court – remember this was written in the late 1980s – was tending more towards protecting sovereignty. Wilkinson avers that "the Court has cut directly against the normal inclinations of Anglo-American judicial decision-making by enforcing laws of another age [treaties and statutes largely written in the nineteenth century] in the face of compelling, pragmatic arguments that tribalism is anachronistic, antiegalitarian, and unworkable in the context of contemporary American society" (Wilkinson, 1987: 5).

Wilkinson's research, while impressive and exhaustive, never leaves the realm of published government documents or Supreme Court opinions. He's interested in showing how law is made at the Supreme Court.

And thus Wilkinson's work raises many questions for the historian seeking to find out how legal history has been made: how did lawyers and Indian activists get these cases to court? Why did they come to the Court when they did? How have Indian people reacted to the power and promise of American law? These questions and others are absent from Wilkinson's work. (Wilkinson's 1999 memoir/history of land and resource development on the Colorado Plateau, *Fire on the Plateau: Conflict and Endurance on the Colorado Plateau*, does explore these kinds of questions.)

There is thus much to be done. And a lot lays buried in the archives. A quick illustration: the records of Justice Department (Record Group 60) are filled with Indian materials. The subject index to the Justice Department files for materials between about 1920 and 1980 is contained on 3 x 5 cards stored in boxes that are roughly three feet deep. Each index card represents a file on a case, whether it be a crime, a trial, a land dispute, what-have-you. There are four boxes devoted to the subject "Indians." That's not four boxes of files; that's four boxes of index cards three feet deep and on each index card is a separate case file. Any time an Indian or a tribe came in contact with the law a new case file, and corresponding number, was created. For example, the files for the Hualapai case amounted to more than six boxes of material but were represented by one index card in the subject catalog. The amount of unmined material is staggering – and this is just in the twentieth-century files of the Justice Department.

So, a strange state of affairs: much work on Indians is not legal history but considers the law as a dominating force in Indian life and much legal scholarship does not involve Indians. In this chapter I have discussed some of the former and none of the latter. I have also left out, generally speaking, work that is policy focused. For example, Donald Fixico's *Termination and Relocation: Federal Indian Policy, 1945–60* (1986) and George Pierre Castile's two books on postwar policy, *To Show Heart: Native American Self-Determination and Federal Indian Policy, 1960–1975* (1999) and *Taking Charge: Native American Self-Determination and Federal Indian Policy, 1975–1993* (2006), to name just a few, will not be discussed. Reservation casinos are, of course, important. They have generated a large legal literature and much commentary. But they have no historiography.

Most topics in American Indian legal history transcend strict periodization. Treaty rights and land claims, for instance, span the twentieth century and many of the historians who have concerned themselves with such topics, like Larry Nesper's *The Walleye War* (2002), recognize this. The assault on sovereignty, most historians would agree, has been ongoing. That said, the vast majority of historical work on the law has been on the long period between 1800 and World War II. Historians have made inroads into the later period. Charles Wilkinson's survey, *Blood Struggle: The Rise of the Indian Nations* (2005), is an excellent introduction to the complicated legal landscape of the postwar period. And Carolyn N. Long's *Religious*

Freedom and Indian Rights: The Case of Oregon v. Smith (2000) is a detailed and sympathetic account of the controversial Supreme Court case about Native American Church peyote use and religious liberty. But there is still more to be done.

Another omission: While one does not want to construct unnecessary barriers between disciplines it is relatively safe to say that systems of Aboriginal law – that is, legal codes and practices devised and carried out by Native people – have been studied much more by anthropologists than historians. Bruce Miller's *The Problem of Justice: Tradition and Law in the Coast Salish World* (2001), Raymond Austin's *Navajo Courts and the Common Law: A Tradition of Tribal Self-Governance* (2009), E. Adamson Hoebel and Karl Llewellyn's classic *The Cheyenne Way: Conflict and Case Law in Primitive Jurisprudence* (1941), and Justin Richland's *Arguing with Tradition: The Language of Law in Hopi Tribal Court* (2008) all offer nuanced studies of Aboriginal systems of justice. Sidney Harring reviewed much of the literature on Aboriginal law in "Indian Law, Sovereignty, and State Law: Native People and the Law" for the *Blackwell Companion to American Indian History* (2002) and Katherine Hermes has written a useful overview of Indian "jurispractice" in the period before 1815 (Hermes, 2008). I would recommend that interested readers turn to the sources noted above to learn about this rich and fascinating area of legal scholarship. It puts Indian people at the center and is thus very, very different from conventional legal scholarship on Indian people.

*****

While they have antecedents, and some of the ideology that forms their essential findings had been part of legal thinking regarding indigenous people for centuries, the trilogy of cases decided by John Marshall's Supreme Court between 1823 and 1832 – *Johnson v. M'Intosh* (1823), *Cherokee Nation v. Georgia* (1831), and *Worcester v. Georgia* (1832) – ushered in federal Indian law. And it is here that, with a few exceptions, the historiography of American Indian law also begins. As noted elsewhere, some historians of early America have looked at treaties; others have traced European ideas regarding property, for example. But very few have done legal history in any conventional sense.

Yashuhide Kawashima is an exception. In *Puritan Justice and the Indian: White Man's Law in Massachusetts, 1630–1763* (1986) he explored colonial Massachusetts and demonstrated, over the course of the seventeenth century, the path from an accommodation of Indian law to the complete domination of English law over Indians – the erosion of sovereignty, in other words. *Igniting King Philip's War: The John Sassamon Murder Trial* (2001) takes a "clash of cultures" approach and describes the different legal cultures of the Indians and the English. He argues, again, that over the course of the seventeenth century Indian legal practices were continually eroded by the English and that, finally, in the murder trial of John Sassamon's killers, Indians had had enough. When the English convicted Sassamon's Indian killers – and it was not even clear a murder had taken place – King Philip's War became inevitable.

Aside from treaties – and even they have not been exhausted – the colonial period's legal history remains largely unexplored. Katherine Hermes's overview of the period before 1815, in the *Cambridge History of American Law*, makes clear that there are many topics waiting to be explored.

The historiographical landscape is dramatically different when it comes to the nineteenth century and beyond. The Marshall trilogy laid the foundations of Indian property rights and mapped the contours of Indian sovereignty. Their impact and meaning have been the subject of a voluminous literature – by Lindsay Robertson's estimate more than 750 articles and books were written on *Johnson* alone in the 1980s and 90s (2005: xi). Several monographs detail the cases; several surveys, like Charles Wilkinson's *American Indians, Time, and the Law* (1987), David Wilkins' *American Indian Sovereignty and the U.S. Supreme Court: The Masking of Justice* (1997), and Stuart Banner's *How the Indians Lost Their Land* (2005), consider the cases in the context of the entire field; and there are innumerable law review articles that, with a few notable exceptions and while certainly not without their merits, do not have much to offer historians. Lindsay Robertson's *Conquest by Law* (2005), Jill Norgren's *The Cherokee Cases: The Confrontation of Law and Politics* (1996; reprinted in 2004 as *The Cherokee Cases: Two Landmark Federal Decisions in the Fight for Sovereignty*), and Tim Alan Garrison's *The Legal Ideology of Removal: The Southern Judiciary and the Sovereignty of Native American Nations* (2002) are the finest to date on the cases.

Johnson v. M'Intosh (1823) is most well-known for its articulation of the doctrine of discovery. The doctrine of discovery, at its core, meant that upon discovery of a new land a sovereign power, and its successor, gained possession of that land's property; any Native people already living there retained only a right of occupancy. Of course, Marshall did not invent the idea that European powers' property rights were superior to Native peoples'. Scholars such as Robert J. Miller in *Native America, Discovered and Conquered: Thomas Jefferson, Lewis & Clark, and Manifest Destiny* (2006) and especially Robert Williams in *The American Indian in Western Legal Thoughts: The Discourses of Conquest* (1990) have argued that Marshall's decision was a ratification of ideas that had been in circulation for centuries (one could also learn this from reading the opinion). Williams argued that "[p]erhaps most important, *Johnson*'s acceptance of the Doctrine of Discovery into the United States preserved the legacy of 1,000 years of European racism and colonialism directed against non-Western peoples" (1990: 317). Williams's view is tempered somewhat by Stuart Banner. Banner has little to say about the more ancient origins of the doctrine of discovery, but what he does do is make a compelling case that Marshall's decision confused a rather recent invention of American law – "Indian title" – with an age-old process – conquest. That is, Banner shows that between the end of the eighteenth century and *Johnson* an intellectual/legal shift took place regarding Indian property rights. What had once been alienable rights – the true rights of an owner – became a new sort of property right – the rights of occupancy. As Banner put it:

> The crux of Marshall's opinion rested on a historical assertion: that in British North America the Indians had only been accorded a right of occupancy. But this assertion was flat wrong. During the colonial period the government had not granted land before it had been purchased from the Indians. A purchase from the Indians was in practice a *prerequisite* for a land grant. The British government 'have always made an Indian Purchase the Basis or Foundation for all Grants,' declared the Indian Superintendent William Johnson toward the end of the colonial period. The practice of granting land before it had been purchased from the Indians originated only after independence. (Banner, 2005: 183)

Banner's assertion does not counter the work of Williams or Miller, or others such Kent McNeil's *Common Law Aboriginal Title* (1987), which all make clear that the doctrine of discovery, and similar ideas, predate *Johnson*; nor does Banner's work suggest that these ideas were not influential in the United States – of course they were. What Banner has aimed to do is show that what Marshall took for settled law was actually only recently introduced into American jurisprudence. To an extent Banner's book builds on Robertson's meticulous reconstruction of the *Johnson* litigation and his persuasive argument that *Johnson v. M'Intsosh* was a case created out of collusion between the parties, none of whom were Indian, to settle title to land on the western frontier. Additionally, Tim Alan Garrison's (2002) excellent book on the legal ideology of removal, like Banner and Robertson, shows that the doctrine of discovery was in many respects a contravention of the British practice it was ostensibly upholding. That is, prior to the American Revolution, lands had to be bought from Indians; after the Revolution, according to Marshall, Indians only had the right of occupancy. Together, Banner, Robertson, and Garrison have provided the most thorough history of the doctrine of discovery.

The legacy of the Marshall trilogy has been debated by legal scholars and historians for more than a century. Most legal scholars, of course, look at the legacy of the cases from a doctrinal perspective: how have they influenced subsequent Supreme Court rulings. Called a "brilliant compromise" by Nell Jessup Newton ("At the Whim of the Sovereign" (1980)), "judicial mythology" by Howard Berman ("The Concept of Aboriginal Rights in the Early Legal History of the United States" (1977)), and recognized by David Wilkins (*American Indian Sovereignty and the U.S. Supreme Court* (1997)) as at least preserving a modicum of Indian land rights, Marshall's opinion in *Johnson v. M'Intosh* tends to polarize. The decision left Indian people with a property right unique in American law. While the United States had the ultimate fee, and the right to extinguish Indian title, it could only do so with the permission of the tribes. Marshall's decision was really a limitation on European powers, not Indian tribes. Marshall realized the oddity of his decision. In fact, he confessed that his version of the doctrine of discovery was unjust, even, eventually, calling it "pretentious." But Marshall saw no other way out. It was, he thought, the custom of the country. And while Indian title was not to be taken lightly – it was as close to fee simple title as possible – *Johnson* was still an unbridled assertion of power. As Philip Frickey argued in "Marshalling Past and Present: Colonialism, Constitutionalism, and Interpretation in Federal Indian Law" (1993), Marshall could find no other justification for his theory of discovery than his belief in the power of the colonialism.

After *Johnson* came the two Cherokee cases, decided in 1831 and 1832. Like *Johnson*, these two cases are the subject of a large literature. For historians, the two most important are Norgren's *The Cherokee Cases* (1996) and Garrison's *The Legal Ideology of Removal* (2002). Both books detail the Cherokee role in the cases and, unlike the law review literature or Wilkinson's *American Indians, Time, and the Law* (1987) or Wilkins' *American Indian Sovereignty and the U.S. Supreme Court* (1997), Norgren and Garrison are less concerned with the legacy of the decisions than they are with how and why they came to the Court when they did. Historical questions, in other words.

Johnson largely dealt with land and involved no Indians directly; the Cherokee cases are about sovereignty and the Cherokee were key players. First, in 1831, and famous for its declaration that Indian tribes were "domestic, dependent nations," came *Cherokee Nation v. Georgia*. *Worcester* came the following year. While *Cherokee Nation* left Indians as "domestic, dependent nations," wards of the federal government, in *Worcester* the Court ruled that the laws of Georgia did not apply to the sovereign Cherokee, and thus Samuel Worcester broke no law when preaching among the tribe without a permit from the state. In order to establish Indian sovereignty Marshall reworked the conquest aspect of his decision in *Johnson*. Now, Marshall admitted, the conceit that discovery gives the discoverer title was a fiction. Marshall made clear that a European nation could claim title to land only if the Indians consented to sell. He repudiated his earlier belief that discovery and conquest were, in essential respects, synonymous. In *Worcester*, when Marshall made clear that Indian tribes possessed all their aboriginal rights at discovery, and could only relinquish those rights to the sovereign power with their consent, he demolished *Johnson's* conflation of discovery with conquest. And if discovery and conquest were not the same thing then discovery did not automatically confer title on the discoverer. Marshall now circled back to Justice Johnson's dissent in an earlier case, *Fletcher v. Peck* (1810): Indians were masters of the soil until they relinquished those rights to the new sovereign. But, for all its strong words in defense of Indian sovereignty, *Worcester* still endorsed colonialism and left its legacy largely outside the arm of the law. The historical processes of colonialism – alienation of land, for one – were not justiciable, but the "ongoing process of colonialism," as Philip Frickey (1993) puts it, such as Samuel Worcester's trouble with the state of Georgia and Cherokee sovereignty, might be handled in court. *Worcester* was a pivot point. The questionable practices of colonialism up to this point were beyond repair, but, after *Worcester*, colonialism had to answer to a limited Indian sovereignty.

But *Worcester* had little practical effect. States continued to routinely trample Indian sovereignty by trying Native people in state courts.

The historical literature on state law is much less well-developed than that on federal law. This is so for one very good reason: Indian tribes deal almost exclusively with the federal government and thus historically states have had little or no jurisdiction over Indians. Even so, there is a rich history of state-Indian (both tribal and individual) interaction that has gotten some attention from historians who have been interested not only in the effect of state law on Indians. They have also examined where sovereignty lay after *Worcester*: with the tribes, the states, or the federal government. Yet, it remains an area still in need of further excavation – especially in the American West.

Recent work on state law begins with Sidney Harring's 1994 book *Crow Dog's Case: American Indian Sovereignty, Tribal Law, and United States Law in the Nineteenth Century*. Harring looked carefully at state law and showed that the power of states over Indian lives was strong despite the dubious legality of their decisions regarding Indians. This was so for the most quotidian of reasons: no one was watching. States, Harring argues, routinely tried and convicted Indians without ever reporting the cases; Indians served sentences, hung from the gallows, or were acquitted by states which went unchallenged by the federal government (1994: 34). Harring argues that before the Civil War states in the Southeast and New York considered themselves in charge of Indian affairs. States like Georgia went to great lengths to assert their sovereignty in cases like 1830's *State v. George Tassels* in which Georgia claimed jurisdiction over crimes, in this case murder, committed by Indians on Indians in Indian country. Harring argues that *Tassels* was in principal and practice, until the twentieth century, more important than *Cherokee Nation v. Georgia* and *Worcester v. Georgia* because it was more accurately representative of the state of affairs over much of the nineteenth century.

In her 2007 book, *American Indians and State Law: Sovereignty, Race, and Citizenship, 1790–1880*, Deborah Rosen argues Indians were more likely to be circumscribed by state law than federal law. As a result, she argues further, states played a significant role in incorporating Indians into American society. States in the South, the Northeast, and the Midwest and the New Mexico territory (although its status as a territory made the debate there over citizenship both a local and a federal matter) all worked hard to make certain that Native people were subject to their laws. States such as New York and Georgia – to take two well-known examples – did this because they believed equally in two interrelated things: Indian sovereignty did not exist in most matters and the states had supremacy over the federal government in dealing with their Indian inhabitants. States and the federal government, in Rosen's view, tangled over Federalism. The federal government considered itself supreme based on its commerce clause powers while states routinely bucked this view by passing law after law and trying case after case in their own courts based on the opposite belief: the commerce clause regulated only a fraction of Indian affairs. Rosen effectively demonstrates that between 1790 and circa 1880 state law did have an impact on Indian lives in several realms: criminal law, marriage, property and inheritance, voting, schools, Indian testimony at trial, and citizenship. New York, for instance, pioneered a form of proto-allotment by allowing individual Indians to sell land in an effort to break down the collective Indian estate. In Alabama, courts allowed Indian custom marriages to prevail. And in Louisiana and Virginia, those held in slavery routinely appeared in court arguing that their Indian ancestry guaranteed them their freedom. Aside from one chapter on New Mexico, the book is concerned with states east of the Mississippi. Federal law, Rosen acknowledges, was generally supreme in the trans-Mississippi West where it came first and states came next. Indeed, Rosen admits that a state's ability to regulate Indians was strong only as long as the federal government's was weak.

Tim Alan Garrison's *The Legal Ideology of Removal* (2002) is, as well as being excellent on the Cherokee cases, also superb on state law. After detailing the work done by John Marshall's Supreme Court Garrison turns to Tennessee, Georgia, and Alabama to see how *Worcester* was received in state courts. Not well it turns out. Garrison, building upon and acknowledging the pioneering work of Harring, finds that *Worcester*, despite its strong support of sovereignty and the fact that the states were bound to follow it, had almost no effect on southern judiciaries committed to asserting *their* sovereignty over Indians. According to the southern states, Indians were simply individual state residents and thus subject to state law.

Lisa Ford's *Settler Sovereignty: Jurisdiction and Indigenous People in America and Australia, 1788–1836* (2010) argues effectively that what happened in the 1820s, 1830s, and 1840s was a gradual replacing of a kind of primitive legal imperialism on the frontier with absolute state sovereignty by the 1840s. Ford's comparison of Australia and Georgia succeeds in showing that the actions of Georgia, New York, and Alabama were part of a more global trend in the same direction: the destruction of indigenous sovereignty over legal matters.

While it was mostly east of the Mississippi that states asserted authority over Indians, states and territories in the West also attempted to wield jurisdiction over Indians. A quick search in Lexis-Nexis turns up cases on Indian-white marriage and probate law, for example, from Arizona that reveal a hidden history. Brad Asher's *Beyond the Reservation: Indians, Settlers, and the Law in Washington Territory, 1853–1889* (1999) is the only book that looks carefully at the effect local laws had on Indian people in the West. This is not a book about sovereignty or treaty rights or property rights. It is a book about boundary making. Asher details the ways in which local officials and courts, through their application of U.S. liquor laws or barring marriage between Indians and non-Indians, set out to harden racial boundaries at a time and in a place when reservations were not doing the job. The local impulse to separate from Indians and then attempt to control them mirrors the federal efforts to do the same. That is, local people in Washington followed the national zeitgeist: remove or separate Indians from our midst and then attempt to regulate their lives. Asher's book, though not for lack of trying, does not contain much in the way of Indian voice. The sources appear to have simply not been there. That said, one is still left with a vital sense of Indian life. Alexandra Harmon's success in *Indians in the Making* (1998) with finding Indian voices – and she is supremely successful – stems from her writing about a later period when the sources become, if not abundant, more readily available.

The question of sovereignty is of obvious importance. Demonstrating that *Worcester* did little to bolster Indian sovereignty in the American South has been an important contribution to legal history. And Rosen's *American Indians and State Law* showing that, for example, some states recognized Indian marriages is surprising. Asher's efforts to show the increasing effect local law had on Indian people in Washington Territory is important. But out of all this, as is common in much Indian legal history, we have come to know an awful lot about the law and still very little about Indians. Considering the challenges involved in finding sources that contain Indian voices and viewpoints this is not surprising, nor is it something these authors are unaware of. Still, it's worth noting if for no other reason than to point out a void to be, maybe, filled by future research.

Worcester v. Georgia stood for the principle that Indian people were masters of their own affairs and that state laws did not impinge upon their rights to self-rule. But, as noted, *Worcester* was not enforced and in fact the southern states in particular resisted the decision. State law, of course, has not been the only check on Indian sovereignty; the federal government has also made clear that sovereignty has its limits. The Major Crimes Act of 1886 is one of the first and most far reaching examples of a federal check on sovereignty. As Sidney Harring makes clear in *Crow Dog's Case: American Indian Sovereignty, Tribal Law, and United States Law in the Nineteenth Century* (1994), Congress passed the Major Crimes Act in the wake of the Supreme

Court's decision in *Ex Parte Crow Dog* (1883). In that decision the Court ruled that Crow Dog, a Brule Sioux, could not be prosecuted under U.S. law for the murder of another Brule Sioux, Spotted Tail, on Sioux land. The decision, as noted earlier, is part of the line of cases Charles Wilkinson has identified as the sovereignty line. But as Wilkinson noted, the Court, more or less simultaneously, made decisions in support of and antithetical to sovereignty. *Crow Dog* is best seen as an anomaly. Harring argues it was in fact a test case designed to push the issue of Indian sovereignty over criminal matters to court in an effort to weaken sovereignty. It was handed down during a time that was simultaneously a period of decreasing Indian power and population and increasing federal power over Indians. Treaty making had ended in 1871 and allotment and assimilation were dawning. The Major Crimes Act – which set out ten crimes that the federal government had jurisdiction over in Indian country – was more indicative of the era generally than *Crow Dog*. Like many periods in American Indian history this one has been well covered by historians interested in American Indians but not necessarily in the law. (The obvious exceptions are Blue Clark's book on *Lone Wolf* (1994) and David Wilkins' *American Indian Sovereignty and the U.S. Supreme Court* (1997).) Most historians would characterize the period from *Johnson* to *Lone Wolf* and the first two decades of the twentieth century as one of ever increasing federal control and diminishing Indian sovereignty. *Lone Wolf* is in some respects the apex of efforts to crush Indian sovereignty. But, as noted, it of course does not exist in a vacuum; it was handed down by a court firmly in the grip of assimilation. And to understand the period, the best place to turn is still Frederick Hoxie's *A Final Promise: The Campaign to Assimilate the Indians, 1880–1920* (1984).

While historians such as Andrew Fisher, Christian McMillen, and Alexandra Harmon have made clear that Indian people were not quiescent during the nadir of the late nineteenth and early twentieth centuries – treaty rights and land claims activism began in earnest in the years surrounding World War I – it is nonetheless the case that Indian policy and law, over the entirety of the nineteenth century, were almost uniformly hostile to Indians.

****

Treaties are an important element in American Indian legal history. They determine, variously, property boundaries, diplomatic relations and obligations between the U.S. and many Indian tribes. They guarantee sovereignty over many matters; they never expire. American Indian historians have always been interested in treaties. Treaty documents – the treaties themselves and the transcripts of negotiations – have been used to great effect as ethnohistorical documents. Scholars such as Raymond DeMallie ("Touching the Pen: Plains Indian Treaty Councils in Ethnohistorical Perspective" (1980)) have scrutinized treaty council minutes for what can be learned from them about American Indian life. Historians of colonial America, such as James Merrell and Daniel Richter, have examined treaty documents for what they can tell us about a wide range of topics – trade, diplomacy, rhetorical strategies, war and peace, Indian leadership and social structures. Richter's *Facing East from Indian Country: A Native History of Early America* (2001) and Merrell's *Into the American Woods: Negotiators on the Pennsylvania Frontier* (1999) both feature extremely close and detailed readings of eighteenth century treaty council minutes. But neither Demallie, Richter, nor Merrell is terribly concerned with the law as a subject except in so far as the treaties themselves are obviously legal documents – and even then the treaties are not their focus as much as what the treaty documents can tell us about Indian life. The vast majority of historians, with exceptions such as Dorothy V. Jones' *License for Empire: Colonialism by Treaty in Early America* (1982), have taken a similar approach.

There are some exceptions and Robert Williams is one. Williams is the author of three books, and numerous law review articles, on American Indian law. *The American Indian in Western Legal Thought* (Williams, 1990) is his ambitious treatment of European impulse to take indigenous land and the legal reasoning used to support that effort. *Like a Loaded Weapon: The Rehnquist Court, Indian Rights, and the Legal History of Racism in America* (2005) is a relatively brief, and polemical, history of the racism Williams finds embedded in just about the entire history of Indian law. *Linking Arms Together: American Indian Treaty Visions of Land and Peace, 1600–1800* (1997) is his take on treaties and their legal meaning, both in the past and the present. And the present must be stressed, for Williams' goal is to think about how non-Indian made law can be just. He asks:

> Given its history, how does this system of colonizing law imposed on the Indian by the United State – this white man's Indian law – manage to transcend the threat it has historically posed to the perpetuation of Indian cultural identity, existence, and sovereignty? How can such a unilaterally imposed system of colonizing law and power ever manage to assist Indian peoples in their decolonization struggles and achieve justice? (Williams, 1997: 7)

His answer is to look to treaties from the colonial and early American periods. Borrowing heavily from Richard White's *The Middle Ground* (1991) and Daniel Richter's *The Ordeal of the Longhouse* (1992), and doing little primary research of his own, Williams describes a world of mutual accommodation between Indians and whites. In this world, whites could hardly expect to simply foist their own visions of law on to Indians. Rather, on the colonial frontier, Indian people, of course already in possession of well-tuned diplomatic norms designed to forge connections and alliances with Indian allies, brought their own visions of justice to the table. They still had some power.

The rich system of metaphors, symbols, and stories that surrounded inter-Indian alliances in pre-contact America also colored Indian-white diplomatic alliances. Williams argues that because Indians appear to have utilized many of the same practices associated with sacred ritual when making treaties – smoking a pipe (calumet), presenting a wampum belt, or mimicking a mourning ceremony, among other things – that treaties in fact are sacred documents. Sharing these ritual practices with Europeans, entering into alliance through partaking in the calumet "elevated the temporal agreement represented by a treaty to the realm of a sacred obligation" (1997: 47). While there is no doubt that Indians took treaty making seriously Williams is reluctant to ever question their motives or even wonder if their rhetoric might be full of public flourish. For this, he seems naive and renders Indians, ironically, a bit one dimensional – only capable of thinking and speaking in the most ponderous of language. One wonders where Creeks like Alexander McGillivray, so brilliantly characterized by J. Leitch Wright ("Creek-American Treaty of 1790: Alexander McGillivray and the Diplomacy of the Old Southwest" (1967)) as a shrewd negotiator with personal financial interests dependent on the outcome of treaty negotiations, would fit into Williams' framework?

Further, Williams' argument might work for the period up to 1800, but it does not for later decades. When treaty negotiations took place in the West later in the century – with the Navajo in 1868, or Isaac Stevens' flurry of treaty writing across the Pacific Northwest in 1854–1855, for example – the landscape was entirely different. Of course, they considered treaty documents important, but it's hard to find much sacred – from either side's point of view – in the western land cession treaties. Additionally, the "middle ground," so important to Williams' calculus, no longer prevailed – after all, it describes a passing stage in white-Indian relations. After the Treaty of Fort Laramie, in 1851, white Americans quickly gained the upper hand; the system of mutual accommodation that Williams argues existed in the East never prevailed in the West. When treaty making ended in 1871 most who gave the matter any thought at all considered Indians either war-mongering savages or a dependent rather than a sovereign people; engaging them in diplomatic negotiations seemed anathema – and many lamented it had ever been done at all.

The later period of treaty making – from 1800–1871 – still needs much work. There is of course excellent work on Indian history more generally that considers treaties. After all, no historian could or would deny the importance of such an event as the treaty negotiations leading up to the Fort Laramie treaty of 1851. More than ten thousand Plain Indians from the Sioux, Gros Ventre, Cheyennes, Crows and others spent weeks on land surrounding Fort Laramie working out the details of the treaty. All historians of Indian America know that treaties became the method by which land passed from Indian to white hands. And no historians deny their importance. Yet, while colonial era treaty making has been taken seriously by historians, similar work on the nineteenth century is less common.

There are exceptions. Francis Paul Prucha's comprehensive and indispensable *American Indian Treaties: The History of a Political Anomaly* (1994) is the most notable. Prucha is an important figure in American Indian historiography. In addition to *American Indian Treaties*, and other books, he is best known for his two-volume masterwork *The Great Father: The United States Government and the American Indians* (1984). Since its publication, *The Great Father* has remained the standard book on American Indian policy. *American Indian Treaties* is similar in tone and approach – a straightforward march through time, dispassionate, rarely making overt judgments on historical events or actors, and, until the book's fourth section on treaty rights in the twentieth century, focused more on policy makers than Indians. Out of this, however, emerges the best single study of post-colonial American Indian treaties we possess. Very little is left out of the book and Prucha usefully periodizes the history of treaties into four parts – building a treaty-making system; using treaties as a way to foment U.S. policy goals; the breakdown and end of treaty making; and, finally, the legacy and meaning of treaties in the twentieth century.

But to understand the importance of treaties and their power and place in Indian life Prucha's book must be read in conjunction with more fine grained regional or case-based studies that include Indian people. The most important work on treaties has been much less about their creation than it has been with their consequences. Several excellent books exemplify this approach. Like most work discussed in this chapter, most are not by any means strictly or even principally legal history in any conventional sense. This is certainly so with Alexandra Harmon's *Indians in the Making: Ethic Relations and Indian Identities around Puget Sound* (1998) which shows over time the ever shifting contours of Indian identity and demonstrates, too, that mid-nineteenth-century treaties became increasingly important symbols of Indianness as the twentieth century wore on. Several other books also look at treaty fishing rights. Katherine Barber's, *The Death of Celilo Falls* (2005) is concerned with the clash between Indian water and treaty rights and hydropower and *The Si'lailo Way: Indians, Salmon and the Law on the Columbia River* (2006) by Joseph C. Dupris, Kathleen S. Hill, and William H. Rodgers, Jr. is detailed examination of Columbia River Indians' asserting their treaty rights to the Columbia River. Larry Nesper's *The Wallaye War: The Struggle for Ojibwe Spearfishing and Treaty Rights* (2002) is similar to Harmon's in its focus on the importance of treaty fishing rights in the second half of the twentieth century. While Harmon and Nesper deal with the resurgence of treaty rights – by no means an easy struggle – Blue Clark's *Lone Wolf v. Hitchcock: Treaty Rights and Indian Law at the End of the Nineteenth Century* (1994) tackles treaty rights at their nadir. His is a grim story that demonstrates the legal violence done to Indian property rights at the end of the nineteenth and beginning of the twentieth centuries – a time when allotment was in full swing; assimilation was the official policy of the Bureau of Indian Affairs; and most thought treaties meaningless holdovers from an earlier time. Clark probes the ways in which the Bureau of Indian Affairs and the Supreme Court so easily tossed treaty rights to the side in favor of the U.S. government's "plenary powers" over Indians in 1903's *Lone Wolf v. Hitchcock*. Clark's book makes clear the Kiowa knew exactly what was being attempted when the U.S. government tried to swindle them out of land and their protests, and the evidence they presented to show that their treaty was being violated, meant little to a court eager to help distribute Indian land to non-Indians.

To read these books together – one a massive overview of the entire system of treaty making and its repercussions; the others fine grained histories of Indians and treaties – is to see treaties as policy documents and as integral pieces of American Indian life. Prucha's book is necessarily superficial on individual treaties and tribes; the others correspondingly in-depth. Where Prucha does not offer much that will surprise readers familiar with Indian history and hews to a fairly conventional chronological approach, Harmon, Clark, and Nesper and others reveal worlds previously unknown to outsiders. What's more, reading them together places treaties at different places in historical time: Prucha when they were being made; Clark at their most meaningless; and Nesper and Harmon as they became symbols of what it means to be an Indian tribe.

More and more work keeps appearing on treaties; most of it is on their legacy and not their making. A recent collection of essays, edited by Alexandra Harmon (*The Power of Promises: Rethinking Indian Treaties in the Pacific Northwest* (2008)), showcases some of the best new work by top scholars from the field in both the U.S. and Canada. For example, Andrew Fisher's essay details the ways in which Columbia River Indians were able, between 1880 and 1920, to defend their treaty fishing rights in the face of settler and state intrusion. Getting several important cases to the state and federal levels – especially 1905's *U.S. v. Winans* – was critical in securing treaty rights. Other articles such as those by Arthur Ray and Robert Anderson, respectively, deal with the "history wars" in Canada over land claims and treaty rights as well as "treaty substitutes" in contemporary times. The essays in this collection make clear that the historiography of treaties is still one of the most dynamic and promising subfields in American Indian history.

****

A topic recently given great attention, and that picks up on some of the themes discussed above, has been the relationship between American Indians and natural resources. National Parks and water have captured most of the attention. Taking their cues in part from books on the British Empire such as John Mackenzie's *The Empire of Nature: Hunting, Conservation, and British Imperialism* (1988) American historians began, in the 1990s, to see similar developments in American history – restrictions placed on Native land use, prohibitions on subsistence hunting, and active management by the state. The creation of National Parks (and other types of land holdings like National Forests) in the American West provided a new site of struggle between Indians and the U.S. government, state governments, and local people over property rights and land use. Set aside at a time when Indian peoples' population and military power were waning, and Americans' interest in conservation and wilderness was waxing, National Parks became places where a new round of Indian removal took place. But this was removal of a different sort. It was both physical and imagined. That is, Indians were both physically removed from places or restricted from using them in ways they always had, as well as written out of the landscape as if they had never been there.

Karl Jacoby's *Crimes Against Nature: Squatters, Poachers, Thieves, and the Hidden History of American Conservation* (2001), Rebecca Solnit's *Savage Dreams: A Journey into the Landscape Wars of the American West* (1994), Mark Spence's *Dispossessing the Wilderness: Indian Removal and the Making of the National Parks* (1999), and Louis Warren's *The Hunter's Game: Poachers and Conservationists in Twentieth-Century America* (1997) all revolved around some very similar concerns: they were all investigating changing ideas about the natural world in the late nineteenth and early twentieth centuries as manifested in the setting aside of large chunks of land. The questions they were interested in were as much about Indian history as they were about environmental history. Indeed, all of their work came less out of American Indian historiography as it did out of environmental history. The environmental history perspective enlivened American Indian historiography and opened up a new area of investigation: the removal or exclusion of Indians from National Parks.

Water rights have inspired an important, if not voluminous, body of historical literature. (There is a massive legal literature that is not considered here.) Since 1978, when Norris Hundley published his seminal article, "The Dark and Bloody Ground of Indian Water Rights: Confusion Elevated to Principle" (1978), and noted that almost no historical work had been done on Indians and water, some work has been done. Hundley was the pioneer. In two articles – in addition to "The Dark and Bloody Ground" Hundley published "The 'Winters' Decision and Indian Water Rights: A Mystery Reexamined" in 1982 – Hundley opened the field to serious historical inquiry. Ever since, the history of Indians and water has been an important topic. That said, like much else in American Indian history, very little of it is strictly, or even mainly, legal history in any conventional sense and little of it involves Indians directly.

Hundley, like many working in the field of Indian law, noted the courts' somewhat Janus-faced stance when it came to Indians. There have been decisions favorable to Indians; there have been unfavorable ones. Of course, that bland characterization could apply to almost any area of law, but in the case of Indians the schizophrenia of the courts is truly bewildering. Unsurprisingly, Hundley identified 1908's *Winters v. United States* as the beginning of Indian water rights. In that case, the U.S. Supreme Court declared that the Gros Ventre and Assiniboine tribes living on the Fort Belknap reservation in central Montana had a right of prior appropriation – Indian reserved water rights – to the waters of the Milk river. The Court found that in the creation of the reservation the right to have water over and above other users was secured to Indians, forever. It was a guaranteed right. But Hundley found that it did not lead to much water use by Indians nor Indian control of Indian water. According to Hundley, Indian reserved water rights lay dormant until the 1960s.

But John Lyle Shurts, in *Indian Reserved Water Rights: The* Winters *Doctrine in its Social and Legal Context, 1880s–1930s* (2000), has to an extent found otherwise. In addition to determining that some non-Indian water users in the Milk river valley actually supported Indian reserved rights because it loosened the stranglehold prior appropriation had on water in Montana, Shurts dug into archival material and found U.S. attorneys and reservation agents, but no Indians, latching on to reserved water rights to preserve Indian water for Indians. Whereas Hundley largely stuck to published court decisions – and did indeed find that the case was ignored at the judicial level – Shurts' archival research revealed a slightly different story. He found that officials within the BIA and the Department of Justice found in *Winters* a way to preserve Indian reservation water rights in the face of non-Indian encroachment. For example, on the Klamath Reservation, in 1913, as the Bureau of Reclamation was planning a project and settlers claimed water on the Klamath river, reservation agents put up notices, based on their understanding of *Winters*, that Indians possessed superior rights. Shurts argues that these kinds of efforts kept *Winters* alive but resulted in almost no litigation. Shurts offers a detailed case study of such efforts on the Uintah reservation in Utah. While Shurts has not overturned Hundley – likely no one will – he did offer a more nuanced view of the *Winters* litigation as well as a careful treatment of its use in the immediately subsequent decades. Further, through his detailed archival research, Shurts has made clear what can be learned about the law when one leaves the realm of published opinions. Similar work on water – deep, detailed, on the ground and archival based – on the decades after 1930 is scant.

Considering what Shurts has revealed, and what historians working on treaty fishing rights have found, one wonders what lies buried in the archives – a history of *Arizona v. California* (1963) and its effects on Indian water, for instance, could be of great value. To this end, Michael Lawson's *Dammed Indians: The Pick-Sloan Plan and the Missouri River Sioux, 1944–1980* (1982) on the damming of the Missouri river by the Army Corps of Engineers and the flooding of Indian land on the Missouri river, demonstrates that Indian water, treaty, and property rights are fragile in the face of federal power. Political scientist Daniel McCool's two books on water rights in the West (*Native Waters: Contemporary Indian Water Settlement and the Second Treaty Era* (2002) and *Command of the Waters: Iron Triangles, the Federal Water Development Program, and Indian Water* (1987)), and Donald Pisani's work on the Bureau of Reclamation and Indians (*Water and American Government: The Bureau of Reclamation, National Water Policy, and the West, 1902–1935* (2002)) suggest that there is a wealth of historical material out there for the historian willing to sift through it.

****

The Indian New Deal – conventionally considered to be those years (1933–1945) when John Collier was Commissioner of Indian Affairs – was a time of reform in Indian Affairs. It was not a wholesale break with the past and Indian people themselves had been agitating for change on a number of fronts – treaty rights and land claims, for example – for more than a decade. Yet the Indian New Deal was a decisive change: more than any other the Collier administration took Indian rights seriously.

Dozens of books and articles consider the Indian New Deal and its policy changes; many look at specific tribes, and involve actual Indian people, while others keep the focus on Washington and John Collier. Elmer R. Rusco's *A Fateful Time: The Background and Legislative History of the Indian Reorganization Act* (2000) is a comprehensive history of what was surely the era's most sweeping legal change. The Indian Reorganization Act did away with the allotment policy and created tribal governance structures among other things. Historians do not consider the Indian New Deal perfect; some consider it a period, in fact, when more, not less, federal control was given to the federal government. But most would agree that the era of modern tribal sovereignty began during the Indian New Deal. Further, most would also agree that it began with Felix Cohen. In *American Indians, American Justice* (1983) Vine Deloria, Jr. and Clifford M. Lytle called Cohen's work "revolutionary"; in their 1980 book, *The Road: Indian Tribes and Political Liberty* (1980), Russell Barsh and James Youngblood Henderson wrote that Cohen's work was the foundation of modern federal Indian law; finally, David Getches, Charles Wilkinson, and Robert Williams, in their casebook on Indian law (1998), said that Cohen had written what is "without question the single most influential passage ever written by an Indian law scholar." Cohen wrote that "the most basic principle of all Indian law, supported by a host of decisions ..., is the principle that those powers which are lawfully vested in an Indian tribe are not, in general, delegated powers granted by express acts of Congress, but rather inherent powers of a limited sovereignty which has never been extinguished ... What is not expressly limited [by treaty or statute] remains within the domain of tribal sovereignty." Cohen's formulation, first articulated in a 1934

Solicitor's Memo (attributed to Nathan Margold but written by Cohen) called "The Powers of Indian Tribes" has remained the cornerstone of Indian sovereignty.

Cohen's work on the Indian Reorganization Act, the *Handbook of Federal Indian Law* (1942), and the Indian Claims Commission Act, among many other achievements, have all recently been discussed in *Architect of Justice* (2007) Dalia Tsuk Mitchell's biography of Cohen. While the Indian New Deal has a rich and well developed historiography there is still work to be done on the law.

One area that has seen some attention during this period is land claims. Indian land claims are a twentieth century phenomenon and are, for the most part, like treaty rights, an Indian generated legal issue. That is, it was Indians who spurred interest in these cases. Land claims cases came about for a variety of reasons, but most arose out of disputes over treaty rights violations or alleged illegal taking of land. Like Alexandra Harmon, Andrew Fisher, and others, who locate the origins of Indian treaty rights activism in the years surrounding World War I, Christian McMillen argues that land claims activism started then too. In *Making Indian Law* (2007), a detailed study of the Hualapai tribe's long-term effort to save their reservation from both the government and the Santa Fe Pacific Railroad, McMillen demonstrates that dozens of land claims came to Congress and the Court of Claims before World War II. These historians' work revealed an unknown strain of Indian activism that predates by decades the Red Power movement of the 1960s and 1970s. McMillen showed that in the 1920s and 1930s, using historical research the Hualapai and their attorneys – most notably Felix Cohen – were able to overturn the notion that Indians had no provable property rights based on occupancy. This was so because when the foundational Indian property rights cases were decided, recognition of occupancy was an entirely different matter; the Indian presence was obvious. *Worcester v. Georgia*, for example, revolved around current rights derived from current occupancy, not rights based on historic occupancy – as in the Hualapai case. When the Hualapai and other tribes began to think about their land in the years after World War I, they no longer practiced their aboriginal lifestyle, and as the years went by, of course, they moved still further away from pre-contact ways; long-term occupancy was not a readily obvious fact.

The history of land claims, as distinct from the history of property rights, has been the subject of a large journal literature, but almost no historians have given claims sustained book-length treatment. Two books by non-professional historians – Mike Lieder and Jake Page's *Wild Justice: The People of Geronimo vs. the United States* (1997) and Edward Lazarus' *Black Hills/White Justice: The Sioux Nation versus the United States, 1775 to the Present* (1991) – offer detailed tribal case studies and *Wild Justice* provides an excellent overview of claims more generally. Harvey Rosenthal's *Their Day in Court: A History of the Indian Claims Commission* (1990) is a very useful administrative history of the ICC and is indispensable for understanding the ICC's claims process. Russell Lawrence Barsh's "Indian Land Claims in the United States" (1982) is also a good introduction to Indian claims across U.S. history. The Indian Claims Commission (1946–1978) has generated some excellent articles by Arthur Ray (2003) and David Wishart (2001) comparing claims in the United States with claims in Canada, Australia, and New Zealand. Arthur Ray and Bain Attwood offer the best introductions to the abundant historical and anthropological literature on land claims coming from scholars outside the United States. There is a lot of work that can still be done on claims. The more than one hundred cases pending in the Court of Claims by 1940 – cases that generated a massive amount of documentation – have all but been ignored by historians. Almost no one has gone into the records of the Justice Department or the Indian Claims Commission or the Great Lakes-Ohio Valley Ethnohistorical Research Project records at Indiana University and done fine grained archival research; most work on the ICC relies on published opinions and other types of accessible materials. One potentially fruitful area of research is the effect of land claims litigation on tribal communities: how did historical research unite or divide communities? How did tribes distribute their earnings from judgements? Pamela Wallace ("Indian Claims Commission: Political Complexity and Contrasting Concepts of Identity" (2002)) provides an excellent example of the kinds of questions a historian might be able to answer. One might also wonder if there is evidence of chicanery in the legal proceedings. Because so little has been done, the possibilities are quite abundant.

Tribal recognition is similar to land claims in that winning recognition depends on history. Because tribal recognition is relatively recent formal process it has a very limited historiography. But as Mark Edwin Miller shows in *Forgotten Tribes: Unrecognized Indians and the Federal Acknowledgment Process* (2004) deciding just what constitutes a recognized Indian tribe is a very old question. *Forgotten Tribes* is both an overview of federal recognition and a series of case studies detailing the process in the twentieth century.

References

Asher, Brad (1999). *Beyond the Reservation: Indians, Settlers, and the Law in Washington Territory, 1853–1889.* University of Oklahoma Press, Norman.

Austin, Raymond (2009). *Navajo Courts and the Common Law: A Tradition of Tribal Self-Governance.* University of Minnesota Press, Minneapolis.

Banner, Stuart (2005). *How the Indians Lost their Land: Law and Power on the Frontier.* Harvard University Press, Cambridge.

Barber, Katherine (2005). *The Death of Celilo Falls.* University of Washington Press, Seattle.

Barsh, Russel Lawrence (1982). "Indian Land Claims Policy in the United States." *North Dakota Law Review* 58: 7–82.

Barsh, Russell and Henderson, James Youngblood (1980). *The Road: Indian Tribes and Political Liberty*. University of California Press, Berkeley.

Berman, Howard (1977). "The Concept of Aboriginal Rights in the Early Legal History of the United States." *Buffalo Law Review* 27: 637–688.

Castile, George Pierre (1999). *To Show Heart: Native American Self-Determination and Federal Indian Policy, 1960–1975*. University of Arizona Press, Tucson.

Castile, George Pierre (2006). *Taking Charge: Native American Self-Determination and Federal Indian Policy, 1975–1993*. University of Arizona Press, Tucson.

Clark, Blue (1994). *Lone Wolf v. Hitchcock: Treaty Rights and Indian Law at the End of the Nineteenth Century*. University of Nebraska Press, Lincoln, NE.

Cohen, Felix S. (1942). *Handbook of Federal Indian Law*. Government Printing Office, Washington, D.C.

Cohen, Felix S. (1948). "Petition to the Congress and the President of the United States, Requesting Disapproval of H.R. 1113, the so-called Indian Emancipation Bill," Correspondence Files, Folder 5, Box 36, Records of the Association on American Indian Affairs, Seeley Mudd Library, Princeton University.

Cohen, Felix S. (1963). "Original Indian Title." In Cohen, ed., *The Legal Conscience: Selected Papers of Felix S. Cohen*, 273–304. Yale University Press, New Haven.

Deloria, Jr., Vine and Lytle, Clifford M. (1983). *American Indians, American Justice*. University of Texas Press, Austin.

Demallie, Raymond (1980). "Touching the Pen: Plains Indian Treaty Councils in Ethnohistorical Perspective." In Leubke, ed., *Ethnicity on the Great Plains*. University of Nebraska Press, Lincoln.

Dupris, Joseph C., Hill, Kathleen S., and Rodgers, Jr., William H. (2006). *The Si'lailo Way: Indians, Salmon and the Law on the Columbia River*. Carolina Academic Press, Durham.

Ford, Lisa (2010). *Settler Sovereignty: Jurisdiction and Indigenous People in America and Australia, 1788–1836*. Harvard University Press, Cambridge.

Fixico, Donald (1986). *Termination and Relocation: Federal Indian Policy, 1945–60*. University of New Mexico Press, Albuquerque.

Frickey, Philip P. (1993). "Marshalling the Past and Present: Colonialism, Constitutionalism, and Interpretation in Federal Indian Law." *Harvard Law Review* 107: 381–440.

Garrison, Tim Alan (2002). *The Legal Ideology of Removal: The Southern Judiciary and the Sovereignty of Native American Nations*. University of Georgia Press, Athens, GA.

Getches, David H., Wilkinson, Charles F., and Williams, Jr., Robert A. (1998). *Cases and Materials on Federal Indian Law*. West Group, St. Paul.

Harmon, Alexandra (1998). *Indians in the Making: Ethnic Relations and Indian Identities around Puget Sound*. University of California Press, Berkeley.

Harmon, Alexandra, ed. (2008). *The Power of Promises: Rethinking Indian Treaties in the Pacific Northwest*. Center for the Study of the Pacific Northwest, in association with University of Washington Press, Seattle.

Harring, Sidney L. (1994). *Crow Dog's Case: American Indian Sovereignty, Tribal Law, and United States Law in the Nineteenth Century*. Cambridge University Press, New York.

Harring, Sidney L. (2002). "Indian Law, Sovereignty, and State Law: Native People and the Law." In Deloria and Salisbury, eds, *A Companion to American Indian History*. Blackwell Publishers, Malden, MA.

Hermes, Katherine (2008). "The Law of American Indians to 1815." In Grossberg and Tomlins, eds, *The Cambridge History of Law in America, Volume 1*. Cambridge University Press, Cambridge, UK.

Hoebel, E. Adamson and Llewellyn, Karl (1941). *The Cheyenne Way: Conflict and Case Law in Primitive Jurisprudence*. University of Oklahoma Press, Norman.

Hoxie, Frederick (1984). *A Final Promise: The Campaign to Assimilate the Indians, 1880–1920*. University of Nebraska Press, Lincoln.

Hundley, Norris (1978). "The Dark and Bloody Ground of Indian Water Rights: Confusion Elevated to Principle." *Western Historical Quarterly* 9(4): 454–482.

Hundley, Norris. (1982). "The 'Winters' Decision and Indian Water Rights: A Mystery Reexamined." *Western Historical Quarterly* 13(1): 17–42.

Jacobs, Margaret D. (1999). *Engendered Encounters: Feminism and Pueblo Cultures, 1879–1934*. University of Nebraska Press, Lincoln.

Jacoby, Karl (2001). *Crimes against Nature: Squatters, Poachers, Thieves, and the Hidden History of American Conservation*. University of California Press, Berkeley.

Jones, Dorothy V. (1982). *License for Empire: Colonialism by Treaty in Early America*. University of Chicago Press, Chicago.

Kawashima, Yasuhide (1986). *Puritan Justice and the Indian: White Man's Law in Massachusetts, 1630–1763*. Wesleyan University Press, Middletown, CT.

Kawashima, Yasuhide (2001). *Igniting King Philip's War: The John Sassamon Murder Trial*. University Press of Kansas, Lawrence.

Lawson, Michael (1982). *Dammed Indians: The Pick-Sloan Plan and the Missouri River Sioux, 1944–1980*. University of Oklahoma Press, Norman.

Lazarus, Edward (1991). *Black Hills/White Justice: The Sioux Nation Versus the United States: 1775 to the Present*. HarperCollins, New York, NY.

Lieder, Michael and Page, Jake (1997). *Wild Justice: The People of Geronimo vs. the United States*. Random House, New York.

Long, Carolyn N. (2000). *Religious Freedom and Indian Rights: The Case of Oregon v. Smith*. University Press of Kansas, Lawrence.

Mackenzie, John (1988). *The Empire of Nature: Hunting, Conservation, and British Imperialism*. Manchester University Press, Manchester, UK.

McCool, Daniel (1987). *Command of the Waters: Iron Triangles, the Federal Water Development Program, and Indian Water*. University of California Press, Berkeley.

McCool, Daniel (2002). *Native Waters: Contemporary Indian Water Settlement and the Second Treaty Era*. University of Arizona Press, Tucson.

McMillen, Christian (2007). *Making Indian Law: The Hualapai Land Case and the Birth of Ethnohistory*. Yale University Press, New Haven.

McNeil, Kent (1989). *Common Law Aboriginal Title*. Clarendon Press, Oxford.

Merrell, James (1999). *Into the American Woods: Negotiators on the Pennsylvania Frontier*. W.W. Norton, New York.

Miller, Bruce (2001). *The Problem of Justice: Tradition and Law in the Coast Salish World*. University Nebraska Press, Lincoln.

Miller, Mark Edwin (2004). *Forgotten Tribes: Unrecognized Indians and the Federal Acknowledgment Process*. University of Nebraska Press, Lincoln.

Miller, Robert J. (2006). *Native America, Discovered and Conquered: Thomas Jefferson, Lewis and Clark, and Manifest Destiny*. Praeger Publishers, Westport, CT.

Mitchell, Dalia Tsuk (2007). *Architect of Justice: Felix S. Cohen and the Founding of American Legal Pluralism*. Cornell University Press, Ithaca.

Nesper, Larry (2002). *The Walleye War: The Struggle for Ojibwe Spearfishing and Treaty Rights*. University of Nebraska Press, Lincoln.

Newton, Nell J. (1980). "At the Whim of the Sovereign: Aboriginal Title Reconsidered." *Hastings Law Journal* 31: 1215–1286.

Norgren, Jill (1996). *The Cherokee Cases: The Confrontation of Law and Politics*. McGraw-Hill, New York.

Pisani, Donald (2002). *Water and American Government: The Bureau of Reclamation, National Water Policy, and the West, 1902–1935*. University of California Press, Berkeley.

Prucha, Francis Paul (1984). *The Great Father: The United States Government and the American Indians*. University of Nebraska Press, Lincoln.

Prucha, Francis Paul (1994). *American Indian Treaties: The History of an Anomaly*. University of California Press, Berkeley.

Ray, Arthur J. (2003). "Aboriginal Title and Treaty Rights Research: A Comparative Look at Australia, Canada, New Zealand and the United States." *New Zealand Journal of History* 37(1): 5–21.

Richland, Justin (2008). *Arguing with Tradition: The Language of Law in Hopi Tribal Court*. University of Chicago Press, Chicago.

Richter, Daniel (1992). *The Ordeal of the Longhouse: The Peoples of the Iroquois League in the Era of European Colonization*. University of North Carolina Press, Chapel Hill.

Richter, Daniel (2001). *Facing East from Indian Country: A Native History of Early America*. Harvard University Press, Cambridge.

Robertson, Lyndsay (2005). *Conquest By Law: How the Discovery of America Dispossessed Indigenous People of their Lands*. Oxford University Press, New York.

Rosen, Deborah (2007). *American Indians and State Law: Sovereignty, Race, and Citizenship, 1790–1880*. University of Nebraska Press, Lincoln.

Rosenthal, Harvey (1990). *Their Day in Court: A History of the Indian Claims Commission*. Garland Publishing, New York.

Rusco, Elmer R. (2000). *A Fateful Time: The Background and Legislative History of the Indian Reorganization Act*. University of Nevada Press, Reno.

Singer, Joseph William (1994). "Well Settled? The Increasing Weight of History in Indian Land Claims." *Georgia Law Review* 28: 482–532.

Shurts, John Lytle (2000). *Indian Reserved Water Rights: The Winters Doctrine in Social and Legal Context, 1880s–1930s*. University of Oklahoma Press, Norman.

Solnit, Rebecca (1994). *Savage Dreams: A Journey into the Landscape Wars of the American West*. University of California Press, Berkeley.

Spence, Mark (1999). *Dispossessing the Wilderness: Indian Removal and the Making of the National Parks*. Oxford University Press, New York.

Warren, Louis (1997). *The Hunter's Game: Poachers and Conservationists in Twentieth Century America*. Yale University Press, New Haven.

Wallace, Pamela (2002). "Indian Claims Commission: Political Complexity and Contrasting Concepts of Identity." *Ethnohistory* 49(4): 743–767.

White, Richard (1991). *The Middle Ground: Indians, Empires, and Republics in the Great Lakes Region, 1650–1815.* Cambridge University Press, New York.

Wilkins, David E. (1997). *American Indian Sovereignty and the U.S. Supreme Court: The Masking of Justice.* University of Texas Press, Austin.

Wilkins, David E. and Lomawaima, K. Tsianina (2001). *Uneven Ground: American Indian Sovereignty and Federal Law.* University of Texas Press, Austin.

Wilkinson, Charles F. (1987). *American Indians, Time, and the Law: Native Societies in a Modern Constitutional Democracy.* Yale University Press, New Haven.

Wilkinson, Charles F. (1999). *Fire on the Plateau: Conflict and Endurance on the Colorado Plateau.* Island Press, Washington, D.C.

Wilkinson, Charles F. (2005). *Blood Struggle: The Rise of the Indian Nations.* Norton, New York.

Williams, Robert A. (1990). *The American Indian in Western Legal Thought: The Discourses of Conquest.* Oxford University Press, New York.

Williams, Robert A. (1997). *Linking Arms Together: American Indian Treaty Visions of Law and Peace, 1600–1800.* Oxford University Press, New York.

Williams, Robert A. (2005). *Like a Loaded Weapon: The Rehnquist Court, Indian Rights, and the Legal History of Racism in America.* University of Minnesota Press, Minneapolis.

Wishart, David (2001). "Belated Justice? The Indian Claims Commission and the Waitangi Tribunal." *American Indian Culture and Research Journal* 25(1): 81–111.

Wright, J. Leitch (1967). "Creek-American Treaty of 1790: Alexander McGillivray and the Diplomacy of the Old Southwest." *Georgia Historical Quarterly* 51(4): 379–400.

Further Reading

Deloria, Jr., Vine and Lytle, Clifford M. (1998). *The Nations Within: The Past and Future of American Indian Sovereignty.* University of Texas Press, Austin.

Williams, Nancy M. (1986). *The Yolngu and Their Land: A System of Land Tenure and the Fight for Its Recognition.* Australian Institute of Aboriginal Studies, Canberra.

Chapter Eight

AFRICAN AMERICANS IN SLAVERY

Thomas J. Davis

Writing on the history of African Americans in slavery has long split toward two foci. Lived experience has lurked in one. Law has dominated the other. It ascended in the agitated antebellum writing on the so-called Slavery Controversy. The title of William Goodell's 1853 *The American Slave Code in Theory and Practice* exemplified the approach. The persistent, underlying question then and since has in many guises been: How did the American legal system embrace American Negro slavery? The frame of the question implied an essential inconsistency clear in John C. Hurd's 1858 *The Law of Freedom and Bondage in the United States*. Critiquing statutes and judicial decisions on slavery, the antislavery Hurd probed conflicts between the natural law of freedom and the positive law of slavery. Attention fell also on arguments about divine law, particularly on whether, or to what degree, Scripture sanctioned slavery. Abolitionist Theodore Dwight Weld's 1838 *The Bible against Slavery* presented part of the antebellum argument. Slavery's defenders countered that the Bible, the Constitution, and the law supported the institution.

A generation after the Civil War, Johns Hopkins University's series of institutional histories, such as James C. Ballagh's *A History of Slavery in Virginia* (1902), further fixed the focus on slavery's legal framework, showing its foundation and structure in and outside the South. Documentary collections in the early 1900s added impetus. The most notable was Helen Tunnicliff Catterall's monumental five-volume documentary collection *Judicial Cases Concerning American Slavery and the Negro* (1926–1937). In the mid-1970s, more contemporary legal historians such as William M. Wiecek (1977a; 1977b)

A Companion to American Legal History, First Edition.
Edited by Sally E. Hadden and Alfred L. Brophy.
© 2013 John Wiley & Sons Ltd. Published 2021 by John Wiley & Sons Ltd.

and A. Leon Higginbotham (1978) refocused on surveying statutes and cases to illuminate slavery's institutional structures and tendencies.

Recent literature has pressed beyond the letter and logic of statutes and judicial opinions, into how law operated. Thomas D. Morris, for example, has notably advanced understanding of the American law of slavery's doctrinal sources and reach. Morris examined legal categories and principles deployed to encage blacks as slaves. His four-part work *Southern Slavery and the Law, 1619–1860* moved from sources of slave law, to "slaves as property," to "slaves as persons" in the context of crime and punishment, and finally to "manumission" as a legal release. He looked at law as "practice as well as doctrine" (Morris, 1996: 3). Yet he seldom brought to life any African Americans in slavery. Law formed the fundamental reality of the slavery Morris presented. Slaves, however, often seemed simply shadows. They appeared mostly in what might be likened to the scenario in the cave allegory in Book VII of Plato's 380 BCE Socratic dialogue *The Republic*. The ancient Greek philosopher described people chained for life to the wall of a cave. They saw the world outside only as shadows projected on the cave's wall. They never saw the persons or things that cast the shadows. In Morris' work, enslaved African Americans almost invariably appeared as shadows and hardly ever as people. The reality of their living ever remained dim, beyond direct view.

Morris' approach emphasized slavery, the institution which has customarily overshadowed the lived experience. The result has showered much attention on slavery and too little attention on slaves. It has been as if the inhumanity of enslavement has continued to rob the enslaved of their humanity, disregarding or discounting their personalities, initiatives, and individualities.

Black bondage shaped much in the American law of crime and punishment, as Flanigan (1987) and Schwarz (1988) have illustrated. Also it influenced much in property law. After all, slavery touched and concerned real and personal property, tangible and intangible property, and present and future interests. It affected mortgage practices, contracts, and general commercial law. It molded much in U.S. employment law – the old common law relation described as "master-servant" in part reflected in the struggles Christopher Tomlins detailed in *Freedom Bound* (2010).

The slaves' manifold personal, practical, and quotidian experiences – the real stuff of American Negro slavery and the roots of much of its terrible legal and extralegal legacy – has too seldom appeared in legal history literature. When work in legal history has personalized discussions of slavery, it has most often been on the white side rather than the black side. Slaveholders, rather than slaves, have long been the more likely subjects. That has reflected the usual historiographic focus on the privileged few more than on the disfavored many. Robert Cover's 1975 classic *Justice Accused: Antislavery and the Judicial Process* illustrated the trend. Cover personalized the rationales antislavery judges frequently offered on issues of proslavery law as they explained that law compelled inhumanity and injustice. Yet even Cover offered little to personalize the enslaved, and he was not alone. Many, like Cover, even when they have described the inhumanity of law or choices individuals made within it have found it difficult to reach the experience of African Americans as they related to law.

The historiographic tendency to neglect slaves in large part was predictable. Neglect has plagued the mass of humanity throughout history. Historiography has usually been top down not bottom up, attending to elites who typically have supplied the doctrines and documents for writing history – to say nothing of the writers themselves. That tradition has tended to abstract or attenuate the substance and significance of the developing and vested human relations, as well as the everyday experiences, of people such as African Americans in slavery. But changing practitioners and priorities over the years have pointed the way to reclaiming the attention due slaves as people and correcting the too often confused narrative institutional emphasis has imposed.

Writers early pursued American Negro slavery through a prescribed formalism that law nicely suited as it enabled writers to categorize and organize slavery as an official set of public relations. Such a view early elevated law not only to controlling but to creating and defining the contents and connotations of slavery. In many eyes law became slavery's substance. Jonathan L. Alpert exhibited the view in writing that "American slavery was above all else a product of the law" (Alpert, 1970: 189). Further, institutionalists typically have looked to legislation and judicial decisions as guides to identify and understand important developments for slavery *and* for slaves.

Institutionalists have tended to see slavery as not starting with the first slaves but with the first slavery statutes. In their eyes only official legal recognition established slavery. The fact of people's being systematically captured and coerced to labor awaited some formal stamp before being cognizable as slavery. The actual course of events served less as evidence than authorized acts. Institutionalists have seemed to conceive of slaves not in terms of flesh and blood but in terms of ink and paper. Edict rather than experience has typically riveted their attention. They have privileged de jure rules inscribed in books over de facto patterns etched in experience.

Institutionalist perspectives have given rise to tedious and often irritating discussions about whether Africans dragged into English America initially were slaves. Oscar and Mary Handlin crystallized the contention in 1950. Discoursing on "The Origins of the Southern Labor System," the couple asserted that "the status of Negroes was that of servants and so they were identified and treated down to the 1660's" (Handlin and Handlin, 1950: 203). Many have followed the Handlins to deny the actuality of slavery in Virginia before the colony's initial slave statute of 1662.

Carl N. Degler echoed the contention in 1959. When "the Negroes were first imported into the English colonies," he wrote, "there was no law of slavery and therefore whatever status they were to have would be the work of the future" (Degler, 1959: 51). Such a conclusion has imposed convoluted categories on captive coffles chained in Africa and dragged away and sold to drudge in the Americas. Institutionalists have hardly nodded at the simple difference between servants' choice and slaves' coercion. In the absence of legislative or judicial pronouncements, institutionalists have tended to conclude that because no status of slave existed no slaves existed.

Africans' actual experience in early America played no role for institutionalists who accepted legal pronouncement as lived reality and so triggered a servant-or-slave debate that has distorted understanding of both servitude and slavery. Blacks' wholly involuntary entry as commodities in colonial America's labor markets counted for little to mark them as slaves for the likes of the Handlins. Nor in that view did blacks' indefinite tenure sufficiently distinguish them from servants, although even white prisoners introduced into the English colonies in involuntary servitude served definite terms. Only nonwhites served indefinite terms that might extend to the entirety of their life. Yet serving for less than life in no way made a slave other than a slave while enslaved. The condition was what it was while it lasted. Its duration was unfixed and unlimited, except by death, and that essential uncertainty fed the mastery by others and the deprivation of the control of self that distinguished the experience of African Americans in slavery.

Race clearly separated slaves from servants and over time served to entrench structural boundaries and features that law accommodated. Yet institutionalists have hardly accounted for race as a forced within or without the law, although it was what distinguished American Negro slavery. After all, European colonists in English North America did not invent slavery. It was in many places ancient, as Moses I. Finley (1968, 1980), Alan Watson (1987), and others have explained in studying classical Greco-Roman antiquity. David Brion Davis has traced slavery far back as a problem in Western culture. Also he noted innovations in slavery's New World versions. "In no ancient society was the distinction between slave and freeman so sharply drawn as in America," he reported (Davis, 1966: 47). Alexis de Tocqueville early captured the core of changes that distinguished American Negro slavery. The French visitor to the United States in the 1830s commented that "the modern slave differs from his master not only in his condition, but in his origin." Tocqueville explained further that "amongst the moderns, the abstract and transient fact of slavery is fatally united with the physical and permanent fact of color" (Tocqueville: 2007 [1838]: 259).

The institutionalist approach began to break down around the time of World War II, as worldwide revulsion at the racism embedded in the war rekindled debate about attitudes and actions in trafficking and enslaving Africans in the Americas. More and more vocal, angry African American voices in the 1940s called attention to U.S. hypocrisy in championing democracy abroad as the segregationist extensions of slavery denied democracy at home. Others in the Americas hastened to distinguish their heritage. Gilberto Freyre, for instance, insisted that in his native Brazil race prejudice had not persisted beyond slavery as it had in the United States (Freyre, 1945: 96–101). Frank Tannenbaum's seminal 1947 *Slave and Citizen: The Negro in the Americas* extended the claim that American Negro slavery was, indeed, a peculiar institution in its virulent racist overflow. Carl N. Degler in 1959 reiterated the point. Racism, he wrote, "deepened and hardened" the genesis of slavery in American law. In time, he reported, "the correspondence between the black man and slavery would appear so perfect that it would be difficult to believe that the Negro was fitted for anything other than the degraded status in which he was almost always found" (Degler, 1959: 66).

Winthrop D. Jordan's 1968 *White over Black: American Attitudes toward the Negro, 1550–1812* plumbed the channels connecting race and slavery. It opened with English notions of what Jordan described as "the *Negro* before he became preeminently the *slave*" (Jordan, 1968: 43). It then traced how racism and slavery joined to shape European-American thought long before any law appeared to support slavery. Jordan's cultural explanation thus veered from institutional studies of slavery's statutory origins.

Jordan's approach appeared as something of a prequel to C. Vann Woodward's 1955 *The Strange Career of Jim Crow*, which transformed thinking about the origins, timing, and nature of segregation after the Civil War. Jordan wrestled with understandable complexities, and many would come to join in the task. Alden T. Vaughan neatly recounted the discussion before 1989 on "the elusive connection between British America's most lamentable institution and its most deplorable ideology" (Vaughan, 1995: 18).

In the cloak of the careful historian's craft amid his massive research, Jordan left American Negro slavery's origins and development as pretty much an accident, as a monument to the "the power of irrationality in men," to use his words (Jordan, 1968: vii). Betty Wood picked up part of the thread of Jordan's argument that slavery in large part represented "an unthinking decision" (Jordan, 1968: 44). In her brief 1997 synthesis, *The Origins of American Slavery*, Wood agreed with Jordan that early English settlers arrived in the Americas with no "explicit intention of enslaving anyone" (Wood, 1997: 6). Yet they did in fact enslave masses.

Neither Jordan nor Wood explained how it happened that the English, who shook off domestic slavery in the aftermath of the Norman conquest of 1066, came more than half a millennium later to enslave millions. While nodding toward "the complex interaction" of economics and race (Wood, 1997: 8), Wood slipped into the convenience of labor market supply and demand to excuse slavery's start in North America. Planters could not get enough European laborers, so they sought alternatives, Wood argued. She cast the English as simply emulating Spanish and Portuguese models of slavery, induced to do so by "the ready availability of a constant supply of West Africans courtesy of Dutch slave traders" (Wood, 1997: 66).

Slave law emerged to rationalize and reinforce practices in an intricate interplay of cultural heritages and economic interests, as Robin Blackburn argued in his 1997 *The Making of New World Slavery*. Spiraling consumer demand for plantation-based commodities – in the Americas primarily tobacco and sugar, to start, then coffee and cotton – escalated demands that yielded compelling profits, which in turn spurred production, Blackburn argued. The seed of growth lay in labor, which itself became a prime commodity in the form of enslaved Africans in the Americas. The vortex Blackburn described took the shape of an expanding Atlantic system with a plantation complex that joined capital and labor in developing international capital markets.

Nascent capitalism engorged on slavery in the Americas, as Eric Williams argued in his seminal 1944 *Capitalism and Slavery*. "Commercial capitalism of the eighteenth century developed the wealth of Europe by means of slavery and monopoly," he explained (Williams, 1994 [1944]: 210). American law grew to protect exploited slave production. Indeed, Stanley Elkins and Eric McKitrick in two 1957 articles (1957a; 1957b) posited that the dynamics of unopposed capitalism embedded American Negro slavery in law as nowhere else. "Unmitigated capitalism" in North America, they declared, created "unmitigated slavery." Further, they argued that "the drive of the law was to clarify beyond all question, unembarrassed by the complexities of competing interests – to rationalize, simplify, to make more logical and symmetrical – the slave's status in society" (Elkins and McKitrick, 1957a: 19, 21).

Law became instrumental in advancing slavery as a mode of capital formation. It accommodated itself to commodifying slaves, as research on capital and credit markets has illustrated. Richard Pares' 1960 *Merchants and Planters* opened views of slavery's role in such markets. Bonnie Martin has added antebellum U.S. connections to how the law used slaves in local lending networks and in the broader organizing of finances. Pushing past accounting details, Martin pointed to effects slaves experienced. She showed one in four of the 11,436 slaves in Louisiana's St. Landry Parish, for example, working as collateral from 1855 to 1859 (Martin, 2010: 859). Mortgaging further degraded slaves' humanity. It imperiled all their personal relations as it multiplied risks of sale and separation from kith and kin.

Law proved useful in exploiting blacks, but it was not required. The Atlantic slave trade early evidenced that. It operated largely without law. As W.E.B. Du Bois made clear in his 1896 classic *The Suppression of the African Slave-Trade to the United States of America, 1638–1870*, efforts to suppress the trade produced more American legislation and court action than efforts to promote the trade. Elizabeth Donnan's four-volume *Documents Illustrative of the History of the Slave Trade to America* (1930–1935) expanded views of the trade. Progress with computers has exponentially enlarged understanding, as David Eltis, Stephen D. Behrendt, David Richardson, and Herbert S. Klein have illustrated in their projects that produced their CD-ROM *The Trans-Atlantic Slave Trade: A Database* (Eltis et al., 2000).

Law had little to do with the largely unregulated trafficking of Africans throughout the Americas, as Marcus Rediker's 2007 *The Slave Ship: A Human History* brilliantly illustrated. Opening organizational and personal perspectives on the traffic, Rediker showed law as superfluous to the enterprise. Putting the African flow to the Americas in a broader historical and human context with his 1996 *Slave Trades, 1500–1800: Globalization of Forced Labor*, Patrick Manning earlier marked the extralegal base of the traffic.

Slavery exploited law when and where it existed, as it exploited the cultures of its human host communities. Eugene D. Genovese noted in his 1974 *Roll, Jordan, Roll: The World the Slaves Made* that "the forces of custom and local usage so often modified Southern legal arrangements" (Genovese, 1974: 407). His Marxist paradigm mixed paternalism with clashes of culture and class to glimpse something of the robust influences of reciprocal relations between slaves and slaveholders. Their interactions shaped work patterns and much more. Genovese projected the slaves' world as one of personal, sometimes intimate, negotiations between accommodation and resistance. He appeared to straddle paths emphasizing slavery as institution and slavery as experience.

Profit proved the bottom line in slavery, as in the slave trade. And so the economics of African Americans in slavery have elicited much attention. Robert William Fogel and Stanley L. Engerman's 1974 *Time on the Cross: The Economics of American Negro Slavery* has served as a modern, flawed classic of the genre. Its aggregated and disaggregated data helped to reveal ranges of slave experiences from work habits to socialization and family formation. It offered little on identifiable, individual slaves. Essentially, it joined Stanley Elkins' controversial 1959 *Slavery: A Problem in American Institutional and Intellectual Life* in retrenching traditional institutional views of the behavior and beliefs of African Americans in slavery. It reached back in large part to the champion of institutionalists, Ulrich B. Phillips, whose 1918 *American Negro Slavery: A Survey of the Supply, Employment, and Control of Negro Labor as Determined by the Plantation Regime* long served as a touchstone.

Phillips gave little attention to blacks as people. He saw slaves mostly as tools for masters to manage. He offered a slight nod to slave life outside of labor. Yet even there, slaves made only brief appearances as actors. They tended to flit in cameos to support stereotypic roles. Phillips toned down his paternalist white supremacy language in his 1929 sequel, *Life and Labor in the Old South*. Yet, Phillips continued to set much of the foundation and framework for discourse on American Negro slavery. Genovese declared in 1966 that "*American Negro Slavery* is not the last word on the subject; merely the indispensable first" (Genovese, 1966: xxi).

Unraveling the first word from the mire of Phillips' racist interpretation loosened parts of the institutionalist grip. Two one-time University of Maryland, College Park, history department colleagues – Richard Hofstadter and Kenneth M. Stampp – pushed openings against Phillips. Hofstadter's 1944 *Journal of Negro History* article, "U.B. Phillips and the Plantation Legend," raised substantial questions of meaning and methodology in Phillips' skewed view of slavery. Stampp's 1956 *The Peculiar Institution: Slavery in the Ante-Bellum South* offered the first broadly accepted alternative version challenging Phillips. Stampp emphasized the inhumanity of slavery and the humanity of slaves. Recognizing slaves as having personalities, Stampp clashed with Phillips on the power of white paternalism over blacks. Writing in a turbulent era of desegregation, the Wisconsin-born Stampp countered the Georgia-born Phillips' view of slaves as simple "darkies" with a view that "innately Negroes are, after all, only white men with black skins, nothing more, nothing less" (Stampp, 1956: vii).

Carter G. Woodson and Charles H. Wesley, among others writing in the *Journal of Negro History* and elsewhere, particularly challenged Phillips' view of enslaved African Americans as nearly inert ciphers. Woodson, Wesley, and others highlighted blacks' ingenuity, initiative, and organization in struggling against slavery. (This essay has left others to discuss antislavery but notes that Benjamin Quarles' 1969 classic *Black Abolitionists* has remained an excellent introduction to the roles African Americans played there.) Part of that attention focused on slave resistance and rebellion. Joseph C. Carroll's 1938 *Slave Insurrections in the United States, 1800–1865,* and Herbert Aptheker's 1943 classic *American Negro Slave Revolts* documented enslaved African Americans as hardly contented and docile.

Blacks' character, even their essential humanity, long remained at issue in the struggle to correct institutionalist views that imputed inferior natures to enslaved African Americans. In analyzing and rejecting paternalistic benign slavery, Stampp appeared to work mostly from an intuitive reverse psychology pitting clever slaves against insufferable slaveholders. He did not seek to document blacks' thinking, as Carter G. Woodson had in his 1900 *The Mind of the Negro as Reflected in Letters Written during the Crisis, 1800–1860.* John W. Blassingame built on Woodson's work with his 1977 *Slave Testimony: Two Centuries of Letters, Speeches, Interviews, and Autobiographies.* More and more evidence on and from the perspective of enslaved African Americans has continued to appear in the Documenting the American South collections of the digital publishing initiative at the University of North Carolina at Chapel Hill.

Slaves' self-expression rarely surfaced in early institutional studies. Stanley Elkins helped to change that. His 1959 *Slavery: A Problem in American Institutional and Intellectual Life* sparked what smoldered in the tinderbox of the riotous 1960s to become a firestorm. Amid upraised fists and chants of "Black Power," many seethed over Elkins' virtual affirmation of slaves as Phillips' childlike "darkies." While exhibiting enslaved African Americans as typically subservient, Elkins cast himself as building on Stampp's work while, in fact, he reinforced Phillips' institutional misinterpretations.

Elkins concluded that enslaved blacks in Anglo-America were much as Phillips had described: they were characteristically compliant; they grew to accept their slaveholders' controlling paternalism; they typically reflected a Sambo personality; they exhibited "irresponsibility, playfulness, silliness, laziness, and (quite possibly) tendencies to lying and stealing," Elkins wrote (Elkins, 1959: 131). He analogized enslaved African Americans' plight with that of prisoners in World War II era Nazi concentration camps. He suggested both underwent a process of infantilization that he proffered as the other side of paternalism or total institutional control. He attributed the results not to law, but to practice.

Fresh work on slave personalities, psychologies, subcultures, and communities sprang up to refute the impression of Phillips' faceless, depersonalized slaves whom Elkins turned into infantile Sambos. Summoning slaves to testify about their lived experiences in his 1972 *The Slave Community: Plantation Life in the Antebellum South*, John W. Blassingame argued to affirm and dimension the humanity, diversity, and individuality of African Americans in slavery. He showed slaves were no empty ciphers slaveholders simply filled and shaped.

Moving from capture through acculturation, Blassingame emphasized African survivals and African Americans' defiant independence. Yet he accepted that plantations produced slave stereotypes and institutional roles – including Sambo. Blassingame insisted that plantation realities included renegades and runaways in a mix of slave personality types. Among them was the rebel Nat, Blassingame noted. Novelist William Styron's controversial 1966 *The Confessions of Nat Turner*, treating Virginia's bloody 1831 slave uprising, had earlier incited fresh argument about Nat and other slave rebels and incidents.

Scenes of slaves in arms have played in various discussions. They figured in law's consistently repressive responses to blacks' seen as behaving badly. That theme has stretched well beyond slavery, particularly in discussing criminal law and penal policy. They figured also in discussing blacks' roles in America's wars and their effects on changing sentiments and structures, including law. War, after all, has demarcated much in U.S. history and in African American life. The War for Independence gave birth to the nation. The Civil War served slavery's death warrant.

Blacks' actions in wars affected change in slavery. Benjamin Quarles' classic 1961 *The Negro in the American Revolution* depicted African Americans in slavery weighing and considering their chances for freedom in a war they joined to fight against being slaves. They prompted and reflected changing laws of manumission and emancipation and rules for serving under arms. Arthur Zilversmit's 1967 *The First Emancipation: The Abolition of Slavery in the North* detailed effects of the ensuing changes in law. Many, particularly Gary B. Nash, have elaborated the combined legal and social changes that affected African Americans in slavery above the

Mason-Dixon Line in the war's aftermath. Sylvia R. Frey's 1991 *Water from the Rock: Black Resistance in a Revolutionary Age* told how African Americans throughout the South seized the moment to challenge the social order that enslaved them. Nash's *The Unknown American Revolution: The Unruly Birth of Democracy and the Struggle to Create America* (2005) and *The Forgotten Fifth: African Americans in the Age of Revolution* (2006) have deepened perspectives on the moral dimensions trapped with African Americans in slavery at the U.S. founding. Woody Holton's 2007 *Unruly Americans and the Origins of the Constitution* further illustrated the impact of enslaved African Americans' joining rebellious undercurrents.

African Americans shifted legal foundations in the Age of Revolution. Attention to slavery in the U.S. Constitution responded after all to black flesh and blood, not simply to structures and theories of law. Slaveholders' interests clearly swayed the new legal foundation. Attention to slaves' insistent recalcitrance moved the framers to curtail the foreign slave trade and to provide protections against domestic insurrections. David Waldstreicher's 2009 *Slavery's Constitution: From Revolution to Ratification* further advanced discussion of the culturally determined constitutional politics of white male supremacy the framers entrenched in a fundamental law that shaped slavery and more in U.S. law and life.

Turning to slaves' agency rather than slavery's legal dictates opened more discussion of connections among and between African Americans themselves and others. The slave testimonies Blassingame interjected showed slavery operating as a set of volatile reciprocal relations. As it Americanized Africans, for instance, it also Africanized the South. In societies with slaves, as well as within slave societies, American Negro slavery was no one-dimensional institution that totally controlled blacks. Slaves succeeded to carve out their own cultural and social spaces, Blassingame showed. Anthony E. Kaye's 2007 *Joining Places: Slave Neighborhoods in the Old South* challenged and refined Blassingame's slave community by expanding it as a network of adjoining plantations with multiple centers of slave politics, power, and production that mostly operated extralegally.

This kind of writing has helped shift focus from the institution of law to bring into view identifiable, individual African Americans in slavery. It has joined an emerging law and society perspective that better realizes slaves' lived experiences. Such writings are desegregating approaches and results too often confined in categories sealed as cultural, economic, intellectual, legal, political, or social history. One model of such integration is Ira Berlin's 1998 *Many Thousands Gone: The First Two Centuries of Slavery in North America*, which examined how "Black life on mainland North America originated" (Berlin, 1998: 17). His three-part work followed the experience of cohorts of African descent as they negotiated life in becoming African Americans. He put slaves center stage, focusing on their social reproduction to which law contributed but did not construct. Their generational life cycles formed Berlin's framework for understanding how blacks changed and developed from place to place over time with the dynamics of slavery. He probed everyday practices and interpersonal transactions in pursuing the fundamental qualities of human existence in slaves' lives.

Highlighting slaves' agency, Calvin Schermerhorn's 2011 *Money over Mastery, Family over Freedom: Slavery in the Antebellum Upper South* demonstrated how African Americans in slavery worked local markets and their masters to maintain their families above all else. Schermerhorn illustrated how industrialization in the region from the Chesapeake Bay to coastal North Carolina pushed economic diversity that eroded both state and plantation law while simultaneously empowering and extenuating slaves' labor positions. They negotiated outside institutional confines, defeating or disregarding what formal law fixed as their position in the master-slave relationship in their staple-crop setting. Slaves contrived to set their own directions, pursuing their own values to mitigate slavery's institutionalized effects, not so much on their material or monetary poverty as much as on their family life.

Blood ties crossed colorlines and crossed-up law in ways long unaccounted for in institutional histories, as Bernie D. Jones' 2009 *Fathers of Conscience: Mixed-Race Inheritance in the Antebellum South* has imaginatively illustrated. Revealing gaps and inconsistencies in the institutional view of slavery, Jones showed that court decisions not always decreed the social death the letter of law supposedly pronounced. Probate results from southern trial court records and appellate court reports granted more to African Americans in and out of slavery than any simple view of statutes would suggest. No sharp black/white, master/slave edge always carved out the same results. White slaveholders sometimes succeeded in bequeathing to African Americans in slavery property, including the right to self in manumission. Such results changed lives. Also they changed slavery.

Jones illustrated how laws of slavery allowed for more varying interpretations and diverse results for African Americans in slavery than traditionally acknowledged. Applied legal doctrine shifted in application from place to place and over time. Law formed no monolith that everywhere at all times pressed slaves down in the same way. Law proved itself a different instrument in different hands. Also as William W. Freehling (1990–2007), Lacy K. Ford (2009), and others have detailed, the South was not always and everywhere the same. Nor were slaves and slaveholders all the same. Mixed motives appeared in legacies. Honor, hate, love, and more played roles, as Ariela J. Gross (2000), Peggy Pascoe (2009), and Joshua D. Rothman (2003) among others have demonstrated, in complicating the institutional view of slavery as a simple person/property dichotomy.

Laura F. Edwards' 2009 *The People and Their Peace* further illustrated how the rule of law in regard to slavery may well have been variance rather than consistency. In exposing significant differences in legal culture from place to place and over time as the South moved from the 1780s to the 1840s, Edwards explained some of the varying effects of when and where slaves lived. The American Revolution, she showed, shifted thinking about law and liberty. What she termed "localized law" ruled at the start. An uncodified sort of common law communities shaped from their own sense of self determined slaves' positions and prospects. It decided the protections and punishments it saw as best to keep "the people's peace" (Edwards, 2009: 79). It contrasted with centralized and formalized state law white paternalist elites increasingly imposed and rationalized in systematizing inequalities to fortify their position in a rights-based society. Appellate courts helped to enforce the more impersonal, legal system of subordination. Local courts persisted, however, in deciding matters based on neighborhood judgments of a personalized law that credited reputation. The communities of neighbors set the law that governed common everyday interactions for African Americans in slavery and after slavery, Edwards persuasively established. Their experiences thus varied extensively from place to place and over time by ways and means obscured in a rigid institutional view of American Negro slavery that has tended to harmonize contradictions and disparities in projecting more consistency and regularity than existed.

More than missing the world of differences between slave law and slave life, institutional focus long isolated slaves from much of significance in developing their own societies and surroundings. Notions of African Americans acting on their own to make their ways in and out of slavery have transformed discussion. Including what slaves did along with what others did to or for slaves has opened and deepened many lines of inquiry. Discussing rebels and runaways, for instance, shifted attention outside the institutional model of antebellum plantation slavery. Peter H. Wood's 1974 *Black Majority: Negroes in Colonial South Carolina from 1670 through the Stono Rebellion* showed the rich connections available in and through views of slave recalcitrance. Colonial episodes outside the South also garnered attention. The 1712 uprising in New York City and the so-called Great Negro Plot of 1741 there received new looks. Such episodes have invited clearer views of African American life, as illustrated in Thomas J. Davis' 1985 *A Rumor of Revolt: The "Great Negro Plot" in Colonial New York*, focused on the 1741 judicial proceedings that left seventeen blacks and four whites hanged and thirteen blacks burned at the stake.

Slave revolts and rumors of revolt exposed the law's use as backlash. They exhibited part of the resistance that was a basic reality for African Americans in slavery. Their recalcitrance flared in notable episodes, but nowhere was it more persistently on view or more disruptive than with runaways. Sally E. Hadden's 2001 *Slave Patrols: Law and Violence in Virginia and the Carolinas* has displayed how white communities organized from colonial times onward in the South to keep blacks in their place.

She tellingly situated slave patrols within a larger policing framework that included constables and militia, for patrols did more than capture runaways. They enforced a colorline that stretched beyond slavery. They were vigilance committees. They acted as ears and eyes. They worked to sniff out and snuff out suspicious black activity. They operated to terrorize. The Ku Klux Klan extended the patrol ethos after the Civil War, brandishing violence and vulnerability as defining elements of African American life. Hadden well demonstrated how licensing brutality operated at the core of slavery and broader black-white relations.

Fugitive slaves proved more than local problems. They provoked interstate and national legal controversy, as Paul Finkelman has variously elaborated in works such as his 1981 *An Imperfect Union: Slavery, Federalism, and Comity*. Evidence of slaves' flight, particularly in so-called "runaway ads", has furnished much information to detail impulses, features, demeanors, and backgrounds to help put a face on enslaved African Americans.

Ex-slave autobiographies have often detailed fugitives' ordeals. The most famous fugitive slave, Frederick Douglass, illustrated the mode. So did Harriet Jacobs in her 1861 *Incidents in the Life of a Slave Girl, Written by Herself*, published under the pseudonym Linda Brent. Jacobs ran to resist rape. She did not at first run far. She hid for seven years in a cramped attic crawl space. Eventually she made her way to Philadelphia, Pennsylvania, and beyond. Her subsequent writings opened perspectives on enslaved black women's lives.

Jean Fagan Yellin and her team of coeditors and researchers elaborated Jacobs' story into a family saga. Their two-volume 2008 *The Harriet Jacobs Family Papers* (with a searchable CD-ROM) reached backward and forward from Harriet to document the slings and arrows of black female life in and out of slavery. That gendered story further underscored enslaved African American women's remaining too often unaccounted as slaves or as women. David Barry Gaspar and Darlene Clark Hine's 1996 *More than Chattel: Black Women and Slavery in the Americas* persuasively demonstrated "how much scholars have missed or misconstrued when they have used the term *slave* without due regard to gender" (Gaspar and Hine, 1996: ix).

Annette Gordon-Reed's 2008 multiple prize-winning *The Hemingses of Monticello: An American Family* connected the personal and the political for African Americans in slavery at the U.S. foundation. Exemplifying progress in moving beyond American Negro slavery as an institution to reach lived experience, Gordon-Reed's work reached back to the early 1700s and forward to the mid-1800s to reveal distances between law as letter and life as lived. Centering on the enslaved Sally Hemings who bore children for the American icon Thomas Jefferson, Gordon-Reed traced four generations of blood relations and social connections in a complex of kin, family, and caste. She drew back the veil on the *pro forma* to reach the personal in bringing to life Sally Hemings, her children, and her siblings.

Gordon-Reed's focus on humanity laid bare multiple contradictions so long nurtured in the old institutional approach to American Negro slavery as a reality law defined and described. She exposed limits of law and the frailty of race as anything other than a social construct. In thus complicating the connections and interconnections of African Americans in slavery, Gordon-Reed altered the face of African Americans in and out of slavery.

As in Gordon-Reed's work on the Hemingses, the best recent work on African Americans in slavery has transcended statutes and legal structures to treat law as lived experience, as more a negotiation than a decree. Ariela J. Gross' work in southern courtrooms of the 1800s, for example, has displayed the civil and criminal theater where racial identity played out during slavery and after. Litigation on who was or was not white early reflected also who was or was not a slave. Studying such issues has enlarged the context for understanding law and life for African Americans in slavery. Linking statutes, court decisions, and broader experiences has opened to view how legal systems actually functioned to support slavery. They have offered paths to move from imagined institutions to lived experiences.

African American women often played central parts in courtroom confrontations that opened the law of slavery to view. Lea VanderVelde's 2009 *Mrs. Dred Scott: A Life on Slavery's Frontier* illustrated the point. Documenting the deeds and determination of the woman behind the man whose name became a watchword for American Negro slavery, VanderVelde displayed the Harriet who got lost as the "wife of a celebrity" while being the impetus for one of the signal lawsuits in U.S. history (VanderVelde, 2009: 11). Harriet's commonly shrouded independent identity and experience and that of her enslaved black sisters in generations reaching from America back to Africa have long promised to fill the vacuum created when historical writing makes it appear that, as Barbara Y. Welke phrased it in another context, "all the women were white, and all the blacks were men" (Welke, 1995: 261).

The lives of Harriet Scott, Harriet Jacobs, Sally Hemings and other enslaved women have reflected yet again that grasping the complexities of human identities enmeshed in American Negro slavery necessarily draws historical writers beyond the carapace of law and the fictions of race to reach as much as possible the lived experiences of African Americans in and out of slavery. They rightfully strip law of any autonomy and reveal its part in the complex of human life. They remind readers to see *slave* as a status not as a substance. *Slave* stands as a signal, like husband or wife or father or mother. Being a slave described aspects of a person's position. It identified lines of relations. It was a social construct used to classify and distinguish persons from others. It was a gross identifier. It clarified little about character or conduct. It conveyed no uniform circumstances and conditions.

What slavery meant varied by time and place and person, as Ira Berlin so well sketched in his seminal 1980 article "Time, Space, and the Evolution of Afro-American Society on British Mainland North America." More emerging writing has been investigating that variety. The best has been probing the diversity and individuality of experiences among African Americans in slavery. It has been exploring African Americans' personal character and conduct in slavery and focusing on what identified individuals did and how their behavior distinguished them from others. Such writing has eschewed the institutional template scripted with doctrinal law and instead embraced the challenge of understanding the law in regard to African Americans in slavery through their experiences. That task has raised fundamental questions about the meanings of law and slavery and about the lived identities of African Americans in slavery.

References

Alpert, Jonathan L. (1970). "The Origin of Slavery in the United States – The Maryland Precedent." *American Journal of Legal History* 14(3): 189–221.

Aptheker, Herbert (1943). *American Negro Slave Revolts*. Columbia University Press, New York.

Ballagh, James C. (1902). *History of Slavery in Virginia*. Johns Hopkins University Press, Baltimore.

Berlin, Ira (1980). "Time, Space, and the Evolution of Afro-American Society on British Mainland North America." *American Historical Review* 85(1): 44–78.

Berlin, Ira (1998). *Many Thousands Gone: The First Two Centuries of Slavery in North America*. Harvard University Press, Cambridge, MA.

Blackburn, Robin (1997). *The Making of New World Slavery: From the Baroque to the Modern, 1492–1800*. Verso, New York.

Blassingame, John W. (1972). *The Slave Community: Plantation Life in the Antebellum South*. Oxford University Press, New York.

Blassingame, John W. (1977). *Slave Testimony: Two Centuries of Letters, Speeches, Interviews, and Autobiographies*. Louisiana State University Press, Baton Rouge.

Carroll, Joseph C. (1938). *Slave Insurrections in the United States, 1800–1865*. Chapman and Grimes, Boston.

Catterall, Helen Tunnicliff (1926–1937). *Judicial Cases Concerning American Slavery and the Negro*. Carnegie Institution of Washington, Washington, D.C.

Cover, Robert M. (1975). *Justice Accused: Antislavery and the Judicial Process*. Yale University Press, New Haven.

Davis, David Brion (1966). *The Problem of Slavery in Western Culture*. Cornell University Press, Ithaca.

Davis, Thomas J. (1985). *A Rumor of Revolt: The "Great Negro Plot" in Colonial New York*. Free Press, New York.

Degler, Carl N. (1959). "Slavery and the Genesis of American Race Prejudice." *Comparative Studies in Society and History* 2(1): 49–66.

Donnan, Elizabeth (1930–1935). *Documents Illustrative of the History of the Slave Trade to America.* Carnegie Institution of Washington, Washington, D.C.

Du Bois, W.E.B. (1896). *The Suppression of the African Slave-Trade to the United States of America, 1638–1870.* Longmans, Green and Co., New York.

Edwards, Laura F. (2009). *The People and Their Peace: Legal Culture and the Transformation of Inequality in the Post-Revolutionary South.* University of North Carolina Press, Chapel Hill.

Elkins, Stanley M. (1959). *Slavery: A Problem in American Institutional and Intellectual Life.* University of Chicago Press, Chicago.

Elkins, Stanley M. and McKitrick, Eric (1957a). "Institutions and the Law of Slavery: The Dynamics of Unopposed Capitalism." *American Quarterly* 9(1): 3–21.

Elkins, Stanley M. and McKitrick, Eric (1957b). "Institutions and the Law of Slavery: Slavery in Capitalist and Non-Capitalist Cultures." *American Quarterly* 9(2): 159–179.

Eltis, David, Behrendt, Stephen D., Richardson, David and Klein, Herbert S. (2000). *The Trans-Atlantic Slave Trade: A Database on CD-ROM.* Cambridge University Press, New York.

Finkelman, Paul (1981). *An Imperfect Union: Slavery, Federalism, and Comity.* University of North Carolina Press, Chapel Hill.

Finley, Moses I. (1968). *Aspects of Antiquity: Discoveries and Controversies.* Viking Press, New York.

Finley, Moses I. (1980). *Ancient Slavery and Modern Ideology.* Chatto and Windus, New York.

Flanigan, Daniel J. (1987). *The Criminal Law of Slavery and Freedom, 1800–1868.* Garland Publishers, New York.

Fogel, Robert William and Engerman, Stanley L. (1974) *Time on the Cross: The Economics of American Negro Slavery.* Little, Brown, Boston.

Ford, Lacy K. (2009). *Deliver Us from Evil: The Slavery Question in the Old South, 1787–1840.* Oxford University Press, New York.

Freehling, William W. (1990–2007). *The Road to Disunion.* Oxford University Press, New York.

Frey, Sylvia (1991). *Water from the Rock: Black Resistance in a Revolutionary Age.* Princeton University Press, Princeton.

Freyre, Gilberto (1945). *Brazil: An Interpretation.* Alfred A. Knopf, New York.

Gaspar, David Barry and Hine, Darlene Clark (1996). *More Than Chattel: Black Women and Slavery in the Americas.* Indiana University Press, Bloomington, IN.

Genovese, Eugene D. (1966). "Ulrich Bonnell Phillips & and His Critics." Foreword to U.B. Phillips, *American Negro Slavery: A Survey of the Supply, Employment and Control of Negro Labor as Determined by the Plantation Regime.* Louisiana State University Press, Baton Rouge.

Genovese, Eugene D. (1974). *Roll, Jordan, Roll: The World the Slaves Made.* Random House, New York.

Goodell, William (1853). *The American Slave Code in Theory and Practice: Its Distinctive Features Shown by Its Statutes, Judicial Decisions, & Illustrative Facts.* American and Foreign Anti-Slavery Society, New York.

Gordon-Reed, Annette (2008). *The Hemingses of Monticello: An American Family.* W.W. Norton, New York.

Gross, Ariela (2000). *Double Character: Slavery and Mastery in the Antebellum Southern Courtroom*. Princeton University Press, Princeton.

Hadden, Sally (2001). *Slave Patrols: Law and Violence in Virginia and the Carolinas*. Harvard University Press, Cambridge, MA.

Handlin, Oscar and Handlin, Mary (1950). "The Origins of the Southern Labor System." *William and Mary Quarterly* 77(2): 199–222.

Higginbotham, A. Leon (1978). *In the Matter of Color: The Colonial Period*. Oxford University Press, New York.

Hofstadter, Richard (1944). "U.B. Phillips and The Plantation Legend." *Journal of Negro History* 29(2): 109–124.

Holton, Woody (2007). *Unruly Americans and the Origins of the Constitution*. Hill and Wang, New York.

Hurd, John C. (1858). *The Law of Freedom and Bondage in the United States*. Little and Brown, Boston.

Jacobs, Harriet (2009 [1861]). *Incidents in the Life of a Slave Girl*. Harvard University Press, Cambridge, MA.

Jones, Bernie D. (2009). *Fathers of Conscience: Mixed-Race Inheritance in the Antebellum South*. University of Georgia Press, Athens, GA.

Jordan, Winthrop D. (1968). *White Over Black: American Attitudes Toward the Negro, 1550–1812*. University of North Carolina Press, Chapel Hill.

Kaye, Anthony E. (2007). *Joining Places: Slave Neighborhoods in the Old South*. University of North Carolina Press, Chapel Hill.

Manning, Patrick (1996). *Slave Trades, 1500–1800: Globalization of Forced Labour*. Variorum, Hampshire.

Martin, Bonnie (2010). "Slavery's Invisible Engine: Mortgaging Human Property." *Journal of Southern History* 76(4): 817–866.

Morris, Thomas D. (1996). *Southern Slavery and the Law, 1619–1860*. University of North Carolina Press, Chapel Hill.

Nash, Gary B. (2005). *Unknown American Revolution: The Unruly Birth of Democracy and the Struggle to Create America*. Penguin Publishers, New York.

Nash, Gary B. (2006). *The Forgotten Fifth: African Americans in the Age of Revolution*. Harvard University Press, Cambridge, MA.

Pares, Richard (1960). *Merchants and Planters*. Cambridge University Press, Cambridge, UK.

Pascoe, Peggy (2009). *What Comes Naturally: Miscegenation Law and the Making of Race in America*. Oxford University Press, New York.

Phillips, Ulrich Bonnell (1929). *Life and Labor in the Old South*. Little, Brown, Boston.

Phillips, Ulrich Bonnell (1966 [1918]). *American Negro Slavery: A Survey of the Supply, Employment and Control of Negro Labor as Determined by the Plantation Regime*. Louisiana State University Press, Baton Rouge.

Quarles, Benjamin (1961). *The Negro in the American Revolution*. University of North Carolina Press, Chapel Hill.

Quarles, Benjamin (1991 [1969]). *Black Abolitionists*. Oxford University Press, New York.

Rediker, Marcus (2007). *The Slave Ship: A Human History*. Viking, New York.

Rothman, Joshua (2003). *Notorious in the Neighborhood: Sex and Families across the Color Line in Virginia, 1787–1861*. University of North Carolina Press, Chapel Hill.

Schermerhorn, Calvin (2011). *Money over Mastery, Family over Freedom: Slavery in the Antebellum Upper South*. Johns Hopkins University Press, Baltimore.

Schwarz, Philip J. (1988). *Twice Condemned: Slaves and the Criminal Laws of Virginia, 1705–1865*. Louisiana State University Press, Baton Rouge.

Stampp, Kenneth Milton. (1956). *The Peculiar Institution: Slavery in the Ante-Bellum South*. Random House, New York.

Styron, William (1966). *The Confessions of Nat Turner*. Random House, New York.

Tannenbaum, Frank (1947). *Slave and Citizen: The Negro in the Americas*. Alfred A. Knopf, New York.

Tocqueville, Alexis de (2007 [1838]). *Democracy in America*. George, Dearborn and Co., New York.

Tomlins, Christopher (2010). *Freedom Bound: Law, Labor, and Civic Identity in Colonizing English America, 1580–1865*. Cambridge University Press, New York.

VanderVelde, Lea (2009). *Mrs. Dred Scott: A Life on Slavery's Frontier*. Oxford University Press, New York.

Vaughan, Alden T. (1995 [1989]). "The Origins Debate: Slavery and Racism in Seventeenth Century Virginia." In *Roots of American Racism: Essays on the Colonial Experience*. Oxford University Press, New York.

Waldstreicher, David (2009). *Slavery's Constitution: From Revolution to Ratification*. Hill and Wang, New York.

Watson, Alan (1987). *Roman Slave Law*. Johns Hopkins University Press, Baltimore.

Weld, Theodore Dwight (1838). *The Bible against Slavery: An Inquiry Into the Patriarchal and Mosaic Systems on the Subject of Human Rights*. American Anti-Slavery Society, New York.

Welke, Barbara (1995). "When All the Women Were White, and All the Blacks Were Men: Gender, Class, Race, and the Road to *Plessy*, 1855–1914." *Law and History Review* 13(2): 261–316.

Wiecek, William M. (1977a). *The Sources of Antislavery Constitutionalism in America, 1760–1848*. Cornell University Press, Ithaca, NY.

Wiecek, William M. (1977b). "The Statutory Law of Slavery and Race in the Thirteen Mainland Colonies of British America." *William and Mary Quarterly* 34(2): 258–280.

Williams, Eric (1994 [1944]). *Capitalism and Slavery*. University of North Carolina Press, Chapel Hill.

Wood, Betty (1997). *The Origins of American Slavery: Freedom and Bondage in the English Colonies*. Hill and Wang, New York.

Wood, Peter H. (1974). *Black Majority: Negroes in Colonial South Carolina from 1670 through the Stono Rebellion*. W.W. Norton, New York.

Woodson, Carter G. (1900). *The Mind of the Negro as Reflected in Letters Written during the Crisis, 1800–1860*. Russell & Russell, New York.

Woodward, C. Vann (1955). *The Strange Career of Jim Crow*. Oxford University Press, New York.

Yellin, Jean Fagan (2008). *The Harriet Jacobs Family Papers*. University of North Carolina Press, Chapel Hill.

Zilversmit, Arthur (1967). *The First Emancipation: The Abolition of Slavery in the North*. University of Chicago Press, Chicago.

Chapter Nine

AFRICAN AMERICANS IN FREEDOM

James Campbell

The abolition of slavery in 1865 marked a transformation in the relationship between African Americans and the law. No longer categorized according to the dual status of person and property, during the years of Reconstruction African Americans obtained the legal standing of citizens, but the meaning and implications of this change long remained subject to fierce contestation not only within the legal system, but also in wider American society, culture, and politics. Consequently, while it has become a primary concern of legal historians in all fields of study to understand law within and as a product of social context, this pursuit assumes particular resonance in African American legal history due to the extreme disjuncture between legal theory and practice in issues of race, civil rights, and criminal justice, and the diverse ways that law has been used both to support and challenge white supremacy.

The centrality of legal history to the African American past has been reflected in the intense politicization of the subject's historiography, which has evolved in dialogue with developments in American race relations and civil rights. In the late nineteenth- and early twentieth-century, for example, major studies were penned by white supremacist writers committed to the racial status quo of the segregation era, while in the later-twentieth century the achievements of the long Black freedom struggle and the increased diversity of the historical profession were critical factors in broadening scholarly interest in the Black legal past and engaging with new questions about African American legal agency. At the same time, historiographical change was also fuelled by external factors, such as the emerging concern of social historians to recover the "lost voices" of traditionally marginalized groups, as well as developments in the

A Companion to American Legal History, First Edition.
Edited by Sally E. Hadden and Alfred L. Brophy.
© 2013 John Wiley & Sons Ltd. Published 2021 by John Wiley & Sons Ltd.

field of legal history itself, including a growing interest in the relationship between society and law, and the notion embodied in critical legal studies scholarship that law is not only a product of specific social values and structures, but also supports the interests of particular groups. Through questioning how "ordinary" Black men and women sought to use law and the ways that gender and class concerns informed their struggles at the local level, recent scholarship has highlighted the complexity of the relationship between law and racial change and the multiplicity of Black legal histories. This chapter explores these broad developments in the historiography of African Americans and law since the Civil War through analysis of four main topics: Reconstruction and the origins of Jim Crow segregation laws, criminal justice and racial violence, the long Black freedom struggle, and the development of a color-blind jurisprudence in the post-civil rights era.

Reconstruction and the Origins of Jim Crow

Law pervaded early post-Civil War Black history, yet legal issues in themselves were rarely the primary concern of scholarly or popular historical attention. Through the first decades of the twentieth century, dominant narratives of African Americans and law were instead entwined with the heavily politicized historiography of Reconstruction and its aftermath. Influential scholars such as John Burgess (1902), William Dunning (1907), and James Rhodes (1920), wrote histories that were sympathetic to the white South, defended the restrictive racial provisions of the southern Black Codes of 1865–1866, and condemned the Freedmen's Bureau and congressional Reconstruction legislation. In these studies, African Americans were depicted mostly as corrupt and ignorant lawmakers who were exploited by cynical and "radical" white Republicans, or as criminals threatening the peace and property of the white South and the sexual purity of white women. This interpretation was consistent with and fuelled the Lost Cause vision of Reconstruction that enjoyed broad public acceptance as white Americans sought to move beyond the sectional divisions of the Civil War era. Arguably reaching its fullest expression in Thomas Dixon's novel *The Clansman* (1905)–later filmed as *Birth of a Nation* (1915)–Lost Cause rhetoric supported ideologies of white supremacy that underpinned segregation, the disfranchisement of Black voters, lynching and race riots. In David Blight's analysis, white Americans reached a consensus in which "Jim Crow laws replaced the Fourteenth Amendment in [its place] of honor in national memory" (2001: 361).

White supremacist sentiments also pervaded early interpretations of post-Reconstruction Black legal history. Philip Alexander Bruce (1911: 386) credited late-nineteenth century southern lawmakers with "five great enactments": African American disfranchisement, the prohibition of interracial marriages, and legalized segregation in education, housing, and public conveyances. These measures, Bruce contended, constituted a solution to "the Negro problem" that repaired the damage of Reconstruction and paved the way for "harmonious" race relations in the South. White racial paternalists also deployed legal history to endorse segregation and Black disfranchisement. North Carolina historian Stephen B. Weeks described voter registration laws in 1894 as "beyond [the] comprehension" of average Black voters and consequently an effective guard against electoral corruption. Like John Dos Passos, writing in the *Yale Law Journal* ten years later, Weeks also cited Black educational progress towards "a real comprehension of the uses and ends of government" as a prerequisite to the restoration of the franchise (Weeks, 1894: 702; Dos Passos, 1903: 483). Gilbert Stephenson reached comparable conclusions about the value of segregation in his *Race Distinctions in American Law* (1910), a comprehensive examination of constitutional, statutory and judicial decisions concerning race since 1865 that was described by one reviewer as "the first through-going attempt" to outline the development of race laws in the United States in the decades following emancipation (Mathews, 1911: 652). Taking as his benchmark the constitutional amendments and civil rights legislation of the Reconstruction era, Stephenson sought to establish how far law constrained African American citizenship. He differentiated between racial distinctions and discrimination, arguing that the latter was invidious and should be purged from American statute books, but the former–including segregation statutes–were a natural product of race consciousness and differentiation that mitigated "race friction" and were consequently in the best interests of both races. Stephenson further concluded that racial distinctions in law were commonplace nationwide rather than unique to the South and called for broader recognition of this fact to promote sectional reconciliation between northern and southern whites.

African American scholars and activists were at the forefront of the development of alternative interpretations of race and law in this era. With W.E.B. Du Bois (1899; 1935) their most notable representative, Black historians and sociologists wrote about the racial injustices of the American legal system, the violence that had perpetuated white supremacy during and after Reconstruction, and the achievements of Black legislators and lawyers. In *The Aftermath of Slavery*, former slave William Sinclair hailed Reconstruction's legacy of "[e]quality of rights for all men before the law" (1905: 38) and decried that southern whites had "place[d] themselves above the law, and force[d] the colored people below it" (1905: 218). Ten years later, John Lynch, a former slave and congressman from Mississippi, praised the work of Reconstruction-era Black legislators and condemned the Supreme Court's failure to uphold Republican civil rights legislation (1915). In the short-term, however, this work was widely neglected and through the 1940s the historiography of African Americans and the law after emancipation remained dominated by works that supported Jim Crow segregation and disfranchisement laws as necessary and inevitable and refuted the notion that law could serve as a force for racial progress. Charles Magnum argued in his 1940 study *The Legal Status of the Negro*, for example, that race distinctions in law were largely immutable and, in any case, that legal change could scarcely alter race relations in practice without a fundamental shift in popular attitudes. Yet, as organizations such as the National Association for the Advancement of Colored People (NAACP) made legal arenas increasingly critical battlegrounds in the Black freedom struggle, so historians, sociologists, and political scientists began to reconsider the role and possibilities of law in African American life and develop new interpretative histories that would constitute a more usable past for the civil rights movement. When the Swedish sociologist Gunnar Myrdal published his magnum opus on American race relations, *An American Dilemma*, in 1944, for example, he described disfranchisement and segregation as unstable systems "gradually losing [their] legal sanctions," and undermined by "an onslaught of legal action" (1944 [1962]: 629).

Within fifteen years, faith in the transformative power of law in the field of race relations dominated historical scholarship. In a study of civil rights legislation from 1862 to 1952, Will Maslow and Joseph Robison (1953) concluded that it was "reasonably clear that legislation not only affects patterns of behavior but, by changing the situations in which we live, may also change beliefs and attitudes." More prominently, in *The Strange Career of Jim Crow*, first published in 1955, C. Vann Woodward argued that following the abolition of slavery there was a period of experimentation in southern race relations that lasted until the 1890s. While recognizing that African Americans suffered discrimination and exploitation during Reconstruction, and especially after the Democratic Party redeemed the South in the 1870s, in Woodward's analysis there was nothing inevitable about the segregation and disfranchisement laws that were enacted at the end of the century. Instead, there were particular economic and political reasons for the passage of this legislation, including the economic crisis of the 1880s, Supreme Court rulings in support of segregation, and "a relaxation of the opposition" that northern liberals and southern conservatives and radicals, notably the Populist movement, had previously mounted against "extreme racism" (1974: 67–109).

The Woodward thesis has proved resilient and influential; as Howard Rabinowitz noted, it is more subtle, qualified, and narrow than its many critics often acknowledge. Yet, it is also controversial. Even though Woodward emphasized that *"laws are not an adequate index of the extent and prevalence of segregation and discriminatory practices in the South"* (italics in original), he nonetheless ranked "the existence of law enforcing segregation" as "the key variable in evaluating the nature of race relations" (Rabinowitz, 1988: 844). By contrast, Woodward's early critics, including Joel Williamson and John Cell argued that segregation law "merely ratified what had been put into practice long before" (Mack, 1999: 380). Writing on South Carolina, Williamson (1965: 275) concluded that "[w]ell before the end of Reconstruction, separation had crystallized into a comprehensive pattern which, in its essence, remained unaltered until the middle of the twentieth century." The reason for this development was not law, but "the philosophies and attitudes each race adopted toward the other." Rabinowitz ploughed a third furrow, arguing that segregation arose not as an alternative to integration, but rather as a replacement for the complete exclusion of African Americans from public spaces, which he presented as the "norm in southern race relations" in the antebellum period and immediate post-war years. Moreover, Rabinowitz suggested that the catalyst for this shift was growing Black autonomy, activism, and perceived disorder that whites viewed as a new threat to the established racial hierarchy.

In new studies of the origins of Jim Crow since the 1990s, gender has emerged as a key analytical category that complicates traditional analyses and demonstrates that *de jure* segregation was "never the stable world of white over Black that its architects envisioned" (Mack, 1999: 403). As Barbara Welke (2001: 329–333) explains, segregation on American railroads first arose in the form of separate cars for women, and legal clashes over Black women's right to this "privilege of their sex" were common in the final decades of the nineteenth century. Often these cases turned on issues of class identity and respectability. Middle-class African American women, for example, went to court to protest their exclusion from first-class railroad cars. The litigants in these cases laid claim to notions of respectability in demanding protection from the coarse culture and sexual exploitation that they might encounter in second-class smoking carriages. By contrast, in contesting these claims, railroad companies and their legal representatives depicted Black women as immoral "jezebels" and identified virtuous womanhood as an inherently white characteristic.

The instability of the Jim Crow legal system reached far beyond railroad segregation. It was strikingly apparent, too, for example, in legal disputes over questions of racial identity, which arose particularly in relation to interracial marriage and moves initiated in the Progressive era to define whiteness in ever more restrictive terms that culminated in the "one-drop" laws of the 1920s (Robinson, 2003: 101). These laws rested on and reinforced popular and pseudo-scientific conceptions of race as a measurable biological fact, yet in practice miscegenation-related civil and criminal court cases time and again revealed the inherent instability of racial categories. If segregation rested on the assumption that the law could tell who was Black and who was white, recent legal histories have demonstrated clearly that attorneys, judges, and jurors routinely struggled to resolve disputes over racial identity and often were forced to wrestle with farcical evidence and rely on the most dubious legal logic in an attempt to do so (Gross, 2008).

Apart from reframing the debate over the origins of segregation, gender analysis has also influenced recent legal histories of freedpeople's working arrangements, intimate relationships, and emerging status as citizens in the aftermath of emancipation. Freedom conferred new rights on African Americans, including the right to own property, marry, and enter into labor contracts, but from their earliest enforcement in the mid-1860s these rights were readily transformed into mechanisms for shaping and constraining Black citizenship. Historians Amy Dru Stanley (1998), Katherine Franke (1999), and others, have shown that prevailing nineteenth-century notions of citizenship informed by Victorian moral values and political and legal discourse about contract and the market worked alongside the demands of southern planters for cheap Black labor and white racial supremacy to fuel the vigorous prosecution of African Americans under fornication, adultery, and vagrancy statutes. This coercive relationship between the state and freedpeople had distinctly gendered implications. Reconstituting their intimate relationships as legally sanctioned marriages, African American wives conceded control of their wages, property, and bodies to their husbands under the doctrine of coverture. Yet, compelled by poverty and vagrancy laws to work outside the home, Black women were simultaneously removed from the domestic sphere where white women laid claim to feminine respectability.

Notwithstanding the intrusion of law into the private sphere of Black households and personal relationships, the gendered construction of Black citizenship, and the discriminatory operation of local courts, freedwomen routinely appealed to legal authorities to regulate family relations, labor contracts, and property claims, and to defend themselves against crime and violence. In doing so, they asserted the status and rights of citizens. However, Laura Edwards (2007: 367) argues that post-Civil War Black legal agency was also rooted in an understanding of southern law as a local and accessible system developed in the antebellum era. Even marginalized poor whites, women, and free African Americans viewed law as a mechanism for resolving the myriad disputes and conflicts of their daily lives and, for Edwards, this was precisely how freedpeople, too, understood and used law and legal institutions after slavery. For Dylan Penningroth (2003: 112), African Americans after slavery engaged with law pragmatically, taking "their concerns from the yard and the church into the courtroom, and sometimes back again, pursuing their interests wherever they saw an advantage." As they did so, they drew less on new rights to property established under the auspices of Republican Reconstruction policies, than on extralegal conceptions of property ownership rooted in the complex dynamics of community and kinship ties forged during slavery.

The history of Jim Crow is usually related as a southern narrative, but historians have shown that in practice segregation was a local matter that varied in law and custom across the former Confederate states and reached far beyond that region. For example, the enforcement of segregation laws was mostly a matter for the urban South (Rabinowitz, 1978). By contrast,

Mark Schultz argues that in rural Georgia, white supremacy rested on the very different foundations of "paternalism and racial etiquette" backed by violence. Far from separation, this highly personal form of racial control was built on "intimacy" between Blacks and whites (Schultz, 2005: 131). There were also considerable variations among southern states. In Mississippi, arguably the South's most racially repressive state, Neil McMillen argues that "the process of formally transcribing custom into law was fitfully pursued and never finished." In most areas of the state's public life, Jim Crow statues were simply unnecessary, McMillen explains, because "the forces of social habit and white opinion were in themselves usually sufficient to ensure that the races knew their places" (1990: 9–10). J. Douglas Smith depicts very different conditions in Virginia, where race relations were increasingly "managed" by law, rather than violence and custom, during the first half of the twentieth century. Virginia's distinctive course was in part a result of Black resistance to white supremacy, but it also stemmed from the Virginia elite's commitment to order, stability, and an "empty paternalism" that encouraged Black progress while resisting its inevitable consequence of growing demands for racial equality (Smith, 2002: 4–15). The situation was different again in the northern states. Jim Crow was less pervasive and extreme above the Mason-Dixon Line and was prohibited by law in most states by the late nineteenth century. Nonetheless, studies of schooling, housing, welfare, and municipal courts have demonstrated the struggles that Black men, women, and children faced in the North to secure equal rights and resources. Davison Douglas (2005), for example, argues that laws prohibiting school segregation in the North were ineffective and persistent racial separation in northern schools proved difficult to challenge for reasons ranging from cost, to divisions between segregationists and integrationists in the Black community, and white judicial and political apathy.

Crime, Punishment and Racial Violence

In the antebellum era, criminal justice systems across the South were fundamentally divided along racial lines. In the wake of abolition, former slaveholders moved swiftly to reaffirm these divisions and reconstitute criminal law as a "functional replacement for slavery" (Adamson, 1983). They constructed systems of crime and punishment that imposed a dual burden on African American citizens by undermining protection for the person and property of Black victims and disregarding the rights of Black defendants.

Debates about lynching provided the context for some of the earliest historical interpretations of African Americans and criminal law after emancipation. In striking contrast to white supremacists' positive interpretations of segregation and disfranchisement laws, turn-of-the-century pro-lynching rhetoric focused on criminal law's limitations in mediating southern race relations. Thomas Nelson Page (1904) argued that, by the turn of the century, legal processes had proved an ineffective deterrent against the rape of white women by Black men, which he identified as lynching's primary cause. Law was slow, punishment uncertain, and securing convictions could require the alleged white women victims of Black rapists to "relate in public the story of the assault–an ordeal which was worse than death." Increasingly savage and ferocious lynchings held "a deeper terror," Page concluded, and were a necessary antidote to African American lawlessness, which he in turn attributed to ignorance and inflammatory "talk of social equality." In an ironic echo of such white supremacist justifications of mob rule, Black anti-lynching activists also constructed arguments that turned on claims concerning the incapacity of law, as they highlighted the acquiescence of lawmakers, legal institutions, and the public at large in the perpetration of racial violence against African Americans (Douglass, 1895: 3). Anti-lynching crusader Ida B. Wells documented in works such as *A Red Record* (1894) how African Americans after Reconstruction were "lynched for almost any offense" in the interests of white supremacy. This work chimed with sociological studies of the time that uncovered structural causes of Black crime and discrimination by the police and in the courts that refuted mainstream white analyses of disproportionately high African American incarceration rates as evidence of inherent criminality.

Although lynching continued to scar American communities into the middle decades of the twentieth century, historians neglected the topic. James Chadbourn's 1933 study *Lynching and the Law* documented state anti-lynching legislation and its overwhelmingly limited effectiveness in bringing mobs to justice. Robert Zangrando (1980) and George Rable (1985) later focused on the long struggle waged by groups including the NAACP to enact federal anti-lynching laws and the successful efforts of southern senators to block legislation. More recent, historians have begun to explore other mechanisms through which African Americans and whites at the local level, as well as the federal government, did challenge southern racial violence. Dominic Capeci (1986) explained the unprecedented response of the Department of Justice to the 1942 lynching of Cleo Wright in Missouri in the context of wartime political expediency, while Kari Frederickson (1997) has connected the post-war acquittal of lynch-mob participants in South Carolina to Truman's executive order establishing the President's Committee on Civil Rights. As Christopher Waldrep (2008) notes, federal investigations of southern lynchings during the 1940s were undermined by local white opposition, but they nonetheless contributed to a cultural shift in popular attitudes that increasingly viewed questions of race, law and violence as national rather than state concerns.

In recent decades, historians have studied the diverse ways that the history of African American criminal law was entwined with questions of political economy, white supremacy, and racial violence. As Howard Rabinowitz argued in 1978, in the years after emancipation, law served not to protect African Americans, but to "discipline them." Edward Ayers' pioneering *Vengeance and Justice* (1984) explored how the market economy shaped the ways that southern whites adapted criminal law and the penal system to this purpose and revealed how the vagaries of local politics and race relations shaped post-Civil War criminal justice. Nieman (1989) likewise stressed the fairness that pervaded judicial procedures in parts of Texas where Black and white Republicans exercised an unusual degree of political power during Reconstruction, while Waldrep (1998) argued that the events of the post-Civil War decade demonstrated to white Mississippians that "law could never be made oppressive enough to effectively control African Americans." These studies demonstrate that African Americans could exercise influence on criminal law in rare circumstances, but histories of convict leasing and peonage are replete with evidence that by the late nineteenth century, notions of justice in southern law enforcement were violently subsumed beneath the insatiable demands of white employers for cheap and pliant Black labor (Daniel, 1990; Lichtenstein, 1996; Mancini, 1996; Curtin, 2000).

As in southern convict leasing camps and at the sites of mob killings, law and lawlessness blurred in American courtrooms when African Americans stood trial. The disregard for due process in twentieth-century criminal proceedings involving Black defendants has been explored in case studies of prominent trials, most notably the "Scottsboro Boys" case of the 1930s. Works on Scottsboro have focused in particular on the role of local and national NAACP activists and lawyers, as well as conflicts between the NAACP and the International Labor Defense, a communist organization that promoted popular agitation to pressurize the Alabama authorities and linked the case to working class and anti-colonial movements across the globe (Carter, 1979; Goodman, 1995). By the mid-1930s, lawyers representing Black defendants had won major victories in the United States Supreme Court against mob-dominated trials, all-white juries, confessions extracted through torture, and inadequate legal counsel. Racial injustice in southern courtrooms nonetheless persisted, notably as a result of the routine neglect of federal due process rulings by local judicial authorities in the southern states, and the refusal of the Supreme Court to engage with the discriminatory administration of the death penalty that was common across the South (Klarman, 2000: 95). Consequently, Glenda Gilmore concludes that for African American defendants before the 1960s there was only an "evolution of injustice: from lynching to a mob-dominated trial to a perfunctory trial" (2008: 335).

When change did come to the administration of law at the local level in the South it was sporadic and driven by extralegal forces, principally the strength and resistance of Black communities. Stephen Tuck (2010) describes the first southern towns and cities that appointed Black police officers after World War II as "islands of progress" distinguished from the region as a whole by the scale of local African American political organization and influence. Danielle McGuire (2004), meanwhile, argues that as civil rights activism grew in the mid-twentieth century, Black women's long-standing "refusal ... to remain silent about sexualized violence" sparked protests that for the first time forced southern courts to take seriously rape charges against white men. A multitude of factors were at work in these cases, as racial politics and protest intersected with considerations of gender, class, and international affairs. Indeed, as Mary Berry (2000: 208–213) has persuasively shown, the concerns of white patriarchy could also shape the administration of criminal law such that even Black men suspected of raping white women might be protected by elites who valued the labor of the accused more highly than their alleged victims' virtue. Appellate courts "eagerly accepted" that lower class alleged rape victims had consented to sex, and regularly overturned convictions even of Black defendants accused by white women. This is consistent with Lisa Dorr's research on Virginia, which indicates that the outcome of Black-on-white rape trials was rarely predictable and not always consistent with expressions of popular white outrage (Dorr, 2004).

In complicating understandings of African Americans and criminal law, recent research has laid bare that the entanglement of law, racial violence, and injustice that characterized African American experiences of crime and punishment in the Jim Crow South was not limited to that region. Instead, historians have begun to explore how African American experiences of crime and punishment nationwide existed along a continuum of law and popular justice, incorporating police brutality, mob killings, "legal lynchings," and state executions. As in the South, rates of Black imprisonment in the North were disproportionately high, Black involvement in the administration of justice rare, and the failure of law officers to bring lynching parties to justice unexceptional. Recent studies also illustrate that northern and western cities were scarred by widespread and unchecked police brutality and that discriminatory conceptions of criminality pervaded the popular press and the courtroom (Gross, 2006; Johnson, 2003; Dale, 2001; Muhammad, 2010).

The Black Freedom Struggle

As white supremacy rested on the integration of legal and extralegal forms of tyranny, so the Black challenge to segregation and racial discrimination involved connected protests within and outside the courtroom. The NAACP stood at the forefront of Black litigation in the mid-twentieth century. Led by a cadre of attorneys in its national office, including Charles Hamilton Houston and Thurgood Marshall, the NAACP crafted successful legal challenges to inequality and discrimination in housing, higher education, transportation, voting, and peonage, as well as criminal procedure cases. The Association's greatest legal victory was *Brown v. Board of Education* (1954), a landmark ruling that declared separate schools for Black and white children inherently unequal, thereby reversing *Plessy* and rendering segregation unconstitutional. The scholarship on *Brown* is voluminous. Richard Kluger (1977) argued that the ruling reflected the convictions and political skill of the justices, notably Chief Justice Earl Warren, Felix Frankfurter, and Robert Jackson, who worked to ensure a unanimous ruling despite divisions on the bench. Mark Tushnet, by contrast, highlighted the political and legal skill of the NAACP's attorneys in pragmatically responding to external and internal pressures to develop a legal strategy that evolved in the late 1940s from an indirect challenge to the inequality of segregated education to a direct attack on the principle of segregation itself (1987: 105–137).

Early histories of *Brown* interpreted the case as a catalyst for the modern civil rights movement that inspired support for racial change and activism among both northern whites and African Americans and culminated a decade later in the Civil Rights Act (1964) and the Voting Rights Act (1965). As the hope of *Brown* faded amidst the limitations of its implementation and the ferocity of white massive resistance, however, historians began to reevaluate its significance and the broader role of law in driving racial progress. This development was related to important changes in civil rights historiography. Whereas the first accounts of the modern civil rights movement centered on national politics and the prominent role of Black community leaders and organizations such as the Southern Christian Leadership Conference (SCLC), in the 1980s focus shifted to the grassroots activism and local organizing of "ordinary" African Americans. In Aldon Morris' assessment, the modern civil rights movement that emerged in the 1950s broke with the legal strategies of past Black freedom struggles and deployed instead nonviolent, direct action tactics, such as economic boycotts, marches, and sit-ins that drew on the strength of Black community resources and organizational structures (1984: ix). As social and political historians investigated the dynamics of grassroots civil rights movements (Dittmer, 1995; de Jong, 2002; Payne, 1995), the role of litigation in the struggle remained compartmentalized as part of a national, top-down story involving the Black elite. As Tomiko Brown-Nagin (2004: 227) wrote, "studies tend to focus on the thrust and parry of legal argument or on the social history of communities in which struggles for political and civil rights were fought–not both." For social historians of civil rights, therefore, law was usually "epiphenomenal, not that important to local movement actors, and sometimes even corrosive of local community organizing" (Mack, 2009: 658).

Writing from a perspective of legal rather than social or political history, Michael Klarman also questioned the significance of *Brown* to the course of the modern civil rights movement. Focusing on the rulings of the

Supreme Court, Klarman argued that legal change in the field of race and rights stemmed throughout the twentieth century from "deep background forces" (Klarman, 2004: 377). At various times, these included the large-scale movement of African Americans to cities, both in the South and in the northern states which increased the economic and political power of the Black community and made segregation a national issue. They also encompassed the experiences of Black soldiers in the two World Wars and the ideological issues at stake in those conflicts which spurred domestic civil rights militancy; the economic depression of the 1930s that shattered confidence in American capitalism and led the Roosevelt administration and the Supreme Court to expand federal powers of economic regulation; and the transformed political landscape of the New Deal that saw Republicans and Democrats campaigning for Black votes more competitively than for a generation previously. With specific reference to *Brown*, Klarman's "backlash thesis" interpreted the decision's primary significance as the "massive resistance" it provoked from southern whites, which in turn instigated civil rights activism and federal intervention to protect Black rights. Additionally, Klarman argued that the process and attendant publicity of *Brown* had such important ramifications as "educating Blacks about their rights, providing occasions for organizing local communities, featuring Black lawyers ... as role models for southern Blacks, and informing northern whites (and judges) about southern Jim Crow conditions" (Klarman, 2002: 120).

The legal history of the civil rights movement continues to branch in many new directions. New perspectives have developed, for example, from the extensive body of revisionist historical scholarship that roots the origins of the Black freedom struggle in the early twentieth century rather than the post-World War II era. The notion of a "long civil rights movement" incorporating the interracial popular front politics of the 1930s has gained currency through the work of historians such as Jacquelyn Dowd Hall (2005) and Robert Korstad (2003). In Glenda Gilmore's analysis (2008: 9), "giving the movement a 1950s start ... privilege[s] its religious, middle-class, and male roots ...[,] suggests that African Americans simply wanted desegregation and highlights NAACP school litigation and the Montgomery bus boycott. On the contrary, African Americans had worked for decades to secure social justice in broader terms." Robin Kelly (1990) has shown how labor and communist organizations played a central role in this project in Alabama during the 1930s and 1940s, appealing to poor Blacks through policies that promised radical economic and social reform in contrast to the middle-class oriented racial-uplift rhetoric and legal strategy of the NAACP. Recent work, however, has questioned the moderate, liberal interpretation of NAACP legal activism implicit in this approach. Kenneth Mack argues that the powerful legacy of *Brown* has caused historians to view earlier African American advocacy, erroneously, as primarily concerned with challenging segregation. Rather, Mack argues, from the 1920s to the 1940s Black lawyers within and outside the NAACP were skeptical about the capacity of courts to transform society (2005: 352). Instead, they believed in racial uplift through "the support of [Black] businesses and local institutions," rather than "transformative litigation". Moreover, Mack (2006: 38–39) contends that prior to *Brown* NAACP lawyers did not represent a conservative alternative to communist-affiliated organizations preoccupied with narrow legalism, but rather sympathized with aspects of the radical agenda which they worked "to fuse ... into a new civil rights paradigm." Risa Goluboff (2007) similarly argues that rather than initiating Black protest, *Brown* marked an end point in a debate over the very meaning of civil rights. Demonstrating that in the 1940s civil rights lawyers fought not only state-sponsored segregation, but also labor discrimination and the economic exploitation of Black workers that formed a second pillar of Jim Crow, Goluboff depicts *Brown* as marking the triumph of a narrower, liberal conception of civil rights that excluded socio-economic considerations. In her study of law and the civil rights movement in Atlanta, meanwhile, Brown-Nagin (2011) has revealed the significance of local context and Black community institutions and resources in shaping courtroom activism, uncovered myriad divisions and conflicts within Black communities over legal strategies, and pointed towards a legal history of the civil rights movement that is more inclusive of the demands and legal activism of the poorest and most marginalized African Americans than is recognized in earlier studies centered on *Brown* and the battle against segregation.

Complementing enquiries into the long-term roots of the civil rights movement, historians have begun to recognize that African Americans engaged in an ongoing legal struggle to shape the meaning, enforcement, and implications of the 1960s civil rights legislation in areas such as housing, schooling, and employment (Hall, 2005: 51–55). Acknowledging the neglect of law in histories of civil rights struggles in the 1960s, Timothy Minchin (2001) explored the work of the NAACP to secure enforcement of the 1964 Civil Rights Act provisions on desegregation, schooling, and employment, while Nancy MacLean (2006) has written on the tens of thousands of Black workers who filed suits demanding fair and equal treatment in the workplace under Title VII of the Civil Rights Act. Coupled with work on anti-poverty campaigns and programs launched in Black communities in the second half of the 1960s and 1970s, this work has encouraged studies of civil rights legal history to address new questions about the movement's links to human rights law and has also opened up new possibilities for exploring the connections between the legal history of African American civil rights and the campaigns for racial justice waged by other minority groups both in the United States and internationally (Brilliant, 2010).

African Americans and the Law since the Civil Rights Movement

Histories of African Americans and law since 1965 have pursued a number of disparate themes, but often are characterized by an overarching concern with questions of continuity and change. Randall Kennedy (1994) has criticized legal scholars who proceed "as if there existed no dramatic discontinuities in American history, as if there existed little difference between the practices and sentiments that characterized the eras of slavery and de jure segregation and those prevalent today" (1994: 1258). For Kennedy, late twentieth-century scholarship and political activism that identified with the struggles of Black defendants and convicts and called for constraints on the powers of law enforcement was detrimental to the interests of Black America and undermined attempts to deal with more pressing legal concerns, principally the under-enforcement of law in Black communities ravaged by illegal drugs and intraracial violence. Lawrence Friedman (2002) was similarly dismissive of critical legal studies approaches that he criticized as neglecting empirical research. Adopting a more polemical stance, Thomas Sowell maintained that the "battle for civil rights was fought and won" in the past and dismissed continued African American agitation as representing the socially destabilizing "politicization" of law (Sowell cited in Crenshaw, 1988: 1339–1340).

By contrast, most recent scholarship is less sanguine about the evolving Black experience of law. As characterized by former federal judge and historian Leon Higginbotham (1996: xxiii–xxiv), African American legal history has been a "journey" from "total racial oppression" to only "muted shades of freedom." The limitations of progress are nowhere more apparent than in criminal law where, since the 1960s, racism has, in Doris Provine's assessment, "morphed ... rather than disappeared" (2007: 127). A tough law and order agenda was first promoted by Republicans in the late 1960s as a political strategy to win the South and a conscious backlash against the achievements of the Black freedom struggle. Loïc Wacquant (2002: 41–60) argues that by the early twenty-first century, mass incarceration, driven by new drugs laws, sentencing reforms, and prison privatization, had developed into a replacement for earlier forms of racial control from slavery, through segregation, to urban ghettos. In an era of economic globalization and deindustrialization that hit lower class Black neighborhoods with particular ferocity, criminal law was used to regulate the Black workforce–particularly young men–to perform casual, deskilled, low wage jobs. It also undermined many of the political and socio-economic gains of the Civil Rights era. As Jeff Manza and Christopher Uggen (2006) note, in most American states, convicted felons are denied the right to vote not only when incarcerated, but for years after their release from prison and in some cases for life.

Across a range of policy areas, including jury selection (Bell, 2000: 545–546), the death penalty (Bright, 1995: 62–63), and the so-called "war on drugs" the U.S. Supreme Court has subscribed to an ideology of color blindness that engrains racial difference and Black disadvantage by neglecting to act on either "unconscious racism born of stereotypical thinking or irrational racial fears" or "structural constraints or institutional practices that can bias outcomes" (Provine, 2007: 127). As legal historians begin to reconsider the African American legal past and future in the light of Barack Obama's election as the first Black president of the United States, Ian López argues that color-blind jurisprudence masks and, indeed, upholds structural racism in legislative and judicial decision-making so as to constitute, in Michelle Alexander's powerful description, a "new Jim Crow" (2009).

References

Adamson, Christopher R. (1983). "Punishment after Slavery: Southern State Penal Systems, 1865–1890." *Social Problems* 30.5: 555–569.

Alexander, Michelle. (2009). *The New Jim Crow: Mass Incarceration in the Age of Colorblindness*. New Press, New York.

Ayers, Edward L. (1984). *Vengeance and Justice: Crime and Punishment in the 19th Century American South*. Oxford University Press, New York.

Bell, Derrick (2000). *Race, Racism, and American Law*. Aspen, New York.

Berry, Mary F. (2000). *"The Pig Farmer's Daughter" and Other Tales of American Justice: Episodes of Racism and Sexism in the Courts from 1865 to the Present*. Vintage, New York.

Blight, David W. (2001). *Race and Reunion: The Civil War in American Memory*. Belknap Press of Harvard University Press, Cambridge.

Bright, Stephen B. (1995). "Discrimination, Death and Denial: The Tolerance of Racial Discrimination in Infliction of the Death Penalty." *Santa Clara Law Review* 35: 433–483.

Brilliant, Mark (2010). *The Color of America Has Changed: How Racial Diversity Shaped Civil Rights Reform in California, 1941–1978*. Oxford University Press, New York.

Brown-Nagin, Tomiko (2004). "The Impact of Lawyer-Client Disengagement on the NAACP's Campaign to Implement *Brown v. Board of Education*." In Lau, ed., *From the Grassroots to the Supreme Court: Brown v. Board of Education and American Democracy*, 227–244. Duke University Press, Durham.

Brown-Nagin, Tomiko (2011). *Courage to Dissent: Atlanta and the Long History of the Civil Rights Movement*. Oxford University Press, New York.

Bruce, Philip A. (1911). "Evolution of the Negro Problem." *The Sewanee Review* 19.4: 385–399.

Burgess, John (1902). *Reconstruction and the Constitution, 1866–1876*. Scribner, New York.

Capeci, Dominic (1986). "The Lynching of Cleo Wright: Federal Protection of Constitutional Rights during World War II." *Journal of American History* 72.4: 869–887.

Carter, Dan T. (1979). *Scottsboro: A Tragedy of the American South.* Louisiana State University Press, Baton Rouge.

Chadbourn, James H. (1933). *Lynching and the Law.* University of North Carolina Press, Chapel Hill.

Crenshaw, Kimberlé W. (1988). "Race, Reform, and Retrenchment: Transformation and Legitimation in Anti-discrimination Law." *Harvard Law Review* 101.7: 1331–1387.

Curtin, Mary E. (2000). *Black Prisoners and their World, Alabama, 1865–1900.* University Press of Virginia, Charlottesville.

Dale, Elizabeth (2001). *The Rule of Justice: The People of Chicago versus Zephyr Davis.* Ohio State University Press, Columbus.

Daniel, Peter R. (1990). *The Shadow of Slavery: Peonage in the South, 1901–1969.* University of Illinois Press, Urbana.

Dittmer, John (1995). *Local People: The Struggle for Civil Rights in Mississippi.* University of Illinois Press, Urbana.

Dixon, Thomas (1905). *The Clansman: An Historical Romance of the Ku Klux Klan.* Doubleday, New York.

Dorr, Lisa L. (2004). *White Women, Rape, and the Power of Race in Virginia, 1900–1960.* University of North Carolina Press, Chapel Hill.

Dos Passos, John R. (1903). "The Negro Question." *The Yale Law Journal* (12)8: 467–483.

Douglas, Davison M. (2005). *Jim Crow Moves North: The Battle Over Northern School Segregation, 1865–1954.* Cambridge University Press, New York.

Douglass, Frederick (1895). *Why is the Negro Lynched?* Whitby, Bridgwater.

Du Bois, W.E.B. (1899). *The Philadelphia Negro: A Social Study.* University of Pennsylvania Press, Philadelphia.

Du Bois, W.E.B. (1935). *Black Reconstruction: An Essay toward a History of the Part which Black Folk Played in the Attempt to Reconstruct Democracy in America, 1860–1880.* Harcourt, New York.

Dunning, William A. (1907). *Reconstruction: Political and Economic, 1865–1877.* Harper, New York.

Edwards, Laura F. (2007). "Status Without Rights: African Americans and the Tangled History of Law and Governance in the Nineteenth-Century U.S. South." *American Historical Review* 112: 365–393.

Franke, Katherine M. (1999). "Becoming a Citizen: Reconstruction Era Regulation of African American Marriages." *Yale Journal of Law and the Humanities* 11: 251–309.

Frederickson, Kari (1997). "'The Slowest State and Most Backward Community': Racial Violence in South Carolina and Federal Civil Rights Legislation, 1946–1948." *South Carolina Historical Magazine* (98)2: 177–202.

Friedman, Lawrence M. (2002). *American Law in the Twentieth Century.* Yale University Press, New Haven.

Gilmore, Glenda (2008). *Defying Dixie: The Radical Roots of Civil Rights, 1919–1950.* W.W. Norton, New Haven.

Goluboff, Risa (2007). *The Lost Promise of Civil Rights.* Harvard University Press, Cambridge.

Goodman, James E. (1995). *Stories of Scottsboro.* Pantheon, New York.

Gross, Ariela (2008). *What Blood Won't Tell: A History of Race on Trial in America.* Harvard University Press, Cambridge.

Gross, Kali (2006). *Colored Amazons: Crime, Violence, and Black Women in the City of Brotherly Love.* Duke University Press, Durham.

Hall, Jacqueline D. (2005) "The Long Civil Rights Movement and the Political Uses of the Past." *Journal of American History* 91: 1233–1263.

Higginbotham, A. Leon (1996). *Shades of Freedom: Racial Politics and Presumptions of the American Legal Process.* Oxford University Press, New York.

de Jong, Greta (2002). *A Different Day: African American Struggles for Justice in Rural Louisiana, 1900–1970.* University of North Carolina Press, Chapel Hill.

Johnson, Marilynn S. (2003). *Street Justice: A History of Police Violence in New York City.* Beacon, Boston.

Kelly, Robin (1990). *Hammer and Hoe: Alabama Communists and the Great Depression.* University of North Carolina Press, Chapel Hill.

Kennedy, Randall (1994). "The State, Criminal Law, and Racial Discrimination: A Comment." *Harvard Law Review* 107: 1255–1278.

Klarman, Michael J. (2000). "The Racial Origins of Modern Criminal Procedure." *Michigan Law Review*, (99)1: 48–97.

Klarman, Michael J. (2002). "Is the Supreme Court Sometimes Irrelevant? Race and the Southern Criminal Justice System in the 1940s." *Journal of American History* 89: 119–153.

Klarman, Michael J. (2004). *From Jim Crow to Civil Rights: The Supreme Court and the Struggle for Racial Equality.* Oxford University Press, New York.

Kluger, Richard (1977). *Simple Justice: The History of* Brown v. Board of Education. Alfred A. Knopf, New York.

Korstad, Robert (2003). *Civil Rights Unionism: Tobacco Workers and the Struggle for Democracy in the Mid-Twentieth-Century South.* University of North Carolina Press, Chapel Hill.

Lau, Peter F., ed. (2004). *From the Grassroots to the Supreme Court:* Brown v. Board of Education *and American Democracy.* Duke University Press, Durham.

Lichtenstein, Alex C. (1996). *Twice the Work of Free Labor: The Political Economy of Convict Labor in the New South.* Verso, London.

López, Ian F. H. (2009). "Post-Racial Racism: Crime Control and Racial Stratification in the Age of Obama." http://ssrn.com/abstract=1418212(last accessed September 28, 2012).

Lynch, John (1915). *The Facts of Reconstruction.* Neale, New York.

Mack, Kenneth W. (1999). "Law, Society, Identity and the Making of the Jim Crow South: Travel and Segregation on Tennessee Railroads, 1875–1905." *Law and Social Inquiry* 24: 377–409.

Mack, Kenneth W. (2005). "Rethinking Civil Rights Lawyering and Politics in the Era before 'Brown.'" *Yale Law Journal* 115: 256–354.

Mack, Kenneth W. (2006). "Law and Mass Politics in the Making of the Civil Rights Lawyer." *Journal of American History* 93: 37–62.

Mack, Kenneth W. (2009). "Bringing the Law Back into the History of the Civil Rights Movement." *Law and History Review* 27: 657–679.

MacLean, Nancy (2006). *Freedom is Not Enough: The Opening of the American Work Place.* Harvard University Press, Cambridge.

Magnum, Charles S. (1940). *The Legal Status of the Negro.* University of North Carolina Press, Chapel Hill.

Mancini, Matthew (1996). *One Dies Get Another: Convict Leasing in the American South, 1866–1928.* University of South Carolina Press, Columbia.

Manza, Jeff and Uggen, Christopher (2006). *Locked Out: Felon Disenfranchisement and American Democracy.* Oxford University Press, New York.

Maslow, Will and Robison, Joseph (1953). "Civil Rights Legislation and the Fight for Equality, 1862–1952." *University of Chicago Law Review* 20: 363–413.

Mathews, J.M. (1911). "Review: Race Distinctions in American Law." *American Political Science Review* (5)4: 651–653.

McGuire, Danielle L. (2004). "'It Was Like All of Us Had Been Raped': Sexual Violence, Community Mobilization, and the African American Freedom Struggle." *Journal of American History* (91)3: 906–931.

McMillen, Neil (1990). *Dark Journey: Black Mississippians in the Age of Jim Crow.* University of Illinois Press, Urbana.

Minchin, Thomas (2001). *The Color of Work: The Struggle for Civil Rights in the Southern Paper Industry, 1945–1980.* University of North Carolina Press, Chapel Hill.

Morris, Aldon D. (1984). *The Origins of the Civil Rights Movement: Black Communities Organizing for Change.* Free Press, New York.

Muhammad, Khalil G. (2010). *The Condemnation of Blackness: Race, Crime, and the Making of Modern Urban America.* Harvard University Press, Cambridge.

Myrdal, Gunnar (1944 [1962]). *An American Dilemma: The Negro Problem and Modern Democracy.* Harper, New York.

Nieman, Donald (1989). "Black Political Power and Criminal Justice: Washington County, Texas, 1868–1884." *Journal of Southern History* 55: 391–420.

Page, Thomas N. (1904). *The Negro: The Southerner's Problem.* Scribner's, New York.

Payne, Charles (1995). *I've Got the Light of Freedom: The Organizing Tradition and the Mississippi Freedom Struggle.* University of California Press, Berkeley.

Penningroth, Dylan (2003). *The Claims of Kinfolk: African American Property and Community in the Nineteenth-Century South.* University of North Carolina Press, Chapel Hill.

Provine, Doris M. (2007). *Unequal Under Law: Race in the War on Drugs.* University of Chicago Press, Chicago.

Rabinowitz, Howard N. (1978). *Race Relations in the Urban South, 1865–1890.* Oxford University Press, New York.

Rabinowitz, Howard N. (1988). "More than the Woodward Thesis: Assessing the Strange Career of Jim Crow." *Journal of American History* 75: 843–856.

Rable, George C. (1985). "The South and the Politics of Antilynching Legislation, 1920–1940." *Journal of Southern History* 51: 201–220.

Rhodes, James (1920). *History of the United States from the Compromise of 1850 to the McKinley-Bryan Campaign of 1896.* Macmillan, New York.

Robinson, Charles F. (2003). *Dangerous Liaisons: Sex and Love in the Segregated South.* University of Arkansas Press, Fayetteville.

Schultz, Mark (2005). *The Rural Face of White Supremacy: Beyond Jim Crow.* University of Illinois Press, Urbana.

Sinclair, William A. (1905). *The Aftermath of Slavery: A Study of the Condition and Environment of the American Negro.* Small, Boston.

Smith, J. Douglas (2002). *Managing White Supremacy: Race, Politics, and Citizenship in Jim Crow Virginia.* University of North Carolina Press, Chapel Hill.

Stanley, Amy Dru (1998). *From Bondage to Contract: Wage Labor, Marriage, and the Market in the Age of Slave Emancipation.* Cambridge University Press, New York.

Stephenson, Gilbert (1910) *Race Distinctions in American Law.* D. Appleton, New York.

Tuck, Stephen (2010). *We Ain't What We Ought To Be: The Black Freedom Struggle from Emancipation to Obama.* Harvard University Press, Cambridge.

Tushnet, Mark V. (1987). *The NAACP's Legal Strategy against Segregated Education: 1925–1959.* University of North Carolina Press, Chapel Hill.

Wacquant, Loïc (2002). "From Slavery to Mass Incarceration: Rethinking the 'race question' in the US." *New Left Review* 13: 41–60.

Waldrep, Christopher (1998). *Roots of Disorder: Race and Criminal Justice in the American South, 1817–1880.* University of Illinois Press, Urbana.

Waldrep, Christopher (2008). *African Americans Confront Lynching: Strategies of Resistance from the Civil War to the Civil Rights Era.* Rowman and Littlefield, Lanham.

Weeks, Stephen B. (1894). "The History of Negro Suffrage in the South." *Political Science Quarterly* (9)4: 671–703.

Wells, Ida B. (1894). *A Red Record: Tabulated Statistics and Alleged Causes of Lynchings in the United States, 1892–1893–1894.* Donohue and Henneberry, Chicago.

Welke, Barbara Y. (2001). *Recasting American Liberty: Gender, Race, Law, and the Railroad Revolution.* Cambridge University Press, New York.

Williamson, Joel (1965). *After Slavery: The Negro in South Carolina during Reconstruction, 1861–1877.* University of North Carolina Press, Chapel Hill.

Woodward, C. Vann (1974 [1955]). *The Strange Career of Jim Crow.* Oxford University Press, New York.

Zangrando, Robert L. (1980). *The NAACP Crusade Against Lynching, 1909–1950.* Temple University Press, Philadelphia.

Chapter Ten

Women's Legal History

Felice Batlan

Over the past three decades, the field of women's legal history has been slowly coming to fruition. Yet only recently was the first volume of essays solely devoted to women's legal history published (Boisseau, 2011). This is at least some indication that women's legal history is slowly but steadily moving from the margins to the center of the field. A number of themes in recent women's legal history scholarship include: how gender constructed ideological categories affecting judicial interpretation and legislative action, how law has denied full citizenship to women, how women functioned as legal actors throughout history, and how gender and race were deeply intertwined.

Although scholars of women's legal history employ different methodologies, they tend to draw upon social history, departing from an analysis that sees law as primarily generated by appellate courts, treatise writers, and the elite bar. Instead, they use a multiplicity of primary sources to try to understand how different iterations of law shaped gender and how gender was constitutive of law. Furthermore, some of these scholars focus on explicating stories of the oppressed. Yet who constitutes the oppressed becomes complicated, especially when race, class, and gender are analyzed. Likewise law could act as a powerful means of social control used to enforce gender norms, contributing to and shaping patriarchy and women's oppression. Simultaneously law could empower some women and women themselves used law as a means to control others. Women's legal history frequently centers these constitutive ironies, emphasizing how law allowed women to be agents while constricting their agency. Historians of women also

A Companion to American Legal History, First Edition.
Edited by Sally E. Hadden and Alfred L. Brophy.
© 2013 John Wiley & Sons Ltd. Published 2021 by John Wiley & Sons Ltd.

challenge the periodization of traditional U.S. legal history, querying how great events such as the Revolution, the ratification of the Fourteenth Amendment, and the New Deal actually affected women's lives. Some scholarship creates declension narratives, arguing that these transformative events decreased equality and freedom for women as a whole. Thus the periodization of women's legal history is frequently dramatically different from mainstream legal history.

The Colonial Period

Any understanding of women's legal history and its underlying debates requires recognizing coverture's central role. Coverture, a legal concept inherited from England, removed a woman's separate legal identity upon marriage. As a feme covert, a wife was unable to contract in her own name, own property, sue, make a will, or claim her own wages. When married, a woman's property became her husband's. Upon widowhood, however, a feme covert was transformed back into a feme sole. Scholars studying women in the colonial era frequently focus upon coverture and whether it actually prevented women from participating in the economy, how women used a variety of legal forums to maneuver around coverture, and the role of widows. This literature demonstrates significant variation in women's legal status from colony to colony which was the result of ideological, social, economic, and religious diversity.

An older body of scholarship saw the colonial period as a "golden age" for women, in which women had more freedom than they would have after the Revolution. These scholars claimed that coverture was seldom fully enforced (Morris, 1930; Beard, 1946; Dexter; 1924). More recent scholarship argues that this older literature is not nuanced enough. Deborah Rosen's groundbreaking work, *Courts and Commerce* (1997), analyzes legal documents from colonial New York and concludes that coverture severely disabled women. As the colonial era progressed and as contracts became more important, restrictions on women's market and legal activities increased. Nonetheless, women still participated as legal actors in many different forums. For example, women used more informal legal methods to enforce legal claims such as petitioning governors. Doing so was inexpensive, and allowed flexible outcomes because governors were not bound by coverture and the common law. Additionally, petitions corresponded with gender ideology as women pleaded for relief rather than asserting rights. However, as the legal system became more formalized during the eighteenth century, the ability to claim petitionary justice and maneuver around the common law declined.

Examining colonial era Connecticut, Cornelia Dayton, in *Women Before the Bar* (1995), finds that Puritan ideology's emphasis on each individual's obedience to God resulted in punishment of men for abuses of power and the equal application of law to men and women for moral violations. Women used courts to sue over slander, inheritances, and debts. Deserted women brought divorce petitions and courts seriously considered women's charges of rape. Like Rosen's declension narrative, Dayton posits that women's access to courts decreased as the importation of English law occurred and legal formality increased.

Other historians, such as Marlynn Salmon in *Women and the Law of Property in Early America* (1986), have found considerable variance in the enforcement of coverture. At times courts upheld married women's contracts when their husbands approved them or when wives acted as agents for husbands. A few colonies had feme sole trader statutes permitting married women to own businesses. Chancery courts, where they existed, were more hospitable to women's claims and tempered coverture through the use of trusts (Virginia, Carolinas). Similarly Linda Sturtz, in *Within Her Power* (2002), finds that some husbands gave powers of attorney to their wives before departing on journeys, enabling women to manage businesses and appear in court. Yet whether and how coverture functioned depended greatly on local and regional factors.

Significant debate also surrounds the condition and role of widows. Colonial women were frequently widowed, especially in the South, and historians focus upon how much agency widows possessed and their material conditions. Once again, an older generation of historians found that widows exercised significant power – so much so that historian Edmund Morgan labeled Virginia a "widowarchy" (Morgan, 1975: 407–408). Recently, historians have challenged this thesis, finding that many widows had scant knowledge of family businesses and that as the colonial period progressed what power widows possessed declined. Rosen argues that urban widows faced particular hardships like low wages and poverty. Widows who did inherit property were not powerful economic and legal actors. Rather the law forced them to conserve their property for future generations of men. Salmon likewise emphasizes that widows seldom maintained their standard of living. Unable to support their families, many widows (given the opportunity) quickly remarried.

In contrast to Salmon and Rosen, some historians have found that southern widows often owned and managed considerable property, behaving as savvy legal actors. Vivian Bruce Conger, in *The Widows' Might* (2009), finds women who refused to remarry in order to "lead independent and financially secure lives" (Conger, 2009: 5). Conger provides evidence that widows managed plantations, shops, and taverns, manipulating law to their benefit. Moreover husbands' wills often named their wives as executors and women appeared in courts, proving wills, presenting estate accounts, and recovering, or paying debts.

Although scholarship on colonial women offers conflicting views, few would still argue that it was a golden age for women. Women functioned at law's margins, often manipulating coverture's disabilities. Moreover, as the colonial period progressed, women lost much legal maneuvering room. Such losses stemmed from secularization, the adoption of British common law, the growing commercial economy, and the decline of chancery courts.

As colonial women attempted to manipulate coverture in order to own property, other women were property. Several scholars have addressed how gender and race functioned together in the creation of slavery. Kathleen Brown's *Good Wives, Nasty Wenches, and Anxious Patriarchs* (1996) examines how Virginia's slave laws became gendered and racialized. By the second half of the seventeenth century, laws associated white women with domestic work, while African women were constructed as suited for fieldwork. In 1662, laws made slavery inherited from the mother rather than the father. This made enslaved women particularly vulnerable to sexual assault by white men who no longer feared the potential of being named in paternity cases. After Bacon's rebellion of 1676, white women's sexuality was carefully controlled while providing white men continued sexual access to women of African descent. As would be the case throughout the South, slaves were unable to marry legally.

Yet slavery in the South and slavery in New England looked quite different. Catherine Adams and Elizabeth Pleck's *Love of Freedom* (2010) explores the legal framework and constitutive ironies shaping free and enslaved Black women's lives in New England. In contrast to the South, slaves could legally marry in many New England states and in a bold historical move the authors demonstrate that coverture affected free, freed, and enslaved women. For example, it prevented married enslaved and freed women from suing for their own or their children's freedom. Legally, the marriages of Black free and freed people looked very similar to those of whites. In another constitutive irony enslaved and freed women longed for domestic lives of gendered norms that paradoxically, through coverture, also restricted their freedom.

The Revolution that Was Not

Given the founders' belief in natural rights, representation, and liberty, one would expect that women following the American Revolution would have gained legal rights and that coverture would be abolished. Yet the Revolutionary era did not usher in any significant change in women's legal rights. As a number of scholars such as Barbara Welke (2010) emphasize, the founders did not forget about women in an act of benign neglect; rather they intentionally excluded women from the Revolution's legal affects.

Debate continues among scholars regarding precisely how the Revolution affected women. Linda Kerber (1980), Mary Beth Norton (1980), Ruth Bloch (1978) and Carol Berkin (2005) have focused upon women's increased presence in the public sphere and the role of the Republican

Mother, who was responsible for raising sons as virtuous citizens. Yet Republican Motherhood fused women's citizenship to maternity and home, and women's relationship to the state was mediated through sons and husbands. Linda Kerber's *No Constitutional Right to be Ladies* (1998) posits that republican virtue, a necessity for citizenship, was a masculine trait based upon independence. Women, economically and legally dependent upon men, could not possess such seeming autonomy. Sandra VanBurkleo (2001) writes that the Revolution had negative effects on women's legal status as an enhanced domestic sovereignty became lodged in men. Bloch (2007) likewise argues that idealization of the family and an emergent idea of family privacy increased legal toleration of wife-beating. Indeed as Barbara Welke (2010) asserts in *Law and the Borders of Belonging in the Long Nineteenth Century United States*, post-Revolutionary laws enshrined privileges of white able-bodied men, allowing them to solidify their property rights in women, slaves, and children.

The most dramatic legal change for women after the Revolution was the increased ability to divorce. Norma Basch writes in *Framing American Divorce*, "No sooner, it seems, did Americans create a rationale for dissolving the bonds of empire than they set about creating rules for dissolving the bonds of matrimony" (Basch, 2001: 21). Divorce was a woman's remedy for a failed marriage, whereas husbands often simply abandoned wives. The women who fared best financially in divorces were those who already had some financial independence, as divorce freed woman from coverture. Yet divorced women, like widowed women, often faced poverty. Moreover, the space that the Revolution provided for divorce quickly faded.

Married Women's Property Acts

In women's legal history, the 1840s are a watershed decade. Two events of extraordinary significance occurred – passage of the first Married Women's Property Acts (MWPA) and the Seneca Falls convention. MWPAs were state statutes that eroded coverture by allowing married women to maintain some separate property. Norma Basch's *In the Eyes of the Law* (1982) demonstrates that MPWAs were not passed to increase women's equality and did not revolutionize women's legal status. Basch explains that legislatures passed MWPAs primarily to protect debtors, and as a reaction against the common law towards codification. Early MWPAs were a response to economic boom and bust cycles, protecting a wife's property from a husband's creditors. Yet by the 1860s women's rights activists lobbied for the expansion of MWPAs to include the ability for married women to retain their earnings, bring suit in their own name, be joint guardians of children, and have equalized intestacy shares. As Basch and Reva Siegel (1994) demonstrate, however, courts often refused to enforce MWPAs and coverture lingered well into the twentieth century.

Historians have also begun positioning the first generation of women's rights activists as legal actors. Nancy Isenberg in *Sex and Citizenship in Antebellum America* (1998) sees women activists as creating a cogent and sophisticated critique of law, rights, and citizenship. Imbued with abolitionist sentiments, women's rights advocates demanded self-ownership which encompassed control over their bodies, ending coverture, equal parental rights, the right to jury service, protection against domestic violence, and suffrage. As Barbara Welke writes of these women, "[L]aw offered a vehicle for making their claims comprehensible . . . they spoke in terms of law because law was the idiom of the nation" (Welke, 2010: 106).

The Post-Civil War Suffrage Movement

Although the post-Civil War women's suffrage movement is a centerpiece in women's history (and this chapter does not explore this rich body of scholarship), it is not prominent in mainstream legal histories. In "She the People" Siegel writes, "Today, women's struggle for enfranchisement plays no role in the ways we understand or interpret the Constitution even though the quest for the vote spanned generations and provoked the most sustained dialogue about women's position in the constitutional community that the nation has ever conducted" (2002: 950). The constitutional story regarding suffrage following the Civil War begins with the purposed Fourteenth and Fifteenth Amendments and the ruptures within the suffrage movement over support for them.

Women's historians have long discussed the anger of suffragists regarding ratification of the Fourteenth and Fifteenth Amendments as they seeming only provided men with the vote. Some women's suffrage advocates embraced racial equality and supported the Amendments while others appeared to sympathize with white racists' opposition to the Amendments (Kraditor, 1965). Whatever their position, women's rights advocates after their passage used the Amendments in affirming women's full citizenship, including suffrage. Ellen DuBois in *Woman Suffrage and Women's Rights* (1998) traces the jurisprudential contours of this constitutional strategy including the Supreme Court's rejection of this argument in *Minor v. Happersett* (1874). The Supreme Court's rebuff was a turning point for the suffrage movement. Now, the best hope for women's enfranchisement was a federal constitutional amendment as well as state referendums and amendments which would provide women with the right to vote.

As advocates began a seemingly unending series of campaigns, they were constantly confronted with anti-suffragists' arguments, including that they were already represented by husbands who cast votes for the entire household, that suffrage would harm marriages by bringing the political into the domestic, and that women's suffrage was a state's rights issue. Opponents further pressed that voting violated gender norms, upset the domestic sphere where women naturally belonged, and would distract women from their motherly and wifely duties. Suffrage, in fact, would re-situate women in an unmediated relationship with the state and disrupt ideas of marital unity in which the wife's legal identity was subsumed by her husband.

During the decade before the Nineteenth Amendment was passed, suffragists engaged in civil disobedience, staged suffrage parades, and laid siege to President Wilson. Although the Nineteenth Amendment was a victory, women's historians are divided over its significance. As Siegel (2002) underscores, courts and legislatures could interpret the Nineteenth Amendment either broadly or narrowly. A narrow reading saw the Amendment as solely related to the vote. An expansive interpretation viewed it as providing full political citizenship for women, including the right to hold political office and sit on juries. Courts, however, consistently adopted a narrow interpretation.

Women and the Practice of Law

There is a growing literature on the first generation of women lawyers and their struggles to be admitted to law schools and bars. Scholarship by Karen Morello, Virginia Drachman, Barbara Babcock, and Jill Norgren presents a picture of the obstacles women faced becoming lawyers and their difficulties creating financially viable law practices. These works also demonstrate the significant role that women lawyers played in suffrage and other reform movements.

Morello's *The Invisible Bar* (1986) excavates women's long history of engaging in the practice of law, even if they were not always identified as lawyers. Starting in the seventeenth century, there were a few women who offered legal services or who represented their own interests in court. In part, women could do this because the practice of law had not yet been entirely professionalized nor was it state regulated. Drachman's *Sisters in Law* (1998) and *Women Lawyers and the Origins of Professional Identity in America* (1993) show that after the Civil War small numbers of women began to become lawyers due to increasing opportunities for women to attend college and the creation of new law schools. The appearance of women lawyers was radical as it ruptured the idea that women belonged in the domestic sphere and reconceptualized women's relationship to the state. Moreover, scholars generally agree that efforts to integrate law schools and the bar were coordinated with the larger women's rights movement.

Women's efforts to become lawyers generated multiple lawsuits. In *Bradwell v. Illinois* (1874), the Supreme Court made clear that the Privileges and Immunities Clause of the Fourteenth Amendment did not apply to the practice of law nor would it protect women from discrimination. State courts were likewise often unsympathetic to such claims, citing the ideology of separate spheres, natural law, custom, that women could not be lawyers because they could not vote, and coverture (even though MWPAs had supposedly dismantled coverture). After 1893, however, courts, according to Drachman, became more sympathetic to women's cases and began to discard the argument that women's admission to the bar was a purely legislative question. They also began to view separate spheres as a relic, and rejected the understanding that an attorney was a public officer.

After admission to the bar, women lawyers confronted and constructed their similarities to and differences from male lawyers. Drachman's *Women Lawyers* examines a remarkable cache of letters from the Equity Club – a correspondence club for women attorneys (1887–1890). Women lawyers struggled with how they could be ladies and lawyers, when the essence of being a lawyer involved performances of masculinity. Early women lawyers also debated whether it was appropriate for them to try cases in the courtroom – a traditional bastion of masculinity.

Norgren's *Belva Lockwood: The Woman Who Would Be President* (2007) follows the life of one woman who gained admittance to the bar, despite many obstacles. Denied her law school diploma, Lockwood agitated until she received it. Initially refused admission to the all-male D.C. bar, she eventually gained the right to practice there. In 1879, Lockwood persuaded Congress to pass a bill that prohibited discrimination against female attorneys in regard to federal bar admission. Norgren writes that this was the first federal statute to prohibit discrimination against women. In 1880, Lockwood became the first woman to argue before the Supreme Court. Ultimately, she ran for president, dividing the suffrage movement and earning her criticism from Susan B. Anthony. Likewise Clara Foltz, an early women lawyer whose life Barbara Babcock explores in *Woman Lawyer* (2011) demonstrates the enormous difficulties women lawyers confronted. Lockwood and Foltz continually stood on the precipice of financial ruin. A theme that emerges from these works, and which deserves further attention, is that even when legal barriers to women practicing law fell, market mechanisms remained which seriously hampered women lawyers' success.

Kenneth Mack's "A Social History of Everyday Practice: Sadie T.M. Alexander and the Incorporation of Black Women into the American Legal Profession" (2002) addresses how race, gender, and class functioned in lawyers' professional lives by examining the life of Sadie Alexander, Pennsylvania's first African-American woman attorney. Rather than writing a story of the exclusion of Black women from the legal profession, Mack focuses on how Alexander's practice and class position allowed her to gain power and prestige within first the local bar and then a wider arena. Mack concludes that the first generation of African-American women lawyers accepted low-status women's legal work, like family law and trusts and estates. In contrast, the second generation protested their exclusion from elite legal institutions on grounds of gender and race discrimination.

Mary Jane Mossman's *The First Women Lawyers* (2006) presents a transnational study of the first generation of women lawyers in Canada, Britain, the U.S., New Zealand, India, and Continental Europe. She points out that although women were admitted to the bar in the U.S. quite early, U.S. women still would be fighting to integrate elite law schools long after women in other countries had achieved such victories. Mossman also challenges historians' assessment that women lawyers were involved deeply in the broader women's rights movement either in the U.S. or elsewhere. Rather, some women lawyers were "inclined to eschew connections with the women's movement in favour of strictly professional identities" (Mossman, 2006: 21).

All of the above authors demonstrate how women's struggles to be admitted to the profession were often supported by powerful male allies. In contrast, after women were admitted to the bar, there is little evidence that male lawyers who were not relatives were especially supportive as women attorneys attempted to build their practices. Yet why this pattern emerges cries out for further study and explanation.

The Progressive Era through the New Deal

The narratives told by mainstream legal historians and women's historians regarding the Progressive Era significantly differ. Legal historians generally view legal progressives as launching a powerful critique of legal formalism. In such narratives women, excluded from the judiciary and the professoriate of law schools, are not considered legal progressives and do not play a significant role. In contrast, for women's historians, the progressive period is a high water mark for women's reform activities, which were often inseparable from legal reform. Women's organizations supported almost every major reform that occurred during the progressive period, from zoning, pure food, truancy, and labor legislation, to the creation of juvenile courts, probation, and prison reform. Long before legal luminary Roscoe Pound called for a sociological jurisprudence, women reformers were already engaged in it (Batlan, 2006, 2010).

One of the key areas of progressive reform involved labor legislation and as Kathryn Kish Sklar's *Florence Kelley and the Nation's Work: The Rise of Women's Political Culture, 1830–1900* (1995) elucidates, Florence Kelley was a crucial figure involved in legal reform who studied the conditions of labor, drafted and lobbied for various labor laws, and then defended such laws from constitutional challenge. Kelley was a radically original legal thinker and through her position as Illinois' first factory inspector, she further enforced and defended from constitutional challenge laws which prohibited child labor and limited the hours of women's employment. Later, as head of the National Consumers League (NCL), Kelley was involved in some of the most important Supreme Court cases of the twentieth century which involved the ability of the state to regulate labor.

A host of scholars, including Julie Novkov in *Constituting Workers, Protecting Women* (2001), have demonstrated how gender was central to whether the courts would uphold labor regulation under the state's police power or strike it down as a violation of the Fourteenth Amendment. The 1908 *Muller* case tested Oregon's new women's labor laws, and the NCL directed the case on appeal. Scholars including Nancy Woloch (1996) have devoted considerable attention to the *Muller* brief written for the NCL by Louis Brandeis and Josephine Goldmark. They point to the brief as the first work of sociological jurisprudence as it contained limited legal arguments and close to a hundred pages of "facts" from various experts about the danger of overwork for women, especially to their reproductive health. Sybil Lipschultz in "Hours and Wages: The Gendering of Labor Standards in America" (1996) argues that the *Muller* brief's arguments which rested on women's potential maternity was the result of male attorneys who used the NCL's data but refashioned their arguments. Lipschultz's conclusion may, however, underestimate the power and legal acumen of Florence Kelley and other women at the NCL.

Following *Muller*, the NCL intensified its study of women's labor and distributed such information widely so that lawyers could use it in legal briefs. From 1911 to 1923, Novkov argues, "the main [constitutional] focus was on women's legislation as the courts ... addressed the various justifications for protecting female laborers. In a reversal of the earlier pattern, the cases involving general measures gradually became a sideshow to the main event: consideration of the legitimacy of limits on women's hours and minimum wages" (Novkov, 2001: 135). Legal historians seldom connect *Muller* to the New Deal's constitutional revolution, although the Supreme Court's decision in *West Coast Hotel* (1937), which upheld a minimum wage law for men and women, must be understood not as a dramatic legal revolution but rather as the slow expansion of women's protective legislation to men. Likewise, given the central role of the NCL in constitutional history, it is quite remarkable that, with the exception of Landon Storrs' *Civilizing Capitalism* (2000), no major scholarship explores its work and impact.

As concepts of motherhood and reproduction played significant roles in constructing women as needing protective labor legislation, scholars such as Linda Gordon (1990, 1994), Theda Skocpol (1995), and Robyn Muncy (1991) have labeled some Progressive Era women's reform organizations "maternalist." Such organizations attempted to extend women's domestic roles into public life by lobbying for legislation and services, which primarily benefited women and children. As explored in Gordon's *Women, the State, and Welfare* (1990), elite and middle-class women reformers in the late nineteenth and early twentieth century created a political and public space for themselves, using a universalized concept of motherhood that expanded the domestic to include a plethora of reforms.

Maternalism played a major role in the creation of multiple types of legal institutions. Estelle Freedman' *Maternal Justice* (1996) examines middle class women's roles in creating and staffing institutions for juvenile delinquents including courts, probation departments, and reformatories. Where such institutions provided power and authority to middle class women, they simultaneously made working class girls and women the subject of social control. Historians, including Mary Odem in *Delinquent Daughters* (1995), discuss how juvenile courts labeled delinquent and sent to reformatories girls from working class families who engaged in sexual experimentation or even popular amusements. Thus middle class women's new found positions within the state had complicated ramifications for the poor and working class who were now subject to new types of disciplinary power.

While mainstream legal history celebrates the New Deal as a time of momentous transformation, for some women's historians it is more ambiguous. The most famous and generous of New Deal programs such as the Works Progress Administration hired few women. What constituted work was built primarily around traditionally male jobs such as construction. Moreover, the federal government allowed only one federally funded job per family resulting in termination of some women's employment. In addition, women who had been brought into the government during the progressive period, such as those in the Children's Bureau, lost power. In *Pitied but not Entitled* (1994), Gordon remarks that as long as welfare dealt with the poor and marginalized it was fine for women to be in control. It was, however, an entirely new matter when it became a central focus of the federal government.

Some women's historians have been particularly critical of the Social Security Act of 1935 and have uncovered its gendered dimensions. Old age pensions and unemployment compensation, premised upon insuring male wage earners, were generous and rights based. In contrast, Aid to Dependent Children (ADC) was based on Progressive Era mothers' pensions, used a means-tested welfare model, made morality-based claims, provided stingy benefits, and used case workers to supervise recipients. Suzanne Mettler's *Dividing Citizens* (1998) concludes that New Deal welfare programs created a dual track of citizenship. White men's federal citizenship was centralized, standardized, and part of the liberal state. Women and minorities had local or state citizenship which was administered with discretion. Mettler also challenges scholars' understanding of the New Deal as a constitutional revolution, arguing that it had little such affect for women. New and expanded concepts of interstate commerce still excluded women who were primarily housewives, domestics, and part-time workers. She concludes that this exclusion was intentional as policy makers sought to undergird the norm of a male family breadwinner. Like Gordon, Mettler also recognizes that there was no strong organized women's movement that could fight for the interests of women as there was in the Progressive Era.

The Revolution that Was: Second Wave Feminism

The importance of second wave feminism to legal change cannot be overestimated. As Linda Kerber writes, only in the 1970s would the blueprint set forth by the founders be overturned regarding the relationship between women, men, and the state (2002: 98). Historians have long recognized that the Civil Rights Movement was a significant impetus for second wave feminism. Yet, until recently, scholars viewed the feminist movement as predominately composed of white women. Over the last decade, however, historians have begun to explore more fully the relationship between the Civil Rights Movement, second wave feminism, and the significant contributions of African-American women lawyers and legal activists. It is now impossible to narrate the story of second wave legal feminism without discussing Pauli Murray, an African-American activist and lawyer, who created much of the legal architecture of the feminist agenda.

As a law student in the 1940s, Murray began developing the paradigm of "Jane Crow," to refer to the structural legal discrimination that women faced. Later Murray's goal was to create a momentous case like *Brown v. Board of Education* (1954) that would apply the Fourteenth Amendment to state discrimination against women, something the courts had consistently failed to do since *Bradwell* and *Minor*. Linda Kerber explains in *No Constitutional Right* that the creation by President Kennedy in 1961 of the President's Commission on the Status of Women (PCSW) was a turning point for the law's treatment of women. Murray's Jane Crow analysis was included in the PCSW report, which highlighted how sex discrimination was embedded in law permeating everything from divorce, credit, and employment to access to government benefits. The report prompted states to engage in their own surveys of women's legal disabilities. Murray's Fourteenth Amendment analysis provided a clear link between the Civil Rights Movement and the Women's Movement (Mayeri, 2011).

During the same period, Title VII also became a focus of attention for feminists. Title VII was intended by Congress to combat race discrimination in employment. Sex discrimination was added only at the last minute. John Skrentny writes in *The Minority Rights Revolution* (2002), that "sex" was added to Title VII by Congressman Howard Smith to *prevent* its passage. Such a tactic had successfully thwarted other civil rights bills and many in Congress found the inclusion of women ridiculous. Skrentny further argues that feminists did not vocally advocate for Title VII. Unlike Skrentny, Nancy MacLean in *Freedom is Not Enough* (2008) gives a greater role to women's activism regarding Title VII. Congressman Martha Griffith and other female House members took the opportunity to raise the issue of sex discrimination in congressional debates. Serena Mayeri, in "Constitutional Choices: Feminism and the Historical Dynamics of Change" (2004), emphasizes the role played by the National Women's Party and white segregationists who supported the amendment. In her account, the NWP argued that without the addition of sex to Title VII, white, Christian women would be left without protection from discrimination.

The passage of Title VII heralded significant change. Since the 1920s, women activists had been split between arguing for complete legal equality, and supporting women's protective labor legislation. MacLean writes that "Title VII cut the Gordian Knot" by doing away with protective legislation, promising women equality with men in the work place, and allowing women to define themselves as full breadwinners (MacLean, 2008: 118).

Title VII's enforcement, however, depended upon the Equal Employment Opportunity Commission (EEOC) and it was not particularly interested in bringing sex discrimination cases. Under the guidance of Pauli Murray, and in response to the need for an organization to exert pressure on Congress and the EEOC, the National Organization for Women (NOW), modeled after the NAACP, was founded as a civil rights organization for women. By 1968, the EEOC began cooperating with NOW, issuing guidelines and decisions in connection with sex discrimination. *Freedom is Not Enough* provides an excellent account of feminist action surrounding Title VII and how the EEOC developed sex discrimination law.

Susan Hartmann, in *The Other Feminists* (1998), explores how women advocates within the ACLU, including long-time activists and lawyers Dorothy Kennon, Pauli Murray, and Suzanne Post, pressured the ACLU to make women's rights a priority. Murray, along with others, convinced the ACLU Board to create the Women's Rights Project (WRP) with Ruth Bader Ginsberg and Feigen Fasteau as co-heads. The WRP would become the most active litigator for gender equity. Hartman's fascinating work also documents how feminist organizations funded their legal battles.

A number of works pay particular attention to the long list of cases in the 1970s which were brought under the Fourteenth Amendment to challenge laws that discriminated on the basis of sex. Joan Hoff's *Law, Gender, and Injustice* (1991) analyzes many U.S. Supreme Court groundbreaking cases from the 1970s, when the Court first recognized that the Fourteenth Amendment encompassed sex, to the court later applying "intermediate scrutiny" to issues involving gender. Mayeri's, *Reasoning From Race*, examines how feminists borrowed from and built upon the jurisprudence of race discrimination in constructing their own legal arguments and Kerber's *No Constitutional Right* focuses on suits about jury and military service – two areas from which women were historically excluded and which she posits as foundational obligations of citizenship.

New scholarship further corrects assumptions that feminist litigation was a white, elite, top-down endeavor directed by a handful of lawyers. Carrie Baker's *The Women's Movement against Sexual Harassment* (2008) explores how women on a grassroots level began articulating their experiences of sexual harassment which were translated by feminist lawyers into legal claims. A diverse group of actors collectively combated sexual harassment. African-American women brought many of the first claims, middle-class white women founded organizations devoted to fighting sexual harassment, and working class women, especially those breaking into male dominated industries, fought alongside their unions, to attack hostile work environments. The movement against sexual harassment drew from the Civil Rights Movement, the sexual revolution, the lesbian and gay rights movement, and the labor movement, combining litigation, collective action, education, and consciousness raising. These actions ultimately convinced courts that sexual harassment was a violation of Title VII. Baker argues that this vibrant social movement eventually bureaucratized and lost sight of feminist goals.

Deborah Dinner (2010) also situates pregnancy discrimination litigation within the context of grassroots and union activity. *Cleveland v. Board of Education* (1974), which challenged school policies prohibiting women from teaching during pregnancy, arose from the actions of feminists within the American Federation of Teachers (AFT). In challenging such leaves, the AFT combined collective bargaining, bringing actions through administrative agencies, and ultimately litigation. Dinner, like Baker, exposes the actors behind the AFT's actions such as Marjorie Stern, chair of its Women's Right's Committee, who made the elimination of mandatory leave policies her top priority. As Dinner emphasizes, many AFT members were feminists and, at least for a short time, organized around feminist understandings of women's subordination.

Where feminists achieved remarkable victories under the Fourteenth Amendment and Title VII, one of the thorniest and most historically laden issues remained – the Equal Rights Amendment (ERA), which had been on the table since the 1920s. Mayeri's *Constitutional Choices* (2004) and *Reasoning from Race* (2011) provides fresh insights into second-wave feminist organizations' stances regarding the ERA. As she sets forth, NOW's eventual support of the ERA committed feminists to a dual constitutional strategy – litigation under the Fourteenth Amendment and advocacy for the ERA. NOW's support of the ERA alienated some labor unions and activists such as Pauli Murray, who long feared what would happen to women's hard-won protective labor legislation. Further, the more it appeared that the ERA would pass, the less pressure courts felt to apply the Fourteenth Amendment in innovative ways. Simultaneously, the more courts interpreted the Fourteenth Amendment to prohibit sex discrimination, the less perceived need there was for the ERA.

Intertwined with the feminist movement and the Civil Rights Movement was the powerful welfare rights movement and several scholars have focused on how poor women organized, became legal actors, and created new and radical claims to citizenship. Permilla Nadasen's *Welfare Warriors* (2005) and Felicia Kornbluh's *The Battle for Welfare Rights* (2007) build upon Cloward and Piven's *Poor People's Movements* (1979), presenting sophisticated and gendered accounts of the welfare rights movement of the 1960s and 1970s. In 1966, African-American women activists, many who had worked in the Civil Rights Movement, created the National Welfare Rights Organization (NWRO) which staged protests, filed law suits, lobbied legislatures, exposed the often discriminatory tactics of state welfare administrators, and empowered welfare recipients to demand just treatment. In the process, these women challenged normative constructions of family, gender, sexuality, and citizenship. Likewise, Eileen Boris and Jennifer Klein (2012) write in great detail of how home health care workers spent decades trying to be included in the growing welfare state as both workers and recipients of benefits.

Of course, a crucial demand of the feminist movement was for reproductive rights and there is a vast literature on the issue. Not only were reproductive rights a central issue for second-wave feminism, but the history of reproductive rights took on added importance as courts in the 1980s and 1990s began to dismantle the framework created by *Roe v. Wade* (1973). Although the history of reproductive rights is beyond the scope of this chapter, Linda Gordon's *Woman's Body, Woman's Right* (1977) and *The Moral Property of Women: A History of Birth Control in America* (2007) remain canonical works as does David Garrow's massive history of reproductive rights (1994).

Recent scholarship has also begun to analyze how the feminist movement, organizations such as NWRO, and cases like *Roe* generated significant backlash. Linda Kerber in *No Constitutional Right to be Ladies* discusses the significant fear that if the ERA passed, women would be drafted into the military and placed in combat positions. ERA opponents, such as Kathleen Teague, argued that women had a constitutional right to be protected – in other words to be different from men and "treated as ladies." More generally opponents feared that the ERA would seismically shift gender norms. Beyond opposition to the ERA, conservative women rallied around other causes as well.

Sarah Barringer Gordon's *The Spirit of the Law* (2010) examines evangelical women as legal actors whose explicit agenda was opposing feminism. To them, feminism undermined the family and women's traditional roles. In 1979, Beverly LaHaye formed Concerned Women for America (CWA). CWA soon began challenging legal structures of secularism in order to protect women's traditional family roles. Again a constitutive irony existed as conservative women left home and engaged in public and legal activism, to protect women's domestic roles. The CWA claimed a membership of 500,000, and as Gordon writes, was "uniquely powerful," bringing a "new legal consciousness" to conservative women (Gordon, 2010: 134). LaHaye drew upon tradition and innovation, arguing that women's duty to god required them to engage in activism in order to defeat the agenda of organizations like NOW and Planned Parenthood. In the coming years, we can expect a spate of new works that further will explore how conservative women used the law to defeat the gains of feminism.

Conclusion

As Linda Kerber and Barbara Welke suggest, the meta-narrative of women's legal history is about how women have fought for centuries to gain full first-class citizenship. This question of citizenship animates the narratives of a great deal of recent scholarship on women and the law and brings to the fore the question of what constellation of rights and obligations create full citizenship. Throughout U.S. history, women collectively and as individual legal actors often had to make complicated choices which were constrained and which created constitutive ironies that could be subversive while simultaneously reifying traditional structures of power. Yet, as we have seen, even the most oppressed women, at certain moments, functioned as legal actors. There was never a time when women in one way or another were not legal actors. When we write women into the narratives of legal history, the stories that we tell and their narrative arcs, at times, look dramatically different from mainstream legal history. Although each year women's legal history becomes more robust and moves increasingly into the mainstream, we can only imagine what a fully integrated legal history might look like.

References

Adams, Catherine and Pleck, Elizabeth H. (2010). *Love of Freedom: Black Women in Colonial and Revolutionary New England*. Oxford University Press, Oxford, UK.

Babcock, Barbara Allen (2011). *Woman Lawyer: The Trials of Clara Foltz*. Stanford University Press, Stanford.

Baker, Carrie N. (2008). *The Women's Movement Against Sexual Harassment*. Cambridge University Press, New York.

Basch, Norma (1982). *In the Eyes of the Law: Women, Marriage, and Property in Nineteenth Century New York*. Cornell University Press, Ithaca.

Basch, Norma (2001). *Framing American Divorce: From the Revolutionary Generation to the Victorians*. University of California Press, Berkeley and Los Angeles.

Batlan, Felice (2006). "Law and the Fabric of the Everyday: The Settlement Houses, Sociological Jurisprudence, and the Gendering of Urban Legal Culture." *Southern California Interdisciplinary Law Journal* 15: 235–284.

Batlan, Felice (2010). "Florence Kelley and the Making of Sociological Jurisprudence." In Brophy and Hamilton, eds., *The Transformation of American Legal History II*. Harvard University Press, Cambridge, MA.

Beard, Mary R. (1946). *Woman as Force in History: A Study in Traditions in Realities*. Macmillan, New York.

Berkin, Carol (2005). *Revolutionary Mothers: Women in the Struggle for American Independence*. Alfred A. Knopf, New York.

Bloch, Ruth H. (1978). "American Feminine Ideals in Transition: The Rise of the Moral Mother." *Feminist Studies* 4: 100–126.

Bloch, Ruth H. (2007). "The American Revolution, Wife Beating, and the Emergent Value of Privacy." *Early American Studies* 5: 224–251.

Boisseau, Tracey and Thomas, Tracy, eds (2011). *Feminist Legal History: Essays on Women and the Law*. New York University Press, New York.

Boris, Eileen and Klein, Jennifer (2012). *Caring for America: Home Health Workers in the Shadow of the Welfare State*. Oxford University Press, New York.

Brown, Kathleen (1996). *Good Wives, Nasty Wenches, and Anxious Patriarchs: Gender, Race, and Power in Colonial Virginia*. The University of North Carolina Press, Chapel Hill.

Cloward, Richard A. and Piven, Frances Fox (1979). *Poor People's Movements: Why They Succeed, How They Fail*. Vintage Books, New York.

Conger, Vivian Bruce (2009). *The Widows' Might*. New York University Press, New York.

Dayton, Cornelia Hughes (1995). *Women Before the Bar: Gender, Law and Society in Connecticut, 1639–1789*. University of North Carolina Press, Chapel Hill.

Dexter, Elisabeth Anthony (1924). *Colonial Women of Affairs: A Study of Women in Business and the Professions in America Before 1776*. Houghton Mifflin Company, Boston and New York.

Dinner, Deborah (2010). "Recovering the *LaFleur* Doctrine: Historicizing the Origins of Intermediate Scrutiny in the Feminist Campaign Against Pregnancy Dismissal Policies." *Yale Journal of Law and Feminism* 22: 343–406.

Drachman, Virginia G. (1993). *Women Lawyers and the Origins of Professional Identity in America*. The University of Michigan Press, Ann Arbor.

Drachman, Virginia G. (1998). *Sisters in Law: Women Lawyers in Modern American History*. Harvard University Press, Cambridge, MA.

DuBois, Ellen (1998). *Woman Suffrage and Women's Rights*. New York University Press, New York.

Freedman, Estelle B. (1996). *Maternal Justice: Miriam Van Waters and the Female Reform Tradition*. The University of Chicago Press, Chicago.

Garrow, David (1994). *Liberty and Sexuality: The Right to Privacy and the Making of Roe v. Wade*. Macmillan, New York.

Gordon, Linda (1977). *Woman's Body, Woman's Right: A Social History of Birth Control in America*. Penguin Books, New York.

Gordon, Linda, ed. (1990). *Women, the State, and Welfare*. University of Wisconsin Press, Madison.

Gordon, Linda (1994). *Pitied But Not Entitled: Single Mothers and The History of Welfare, 1890-1935*. The Free Press, New York.

Gordon, Linda (2007). *The Moral Property of Women: A History of Birth Control in America*. The University of Illinois Press, Champaign.

Gordon, Sarah Barringer (2010). *Spirit of the Law: Religious Voices and the Constitution in Modern America*. Harvard University Press, Cambridge.

Hartmann, Susan M. (1998). *The Other Feminists: Activists in the Liberal Establishment*. Yale University Press, New Haven.

Hoff, Joan (1991). *Law, Gender, and Injustice: A Legal History of U.S. Women*. New York University Press, New York.

Isenberg, Nancy (1998). *Sex and Citizenship in Antebellum America*. The University of North Carolina Press, Chapel Hill.

Kerber, Linda K. (1998). *No Constitutional Right to Be Ladies*. Hill and Wang, New York.

Kerber, Linda K. (2002 [1980]). *Women of the Republic: Intellect and Ideology in Revolutionary America*. The University of North Carolina Press, Chapel Hill.

Kornbluh, Felicia (2007). *The Battle for Welfare Rights*. University of Philadelphia Press, Philadelphia.

Kraditor, Aileen (1965). *Ideas of the Suffrage Movement, 1890-1920*. Columbia University Press, New York.

Lipschultz, Sybil (1996). "Hours and Wages: The Gendering of Labor Standards in America." *Journal of Women's History*, 8: 114–136.

Mack, Kenneth W. (2002). "A Social History of Everyday Practice: Sadie T.M. Alexander and the Incorporation of Black Women into the American Legal Profession." *Cornell Law Review* 87: 1405–1474.

MacLean, Nancy (2008). *Freedom is Not Enough: The Opening of the American Workplace*. Harvard University Press, Cambridge.

Mayeri, Serena (2004). "Constitutional Choices: Legal Feminism and the Historical Dynamics of Change." *California Law Review* 92: 755–839.

Mayeri, Serena (2011). *Reasoning From Race: Feminism, Law, and the Civil Rights Revolution*. Harvard University Press, Cambridge.

Mettler, Suzanne (1998). *Dividing Citizens: Gender and Federalism in New Deal Public Policy*. Cornell University Press, Ithaca.

Morello, Karen (1986). *The Invisible Bar: The Woman Lawyer in America 1638 to Present*. Random House, New York.

Morgan, Edmund S. (1975). *American Slavery, American Freedom*. W.W. Norton, New York.

Morris, Richard B. (1930). *Studies in the Early History of American Law, With Special Reference to the Seventeenth and Eighteenth Centuries*. Columbia University Press, New York.

Mossman, Mary Jane (2006). *The First Women Lawyers: A Comparative Study of Gender, Law and the Legal Professions*. Hart Publishing, Portland, OR.

Muncy, Robyn (1991). *Creating a Female Dominion in American Reform, 1890-1935*. Oxford University Press, New York.

Nadasen, Premilla (2005). *Welfare Warriors: The Welfare Rights Movement in the United States*. Routledge, New York.

Norgren, Jill (2007). *Belva Lockwood: The Woman Who Would Be President*. New York University Press, New York.
Norton, Mary Beth (1980). *Liberties Daughters: The Revolutionary Experience of American Women, 1750–1800*. Little, Brown and Co., New York.
Novkov, Julie (2001). *Constituting Workers, Protecting Women: Gender, Law, and Labor in the Progressive Era and New Deal Years*. The University of Michigan Press, Ann Arbor.
Odem, Mary (1995). *Delinquent Daughters: Protecting and Policing Adolescent Female Sexuality in the United States, 1885–1920*. University of North Carolina Press, Chapel Hill.
Rosen, Deborah A. (1997). *Courts and Commerce: Gender, Law, and the Market Economy in Colonial New York*. Ohio State University Press, Columbus.
Salmon, Marylynn (1986). *Women and the Law of Property in Early America*. The University of North Carolina Press, Chapel Hill.
Siegel, Reva B. (1994). "Home As Work: The First Woman's Rights Claims Concerning Wives' Household Labor, 1850–1880." *Yale Law Journal* 103: 1073–1217.
Siegel, Reva B. (2002). "She the People: The Nineteenth Amendment, Sex Equality, Federalism and the Family." *Harvard Law Review* 115: 947–1046.
Sklar, Kathryn Kish (1995). *Florence Kelley and the Nation's Work: The Rise of Women's Political Culture*. Yale University Press, New Haven.
Skocpol, Theda (1995). *Protecting Soldiers and Mothers: The Political Origins of Social Policy in the United States*. Harvard University Press, Cambridge.
Skrentny, John D. (2002). *The Minority Rights Revolution*. The Belknap Press of Harvard University Press, Cambridge.
Storrs, Landon R.Y. (2000). *Civilizing Capitalism: The National Consumers' League, Women's Activism, and Labor Standards in the New Deal Era*. University of North Carolina Press, Chapel Hill.
Sturtz, Linda L. (2002). *Within Her Power: Propertied Women in Colonial Virginia*. Routledge, New York.
VanBurkleo, Sandra F. (2001). *"Belonging to the World": Women's Rights and Constitutional Culture*. Oxford University Press, New York.
Welke, Barbara Y. (2010). *Law and the Borders of Belonging in the Long Nineteenth Century United States*. Cambridge University Press, New York.
Woloch, Nancy (1996). *Muller v. Oregon: A Brief History with Documents*. Bedford, New York.

Chapter Eleven

FAMILIES

David S. Tanenhaus

Since the publication in the late nineteenth century of Pierre G.F. Le Play's *L'Organisation de la Famille* and Friedrich Engels' *The Origins of the Family, Private Property and the State*, scholars have studied family structures and the relationship of the family to economic change (Le Play, 2010 [1871]; Engels 1972 [1884]). The subfield of family history later became the cornerstone of the social history revolution that flourished after World War II. By the mid-1970s, scholarly production had reached dizzying heights, with more than "800 books and articles on family history" being published between 1972 and 1976 on America, England, and France (Stone, 1981: 51). "From this torrential outpouring of historical investigation," according to Lawrence Stone, it was clear that "there is no such thing as a single national family type at any given period." He elaborated, "There has never been a French Family or an English Family or an American family, but rather a plurality of families" (Stone, 1981: 81). The diversity of families became an organizing principle for histories of American family law, although this subfield of American legal history did not emerge until the 1980s. Whereas French social historians were familiar with legal history because there was a long tradition of French law students writing their doctoral dissertations "on local marriage customs and laws of inheritance," the influence of legal history was "hardly visible elsewhere" (Stone, 1981: 52). Historians of American families had drawn on legal sources, such as wills and probate records, but relied on concepts and methods from anthropology and historical demography, not law, to structure their studies of families in local communities (Morgan, 1966; Demos, 1970; Greven, 1970; Lockridge, 1970).

A Companion to American Legal History, First Edition.
Edited by Sally E. Hadden and Alfred L. Brophy.
© 2013 John Wiley & Sons Ltd. Published 2021 by John Wiley & Sons Ltd.

Social historians of the family were trying to understand what the German sociologist Ferdinand Tönnies famously described in the late nineteenth century as the shift from *gemeinshaft* (community) to *gesellschaft* (society) (1963). In other words, how did traditional societies become modern? And did changing family structures serve as a catalyst in this transformative process? According to Stone, "No other question is more important to historians of the West than the causes, nature, timing, and consequences of this transition." Whereas early modern society "was sparse, with high birth and high mortality rates, and was poor, rural, agrarian, illiterate, small-scale, communitarian, hierarchical, authoritarian, pious, weakly governed, and amateurish," he explained, "[l]ate twentieth-century society is dense, with low birth and death rates, and is rich, urban, industrial, literate, large-scale, individualistic, depersonalized, egalitarian, democratic, agnostic, bureaucratized, and professional" (Stone, 1981: 82). Historians disagreed over the role of the family in this so-called modernization process, including the timing and significance of the nuclear family (parents and their children living together as a single household unit) becoming a core feature of Western civilization.

For example, in *Domestic Revolutions*, a comprehensive and important synthesis of the burgeoning social historical scholarship on American families from colonial to modern times, Steven Mintz and Susan Kellog explained that the family has always been a dynamic and historical institution (1988). "Although the family is seen as the social institution most resistant to change, it is, in fact," they highlighted, "as deeply embedded in the historical process as any other institution" (Mintz and Kellog, 1988: xiv). They emphasized that capitalism, demographics, and new gender roles had all dramatically changed the structure, role, and conception of the family since the seventeenth century. Whereas the early colonial household had been "the fundamental economic, educational, political, and religious unit of society," they observed that the mid-twentieth-century family had "ceased to be a largely autonomous, independent, self-contained, and self-sufficient unit" (Mintz and Kellog, 1988: xv). By the 1950s, the modern family's primary functions had become limited to providing affection and socializing the young – not to mention, keeping sitcom writers and advice columnists busy. By the 1970s, however, the family appeared besieged in the United States and abroad (Lasch, 1977; Hafen, 1983). From 1965 to 1980, for example, household composition in North America, Europe, Japan, Australia and the Soviet Union had changed dramatically (Cott, 2000). "Among the billion people encompassed in these nations," Nancy Cott noted, "rates of formal marriages and of birth tumbled; divorces and the proportion of births outside formal wedlock both shot up. The increases and decreases were substantial and even spectacular, often 50 percent or more" (Cott, 2000: 202). Thus, it was not surprising Mintz and Kellog observed that the United States in the 1980s was a "society without a clear unitary set of family ideals and values." They added, "Many Americans are groping for a new paradigm of

American family life, but in the meantime a profound sense of confusion and ambivalence reigns" (Mintz and Kellog, 1988: xvii). Such confusion helped fuel a brewing culture war over "family values."

During this tense historical moment, Michael Grossberg announced that it was time to study the relationship between families and the law because "a history of the law of the family does not exist" (1986: 799). Social historians, he explained, had focused almost exclusively on the internal workings of families and largely ignored law and public institutions. And legal historians, since the founding of their field in the 1950s, with a few notable exceptions, such as Norma Basch's *In the Eyes of the Law*, had studied commercial transactions, not domestic relations (Basch, 1982). Grossberg proposed that social and legal historians join forces to write the history of family law. "Such a merger," he explained, "can give current debates on abortion, spousal responsibilities, children's rights, and the regulation of sexuality a history. Far too often those debates proceed from assertions about the uniqueness of contemporary conflicts. A glance backward reveals not only how fallacious such assumptions are, but also how the past has helped structure the present" (Grossberg, 1986: 803). Thus, contemporary concerns about the family and public policy helped launch the new subfield, and subsequent debates over federal legislation, such as the Defense of Marriage Act (1996), and U.S. Supreme Court decisions, such as *Lawrence v. Texas* (2003), have kept scholars of American families busy.

At the same time that Grossberg encouraged scholars to provide historical analysis for policy makers, Martha Minow called for scholars to cross the boundaries between social and legal history to challenge the unquestioned, ahistorical assumptions about families embedded in legal casebooks and constitutional law (Minow, 1985). Instead of replicating the conventional narrative that described "a linear evolution from a family law centered on traditional, patriarchal families, toward a family law for egalitarian families, whose individual members enjoyed state-protected rights," Minow urged scholars to study social experience at given historical moments to understand more precisely the contested nature of past practices and concepts (1985: 826). She urged scholars to use the innovative methods being developed in the nascent fields of gender history (Scott, 1986), feminist jurisprudence (MacKinnon, 1979), and critical legal studies (Gordon, 1984) to write the history of American family law. And they listened.

The subfield of family history, which Grossberg and Minow encouraged scholars to establish, is flourishing (Brewer, 2008; Basch, 2008). For instance, there are important studies that examine how colonizers used the ideal of a Christian, monogamous, and patriarchal family structure as an ideological tool in the conquest of North America (Cott, 2000); critical examinations of how Americans used similar concepts to justify a revolution and to build and govern the New Republic (Fliegelman, 1985; Brewer, 2005); insightful studies of particular areas of family law, such as inheritance

(Shammas, Salmon and Dahlin, 1987; Friedman, 2009), married women's property acts (see Batlan chapter in this volume, *A Brief Analysis of Women's Legal History*); divorce (Basch, 1999; Hartog, 2000; Buckley, 2002), child custody (Mason, 1994; Grossberg, 1996) and adoption (Carp, 1998), and a significant body of work that examines how gendered conceptions of marriage and citizenship structured American political development and social policy design (Skocpol, 1992; Gordon, 1994; Fineman, 1995; Isenberg, 1998; Kerber, 1998; Stanley, 1998; Cott, 2000; Witt, 2004; Canaday, 2009).

Much as social historians discovered that the composition of families has varied historically, legal historians have uncovered how elastic the legal definition of the family has been. For example, in a comprehensive study of homestead cases, Alison Morantz found that American state court judges well into the nineteenth century used a capacious definition of a family as people living together in a household. "Remarkably," she noted, "it was not until the postbellum period – the heyday of homestead exemption litigation – that the nuclear family began to appear as one of the definitions of 'family' in legal and popular dictionaries" (2006: 294). Morantz thus concluded that nineteenth-century jurists "permitted some groups of cohabitants that bore a functional resemblance to nuclear families to enjoy the same privileges as husband and wife" (2006: 295). Along similar lines, Ariela Dubler has shown the legitimacy of common law marriage revolved around couples acting like married people (2000).

To provide an introduction to this vibrant and sprawling subfield, this chapter begins with a re-examination of the field's foundational text, Grossberg's *Governing the Hearth: Law and the Family in Nineteenth-Century America* (1985). It then explores how subsequent scholarship built on the insights of this study, including the idea that "the family is in many ways a legal creation" (Grossberg, 1985: ix). The chapter then examines the literature on families and social policy in the twentieth century. A brief conclusion considers the future of the legal history of American families.

Beginnings

Just as the field of legal history itself had begun with J. Willard Hurst's pioneering work on the relationship between law and capitalism in nineteenth-century America (Hurst, 1956; Scheiber, 1970), histories of family law also initially focused on the same period. The subfield also built on Morton Horwitz's influential work on the role of nineteenth-century judges as "instrumentalists" whose appellate court decisions settled public policy decisions about economic growth, such as determining which class of Americans should pay for the costs of industrialization (Horwitz, 1977). In his prizing-winning *Governing the Hearth*, Grossberg analyzed how judges crafted policies to govern what the founders considered "the primary institution of American society" (1985: 3). He argued that the rise of republican theory and culture in the aftermath of the American Revolution had undermined the patriarchal foundations of the colonial household, setting the stage for the nineteenth-century legal battles over "the proper allocation of private and public domestic authority" (Grossberg, 1985: 29).

Drawing on state court appellate decisions, legal treatises, and other published sources, Grossberg reconstructed how nineteenth-century lawmakers had created the law of families from a mosaic of state laws regulating matrimony, parenthood, and divorce. He argued that the power of judges to define individual relationships within families established a new form of male authority: judicial patriarchy. "By seizing the power to define the legal abilities of married women, and other family members," he explained, "judges helped perpetuate, albeit in altered form, patriarchal authority within republican society" (1985: 300). And, as Grossberg later vividly recounted in his second book, *A Judgment for Solomon*, judges created and applied new doctrines, such as "the best interests of the child" and "the tender years rule," so that they could, in effect, dictate and control the lives of men, women and children who became entangled in the web of American custody law (1996). Critics of the children's rights movement make similar arguments about the power of family courts to interfere with parental rights and decision-making (Guggenheim, 2005).

Grossberg's idea of a judicial patriarchy built on an earlier important study of policing families in France and helped structure later studies of socialized courts in the United States, such as juvenile courts and domestic relations courts (Donzelot, 1979; Odem, 1995; Willrich, 2003; Tanenhaus, 2004). It also complemented a historiography on state actors and agencies, such as social workers and public schools, taking over the socialization functions that once belonged to families or households (Lasch, 1977; Polsky, 1991). In addition, historians influenced by E.P. Thompson's *The Making of the English Working Class* and Linda Gordon's *Heroes of Their Own Lives* closely examined how men, women, and children used and shaped the administration of public power, including welfare agencies and the courts (Thompson, 1963; Gordon, 1988; Odem, 1995; Robertson, 2005; Schmidt, 2010). Finally, there is also a related literature on women as state or quasi-state actors who dispensed maternal justice and material aid from the Civil War onwards (Freedman, 1996; Batlan, 2010).

Over the course of the nineteenth century, Grossberg argued, American courts (and to a lesser extent, legislatures) had established "a law for republican families" (1985: vi). This American law of domestic relations assumed "each family member had distinct legal interests and rights drawn from his or her individuality, and the judiciary had the primary duty of resolving conflicts between them" (1985: 29). Thus, he wrote, "in a society that placed great reliance on the law for settling conflicts, fixing status, and protecting wealth and authority, domestic-relations law helped establish the boundaries within which families formed and lived. It did so by occupying a position on the border between the public and private spheres of American society." He added that family law became "the most personal aspect of public law, the most public aspect of private law" (1985: 30). And, as the domestic law treatise writer James Schouler explained in 1895:

> The supremacy of the law of the family should not be forgotten. We come under the dominion of this law at the very moment of birth; whether we will or not. Long after infancy has ceased, the general obligations of parent and child may continue; for these last through life. Again we subject ourselves by marriage to a law of the family; this time to find our responsibilities still further enlarged. And although the voluntary act of two parties brings them within law, they cannot voluntarily retreat when so minded. To an unusual extent, therefore, is the law of family above, and independent of, the individual. Society provides the home; public policy fashions the system; and it remains for each one of us to accustom himself to the rules which are, and must be, arbitrary. (Quoted in Grossberg, 1985: 2)

Grossberg reconstructed this American public law of domestic relations. Twenty years after the publication of *Governing the Hearth*, in a field review essay on law and gender for the *Law & Social Inquiry*, Felice Batlan confirmed the importance of the nineteenth century for legal historians of families because they continued to "confront the porous boundaries between state regulation, the public, the family, and the private" (2005: 826).

Whether the family is a private or quasi-public institution has remained an enduring issue in the literature because the answer to the question is critical to understanding the nature of American governance, especially at the local and state level in the nineteenth century (Novak, 1996; Edwards, 2009). Many of the debates in the field, for example, raise questions about whether family law is a component of classical liberalism that has protected the family as a private institution from state interference and used inheritance law to maintain wealth within families (Friedman, 2009). The idea that the family is a private institution also became embedded in twentieth-century constitutional law and politics. In the 1920s, the U.S. Supreme Court held that the due process clause of the Fourteenth Amendment guaranteed the right of the individual "to marry" and "to establish a home and bring up children" (*Meyer v. Nebraska*, 262 U.S. 390 [1923]; Woodhouse, 1992). Later in the context of the Cold War, the Supreme Court built on earlier decisions, such as *Meyer v. Nebraska*, to establish the constitutional right to privacy that allowed for married couples to purchase contraceptives. That decision, *Griswold v. Connecticut* (1965), ultimately served as a foundation for *Roe v. Wade* (1973), which guaranteed constitutional protection for women's reproductive rights during the early stages of a pregnancy. There is a substantial literature addressing the ensuing controversy over reproductive rights (Hull and Hoffer, 2001).

Yet, as scholars of domestic violence have demonstrated, for much of American history judges had also used the idea of privacy to stop public authorities from intervening in "private homes" to protect women and children from abuse, while simultaneously affirming that a man had a right to chastise his wife and denying the concept of marital rape (Schneider, 1991; Siegel, 1996; Cott, 2000). By the late twentieth century, feminists considered the right to privacy a double-edged sword. It protected a woman's right to make decisions about her own body, but also helped legitimate violence against women.

Significantly, *Governing the Hearth* also addressed the methodological question of how to strike a proper balance between social experience and law. Grossberg, for example, sought to write a general national history of evolving public policy, not an in-depth analysis of one particular community. Due to federalism and the tenacity of localism in American history, calculating the proper scale for historical investigation remains one of the central challenges of legal history (Edwards, 2009). For example, how should scholars write the history of marriage and divorce in America? In *Man & Wife in America: A History*, Hendrik Hartog argues the law of marriage was one of the powers delegated to the states by the founders and became a federal concern only quite recently. "From the middle of the nineteenth century until the constitutional revolution of the 1960s," he pointed out, "there were repeated moments of passionate talk about the need for a national law of marriage and for uniformity, particularly in the face of the threat posed by Mormon polygamy in the Utah territory." He added, "And there were particular institutional responsibilities of the federal government, such as immigration laws, that implicated marriage. Nonetheless, throughout the first 175 years of national government, marriage law was not the business of Washington (Hartog, 2000: 17). Accordingly, his book is not a history of marriage and the nation. It is the histories of couples and the legal process in particular places.

By contrast, in *Public Vows: A History of Marriage and the Nation*, Nancy Cott examines the history of marriage through a national lens (2000). As she points out, "Even though state governments, not federal authorities, have the power to regulate marriage and divorce, a 1996 report from the U.S. General Accounting Office found more than *one thousand* places in the corpus of federal law where legal marriage conferred a distinctive status, right, or benefit" (Cott, 2000: 2, italics in original). These contrasting approaches in important books published the same year on the same topic illustrate the challenges of striking the proper balance between writing the social history of lived legal experience and understanding a nation (or empire) and its legal history.

Too often national histories of nineteenth-century America, such as Morton Horwitz's *The Transformation of American Law*, examined northern legal history at the expense of the South and West (1977). The subfield of family law, by contrast, has been more inclusive from its inception. The charged political debate over African American families, which intensified in the late 1960s, ensured that the subfield of American family law would have to directly address historical questions about slavery, race, and family law. In what became known as the Moynihan Report, Assistant Secretary of Labor Daniel Patrick Moynihan proposed fundamental changes in federal policy toward African Americans (1965). In a chapter on "The Tangle of Pathology," Moynihan relied on scholarship that contrasted black and white familial structures. He stated:

> In essence, the Negro community has been forced into a matriarchal structure which, because it is so out of line with the rest of the American society, seriously retards the progress of the group as a whole, and imposes a crushing burden on the Negro male and, in consequence, on a great many Negro women as well.
>
> There is, presumably, no special reason why a society in which males are dominant in family relationships is to be preferred to a matriarchal arrangement. However, it is clearly a disadvantage for a minority group to be operating on one principle, while the great majority of the population, and the one with the most advantages to begin with, is operating on another. This is the present situation of the Negro. Ours is a society which presumes male leadership in private and public affairs. The arrangements of society facilitate such leadership and reward it. A subculture, such as that of the Negro American, in which this is not the pattern, is placed at a distinct disadvantage. (1965: 29)

From Moynihan's perspective, the institution of slavery had severely damaged the "Negro family" and federal policy going forward had to acknowledge this historical legacy.

"It was the Moynihan controversy," Peter Novick later noted in his history of the American historical profession, "which led Herbert Gutman to set aside his studies in labor history, and begin work on what became *The Black Family in Slavery and Freedom*" (Novick, 1988: 483; Gutman, 1976). Gutman and other historians of the black family emphasized the role of African Americans as resourceful human beings who had resisted slavery and later creatively adapted to new forms of racism and oppression (Penningroth, 2003). By the early 1980s, scholarship on the black family and culture had become a prominent subfield of American family history.

Thus, it made sense that Grossberg analyzed the tension between marriage and slavery as competing forms of patriarchy in antebellum America. As he explained, the incompatibility of slavery and marriage, as commentators from Alexis de Tocqueville to Eugene Genovese had pointed out, meant that slaves could not legally wed (Tocqueville, 1835; Genovese, 1974). Abolitionists, such as Harriet Beecher Stowe in her novels *Uncle Tom's Cabin* and *Dred*, had used slavery's destruction of the family to demonstrate the immorality of "the peculiar institution" (Brophy, 1998). Subsequent scholarship to Grossberg's *Governing the Hearth*, such as Peter Bardaglio's *Reconstructing the Household*, focused more specifically on the question of southern differences in family law, and, more recently, Lea VanderVelde has demonstrated how African American women, such as Mrs. Dred Scott, used the public recognition of their marriages as the basis for filing freedom suits that challenged the legality of their enslavement (Bardaglio, 1995; VanderVelde , 2010).

A sophisticated literature has also explored how law structures the performances of gender roles, race relations, and the definition and regulation of families. This literature crosses the Mason Dixon Line, moves into the American West, and extends well beyond the abolition of chattel slavery to examine the strange career of miscegenation laws, the prohibition of polygamy, and racial passing (Stanley, 1998; Franke, 1999; Gordon, 1999; Wallenstein, 2002; Gross, 2008; Pascoe, 2009; Sandweiss, 2009; Sharfstein, 2011). Several of these studies also reveal how gendered and racial assumptions about families, sexuality, and legitimacy have shaped the administration of federal social programs from the creation of the Freedmen's Bureau after the Civil War to the construction and administration of the modern American welfare state (Gordon, 1990; Stanley, 1998; Davis, 1999; Gordon, 1994; Witt, 2004; Kornbluh, 2007; Tani, 2008).

The Force of Law

Legal historians still work from the basic premise of *Governing the Hearth*–"the family is in many ways a legal creation" (Grossberg, 1985: ix)–while simultaneously applying the theoretical insights of scholars, such as Pierre Bourdieu, who examine the power (or force) of legal systems to universalize and naturalize human existence (Bourdieu, 1987). For example, Holly Brewer has recently re-examined the Anglo-American common law of domestic relations, which served as the backdrop for Grossberg's history of family law in the nineteenth century (Brewer, 2005; 2008). She concluded, "The fundamental change that occurred during the seventeenth and eighteenth century was that the legal powers of masters (or as the legal guides of the seventeenth century called them, Lords) were extended to men as fathers and as husbands" (Brewer, 2008: 290). Thus, the idea of the patriarchal family itself had been a relatively late legal creation.

A central theme of Grossberg's book was using law to distinguish between "legitimate" and "illegitimate" families (1985). He included, for example, a chapter on nineteenth-century legal reforms to establish at least some rights for nonmarital children, who were classified as either "bastards" or "illegitimate" children. In colonial America, as in England, Grossberg explained, "The law used matrimony to separate legal from spurious issue. It defined the latter as 'filius nullius,' the child and heir of no one. The bastard had no recognized legal relations with his or her parents, particularly not those of inheritance, maintenance, and custody. Nor did the couple have any rights or duties toward their spurious issue. The only heirs of bastards were those of their own bodies" (1985: 197). Subsequent nineteenth-century reforms helped to establish legal ties between a mother and her nonmarital children, but family law still treated "illegitimate" children unequally until the late twentieth century (Grossberg, 1985; Bakelar, 2010). In 1968, in *Levy v. Louisiana*, the U.S. Supreme Court held, "We start from the premise that illegitimate children are not 'nonpersons.' They are humans, live, and have their being. They are clearly 'persons' within the meaning of the Equal Protection Clause of the Fourteenth Amendment" (391 U.S. 68, 70). For the first time, the Supreme Court had recognized the status of nonmarital children as family members.

Similarly, the nineteenth-century campaigns against "the twin relics of barbarism" – slavery and polygamy – inscribed the idea of "legitimate" families into national policy and consciousness (Foner, 1988; Gordon, 2002). Birthright national citizenship was incorporated into the U.S. Constitution through the ratification of the Fourteenth Amendment in 1868 to overturn the infamous *Dred Scott v. Sandford* decision (1857). In the 1870s and 1880s, Congress passed laws designed to destroy Mormon polygamy in the Utah Territory and to reorganize the social structure of Indian tribes (Gordon, 2002; Cott, 2000). Federal lawmakers also used conceptions of the family to design the nation's immigration policies, including a Progressive Era law that stripped American women of their citizenship if they married foreigners. Feminists in the early twentieth century fought for passage of the Married Women's Independent Nationality Act of 1922 to ensure that women who married foreigners retained their American citizenship. Later, during the 1960s, civil rights activists successfully used the federal courts to strike down state laws criminalizing interracial marriage and penalizing illegitimate children (*Loving v. Virginia* [1967] and *Levy v. Louisiana* [1968]). As these examples suggest, citizenship and nationhood have been bound up with conceptions of the family since the end of the Civil War.

Legal historians have also demonstrated that perhaps as much as eighty percent of the household wealth in the United States is derived from the law of inheritance (Shammas, Salmon and Dahlin, 1987). Thus, inheritance law perpetuates not only particular family lines but also helps replicate the larger social structure (Friedman, 2009). And, as scholars of the colonial Chesapeake have shown, inadequate support of widows under the common law (wives received only one-third of their husband's realty and had only the right of tenancy) forced women either to remarry or become independent and work to support themselves and their children (Keyssar, 1974; Carr and Walsh, 1977; Norton, 1996; Conger, 2009). The literature on widows, as Ariela Dubler has highlighted, challenges the assumption "the legal regulation of the husband-wife relationship is the key to understanding the development of family law ... and the changing relationship between the family and the state" (Dubler, 2003: 1649). Thus, the force of family law helped constitute households, keep the intergenerational transfer of wealth within families, and establish the conditions under which unmarried women had to carve out independent lives.

The literature on divorce also underscores the importance of law in shaping social experience within as well as outside of the nation's courtrooms (Mnookin and Kornhauser, 1979). Scholars have examined how the framing of divorce has changed since the revolutionary generation and how American couples have negotiated their lives and roles as husbands and wives in a society that embraced coverture, the legal idea that a wife's legal identity was subsumed under her husband's (Basch, 1999; Hartog, 2000; Cott, 2000). Basch, for instance, has examined the tensions between coverture and divorce in the nineteenth century, and Hartog argues that the regime of coverture essentially lasted into the 1950s. Significantly, Hartog also demonstrates that judges should be understood not as instrumentalists, but as "the managers of the legal process: of laws, customs, and inherited practices that incorporated incoherent and contradictory values and histories" (Hartog, 2000: 4).

The intense interest in marital exits partly reflected changing demographics. When social historians in the 1970s were intensely studying household composition, seventy-five percent of adult Americans were married. By the turn of the twenty-first century, when Basch, Hartog, and Cott were writing about marriage and divorce, fewer than sixty percent of American adults were married, and more than fifty percent of marriages ended in divorce (Cott, 2000: 203). This cultural change was related to the widespread adoption of no-fault divorce laws since 1969. By 1985, for example, every state allowed married couples to separate because of incompatibility. Moreover, in some regions of the United States by the late 1990s, nearly seven in ten marriages ended in divorce (Cott, 2000: 203).

Families and Social Policy

In light of the nation's high divorce rate at the end of the twentieth century, it is ironic that family preservation had been one the pillars of twentieth-century U.S. social policy. Progressive Era reformers, for example, championed the idea that women should not be separated from their offspring due to poverty in order to secure passage of mothers'-pension legislation at the state level (Leff, 1973; Skocpol, 1992; Goodwin, 1997; Tanenhaus, 2004).

The ideal of family preservation had also animated the 1909 White House Conference on Dependent Children that led to the establishment of the Federal Children's Bureau in 1912 (Wald, 1909; Muncy, 1991; Lindemeyer, 1997), which compiled essential data on American families and launched successful educational programs focusing on prenatal care and child wellness. Ultimately, such Progressive Era reforms dramatically lowered the nation's infant mortality rate by more than fifty percent, which still ranks as one of the most significant accomplishments in the history of American social policy (Mintz, 2004: 173).

The emphasis on family preservation also undermined the common practice for more than a century of placing children temporarily in orphanages until they could be reunited with their parents (Hacsi, 1997; Crenson, 2001). During the crisis of the Great Depression, the federal government included the Aid to Dependent Children program (later changed to Aid to Families with Dependent Children) as part of the Social Security Act. Based on the idea of family preservation, New Deal programs wove gendered notions of citizenship into the nation's safety net. As Linda Gordon explained, mothers were pitied but not entitled, while husbands as workers had earned their entitlements and social security (Gordon, 1994). And, as Margot Canaday, has shown, New Deal programs intended as family support received more support than those aimed at single men (Canaday, 2009).

Finally, family preservation has been a core feature of modern American law since the adoption of the Immigration Act of 1965, which made family preferences a basis for bringing relatives to the United States and helped bolster the nation's Asian American population in the late twentieth century (Ngai, 2004).

The Future of Families

American families have changed over time, and continue to do so. As Nancy Cott explained, "the number of unmarried-couple households recorded by the Census Bureau multiplied by ten times from 1960 to 1998. It grew more than five times as fast as the number of households overall." Moreover, "the birth rate dropped, from more than 3.5 births per woman in 1960 to about 2 births per woman in the mid-1990s. The household without children, rather than with children, was the norm (62 percent) in the United States. What had been typical adult status in the long past – married, with minor children – described barely more than one quarter of adults in 1999" (Cott, 2000: 203–204). How the changing composition of families affects public policy at the local, state and national level will surely continue to be a topic for future investigation, especially since the Great Recession of the early twenty-first century has refocused scholarly attention on social policy and the welfare state, much as the Great Depression and War on Poverty had done so previously (Vernier, 1931; Breckinridge, 1934; Abbott, 1938; TenBroek, 1964a; 1964b).

Because the subfield of family law has been so intertwined with contemporary policy debates, it should continue to provide histories for what might appear at first glance to be new issues. Battles over universal childcare in the 1960s and 1970s and the Defense of Marriage Act and the Personal Responsibility and Economic Opportunity Acts of 1996, for example, were only recent chapters in a long history of using the force of law to define American families and social obligations (Dinner, 2010; Cott, 2000). These battles also continued the ongoing struggle to define the nature of modern American governance (Novak, 2008; 2010). If past behavior is the best indicator of future action, then Americans will provide contradictory answers to whether family law functions best when the state is supportive, intrusive, or hands off, and continue to argue about which families should be recognized as legitimate.

The next generation of scholarship will likely include more attention to the intersection between immigration and family law (Augustine-Adams, 2011; Girard and Philips, 2011), more analysis of family law across national borders (Glendon, 1989; Myers, 2006), important studies of child and youth history (Bremner, 1971; Hawes, 1991; Mintz, 2004; Brewer, 2005; Robertson, 2005; Schmidt, 2010), and histories of gay marriage (Chauncey, 2005; Gordon, 2010).

Acknowledgements

I would like to thank the editors, Sally Hadden and Al Brophy, for their guidance, patience and most helpful comments on several drafts of this chapter. Mike Green and Mary Wammack also provided valuable feedback on the penultimate version.

References

Abbott, Grace (1938). *The Child and the State*. 2 Vols. University of Chicago Press, Chicago.

Augustine-Adams, Kif (2011). "Marriage and *Mestizaje*, Chinese and Mexican: Constitutional Interpretation and Resistance in Sonora, 1921–1935." *Law and History Review* 29(2): 419–463.

Bakelar, Sherrie Anne (2010). "From 'Baggage' to Not 'Non-Persons': *Levy v. Louisiana* and the Struggle for Equal Rights for 'Illegitimate' Children." M.A. Thesis, University of Nevada, Las Vegas.

Bardaglio, Peter W. (1995). *Reconstructing the Household: Families, Sex, and the Law in the Nineteenth-Century South*. University of North Carolina Press, Chapel Hill.

Basch, Norma (1982). *In the Eyes of the Law: Women, Marriage, and Property in Nineteenth-Century New York*. Cornell University Press, Ithaca, NY.

Basch, Norma (1999). *Framing American Divorce: From the Revolutionary Generation to the Victorians*. University of California Press, Berkeley and Los Angeles.

Basch, Norma (2008). "Marriage and Domestic Relations." In Grossberg and Tomlins, eds, *The Cambridge History of Law in America*, Volume 2. Cambridge University Press, New York.

Batlan, Felice (2005). "Engendering Legal History." *Law & Social Inquiry* 30(4): 823–851.

Batlan, Felice (2010). "The Birth of Legal Aid: Gender Ideologies, Women, and the Bar in New York City, 1863–1910." *Law and History Review* 28(4): 931–971.

Bourdieu, Pierre (1987). "The Force of Law: Toward a Sociology of the Juridical Field." *The Hastings Law Journal* 38(5): 814–853.

Breckinridge, Sophonisba P. (1934). *The Family and the State: Select Documents*. University of Chicago Press, Chicago.

Bremner, Robert (1970–1974). *Children and Youth in America: A Documentary History*. 3 volumes. Harvard University Press, Cambridge, MA.

Brewer, Holly (2005). *By Birth or Consent: Children, Law and the Anglo-American Revolution in Authority*. University of North Carolina Press, Chapel Hill.

Brewer, Holly (2008). "The Transformation of Domestic Law." In Grossberg and Tomlins, eds, *The Cambridge History of Law in America*, Volume 1. Cambridge University Press, New York.

Brophy, Alfred L. (1998). "Humanity, Utility, and Logic in Southern Legal Thought: Harriet Beecher Stowe's Vision in *Dred*: *A Tale of the Great Dismal Swamp*." *Boston University Law Review* 78(4): 1113–1161.

Buckley, Thomas E. (2002). *The Great Catastrophe of My Life: Divorce in the Old Dominion*. University of North Carolina Press, Chapel Hill.

Canaday, Margot (2009). *The Straight State: Sexuality and Citizenship in Twentieth-Century America*. Princeton University Press, Princeton.

Carp, E. Wayne (1998). *Family Matters: Secrecy and Disclosure in the History of Adoption*. Harvard University Press, Cambridge, MA.

Carr, Lois Green and Walsh, Lorena (1977). "The Planter's Wife: The Experience of White Women in Seventeenth-Century Maryland." *William and Mary Quarterly* 3rd series, 34(4): 542–571.

Chauncey, George (2005). *Why Marriage? The History Shaping Today's Debate Over Gay Equality*. Basic Books, New York.

Conger, Vivian (2009). *The Widows' Might: Widowhood and Gender in Early British America*. New York University Press, New York.

Cott, Nancy F. (2000). *Public Vows: A History of Marriage and the Nation*. Harvard University Press, Cambridge, MA.

Crenson, Matthew (2001). *Building the Invisible Orphanage: A Prehistory of the American Welfare State*. Harvard University Press, Cambridge, MA.

Davis, Adrienne D. (1999). "The Private Law of Race and Sex: An Antebellum Perspective." *Stanford Law Review* 51(2): 221–288.

Demos, John (1970). *A Little Commonwealth: Family Life in Plymouth Colony.* Oxford University Press, New York.

Dinner, Deborah (2010). "The Universal Childcare Debate: Rights Mobilization, Social Policy, and the Dynamics of Feminist Activism, 1966 to 1974." *Law and History Review* 28(3): 577–628.

Donzelot, Jacques (1979). *The Policing of Families.* Pantheon, New York.

Dubler, Ariela (2000). "Wifely Behavior: A Legal History of Acting Married." *Columbia Law Review* 100(4): 957–1021.

Dubler, Ariela (2003). "In the Shadow of Marriage: Single Women and the Legal Construction of the Family and the State." *Yale Law Journal* 112(7): 1641–1715.

Edwards, Laura (2009). *The People and Their Peace: Legal Culture and the Transformation of Legal Inequality in the Post-Revolutionary South.* University of North Carolina Press, Chapel Hill.

Engels, Friedrich (1972). *The Origins of the Family, Private Property and the State.* International Publishers, New York.

Fineman, Martha Alberston (1995). *The Neutered Mother, The Sexual Family and Other Twentieth Century Tragedies.* Routledge, New York.

Foner, Eric (1988). *Reconstruction: America's Unfinished Revolution, 1863–1877.* Harper, New York.

Fliegelman, Jay (1985). *Prodigals and Pilgrims: The American Revolution against Patriarchal Authority, 1750–1800.* Cambridge University Press, New York.

Franke, Katherine M. (1999). "Becoming a Citizen: Reconstruction Era Regulation of African American Marriages." *Yale Journal of Law and the Humanities* 11(2): 251–310.

Freedman, Estelle (1996). *Maternal Justice: Miriam Van Waters and the Female Reform Tradition.* University of Chicago Press, Chicago.

Friedman, Lawrence M. (2009). *Dead Hands: A Social History of Wills, Trusts, and Inheritance Law.* Stanford University Press, Stanford.

Genovese, Eugene (1974). *Roll, Jordan, Roll: The World the Slaves Made.* Pantheon Books, New York.

Girard, Philip, with Philips, Jim (2011). "Rethinking 'the Nation' in National Legal History: A Canadian Perspective." *Law and History Review* 29(2): 607–626.

Glendon, Mary Ann (1989). *The Transformation of Family Law: State, Law and Family in the United States and Western Europe.* University of Chicago Press, Chicago.

Goodwin, Joanne L. (1997). *Gender and the Politics of Welfare Reform: Mothers' Pensions in Chicago, 1911–1929.* University of Chicago Press, Chicago.

Gordon, Linda (1988). *Heroes of Their Own Lives: The Politics and History of Family Violence in Boston, 1880–1960.* Viking, New York.

Gordon, Linda (1990). *Women, the State, and Welfare.* University of Wisconsin Press, Madison, WI.

Gordon, Linda (1994). *Pitied but Not Entitled: Single Mothers and the History of Welfare.* Free Press, New York.

Gordon, Linda (1999). *The Great Arizona Orphan Abduction.* Harvard University Press, Cambridge, MA.

Gordon, Robert W. (1984). "Critical Legal Histories." *Stanford Law Review* 36: 57–125.

Gordon, Sarah Barringer (2002). *The Mormon Question: Polygamy and Constitutional Conflict in Nineteenth-Century America*. University of North Carolina, Chapel Hill.

Gordon, Sarah Barringer (2010). *The Spirit of the Law: Religious Voices and the Constitution in Modern America*. Belknap Press of Harvard University Press, Cambridge, MA.

Greven, Philip J. (1970). *Four Generations: Population, Land and Family in Colonial Andover, Massachusetts*. Cornell University Press, Ithaca.

Gross, Ariela (2008). *What Blood Won't Tell: A History of Race on Trial*. Harvard University Press, Cambridge, MA.

Grossberg, Michael (1985) *Governing the Hearth: Law and the Family in Nineteenth-Century America*. University of North Carolina Press, Chapel Hill.

Grossberg, Michael (1986). "Crossing Boundaries: Nineteenth-Century Domestic Relations Law and the Merger of Family and Legal History." *American Bar Foundation Research Journal* 10(4): 799–847.

Grossberg, Michael (1996). *A Judgment for Solomon: The DeHauteville Case and Legal Experience in Antebellum America*. Cambridge University Press, New York.

Guggenheim, Martin (2005). *What's Wrong with Children's Rights*. Harvard University Press, Cambridge, MA.

Gutman, Herbert (1976). *The Black Family in Slavery and Freedom, 1750–1925*. Pantheon, New York.

Hacsi, Timothy (1997). *Second Homes: Orphan Asylums and Poor Families in America*. Harvard University Press, Cambridge, MA.

Hafen, Bruce C. (1983). "The Constitutional Status of Marriage, Kinship, and Sexual Privacy–Balancing the Individual and Social Interests." *Michigan Law Review* 81: 463–574.

Hartog, Hendrik (2000). *Man & Wife in America: A History*. Harvard University Press, Cambridge, MA.

Hawes, Joseph (1991). *The Children's Rights Movement: A History of Advocacy and Protection*. Twayne Publishers, Boston.

Horwitz, Morton J. (1977). *The Transformation of American Law, 1780–1960*. Harvard University Press, Cambridge, MA.

Hull, N.E.H. and Hoffer, Peter C. (2001). *Roe v. Wade: The Abortion Rights Controversy in American History*. University Press of Kansas, Lawrence.

Hurst, J. Willard (1956). *Law and the Conditions of Freedom in the Nineteenth-Century United States*. University of Wisconsin Press, Madison.

Isenberg, Nancy (1998). *Sex and Citizenship in Antebellum America*. University of North Carolina Press, Chapel Hill.

Kerber, Linda (1998). *No Constitutional Right to be Ladies: Women and the Obligations of Citizenship*. Hill and Wang, New York .

Keyssar, Alexander (1974). "Widowhood in Eighteenth-Century Massachusetts: A Problem in the History of the Family." *Perspectives in American History* 8: 83–119.

Kornbluh, Felicia (2007). *The Battle for Welfare Rights: Politics and Poverty in Modern America*. University of Pennsylvania Press, Philadelphia.

Lasch, Christopher (1977). *Haven in a Heartless World: The Family Besieged.* Basic Books, New York.
Le Play, Frédéric (2010 [1871]). *L'Organisation de la Famille.* Téqui, Bibliothecaire de l'oeuvre Saint-Michel, Paris.
Leff, Mark H. (1973). "Consensus for Reform: The Mothers' Pensions Movement in the Progressive Era." *Social Service Review* 47(3): 397–417.
Lindemeyer, Kristie (1997). *A Right to Childhood: The U.S. Children's Bureau.* University of Illinois Press, Urbana.
Lockridge, Kenneth (1970). *A New England Town: The First Hundred Years, Dedham, Massachusetts, 1636–1736.* W.W. Norton, New York.
MacKinnon, Catherine (1979). *Sexual Harassment of Working Women: A Case of Sex Discrimination.* Yale University Press, New Haven.
Mason, Mary Ann (1994). *From Father's Property to Children's Rights: A History of Child Custody in the United States.* Columbia University Press, New York.
Minow, Martha (1985). "'Forming Underneath Everything That Grows': Toward a History of Family Law." *Wisconsin Law Review,* 819–898.
Mintz, Steven and Kellog, Susan (1988). *Domestic Revolutions: A Social History of American Family Life.* Free Press, New York.
Mintz, Steven (2004). *Huck's Raft: A History of American Childhood.* Belknap Press of Harvard University Press, Cambridge, MA.
Mnookin, Robert H. and Kornhauser, Lewis (1979). "Bargaining in the Shadow of the Law: The Case of Divorce." *Yale Law Journal* 88(5): 950–997.
Morantz, Alison D. (2006). "There's No Place Like Home: Homestead Exemption and Judicial Constructions of Family in Nineteenth-Century America." *Law and History Review* 24(2): 245–295.
Morgan, Edmund S. (1966). *The Puritan Family: Religious and Domestic Relations in Seventeenth-Century New England.* Revised Edition. Harper Perennial, New York.
Moynihan, Daniel Patrick (1965). *The Negro Family: A Case for Action.* Department of Labor, Washington, DC.
Muncy, Robyn (1991). *Creating a Female Dominion in American Reform, 1890–1935.* Oxford University Press, New York.
Myers, Tamara (2006). *Caught: Montreal's Modern Girls and the Law, 1868–1945.* University of Toronto Press, Toronto.
Ngai, Mae M. (2004). *Impossible Subjects: Illegal Aliens and the Making of Modern America.* Princeton University Press, Princeton.
Norton, Mary Beth (1996). *Liberty's Daughters: The Revolutionary Experience of American Women, 1750–1800.* Cornell University Press, Ithaca.
Novak, William (1996). *The People's Welfare: Law and Regulation in Nineteenth-Century America.* University of North Carolina Press, Chapel Hill.
Novak, William (2008). "The Myth of the 'Weak' American State." *American Historical Review* 113(3): 752–772.
Novak, William (2010). "AHR Exchange: Long Live the Myth of the Weak State? A Response to Adams, Gerstle, and Witt." *American Historical Review* 115(3): 792–800.
Novick, Peter (1988). *That Noble Dream: The "Objectivity Question" and the American Historical Profession.* Cambridge University Press, New York.

Odem, Mary E. (1995). *Delinquent Daughters: Policing and Protecting Adolescent Female Sexuality in the United States, 1885 to 1920.* University of North Carolina Press, Chapel Hill.

Pascoe, Peggy (2009). *What Comes Naturally: Miscegenation Law and the Making of Race in America.* Oxford University Press, New York.

Penningroth, Dylan (2003). *The Claims of Kinfolk: African American Property and Community in the Nineteenth-Century South.* University of North Carolina Press, Chapel Hill.

Polsky, Andrew (1991). *The Rise of the Therapeutic State.* Princeton University Press, Princeton.

Robertson, Stephen (2005). *Crimes against Children: Sexual Violence and Legal Culture in New York City, 1880 to 1960.* University of North Carolina, Chapel Hill.

Sandweiss, Martha A. (2009). *Passing Strange: A Gilded Age Tale of Love and Deception Across the Color Line.* Penguin Press, New York.

Scheiber, Harry N. (1970). "At the Borderland of Law and Economic History: The Contributions of Willard Hurst." *American Historical Review* 75(3): 744–756.

Schmidt, James D. (2010). *Industrial Violence and the Legal Origins of Child Labor.* Cambridge University Press, New York.

Schneider, Elizabeth M. (1991). "The Violence of Privacy." *Connecticut Law Review* 23(4): 973–999.

Schouler, James (1895). *A Treatise on the Law of Domestic Relations.* 5th Edition. Little, Brown, Boston.

Scott, Joan W. (1986). "Gender: A Useful Category of Historical Analysis." *American Historical Review* 113(5): 1053–1075.

Shammas, Carole, Salmon, Marylynn and Dahlin, Michel (1987). *Inheritance in America: From Colonial Times to the Present.* Rutgers University Press, New Brunswick.

Sharfstein, Daniel J. (2011). *The Invisible Line: Three American Families and the Secret Journey.* Penguin, New York.

Siegel, Reva (1996). "'The Rule of Love': Wife Beating as the Rule of Prerogative and Privacy." *Yale Law Journal* 105(8): 2117–2207.

Skocpol, Theda (1992). *Protecting Soldiers and Mothers: The Political Origins of Social Policy in the United States.* Belknap Press of Harvard University Press, Cambridge, MA.

Stanley, Amy Dru (1998). *From Bondage to Contract: Wage Labor, Marriage, and the Market in the Age of Slave Emancipation.* Cambridge University Press, Cambridge, UK.

Stone, Lawrence (1981). "Family History in the 1980s: Past Achievements and Future Trends." *Journal of Interdisciplinary History* 12(1): 51–87.

Tanenhaus, David S. (2004). *Juvenile Justice in the Making.* Oxford University Press, New York.

Tani, Karen (2008). "*Flemming v. Nestor*: Anticommunism, the Welfare State, and the Making of 'New Property.'" *Law and History Review* 26(2): 379–414.

TenBroek, Jacobus (1964a). "California's Dual System of Family Law: Its Origin, Development, and Present Status: Part I." *Stanford Law Review* 16(2): 257–317.

TenBroek, Jacobus (1964b). "California's Dual System of Family Law: Its Origin, Development, and Present Status: Part II." *Stanford Law Review* 16(4): 900–982.

Thompson, E.P. (1963). *The Making of the English Working Class*. Pantheon Books, New York.

Tocqueville, Alexis de (1835). *Democracy in America*. 2 volumes. Saunders and Otley, London.

Tönnies, Ferdinand (1963). *Community & Society (Gemeinschaft und Gesellschaft)*. Harper & Row, New York.

VanderVelde, Lea (2010). *Mrs. Dred Scott: A Life on Slavery's Frontier*. Oxford University Press, New York.

Vernier, Chester Garfield (1931). *American Family Laws: A Comparative Study of the Family Laws of the Forty-Eight American States, Alaska, the District of Columbia and Hawaii*. 5 volumes. Stanford University Press, Stanford.

Wald, Lillian (1909). *The Federal Children's Bureau: A Symposium*. National Child Labor Committee, New York.

Wallenstein, Peter (2002). *Tell the Court I Love My Wife: Race, Marriage, and Law: An American History*. Palgrave MacMillan, New York.

Willrich, Michael (2003). *City of Courts: Socializing Justice in Progressive Era Chicago*. Cambridge University Press, New York.

Witt, John Fabian (2004). *The Accidental Republic: Crippled Workingmen, Destitute Widows, and the Remaking of American Law*. Harvard University Press, Cambridge, MA.

Woodhouse, Barbara Bennett (1992). "Who Owns the Child?: *Meyer and Pierce* and the Child as Property." *William & Mary Quarterly* 3rd series. 33(4): 996–1122.

Chapter Twelve

WHO BELONGS? IMMIGRANTS AND THE LAW IN AMERICAN HISTORY

Allison Brownell Tirres

John Larson and Moy Dong Kee shared much in common. Born on different sides of the globe (Larson in Sweden and Moy in China), both were raised in mid-nineteenth century farming families, sought new opportunities in the United States, and risked traveling there as young men. They both expected a short, profitable sojourn in the land of opportunity. That was not to be; the U.S. became their permanent home. Moy settled in New York City, opened a store, and later brought his wife and children to join him. Larson settled with his two older sisters in New Haven (Stave, *et al.*, 1994; Lee, 2003).

In many ways, the lives of Larson and Moy were parallel, yet there were key differences in their experiences. After arriving in the U.S., Larson could freely travel outside the U.S. and return, apply for naturalization to become a U.S. citizen, and sponsor other family members to join him in his adopted homeland. He faced few bars to owning property, choosing what clothing or hairstyles to adopt, or marrying whom he liked. Moy's "immigrant experience" was altogether different. Moy and his fellow Chinese migrants encountered laws that prohibited them from naturalizing, forced them to apply for certificates of return for travel outside the U.S., and controlled if not prohibited the sponsoring of family members. Such differential treatment of ostensibly similar immigrants not only was embedded in immigration law but also found its way into criminal law, municipal regulations, and other domestic regulation. Moy, a merchant living in the relatively tolerant state of New York, escaped the worst of this discrimination, but many laboring Chinese migrants were not so fortunate.

A Companion to American Legal History, First Edition.
Edited by Sally E. Hadden and Alfred L. Brophy.
© 2013 John Wiley & Sons Ltd. Published 2021 by John Wiley & Sons Ltd.

Why did these two migrant experiences differ? This chapter explores this question from the perspective of legal history. Both Larson and Moy were "migrants" – natives of another land who traveled to the U.S. – but their identities as "immigrants" were legal constructs. They differed not in actions or expectations but rather in their treatment under the law. Unequal immigration laws, coupled with discriminatory alienage laws, had a dramatic effect on their otherwise similar experiences.

Ultimately, any scholarly study of the "immigrant" examines the creation, deployment, influence or challenging of a legal category. Unlike some other types of status, such as race and gender, that of alienage is not immutable. As a creation of law, the status of "immigrant" can vary depending on applicable laws. Immigrants might be immigrants only temporarily, eventually becoming citizens. Or they might lose their status by overstaying a visa or committing certain crimes. Immigrant status is transitory, shifting, and impermanent, dependent on laws as well as on interpretations of actions of immigrants themselves.

One of the challenges of studying immigrants and immigration law is grappling with contradictions in this politically-charged category. Immigration law is a window onto perceptions of national identity. Classically, the U.S. is a "nation of immigrants," defined by waves of migrants who came, and continue to come, to its shores seeking the mythical "American Dream." Yet alongside that constitutive story of inclusion is an equally strong story of exclusion, typically along lines of race, class, and political ideology. Law played a pivotal role in both stories, a mechanism for drawing in immigrants and a tool for excluding and marginalizing them.

Colonial and Early National Immigration Regulation

The Constitution is relatively silent when it comes to matters of citizenship. There are only a few scattered references to the term and no overall definition or description of the rights and duties of citizens. The power to regulate immigration and immigrants is even harder to find in the Constitution. The "migration and importation clause" clearly describes migrants, but commentators agree this provision referred to the international slave trade. The document gives Congress power "to establish an Uniform Rule of Naturalization," but gives no further specifics. In the early years of the polity, immigration was considered to fall under the Commerce Clause, which is an imperfect fit (Parker, 2008).

The relative constitutional silence on citizenship and immigration left a conundrum for both scholars and state and federal governments regarding jurisdiction. Is immigration regulation purely a federal task, or can states be involved too? What rights pertain exclusively to citizens, and what rights belong to all persons, regardless of alienage status? The Supreme Court did not address these questions until 1889, in the *Chinese Exclusion Case*. This case established the plenary power of Congress over immigration, limiting the courts' ability to intervene based on interpretations of sovereignty and international law.

Sociologists and economists in the early twentieth century studied immigration, but it did not attract significant attention from historians until the 1950s, with the publication of seminal works by Oscar Handlin (1959) and John Higham (1955). This first scholarly wave assumed immigration law had its origins in the late nineteenth century. In theory, before the Gilded Age influx of southern and eastern European migrants, there was little or no American regulation of migration. According to this narrative, before the 1870s the U.S. needed settlers and therefore had little interest in restricting migrants; but an influx of "unassimilable" migrants in the late nineteenth century spawned immigration restrictions – and immigration law (Hutchinson, 1981; Schuck and Smith, 1985).

Recent work by historians and legal scholars has revealed that this story of colonial and antebellum "open borders" is inaccurate. Broadly speaking, scholars have revised understandings about this era in one of two ways: by offering new interpretations of the meanings of immigration and naturalization law during the founding era, or by revealing immigration regulation that existed at local and state levels.

James Pfander and Teresa Wardon argue that courts have misread the early Congress' intentions about immigration law (2010). Examining drafts of laws relating to naturalization and citizenship in the founding era and the early national period, and the related political and cultural context of the era, they argue that Congress had clear assumptions about procedural fairness and immigrant rights. If applied today, these approaches to immigration law would weaken plenary power doctrine, especially by prohibiting the passage of retroactive laws (currently allowed in immigration law and policy). Hiroshi Motomura describes the wide range of rights that immigrants enjoyed once they declared their intention to become citizens (2006; Neuman, 1996). This discovery undermines modern-day assumptions about the strict demarcation between citizens and non-citizens in voting and other forms of political participation (Hayduk, 2006).

Other scholars have revealed the bevy of local and state immigration regulations that existed before the assertion of federal control in the nineteenth century. Gerald Neuman, in "The Lost Century of Immigration Law," was among the first to demonstrate the usefulness of expanding the time frame of the legal history of immigration (1993). By thinking of immigration law as not only a federal administrative apparatus but as any law that "seeks to prevent or discourage the movement of aliens across an international border ... or movement across interstate borders," he demonstrated the prevalence of immigration laws at state and local levels, beginning with the colonial era (1996: 20). Colonization itself was governed by royal rules and practices that determined how people should migrate, where they could migrate, and how they should live once they got there (Meining, 1986). As colonies became more established, they developed their own regulations governing the migration and incorporation of outsiders, including freemen, indentured servants, and slaves (Bailyn, 1986; Baseler, 1998). Such colonial communities have not traditionally been included as part of immigration history, and yet they were essential precursors for regulating immigration in the early national period.

After independence, states and municipalities came up with their own mechanisms for regulating migration, including laws regarding the poor, the sick, criminals, and freed slaves (Parker, 2001; 2008). Such regulation was not only about restricting movement of migrants but also about encouraging it (Abrams, 2009). States and the federal government used a variety of incentives to draw migrants to them, including passing favorable property laws and providing for non-citizen suffrage. Aristide Zolberg demonstrates that the approach to immigration policy was not laissez faire in this period but rather intentional and deliberate, aimed at recruiting the "right" kind of migrants to settle the vast public lands. Immigration policy, he argues, was a "major instrument of nation building" from the colonial period onward (2008: 1).

Scholarship on the colonial and early national periods helps place the changes of the nineteenth century into better context. The late nineteenth-century approach to immigration regulation did not arise from thin air but drew on methods of control created by colonial and then state and local governments. For example, the current exclusion of migrants who may be or may become "public charges" has deep roots in colonial town and county poor laws (Herndon, 2001). Federal government efforts to reject undesirable migrants were copied from states like New York and Massachusetts, which made ship captains liable for bringing unwanted immigrants into their ports and fined them accordingly (Neuman, 1993; 1996; Parker, 2001).

Several historians working in this period have noted the overlap between legal histories of slavery – and race more generally – and immigration. Many Americans-to-be in the colonial and early national periods migrated not as willing and ambitious individuals but as forced labor, as slaves or indentured servants (Wokeck, 1999). The forced migration of millions of Africans, and the nation's struggle to control and later incorporate this migrant population, is not just a slavery story but also an immigration story. As Kitty Calavita has noted, in the case of both a slave and a contract laborer, what was sought was the labor power itself; the employers merely used different methods (Calavita, 1984). Keeping these narratives parallel to each other exposes the role of capitalist economic development in creating migration streams (Tomlins, 2010).

The overlap between legal histories of slavery and immigration does not end with the colonial and early national periods, but extends into the mid- to late-nineteenth century as well. Reconstruction was, by most accounts, primarily a process of reestablishing federal control over rebel states and deciding how to incorporate newly freed slaves into the constitutional framework. But the Fourteenth Amendment was of critical importance not just to freed slaves but also to two other key populations: immigrants and Native Americans. The Fourteenth Amendment asserted what was common practice but unstated in the Constitution: birthright citizenship. Individuals born within the jurisdiction of the United States would be U.S. citizens. There continue to be proposals to limit birthright citizenship, such as withholding citizenship from children born on U.S. soil to parents who entered the country without authorization (Schuck and Smith, 1985).

The revised naturalization law of 1870 drew new lines between former slaves and immigrants. The 1790 naturalization law permitted "free white persons" of "good moral character" to naturalize. The 1870 law added that persons of "African descent" could become naturalized citizens, omitting migrants from Asia (arriving in record numbers to labor on railroads) and Native Americans, who were not comprehensively granted federal citizenship until 1921. The intersection of these historical moments – the end of slavery and growth of immigration – allowed legislators to determine how race would come into play in a new way.

One of the first scholars to combine these different stories about citizenship laws in one text was political scientist Rogers Smith. In his book *Civic Ideals*, Smith clarifies the connecting, overlapping discourses on immigrants, women, African Americans, Native Americans, and other minorities (1997). Discussion of the rights and obligations of aliens was tied to discussions of the status of other non-citizens during the colonial and early national periods. Surprisingly, Smith and other scholars who write about citizenship in this period tend to downplay the negative aspects of citizenship (a position Smith later reversed, 2001). As Rogers Brubaker noted, citizenship is a "powerful instrument of social closure," enabling nation-states to restrict the rights of others to enter their territory (1992). Most historians of American citizenship underemphasize exclusion and highlight instead the positive attainment of political and social rights. Other historians have lodged a critique of this shortsightedness, including Christina Duffy Burnett (2008), Lucy Salyer (2004), and Kunal Parker (2001). Parker argues that the "hegemonic liberal historiography of American citizenship" has paid too much attention to individuals already "inside" the nation and far too little to those excluded from the nation (2001: 534). By increasing attention to immigrants and immigration laws, historians of citizenship can give a more accurate and nuanced account of this core American ideal.

Attention to earlier immigration regulation can destabilize the current framework of constitutional immigration law, which assumes that plenary power existed all along. As historians have shown, an immigration legal framework was not created out of thin air. When viewed in the light of nearly two centuries of local and state regulation, federal plenary power seems less a given and more a departure.

Foundations of the Modern System: 1870s–1920s

The historiographical impression of the 1870s to the 1920s as foundational is in many ways justifiable. At the start there were no *federal* immigration laws (with the exception of the international slave trade ban), no immigration enforcement bureaucracy, and little popular consensus about the need or the desire to regulate migration as a national (rather than state or local) problem. By the 1920s, there had been a long progression of ever more elaborate immigration laws which placed numerical limits on immigration. It would be enforced by a burgeoning immigration bureaucracy, housed in the Bureau of Immigration (created in 1891), which included the first iteration of today's Border Patrol, known then as "Chinese Inspectors." Immigration itself became a hotly contested issue, spawning national political parties and igniting political campaigns.

The politicization of immigration coincided with a rapid rise in migration. Between 1880 and the 1920s, more than 23.5 million immigrants arrived in the United States. The upswing began in the 1840s, with the increase in northern and western European migration. These populations were not easily woven into the social fabric. Irish migration – and rising anti-Catholic sentiment – sparked the first nativist political party, the "Know Nothings," in the 1840s and 1850s (Higham, 1955; Ignatiev, 1995). Nativists labeled Irish immigrants as "unsuitable for American citizenship." This was a claim that nativists would make about subsequent groups of Chinese and southern and eastern European migrants in the nineteenth century (Perea, 1997; Smith, 1997; Gross, 2010).

As immigrant numbers increased, so did some citizens' fears of America's inability to "assimilate" these communities. In 1875, Congress passed the first federal legislation regulating immigrant admissions, barring prostitutes and convicts. By 1917 inadmissible migrants included those who were (or were alleged to be) sick, poor, mentally impaired, or morally suspect, as well as laborers who were of either Chinese or Japanese origin. Despite restrictions, immigration continued unabated, prompting Congress to create quantitative restrictions rather than merely qualitative ones. In 1924, the Johnson-Reed Immigration Act established the national origins quota system, limiting the number of permissible immigrants based on their country of origin. The United States had transitioned from a "nation of immigrants," relatively open to foreign settlement, to what Erika Lee calls a "gatekeeping nation," preoccupied with restricting the entry of foreigners (Lee, 2006: 5).

Not until the 1950s did immigration history begin to be taken seriously in high-profile academic settings. Essential texts like John Higham's *Strangers in the Land* (1955) and Oscar Handlin's *Boston's Immigrants* (1959) were the first to explore immigration as a facet of American history. These earliest examinations tended to be intellectual, political, or social histories; if they focused on law at all, it was in the form of legislative history, tracking various Congressional policies (Hutchinson, 1981).

Starting in the 1990s, historians began to reconsider this era, seeking to understand not just the political climate but also immigration regulation as a whole, its enforcement (or lack thereof), and its interpretation in the courts. This approach revealed how immigrants themselves push the development of immigration law, as well as how immigrant communities are shaped by laws. Some scholars have examined specific categories of exclusion, tracking them from their beginnings in the foundational era (or earlier) to the present day. For example, Alan Kraut reveals the long and tortuous relationship between disease and immigration, including the development of the public health exclusion, while Eithne Luibhéid explores the complicated role of sexuality, including exclusions of prostitutes and homosexuals (Kraut, 1994; Luibhéid, 2002; Shah, 2001). The exclusion of prostitutes and those with communicable diseases is still law today, while the exclusion of gays and lesbians was repealed in 1990.

Other historians have taken a broader approach, tracking the influence of changes originating in the foundational era on later immigration regulation. On the forefront of this approach is Mae Ngai's *Impossible Subjects*, published in 2004. This work recasts both the foundational era and the twentieth century, demonstrating that the modern problem of "illegal" migration was born out of policies of the 1920s. Restrictive policies of that era, intended to limit immigration, actually resulted in more illegal immigration. Factors pushing migrants from their home countries – war, famine, economic hardship – and pulling them to the United States – economic opportunity, the chance to reunite with family members, relative peace and freedom – remained unchanged, but 1920s policies made little effort to account for relentless demand. Congress in 1929 for the first time made unauthorized entry a crime, punishable by fines and/or imprisonment, and illegal entrants could be deported at any time after entry, with no statute of limitations. Congress also created the Border Patrol. As Ngai explains, these restrictions "produced the illegal alien as a new legal and political subject, whose inclusion within the nation was simultaneously a social reality and a legal impossibility – a subject barred from citizenship and without rights" (Ngai, 2004: 4).

Ngai is among those who have emphasized looking beyond Ellis Island, that familiar marker of the nineteenth-century immigrant experience, to Angel Island off the coast of San Francisco. It was the official entry point for immigrants from Asia, most commonly from China and Japan. Ellis

Island and Angel Island are on opposite coasts and opposite ends of an historiographical divide, between the mythic immigrant experience of sailing past the Statute of Liberty into the open arms of New York City and the alternate immigrant experience of harsh and arbitrary treatment due only to one's racial or ethnic identity. Only on Angel Island were migrants detained for months or even years at a time in deplorable conditions. Inspections and interviews there were far more invasive, as officials attempted to find any possible reason to exclude each migrant (Takaki, 1989; Lee, 2003).

In the past two decades historians have begun investigating the significance of the Asian migration experience (Chin and Cole, 1999). Numerically speaking, Asian migration was minor compared to European migration. However, the issue of Asian migration contributed to the development of law in a manner that far surpasses its numerical importance. Modern immigration jurisprudence is built upon cases that arose from attempts to restrict Asian migration. The arrival of these so-called "unassimilable" migrants sparked a legal debate about the identity of the United States. Was it ultimately a nation of immigrants, or was it an Anglo-Saxon territory with a white culture to preserve?

In 1882, Congress passed the first Chinese Exclusion Act, which barred Chinese laborers and prohibited the naturalization of all those of Chinese origin. It reaffirmed their exclusion in 1891 and 1903. In 1907 the United States signed a diplomatic agreement with Japan to greatly restrict Japanese immigration as well. In 1917, Congress created the "Asiatic Barred Zone," which barred entrants from China and Japan as well as India, Afghanistan, Turkey, Saudi Arabia, and the Polynesian Islands, among other countries.

The influence of Chinese Exclusion Laws, and later the Asiatic Barred Zone, on the development of immigration law was enormous. Migrants challenged these laws, with the result that they were litigated more frequently than other restrictions. At least four important legal developments arose from challenges to restrictive laws against Asian migrants: the establishment of the plenary power doctrine; the build-up of the administrative apparatus of immigration enforcement; constitutional support for the rights of aliens within U.S. borders (outside of the immigration context); and the litigation of "whiteness," stemming from racial aspects of naturalization laws.

Several historians have chronicled these interactions between immigration law and issues of Asian migration, most notably Lucy Salyer, Charles McClain (1996), Erika Lee (2003), and Bill Ong Hing (1993). Salyer, in *Laws Harsh as Tigers*, demonstrates how Chinese migrants challenged the laws and found a receptive audience in California federal district courts (1995). In high-profile cases defendants were ably represented by what Gabriel Chin has called a "'Dream Team' of elite lawyers of the day," thanks to the support of Chinese mutual aid societies which paid their fees (Chin, 2005: 9). Surprisingly, many petitioners were successful at the district court level, receiving favorable rulings from judges who could not in good conscience comply with questionable procedures used by immigration authorities to detain and deport migrants.

The favorable rulings presented a problem for the nascent immigration authorities in the federal government, housed at that time in the treasury department, who felt their power was undermined by these efforts at granting relief. Congress responded by expanding the regulatory bureaucracy. The contest over the federal government's ability to restrict Asian migration gave rise to new administrative and enforcement apparatus, connected to the expanding administrative state.

When challenges to the Chinese exclusion laws reached the Supreme Court, justices confronted the questions of jurisdiction over immigration and the individual rights of migrants. In two foundational cases, *Chae Chan Ping v. United States* (1889) and *Fong Yue Ting v. U.S.* (1893), the Court created the plenary power doctrine, placing power over immigration in Congressional hands with little to no judicial oversight.

Yet during this era the Court also introduced another lasting foundation to the modern system: the notion that even non-citizen aliens, as long as within U.S. territory, were protected by the Constitution. In *Yick Wo v. Hopkins* (1886), a unanimous Court ruled that a law applied in a discriminatory fashion against Chinese laundry owners violated the plaintiff's right to equal protection under the Fourteenth Amendment. The Court held that the Fourteenth Amendment applies "to all persons within the territorial jurisdiction, without regard to any differences of race, of color, or of nationality." Ten years after *Yick Wo*, the Court extended constitutional protection for aliens in *Wong Wing v. U.S.*, declaring that the Bill of Rights protects non-citizens from arbitrary action by the federal government (Neuman, 2005). A federal law required that unlawful migrants from China be sentenced to hard labor before their deportation. The Court held that such a punishment could not be imposed, even on a non-citizen, without due process, as guaranteed by the Fifth and Sixth Amendments. The significance of *Yick Wo* and *Wong Wing* cannot be overstated, since they continue to serve as a bulwark against the erosion of non-citizens' rights within U.S. borders.

Throughout the story of Asian exclusion is an elemental tension in immigration and nationality law more generally. Most migrants from Asian countries were banned from entering the United States entirely; for those who did enter, the path to citizenship was foreclosed, since the 1882 law declared that Chinese persons could not naturalize. Yet, because of the Fourteenth Amendment and the commitment to birthright citizenship, all children of those migrants were American citizens. Several scholars have highlighted the lasting influences these contradictory laws had on Asian communities in the United States well into the mid-twentieth century. As Erika Lee has shown, American citizens could be detained, questioned, and possibly deported due to their Chinese appearance. Such threats created a pervasive climate of fear, or what one Chinese-American group called "a veritable Reign of Terror" (Lee, 2003: 231). The influence of Chinese exclusion laws can also be seen on a macro-level. There was a marked gender imbalance among Chinese immigrant communities for almost a century, due to immigration authorities, who assumed all Chinese women not of the merchant class were prostitutes and thus excludable. Low numbers of Chinese women, combined with anti-miscegenation laws, greatly limited the ability of Chinese laboring men to start families in the U.S. (Chan, 1991; Hing, 1993).

Litigation about Asian exclusionary laws, in addition to laying the foundations of our current constitutional law of immigration, also led to a series of Supreme Court cases defining race in the context of citizenship (commonly called racial prerequisite cases) (Haney-López, 1996). Each petitioner claimed to come within the language of naturalization laws, which at that time limited naturalization to "free white persons" or persons of "African descent." Some Asian petitioners succeeded in defining themselves as "white" in state and federal district courts, but the Supreme Court drew a hard line against Asian migrants, refusing to find that they were "Caucasian," no matter how highly-educated or light-skinned. As Ariela Gross notes, these cases expose the era's links between race and nationhood; a migrant's perceived racial identity was thought to affect his ability, or inability, to be a good American citizen (Gross, 2010: 252). These cases further illustrate the myriad ways in which discourses of race and migration have intersected in American history.

The mythic tale of Ellis Island and the revisionist corrective of Angel Island provide two poles to the immigration story during this era, but they are not enough. Not all migrants in the nineteenth and twentieth centuries entered the U.S. by sailing on a ship to a port of entry. Many new citizens or nationals became Americans not because of their own migration but as the result of American imperialism. In 1848, the United States incorporated approximately 80,000 new citizens living along the new U.S.-Mexico border (Nostrand, 1975); in 1898, the government gained control over Puerto Rico, Guam, and the Philippines. With new territories came new legal questions. What would be the status of these islands in relation to the United States? What would be the status of the people residing there?

The Supreme Court provided a partial answer via a collection of decisions now known as the *Insular Cases*, which determined that the U.S. government could maintain these islands as unincorporated territories, with no guarantees of either statehood or independence (Burnett and Marshall, 2001). The Court granted Congress plenary power over these new territories and the people living there, free of judicial oversight. Congress could decide how many rights – if any – these new colonial subjects would have.

Recently, historians have begun unraveling the motivations for these choices and exposing the prominent place that race and racism played in the decisions (Ngai, 2004; Gómez, 2007; Burnett and Marshall, 2001; Smith, 1997). As this scholarship demonstrates, imperialism was intimately connected to immigration and immigration law, since geographic expansion forced the polity to incorporate – or not incorporate – newly colonized peoples. In so doing, the government created differing legal statuses based on diverse political relationships between the United States and the territories. Importantly, the answer was not always the same. So for Mexico, incorporation theoretically meant full, treaty-guaranteed American citizenship; however, citizenship was not always granted, and those of Mexican descent faced numerous barriers to fair and equal treatment (Sánchez, 1993; Montejano, 1987; Gross, 2010). Although all territory ceded under the 1848 Treaty of Guadalupe Hidalgo eventually achieved statehood, New Mexico and Arizona were not granted statehood until 1911. The delay, as Laura Gómez demonstrates in her book *Manifest Destinies*, was largely due to legislators' fears that the majority Mexican-American population would not be capable of self-government (Gómez, 2007).

Until 1911, Mexican-American residents of Arizona and New Mexico had federal, but not state, citizenship. The issue of the Mexican cession was therefore alive and well when Congress and the Court were discussing the status of territories gained from Spain in 1898. For those islanders, congressional debates raised similar arguments against full incorporation: the "mongrel" and "savage" races, if granted full American citizenship, might degrade the polity. The government chose to treat these territories as perpetual colonies, and residents received a new status of "U.S. national," somewhere between citizen and alien, without rights of political representation. Residents could travel to and from the United States without being subjected to the numerical restrictions put in place in 1924. Yet they were simultaneously treated as aliens, without full rights and unable to naturalize (Burnett, 2008).

Mexican-Americans eventually attained both state and federal citizenship, but Puerto Ricans did not. Puerto Rico remains an unincorporated territory, and although Puerto Ricans are considered U.S. citizens, they cannot vote in U.S. elections unless they are resident within one of the fifty states. The Philippines eventually was granted independence, with the result that Filipinos could no longer freely migrate to the United States. The historical relationship of the U.S. with the Philippines and Mexico continues to affect migration today; citizens from either country who seek to enter as permanent residents face one of the longest backlogs in the system, waiting in some cases more than ten years for admission.

The idiosyncratic treatment of peoples from Mexico and former Spanish colonies during imperialism's heyday helps explain the origins and legacy of two major migrant groups during the remainder of the twentieth century, as well as address the unique position of Puerto Ricans as, in a sense, citizen aliens. Furthermore, comparing the discourses of immigration law and imperialism reveals common themes in both: fear of the unassimilable other; deployment of ideas about racial inferiority in political decisions; and the remarkable power granted in these two areas to the legislative and executive branches, free of judicial oversight.

Challenges of Wartime and Economic Depression: 1920s–1960s

The 1924 national origins quota system was not fully repealed until 1965. Immigration law did not remain static, however. Legislators passed amendments to the law, and the Immigration and Naturalization Service (INS) created new practices that changed the nature of migration. Unlike the foundational era, this next stage has been less comprehensively addressed by legal historians, due to the piecemeal nature of legal change during these middle decades. Immigration historians grappling with this era have focused on two areas as the primary drivers of legal change: war and the economy.

War opened new opportunities for inclusion of immigrant communities. Military service could be a boon; those who volunteered to serve might receive an expedited path to citizenship (Samito, 2009; Salyer, 2004). During World War II, Congress repealed the Chinese Exclusion Laws, which were at odds with the relationship between the U.S. and China as wartime allies. Congress also passed laws advantageous to foreign brides of U.S. soldiers (Zeiger, 2010: 5).

Between 1945 and 2000, more than 4 million refugees arrived in the United States, fifteen percent of the total 28 million immigrant arrivals (Bon Tempo, 2008). The distinct category of "refugee" – as a subset of "immigrant" – has its own historical trajectory. Refugees must meet a threshold test, demonstrating that they are fleeing persecution in their home country. The 1930s provided the first major opportunity for the United States to admit refugees, in this case individuals fleeing Hitler's policies. In 1948, Congress passed the Displaced Persons Act, which admitted 200,000 refugees from postwar Europe.

Wartime thus provided novel opportunities for the admission and inclusion of immigrants. Yet wartime also triggered rights deprivations and the creation of new ideological restrictions on migration. Government officials used these restrictions to deport migrants based on political persuasion. Congress passed the first such laws well before the twentieth century, in 1798. The Alien and Sedition Acts were composed of four separate laws, each giving the federal government power to control and punish enemy aliens. One, known as the Enemy Alien Act, remains good law today. It gives the executive branch unreviewable powers to detain, intern, and expel any citizen of any country with which the United States is at war (Cole, 2003).

At the turn of the twentieth century, political persuasion for the first time became an explicit ground of inadmissibility within immigration law. Efforts to exclude and deport those considered "subversive" intensified prior to World War I, when "enemy alien" and "labor radical" were often assumed by nativist politicians and government officials to be one and the same. Unable to prosecute such "subversives" through other legal channels, federal officials increasingly turned to immigration law, which gave greater latitude in punishing persons – through deportation – for their beliefs. World War II also triggered its share of threats to immigrants and citizens alike, on the basis of perceived disloyalty. Japanese internment is the most notorious example: the government interned 110,000 persons of Japanese descent, 70,000 of whom were U.S. citizens.

During and after World War II, Congress passed laws aimed at current or former members of the Communist Party, and courts enforced these laws with remarkable deference. In *Harisiades v. Shaughnessy* (1952), the Supreme Court affirmed the deportation of three permanent residents for their former communist affiliation, despite the fact that the deportation provision under which they were charged was not in effect at the time they were members (Neuborne, 2005).

Legal changes in the 1980s and 1990s shifted the language of the Immigration and Nationality Act from a focus on Communism to a focus on terrorism. Today, former communists can be admitted under an exception for past membership, but any person who has ever committed "terrorist activity" is inadmissible. In theory, the statute now emphasizes national security threats, a shift from excluding people for their ideas to excluding them for potentially dangerous acts. Yet ideological exclusion remains, as even those who have innocently given money to a seemingly benevolent charity can be excluded, deported, or placed in prison if the charity has terrorist connections.

The effects of economic fluctuations on immigration law is the other major theme of works covering this mid-century era, and perhaps nowhere is this relationship more evident than with regard to Mexican migration. The literature on Mexican migration shows that economic pressures – like war – could provide great opportunities for some immigrants while inflicting severe costs on others. With their long tradition of working and living in the borderlands, their close economic, cultural, and social connections to the Southwest, and their proximity to the U.S., Mexican migrants proved to be an essential part of America's workforce. Yet they have been easy scapegoats during the twentieth century, especially during times of economic hardship, subjected to what Daniel Kanstroom aptly labels "a recurrent pattern of recruitment, restriction, and expulsion" (2007: 215). Some animus has been expressed through politics and culture, but it has also been expressed through law. Mexicans were excluded and deported in ever-increasing numbers during the 1920s, oftentimes on the grounds that they were "likely to become a public charge." During the Great Depression use of deportation skyrocketed, as more than 1 million persons of Mexican descent, some of them American citizens, were forcibly removed in an effort to rid the country of persons perceived as a drain on the malfunctioning economy. Government officials used both legal and extralegal means of removal (Kanstroom, 2007; Balderrama and Rodriguez, 1995; Ngai; 2004). Whole communities were rounded up by local and state officials and put on trains, sent "home" to a country that some had never seen.

As the economy rebounded in the 1940s, the U.S. government did an about-face, recruiting Mexican workers to fill labor shortages. In 1942, Congress lifted the long-standing ban on contract labor and created the Bracero Program, the first temporary guest worker plan, in hopes of bringing in migrant laborers who could then be sent home at the end of their stay (Calavita, 1992). The program involved more than 4 million workers in a twenty-year span and bolstered long-standing traditions of Mexican migrant labor. Intended to terminate illegal immigration, it instead contributed to it, since labor demand still exceeded supply, poverty in Mexico remained high, and growers capitalized on the recruitment of those who wanted to become braceros but were refused.

As the economy's pendulum swung back, the Justice Department began the infamously-named "Operation Wetback" in 1954, a large-scale effort to round up and deport Mexican laborers. Recent work by Kelly Lytle Hernández has demonstrated the integral role that the federal Border Patrol played throughout the twentieth century in mediating and enforcing conflicted responses towards Mexican labor migration (2010). At first glance, it would seem the Border Patrol's task was simple: enforcing immigration control measures along territorial boundaries. Yet, as Hernández, Peter Andreas (2000), Timothy Dunn (1996), Mae Ngai (2004), and Joseph Nevins (2010), among others, have demonstrated, the Border Patrol's role was far more complex, operating at times in the interests of southwestern agribusiness through selective enforcement and outright collusion. In one infamous example, agents in El Paso allowed more than seven thousand Mexicans to enter illegally, arrested them, and then paroled them to the custody of growers (Ngai, 2004). As Hernández notes, an obsession with U.S.-Mexico border enforcement "effectively Mexicanized the set of inherently and lawfully unequal social relations emerging from the legal/illegal divide" (2010: 10). Once again, the legal history of immigration demonstrates the tangled relationship between race and immigrant status.

The Civil Rights Era and Beyond

The Immigration Act of 1965 ushered in a new era of immigration law by ending the 1924 national origins quota system. Historians generally agree about why the bill became law: concerns about America's image to the world in the Cold War era; mobilization by powerful immigrant groups, especially European Americans; and the push toward racial egalitarianism in other venues, namely civil rights (Reimers, 1992). The Hart-Celler Act, as it is also known, removed race as an explicit part of the admissions framework. It also affirmed two primary avenues for accepting legal permanent residents: family reunification and employment. Almost any migrant wishing to become a permanent resident must fit these categories (excepting refugees and asylees). The Act retained a numerical limitation, but did so by creating per-country and per-category caps. "Immediate relatives" of American citizens – spouses, parents, and unmarried sons or daughters – could enter without limitation (Ngai, 2004). The demographic profile of immigration changed: Asia, Latin America, and the Caribbean sent the vast majority of migrants by the 1970s (Tichenor, 2002: 219–220).

The post-1965 era of immigration law is ripe for treatment by historians. There is a noticeable gap in the literature when it comes to the sociolegal history of immigrants and immigrant communities in the post-1965 era, with a few exceptions (Hing, 1993; Bon Tempo, 2008). Important laws passed in the 1980s and 1990s have yet to receive treatment by legal historians. In 1986, Congress passed the Immigration Reform and Control Act (IRCA), which granted amnesty to approximately 3 million undocumented immigrants and established a system of employer sanctions to punish those who employ aliens ineligible to work. The attacks of September 11, 2001, triggered a reorganization of immigration matters; the Homeland Security Act of 2002 and the USA PATRIOT Act placed jurisdiction over migrants in the newly-created Department of Homeland Security and expanded the terrorist grounds of inadmissibility (Cole, 2003). The so-called "War on Terror" era will no doubt provide rich fodder for historical interpretation.

Conclusion: New Directions

Cutting-edge work in the legal history of immigrants is beginning to expand our idea of what counts as immigration law. Scholars are exploring the law "on the ground," in border patrol stations, inspection posts, and work sites (Hernández, 2010). Deportation is now beginning to receive the same sort of scholarly attention as laws that determine whether an immigrant will be admitted (Lee, 2003; Kanstroom, 2007).

Immigration law continues to change, and immigrants face a shifting legal landscape. Two themes in contemporary legal scholarship would benefit from historians' attention: the increasing criminalization of immigration law (aptly termed "crimmigration" law (Stumpf, 2006)), and the conflict between states, municipalities, and the federal government over enforcement. These topics are reminiscent of struggles in the eighteenth and nineteenth centuries, so renewed investigation will demonstrate what has changed in the contemporary period. Historians should also pay attention to lesser-known state and local laws that turn on alienage status, including laws relating to voting, holding property, and licensing (Hayduk, 2006; Motomura, 2006). How have alienage laws changed over time, and what have been the driving forces of change?

Finally, immigration history also benefits from increasing attention to transnational dimensions. Globalization presents unique issues in this field; as countries have become more economically, culturally, and socially connected, how have notions of citizenship and alienage status changed? What becomes of people who are caught between sovereigns, or, as Linda Kerber terms it, the "stateless" persons among us (Kerber, 2006)? There is rich new ground to break here.

References

Abrams, Kerry (2009). "The Hidden Dimensions of Nineteenth-Century Immigration Law." *Vanderbilt Law Review* 62(5): 1353–1418.

Andreas, Peter (2000). *Border Games: Policing the U.S.-Mexico Divide*. Cornell University Press, Ithaca.

Bailyn, Bernard (1986). *Voyagers to the West: A Passage in the Peopling of America on the Eve of the Revolution*. Knopf, New York.

Balderrama, Francisco E. and Rodriguez, Raymond (1995). *Decade of Betrayal: Mexican Repatriation in the 1930s*. University of New Mexico Press, Albuquerque.

Baseler, Marilyn C. (1998). *"Asylum for Mankind": America, 1607–1800*. Cornell University Press, Ithaca and London.

Bon Tempo, Carl J. (2008). *Americans at the Gate: The United States and Refugees During the Cold War*. Princeton University Press, Princeton.

Brubaker, Rogers (1992). *Citizenship and Nationhood in France and Germany*. Harvard University Press, Cambridge, MA.

Burnett, Christina Duffy (2008). "'They Say I am Not an American...': The Noncitizen National and the Law of American Empire." *Virginia Journal of International Law* 48(4): 659–718.

Burnett, Christina Duffy and Marshall, Burke, eds (2001). *Foreign in a Domestic Sense: Puerto Rico, American Expansion, and the Constitution*. Duke University Press, Durham.

Calavita, Kitty (1984). *U.S. Immigration Law and the Control of Labor, 1820–1924*. Academic Press, London.

Calavita, Kitty (1992). *Inside the State: The Bracero Program, Immigration, and the I.N.S.* Routledge, New York.

Chan, Sucheng (1991). "The Exclusion of Chinese Women, 1870–1943," in Chan, ed., *Entry Denied: Exclusion and the Chinese Community in America, 1882–1943*, 94–146. Temple University Press, Philadelphia.

Chin, Gabriel J (2005). "Chae Chan Ping and Fong Yue Ting: The Origins of Plenary Power." In Martin and Schuck, eds, *Immigration Stories*. Foundation Press, New York.

Chin, Gabriel J. and Cole, Richard P. (1999). "Emerging from the Margins of Historical Consciousness: Chinese Immigrants and the History of American Law." *Law and History Review* 17(2): 325–364.

Cole, David (2003). *Enemy Aliens: Double Standards and Constitutional Freedoms in the War on Terrorism*. New Press, New York.

Dunn, Timothy (1996). *The Militarization of the U.S.-Mexico Border, 1978–1992: Low-Intensity Conflict Doctrine Comes Home*. University of Texas Press, Austin.

Gómez, Laura E. (2007). *Manifest Destinies: The Making of the Mexican American Race*. New York University Press, New York.

Gross, Ariela J. (2010). *What Blood Won't Tell: A History of Race on Trial in America*. Harvard University Press, Cambridge, MA.

Handlin, Oscar (1959). *Boston's Immigrants: A Study in Acculturation*. Atheneum, New York.

Haney-López, Ian (1996). *White by Law: The Legal Construction of Race*. New York University Press, New York.

Hayduk, Ron (2006). *Democracy for All: Restoring Immigrant Voting Rights in the United States*. Routledge, New York.

Hernández, Kelly Lytle (2010). *Migra!: A History of the U.S. Border Patrol*. University of California Press, Berkeley.

Herndon, Ruth (2001). *Unwelcome Americans: Living on the Margin in Early New England*. University of Pennsylvania Press, Philadelphia.

Higham, John (1955). *Strangers in the Land: Patterns of American Nativism, 1860–1925*. Rutgers University Press, New Brunswick, NJ.

Hing, Bill Ong (1993). *Making and Remaking Asian America through Immigration Policy, 1850–1990*. Stanford University Press, Stanford, CA.

Hutchinson, Edward P. (1981). *Legislative History of American Immigration Policy, 1798–1965*. University of Pennsylvania Press, Philadelphia.

Ignatiev, Noel (1995). *How the Irish Became White*. Routledge, New York.

Kanstroom, Dan (2007). *Deportation Nation: Outsiders in American History*. Harvard University Press, Cambridge, MA.

Kerber Linda K. (2006). "Toward a History of Statelessness in America." In Dudziak and Volpp, eds, *Legal Borderlands: Law and the Construction of American Borders*, 135–157. Johns Hopkins University Press, Baltimore, MD.

Kraut, Alan M. (1994). *Silent Travelers: Germs, Genes and the "Immigrant Menace"*. Basic Books, New York.

Lee, Erika (2003). *At America's Gates: Chinese Immigration During the Exclusion Era, 1882–1943*. University of North Carolina Press, Chapel Hill.

Lee, Erika (2006). "A Nation of Immigrants and a Gatekeeping Nation: American Immigration Law and Policy." In Ueda, ed., *A Companion to American Immigration*, 5–35. Blackwell Publishing, Malden, MA.

Luibhéid, Eithne (2002). *Entry Denied: Controlling Sexuality at the Border*. University of Minnesota Press, Minneapolis.

McClain, Charles J. (1996). *In Search of Equality: The Chinese Struggle against Discrimination in Nineteenth-Century America*. University of California Press, Berkeley.

Meining, D.W. (1986). *The Shaping of America: A Geographical Perspective on 500 Years of History, Volume 1: Atlantic America, 1492–1800*. Yale University Press, New Haven.

Montejano, David (1987). *Anglos and Mexicans in the Making of Texas, 1836–1986.* University of Texas Press, Austin.

Motomura, Hiroshi (2006). *Americans in Waiting: The Lost Story of Immigration and Citizenship in the United States.* Oxford University Press, New York.

Neuborne, Burt (2005). "*Harisiades v. Shaughnessy*: A Case Study in the Vulnerability of Resident Aliens." In Martin and Schuck, eds, *Immigration Stories*, 87–112. Foundation Press, New York.

Neuman, Gerald L. (1993). "The Lost Century of American Immigration Law (1776–1875)." *Columbia Law Review* 98(8): 1833–1901.

Neuman, Gerald L. (1996). *Strangers to the Constitution: Immigrants, Borders, and Fundamental Law.* Princeton University Press, Princeton, NJ.

Neuman, Gerald L. (2005). "*Wong Wing v. United States*: The Bill of Rights Protects Illegal Aliens." In Martin and Schuck, eds, *Immigration Stories*, 31–50. Foundation Press, New York.

Nevins, Joseph (2010). *Operation Gatekeeper and Beyond: The War on "Illegals" and the Remaking of the U.S.-Mexico Boundary.* Routledge, New York.

Ngai, Mae M. (2004). *Impossible Subjects: Illegal Aliens and the Making of Modern America.* Princeton University Press, Princeton, NJ.

Nostrand, Richard L. (1975). "Mexican Americans Circa 1850." *Annals of the Association of American Geographers* 65(3): 378–390.

Parker, Kunal M. (2001). "State, Citizenship, and Territory: The Legal Construction of Immigration in Antebellum Massachusetts." *Law and History Review* 19: 583–644.

Parker, Kunal M. (2008). "Citizenship and Immigration Law, 1800–1924: Resolutions of Membership and Territory." In Grossberg and Tomlins, eds, *The Cambridge History of Law in America*, Volume 2, 168–202. Cambridge University Press, Cambridge, UK.

Perea, Juan (1997). *Immigrants Out! The New Nativism and the Anti-Immigrant Impulse in the United States.* New York University Press, New York.

Pfander, James E. and Wardon, Teresa R. (2010). "Reclaiming the Immigration Constitution of the Early Republic: Prospectivity, Uniformity, and Transparency." *Virginia Law Review* 96: 359–441.

Reimers, David M. (1992). *Still the Golden Door: The Third World Comes to America.* 2nd Edition. Columbia University Press, New York.

Salyer, Lucy E. (1995). *Laws Harsh as Tigers: Chinese Immigrants and the Shaping of Modern Immigration Law.* University of North Carolina Press, Chapel Hill.

Salyer, Lucy E. (2004). "Baptism by Fire: Race, Military Service, and U.S. Citizenship Policy." *Journal of American History* 91(3): 847–876.

Samito, Christian G. (2009). *Becoming American Under Fire: Irish Americans, African Americans, and the Politics of Citizenship during the Civil War Era.* Cornell University Press, Ithaca, NY.

Sánchez, George J. (1993). *Becoming Mexican American: Ethnicity, Culture, and Identity in Chicano Los Angeles, 1900–1945.* Oxford University Press, New York.

Schuck, Peter H. and Smith, Rogers M. (1985). *Citizenship without Consent: Illegal Aliens in the American Polity.* Yale University Press, New Haven.

Shah, Nayan (2001). *Contagious Divides: Epidemics and Race in San Francisco's Chinatown.* University of California Press, Berkeley.

Smith, Rogers M. (1997). *Civic Ideals: Conflicting Visions of Citizenship in U.S. History.* Yale University Press, New Haven.

Smith, Rogers M. (2001). "The Bitter Roots of Puerto Rican Citizenship." In Burnett and Marshall, eds, *Foreign in a Domestic Sense: Puerto Rico, American Expansion, and the Constitution,* 349–371. Duke University Press, Durham and London.

Stave, Bruce M., Salerno, Aldo, and Sutherland, John F. (1994). *From the Old Country: An Oral History of the European Migration to America.* Twayne, New York.

Stumpf, Juliet (2006). "The Crimmigration Crisis: Immigrants, Crime, and Sovereign Power." *American University Law Review* 56(2): 367–420.

Takaki, Ronald T. (1989). *Strangers from a Different Shore: A History of Asian Americans.* Little, Brown, Boston.

Tichenor, Daniel J. (2002). *Dividing Lines: The Politics of Immigration Control in America.* Princeton University Press, Princeton, NJ.

Tomlins, Christopher (2010). *Freedom Bound: Law, Labor, and Civic Identity in Colonizing English America, 1580–1865.* Cambridge University Press, Cambridge and New York.

Wokeck, Marianne (1999). *Trade in Strangers: The Beginnings of Mass Migration to North America.* Pennsylvania State University Press, University Park.

Zeiger, Susan (2010). *Entangling Alliances: Foreign War Brides and American Soldiers in the Twentieth Century.* New York University Press, New York.

Zolberg, Aristede R. (2008). *A Nation by Design: Immigration Policy in the Fashioning of America.* Harvard University Press, Cambridge, MA.

Chapter Thirteen

THE LEGAL PROFESSION

Mark E. Steiner

Most historiographic essays are a variant of Whig history: older scholarship – at best, uneven, and, at worst, fatally flawed – has given way to the enlightened and progressive scholarship of the present day. With the subfield of the history of the legal profession, this ain't necessarily so. In fact, this subfield may have peaked in the 1980s. Consider that after the legal papers of Daniel Webster were published in 1982, four outstanding essay-reviews by prominent legal historians were published (Botein, 1985; Gordon, 1984a; Hartog, 1984; Konefsky, 1988; Newmyer, 1983). But the publication of the legal papers of Abraham Lincoln in an electronic edition in 2000 and a letterpress edition in 2008 occasioned no such reviews (Benner and Davis, 2000; Stowell, 2008). While Morton J. Horwitz devoted a chapter on the legal profession in The *Transformation of American Law, 1780–1860 (Transformation I)*, published in 1979, lawyers effectively disappeared from The *Transformation of American Law, 1870–1860 (Transformation II)*, published in 1992 (Horwitz, 1979; 1992). As a subfield that has attracted relatively few scholars, it may have never recovered from the untimely death of Stephen Botein in 1986, its most promising historian. The interest of most of the current scholars in this subfield comes from teaching professional responsibility courses in law schools. With some exceptions, their work focuses on the history of legal ethics (Carle, 1999; Pearce, 2001; Spaulding, 2003).

The failure to attract more scholars is somewhat understandable. American legal historians have long been associated with law schools. There, the history of the legal profession probably is linked to the self-congratulatory works by law professors like Charles Warren, Roscoe Pound, and Anton-Hermann

A Companion to American Legal History, First Edition.
Edited by Sally E. Hadden and Alfred L. Brophy.
© 2013 John Wiley & Sons Ltd. Published 2021 by John Wiley & Sons Ltd.

Chroust (Warren, 1911; Pound, 1953; Chroust, 1965). The work of Pound and Chroust, in particular, was excoriated by Horwitz in his famous essay on the "conservative tradition" in legal historiography: Pound was the "single most influential representative of orthodox lawyer's legal history" and Chroust's book on the legal profession was "one of the most notorious examples of the dominant form of conservative legal history" (Horwitz, 1973: 276, 278). Horwitz criticized their studies of the legal profession for emphasizing "patterns of recruitment and training for the bar" while ignoring "the relationship between what lawyers do and their political function" (Horwitz, 1973: 275). In addition to writing in what Horwitz termed a "conservative tradition," these law professors also wrote in an amateurish one. Their books have not aged well.

Studies of the legal profession no longer deserve this obloquy. Historians like Maxwell Bloomfield also wrote essentially "conservative" legal history but it was informed by historical training; others have contributed revisionist accounts of the recruitment and training of lawyers (Bloomfield, 1976; Abel, 1989; Auerbach, 1976b; Steiner, 1997). But other obstacles face this subfield beyond its now inaccurate association with conservative, celebratory "lawyer's history." Most law school professors left the practice of law because it was intellectually unfulfilling. These recovering lawyers aren't attracted to the study of the profession they fled. Moreover, most law school professors were trained as lawyers; consequently, they have little experience in the archival research that this subfield demands.

There are two towering figures in this subfield: Alexis de Tocqueville and J. Willard Hurst. The most famous commentary about the American bench and bar is found in Tocqueville's *Democracy in America*. What Daniel J. Boorstin once called "the standard source for generalizing about America" is also the standard source for generalizing about American lawyers (Tocqueville, [1835] 1990, I: vii). Tocqueville's comments appear in a chapter on "causes which mitigate the tyranny of the majority in the United States." The most quoted passage is Tocqueville's description of lawyers as the "American aristocracy":

> In America there are no nobles or literary men, and the people are apt to mistrust the wealthy; lawyers consequently form the highest political class and the most cultivated portion of society. They have therefore nothing to gain by innovation, which adds a conservative interest to their natural taste for public order. If I were asked where I place the American aristocracy, I should reply without hesitation that it is not among the rich, who are united by no common tie, but that it occupies the judicial bench and the bar.

Tocqueville described how American lawyers provide the "most powerful existing security against the excesses of democracy." Lawyers are by training conservative; they possess "certain habits of order" and "a taste for formalities" that make them hostile to "the revolutionary spirit and the unreflecting passions of the multitude." Lawyers hold immense political power. They serve as a mediating force – "lawyers belong to the people by birth and interest, and to the aristocracy by habit and taste; they may be looked upon as the connecting link between the two great classes of society" (Tocqueville [1835] 1990, I: 272–280).

Tocqueville is often referenced but seldom engaged. Robert W. Gordon notes that Tocqueville's famous passage about lawyers as the American aristocracy is now part of professional ritual, quoted at law school commencements and bar association meetings. While Gordon advocates this ideal of engaged lawyering for contemporary lawyers, he also has examined its historicity. Gordon argued that Tocqueville's ideal fell short of realization but those who believed in it actually accomplished a lot. Gordon pointed "to the triumph of the idea of the Constitution as law and the acceptance of judicial review"; Webster's success in promoting law and the Constitution as unifying symbols of nationhood; the legal professions' continued domination of office holding; and the assumption of responsibility by the bench and bar to define and enforce the rules of property rights and exchange (Gordon, 1985: 79).

Leaving aside the accuracy of Tocqueville's description of the American bar, he certainly described elite lawyers' understanding of their role. Russell G. Pearce has described how "the legal elite's original and uniquely American understanding of the lawyer's role was that lawyers were America's governing class." (Pearce does not address whether the conduct of this elite matched its professed beliefs.) Throughout most of the nineteenth century, this governing class ideal was grounded upon republican principles whereby lawyers engaged in the disinterested pursuit of the common good. In the late nineteenth century, republicanism was replaced with professionalism; however, the commitment to the ideal remained. According to Pearce, it wasn't until the 1960s that the hired gun ethic took over. Pearce suggests four factors for the decline in the governing class ideal: (1) the growing distrust of disinterested expertise, (2) increased individualism throughout American society, (3) the emergence of the public interest bar, and (4) the development of the pro bono ethical duty (Pearce, 2001: 383).

Willard Hurst remains the "near official" historian of the American legal profession, challenged only by Robert W. Gordon. Hurst covered the history of the bar in his classic work, *The Growth of American Law: The Law Makers* (1950). Hurst covered a 150-year period from 1790 to 1940, relying primarily on secondary sources. That much of Hurst's interpretation of this material remains useful over sixty years later says something about both his skill and the lack of subsequent attention the study of the legal profession has drawn.

Hurst proposed the character or identity of American lawyers could be traced by examining several elements: (1) popular attitudes toward the bar, (2) the position in class structure, (3) legal education, (4) admission, and

(5) internal organization of the bar. Hurst found relative continuity in popular attitudes (ambiguity) and in the legal profession's place in class structure (middle class). He found that legal education, admission, and internal organization were interrelated in development and tended to be strong or weak together.

On the evolution of law practice, he was interested in the work done by lawyers. Hurst traced the change in law practice from generalists to specialists and from advocate to counselor. He also examined the economics of the profession, considering changes in the size of firms, overhead costs, division of labor, income, and lay competition. Hurst outlined the "social functions of the bar," the jobs and skills identified with lawyers. Hurst suggested that after 1870 a revolution in law practice occurred as lawyers became corporate directors and advisors. Lawyers were no longer cleaning up messes; they were advising on how to avoid them. Their objectivity, not their partisanship, was valued. Another social function provided by lawyers was their participation in politics (Hurst, 1950). The biggest drawback to this study of the bar is that it is over sixty years old; however, Robert Gordon admirably has updated it (Gordon, 2002).

Hurst's work has been hailed as the "best general history of the bar" and Hurst's concerns continue to guide the subfield (Maru, 1986). The subfield still lacks an adequate one-volume history of the profession. Although Richard L. Abel has published *American Lawyers* (1989), its narrow focus on the historical sociology of the "modern" profession from the 1880s to the 1980s limits its usefulness as a general history of the bar. Moreover, Abel is primarily interested in the economic aspects of legal practice in terms of the "professional project" of lawyers to control the market for legal services and enhance their professional status. Abel suggests the formative years of this project occurred in the last third of the nineteenth century. Lawyers became a profession by limiting entry and by structuring the market to prevent competition from non-lawyers (Abel, 1989).

Synthesis is becoming more difficult as more work explores regional differences and the lack of homogeneity in the profession (Munger, 1994; Wald, 2008; 2009). Lawrence Friedman has produced the best synthesis of the work done on the American legal profession since Hurst. The picture that emerges is this: The colonial period was marked by a gradual acceptance of lawyers and increased professionalization at the bar. Lawyers became a necessary evil as colonial society became more complex and commercial. The nineteenth century saw the end of the hegemony of the courtroom. As the number of lawyers grew steadily, their functions changed; the corporation lawyer, the new figure of the profession, was much less focused on courtroom work. According to Friedman, the "rise of the Wall Street lawyer was the most important event in the life of the profession during this period." Corporate lawyers did not supplant other lawyers; they supplemented them. Corporate lawyers also ran in packs; accompanying the rise of corporate lawyers was the rise of corporate law firms, with the Cravath firm becoming the model. Like Abel and others, Friedman depicted the late nineteenth century and early twentieth century as critical to the development of the American legal profession. This crisis was not only a crisis in decency (which called for the promulgation of codes of conduct) but a "real sense of business crisis" (which called for restrictions to access to the bar). The second half of the twentieth century also saw the American legal profession change from a "white male preserve" to a much more diverse group of lawyers (Friedman, 2005: 485, 496, 538).

Synthesis is harder to achieve when research has tended to focus on either individual lawyers whose fame makes them hardly representative or unsystematic groupings of lawyers. Stephen Botein advised that a "full program of prosopographical research" would be required to better understand the history of the legal profession. Botein called for "well-defined sequences of research into the common background and behavioral characteristics of various groups of legal actors." In 1977, Botein could only point to Daniel Calhoun's study of antebellum Tennessee lawyers as a model for such research (Botein, 1977: 68–69). Calhoun brilliantly had used docket books from a handful of circuit courts to discover a decline of circuit riding, specialization of lawyers representing either plaintiffs or defendants, and how the handling of debt suits led to the domination of practice by one or two lawyers in each county (Calhoun, 1965). Botein overlooked Gary B. Nash's study of the antebellum bar in Philadelphia, which also serves as a pretty good model of systematic research of legal cohorts. Looking at two generational groups of lawyers, Nash found easier access to the legal profession from middle- and lower-class ranks in 1860 than in 1800–1805, when a homogenous bar consisted of the sons of the upper-class elite (Nash, 1965).

Botein's 1977 call for more prosopographical research has gone largely unheeded. The most thoroughly prosopographical research was done by Kermit Hall, who studied nineteenth-century judges. Hall, for example, found the lawyers from middle-class backgrounds most frequently reached the federal bench; he concluded the judges hardly constituted a hegemonic ruling class (Hall, 1980). Less research on defined cohorts has been done on lawyers in the twentieth century. Auerbach and Bardach looked at the career patterns of law review editors from three Ivy League schools from 1919 to 1941 and concluded that the increase in federal government employment reflected a shift in values (Auerbach and Bardach, 1973). Wald examined elite firms in Colorado and found recruitment differed significantly from the "Cravath model" (Wald, 2009). Mack has written a "collective biography" of modern civil rights lawyers (Mack, 2012).

The typical periodization employed by historians of the legal profession should be noted. Legal historians have generally constructed three periods: a roughly 150-year colonial period, an 80-year middle period dated from the Revolution to the Civil War, and a roughly 50-year modern period that lasted from 1870 until 1920. Not all scholars have maintained these strict boundaries. (Gawalt, 1979; Roeber, 1981; O'Brien, 1986).

The colonial period is generally portrayed as one of gradual professionalization. The work on the colonial bar has been published primarily as articles or book chapters, only a few need be noted here. John M. Murrin, in an influential essay on the "legal transformation" in eighteenth-century Massachusetts, portrayed a steady advance of the legal profession from the 1740s to the 1760s as the bench and bar became more English and more formal. The Massachusetts bar between 1760–1775 "consciously restructured itself along English lines" (Murrin, 1983: 565). Botein found the same general pattern throughout the colonies. Before 1700, there were "only occasional glimpses of legal professionalism." After 1700, changes in mercantile activity and imperial governance created favorable opportunities for lawyers. While the practice of law became more lucrative and more English, the colonial bar did not develop the functional divisions of practice along English lines (Botein, 1981: 132). More recently, Mary Sarah Bilder argued that the commonly accepted dichotomy of a seventeenth-century colonial society without lawyers and an eighteenth-century society with them was too dependent on modern conceptions of professionalism. Bilder instead used a functional description of "legal literacy" and found accomplished "legal practitioners" in early Rhode Island legal culture (Bilder, 1999).

The antebellum period has been portrayed as either a formative or transformative era for the American legal profession. The most significant works are Perry Miller's work on the "legal mind" and Morton J. Horwitz's chapter on the legal profession in *Transformation of American Law* (Horwitz, 1979). Interestingly, what is most important about these works is the criticism they have drawn.

In his posthumously published *The Life of the Mind in America*, intellectual historian Perry Miller included an examination of the "legal mind." Miller presented a struggle in the early republic between head and heart, a struggle apparently won by the sheer intellectual force of such writers as Kent and Story. By winning the intellectual battle, the legal profession secured its position of political and intellectual domination. Arguments advanced by treatise writers and judges overcame the popular mistrust of law and lawyers and antagonism toward English common law. Having convinced Americans that law did not represent tyranny, lawyers won a second round that centered on the proper role of attorneys (Miller, 1965).

Miller's work was not particularly well received. Lawrence M. Friedman criticized his "strained and strange view of American law and the legal profession" (Friedman, 1968: 1244). Friedman, Stanley Katz, and Stephen Botein all complained about the size of the vineyard where Miller toiled. For sources, Miller relied too heavily on the "rhetoric of professional speeches and other self-justifying public statements" of relatively few lawyers (Botein, 1977: 62); "formal literary" sources instead of the working papers of lawyers (Katz, 1966: 877); and "windy prefaces and orations" and "the literary remains of a small group of eminent jurists" (Friedman, 1968: 1254, 1257). Miller had little to say about the actual behavior of the elite lawyers and judges he studied; he had nothing to say about the rest of the (non-elite) bar (Friedman, 1968; Botein, 1977). While Miller's interpretative framework of the "legal mind" bears little influence on current scholarship, his collection of documents published in 1962 continues to shape what voices are heard from the antebellum bar (Miller, 1962).

Horwitz asserts that the major transformation of the legal system that took place during the eighty years after the American Revolution "reflected aspects of social struggle." This legal transformation "enabled emergent entrepreneurial and commercial groups to win a disproportionate share of wealth and power in American society." The transformation thus was the result of the "forging of an alliance between legal and commercial interests." Lawyers conspired with commercial interests to redistribute wealth in a "reverse-Robin Hood" manner (Horwitz, 1979: xvi, 140).

Horwitz's depiction of the legal profession's instrumental role in changing legal doctrine to accommodate the "needs" of market capitalism has not attracted the same amount of attention as the rest of the book. Mark Tushnet complained that Horwitz had advanced too narrow a conception of the bar's interests and had failed to tell the entire story. Tushnet attempted to recast the antebellum bar in Gramscian terms: "the development of American law embodied a process by which 'organic' lawyers of the emergent bourgeoisie won over 'traditional' lawyers" (Tushnet, 1978: 107).

Other scholars have questioned Horwitz's portrait of a unified antebellum bar. John Phillip Reid, for example, criticized Horwitz's "tendency of attributing unanimity to events" (Reid, 1977: 1311). Alfred S. Konefsky faulted Horwitz for using changes in legal doctrine to prove an alliance between lawyers and commercial interests. Konefsky studied the antebellum Boston bar, detailing the "interconnected nature of the social visions expressed and the social ties woven by lawyers and other elites." Konefsky found that elite lawyers and members of other elite groups in Boston shared both social space and basic values (Konefsky, 1988: 1121).

The publication of legal papers answers a critical need for the study of the legal profession. Clearly, the greatest deficiency of work on American lawyers is its overall neglect of everyday practice. As Kenneth Mack notes, almost nothing is known about day-to-day law practice before the 1960s for most demographic groups of lawyers, except lawyers at large law firms and a few lawyer-politicians like Abraham Lincoln (Mack, 2002). John Henry Schlegel similarly noted how the lawyer was the "key, neglected actor" in twentieth-century legal history. Schlegel posed these questions for future research: "Just what have lawyers done all day? And how has it changed? As long as these baseline questions go unanswered we shall never come close to knowing the important why?" (Schlegel, 1988: 974).

The neglect of the lives of working lawyers is not limited to the twentieth century. Lawrence Friedman observed that "rare indeed are books that open the door to the lawyer's office" (Friedman, 2005: 589).

The failure to recapture the working lives of lawyers has several causes. Sources are either ephemeral, inaccessible, or unyielding (Konefsky, 1976). For example, Milton M. Klein found the surviving papers of New York lawyer William Livingston "help to establish the extent of his practice but disclose little concerning the nature of his cases or his working methods" (Klein, 1958: 342). Some historians have used extant fee books to capture some glimpses of the everyday practice of colonial and antebellum lawyers. The records of the pre-revolutionary bar in Massachusetts, New York, and Virginia reveal lawyers who had to seek alternative sources of income in land speculation and political office; the bulk of an attorney's practice was debt collection and real property litigation; and fees were limited by statute (McKirdy, 1976; Eaton, 1951; Klein, 1958). After the Revolution, lawyers in South Carolina also spent most of their efforts in debt collection (Hadden, 2009). In nineteenth-century Kansas, minimum fee schedules were used to address overcrowding; in antebellum Virginia, young lawyers found it increasingly important to associate with older attorneys to "break into the profession" (Hoeflich, 2000; Shepard, 1982).

One part of the colonial and antebellum lawyer's office has been fairly well scrutinized: the bookshelves. Long a staple of scholarly research, there has been renewed interest in lawyer's libraries as part of the "history of the book" (Bilder, 1999; Brophy, 2003). More than traditional legal treatises have received increased attention. Recent work has examined the use of justice of the peace manuals in colonial Virginia and the importance of form books and law blanks for nineteenth-century lawyers (Conley, 1985; Hoeflich, 2008). There also has been some effort to recreate how lawyers actually used their books in practice (Steiner, 2010).

Biographies of individual lawyers and judges have always constituted a substantial portion of the work done on the legal profession. These biographies inevitably have an elite bias; would-be biographers are not drawn to obscure lawyers. But the subjects of these biographies tend to be lawyers who were generally even more famous as politicians or judges. Consequently, their biographers largely avoid discussing the law practice of their subjects. Scholars also hoped to avoid "the frequent obscurities and intermittent venality of private practice" (Botein, 1976: 456) or the "trivial, repetitious, and boring" details of day-to-day practice (Gordon, 1984a: 446). Robert W. Gordon noted how biographers of lawyers tend to address "about almost any aspect of their careers other than how they made a living" (Gordon, 1984a: 445). Stephen Botein suggested that scholars choose lawyers who oriented toward public service or those who left some evidence of "vigorous intellectual activity," which has led to a preponderance of judicial biographies (Botein, 1976: 456). With rare exceptions, judicial biographies are about justices on the United States Supreme Court (Reid, 1995).

This pattern of neglect of the everyday practice of lawyers is evidenced in such biographies of nineteenth-century lawyers such as Rufus Choate, Felix Grundy, James Louis Petigru, and Hugh Legaré, where details of their professional lives are scant (Matthews, 1980; Pease and Pease, 2002; Heller, 2010; O'Brien, 1985). One notable exception is John Moretta's biography of Texas lawyer William Pitt Ballinger. Moretta examined the gritty details of Ballinger's practice: land claims, collection work for Northern firms, and railroad litigation, where Ballinger felt a loss of autonomy as a "division attorney" (Moretta, 2000).

This brings us back to the publication of legal papers. Because many American statesmen of the early republic and antebellum era were lawyers, their professional papers have survived to a far greater extent than those of their lesser known colleagues at the bar and their professional lives have garnered more interest. In the last fifty years, editions of the legal papers of John Adams, Alexander Hamilton, Daniel Webster, Andrew Jackson, and Abraham Lincoln have been published (Wroth and Zobel, 1965; Goebel, 1964–1981; Konefsky and King, 1982; Ely and Brown, 1987; Benner and Davis, 2000; Stowell, 2008). The most influential edition is the *Legal Papers of Daniel Webster*. The editors presented a conceptual framework for understanding the changes in Webster's practice from a rural environment to an elite urban setting. Webster balanced the interests of the community in his early practice while in his later practice he was less autonomous and more directed toward the needs of his individual clients (Konefsky and King, 1982).

The publication occasioned a remarkable set of essay-reviews by noted legal historians Hendrik Hartog, Stephen Botein, Robert W. Gordon, and Kent Newmyer. Hartog noted the difficulty of using legal biography to explain the social history of the legal profession, asking whether one lawyer's career can "represent significant features of the history of the legal profession"–particularly Webster's rather singular career (Hartog, 1984: 1109). R. Kent Newmyer was more receptive to the representativeness of Webster's career, believing that Webster was like most of the outstanding lawyers of the early republic "when he was drawn willingly into the urban orbit of commercial capitalism." Newmyer argued that Webster didn't have "a grand plan for the modernization of the New England commercial law" because the "case-by-case, day-by-day nature of lawyering militated against long-range strategy" (Newmyer, 1983: 825, 827). Botein welcomed Konefsky and King's use of Webster's practice to make generalizations about the practice of law in the early republic. While other editions of legal papers had avoided "routine actions of debt or ejectment, then the bread and butter of practice," Konefsky and King instead embraced "the grubby details of rural debt collection." Botein suspected that Webster's early rural practice may have been typical but his later Boston practice "looks suspiciously unique" (Botein, 1985: 222, 225). Robert W. Gordon hailed the publication of the Webster papers along with the earlier publication of the legal papers of Adams and Hamilton. All three collections served as exhaustive guides to the routine business of successful lawyers from the mid-eighteenth to mid-nineteenth century. Like Botein, Gordon accepted the contours of Webster's career as presented by Konefsky and King. Webster's climb upward illuminated how legal business came to be divided by the early nineteenth-century bar (Gordon, 1984a).

The development of the "modern" legal profession is often traced to the end of the nineteenth century and beginning of the twentieth (Abel, 1989; Auerbach, 1976b; Gawalt, 1984). This period witnessed the rise of large law firms, the shift by elite lawyers from trial practice to transactional work, and the increased stratification of the profession. The two key works are Jerold S. Auerbach's *Unequal Justice: Lawyers and Social Change in Modern America* (1976) and *The New High Priests: Lawyers in Post-Civil War America*, a collection of influential essays published in 1984 (Gawalt, 1984).

The New High Priests contains several influential essays on the development of the modern legal profession. The most cited is probably Robert W. Gordon's "'The Ideal and the Actual in the Law': Fantasies and Practices of New York City Lawyers, 1870–1910." Gordon described the attempt by elite lawyers to work on behalf of the "ideology of scientific reform." While these efforts to develop "legal science" and institute legal reforms may have served their material interests, Gordon insisted that they were also motivated by "ideal interests." Unfortunately, the character of practice changed as these lawyers now were doing "essentially business jobs," and were no longer doing work that required the "repositories and oracles of legal science." Elite lawyers gave up on their practical attempts to unify public and private roles, taking divergent paths as classical-liberal reactionaries, schizophrenics who alternated between public and private roles, and "apolitical technicians" (Gordon, 1984b: 53, 61). Wayne K. Hobson described the emergence of the large law firm in the period from the 1870s to the 1920s. He quantified the growth of "large firms" (more than five partners and associates) and "law factories" (more than ten partners and associates) in five cities. Like Auerbach, Hobson stressed the importance of the Cravath model (Hobson, 1984).

While *Unequal Justice* covered roughly from the 1870s to the 1970s, its portrait of "how a stratified bar" emerged in the early twentieth century has had the most influence. Auerbach suggests that the structure of the modern legal profession was built in the period from 1905 to 1925. Oddly for a book about stratification, Auerbach primarily examined "the response of elite lawyers to social change"; the voices of non-elite lawyers are largely missing. Like most historians writing about lawyers, Auerbach also neglected the day-to-day practice of law. What he does present though is a devastating portrait of the arrogance and ethnic and class bias of elite lawyers and law professors.

These lawyers and professors were predominately white Anglo-Saxon Protestants reacting to changing immigration and demographic patterns. For most of the nineteenth century, lawyers had shared "ethnic homogeneity." Industrialization, urbanization, and immigration changed that. The bar became stratified as WASP lawyers retreated to corporate enclaves – the "corporate law firm was their fortress." Following the Cravath model, these firms hired graduates who had the right ethnic, social, and law school credentials.

The corporate lawyers became the leaders of bar associations that, in turn, led the way for changes in education, admission, ethics and lawyer discipline. Newly enacted canons of ethics reflected and reinforced a stratified bar. They sought to regulate and restrict the activities of non-elite lawyers – sole practitioners in urban areas, many of whom were foreign-born. New rules on contingent fees and solicitation restricted the practice of personal injury lawyers. Elite lawyers sought to raise educational standards and bar admission requirements. Barriers to entry were needed to block access to the profession from immigrants and Jews. Disgusted by the flood of lawyers with "foreign names," elite lawyers wanted to put more obstacles on the path to a legal career. By toughening bar examinations, more would-be lawyers would have to attend law school. When night schools provided affordable and effective education to poor immigrants, educational requirements for admission were raised. These efforts had limited success on closing the door of opportunity and the New Deal presented new careers for lawyers shunned by elite law firms (Auerbach, 1976b: 107).

Unequal Justice is a great book with some serious flaws. Auerbach assumed that all professional developments in New York City influenced the rest of the country. He also admittedly failed to depict the everyday practice of either elite or non-elite lawyers. What elite lawyers actually did for American business was not explored. Other historians have examined the relationship between business and lawyers in this period and have developed a far more nuanced portrait.

Frank Munger's work on law practice in West Virginia does not support Auerbach's depiction of class divisions among clients being quickly reflected in the social and political hierarchy in the profession itself. Apparently, Fayette County, West Virginia is not the same as New York City. Almost all attorneys between 1880 and 1900 represented both workers and employers; in 1910, the county's largest firm continued to represent both injured workers and coal companies. Munger suggests that "the homogeneity of the lawyers, the limited client base, or the opportunities for more close-knit professional social networks may have made the changes in small town or rural law practice quite different from those in large cities" (Munger, 1994: 188).

Kenneth Lipartito, a business historian, examined the role of the Houston firm of Baker & Botts in the early twentieth century. Lipartito found that those lawyers solved the problems of corporate organization, mediated the relationship between their clients and the state, and served as a go-between for investors and entrepreneurs. The role of regional and local lawyers – not the corporate law firms in New York – was stressed by Lipartito, who argued that these lawyers "spearheaded the effort" against "legal localism." Firms like Baker & Botts in Houston were outposts of Wall Street values in what was still largely a rural, agrarian society. Lipartito describes how railroads called upon local lawyers to defend personal-injury lawsuits, and co-opted lawyers by the extensive distribution of small-town free passes, which came with a promise not to sue the railroads; other lawyers were retained by railroads. Lawyers as "mobilizers of capital" put together deals, bringing together capital and capitalists (Lipartito, 1990).

Lawyers in nineteenth-century El Paso played a direct role in that city's transformation from an isolated frontier community to a burgeoning border metropolis. Allison Brownell Tirres found that prior scholarship on western development had either underestimated the role of lawyers or had treated lawyers as more agents of capitalists and cattle ranchers. Tirres portrayed El Paso lawyers as playing active roles as land brokers, boosters, and social engineers. Lawyers were the main engine of change for western towns in the late nineteenth century, playing critical roles in the arrival of railroads, the dramatic increase in white settlement, and the consolidation of land into fewer hands (Tirres, 2010).

Eli Wald has decried the "standard story" of the American legal profession for its multiple biases: it is the story of large law firms specializing in corporate law located in large cities in the Northeast. In contrast to elite firms in New York City, Wald found that elite firms in Colorado didn't adopt the Cravath system. They instead practiced nepotism. These firms established diverse practice areas and recruited attorneys from non-elite law schools (Wald, 2009). While Auerbach and others portrayed Jewish lawyers seemingly relegated to "non-elite" practice such as personal injury and criminal defense, Wald has written about the rise (and fall) of Jewish law firms that handled transactional and corporate law work. In the 1950s and 1960s, large law firms were segregated along religious and cultural lines between WASP and Jewish firms (Wald, 2008).

Wald's work suffers a bias of its own: it too is limited to the world of large law firms and elite lawyers. Kenneth W. Mack has more directly challenged the dominance of elite lawyers in the historiography of the American legal profession. Mack also has noted how most analyses of the bar in the early twentieth century focused on elite lawyers. Mack examined "doubly marginalized" black women lawyers through the practice of Philadelphia lawyer Sadie T.M. Alexander, paying particular attention to Alexander's correspondence with her sisters in law. He found a "rich and complex professional world where black women lawyers' identities were constituted as much by everyday interactions with professional colleagues, judges, clients, and opponents as by the structural features of an exclusionary bar." Black women lawyers like

Alexander were able to obtain a "surprising, and often ironic, degree of power and prestige." Mack's portrait of Sadie Alexander thus contributes greatly to "the social history of the American legal profession" (Mack, 2002: 1409). Additionally, Virginia G. Drachman's collection of the letters from the Equity Club sheds considerable light on women lawyers' quest for professional identity in the late nineteenth century (Drachman, 1993).

While the work on elite lawyers traditionally neglected the details of their law practices, they fare better than the work on non-elite lawyers, who have been mostly ignored altogether. Alfred Konefsky once urged legal historians to "move beyond just the elite bar and spread the net wider." He noted, "What we have never really adequately had in this country is a legal history from the bottom up – a view of the invisible bar toiling away underneath the most prominent and accessible elite bar." Konefsky gave two examples of neglect: legal aid and personal injury lawyers (Konefsky, 1976: 308).

Since Konefsky's 1976 exhortation, some valuable work on non-elite lawyers has appeared. The early history of legal aid has been examined by Felice Batlan and Michael Grossberg. Grossberg studied the national movement for legal aid as part of the bar's larger political project to reconstruct the liberal state and preserve the place of lawyers in it. Grossberg argued that legal aid lawyers in the early twentieth century used their newly created role of representing poor clients to "police the profession's lower reaches." This new role also affected their "everyday professional practices" by emphasizing compromise and education rather than adversarial conflict (Grossberg, 1997: 307). Batlan argued that "gender was foundational to the development of legal aid and that women played crucial roles as lawyers, benefactors, and clients" (Batlan, 2010: 932–933).

Some initial work on the development of the personal injury bar has been done. William G. Thomas' study of railroad lawyers in the South also portrayed the emergence of their bêtes noires – "a specialized and successful personal injury bar" (Thomas, 1999: 45). While railroads tried to monopolize the best lawyers through the use of retainers and free passes, they had only marginal success because suing railroads proved as lucrative as representing them. Louis Anthes recreated the "social world of personal injury law" in 1920s Brooklyn. He found an "on-going social network" of immigrants, runners, doctors, police officers, and lawyers (Anthes, 2003: 133, 151).

The classic study of the modern Chicago bar found "two hemispheres" of the legal profession. Within these two hemispheres were separate professions, differentiated by lawyers who represent large organizations and those who represent individuals. The status and prestige of lawyers depends upon their distance from human suffering. Those lawyers who deal with the personal plight of low-status clients are afforded the least amount of status (Heinz, 1982). Those lawyers have been given relatively greater attention by sociologists than by legal historians, who seemingly reproduce the hierarchy of the legal profession by continuing to focus primarily on elite lawyers.

Sociologists Richard L. Abel and Philip S.C. Lewis have observed, "[W]e know more (if still very little) about lawyers representing individuals than about those serving companies and the state" (Abel and Lewis, 1995: 292). Sociologists have concentrated on such non-elite lawyers as divorce lawyers (Sarat and Felstiner, 1995), rural lawyers (Landon, 1990), and sole practitioners (Carlin, 1962), while legal historians have focused primarily on elite lawyers (Gordon, 1983; Horwitz, 1979; Miller, 1965; Shamir, 1995).

That legal historians and sociologists map different hemispheres of the profession may be because historians lack easily accessible archival material. The abundant work on cause lawyers, particularly those associated with the National Association for the Advancement of Colored People (NAACP), may reflect the existence of accessible archives of the organizations for which those lawyers worked (Carle, 2002; Ernst, 1995; Tushnet, 1987; Meier and Rudwick, 1976). But the problem with sources may be overstated. Jerold S. Auerbach noted in 1976 how he was unable to discover any collection of papers from "a country lawyer, an urban solo lawyer, an ambulance chaser, or a night school law teacher"; however, sources do exist that illuminate non-elite training and practice (Auerbach, 1976a: 312). Anthes used the records of disciplinary proceedings to reconstruct the world of "ambulance chasers" and records from proprietary law schools are extant (Anthes, 2003; Steiner, 1997).

The study of the history of the legal profession in America will be in good shape if certain trends continue. The variety of work on twentieth-century lawyers that has appeared in the last few years is encouraging (Mack, 2012; Mehrotra, 2010; Wald, 2008). The increasingly imaginative and sophisticated use of available sources by such scholars as Mary Sarah Bilder, Michael Grossberg, and Hendrik Hartog should inspire others to follow their path or make their own (Bilder, 1999; Grossberg, 1990; Hartog, 1997). And if we are really lucky, somebody will use all this rich scholarship to write the long overdue history of the profession.

References

Abel, Richard L. (1989). *American Lawyers.* Oxford University Press, New York.
Abel, Richard L. and Phillip, Lewis, S.C. (1995). "Putting Law Back into the Sociology of Lawyers." In Abel and Phillip, eds, *Lawyers in Society: An Overview.* University of California Press, 281–329, Berkeley.
Anthes, Louis (2003). *Lawyers and Immigrants, 1870–1940: A Cultural History.* LFB Scholarly Publishing LLC, Levittown, PA.
Auerbach, Jerold S. and Bardach, Eugene (1973). "'Born to an Era of Insecurity': Career Patterns of Law Review Editors, 1918–1941." *American Journal of Legal History* 17: 3–26.
Auerbach, Jerold S. (1976a). "Lawyers' Papers as a Source of Legal History: The 20th Century." *Law Library Journal* 69: 310–313.

Auerbach, Jerold S. (1976b). *Unequal Justice: Lawyers and Social Change in Modern America*. Oxford University Press, New York.

Batlan, Felice (2010). "The Birth of Legal Aid: Gender Ideologies, Women, and the Bar in New York City, 1863–1910." *Law and History Review* 28: 931–972.

Benner, Martha, and Davis, Cullom, eds (2000). *The Law Practice of Abraham Lincoln: Complete Documentary Edition*. 3 volumes. University of Illinois Press, Urbana.

Bilder, Mary Sarah (1999). "The Lost Lawyers: Early American Literates and Transatlantic Legal Culture." *Yale Journal of Law and the Humanities* 11: 47–117.

Bloomfield, Maxwell (1976). *American Lawyers in a Changing Society, 1776–1876*. Harvard University Press, Cambridge, MA.

Botein, Stephen (1976). "Biography in Legal History." *Law Library Journal* 69: 456–459.

Botein, Stephen (1977). "Professional History Reconsidered." *American Journal of Legal History* 21: 60–79.

Botein, Stephen (1981). "The Legal Profession in Colonial North America." In Prest, ed., *Lawyers in Early Modern Europe and America*, 129–146. Holmes & Meier, New York.

Botein, Stephen (1985). "Love of Gold and Other Ruling Passions: The Legal Papers of Daniel Webster." *American Bar Foundation Research Journal* 1985: 217–229.

Brophy, Alfred L. (2003). "The Law Book in Colonial America." *Buffalo Law Review* 51: 1119–1143.

Calhoun, Daniel H. (1965). *Professional Lives in America: Structure and Aspiration 1750–1850*. Harvard University Press, Cambridge, MA.

Carle, Susan B. (1999). "Lawyers' Duty to Do Justice: A New Look At the History of the 1908 Canons." *Law and Social Inquiry* 24: 1–44.

Carle, Susan B. (2002). "Race, Class, and Legal Ethics in the Early NAACP (1910–1920)." *Law and History Review* 20: 97–146.

Carlin, Jerome E. (1962). *Lawyers on Their Own: A Study of Individual Practitioners in Chicago*. Rutgers University Press, New Brunswick, NJ.

Chroust, Anton-Hermann (1965). *The Rise of the Legal Profession in America*. 2 volumes. University of Oklahoma Press, Norman.

Conley, John A. (1985). "Doing it by the Book: Justice of the Peace Manuals and English Law in Eighteenth Century America." *Journal of Legal History* 6: 257–298.

Drachman, Virginia G. (1993). *Women Lawyers and the Origins of Professional Identity in America: The Letters of the Equity Club, 1887 to 1890*. University of Michigan Press, Ann Arbor.

Eaton, Clement (1951). "A Mirror of the Southern Colonial Lawyer: The Fee Books of Patrick Henry, Thomas Jefferson, and Waightstill Avery." *William and Mary Quarterly* 8: 520–534.

Ely, Jr., James W. and Brown, Jr., Theodore, eds (1987). *Legal Papers of Andrew Jackson*. University of Tennessee Press, Knoxville.

Ernst, Daniel R. (1995). *Lawyers Against Labor: From Individual Rights to Corporate Liberalism*. University of Illinois, Urbana.

Friedman, Lawrence M. (1968). "Heart Against Head: Perry Miller and the Legal Mind." *Yale Law Journal* 77: 1244–1259.

Friedman, Lawrence M. (2005). *A History of American Law*. 3rd Edition. Simon & Schuster, New York.

Gawalt, Gerard W. (1979). *The Promise of Power: The Emergence of the Legal Profession in Massachusetts, 1760–1840*. Greenwood Press, Westport, CN.

Gawalt, Gerard W., ed. (1984). *The New High Priests: Lawyers in Post-Civil War America*. Greenwood Press, Westport, CT.

Goebel, Julius, ed. (1964–1981). *The Law Practice of Alexander Hamilton*. 5 volumes. Columbia University Press, New York.

Gordon, Robert W. (1983). "Legal Thought and Legal Practice in the Age of American Enterprise 1870–1920." In Geison, ed., *Professions and Professional Ideologies in America*, 70–110. University of North Carolina Press, Chapel Hill.

Gordon, Robert W. (1984a). "The Devil and Daniel Webster." *Yale Law Journal* 94: 445–460.

Gordon, Robert W. (1984b). "'The Ideal and the Actual in the Law': Fantasies and Practices of New York City Lawyers, 1870–1910." In Gawalt, ed., *The New High Priests: Lawyers in Post-Civil War America*, 51–74. Greenwood Press, Westport, CT.

Gordon, Robert W. (1985). "Lawyers as the 'American Aristocracy': A Nineteenth-Century Ideal That May Still be Relevant." *Stanford Lawyer* 20: 2–7.

Gordon, Robert W. (2002). "The Legal Profession." In Sarat, Garth and Kagan, eds, *Looking Back at Law's Century*, 287–336. Cornell University Press, Ithaca.

Grossberg, Michael (1990). "Institutionalizing Masculinity: The Law as a Masculine Profession." In Carnes and Griffen, eds, *Meanings for Manhood: Constructions of Masculinity in Victorian America*, 133–151. University of Chicago Press, Chicago, IL.

Grossberg, Michael (1997). "The Politics of Professionalism: The Creation of Legal Aid and the Strains of Political Liberalism in America, 1900–1930." In Halliday and Karpik, eds, *Lawyers and the Rise of Western Political Liberalism*, 305–347. Oxford University Press, New York.

Hadden, Sally E. (2009). "DeSaussure and Ford: A Charleston Law Firm of the 1790s." In Hamilton and Brophy, eds, *Transformations in American Legal History: Essays in Honor of Professor Morton J. Horwitz*, 85–108. Harvard Law School, Cambridge, MA.

Hall, Kermit L. (1980). "The Children of the Cabins: The Lower Federal Judiciary, Modernization, and the Political Culture, 1789–1899." *Northwestern University Law Review* 75: 423–471.

Hartog, Hendrik (1984). "The Significance of a Singular Career: Reflections on Daniel Webster's Legal Papers." *Wisconsin Law Review* 1984: 1105–1119.

Hartog, Hendrik (1997). "Lawyering, Husbands' Rights, and 'the Unwritten Law' in Nineteenth-Century America." *Journal of American History* 84: 67–96.

Heinz, John P. and Laumann, Edward O. (1982). *Chicago Lawyers: The Social Structure of the Bar*. Russell Sage Foundation, New York.

Heller, III, J. Roderick (2010). *Democracy's Lawyer: Felix Grundy of the Old Southwest*. Louisiana State University Press, Baton Rouge.

Hobson, Wayne K. (1984). "Symbol of the New Profession: Emergence of the Large Law Firm, 1870–1915." In Gawalt, ed., *The New High Priests: Lawyers in Post-Civil War America*, 3–27. Greenwood Press, Westport, CT.

Hoeflich, M.H. (2000). "Legal Fees in Nineteenth-Century Kansas." *University of Kansas Law Review* 48: 991–1003.

Hoeflich, M.H. (2008). "Law Blanks & Form Books: A Chapter in the Early History of Document Production." *Green Bag 2d* 11: 189–201.

Horwitz, Morton J. (1973). "The Conservative Tradition in the Writing of American Legal History." *American Journal of Legal History* 17: 275–294.

Horwitz, Morton J. (1979). *The Transformation of American Law, 1780–1860*. Harvard University Press, Cambridge, MA.

Horwitz, Morton J. (1992). *The Transformation of American Law, 1870–1960: The Crisis of Legal Orthodoxy*. Oxford University Press, New York.

Hurst, James Willard (1950). *The Growth of American Law: The Law Makers*. Little, Brown, Boston.

Katz, Stanley N. (1966). "Looking Backward: The Early History of American Law." *University of Chicago Law Review* 33: 867–884.

Klein, Milton M. (1958). "The Rise of the New York Bar: The Legal Career of William Livingston." *William and Mary Quarterly* 15: 334–358.

Konefsky, Alfred S. (1976). "Lawyers' Papers as a Source of Legal History: The 19th Century." *Law Library Journal* 69: 307–309.

Konefsky, Alfred S. (1988). "Law and Culture in Antebellum Boston." *Stanford Law Review* 40: 1119–1159.

Konefsky, Alfred S. and King, Andrew J., eds (1982). *The Papers of Daniel Webster: Legal Papers*. 2 volumes. Dartmouth College, Hanover, NH.

Landon, Donald D. (1990). *Country Lawyers: The Impact of Context on Professional Practice*. Praeger, New York.

Lipartito, Kenneth (1990). "What Have Lawyers Done for American Business? The Case of Baker & Botts of Houston." *Business History Review* 64: 489–526.

McKirdy, Charles (1976). "Before the Storm: The Working Lawyer in Pre-Revolutionary Massachusetts." *Suffolk University Law Review* 11: 46–60.

Mack, Kenneth W. (2002). "A Social History of Everyday Practice: Sadie T.M. Alexander and the Incorporation of Black Women into the American Legal Profession, 1925–1960." *Cornell Law Review* 87: 1405–1474.

Mack, Kenneth W. (2012). *Representing the Race: The Creation of the Civil Rights Lawyer*. Harvard University Press, Cambridge, MA.

Maru, Olavi (1986). *Research on the Legal Profession: A Review of Work Done*. 2nd Edition. American Bar Foundation, Chicago.

Matthews, Jean V. (1980). *Rufus Choate: The Law and Civic Virtue*. Temple University Press, Philadelphia.

Mehrotra, Ajay K. (2010). "Lawyers, Guns, and Public Monies: The U.S. Treasury, World War One, and the Administration of the Modern Fiscal State." *Law and History Review* 28: 173–225.

Meier, August and Rudwick, Elliott (1976). "Attorneys Black and White: A Case Study of Race Relations Within the NAACP." *Journal of American History* 62: 913–946.

Miller, Perry, ed. (1962). *The Legal Mind in America: From Independence to the Civil War*. Cornell University Press, Ithaca, NY.

Miller, Perry (1965). *The Life of the Mind in America: From the Revolution to the Civil War*. Harcourt, Brace, World, New York.

Moretta, John (2000). *William Pitt Ballinger: Texas Lawyer, Southern Statesman, 1825-1888*. Texas State Historical Association, Austin.

Munger, Frank (1994). "Miners and Lawyers: Law Practice and Class Conflict in Appalachia, 1872-1920." In Cain and Harrington, eds, *Lawyers in a Postmodern World: Translation and Transgression*, 185-228. New York University Press, New York.

Murrin, John M. (1983). "The Legal Transformation: The Bench and Bar of Eighteenth-Century Massachusetts." In Katz and Murrin, eds, *Colonial America: Essays in Politics and Social Development*, 540-572. 3rd Edition. Knopf, New York.

Nash, Gary B. (1965). "The Philadelphia Bench and Bar, 1800-1861." *Comparative Studies in Society and History* 8: 203-220.

Newmyer, Kent R. (1983). "Daniel Webster and the Modernization of American Law." *Buffalo Law Review* 32: 819-858.

O'Brien, Gail Williams (1986). *The Legal Fraternity and the Making of a New South Community, 1878-1882*. University of Georgia Press, Athens.

O'Brien, Michael (1985). *A Character of Hugh Legaré*. University of Tennessee Press, Knoxville.

Pearce, Russell G. (2001). "Lawyers as America's Governing Class: The Formation and Dissolution of the Original Understanding of the American Lawyer's Role." *University of Chicago Law School Roundtable* 8: 381-421.

Pease, William H. and Pease, Jane H. (2002). *James Louis Petigru: Southern Conservative, Southern Dissenter*. University of South Carolina Press, Columbia.

Pound, Roscoe (1953). *The Lawyer From Antiquity to Modern Times*. West Publishing, St. Paul, MN.

Reid, John Phillip (1977). "A Plot too Doctrinaire." *Texas Law Review* 55: 1307-1321.

Reid, John Phillip (1995). "Beneath the Titans." *New York University Law Review* 70: 653-676.

Roeber, A.G. (1981). *Faithful Magistrates and Republican Lawyers: Creators of Virginia Legal Culture 1680-1810*. University of North Carolina Press, Chapel Hill.

Sarat, Austin and Felstiner, William L. F. (1995). *Divorce Lawyers and Their Clients: Power and Meaning in the Legal Process*. Oxford University Press, New York.

Schlegel, John Henry (1988). "The Line Between History and Casenote." *Law & Society Review* 22: 969-985.

Shamir, Ronen (1995). *Managing Legal Uncertainty: Elite Lawyers in the New Deal*. Duke University Press, Durham, NC.

Shepard, E. Lee (1982). "Breaking into the Profession: Establishing a Law Practice in Antebellum Virginia." *Journal of Southern History* 48: 393-410.

Spaulding, Norman W. (2003). "The Myth of Civic Republicanism: Interrogating the Ideology of Antebellum Legal Ethics." *Fordham Law Review* 71: 1397-1460.

Steiner, Mark E. (1997). "The Secret History of Proprietary Legal Education: The Case of the Houston Law School." *Journal of Legal Education* 47: 341–368.

Steiner, Mark E. (2010). "Abraham Lincoln and the Rule of Law Books." *Marquette Law Review* 93: 1283–1324.

Stowell, Daniel W., ed. (2008). *The Papers of Abraham Lincoln: Legal Documents and Cases*. 4 volumes. University of Virginia Press, Charlottesville.

Thomas, William G. (1999). *Lawyering for the Railroad: Business, Law, and Power in the New South*. Louisiana State University Press, Baton Rouge.

Tirres, Allison Brownell (2010). "Lawyers and Legal Borderlands." *American Journal of Legal History* 50: 157–199.

Tocqueville, Alexis de (1990 [1835]). *Democracy in America*. Daniel J. Boorstin, introduction, Bradley Phillips, ed., Henry Reeve, trans. 2 volumes. Vintage Books, New York.

Tushnet, Mark (1978). "A Marxist Analysis of American Law." *Marxist Perspectives* 1: 96–113.

Tushnet, Mark (1987). *The NAACP's Strategy Against Segregated Education, 1925–50*. University of North Carolina Press, Chapel Hill.

Wald, Eli (2008). "The Rise and Fall of the WASP and Jewish Law Firms." *Stanford Law Review* 60: 1803–1866.

Wald, Eli (2009). "The Other Legal Profession and the Orthodox View of the Bar: The Rise of Colorado's Elite Law Firms." *University of Colorado Law Review* 80: 605–683.

Warren, Charles (1911). *A History of the American Bar*. Little, Brown, Boston.

Wroth, L. Kinvin and Zobel, Hiller B., eds (1965). *Legal Papers of John Adams*. 3 volumes. Harvard University Press, Cambridge, MA.

Part III

Subject Areas

Chapter Fourteen

LAW AND THE ECONOMY OF EARLY AMERICA: MARKETS, INSTITUTIONS OF EXCHANGE, AND LABOR

Christine Desan

Law has long played an essential part in histories of American economic change, modernization, and labor. If economists can imagine markets as a natural matter and exchange as an untethered affair, legal scholars have seen them instead as patterns made possible by property and contract, arrangements contrived by people who dwell in governed communities and who produce within webs of obligation, employment, service or debt. In each of these aspects, law is indispensible, an instrument of political power and an expression of social relations. In some accounts a constructive actor and in others an apologetic one, for decades law has been portrayed as a complex vehicle for the workings of material value, a vessel for American action and ideology that it could in turn influence. Given its critical role, law becomes a contentious technology, the medium for progress or exploitation, the blessings of development or its burdens.

Recent historiography goes beyond this rich baseline. For contemporary authors, law does more than promote economic activity or distribute its costs. Rather than instrumental, law is performative, creative, conceptual. While earlier historians were likely to consider law as a means deployed by contending groups, current scholars overwhelmingly approach law as fundamentally constitutive, as infrastructural or architectural, as formative of the very binaries and boundaries of analysis. In today's scholarship, law is the vocabulary of daily action, including consumption, exchange, and work.

This chapter describes the dynamic sensibility and vast capacity of contemporary histories. The review begins with background on earlier legal scholarship on the American political economy. That setting exposes the innovative

A Companion to American Legal History, First Edition.
Edited by Sally E. Hadden and Alfred L. Brophy.
© 2013 John Wiley & Sons Ltd. Published 2021 by John Wiley & Sons Ltd.

nature of recent work, here loosely grouped into three substantive areas. The first cluster might be called "market studies" – histories focusing on capital and consumption, the activities of merchants and entrepreneurs, the market-making efforts of ordinary people, their demands, and their interest in goods that economic exchange made more accessible. While these accounts are written by historians from many subfields (economic, social, and cultural among them), they are all sensitive to the legal constituents of practice and to the close relationship between economic organization and governance.

The second cluster of studies explores institutions of exchange, including public debt and banks, as well as money, credit, property and land, proprietorships and corporations. These histories recognize that the logistics of economic activity are themselves invented; they are possibilities written into rules and practices that are enacted, adopted, and challenged. According to some of these authors, modern markets arrived when exchange was innovatively engineered.

The final cluster explored here is scholarship on labor and work. That foray suggests the ambiguity of "production" in the canon of legal work on the economy. On the one hand, the category remains foundational to scholarly approaches to modernization, whether those accounts screen for wage labor as the talismanic indicator of capitalism or evoke laborers who enter the market as representatives of its democratic reach. On the other hand, the iconic category of "wage labor" has obscured studies that, with increasing sophistication, dismantle the very coherence of the line between "free" and "unfree" or, unnervingly, document the deep dependence of "economic enfranchisement" for part of the American population on the concerted disenfranchisement of others.

As the chapter concludes, there is no question that the recent historiography of law and the economy in early America sheds new light on long-standing debates over matters of material value. The question is whether we can move beyond that familiar contest to explore what we mean by the drama and its constituents – including markets, exchange, and labor.

Progress Narratives and Their Radical Critique in Law

The great institutional narratives of the early twentieth century were not conceived as economic histories. Scholars like Charles McLean Andrews, Herbert Osgood, and Evarts Boutell Greene intended to produce panoramic accounts of colonial Americans' representative institutions, resistance to British rule, eventual autonomy, and new governance projects (Andrews, 1934; Osgood, 1904; Greene, 1906). But their portraits of enterprising individuals fashioning strong and free states – and ultimately a nation-state – comported with the models of progress and material development crafted by classical economists and their marginalist successors. Indeed, the political economic story those scholarships told together held the normative promise of liberal society: democratic self-governance met economic prosperity. Law figured heavily in that story. Whether through the "genius" of common law, the popular product of legislative assemblies, or the unfolding constitution, law supported the actions and exchanges of empowered agents.

Law also figured heavily in critiques of those decidedly celebratory stories. The leading edge of that critique, Charles Beard's *An Economic Interpretation of the Constitution of the United States*, mapped America's founding architecture (Beard, 1986). The constraints it imposed on state fiscal and monetary power, the authority it allocated a federal judiciary, the protection from local demands it accorded interstate commerce – all were part of the elite's self-serving design for economic development. Beard's assault, reinforced by legal-institutional work of scholars like John Commons, Wesley Hohfeld, and Robert Hale, fueled a barrage of Progressive history (Commons, 1924; Hohfeld, 1913; Hale, 1923). Like its Beardian exemplar, early American historians including Robert Brunhouse, Merrill Jensen, Oscar and Mary Handlin, Jackson Turner Main, and E. James Ferguson, were keenly attuned to how powerful groups, including financiers, merchants, and businessmen, shaped legal and political structures to suit their own interests (Brunhouse, 1942; Jensen, 1950; Handlin and Handlin, 1947; Main, 1961; Ferguson, 1961). Their scholarship sat comfortably close to the accounts of scholars with specifically legal historical training like Richard Morris and George Haskins. These accounts cast rules, from the constitutional to the common law, as both critical to economic activity and as chronically susceptible to manipulation by dominant actors (Morris, 1946; Haskins, 1960).

A less conflicted reading gained ground by mid-century, drawing upon a developing sense that Americans had been blessed with material wealth from the early years of settlement. Scholars like Louis Hartz and Richard Hoftstader maintained a critical attitude towards the effect abundance had had on American politics and culture. But they joined authors like Robert E. Brown, David M. Potter, Daniel Boorstin, and James T. Lemon, who concluded that economic opportunity had united men (at least) of many classes in a liberal worldview (Hartz, 1955; Hofstadter, 1948; Potter, 1954; Brown, 1955; Boorstin, 1958; Lemon, 2002). Like their Progressive colleagues, many "Consensus" historians carefully mapped regulatory and institutional dimensions in their work. Willard Hurst expertly refined that project, casting the nineteenth century as a burst of entrepreneurial energy, projected through law and legislation to create American economic dynamism (Hurst, 1956). Finally, constitutional histories produced in the 1960s reinforced a Whiggish view of American political progress, mapping the structural design of self-governance by enterprising individuals who sought voluntaristic modes of economic and civic organization (Bailyn, 1967; Wood, 1969).

The sense of American abundance, happily supported by the U.S. renaissance after World War II, also drew on another strand of economic history, one developing somewhat separately in economics departments. "The new economic history" was quantitatively oriented research that documented American economic growth over the centuries. Scholars in that tradition explored "the staples thesis," a hypothesis earlier articulated by Canadian historian Harold Innis (1933) that colonial staple exports drove not only trade but also internal economic activity and overall growth. John McCusker and Russell Menard's magisterial account, *The Economy of British America, 1607–1789* (1985), synthesized existing work and framed an agenda for further research with that methodology.

By the time McCusker and Menard published their opus however, the fragile confluence of opinion about early American economic experiences had fallen apart. The questions came from many angles, including charges that liberal models and narratives failed to recognize (even as "costs") the destruction of indigenous communities and exploitation of workers, the local, uneven nature of development, and the dependence of commercial centers on extractive relationships with peripheral areas. Marxist and world systems theories were especially influential here (Braudel, 1974; 1981; Wolf, 1982; Wallerstein, 1974).

Others objected that liberal accounts employed a reductionist view of human agency as narrowly materialist and self-interested. Those historians challenged the assumption that many farmers or small tradesmen produced for profit, as opposed to obtaining a sufficiency, preserving family structures or communal bonds, or avoiding risk and innovation. While "moral economy" scholars often hailed from social and cultural history, a number wrote with particular attention to the law, including the way local governance instantiated patterns of customary behavior, legal forms of property and labor shaped settler interests and identities, and aspects of constitutional design functioned to further "capitalist" elites (Clark, 1979; Kulikoff, 1992; Merrill, 1990). Historians Charles Sellers and Steven Hahn carried the argument deep into the nineteenth century, tracing how agrarian communities resisted commercializing trends (Sellers, 1991; Hahn, 1983). For these authors, the "transition to capitalism" occurred only as farmers were forced by debt and falling prices, demographic pressures on land, and new political constraints to begin commercial production.

Morton Horwitz's landmark legal history, *Transformation of American Law, 1780–1860*, appeared in the midst of this debate over the transition to capitalism (Horwitz, 1977). It articulated an eighteenth-century world, both legal and lay, profoundly attached to customary norms that used substantive, non-market-oriented notions of worth to evaluate fair exchange. From that baseline, Horwitz tracked changing common law jurisprudence, tying doctrinal shifts that benefited market-oriented innovation and economic development to the judicial elites who were sympathetic to such efforts. Patrick

Atiyah's important study of contract reinforced that reading, as did William Nelson's narrative of doctrinal change eroding the priority of economic stability in Massachusetts and Bruce Mann's influential account of the turn by Connecticut colonists towards increasingly formal adjudication to manage their sales, loans, and trades (Atiyah, 1979; Nelson, 1975; Mann, 1987).

Horwitz's work drew on critical legal studies and Legal Realist works that understood law as both an ideological and a professional project. Its considerable if not complete autonomy became, in these accounts, a source of power and legitimacy. Legal doctrine thus acted in more structured, if also conflicted, ways to historicize the shape of exchange (Kennedy, 1978–1979; Mensch, 1982). Indeed, instrumentalism in law became itself a matter of judicial consciousness – witness its arrival only in the nineteenth century. Nevertheless, Horwitz's approach, like that of Nelson and Mann, was easily read to cast law as reactive: it remained a tool, "functioning" as it had earlier accounts.

The debate over the transition to capitalism stalemated in the early 1990s, enmeshed in the mutual recognition that people's entrance into the modern economy occurred differently across time and space. On the one hand, Winifred Rothenberg published strong evidence about the convergence of prices and the elaboration of credit networks in the Massachusetts countryside of the 1780s and 1790s (Rothenberg, 1992). That phenomenon suggested that early Americans entered "market" relations by the end of the eighteenth century, embracing the opportunities they offered. For Naomi Lamoreaux and others, Rothenberg's work was persuasive, especially if seasoned with a more nuanced approach to human agency than that assumed by early neoclassical authors, one that valued social and institutional frameworks for individual decision-making (Lamoreaux, 2003).

On the other hand, Merrill and a series of authors working on the nineteenth century responded that price data did not illuminate the behaviors that produced it. Economic activity could flow from deeply contested processes in which elites monopolized opportunity and controlled legal and constitutional dynamics (Merrill, 1995). Work on labor powerfully anchored that darker reading, arguing that the liberal vocabulary of work cast employment as a freely sought and fair relationship while insulating material disparities from redress. More striking yet for legal historians, law was central to the relations inequality instituted – it was a modality of rule, an edifice of categories including rights, claims, and remedies that created a regime of domination (Tomlins, 1993).

If the debate over matters of material value in early America deadlocked in the early 1990s, that very stand-off produced a newly chastened kind of convergence. Scholars had overwhelmingly identified the emergence of the modern market as the crucial drama. That transformation included the rise of production for discrete and impersonal exchange, increasing consumption, an orientation towards profit, and the conceptualization of human desires as interests that could be measured in transactional terms. According to its historians, law moved in concert with the modernizing shift. It engendered doctrines well-suited for enterprising actors who took initiatives, calculated outcomes and uncertainties, and interacted with each other in a private sphere that could be regulated by a well-ordered public. Law still figured, then, as an essential medium of economic change, even as the argument stalemated about the timing and character of development, as well as its relationship to a democratic politics. The contest over modernization had re-emerged and was being fought anew.

Consumption and Commodity Studies

As Cathy Matson points out in an insightful overview of economic history, Henry Clay invoked a particular vision of Americans on the eve of the War of 1812. They were a "hard-working people of rising means, producing and consuming an ever-expanding variety of goods" (Matson, 2006: 62). They warranted an "American System of Manufactures" – a program of government protection for infant American industry. That program and the people it assumes capture a theme in recent studies of the early political economy – the burgeoning appeal of goods to the American public and the active construction of the market to deliver them. Law appears here as integral to that bustling, penetrating movement.

The focus on goods flows neatly from the confluence of the new economic history described above with interests of social and cultural historians. Staples studies and related work indicated that colonial America enjoyed a healthy rate of economic growth, especially after the 1740s, along with a rising standard of living. That finding provoked historians like Timothy Breen, Laurel Ulrich, John Crowley, and Anne Smart Martin to ask how early Americans made sense of associated changes in material life. Their accounts portrayed people turning to consumption for new sources of satisfaction, especially defined by fashion, social performance, and aspirations to local and national improvement (Breen, 2004; Ulrich, 2001; Crowley, 2001; Martin, 2008). Although not legal histories in a disciplinary sense, many of these studies are extraordinarily sensitive to law, writ large or small. Ulrich's women weavers were pervasively informed by gendered opportunities and disabilities instantiated in legal categories like coverture. Breen's work engages law at the public level, with "consumption" as a catalyst of revolution and identity formation. As his subjects became immersed and attached to the market for British goods, they reacted to imperial ineptitude in managing trade. Their shared experience in consuming created the unity essential for political mobilization and allowed them to deploy a new weapon – non-importation and non-consumption, boycotts – to dramatic effect. Moreover, consumer protest involved the disenfranchised and unlearned; engagement in revolutionary activity went viral when it entered the marketplace. In Breen's account, ordinary people engaged in an ordinary act – spending – sparked constitutional crisis.

John Crowley offers another example, as he illuminates the transformative role of "consuming" within the political economy of liberalism and how that change may have involved law. Before it became an acceptable aspiration for middling and working class people, hoping for "comfort" invoked a much more modest baseline – minimal food and medicine. English Enlightenment political theorists only later legitimated the desire for material improvement as a social good, along with the spending it entailed. "Rights" then attached more widely to a consuming public, especially in market exchanges. The ingredients of liberal legality flow, in this history, from changes in people's attitudes towards goods.

Work on consumption relates to research on the commercial enterprises that delivered commodities and credit to American appetites. Until well into the nineteenth century, those webs connected Americans with predominantly external suppliers. Drawing from scholarship on the Atlantic world, recent histories reconstruct trade relations from the ordinary to the imperial level. They find export opportunities that, in the mid-Atlantic and to a lesser extent New England, encouraged local shipbuilding, fishing, and farming efforts. From these, credit flowed into early America and radiated outward through local merchants and shopkeepers. Increasingly ambitious urban entrepreneurs, artisans, and shopkeepers populate America after the Revolution. Merchant capital would finance the development of internal manufactures, mills, and mines (Rilling, 2006; Appleby, 2000; Lamoreaux, 1994). These developments, lucidly reviewed by Matson (Matson, 2006: 60–62), suggest a more dynamic American North than earlier accounts, while confirming the sense that the South remained dependent on English purchases of staples like rice, indigo, tobacco, and, eventually, cotton, and on slave labor to produce those exports. Those commitments would also expand in the nineteenth century.

The patterns produced were more than material. As Thomas Doerflinger observed in his path-breaking account of Philadelphia's merchant community, discerning how communities shaped their political economies requires "a comprehensive approach," one that sees it as "a cultural expression and a social process, a distinctive manifestation of the values of a people" (Doerflinger, 1986: 4). Doerflinger could easily have added "a movement embedded in a community's law" to those perspectives as his own account suggests, with its insightful narrative of the way merchants sought order in the chaotic aftermath of Revolution. Stephen Innes' work is similarly striking here. It finds a Protestant ethic of work and enterprise inculcated in early Massachusetts communities through a plethora of legal practices like contract law that reinforced covenant theology (Innes, 1995).

Governance structures likewise informed strategies of American farmers, merchants, and plantation owners. Mercantilism has attracted particular notice, given the interest in Atlantic studies and a sensitivity to how empire shaped economic development. Work tracing English strategies to elaborate long-term domestic debt, attract foreign investment, channel commercial exchange, and prevail militarily in the eighteenth and nineteenth centuries raises the issue of how closely Americans attended to those tactics and copied them (Priest, 2008; Ferguson, 2004; Wilson, 2002). That question is as much philosophical as practical, as demonstrated by the debate – now more than four decades old – over the power in America of classical republicanism as compared to liberal political economy (Appleby, 1984; McCoy, 1980; Pocock, 1975). Wrapped into the argument over the aims of Federalists and Jeffersonians – to build trade with independent sovereigns, exploit relations with dependent peoples, or prioritize political to economic goals – is a disagreement about the attachment those politicians felt to Smithian prescriptions, including the role of human agency. John Crowley's historiographic essay, tacked on to an incisive account of early policy debates as intellectual history, invaluably surveys the rich literature in the area as does David Hancock's more recent essay (Crowley, 1993; Hancock, 2006).

But mercantilism is only one approach taking political economy to the constitutional level. Eschewing the orientation of Beard and his successors towards elites, Joyce Appleby and Gordon Wood instead identify liberalism in people's orientation towards empowering themselves economically in everyday exchange. Appleby's definition of "capitalism" as "a system that depends upon private property and the relatively free use of it in economic endeavors" allows her to find it in the enterprise of individuals populating the new market studies. And once located in "the habits, values, preference, desires, talents, and predispositions of a sizeable proportion of young white northern men," Appleby equates capitalism with liberal democracy itself (Appleby, 2001: 1, 8; Wood, 1993; 1996).

According to these scholars, middling men used banks, requested credit, and participated in investment, thus demonstrating their support for characteristically modern and entrepreneurial institutions. As in England, such actions were part of a "larger program of personal liberation," one with a radically egalitarian and socially fluid tone that allowed people to free themselves from old hierarchies and traditions and to claim representative institutions (Appleby, 2001: 13). Insofar as the U.S. Constitution protected the material aspirations of Americans, it made them citizens in a commercial, liberal republic. In the coming decades, Jeffersonians met Federalists, or rather outdid them, in the Schumpeterian conditions for innovation and growth they supported (Appleby, 2000; Kornblith, 1995).

Insofar as scholarship on "market studies" assumes a story of growth and freedom, it provokes a chorus of dissents. One problem is suggested by the political writing of William Manning, a propertied 1790s farmer who authored a stinging critique of Federalist finance. While Manning aspired to prosperity, his prescriptions for America's political economy rejected banks and national debt. They embraced inflationary finance and distributive concerns oddly discordant with our conception of a liberal commercial republic. In their complex detail, Manning's prescriptions remind us that "markets" and "exchange" can be organized in myriad ways. The aspiration to "commercial" ends and "prosperity" itself may reveal very little about the way Americans wanted those relationships to work (Manning, Merrill, and Wilentz, 1993).

Elaborating that insight, a variety of writers recast the consumption constitutionalism of more optimistic writers. Inspired by Progressive critiques, they explore distributional issues that financial and monetary structures advocated by elites posed for less wealthy settlers. That focus reveals burdens that the turn to specie-backed money placed on farmers and laborers, many of them former revolutionary soldiers. The shift meant that public debt incurred by making wartime paper promises would be largely repaid in money scarcer and more valuable. Bonds had been bought up by speculators, while higher taxes to retire that debt were levied on a poorer population (Bouton, 2007; Grubb, 2006; Holton, 2004).

The federal Constitution was designed to intervene into the controversy; it prohibited currency alternatives deployed by many states. In a painstaking re-examination of Beard's 1913 thesis, Robert McGuire has recently concluded that Federalist support for the Constitution came disproportionately from individuals, including those owning securities, who would benefit by the way it structured commercial life, finance, and money (McGuire, 2003). Other authors explore the federal judiciary's use of the Constitution to satisfy creditors (Steinfeld, 2010; Desan, 2002). As Terry Bouton points out, in Pennsylvania, popular engagement with banks and efforts to participate in the economic opportunities they offered occurred in part because alternatives like those advocated by William Manning were taken off the table. That engagement leaves unclear whether banks actually benefited farmers, a population they clearly neglected in their early years (Bouton, 2006).

A related objection comes from scholars who fear that the focus on consumption obscures wide discrepancies in material conditions experienced by early Americans. While economic growth continued in the early Republic, inequality rose as well and, as Cathy Matson notes, if some fraction (perhaps fifteen percent) of artisans were upwardly mobile, more than half could not make ends meet. While some communities flourished before and after the Revolution, others faced pressures on the land, challenges to familial modes of social organization and work, and deepening wealth disparities. The larger point is that a limited focus on production or growth does not reach critical issues concerning "political stability, elite formation, cultural distinctions, and family dynamics" (Matson, 2006: 20, 59; Rockman, 2006: 344).

The selective ambit of market studies drives a last objection by scholars of labor and slavery. As explored below, the "unfreedom" of many American workers enabled the capacity of others to consume – yet remains perennially unmeasured.

Institutions of Exchange

As exemplified by scholars of consumption, new approaches to capitalism emphazise its performance by participants. That focus raises questions about how production, purchases, or exchange happened, or more generally, how institutions that "make" markets function. That puzzle is catalyzing rich new, if also deeply divided, legal studies.

Property remains the compass for those mapping market exchange. Two new accounts explode conventional accounts of Native Americans' dispossession. Robert Williams reconstructs early Indian traditions of treaty negotiation, while Ned Blackhawk moves beyond the localism that long defined East Coast populations as alone relevant in the saga of European settlement (Williams, 1997; Blackhawk, 2006). These accounts assert the selective nature of Anglo-American doctrinal categories and the brute nature of their imposition.

Capital's subsequent efflorescence may depend on another rupture, an American Revolution that redounded to bourgeois effect, ushering in protections for monetary value and infant manufactures (Kulikoff, 1992; 2000). Alternatively, doctrines about ownership arguably transcended class, allowing property to function as collateral for many individuals (Priest, 2006).

Both approaches expose the importance of credit, a mechanism early Americans recognized could awaken "dead stock," engender new opportunity, and open individuals to unprecedented risk. Bruce Mann's history traces the way legal instruments of credit and approaches to debt shifted over the course of the eighteenth century. Movement was often experimental and erratic, but both laws of obligation (e.g., contract) and law of failure (e.g., bankruptcy) changed. Mann's account virtually equates modernity with a transactional economy, itself identified with the legally engineered credit that allowed and defined it (Mann, 2008; 2002). Other studies complicate the trajectory of increasingly impersonalized exchange. Credit in the early Republic appears to have been a familially rooted project, one that embedded early liberalism in a culture of social relation (Lamoreaux, 1994; Gervais, 2004; Sandage, 2005). From that setting, the reconceptualization of exchange as a more profit-oriented affair, calculated in increasingly atomistic terms, was informed by a realignment of legal thought and doctrine (Kreitner, 2007; Rogers, 1995).

Liquidity was more than a matter of private debt and obligation. Scholars are exploring the collective creation of money, building on foundations laid by Joseph Ernst and Leonard Brock (Brock, 1975; Ernst, 1973). Intrigued by successful early American "bills of credit," economists in the 1980s reopened the debate about whether and how circulating public credit worked (Smith, 1987; Calomiris, 1988). Claire Priest finds that currency levels dramatically affected patterns of debt litigation in Massachusetts, while Margaret Newell identifies monetary policy as central to rising economic ambition and activity. In Newell's account, the turn to money ushered in a liberal market culture (Priest, 2001; Newell, 1998). By contrast, early paper money, printed by colonial assemblies and issued as direct public I.O.U.s (without commercial banks), may have engendered a distinctive political economy. Its emphasis on market access and public liquidity would make the later advent of bank-based liquidity a dramatic event (Desan, 2008).

Increasingly, scholars question rather than accept the transition from public credit money to specie and commercial banknotes (Bouton, 2006; Grubb, 2003; McGuire, 2003). Working from an understanding of the power and fragility of early paper money, they contest accounts that assume the economic efficiency of financial innovation and commercial banking. That premise, by contrast, undergirds a number of studies describing America's financial revolution as a remedy for the liquidity crises and tax protests of the post-Revolutionary period. Hamilton's commitment to a public debt drew foreign and domestic investors, stabilized federal revenues, and influenced the constitutional allocation of judicial and legislative powers. Americans soon vested money creation in banks, both national and state-chartered. As sources of money and credit, banks would transform the commercial expansion of the United States and its politics, as well as the body of law that articulated the changing economic landscape (Sylla, 1999; Wright, 2001; 2002; MacDonald, 2003).

In the early nineteenth century, Americans experimented with forms of public finance and business instrumentalities. Corporate governance became contested, as securities markets developed (Dunlavy, 2006; Banner, 1998). The insurance industry and credit agencies took root (Carruthers and Ariovich, 2010; Larson, 2001; Klein and Majewski, 1992). All informed the entrepreneurial trajectory traced above, inviting historical inquiry about the distributive effects of new forms of liquidity and business, their impact on federal-state relations, investment patterns across borders, and the character of the changing legalities that now delineated public and private territories.

The Ambiguous Place of Labor

In *Freedom Bound: Law, Labor, and Civic Identity in Colonizing English American, 1580–1865*, Christopher Tomlins frames American history around labor. That elemental resource drives the "manning" and making of a continent – and it is irreducibly legal (Tomlins, 2010). Productive work justifies conquest and creates property from land. Securing labor power drives the internecine combat that orders settlers and enslaves Africans. Defining what is earned and who can claim it deals out abundance, dearth, and the richly segmented hierarchy of American identities. Tomlins' logic folds migration, settlement, governance, and an evanescent freedom into the legal world of work.

Tomlins' insight is arresting given the current historiography's emphasis on "the world of goods." On the one hand, that historiography acknowledges production. It attends artisanal work, home crafts, and informal or familial labor, and is attuned to farming as the dominant early American livelihood. The entry of "middling" populations into consumption and, later, borrowing from commercial banks, stock ownership, and investment, are important in the narrative. "The market" gains purchase, even democratic stature, through the choice of ordinary working people to engage a commercial life: their voluntarism is its legitimation.

On the other hand, that orientation toward labor distorts it, according to scholars like Tomlins. First, histories assuming that wage labor arrived with the Revolution and the widespread experience of freedom, draw on old, outdated conventions. In fact, many Americans worked for wages far earlier in the eighteenth century, displacing indentured servitude more quickly than older histories held (Tomlins, 2006). But although waged work increased, it did not carry with it the experience of freedom. Law, by the way it defined property, trespass, inheritance, vagrancy, gender roles, and other conditions of life, constrained many opportunities. And law, by the way it balanced power between employers and employees, handicapped workers with threats of wage forfeiture, criminal conspiracy for collective action, and other prohibitions (Tomlins, 2008; Rockman, 2006; Steinfeld, 2001; Steinfeld and Engerman, 1997). Additional studies consider the workers – women, children, immigrants, free blacks, and unskilled white men – that, along with slaves, made up the majority of the workforce (Roediger, 2007; Gilje, 2004).

Second, although some Americans reached the economic enfranchisement celebrated in some market studies, they did so standing on the backs of those denied entrance. As Seth Rockman's study of urban labor in early Baltimore argues, prosperity and privation were not independent stories. Rather, "prosperity came to Americans who could best assemble, deploy, and exploit the physical labor of others" (Rockman, 2009: 3). Slavery endures as the extremity that defies line-drawing here. The enslaved – a category that expanded enormously in the early Republic – became essential "labor" in the ascendance of those who owned or hired them, sold or spun the cotton they produced. Recent studies explore the slave market, the binaries of slavery and freedom, and the legal constitution of race (Johnson, 1999; Stanley, 1998; Waldstreicher, 2006; Gross, 2008). The importance of such studies undermines the conflation of Revolution, commercial development, democracy, and liberty.

Historiographic fashion also suggests that critical research on the experience and context of work remains undone. A recent conference on capitalism produced approximately twenty graduate student proposals on consumption, advertising, merchant networks, credit, and credit reporting – and one on labor. That apparent imbalance underscores the importance of recent histories of mobility and governance, slave policing, immigration and welfare, to name a few (Hulsebosch, 2005; Hadden, 2001; Parker, 2001). Those ventures merit much more company.

Finally, while the ascendance of wage labor traditionally indicated the rise of "capitalism," the turn towards consumption studies may reflect a shift in that assumption. Some may hold with Appleby's focus on private property and its "free use," others seem to trawl more loosely for a set of "effects," like rising commercial exchange and price convergence (Rockman, 2006: 344). But that diffusion submerges rigorous debate about how labor, consumption, liquidity, and exchange fit together. Whatever the fate of traditional definitions, the debate over them would clarify the stakes and the claims of the new histories.

Conclusion

Modernization remains the focal economic drama of early America. But recent approaches open up innovative ways to think about that project as a legal matter. Rather than an instrument deployed towards independent ends, law in these accounts becomes part of the working vocabulary that informed people, limited them, and allowed them to recombine meanings and practices to innovative effects. That methodology deepens the perspective we have on the way Americans worked with and occasionally against legal categories to conceive new claims, modes of exchange, and ways to work and hire.

Can our innovation go further? Current work relies heavily upon conventions about commodities, exchange, and labor that have long informed debates about "the market." Indeed, current work may perpetuate those conventions; they form three familiar dimensions that organize, perhaps too neatly, the drama we try to understand.

Insofar as we recognize economic phenomena as deeply legal, we also identify them as deployments of power and claims about authority. The issue is not whether there are commodities (aka "private property") or not, liquidity (aka money or credit) or not, waged labor or not. Rather, it is what legal relations these categories evoke – clearly a complex and changing constellation.

We might de-reify "modernization" by following the lead of current work to second-guess the dimensions we assume. Does capitalism turn on the waged form of labor or, instead, on its ability to convert workers into investors, bond-holders, and pensioners? Does "money" simply liquefy exchange, creating an abstract commodification, or does it depend on how currency is orchestrated and sustained by contract, tax liabilities, and negotiability? Does the analytic of consumption capture a basic impulse, or format modern models of exchange into rights and interests? With luck, we might follow such issues right off the known map.

References

Andrews, Charles McLean (1934). *The Colonial Period of American History.* 4 volumes. Yale University Press, New Haven.

Appleby, Joyce Oldham (1984). *Capitalism and a New Social Order: The Republican Vision of the 1790s.* New York University Press, New York.

Appleby, Joyce Oldham (2000). *Inheriting the Revolution: The First Generation of Americans.* Belknap Press of Harvard University Press, Cambridge, MA.

Appleby, Joyce Oldham (2001). "The Vexed Story of Capitalism Told by American Historians." *Journal of the Early Republic* 21(1): 1–18.

Atiyah, P.S. (1979). *The Rise and Fall of Freedom of Contract.* Oxford University Press, Oxford.

Bailyn, Bernard (1967). *The Ideological Origins of the American Revolution.* Belknap Press of Harvard University Press, Cambridge.

Banner, Stuart (1998). *Anglo-American Securities Regulation, Cultural & Political Roots, 1690–1860.* Cambridge University Press, Cambridge, UK.

Beard, Charles Austin (1986). *An Economic Interpretation of the Constitution of the United States.* MacMillan, New York.

Blackhawk, Ned (2006). *Violence Over the Land: Indians and Empires in the Early American West.* Harvard University Press, Cambridge, MA.

Boorstin, Daniel J. (1958). *The Americans: The Colonial Experience.* Random House, New York.

Bouton, Terry (2006). *Moneyless in Pennsylvania: Privatization and the Depression of the 1780s.* In Matson, ed., *The Economy of Early America: Historical Perspectives and New Directions*, 218–235. Pennsylvania State University Press, University Park, PA.

Bouton, Terry (2007). *Taming Democracy: "The People," The Founders, and the Troubled Ending of the American Revolution.* Oxford University Press, Oxford, UK.

Braudel, Fernand (1974). *Capitalism and Material Life, 1400–1800.* Fontana, London.

Braudel, Fernand (1981). *The Structures of Everyday Life: The Limits of the Possible. Civilization and Capitalism, 15th–18th Century,* Volume 1. 1st U.S. Edition. Harper & Row, New York.

Breen, T.H. (2004). *The Marketplace of Revolution: How Consumer Politics Shaped American Independence.* Oxford University Press, Oxford.

Brock, Leslie V. (1975). *The Currency of the American Colonies, 1700–1764, A Study in Colonial Finance and Imperial Relations, Dissertations in American Economic History.* Arno Press, New York.

Brown, Robert Eldon (1955). *Middle-Class Democracy and the Revolution in Massachusetts, 1691–1780.* Cornell University Press, Ithaca, NY.

Brunhouse, Robert Levere (1942). *The Counter-Revolution in Pennsylvania, 1776–1790.* Pennsylvania Historical Commission, Harrisburg.

Calomiris, Charles W. (1988). "Institutional Failure, Monetary Scarcity, and the Depreciation of the Continental." *Journal of Economic History* 48(1): 47–68.

Carruthers, Bruce G. and Ariovich, Laura (2010). *Money and Credit: A Sociological Approach.* Polity, Cambridge, Malden, MA.

Clark, Christopher (1979). "Household Economy, Market Exchange and the Rise of Capitalism in the Connecticut Valley, 1800–1860." *Journal of Social History* 13: 169–189.

Commons, John Rogers (1924). *Legal Foundations of Capitalism.* The Macmillan Company, New York.

Crowley, John E. (1993). *The Privileges of Independence: Neomercantilism and the American Revolution, Early America.* Johns Hopkins University Press, Baltimore.

Crowley, John E. (2001). *The Invention of Comfort: Sensibilities and Design in Early Modern Britain & Early America.* Johns Hopkins University Press, Baltimore.

Desan, Christine A. (2002). "Contesting the Character of the Political Economy in the Early Republic: Rights and Remedies in Chisholm v. Georgia." In Bowling and Kennon, eds, *The House and Senate in the 1790s: Petitioning, Lobbying, and Institutional Development.* Ohio University Press, Athens, OH.

Desan, Christine A. (2008). "From Blood to Profit: Making Money in the Practice and Imagery of Early America." *Journal of Policy History* 20(1): 26–46.

Doerflinger, Thomas M. (1986). *A Vigorous Spirit of Enterprise: Merchants and Economic Development in Revolutionary Philadelphia.* University of North Carolina Press, Chapel Hill.

Dunlavy, Colleen (2006). "Social Conceptions of the Corporation: Insights from the History of Shareholder Voting Rights." *Washington and Lee Law Review* 63(4): 1347–1388.

Ernst, Joseph Albert (1973). *Money and Politics in America, 1755–1775: A Study in the Currency Act of 1764 and the Political Economy of Revolution.* University of North Carolina Press, Chapel Hill.

Ferguson, E. James (1961). *The Power of the Purse: A History of American Public Finance, 1776–1790.* University of North Carolina Press, Chapel Hill.

Ferguson, Niall (2004). *Colossus: The Price of America's Empire.* Penguin Press, New York.

Gervais, Pierre (2004). *Les Origines de la Revolution Industrielle aux Etats-Unis: Entre Economie Marchande et Capitalisme Industriel, 1800–1850.* Ecole des Hautes Etudes en Sciences Sociales, Paris.

Gilje, Paul A. (2004). *Liberty on the Waterfront: American Maritime Culture in the Age of Revolution.* University of Pennsylvania Press, Philadelphia.

Greene, Evarts Boutell (1906). *The Provincial Governor in the English Colonies of North America,* Harvard Historical Studies, Volume 7. Harvard University Press, Cambridge.

Gross, Ariela Julie (2008). *What Blood Won't Tell: A History of Race on Trial in America.* Harvard University Press, Cambridge, MA.

Grubb, Farley (2003). "Creating the U.S. Dollar Currency Union, 1748-1811: A Quest for Monetary Stability or a Usurpation of State Sovereignty for Personal Gain?" *The New American Economic Review* 93: 1778-1779.

Grubb, Farley (2006). "The US Constitution and Monetary Powers: An Analysis of the 1787 Constitutional Convention and the Constitutional Transformation of the US Monetary System." *Financial History Review* 13: 43-71.

Hadden, Sally E. (2001). *Slave Patrols: Law and Violence in Virginia and the Carolinas.* Harvard University Press, Cambridge, MA.

Hahn, Steven (1983). *The Roots of Southern Populism: Yeoman Farmers and the Transformation of the Georgia Upcountry, 1850-1890.* Oxford University Press, New York.

Hale, Robert L. (1923). "Coercion and Distribution in a Supposedly Non-Coercive State." *Political Science Quarterly* 38(3): 470-494.

Hancock, David (2006). "Rethinking The Economy of British America." In Matson, ed., *The Economy of Early America: Historical Perspectives and New Directions,* 71-106. Pennsylvania State University Press, University Park, PA.

Handlin, Oscar and Handlin, Mary Flug (1947). *Commonwealth: A Study of the Role of Government in the American Economy: Massachusetts, 1774-1861.* New York University Press, New York.

Hartz, Louis (1955). *The Liberal Tradition in America: An Interpretation of American Political Thought Since the Revolution.* 1st Edition. Harcourt Brace, New York.

Haskins, George Lee (1960). *Law and Authority in Early Massachusetts: A Study in Tradition and Design.* Macmillan, New York.

Hofstadter, Richard (1948). *The American Political Tradition and the Men Who Made It.* Vintage Books, New York.

Hohfeld, Wesley Newcomb (1913). "Some Fundamental Legal Conceptions as Applied in Judicial Reasoning." *Yale Law Journal* 23(1): 16-59.

Holton, Woody (2004). "'From the Labours of Others': The War Bonds Controversy and the Origins of the Constitution in New England." *The William and Mary Quarterly* 61(2): 271-316.

Horwitz, Morton J. (1977). *The Transformation of American Law, 1780-1860, Studies in Legal History.* Harvard University Press, Cambridge, MA.

Hulsebosch, Daniel Joseph (2005). *Constituting Empire: New York and the Transformation of Constitutionalism in the Atlantic World, 1664-1830.* University of North Carolina Press, Chapel Hill.

Hurst, James Willard (1956). *Law and the Conditions of Freedom in the Nineteenth-Century United States.* University of Wisconsin Press, Madison.

Innes, Stephen (1995). *Creating the Commonwealth: The Economic Culture of Puritan New England.* 1st Edition. W.W. Norton, New York.

Innis, Harold Adams (1933). *Problems of Staple Production in Canada.* The Ryerson Press, Toronto.

Jensen, Merrill (1950). *The New Nation: A History of the United States during the Confederation, 1781-1789.* 1st Edition. Knopf, New York.

Johnson, Walter (1999). *Soul by Soul: Life Inside the Antebellum Slave Market.* Harvard University Press, Cambridge, MA.

Kennedy, Duncan (1978–1979). "The Structure of Blackstone's Commentaries." *Buffalo Law Review* 28: 205–382.

Klein, Daniel B. and Majewski, John (1992). "Economy, Community, and Law: The Turnpike Movement in New York, 1797–1845." *Law and Society Review* 26(3): 469–512.

Kornblith, Gary J. (1995). "Becoming Joseph T. Buckingham: The Struggle for Artisanal Independence in Early-Nineteenth-Century Boston." In Rock, Gilje, and Asher, eds, *American Artisans: Crafting Social Identity, 1750–1850*. Johns Hopkins University Press, Baltimore.

Kreitner, Roy (2007). *Calculating Promises: The Emergence of Modern American Contract Doctrine*. Stanford University Press, Stanford.

Kulikoff, Allan (1992). *The Agrarian Origins of American Capitalism*. University Press of Virginia, Charlottesville.

Kulikoff, Allan (2000). *From British Peasants to Colonial American Farmers*. University of North Carolina Press, Chapel Hill.

Lamoreaux, Naomi R. (1994). *Insider Lending: Banks, Personal Connections, and Economic Development in Industrial New England*. Cambridge University Press, Cambridge, UK.

Lamoreaux, Naomi R. (2003). "Rethinking the Transition to Capitalism in the Early American Northeast." *Journal of American History* 90: 437–461.

Larson, John Lauritz (2001). *Internal Improvement: National Public Works and the Promise of Popular Government in the Early United States*. University of North Carolina Press, Chapel Hill.

Lemon, James T. (2002). *The Best Poor Man's Country: Early Southeastern Pennsylvania*. Johns Hopkins University Press, Baltimore, MD.

MacDonald, James (2003). *A Free Nation Deep in Debt: The Financial Roots of Democracy*. 1st Edition. Farrar Straus and Giroux, New York.

Main, Jackson Turner (1961). *The Antifederalists: Critics of the Constitution, 1781–1788*. Published for the Institute of Early American History and Culture at Williamsburg, VA by the University of North Carolina Press, Chapel Hill.

Mann, Bruce H. (1987). *Neighbors and Strangers: Law and Community in Early Connecticut*. University of North Carolina Press, Chapel Hill.

Mann, Bruce H. (2002). *Republic of Debtors: Bankruptcy in the Age of American Independence*. Harvard University Press, Cambridge, MA.

Mann, Bruce H. (2008). "The Transformation of Law and Economy in Early America." In Tomlins and Grossman, eds, *The Cambridge History of Law in America*. Cambridge University Press, Cambridge, UK.

Manning, William, Merrill, Michael, and Wilentz, Sean (1993). *The Key of Liberty: The Life and Democratic Writings of William Manning, "A Laborer," 1747–1814*. Harvard University Press, Cambridge, MA.

Martin, Ann Smart (2008). *Buying Into the World of Goods: Early Consumers in Backcountry Virginia, Studies in Early American Economy and Society from the Library Company of Philadelphia*. Johns Hopkins University Press, Baltimore.

Matson, Cathy (2006). "A House of Many Mansions: Some Thoughts on the Field of Economic History." In Matson, ed., *The Economy of Early America: Historical Perspectives and New Directions*, 1–70. Pennsylvania State University Press, University Park, PA.

McCoy, Drew R. (1980). *The Elusive Republic: Political Economy in Jeffersonian America*. University of North Carolina Press, Chapel Hill.

McCusker, J.J. and Menard, R.R. (1991). *The Economy of British America, 1607–1789*. University of North Carolina Press, Chapel Hill.

McGuire, Robert A. (2003). *To Form a More Perfect Union: A New Economic Interpretation of the United States Constitution*. Oxford University Press, Oxford.

Mensch, Elizabeth (1982). "The Colonial Origins of Liberal Property Rights." *Buffalo Law Review* 31: 635–735.

Merrill, Michael (1990). "The Anticapitalist Origins of the United States." *Fernand Braudel Review* 13: 465–497.

Merrill, Michael (1995). "Putting 'Capitalism' in Its Place: A Review of Recent Literature." *The William and Mary Quarterly* 52(2): 315–326.

Morris, Richard Brandon (1946). *Government and Labor in Early America*. Columbia University Press, New York.

Nelson, William Edward (1975). *Americanization of the Common Law: The Impact of Legal Change on Massachusetts Society, 1760–1830*. Harvard University Press, Cambridge, MA.

Newell, Margaret Ellen (1998). *From Dependency to Independence: Economic Revolution in Colonial New England*. Cornell University Press, Ithaca.

Osgood, Herbert L. (1904). *The American Colonies in the Seventeenth Century*. Macmillan & Co. Ltd., New York.

Parker, Kunal (2001). *State, Citizenship, and Territory: The Legal Construction of Immigration in Antebellum Massachusetts*. Law and History Review 19: 583–661.

Pocock, J.G.A. (1975). *The Machiavellian Moment: Florentine Political Thought and the Atlantic Republican Tradition*. Princeton University Press, Princeton, NJ.

Potter, David Morris (1954). *People of Plenty: Economic Abundance and the American Character*. Charles R. Walgreen Foundation lectures. University of Chicago Press, Chicago.

Priest, Claire (2001). "Currency Policies and Legal Development in Colonial New England." *Yale Law Journal* 110(8): 1303–1405.

Priest, Claire (2006). "Creating an American Property Law: Alienability and its Limits in American History." *Harvard Law Review* 120(2): 385–458.

Priest, Claire (2008). "Law and Commerce, 1580–1815." In Tomlins and Grossman, eds, *The Cambridge History of Law in America*, 1: 400–446. Cambridge University Press, Cambridge.

Rilling, Donna J. (2006). "Small-Producer Capitalism in Early National Philadelphia." In Matson, ed., *The Economy of Early America: Historical Perspectives and New Directions*, 317–334. Pennsylvania State University Press, University Park, PA.

Rockman, Seth (2006). "The Unfree Origins of American Capitalism." In Matson, ed., *The Economy of Early America*, 335–361. Pennsylvania State University Press, University Park, PA.

Rockman, Seth (2009). *Scraping By: Wage Labor, Slavery, and Survival in Early Baltimore*. Johns Hopkins University Press, Baltimore.

Roediger, David R. (2007). *The Wages of Whiteness: Race and the Making of the American Working Class*. Revised Edition, Haymarket series. Verso, London.

Rogers, James Steven (1995). *The Early History of the Law of Bills and Notes: A Study of the Origins of Anglo-American Commercial Law*, Cambridge Studies in English Legal History Index. Cambridge University Press, Cambridge.

Rothenberg, Winifred Barr (1992). *From Market-Places to a Market Economy: The Transformation of Rural Massachusetts, 1750–1850*. University of Chicago Press, Chicago.

Sandage, Scott (2005). *Born Losers: A History of Failure in America*. Harvard University Press, Cambridge.

Sellers, Charles Grier (1991). *The Market Revolution: Jacksonian America, 1815–1846*. Oxford University Press, New York.

Smith, Bruce D. (1987). "Money and Inflation in the American Colonies: Further Evidence on the Failure of the Quantity Theory." University of Western Ontario Press, London, Ontario.

Stanley, Amy Dru (1998). *From Bondage to Contract: Wage Labor, Marriage, and the Market in the Age of Slave Emancipation*. Cambridge University Press, Cambridge, UK.

Steinfeld, Robert J. (2001). *Coercion, Contract, and Free Labor in the Nineteenth Century, Cambridge Historical Studies in American Law and Society*. Cambridge University Press, Cambridge, UK.

Steinfeld, Robert J. (2010). "The Early Anti-Majoritarian Rationale for Judicial Review." In Hamilton and Brophy, eds, *Transformations in American Legal History – Law, Ideology, and Methods*, 143–164. Harvard Law School, Cambridge, MA.

Steinfeld, Robert J. and Engerman, Stanley L. (1997). "Labor – Free or Coerced? A Historical Reassessment of Differences and Similarities." In Brass and van der Linden, eds, *Free and Unfree Labor: The Debate Continues*. Peter Land, Bern.

Sylla, Richard Eugene (1999). "Shaping the US Financial System, 1690–1913: The Dominant Role of Public Finance." In Sylla, Tilly and Tortella Casares, eds, *The State, the Financial System and Economic Modernization*, 249–270. Cambridge University Press, Cambridge, UK.

Tomlins, Christopher (1993). *Law, Labor, and Ideology in the Early American Republic*. Cambridge University Press, Cambridge, UK.

Tomlins, Christopher (2006). "Indentured Servitude in Perspective: European Migration into North America and the Composition of the Early American Labor Force, 1600–1775." In Matson, ed., *The Economy of Early America: Historical Perspectives and New Directions*, 146–182. Pennsylvania State University Press, University Park, PA.

Tomlins, Christopher (2008). "Law, Population, Labor." In Tomlins and Grossberg, eds, *The Cambridge History of Law in America*, 1: 211–252. Cambridge University Press, Cambridge, UK.

Tomlins, Christopher (2010). *Freedom Bound: Law, Labor, and Civic Identity in English America, 1580–1865*. Cambridge University Press, Cambridge, UK.

Ulrich, Laurel (2001). *The Age of Homespun: Objects and Stories in the Creation of an American Myth*. 1st Edition. Alfred A. Knopf, New York.

Waldstreicher, David (2006). "Capitalism, Slavery, and Benjamin's Franklin's American Revolution." In Matson, ed., *The Economy of Early America: Historical Perspectives and New Directions*, 183–217. Pennsylvania State University Press, University Park, PA.

Wallerstein, Immanuel Maurice (1974). *The Modern World-system: Capitalist Agriculture and the Origins of the European World-economy in the Sixteenth Century*, Studies in Social Discontinuity. Academic Press, New York.

Williams, Robert A. (1997). *Linking Arms Together: American Indian Treaty Visions of Law and Peace, 1600–1800*. Oxford University Press, New York.

Wilson, James G. (2002). *The Imperial Republic: A Structural History of American Constitutionalism from the Colonial Era to the Beginning of the Twentieth Century*. Ashgate, Burlington, VT.

Wolf, Eric R. (1982). *Europe and the People Without History*. University of California Press, Berkeley.

Wood, Gordon S. (1969). *The Creation of the American Republic, 1776–1787*. University of North Carolina Press, Chapel Hill, NC.

Wood, Gordon S. (1993). *The Radicalism of the American Revolution*. 1st Vintage Books edition. Vintage Books, New York.

Wood, Gordon S. (1996). "The Enemy Is Us: Democratic Capitalism in the Early Republic." *Journal of the Early Republic* 16(2): 293–308.

Wright, Robert E. (2001). *Origins of Commercial Banking in America, 1750–1800*. Rowman & Littlefield, Lanham, MD.

Wright, Robert E. (2002). *The Wealth of Nations Rediscovered: Integration and Expansion in American Financial Markets, 1780–1850*. Cambridge University Press, Cambridge, UK.

Chapter Fifteen

LAW AND THE ECONOMY IN THE UNITED STATES, 1820–2000

Harwell Wells

Introduction

In the beginning was the market – or so, it appears, many Americans believe. The popular story of American history seems all too often to assume that there existed before the twentieth century an untrammeled economy, one slowly tamed, or tripped up, by the imposition of legal rules. Whether sold by defenders of "freedom of contract" in the 1890s, opponents of the New Deal in the 1930s, or those who aim to slash government in the twenty-first century, the widespread assumption has been that the nation's economy grew first and the nation's laws caught up later (Novak, 2008; Balogh, 2009). Of course, it's not true that the market precedes law and regulation; law has always been indissolubly linked with economic growth in the United States, structuring our boasted free markets from the earliest days. Yet for legal historians, the popular myth of the law-less free market has been a constant obstacle, to be challenged anew by each succeeding scholarly generation.

This chapter examines historians' accounts of how law structured and even created America's markets, commerce, and business enterprises. It tilts towards private law, recognizing that the public law aspects of this story are told elsewhere in this volume (e.g., chapters on administrative, labor, and tax law). And it is in many ways selective and incomplete, omitting subjects that it could cover (e.g., banking and money, the public lands). Its uneven coverage may just reflect the paradox of the subject "Law and the Economy," for it is a topic that is both small, in that most legal historians have chosen

---

A Companion to American Legal History, First Edition.
Edited by Sally E. Hadden and Alfred L. Brophy.
© 2013 John Wiley & Sons Ltd. Published 2021 by John Wiley & Sons Ltd.

to direct their studies elsewhere, and far too big, since read broadly enough "law and the economy" can cover *everything*. Perhaps this just means there is much left for scholars to do.

Law and Political Economy in Antebellum America

There have always been scholars who recognized that legal regulation was woven through America's free markets, but the modern challenge to the myth of the law-less market can be dated to the post-World War II "Commonwealth" studies, most notably Oscar and Mary Flug Handlin's *Commonwealth: A Study of the Role of Government in the American Economy 1787–1861* ([1947] 1969) – whose title says it all – and Hartz's parallel study *Economic Policy and Democratic Thought: Pennsylvania, 1776–1860* (1948). After what appeared to be unprecedented government intrusion in the economy during the New Deal, the Rockefeller Foundation, through Harvard's Committee on Research in Economic History, funded these and other studies aiming to trace the roots of government economic intervention (Scheiber, 1972). Expecting to find little government involvement in the economy before the twentieth century, the studies' authors instead discovered that state governments had been deeply entangled in antebellum development. According to the Handlins, for instance, the Commonwealth of Massachusetts made "itself felt in every aspect of production" ([1947] 1969: 52). Hartz, the Handlins, and others found states granting exclusive franchises, regulating goods, and issuing corporate charters, all to mobilize private energies for public benefit. Far from state inactivity, the states' energies seemed indispensable for economic growth, though early plans to carefully develop a state's economy could, through the pressures of democracy, turn into programs promising economic benefits to all comers (Scheiber, 1969). Only towards the end of the antebellum period did states retreat from this active role, opening up a space for sharper competition in which private parties became the drivers of economic growth, and creating an economic space with minimal state involvement.

This first telling – of the state as organizer of economic development in the antebellum economy – underwent a subtle shift in the following decade with J. Willard Hurst's *Law and the Conditions of Freedom in the United States* (1956). In this and later works, Hurst depicted nineteenth-century law as an instrument for commercial development, intended, in his well-known phrase, not to restrain or direct economic activity but to enable the "release of energy" by the private efforts of entrepreneurial settlers (1956: 3). In his account, both courts and legislatures bent law and policy to the ends of economic growth, for instance, by expanding the reach of contract into areas such as employment law, granting corporate charters to promote the development of a transportation infrastructure, encouraging bank note issuance, and enabling widespread use of negotiable instruments. For Hurst the desire to expand the market, and so increase options for individuals, was all-encompassing during the nineteenth century; even developments that seemed at first glance to work against a dynamic market, such as the evolution of "vested rights" in property, had at base the desire to protect and thus promote business ventures. Much of Hurst's work is extremely abstract and sociologically inflected; fortunately, those interested in accounts showing how the law actually operated to release private energies can look to Hurst's own monumental legal history of the Wisconsin lumber industry, *Law and Economic Growth* (1964), or the account presented by his student Stanley Kutler in *Privilege and Creative Destruction: The Charles River Bridge Case* ([1971] 1990).

Hurst did not ignore conflict; he wrote of struggles between employers and employees over tort law, and between farmers and railroads over rates. But the conflicts he identified were not over fundamental values: his combatants all seemed to accept "the family of middle-class values which had set the dominant policy tone" of nineteenth-century society, a view which placed him alongside the consensus school of history which dominated the academy during the 1950s (Hurst, 1956: 94). In contrast, conflict, particularly class conflict, was at the heart of Morton Horwitz's *The Transformation of American Law, 1780–1860* (referred to hereafter as *Transformation I*) (1977).

Like Hurst, Horwitz has an instrumental view of law, but in Horwitz's account law, particularly private law, was an instrument wielded by elites. Focusing on the common law, he began by historicizing the very idea of instrumental law, dating it to the early nineteenth century when lawyers and judges abandoned older notions of a settled, discoverable common law in favor of the view that judges made the common law, and that it could serve as a malleable instrument for social policy. Horwitz followed Hurst's broad outlines in seeing most of the nineteenth century's legal developments as oriented to economic development, painting fine-grained accounts of such changes as limits on nuisance doctrines and the abandonment of equitable limitations on contracting, and linking them to the demands of commercial interests. Behind these particular developments lurked a larger and more depressing story: the triumph of commercial interests in the making of legal-economic policy, and their collusion, conscious or not, with judges and the bar. Together, they replaced an eighteenth-century common law shot through with "precommercial and antidevelopmental" values with a legal system "reshaped to serve the interests of the wealthy and the powerful," one that redistributed wealth away from the weakest in society (Horwitz, 1977: 253). This was economic instrumentalism with a vengeance, depicting the law as little more than a tool of the powerful. *Transformation I* ended before the Civil War, as the wealthy and the elite bar, having accomplished their goals of constructing a favorable commercial order, shifted tactics to adopt a new antipolitical and formalist view of the law that would prevent the legal system from further modifying the new distribution of wealth that the law had brought about.

Horwitz's argument was immensely influential, not least in attracting a cadre of energetic critics who went back over the period and themes Horwitz explored, producing a small genre of articles attacking his thesis that the law was marked by a transition from an eighteenth-century quasi-communitarian common law to a rapacious, instrumentalist version in the following century (the best-known of these are perhaps Schwartz's "Tort Law and the Economy in Nineteenth-Century America" (1981) and Simpson's "The Horwitz Thesis and the History of Contract" (1979)). Early in the 1990s, it also produced two works that aimed to upend Horwitz, Novak's *The People's Welfare* (1996) and Karsten's *Heart versus Head* (1997).

The People's Welfare presented a radically different vision of antebellum society and law. Though not always spelled out, the backdrop to works such as Horwitz's was a fragmented society, in which largely autonomous individuals could shape the laws to further their own economic interests. In place of this recognizably modern vision, Novak argued that the antebellum polity was best described as a "well-ordered society," a tight-knit social and political-economic order built around locality or state, possessing broad powers to "enact or enforce public laws regulating or even destroying private right, interests, liberty, or property for the common good" through the ill-defined but pervasive police power (1996: 13). This was a society pervaded by regulation – an order captured in the equitable maxim *salus populi* ("the good of the people"). The common law here was not an instrument for economic development, but both the theory and practice of government, supplying pervasive regulations to anchor a society shaped not by market demands but by a vision of the *common* good. Some fifty years after the Commonwealth school, the battle was still being waged against the myth of the "stateless state" in the early Republic.

Novak backed up his claim with an avalanche of detail on nineteenth-century regulation, documenting how, through the police power, localities – for this is a profoundly local vision – limited and regulated activities ranging from building construction to sale of goods, from public roads to public morals. If not quite as original as Novak claimed – *The People's Welfare* was not the first work to challenge the myth of laissez-faire – it still marked a sharp break from its predecessors.

As did *Heart versus Head*. If there was a "Horwitz thesis," this was its antithesis. Like Novak, Karsten dissented from what he labeled the "economic-oriented reigning paradigm," arguing that there had been no great transformation of private law in the nineteenth century (1997: 298). Judges in this account did not seek to promote economic efficiency or elites; instead their decisions were either constrained by English precedent (produced by the "Head"), or impelled by their Christian beliefs and the era's new reformist sensibilities (guided by the "Heart"). To the extent they departed from precedent, they did so to "*aid* the weak and the poor" (1997: 3). To demonstrate this, Karsten turned well-known episodes of legal history on their head, arguing for instance that the "ancient lights" doctrine was abandoned during the nineteenth century not because it prevented development but (*contra* Horwitz) because it encouraged antisocial behavior, or that the 1839 *Farwell* decision, adopting the "fellow servant rule" shielding employers from negligence claims, was a reluctant decision compelled not by the needs of commerce but by English precedent, and so a product of "Jurisprudence of the Head."

To date, works on antebellum law and political economy offer more thesis and antithesis than synthesis. After decades of withering criticism Horwitz's argument no longer persuades. But the main candidates to replace it, Novak's and Karsten's, stake out their own extremes, and readers can doubt whether the common law polity was quite as monolithic and all-encompassing, or judges quite as uniformly benign, as they appear in these authors' accounts. There must be a middle ground, but it has not yet found its historian.

Political Economy and Law in the Gilded Age and Progressive Era

After the Civil War and Reconstruction – whose huge legal and economic repercussions are addressed elsewhere in this volume – Americans faced a rapidly transforming world. The period between the end of Reconstruction and World War I brought fundamental changes to the nation, as urbanization, industrialization, the construction of a national market, and the growth of railroads and then other giant corporations both sparked and were mediated through legal change. In examining these developments, we work through historiography that began as sunnily Progressive, became more somber with the appearance of theorists of corporatism and its variant, "corporate liberalism," then was challenged anew by the spread of organizational and pluralist theories in the 1970s, before the rise of a new approach intent on bringing the "state back in" to historical analysis.

Here again we enter seemingly in the middle of the story, for by the 1950s historians of the Progressive Era were already writing *against* older accounts of the period that painted it as a time of strife between the Interests and the People which culminated in hard-won victories by beneficent state and Federal governments triumphing over giant corporations run by robber barons. This simplistic history, a bit of a caricature of the actual "Progressive Historians," was nonetheless what many historians rejected in the 1950s, as exemplified by Richard Hofstadter, who cast a skeptical eye on the Populists' and Progressives' motivations in his *Age of Reform* (1955).

A darker account of the Progressive Era, and particularly its push for business regulation, appeared in the 1960s, with the work of "New Left" historians, most notably Gabriel Kolko and Martin Sklar. Kolko's *Railroads and*

Regulation (1965) and *Triumph of Conservatism* (1963) portrayed Progressive business reforms, particularly antitrust law and railroad regulation, as the product not of anti-corporate reformers aiming to tame large corporations but of business elites themselves, intent on managing markets in order to guarantee themselves stability and oligopoly. Sklar's *Corporate Reconstruction of American Capitalism* (1988), which appeared in the 1980s but grew out of ideas developed decades before, likewise presented a skeptical vision, arguing that the reforms were not simply intended to protect large corporations, but helped effect a transition from a viciously competitive to a more managed, corporate capitalism. To Sklar, this resulted in corporations managing the market apart from government involvement. These accounts are similar but not identical; as Morton Keller put it, in Kolko's corporatism the state was "doing the bidding of big business," while in Sklar's corporate liberalism the state was "getting out of the way of big business" (Keller, 1990: 5). In either account, the law was ultimately subservient to corporate needs.

These views soon found critics. In 1970 Galambos, drawing on the work of Alfred Chandler, Max Weber, and Robert Wiebe, proposed an "organizational synthesis," which claimed that the fundamental development during this period was not political or legal but structural, as large, bureaucratic organizations appeared in business, labor, and the professions (with, admittedly, profound political and legal implications) (Galambos, 1970). Further historical refinements appeared in the 1970s and 1980s. In 1977 and 1990, respectively, Morton Keller weighed in with *Affairs of State* and *Regulating a New Economy*, works that focused on the "American polity," including lawmakers and courts, to argue that political and economic life in the Gilded Age and Progressive Era could best be understood not as dictated by a powerful business class but as the product of more discrete and complex interactions between a large number of influential groups. In this account, new regulation emerged from "a roiling aggregate of interests, issues, institutions, ideas: in sum, an increasingly pluralist American polity" (1990: 3).

Skowronek's *Building a New American State* (1982) put forward yet another account. This pioneering work of historical institutionalism tackled Americans' apparent antipathy to the modern state (perhaps a version of the claim that America had an economy without law). Far from there being no state in the nineteenth century, Skowronek argued, the U.S. had a "state of courts and parties," in which national parties and courts knit together the polity. Novel in this account was the claim that this state did not merely respond (for instance) to outside demands by corporations or workers, but that it had its own interests and institutional imperatives, and the persistence of the state of courts and parties helps explain the inconsistent and fragmented modern state that succeeded it. None of these accounts is simply legal history, but each has much to say about the role of the law in the construction of the modern economy. These last-mentioned works also point forward to a new development in twentieth-century America, one that would come to occupy a central place in discussions of law and the economy: the administrative state (see Grisinger elsewhere in this volume).

Constructing a National Market

The law also played a major role in constructing an integrated national economy during the nineteenth century. In an era marked by endemic conflict between locally-oriented small businesses and larger "foreign" (i.e., out-of-state) enterprises, courts, particularly Federal courts, provided significant support for interstate commerce (Freyer, 1994). The Constitution's commerce clause was the most visible measure favoring a national market, and courts wielded it to knock down particularly egregious barriers to interstate trade, exemplified by the Marshall Court's decision in *Gibbons v. Ogden* (Johnson, 2010). Federal courts helped in other ways as well; 1842's *Swift v. Tyson*, which initiated nearly a century of Federal common law, helped create a uniform commercial law (Freyer, 1979), while from the 1870s to the 1930s Federal courts would be perceived as providing a friendly venue for corporations litigating against small opponents (Purcell, 1992). And, while one may think that law led the way in opening the national market for businesses, sometimes causation went the other way; Charles McCurdy has ingeniously argued that in the post-Civil War era the courts' expansive commerce clause jurisprudence was a response to, rather than a precursor of, the rise of giant, vertically integrated corporations and their national marketing arms (McCurdy, 1978).

Though constitutional issues are largely beyond this chapter's reach, it should be noted that the commonplace view that the *Lochner* era of the late nineteenth and early twentieth centuries was a high watermark of judicial solicitude of big business, with courts developing notions of substantive due process and liberty of contract in order to strike down regulation, has faced significant challenge. The simple image of the era's Supreme Court siding with the "Interests" against the "People" is no longer tenable to many historians – after all, even in those decades the Court upheld most regulatory legislation – and has been replaced by a more subtle account of interactions between government regulation and the period's so-called laissez-faire constitutionalism (McCurdy, 1975; Wiecek, 1998; Novak, 2010).

Law and Business Organization: Corporation, Antitrust, Securities Law

The story of the growth of the modern economy is, to a great extent, the story of the giant corporation. Business corporations had begun to appear by the start of the nineteenth century, and state support for them, often through direct investment or the grant of special privileges, was a significant issue in antebellum politics – developments discussed in the works on antebellum law and political economy, *supra*. Growing suspicion of corporate privileges, fueled by the era's Jacksonian democratic ethos, began the move from special to general incorporation, making the corporate form more readily available. Corporations truly took center stage, however, in the decades after the Civil War, as first railroads and then other nation-spanning enterprises powered rapid economic development and created enormous wealth, even as their growth led many to fear a future dominated completely by giant corporations and the wealthy few thought to control them.

But what is the relationship between the corporation and law? The best history of corporation law remains Hurst's *The Legitimacy of the Business Corporation in the Law of the United States* (1970), which answers that question by depicting corporation law as an enabler of the corporation rather than its "prime mover" (1970: 10). In this work men first organized for business and only then fit their enterprises to the law, or tried to change the law to fit their enterprises. While general incorporation made the form widely available, nineteenth-century corporate law still aspired to regulate the corporation by, for example, limiting its lifespan, capital, or purposes, though without great success. By the 1890s that began to change, as corporation law increasingly aimed not to limit but to facilitate a corporation's organizers and managers, and during the twentieth century limits on corporations were no longer built into corporation law itself but assigned to outside regulators and administrative agencies.

This account of corporation law shedding regulatory functions to facilitate the giant corporation fit well with the canonical account of the rise of the modern American corporation, Chandler's *Visible Hand* (1977). Chandler attributed the growth of large-scale multi-unit business enterprise to developments far outside the law: the maturation of a national market, itself the product of the communications and transportation revolutions, and technological imperatives favoring mass production and organizational integration in certain industries. Corporation law's most notable appearance in the *Visible Hand* is in its discussion of the "trust," the legal device developed to detour around corporate law limits on multi-state and multi-unit business enterprises. But the legal form of the trust and its successor, the holding company, did not trump technology as a prime mover; the industrial behemoths that succeeded did so because their production methods encouraged such integration, while those that failed were doomed by different technological imperatives. Corporate law helped them, but it did not make them. Nor was Chandler's the first work depicting the law as peripheral to the growth of the corporation; Berle and Means' *The Modern Corporation and Private Property* (1932), which set the tone for modern analysis of the corporation by identifying the separation of ownership and control as the key development in the modern corporation, similarly downplayed the *causative* force of law in shaping the corporation. To be sure, Berle and Means exhaustively surveyed the legal developments that led to that separation between managers and shareholders – indeed, theirs remains one of the best accounts of these developments – but *The Modern Corporation* depicted the growth of large corporations, and concentration of power in management, as a fundamentally economic development, encouraged by, but not the result of, legal change.

More recent accounts attempt to put law back at the center of the giant corporation's growth. Roe's *Strong Managers, Weak Owners* attributes the separation of ownership and control in the American corporation not to economic necessity but to Americans' dislike of concentrated financial power, an antipathy that gave rise to legal limits preventing financial intermediaries such as banks, insurance companies, or mutual funds from taking large stakes in corporations and challenging their management. In Roe's account, America's management-dominated corporations resulted not from a "natural economic evolution" but the nation's distinctive anti-statist, anti-finance legal culture (Roe, 1994: 3). Roy's *Socializing Capital* (1997) directly challenges Chandler, contending that the "corporate revolution" was not the product of technological-economic imperatives but of a power struggle won by corporate managers and owners who, among other things, manipulated state corporate law to promote their own interests.

Other approaches gave renewed emphasis to the power of legal ideas in the modern corporate economy. Hovenkamp's *Enterprise and American Law* charted the interaction between classical political economy and law from the Jacksonian era to the New Deal, and argued for the centrality of theoretical economics to those periods' legal and political debates. While classical economics held sway, he argued, its belief that the state should largely leave entrepreneurs "free of both regulation and subsidy" guided lawmakers; its erosion around the turn of the century opened the door to new judicial toleration of government regulation (Hovenkamp, 1991: 11). Horwitz's *The Transformation of American Law 1870–1960* (*Transformation II*) (1992), dissected the scholarly debates over "corporate personhood" that raged from the 1880s to the 1930s, arguing that shifts in the seemingly epiphenomenal legal concept of the corporation, from a partnership-like "aggregate theory" to the "real entity theory," helped legitimate the large-scale business corporation and, incidentally, undermine legal theories more favorable to stringent state regulation. Neither author claimed that legal or economic theory produced the modern corporation, but both believed that theory powerfully shaped the response to it.

While the nineteenth century looked to state corporation laws to tame the giant corporation, they proved unequal to the job. States enjoyed some success in regulating railroads in the 1870s, but were either unable or unwilling to challenge corporate combinations at the end of the century (Ely, 2001; Scheiber, 1971). The twentieth century pinned its hopes on

Federal antitrust law (McCurdy, 1979). The rise of nation-spanning trusts in the 1880s, and a merger wave among manufacturers in the late 1890s, spurred calls for Federal action against developments widely perceived to thwart competition. Antitrust law entered the Federal arena in 1890 with the adoption of the Sherman Act.

The Act's early history, and the course of antitrust law from the 1880s to the First World War, occupied the New Left historians Kolko and Sklar, who reached different conclusions as to whether the Act and the antitrust movement were deliberate failures to encourage competition and thwart bigness, or merely inadvertent ones (Kolko, 1963; Sklar, 1988). They agreed, though, that popular hopes for antitrust were not met. Hopes that the Sherman Act would roll back large corporations were extinguished by 1911's *Standard Oil* case, where the Supreme Court adopted the "rule of reason" holding that the Act's prohibitions on "restraint of trade" only barred *unreasonable* trade. (Others have offered different accounts of this period – Hovenkamp (1991), for instance, emphasizing the economic theories underpinning antitrust.) By the 1920s, bigness became an accepted feature of modern American business.

Yet, as Hofstadter pointed out in "What Happened to the Antitrust Movement?" this narrative of failure missed something important: long after the antitrust movement ended, the antitrust enterprise continued, and "became a force of real consequence in influencing the behavior of business" (Hofstadter, 1965: 104). Hawley's *The New Deal and the Problem of Monopoly* (1966) remains the starting point for tracing this antitrust enterprise. A broader work than its title suggests, it examines the New Deal's ambiguous relationship to the giant corporation and the free market economy and its slow abandonment of anti-big business and national planning goals, closing with an account of the unexpected blossoming of antitrust law under Thurman Arnold in the late 1930s. Antitrust's career during the rest of the century is traced by Freyer's *Regulating Big Business* (1992), a comparative study of U.S. and U.K. antitrust which argues that their divergent antitrust policies helped determine the differential development of managerial capitalism in the two nations, and Peritz's *Competition Policy in America* (1992), which examines the development of antitrust law through the lens of rhetorical analysis and is particularly strong on the rise of deregulatory ideologies since 1970.

One legacy of legal historians' focus on the giant corporation is comparative neglect of small business and other business forms. Only recently, for instance, have scholars begun to examine the legal organization of small business (Guinnane et al., 2007; Lamoreaux, 2004), while Woeste's *The Farmer's Benevolent Trust* (1998) remains a rare study of how a non-corporate business form, the agricultural cooperative, grew to power and navigated business and antitrust law to become an accepted part of the business landscape. More also remains to be done on conflicts between small and large business outside the antitrust arena, perhaps following Freyer's *Producers versus Capitalists* (1994), which charted antebellum struggles between small local and large national enterprises, and Schragger's "Anti-Chain Store Movement" (2005), which discussed a similar battle a century later. Finally, surprisingly little has been written on corporate law during the twentieth century (Mark, 2008).

The history of securities law, as distinct from corporate law or the history of Wall Street, is also understudied. Banner's *Anglo-American Securities Regulation* (1998) connects regulation of America's antebellum capital markets to earlier developments in English law and culture, depicting a surprisingly active market for corporate securities during that era. Seligman's *Transformation of Wall Street* (2003) exhaustively narrates Federal securities regulation after 1933, while McCraw's *Prophets of Regulation* (1984) has material on the development of the Federal Securities Acts. Mitchell's *Speculation Economy* (2007) presents a neo-Progressive account in which changes surrounding the turn of the century's "merger mania" fundamentally reoriented business managers from concern with their firm's performance to concern with its stock price.

Bankruptcy

Perhaps because it is the definition of failure in a society devoted to economic success, bankruptcy has received only sporadic study from legal historians. While the Constitution gave Congress power to set uniform bankruptcy laws, such laws existed only intermittently until the twentieth century. Warren's 1935 *Bankruptcy in United States History* remains useful as a compendium of nineteenth-century debates over bankruptcy laws and is a historical document in its own right; reflecting its historical moment, it puts forward a capacious view of Congress' powers under the Bankruptcy Clause to challenge the then-Supreme Court's narrow view of Federal authority. Coleman's 1970 *Debtors and Creditors in America* largely records state-level changes to bankruptcy laws in the eighteenth and nineteenth century, with a particular focus on the slow end of imprisonment for insolvency, while Ely's *Railroads and American Law* (2001) devotes a chapter to an important area of late nineteenth-century bankruptcy, railroad receiverships. Perhaps signaling a renewed interest in the subject, 2001 saw the appearance of Skeel's *Debt's Dominion* and Balleisen's *Navigating Failure*. The former was a detailed history of Federal bankruptcy law in the twentieth century (with a look back to the nineteenth century), drawing on public choice theory to present modern bankruptcy law as the product of shifting interest groups, providing as well an insightful account of the growth of the bankruptcy bar. *Navigating Failure* looked further back, presenting a social, economic, and legal history of the short-lived Bankruptcy

Act of 1841, and of debtors who took advantage of its provisions, to depict the growth of a credit-based economy and its consequences in the nineteenth century. These were followed shortly by Sandage's *Born Losers* (2005), which draws on bankruptcy law (among other things) to present a profound meditation on the idea of failure in American history.

Private Law: Contract

The history of private law (indeed, the very idea of private law and the public/private distinction) was examined in many of the works discussed above, and is a central topic in works such as *Transformation I* and *Heart versus Head*. But we also have accounts more sharply focused on particular areas of private law, notably the core areas of contract, property, and tort.

Contract lay at the heart of nineteenth century law; Friedman described it as the "century of contract" (Friedman, 2002: 381). His *Contract Law in America* remains perhaps the best account of contract's evolution, focusing on appellate decisions in a single jurisdiction, Wisconsin. The book partook of both the Wisconsin Schools of legal history and of contracts, as it attempted to chart the relationship between contract law and the free market. Its results were counterintuitive; here contract law was not the story of high theory and theorists but the law's retreat from these, as Friedman showed courts that preferred to focus on particulars to resolve specific disputes rather than rely on the generalities of the treatises. Indeed, an important thread of the work is how little purchase contract law had on the actual evolution of Wisconsin's economy, as both court and, apparently, litigants sought to evade it in favor of private dispute resolution.

Friedman's painstaking empirical work was, oddly, an inspiration for perhaps the best-known history of contract, Gilmore's *Death of Contract* (1974), which focused on the great contract theorists – Holmes, Langdell, Williston, and Corbin – to argue that the twentieth century had seen the short triumph and long decline of classical contract theory, as contract's liability-restrictive approach was slowly eclipsed by tort's more expansive approach to liability. Since publication *The Death of Contract* has suffered scholarly drubbings, but it remains a provocative account of the field's evolution. More recently, Horwitz traced the "disintegration of the imperial idea of contract" in *Transformation II*, showing how early in the twentieth century contract theorists slowly broadened their view from an exclusively consent-based theory of contract to one including non-consensual elements (Horwitz, 1992: 37). Late nineteenth-century contract theory is the subject of Kreitner's *Calculating Promises* (2006), which provocatively argues that modern contract law was not the product of a centuries-long evolution but was created in the late nineteenth century by a series of scholars who distilled a discordant mass of earlier law into coherent doctrine valorizing a rational, calculating decision-maker capable of making binding promises through exchange of consideration – an individual particularly suited to surviving in the free market. With this sovereign individual at its center, all else once covered by contract law, from contracts based on preexisting status to consideration-free promises, moved to the margins.

The history of contract is not, however, limited to theory and doctrine. Witness Stanley's wide-ranging *From Bondage to Contract* (1998), which as its name suggests takes the Civil War-era abolition of slavery, and the triumph of contract as a basis for labor relationships, as a lens through which to examine debates over freedom and dependence in the Gilded Age. In her study, the ideology and rhetoric of slavery, freedom, and contract shaped understandings of issues as diverse as freedmens' and womens' work, beggary, prostitution, marriage, and women's economic independence.

Private Law: Property

Private property, too, was a prime subject for legal historians, exemplified by Hurst's description of the nineteenth-century's interest in "[d]ynamic rather than static property, property in motion or at risk rather than property secure and at rest" (Hurst, 1956: 24). A ground-level view of property law and politics is provided in McCurdy's *Anti-Rent Era in New York Law and Politics* (2001), a legal and political history of New York's 1840s Anti-Rent movement. McCurdy showed how the battle against New York's remaining "feudal" rents threaded its way through Americans' deep commitment to property and freedom of contract but was largely stymied by a legal-property system that proved more autonomous, and less amenable to change, than some earlier scholars may have made it appear.

Broader, synoptic views of property in American history appear in Alexander's *Commodity and Propriety* (1997) and Ely's *The Guardian of Every Other Right* (2008). The former is a history of legal ideas about property from before the Revolution to today, one that sees ideas about property oscillating between two views: the "commodity" view, related to classical liberalism, which depicts property chiefly as an item of exchange lodged in the private sphere, and the "propriety" view, linked to classical republicanism, that regards property as playing a public function, providing "the private basis for the public good" (1997: 1). The latter is a straightforward history tracing ideas of property rights in constitutional law, providing a sympathetic account of the defenders of strong constitutional protections for property and other economic rights.

Private Law: Tort, Accident, and Insurance

While it draws on older sources, modern tort law is distinctly a product of the late nineteenth and twentieth century, as the growth of industrial society – and industrial accidents – spurred first limits on plaintiffs' ability to seek recompense from large corporations (in the nineteenth century), then a flowering of new theories allowing recovery (in the twentieth). Tort was essayed in some of the works discussed above, including *Transformation I* and *Heart versus Head*. An incisive overview of tort law's growth, focusing on the "Liability Explosion" in personal-injury law during the twentieth century, is provided in a chapter with that title in Friedman's *American Law in the Twentieth Century* (2002). The field's doctrinal development is well covered in White's *Tort Law in America* (2003), which situates tort law's growth primarily in the interactions of judges and academics, against a backdrop of larger trends in American social thought.

Several recent studies have focused on the late nineteenth century, when the question of industrial accidents gave shape to modern tort law. Bergstrom's *Courting Danger* (1992) examines the explosive growth of injury litigation in New York City courts from 1870 to 1910, using the tools of social and economic history to conclude that the rise in litigation was explained neither by an increasing number of accidents nor by changes in the law, but by changing popular perceptions of causality that attached new responsibility to distant actors. Witt's *Accidental Republic* (2004) also begins with the late nineteenth-century's "industrial accident crisis," but moves from there to the consequent development of workers' compensation plans, and to the transformation of thinking about accident – from a "free labor" notion that focused on individual autonomy, or lack thereof, to actuarial models that treated accident as a collective problem to be resolved through social programs. Welke's *Recasting American Liberty* (2001) moves along parallel tracks, putting gender and race at the center of its analysis of how the spread of railroads and streetcars changed notions of "liberty" during this period. As women became passengers (and so accident victims), notions of what was expected of passengers, and what duties corporations owed them, changed; travelers were now seen as vulnerable, and protecting them required having their liberties curtailed, even as corporations were assigned new responsibilities for their well-being.

In the twentieth century, tort law became entwined with insurance and government risk-management. Abraham's *Liability Century* (2008) is a pathbreaking attempt to chart the interconnected development of tort law and liability insurance, showing how these systems grew in tandem, as developments in tort liability spurred the development of new forms of insurance, and how, perhaps less appreciated, the spread of new insurance products paved the way for courts to expand tort liability (e.g., the spread of homeowners' insurance covering family members made it easier for courts to find children liable for certain torts). By the end of the twentieth century, he shows, tort and insurance were locked together in a single, highly imperfect system for compensating accident victims. Moss' *When All Else Fails* (2002) has an even broader scope, depicting government activities over the past two hundred years as a series of attempts to manage risk through interventions as diverse as granting corporations limited liability in the early nineteenth century, the adoption of workers' compensation at the end of that century, and the tort-law products liability revolution at the middle of the twentieth century. Moss presents not only a radically different way to conceptualize government activity, he also argues that such risk-management programs were particularly suited to the American distrust of the intrusive state – that risk management activities were "statism for anti-statists" (2002: 316). Finally, Clarke's *Trust and Power* (2007) illustrates how the history of tort law can be threaded into economic and business history, as it shows how changes in the assignment of tort liability helped structure the relationships between auto makers, dealers, and consumers during the rise of America's automotive industry.

Conclusion

To close with a puzzle: Over the past several decades, the historical interaction of law and the economy has attracted an imposing array of scholars, including the two canonical modern legal historians, Willard Hurst and Morton Horwitz. Yet after all this, so much remains to be done! Along with the rest of the historical profession, legal historians seem to have drifted away from economic questions. The above illustrates just a few of the gaps in the scholarship – picking at random, for instance, not enough has been written on the history of securities laws, twentieth-century corporate law, or the liability revolution. Nor have those legal historians who do study the economy taken full advantage of developments in what should be their natural allied field – economic history (Harris, 2003). Perhaps, though, this neglect is not so bad, at least for future work – for it is in neglected fields that scholars can most easily find important questions yet to be answered.

References

Abraham, Kenneth (2008). *The Liability Century: Insurance and Tort Law from the Progressive Era to 9/11*. Harvard University Press, Cambridge, MA.

Alexander, Gregory S. (1997). *Commodity and Propriety: Competing Visions of Property in American Legal Thought, 1776–1970*. University of Chicago Press, Chicago.

Balleisen, Edward J. (2001). *Navigating Failure: Bankruptcy and Commercial Society in Antebellum America*. University of North Carolina Press, Chapel Hill, NC.

Balogh, Brian (2009). *A Government Out of Sight: The Mystery of National Authority in Nineteenth-Century America*. Cambridge University Press, New York.

Banner, Stuart (1998). *Anglo-American Securities Regulation: Cultural and Political Roots, 1690–1860*. Cambridge University Press, New York.

Bergstrom, Randolph E. (1992). *Courting Danger: Injury and Law in New York City, 1870–1910*. Cornell University Press, Ithaca, NY.

Berle, Jr., Adolf A. and Means, Gardiner C. (1932). *The Modern Corporation and Private Property*. Macmillan, New York.

Chandler, Jr., Alfred D. (1977). *The Visible Hand: The Managerial Revolution in American Business*. Belknap Press, Cambridge, MA.

Chandler, Jr., Alfred D. (1992). *Scale and Scope: The Dynamics of Industrial Capitalism*. Belknap Press, Cambridge, MA.

Clarke, Sally (2007). *Trust and Power: Consumers, the Modern Corporation, and the Making of the United States Automobile Market*. Cambridge University Press, New York.

Coleman, Peter J. (1970). *Debtors and Creditors in America: Insolvency, Imprisonment for Debt, and Bankruptcy, 1607–1900*. State Historical Society of Wisconsin, Madison, WI.

Ely, James W. (2001). *Railroads and American Law*. University of Kansas Press, Lawrence, KS.

Ely, James W. (2008). *The Guardian of Every Other Right: A Constitutional History of Property Rights*. Oxford University Press, New York.

Freyer, Tony (1979). *Forums of Order: The Federal Courts and Business in American History*. JAI Press, Greenwich, CT.

Freyer, Tony (1992). *Regulating Big Business: Antitrust in Great Britain and America, 1880–1990*. Cambridge University Press, New York.

Freyer, Tony (1994). *Producers versus Capitalists: Constitutional Conflict in Antebellum America*. University Press of Virginia, Charlottesville, VA.

Freyer, Tony (2008). "Legal Innovation and Market Capitalism, 1790–1920." In Grossberg and Tomlins, eds, *Cambridge History of Law in America*, Volume 2, 449–482. Cambridge University Press, New York.

Friedman, Lawrence M. (1964). *Contract Law in America: A Social and Economic Case Study*. University of Wisconsin Press, Madison, WI.

Friedman, Lawrence M. (2002). *American Law in the 20th Century*. Yale University Press, New Haven, CT.

Friedman, Lawrence M. (2005). *A History of American Law*. Touchstone, New York.

Galambos, Louis (1970). "The Emerging Organizational Synthesis in Modern American History." *Business History Review* 44: 279–290.

Gilmore, Grant (1974). *The Death of Contract*. Ohio State University Press, Columbus, OH.

Guinnane, Timothy, Harris, Ron, Lamoreaux, Naomi R., and Rosenthal, Jean-Laurent (2007). "Putting the Corporation in its Place." *Enterprise & Society* 8: 687–729.

Handlin, Oscar and Handlin, Mary Flug (1969 [1947]). *Commonwealth: A Study of the Role of Government in the American Economy, 1774–1861*. Belknap Press, Cambridge, MA.

Harris, Ron (2003). "The Encounters of Economic History and Legal History." *Law & History Review* 21: 297–346.
Hartz, Louis (1948). *Economic Policy and Democratic Thought: Pennsylvania, 1776–1860.* Harvard University Press, Cambridge, MA.
Hawley, Ellis W. (1966). *The New Deal and the Problem of Monopoly.* Princeton University Press, Princeton, NJ.
Hofstadter, Richard (1955). *The Age of Reform.* Vintage Books, New York.
Hofstadter, Richard (1965). "What Happened to the Antitrust Movement?" In *The Paranoid Style in American Politics and Other Essays.* Vintage Books, New York.
Horwitz, Morton J. (1977). *The Transformation of American Law 1780–1860.* Harvard University Press, Cambridge, MA.
Horwitz, Morton J. (1992). *The Transformation of American Law 1870–1960: The Crisis of Legal Orthodoxy.* Oxford University Press, New York.
Hovenkamp, Herbert (1991). *Enterprise and American Law 1836–1937.* University of North Carolina Press, Chapel Hill, NC.
Hurst, J. Willard (1956). *Law and the Conditions of Freedom in the Nineteenth-Century United States.* University of Wisconsin Press, Madison, WI.
Hurst, J. Willard (1964). *Law and Economic Growth: The Legal History of the Lumber Industry in Wisconsin 1836–1915.* Belknap Press, Cambridge, MA.
Hurst, J. Willard (1970). *The Legitimacy of the Business Corporation in the Law of the United States, 1780–1960.* University Press of Virginia, Charlottesville, VA.
Johnson, Herbert A. (2010). *Gibbons v. Ogden: John Marshall, Steamboats, and the Commerce Clause.* University of Kansas Press, Lawrence, KS.
Karsten, Peter J. (1997). *Heart Versus Head: Judge-Made Law in Nineteenth-Century America.* University of North Carolina Press, Chapel Hill, NC.
Keller, Morton (1977). *Affairs of State: Public Life in Late Nineteenth-Century America.* Harvard University Press, Cambridge, MA.
Keller, Morton (1990). *Regulating a New Economy: Public Policy and Economic Change in America, 1900–1933.* Harvard University Press, Cambridge, MA.
Kolko, Gabriel (1963). *The Triumph of American Conservatism, 1900–1916.* Free Press, New York.
Kolko, Gabriel (1965). *Railroads and Regulation, 1877–1916.* Princeton University Press, Princeton, NJ.
Kreitner, Roy (2006). *Calculating Promises: The Emergence of Modern American Contract Doctrine.* Stanford University Press, Palo Alto, CA.
Kutler, Stanley I. (1990 [1971]). *Privilege and Creative Destruction: The Charles River Bridge Case.* Johns Hopkins University Press, Baltimore, MD.
Lamoreaux, Naomi (2004). "Partnerships, Corporations, and the Limits on Contractual Freedom in U.S. History: An Essay in Economics, Law, and Culture." In Lipartito and Sicilia, eds, *Constructing Corporate America: History, Politics, Culture.* Oxford University Press, New York.
Mark, Gregory A. (2008). "The Corporate Economy: Ideologies of Regulation and Antitrust, 1920–2000." In Grossberg and Tomlins, eds, *Cambridge History of Law in America,* Volume 3, 613–652. Cambridge University Press, New York.
McCraw, Thomas K. (1984). *Prophets of Regulation.* Belknap Press, Cambridge, MA.

McCurdy, Charles (1975). "Justice Field and the Jurisprudence of Government-Business Relations: Some Parameters of Laissez-Fair Constitutionalism, 1863–1897." *Journal of American History* 61: 970–1005.

McCurdy, Charles (1978). "American Law and the Marketing Structure of the Large Corporation, 1875–1890." *Journal of Economic History* 38: 631–649.

McCurdy, Charles (1979). "The Knight Sugar Decision of 1895 and the Modernization of American Corporation Law, 1869–1903." *Business History Review* 53: 304–342.

McCurdy, Charles (2001). *The Anti-Rent Era in New York Law and Politics*. University of North Carolina Press, Chapel Hill, NC.

Mitchell, Lawrence (2007). *The Speculation Economy: How Finance Triumphed over Industry*. Berrett-Koelher, San Francisco.

Moss, David A. (2002). *When All Else Fails: Government as the Ultimate Risk Manager*. Harvard University Press, Cambridge, MA.

Novak, William J. (1996). *The People's Welfare: Law and Regulation in Nineteenth-Century America*. University of North Carolina Press, Chapel Hill, NC.

Novak, William J. (2008). "The Myth of the 'Weak' American State." *American Historical Review* 113: 752–772.

Novak, William J. (2010). "Law and the Social Control of American Capitalism." *Emory Law Review* 60: 377–405.

Peritz, Rudolph (1992). *Competition Policy in America, 1888–1992*. Oxford University Press, New York.

Purcell, Edward A. (1992). *Litigation & Inequality: Federal Diversity Jurisdiction in Industrial America, 1870–1952*. Oxford University Press, New York.

Roe, Mark (1994). *Strong Managers, Weak Owners: The Political Roots of American Corporate Finance*. Princeton University Press, Princeton, NJ.

Roy, William (1997). *Socializing Capital: The Rise of the Large Industrial Corporation in America*. Princeton University Press, Princeton, NJ.

Sandage, Scott A. (2005). *Born Losers: A History of Failure in America*. Harvard University Press, Cambridge, MA.

Scheiber, Harry N. (1969). *Ohio Canal Era: A Case Study of Government and the Economy, 1820–1861*. Ohio University Press, Athens, OH.

Scheiber, Harry N. (1971). "The Road to *Munn*: Eminent Domain and the Concept of Public Purpose in the State Courts." *Perspectives in American History* 5: 327–402.

Scheiber, Harry N. (1972). "Government and the Economy: Studies of the 'Commonwealth Policy' in Nineteenth-Century America." *Journal of Interdisciplinary History* 3: 135–151.

Schragger, Richard C. (2005). "The Anti-Chain Store Movement, Localist Ideology, and the Remnants of the Progressive Constitution 1920–1940." *Iowa Law Review* 90: 1011–1094.

Schwartz, Gary T. (1981). "Tort Law and the Economy in Nineteenth-Century America: A Reinterpretation." *Yale Law Journal* 90: 1717–1776.

Seligman, Joel (2003). *The Transformation of Wall Street: A History of the Securities and Exchange Commission and Modern Corporate Finance*. Aspen, New York.

Simpson, A.W.B. (1979). "The Horwitz Thesis and the History of Contract." *University of Chicago Law Review* 46: 533–601.

Skeel, David A. (2001). *Debt's Dominion: A History of Bankruptcy Law in America*. Princeton University Press, Princeton, NJ.

Sklar, Martin J. (1988). *The Corporate Reconstruction of American Capitalism, 1890–1916: The Market, Law, and Politics*. Cambridge University Press, New York.

Skowronek, Stephen (1982). *Building a New American State: The Expansion of National Administrative Capacities, 1877–1920*. Cambridge University Press, New York.

Stanley, Amy Dru (1998). *From Bondage to Contract: Wage Labor, Marriage, and the Market in the Age of Slave Emancipation*. Cambridge University Press, New York.

Warren, Charles (1935). *Bankruptcy in United States History*. Harvard University Press, Cambridge, MA.

Welke, Barbara Young (2001). *Recasting American Liberty: Gender, Race, Law and the Railroad Revolution, 1865–1920*. Cambridge University Press, New York.

White, G. Edward (2003). *Tort Law in America: An Intellectual History*. Oxford University Press, New York.

Wiecek, William M. (1998). *The Lost World of Classical Legal Thought: Law and Ideology in America, 1868–1937*. Oxford University Press, New York.

Witt, John Fabian (2004). *The Accidental Republic: Crippled Workingmen, Destitute Widows, and the Remaking of American Law*. Harvard University Press, Cambridge, MA.

Woeste, Victoria Saker (1998). *The Farmer's Benevolent Trust: Law and Agricultural Cooperation in Industrial America, 1865–1945*. University of North Carolina Press, Chapel Hill, NC.

Chapter Sixteen

LAW AND LABOR IN THE NINETEENTH AND TWENTIETH CENTURIES

Deborah Dinner

The question of how law structures power relations between workers, employers, and the state animates the history of law and labor in the nineteenth and twentieth centuries. Historians bring disparate methodologies and theoretical frames to bear on that question. Their analyses enhance our understanding of the historical evolution of labor law as well as the relationship between law, politics, and society.

The critical insight that law is constitutive of social relations shaped a generation of legal historians studying labor in the early republic and antebellum and Reconstruction periods (Gordon, 1984). These historians elucidate the common law's creation of background rules that structured the terms on which workers negotiated with employers, as individuals and as unions. They ask whether court decisions reflected the judiciary's class bias, the demands of industrial capitalism, or judges' theories about the political function of labor and business independent of economic exigencies. The analysis of labor alongside slavery and its legacies leads historians to engage philosophical questions about the meaning of freedom and coercion.

The lines of causation between law and politics lie at the center of many histories addressing labor in the late nineteenth and twentieth centuries. Scholars within the American Political Development School study the origins of labor legislation, which they variously attribute to features of the U.S. administrative state, social movement mobilization, and governance ideologies. Legal scholars devote attention to the question of whether internal jurisprudential or external political factors determined court rulings on state and

A Companion to American Legal History, First Edition.
Edited by Sally E. Hadden and Alfred L. Brophy.
© 2013 John Wiley & Sons Ltd. Published 2021 by John Wiley & Sons Ltd.

federal labor legislation. Critical historians assess the promise and peril that legal recognition of unions held for labor organizing and political action.

The turn to the study of women and people of color in social history, as well as to the use of gender and race as analytical tools, has also influenced labor history. Cognizant of the centrality of the employment relation to the construction of citizenship, historians probe how gender and racial ideologies shaped the definition of work and workers under common law and statutes. Other historians study the relationship between law and social movements. They compare workers' constitutional and legal imagination with movement leaders' litigation strategies and with the consequences of legislative reform. Scholars of the late twentieth century examine the fragmentation of antidiscrimination law and labor law into separate doctrines and institutions.

Several key questions animate the literature on labor and the law in the nineteenth and twentieth centuries: (1) How should we define coerced labor and free labor in the nineteenth century, in light of the centrality of slavery and its abolition to the American experience? (2) How has the state apparatus, including courts, legislatures, and administrative agencies, shaped the identity of the labor movement and its space for action? (3) How have ideas about gender shaped the relationship between work and citizenship? And, (4) What was the relationship between labor organizing and the civil rights movement and what consequences did the advent of antidiscrimination law pose for the pursuit of economic justice? All these inquiries also entertain a common concern with law's capacity to foster or to undermine material inequalities as well as class consciousness.

Labor Coerced and Free

The effort to locate different forms of labor along axes of coercion and freedom animates the historiography of the colonial, founding, and antebellum eras. The endeavor begins with a paradox: How do we account for the coexistence of slavery and freedom as foundational political theories and economic systems? Edmund Morgan's study of colonial Virginia (1975) provided the first resolution of this paradox, arguing that the enslavement of African Americans gave rise to white freedom. In the decades since Morgan's foundational work, social histories, such as Seth Rockman's multi-ethnic labor history of proletarianized workers in Baltimore (2009), have complicated the distinction between slave and free labor. Legal historians have engaged in rich debates about the characteristics that defined slave, indentured, and wage labor, as well as the ways in which these labor forms changed over time.

Historians have evaluated the nature of wage labor in the antebellum period with reference to earlier, pre-industrial periods. They have taken disparate positions on the conditions of labor during the colonial era and early republic. Robert J. Steinfeld (2001) argues that the English settlement of the Americas transplanted common law master-servant rules that laid the foundation for the coercive labor regimes of the nineteenth century. In contrast with Steinfeld, Christopher Tomlins (2010) sees pluralism and possibilities for freedom in the colonization of English America. He argues that indentured servitude did not dominate the culture of work and that indentured servants did not represent as large a proportion of the laboring population in the colonies as previously thought. Furthermore, the regional diversity of English migrants settling the Americas yielded variations in the nature of servitude in the Chesapeake, New England, and the Delaware Valley.

Tomlins (1993) argues that capital's power consolidated during the first half of the nineteenth century, when law replaced mass democracy as the dominant paradigm for republican order. Courts wielded the doctrine of criminal conspiracy to define labor organizing as illegal collective action and thereby foreclose labor's claim to quasi-corporate rights. Common law rules of master and servant expanded to cover not only the particular status of indentured servants from Europe and American-born bound-out apprentices but also all employer-employee relations. The doctrine of entirety provided that an employer owed an employee wages only at the end of the labor contract. If the employee breached, then the employer did not owe any wages for the portion of the work completed (Orren, 1991; Steinfeld, 2001; Tomlins, 1993; Horwitz, 1977). In addition to the denial of quantum meruit, common law doctrines provided for the forfeiture of wages when an employee failed to obey shop rules or declined to give notice before leaving (Steinfeld, 2001; Tomlins, 1993). Anti-enticement laws imposed penalties for hiring other employers' workers during the terms of their contracts (Orren, 1991; Tomlins, 1993).

By midcentury, courts had significantly narrowed employers' liability for industrial accidents. Massachusetts Chief Justice Lemuel Shaw's opinion in *Farwell v. Boston & Worcester Railroad Corporation* (1839) became the leading case applying the "fellow servant rule" to shield employers from liability when harm to an employee resulted from another employee's actions (Tomlins, 1993). Morton Horwitz (1977) understands *Farwell* as evidence of a new market ideology ascendant in the antebellum period. Karen Orren (1991), by contrast, views the decision as evidence that a "belated feudalism" persisted until the period of full-scale industrialization after the Civil War. In her view, not until the late nineteenth century did labor succeed in dismantling feudalism and in paving the way toward a liberal polity in which legislatures and not courts regulate labor.

The history of contract doctrine and ideology is intertwined with the legal history of labor in the antebellum and Reconstruction periods. An early historiographic debate centered on continuities and change in contract law from the eighteenth to the nineteenth centuries. Morton J. Horwitz's classic study (1977) traces a transformation from eighteenth-century legal rules that encompassed substantive standards of fairness toward a "will theory" of contracts, based on subjective definitions of value in a market society. A.W.B. Simpson (1979) challenged the evidence underpinning Horwitz's thesis arguing, for example, that eighteenth-century courts recognized executory contracts and expectation damages (1979).

By the 1880s, courts departed from pure contract theory to adjudicate employer-employee disputes on the basis of the nature of the contract and not the intention of the parties. The development of the "employment at will" rule facilitated the advent of industrial capitalism by giving owners greater control over workers and allowing them to discharge employees without notice (Feinman, 1976). While common law regulation of employment contracts represented default rather than mandatory rules, their complexity and the disparate institutional resources wielded by employers and employees dissuaded potential employees from contracting around these rules (Witt, 2000).

The key questions in the historiography of the postbellum period center on how to understand the ironies and contradictions that accompanied the ascendance of free labor ideology. Steinfeld complicates the dichotomy between free and coerced labor by arguing, first, that pecuniary sanctions sometimes had as coercive an effect on workers as non-pecuniary sanctions. Second, Steinfeld shows that while penal sanctions for breach of contract by native-born adult white workers ended by 1800, such sanctions persisted for imported European workers until the 1830s and for people of color through the end of the century, even after the adoption of the Thirteenth Amendment and the enactment of the 1867 Anti-Peonage Statute.

In the era of slave emancipation, historical actors debated the implications of contract ideologies and doctrines for the freedom of African Americans, wage laborers, and married women (Fox, 2007). Northern wage hirelings interrogated the opposition between chattel slavery and free labor; they claimed that ironclad contracts which prohibited collective bargaining made them "wage slaves." Cultural anxieties surrounded figures who challenged contract's hegemony: the beggar because of his reliance on charity rather than contractual change and the prostitute because she embodied a tension between free contract and the prohibition on traffic in bodies (Stanley, 1998). In the late nineteenth century, workers' acceptance of the ideology of the "living wage" linked working-class cultural and political identity to consumption (Glickman, 1997).

In the South, ideas about gender and race as well as regional political economy shaped a contest over the meaning of freedom for former slaves. Emancipated African Americans understood freedom to entail familial integrity, access to education, an end to corporal punishment, improved work conditions, and, for some, equal rights with whites. Black families also wanted to withdraw the labor of women from the fields, to protect them from sexual exploitation and to enable them to care for their families (Foner, 1988). Large planters, however, possessed an economic interest in returning all former slaves, both men and women, to a disciplined workforce laboring in gangs on cash crops (Woodman, 1995). When it became evident that the freedpeople would not receive land allocations, Freedmen's Bureau officials enforced anti-vagrancy laws and labor contracts as a means to coerce freedpeople to work for planters (Schmidt, 1998).

Convict leasing, which began after the Civil War and continued until Alabama became the last state to abolish the practice in 1928, formed part of the labor struggle in the former Confederate states. Economic considerations as well as racism undergirded the system: states' interest in simultaneously avoiding the cost of holding prisoners and in deriving a new source of capital; private industry's interest in securing a reliable and inexpensive labor source; and planters' interest in the regulation of black laborers (Mancini, 1996). Convict leasing also depressed the wages of white workers, who faced greater threat of job loss during strikes because of employers' capacity to rely on convict labor (Shapiro, 1998). Matthew Mancini (1996) argues that the abolition of convict leasing did not represent a triumph of humanitarianism, but rather resulted from its decreasing profitability to lessees; the increasing cost-efficacy of chain gangs to states; and the desire on the part of reformers to use convict labor to advance public projects rather than private economic interests. While Alex Lichtenstein (1996) concurs with this conclusion, he views the chain gangs that replaced convict leasing as continuous with southern states' use of convict labor as a modernization strategy. As David Oshinsky's account of Parchman Farm in Mississippi (1996) demonstrates, states' use of convicts to produce public revenue proved as brutal a system of racial and labor control as did convict leasing.

Labor and the State

Historians have devoted considerable attention to the relationship between labor and the state, from the Civil War to World War II. From the 1910s through the 1940s, the labor economist John R. Commons and scholars influenced by him analyzed labor from a pluralist perspective (Commons and Andrews, 1936). These scholars believed that class conflict was not inevitable, that disinterested experts could mediate disputes between employers and workers, and that national labor policy should embody the principles of collective laissez-faire (Ernst, 1995; Fleming, 1957). Beginning in the 1960s, critical legal theorists and the "new" labor historians viewed common law and legislative regulation of labor from the perspective of class struggle. Corrective accounts, finally, have argued that courts' recognition of rights for organized labor produced liberating and repressive effects. These histories complicate our understanding of the role of the courts and the federal government in shaping labor's capacity for collective action.

Historians have debated the relationship between labor, corporate power, and the courts during the Gilded Age. As Alan Trachtenberg (1982) has described, business incorporation during this period widened the class rift between employer and employee. The escalating conflict between capital and labor implicated a contest over national identity, in which corporations stood for the value of marketplace competition and unions for workplace mutuality. During this period, the decline in skilled workers' professional independence and the rise of management's ownership of employee innovation undermined economic democracy (Fisk, 2009). Scholars interested in the welfare state endeavor to historicize American exceptionalism: Why did trade unions not join with professional reformers to demand labor regulations and social insurance? Both Theda Skocpol (1993) and William Forbath (1991) answer with reference to the influential concept of the "state of courts and parties" developed by Stephen Skowronek (1982).

American workers did not inherently lack class consciousness. In the 1880s, the American Federation of Labor (AFL) emphasized collective action to transform political economy. In the last decade of the nineteenth century and the first decade of the twentieth century, the AFL evolved toward a voluntarist ideology: a commitment to "private" collective bargaining and disavowal of public political action. As the nineteenth century came to a close, the courts' application of conspiracy law to labor organization largely ended. But courts that had first applied labor injunctions to railroad lines in receivership during the 1877 strikes, now extended injunctions to strikes and boycotts well beyond these lines (Friedman, 1985). In 1895, the U.S. Supreme Court upheld the federal government's power to enjoin striking workers and, in 1908, to hold them liable under the Sherman Antitrust Act; that year, the Supreme Court for the District of Columbia held that the Clayton Act prohibited secondary boycotts. Thus, the power of the judiciary in the United States and its hostility toward labor prompted the AFL's turn away from the associational vision it had earlier espoused (Forbath, 1991; Hattam, 1993).

Even as labor evolved from an associational to a voluntarist ideology, a parallel evolution occurred in the attitudes of the legal class toward labor. Lawyers, judges, and legislators, while fearful of labor's power in the 1880s, by World War I viewed labor as occupying a legitimate and important place in the political order. Part of that acceptance can be explained by intervening government suppression of radical labor, including the Knights of Labor in the 1880s, industrial unionism in the 1890s, and the Industrial Workers of the World in the early twentieth century (Fusfeld, 1984). Daniel Ernst (1995) argues that courts laid the foundation for industrial pluralism by accommodating the rise of national trade unions. Ernst chronicles the activities of the American Anti-Boycott Association (AABA), a group that litigated and lobbied against organized labor from 1902 through 1918. Ernst offers evidence, which the critical labor historians of the 1960s had overlooked, that in the decades before the New Deal courts did not serve as the "reliable ally" of employers. Instead, courts recognized the legitimacy of unions' legal personality.

Historians have studied the courts' treatment of labor legislation as well as labor organization. Revisionist histories shed new light on the well-trod path from the *Lochner* era to the Second New Deal. They challenge the conventional academic notion that laissez-faire merely rationalized common law doctrines that served the economic interests of its proponents. The intellectual origins of *Lochner* era jurisprudence lay in the free labor ideology of the antebellum Republican Party (Foner, 1995; Nelson, 1988). Conservative justices' libertarian antipathy to class legislation expressed a Jacksonian commitment to equal rights and neutrality (Benedict, 1985; McCurdy, 1998). The Court distinguished between states' valid use of the police power to promote public health and safety and invalid legislation on behalf of a particular class (Gillman, 1993). Gilded Age judges' decisions regarding labor strikes and boycotts reflected not legal formalism so much as moralism regarding work and the labor contract (Ernst, 1992).

Scholarly disagreement persists about whether the political New Deal catalyzed a doctrinal revolution in the Supreme Court. Externalist accounts emphasize the Court's response to Franklin Delano Roosevelt's Court-packing plan, popular electoral mobilization, and Congressional legislation (Ackerman, 1998; Leuchtenberg, 1995). Internalist accounts argue that the decisions ratifying the legislation of the Second New Deal represented the culmination of doctrinal evolution over three decades. Barry Cushman (1998) presents evidence that the Supreme Court justices voted on the major cases of the alleged constitutional revolution before Roosevelt announced his Court-packing plan. Cushman places the key decisions ratifying the Second New Deal in the context of the gradual erosion of a public/private distinction that had underpinned laissez-faire principles of federalism, government neutrality, and rights in property and contractual liberty. Julie Novkov (2001) concludes that the New Deal represented an expansion of the belief that women workers merited protective legislation to all workers. By contrast, social and political historians eschew the question of judicial motivation altogether. Instead, they analyze how workers' experiences of popular culture, the Great Depression, and welfare capitalism, as well as Roosevelt's growing need for political support for the Second New Deal as business opposition intensified, transformed the relationship between labor and the state (Cohen, 1990; Dubofsky, 1994).

Historians and political scientists debate the origins of the National Labor Relations Act (NLRA), or Wagner Act, of 1935, which created the National Labor Relations Board (NLRB). Some advance a state-centered explanation for the NLRA. They stress the causal importance of party alignment and lack of administrative capacity to mediate industrial conflict. The Democratic Party's strong win in the 1934 election put labor reform on the agenda. The institutional failure of the National Industrial Recovery Act, even before the Supreme Court held the Act unconstitutional, created a policy vacuum that enabled passage of the NLRA (Finegold and Skocpol, 1984). In contrast, social-movement explanations focus on mass mobilization that placed political pressure on both Congress and the Roosevelt administration. Some point to spontaneous, unorganized protest by industrial workers, the unemployed, and farmers (Piven and Cloward, 1977). Others emphasize the role of the Communist Party and other radical activists in organizing protest (Skocpol, Finegold, and Goldfield, 1990).

Ruth O'Brien (1998) rejects the dominant narratives centered on either the New Deal administrative state or popular mobilization. Instead, she argues that the principles of the major pieces of New Deal labor legislation evolved over the preceding half century of Republican governance. Beginning in the 1890s and continuing through the 1920s, Progressives forged the concept of "responsible unionism" that guaranteed worker representation and granted procedural rights to unions in exchange for heightened state regulation. O'Brien concludes that the Transportation Act of 1920 and the Railway Labor Act of 1926 establishing the Railway Labor Boards, and not the National Industrial Recovery Act, became the blueprint for the Wagner Act. Colin Gordon (1994) offers a more qualified revision of the Wagner Act's origins. Gordon points to business's pursuit of "regulatory unionism" during the two prior decades, a two-year failed experiment in regulation under the National Recovery Administration, and a Keynesian concern with under-consumption and commitment to increasing mass purchasing power.

Historians have also studied the effects of the Wagner Act. Critical legal scholars contend that although the NLRA represented a radical response to the strike wave of 1934, the remainder of the decade and the 1940s constituted a period of deradicalization. In legitimating the institutional structure of collective bargaining, the NLRB aggrandized the power of labor unions at the expense of individual workers' organizing activities (Klare, 1978; Tomlins, 1992). In the postwar period, judges, labor economists and sociologists, and legal theorists subscribed to an industrial pluralist ideology that conceived of the NLRA as granting procedural rather than substantive rights. Postwar liberals entertained a legal fiction that capital and labor negotiated as equals, which legitimated existing inequalities in the workplace (Stone, 1981). The Taft-Hartley Act of 1947, amending the Wagner Act, reinforced the pluralist model and further confined collective bargaining to issues of wages, hours, and benefits alone (Tomlins, 1985).

Gender and the Definition of a "Worker"

In the years between 1920 and 1950, the United States developed a public-private welfare state, and the employment relationship came to play a constitutive role in citizenship (Boris, 2008). Employers and insurers established private health benefits and pension plans attached to the employment relation and simultaneously constrained the expansion of a public welfare state (Klein, 2004). Historians interested in the relationship between gender, race, labor regulation, and public policy have focused on the public half of our nation's hybrid social welfare system. Alice Kessler-Harris (2001) elucidates how a "gendered imagination" has shaped the ways in which legal and policy actors envisioned, debated, and drew meaning from labor legislation and employment discrimination laws as well as social insurance and tax schemes. The sexual division of labor, in particular, has de-legitimated women's presence in the workforce; denied women the government benefits afforded worker-citizens; and resulted in the creation of a liberal welfare state premised on the model of the male breadwinner.

Historians have brought to light the economic value of women's labor in the home as well as the social and legal processes by which that labor came to be understood as something other than "work." As a result of the economic change that proletarianized men during the early republic, manliness developed an association with wage-earning. Non-wage-earning labor in the home – both traditional sustaining activities such as cooking and productive activities that made up the gap between a man's actual wage and a family's needs – no longer gained recognition as work (Boydston, 1990). In the antebellum period, women's rights leaders challenged the pastoralization of women's labor and made claims for joint marital property on the basis of women's contribution to the household economy. Postbellum women's rights leaders began to articulate women's right to work outside the home, but in so doing devalued women's labor within the home. Individual women litigants continued to claim earnings for labor performed within the household. Despite the passage of the Married Women's Property Acts, however, courts treated the work that women performed on behalf of their families and work related to keeping boarders as labors for love, not money (Siegel, 1994).

In contrast to economic sociologists who attribute behavioral change to economic determinants, historians have argued that cultural values regarding gender and the family shaped claims for labor and social welfare reforms in the late nineteenth century. The debate over child labor, for example, implicated a broader social controversy about whether children should hold economic value, or whether they were emotionally priceless and therefore necessarily outside of the market (Zelizer, 1985). Gender ideologies embedded in the family wage and free labor ideals contributed to the development of workers' compensation insurance in the early twentieth century (Witt, 2001; 2004).

The question of women's participation in the workforce divided the women's movement during the Progressive Era. Over time, women's rights leaders advocating for the Equal Rights Amendment (ERA) came to view sex-based protective labor laws as denying women equal access to employment opportunities. In contrast, most women's voluntary associations as well as the labor movement defended protective laws and preferred specific legislation rather than a broadly sweeping ERA. Both groups of activists understood themselves as feminists and advocates for women's economic justice and for the prevention of women's exploitation (Cott, 1987). Historians have since argued that a conservative legal environment forced women activists to funnel a broader rights consciousness into specific constitutional arguments, in a manner that distanced the position of social feminists from that of ERA advocates. Advocates strategically invoked gender difference as a wedge to crack the *Lochner* court's laissez-faire jurisprudence (Hart, 1994; Zimmerman, 1991).

Historians have also analyzed how responses to the Civil War, industrial labor, and changes in family structure shaped the development of a protean welfare state over the latter half of the Long Nineteenth Century. Theda Skocpol (1993) argues that Civil War pensions established an atavistic system of social spending. Charges of patronage and corruption, however, thwarted the development of a paternalist social welfare state led by male bureaucrats for the good of industrial workers. Only the effort to establish social insurance compensating injured workers reached fruition in this period, and efforts to realize old-age, health care, and unemployment insurance failed. By contrast, Skocpol argues, the activities of female civic reformers to establish mothers' pensions, protective labor legislation for women, the Children's Bureau, and the passage of the Sheppard-Towner Act realized a nearly fully-fledged maternalist welfare state. Linda Gordon (1993a; 1993b) suggests that Skocpol's state-centered approach pays insufficient attention to gender ideology and power relations between middle-class reformers and working-class and poor women. Gordon (1994) argues that maternalist social reform culminated in New Deal legislation creating a two-tier welfare state with superior, universal benefits administered by the federal government for men and inferior, means and moral-tested benefits administered by the states for women.

Histories focused on institutions and ideology alike argue that gender as well as race shaped the definition of "worker" under New Deal social and labor legislation. Suzanne Mettler (1998) chronicles how New Deal policies made men into national citizens, via regulatory and redistributive policies administered at the federal level according to liberal principles, and women into state citizens, via policies administered by the state on the basis of non-liberal rationales. Federal Old-Age Insurance (OAI) targeted able-bodied, lifetime participants in the labor force, while states administered Old-Age Assistance programs providing for dependents within the family. The same "divided citizenship" characterized unemployment insurance, disproportionately benefitting men, and Aid to Dependent Children, benefitting single mothers and their children. Only in 1939, with the addition of widows' and wives' benefits to OAI, did women gain access to national citizenship, albeit as unpaid housewives rather than workers.

The NLRA and Fair Labor Standards Act (FLSA) held more promise for white, male workers than for either women or minority, male workers. Part of the explanation lies in the exclusionary character of union organizing. The Congress of Industrial Organizations (CIO), which split from the AFL after the passage of the NLRA, proved far more inclusive of women (Foner, 1980). Still, the CIO directed organizing activities at women workers in industries that also employed large numbers of men and largely ignored wage differentials and labor grievances particular to women workers (Strom, 1983). Between the New Deal and the late 1960s, "labor feminists" used unions as the primary vehicle by which to realize rights to employment opportunity for women as well as social rights that supported women's role as caregivers within the family (Cobble, 2004).

Another factor producing inequalities in labor protections, of enduring significance, is implicit gender and racial bias in statutory design. Because so many of the social benefits and protections in the United States are conditioned on the employment relationship, the question of who counts as an "employee" under the NLRA and FLSA holds considerable importance (Smith, 2007a; Linder, 1989). Southern resistance to labor reform constrained reformers' vision for a federal labor standard setting forth a forty-cent-per-hour minimum wage and forty-hour-per-week maximum (Storrs, 2000). Furthermore, southern whites' commitment to racial hierarchy in the labor force resulted in the exclusion of agricultural and domestic workers from the protection of FLSA (Palmer, 1995). In addition, FLSA implicitly excluded those occupations that did not affect interstate commerce and those jobs within larger commercial operations that remained intrastate in effect (Hart, 1994). Thus, even after the passage of FLSA, disproportionate numbers of women and minority men labored outside of the protection of federal standards. The NLRA's definition of an "employee" excludes categories of workers beyond the model of the traditional male breadwinner: persons working for their spouses, domestic employees, "confidential employees" assisting managers, and independent contractors. Because women disproportionately occupy these sectors of the workforce, the NLRA's gendered definition of work continued to impede union organization of women through the late twentieth century (Crain, 1991).

Labor and Civil Rights

A nascent, yet rich, literature exists on the relationship between race and civil rights. Scholars explore the problem of racism within the labor movement (Bernstein, 1993); the role of class in the civil rights movement (Salmond, 2004); and the promise and limits of federal labor policy in disrupting racial hierarchies (Forbath, 1999; Hill, 1977; McCartin, 1997). They examine the myriad ways in which Title VII of the Civil Rights Act of 1964 – the federal statute that prohibits employment discrimination based on race, color, religion, sex, and national origin – shaped the identities, strategies, and institutional forms of labor, liberal, and conservative movements.

Some of the most exciting recent work on the labor movement analyzes alternative constitutional trajectories rooted in the promise of the Thirteenth Amendment, as well as the popular constitutional aspirations of workers and their advocates. Lea VanderVelde (1989) argues that many of the Congress members who enacted the Thirteenth Amendment believed that it not only eliminated slavery and involuntary servitude but also created an affirmative guarantee of labor autonomy. James Pope (2002) explicates the constitutional vision advanced by unions and workers during the 1920s and 1930s, interpreting the Thirteenth Amendment as a barrier to labor injunctions, yellow-dog contracts, and other restrictions on labor's freedom. Pope argues that Robert Wagner's decision to base the NLRA on the Commerce Clause rather than the Thirteenth Amendment hijacked labor's vision. Laura Weinrib unearths the origins of civil liberties in the labor movement. During the inter-war period, the American Civil Liberties Union moved away from a model of civil liberties that understood free speech as a means to realize working-class power toward a model that celebrated individuals' negative right to expression free from state interference (Weinrib, 2012).

Risa Goluboff (2007) revises the historiography of civil rights by highlighting the grievances of African-American sharecroppers, tenant farmers, and industrial workers in the South. These workers desired rights related to employment relations legally categorized as "private," as well as the extension of New Deal protections to African Americans. The Civil Rights Section (CRS) of the Department of Justice understood the Thirteenth Amendment, which did not have a state action requirement, as the primary constitutional tool to dismantle economic exploitation as well as racial discrimination under Jim Crow. By contrast, the middle-class orientation of the National Association for the Advancement of Colored People (NAACP) Legal Defense and Educational Fund led it to target segregation as Jim Crow's primary injury and pursue desegregation in education as the most significant civil rights objective. Goluboff illustrates the "lost promise" of a construction of civil rights focused on economic subordination, material insecurity, and private exploitation rather than formal equality, psychological injury and social stigma, and government action. Sophia Lee (2008), however, provides a rejoinder to Goluboff's argument that the NAACP abandoned its concern with a working-class agenda and economic issues by the early 1950s. Instead, Lee uncovers evidence that the NAACP challenged the state action doctrine and fought workplace discrimination from 1948 through the early 1960s via administrative agencies, rather than the courts.

The enactment of Title VII offered a powerful tool to African Americans, women, and immigrants fighting for workplace justice (MacLean, 2006). Still, historians have sought to explain the conundrum that, in the half century between the Wagner Act and the mid-1980s, the organized labor movement opened dramatically to African-American participation at the same time as it significantly declined in power (Frymer, 2007). Nelson Lichtenstein (2002) argues that the African-American civil rights movement and its legal manifestations ratified a shift from a political concern with economic inequality, capitalism, and the democratization of the workplace to a concern with statecraft to manage racial divisions. Paul Frymer (2007) emphasizes not an ideological shift from collective to individual rights but rather the fragmentation of labor and civil rights via the Wagner Act and Title VII into separate institutions and bodies of law. Frymer argues that at the same time as courts advanced civil rights through their interpretation of Title VII, courts also weakened the bargaining strength of unions as a result of concurrent structural factors: the development of class actions, increases in damage awards and attorney fees, corporate lawyers' role in litigating Title VII cases, and judges' insensitivity to the growing vulnerability of the labor movement.

In rendering sex-based protective labor laws illegal, Title VII both marked the receding influence of an older generation of labor feminists and created new opportunities for alliances among women (MacLean, 2006). Title VII rendered moot the choice between anti-discrimination paradigms that promised opportunity, or sex-based labor standards that offered security. By the early 1970s, working-class as well as professional women saw Title VII as a means to realize substantive fairness in the workplace. Black women, in particular, who had benefitted little from the family-wage ideology, identified with the promise of legal prohibitions on sex-based employment discrimination (MacLean, 2006).

Women's rights activists grew dependent on Title VII as a means to achieve workplace justice, however, at the same time as it grew less powerful as a tool for change (MacLean, 2006). Just as women began to make inroads into nontraditional lines of work, the economy constricted and the New Right began to use social anxieties regarding the decline of the family wage to gain political leverage. Likewise, organizational changes within the National Organization for Women and its increasing focus on the ERA, abortion, and identity concerns turned liberal feminism away from broader conceptions of workplace justice (Turk, 2010). Feminist legal scholars (Crain, 1994; Crenshaw, 1989) critique antidiscrimination law's capacity to redress the economic subordination of working-class women and women of color. Serena Mayeri (2011) has initiated an investigation into the contingent character of these limitations; whether they were inherent in Title VII's design or a consequence of its institutional implementation and judicial interpretation warrants further historical investigation.

Conclusion: Turns Right and Global

While a rich history exists concerning labor and law in the nineteenth and twentieth centuries, significant areas of inquiry remain for scholars to investigate. The rightward turn in American politics and in the judiciary, during the late twentieth century, offers fruitful avenues for investigation. Nancy MacLean (2006) has initiated inquiry into the relationship between political conservatism and demands by women, African Americans, and immigrants for employment opportunity. MacLean describes how conservatives in the 1970s and 1980s shifted their opposition to affirmative action in employment from reliance on the rhetoric of states' rights, private property, and biological racism to one based on liberal individualism and colorblindness. Even as the Republican Party appropriated the language of civil rights, social conservatives attacked feminism as antagonistic to married white women who still relied on the family wage. In addition to social conservatism, fiscally conservative arguments for privatization had important consequences for the labor movement. Historians have examined the deregulation of homework (Boris, 1994) and the Reagan Administration's breaking of the Professional Air Traffic Controllers Organization strike (McCartin, 2011). Katherine Stone (2004) argues that at the same time as courts and state legislatures used common law and public policy to create job protections in the 1970s and 1980s, employers repudiated the *de facto* practices guaranteeing job security that originated in the early twentieth century to return to a purer at-will model of employment. The complicated story of labor's decline, contests over the meaning of racial equality, resistance to changing gender norms, and the rise of Reagan Democrats remains largely untold. What role did the courts and administrative agencies play in this process? How did the law reflect evolving social mores and constitute the political imagination of liberals, radicals, social and market conservatives disputing the rights of workers?

Scholars have also called for a reexamination of labor law in the context of global migration and markets (Jacoby, 1998). Mae Ngai (2004) examines the experience of Filipinos and Mexican migrants who were exempt from the racial restrictions of the Immigration Act of 1924 because of their respective status as colonial subjects and Western hemisphere residents. Of particular interest, Ngai shows how the development of a Mexican migrant labor force began in the 1920s to serve the needs of a transformed industrial agricultural economy in the West and Southwest. A compilation of essays from U.S., Canadian, Latin American, and Caribbean scholars edited by Leon Fink (2011) represents a pioneering effort to apply the transnational turn in historical scholarship to labor and working-class histories. The chapters range across time periods from the eighteenth through the twenty-first centuries and address topics as disparate as labor and empire, international feminism and reproductive labor, and transnational labor politics.

Legal scholars, too, pose critiques of contemporary law that may serve as a jumping-off point for historians. The intriguing questions raised by these scholars include: the bounds of undocumented migrants' membership in the national community; the function of citizenship in shaping the interaction between low-wage African-American and Latino immigrant workers; the noncompliance of employers in the agricultural and garment industries with FLSA and other protective labor laws; the regulation of home-care workers; the function of labor and immigration law in enabling human trafficking; the insulation of domestic labor law from the influence of international human rights and other nations' labor laws; and the problem of enforcing international labor standards and of legislating domestically to improve working conditions in foreign countries (Bosniak, 1988; Gordon, 2008; Goldstein, 1999; Smith, 2007a; 2007b; Chacon, 2006; Estlund, 2002; Pagnattaro, 2004; Doorey, 2010). A compelling research agenda exists for legal, political, and social historians interested in the global intersections of law, migration, and labor.

References

Ackerman, Bruce (1998). *We the People: Transformations,* Volume 2. Belknap Press of Harvard University Press, Cambridge, MA.

Benedict, Michael Les (1985). "Laissez-Faire and Liberty: A Re-Evaluation of the Meaning and Origins of Laissez-Faire Constitutionalism." *Law and History Review* 3(2): 293–332.

Bernstein, David E. (1993). "Roots of the 'Underclass': The Decline of Laissez-Faire Jurisprudence and the Rise of Racist Labor Legislation." *American University Law Review* 43(1): 85–138.

Boris, Eileen (1994). *Home to Work: Motherhood and the Politics of Industrial Homework in the United States.* Cambridge University Press, Cambridge, UK.
Boris, Eileen (2008). "Labor's Welfare State: Defining Workers, Constructing Citizens." In Grossberg and Tomlins, eds, *The Cambridge History of Law in America, Volume III: The Twentieth Century and After,* 319–358. Cambridge University Press, Cambridge, UK.
Bosniak, Linda S. (1988). "Exclusion and Membership: The Dual Identity of the Undocumented Worker under United States Law." *Wisconsin Law Review* 6: 955–1042.
Boydston, Jeanne (1990). *Home and Work: Housework, Wages, and the Ideology of Labor in the Early Republic.* Oxford University Press, New York.
Chacon, Jennifer M. (2006). "Misery and Myopia: Understanding the Failures of U.S. Efforts to Stop Human Trafficking." *Fordham Law Review* 74(6): 2977–3040.
Cobble, Dorothy S. (2004). *The Other Women's Movement: Workplace Justice and Social Rights in Modern America.* Princeton University Press, Princeton, NJ.
Cohen, Lizabeth (1990). *Making a New Deal: Industrial Workers in Chicago, 1919–1939.* Cambridge University Press, Cambridge, UK.
Commons, John R. and Andrews, John B. (1936). *Principles of Labor Legislation.* 4th Edition. Harper and Bros., New York.
Cott, Nancy (1987). *The Grounding of Modern Feminism.* Yale University Press, New Haven, CT.
Crain, Marion (1994). "Between Feminism and Unionism: Working Class Women, Sex Equality, and Labor Speech." *Georgetown Law Journal* 82(6): 1903–2002.
Crain, Marion (1991). "Feminizing Unions: Challenging the Gendered Structure of Wage Labor." *Michigan Law Review* 89(5): 1155–1221.
Crenshaw, Kimberle (1989). "Demarginalizing the Intersection of Race and Sex: A Black Feminist Critique of Antidiscrimination Doctrine, Feminist Theory and Antiracist Politics." *University of Chicago Legal Forum* 139–168.
Cushman, Barry (1998). *Rethinking the New Deal Court: The Structure of a Constitutional Revolution.* Oxford University Press, New York.
Doorey, David J. (2010). "In Defense of Transnational Domestic Labor Regulation." *Vanderbilt Journal of Transnational Law* 43(4): 953–1010.
Dubofsky, Melvyn (1994). *The State and Labor in Modern America.* University of North Carolina Press, Chapel Hill.
Ernst, Daniel R. (1992). "Free Labor, the Consumer Interest, and the Law of Industrial Disputes." *American Journal of Legal History* 36(1): 19–37.
Ernst, Daniel R. (1995). *Lawyers Against Labor: From Individual Rights to Corporate Liberalism.* University of Illinois Press, Chicago.
Estlund, Cynthia L. (2002). "The Ossification of American Labor Law." *Columbia Law Review* 102(6): 1527–1612.
Feinman, Jay M. (1976). "The Development of the Employment at Will Rule." *The American Journal of Legal History* 20(2): 118–135.
Finegold, Kenneth and Skocpol, Theda (1984). "State, Party, and Industry: From Business Recovery to the Wagner Act in America's New Deal." In Bright and Harding, eds, *Statemaking and Social Movements: Essays in History and Theory,* 159–192. University of Michigan Press, Ann Arbor.

Fink, Leon, ed. (2011). *Workers Across the Americas: The Transnational Turn in Labor History.* Oxford University Press, New York.

Fisk, Catherine L. (2009). *Working Knowledge: Employee Innovation and the Rise of Corporate Intellectual Property, 1800–1930.* University of North Carolina Press, Chapel Hill.

Fleming, R.W. (1957). "The Significance of the Wagner Act." In Derber and Young, eds, *Labor and the New Deal*, 121–155. The University of Wisconsin Press, Madison.

Foner, E. (1988). *Reconstruction: America's Unfinished Revolution, 1863–1877.* Harper & Row, New York.

Foner, E. (1995). "The Idea of Free Labor in Nineteenth-Century America." In Eric Foner, ed., *Free Soil, Free Labor, Free Men: The Ideology of the Republican Party before the Civil War.* Oxford University Press, New York.

Foner, Philip S. (1980). *Women and the American Labor Movement: From World War I to the Present.* Free Press, New York.

Forbath, William E. (1991). *Law and the Shaping of the American Labor Movement.* Harvard University Press, Cambridge, MA.

Forbath, William E. (1999). "Caste, Class and Equal Citizenship." *Michigan Law Review* 98(1): 1–91.

Fox, James W. (2007). "The Law of Many Faces: Antebellum Contract Law Background of Reconstruction-Era Freedom of Contract." *American Journal of Legal History* 49(1): 61–112.

Friedman, Lawrence M. (1985). *A History of American Law*, 2nd Edition. Simon & Schuster, New York.

Frymer, Paul (2007). *Black and Blue: African Americans, the Labor Movement, and the Decline of the Democratic Party.* Princeton University Press, Princeton, NJ.

Fusfeld, Daniel R. (1984). "Government and the Suppression of Radical Labor, 1877–1918." In Bright and Harding, eds, *Statemaking and Social Movements: Essays in History and Theory*, 344–377. The University of Michigan Press, Ann Arbor.

Gillman, Howard (1993). *The Constitution Besieged: The Rise and Demise of Lochner Era Police Powers Jurisprudence.* Duke University Press, Durham, NC.

Glickman, Lawrence B. (1997). *A Living Wage: American Workers and the Making of Consumer Society.* Cornell University Press, Ithaca, NY.

Goldstein, Bruce, Linder, Marc, Norton II, Laurence E., and Ruckelshaus, Catherine K. (1999). "Enforcing Fair Labor Standards in the Modern American Sweatshop: Rediscovering the Statutory Definition of Employment." *UCLA Law Review* 46(4): 983–1164.

Goluboff, Risa L. (2007). *The Lost Promise of Civil Rights.* Harvard University Press, Cambridge, MA.

Gordon, Colin (1994). *New Deals: Business, Labor, and Politics in America, 1920–1935.* Cambridge University Press, Cambridge, UK.

Gordon, Jennifer, and Lenhardt, R.A. (2008). "Rethinking Work and Citizenship." *UCLA Law Review* 55(5): 1161–1238.

Gordon, Linda (1993a). "Gender, State and Society: A Debate with Theda Skocpol" *Contention: Debates in Society, Culture, and Science* 2(3): 139–156.

Gordon, Linda (1993b). "Response to Theda Skocpol" *Contention: Debates in Society, Culture, and Science* 2(3): 185–189.

Gordon, Linda. (1994b). *Pitied But Not Entitled: Single Mothers and the History of Welfare*. Harvard University Press, Cambridge, MA.

Gordon, Robert W. (1984). "Critical Legal Histories." *Stanford Law Review* 36(1&2): 57–126.

Hart, Vivien (1994). *Bound by Our Constitution: Women, Workers, and the Minimum Wage*. Princeton University Press, Princeton, NJ.

Hartman Strom, Sharon (1983). "Challenging 'Woman's Place': Feminism, the Left, and Industrial Unionism in the 1930s." *Feminist studies* 9(2): 359–386.

Hattam, Victoria C. (1993). *Labor Visions and State Power: The Origins of Business Unionism in the United States*. Princeton University Press, Princeton, NJ.

Hill, Herbert (1977). *Black Labor and the American Legal System: Race, Work, and the Law*. Bureau of National Affairs, Washington, D.C.

Horwitz, Morton J. (1977). *The Transformation of American Law, 1780–1860*. Harvard University Press, Cambridge, MA.

Jacoby, Daniel (1998). *Laboring for Freedom: A New Look at the History of Labor in America*. M.E. Sharpe, Armonk, NY.

Kessler-Harris, A. (2001). *In Pursuit of Equity: Women, Men, and the Quest for Economic Citizenship in 20th-Century America*. Oxford University Press, New York.

Klare, Karl E. (1978). "Judicial Deradicalization of the Wagner Act and the Origins of Modern Legal Consciousness, 1937–1941." *Minnesota Law Review* 62(3): 265–340.

Klein, Jennifer (2004). *For All these Rights: Business, Labor, and the Shaping of America's Public-Private Welfare State*. Princeton University Press, Princeton, NJ.

Lee, Sophia Z. (2008). "Hotspots in a Cold War: The NAACP's Postwar Workplace Constitutionalism, 1948–1964." *Law and History Review* 26(2): 327–378.

Leuchtenberg, William E. (1995). *The Supreme Court Reborn: The Constitutional Revolution in the Age of Roosevelt*. Oxford University Press, New York.

Lichtenstein, Alex (1996). *Twice the Work of Free Labor: The Political Economy of Convict Labor in the New South*. Verso, New York.

Lichtenstein, Nelson (2002). *State of the Union: A Century of American Labor*. Princeton University Press, Princeton, NJ.

Linder, Marc. (1989). "What is an Employee – Why it Does, But Should Not, Matter." *Law and Inequality: A Journal of Theory and Practice* 7(2): 155–188.

MacLean, Nancy (2006). *Freedom Is Not Enough: The Opening of the American Workplace*. Russell Sage Foundation Books, Harvard University Press, Cambridge, MA.

Mancini, Matthew J. (1996). *One Dies, Get Another: Convict Leasing in the American South, 1866–1928*. University of South Carolina Press, Columbia, SC.

Mayeri, Serena (2011). *Reasoning from Race: Feminism, Law, and the Civil Rights Revolution*. Harvard University Press, Cambridge, MA.

McCartin, Joseph A. (1997). "Abortive Reconstruction: Federal War Labor Policies, Union Organization, and the Politics of Race, 1917–1920." *Journal of Policy History* 9(2): 155–183.

McCartin, Joseph A. (2011). *Collision Course: Ronald Reagan, the Air Traffic Controllers, and the Strike That Changed America*. Oxford University Press, New York.

McCurdy, Charles W. (1998). "The 'Liberty of Contract' Regime in American Law." In Harry N. Scheiber, ed., *The State and Freedom of Contract*, 161–197. Stanford University Press, Palo Alto, CA.

Mettler, Suzanne (1998). *Dividing Citizens: Gender and Federalism in New Deal Public Policy.* Cornell University Press, Ithaca, NY.

Morgan, Edmund S. (1975). *American Slavery, American Freedom: The Ordeal of Colonial Virginia.* W.W. Norton, New York.

Nelson, William E. (1988). *The Fourteenth Amendment: From Political Principle to Judicial Doctrine.* Harvard University Press, Cambridge, MA.

Ngai, Mae (2004). *Impossible Subjects: Illegal Aliens and the Making of Modern America.* Princeton University Press, Princeton, NJ.

Novkov, Julie (2001). *Constituting Workers, Protecting Women: Gender, Law, and Labor in the Progressive Era and New Deal Years.* University of Michigan Press, Ann Arbor.

O'Brien, Ruth (1998). *Workers' Paradox: The Republican Origins of New Deal Labor Policy, 1886–1935.* University of North Carolina Press, Chapel Hill.

Orren, Karen (1991). *Belated Feudalism: Labor, the Law, and Liberal Development in the United States.* Cambridge University Press, Cambridge, UK.

Oshinsky, David M. (1996). *"Worse than Slavery": Parchman Farm and the Ordeal of Jim Crow Justice.* Free Press, New York.

Pagnattaro, Marisa Anne (2004). "Enforcing International Labor Standards: The Potential of the Alien Tort Claims Act." *Vanderbilt Journal of Transnational Law* 37(1): 203–264.

Palmer, Phyllis (1995). "Outside the Law: Agricultural and Domestic Workers Under the Fair Labor Standards Act." *Journal of Policy History* 7(4):416–440.

Piven, Frances Fox, and Cloward, Richard A. (1977). *Poor People's Movements: Why They Succeed, How They Fail.* Pantheon Books, New York.

Pope, James Gray (2002). "The Thirteenth Amendment Versus the Commerce Clause: Labor and the Shaping of American Constitutional Law, 1921–1957." *Columbia Law Review* 102(1): 1–122.

Rockman, Seth (2009). *Scraping By: Wage Labor, Slavery, and Survival in Early Baltimore.* Johns Hopkins University Press, Baltimore.

Salmond, John A. (2004). *Southern Struggles: The Southern Labor Movement and the Civil Rights Struggle.* University Press of Florida, Gainesville, FL.

Schmidt, James D. (1998). *Free to Work: Labor Law, Emancipation, and Reconstruction, 1815–1880.* University of Georgia Press, Athens.

Shapiro, Karin A. (1998). *A New South Rebellion: The Battle Against Convict Labor in the Tennessee Coalfields, 1871–1896.* University of North Carolina Press, Chapel Hill.

Siegel, Reva B. (1994). "Home as Work: The First Woman's Rights Claims Concerning Wives' Household Labor, 1850–1880." *Yale Law Journal* 103(5): 1073–1218.

Simpson, A.W.B. (1979). "The Horwitz Thesis and the History of Contracts." *University of Chicago Law Review* 46(3): 533–601.

Skocpol, Theda (1992). *Protecting Soldiers and Mothers: The Political Origins of Social Policy in the United States.* Belknap Press of Harvard University Press, Cambridge, MA.

Skocpol, Theda (1993). "Soldiers, Workers, and Mothers: Gendered Identities in Early U.S. Social Policy." *Contention: Debates in Society, Culture, and Science* 2(3): 157–183.

Skocpol, Theda, Finegold, Kenneth, and Goldfield, Michael (1990). "Explaining New Deal Labor Policy." *American Political Science Review* 84(4): 1297–1315.

Skowronek, Stephen (1982). *Building a New American State: The Expansion of National Administrative Capacities, 1877–1920.* Cambridge University Press, Cambridge, UK.

Smith, Peggie R. (2007a). "Aging and Caring in the Home: Regulating Paid Domesticity in the Twenty-First Century." *Iowa Law Review* 92(5): 1835–1900.

Smith, Peggie R. (2007b). "Welfare, Child Care, and the People Who Care: Union Representation of Family Child Care Providers." *University of Kansas Law Review.* 55(2): 321–364.

Stanley, Amy Dru (1998). *From Bondage to Contract: Wage Labor, Marriage, and the Market in the Age of Slave Emancipation.* Cambridge University Press, Cambridge, UK.

Steinfeld, Robert J. (2001). *Coercion, Contract, and Free Labor in the Nineteenth Century.* Cambridge University Press, Cambridge, UK.

Stone, Katherine Van Wezel (1981). "The Post-War Paradigm in American Labor Law." *Yale Law Journal* 90(7): 1509–1580.

Stone, Katherine Van Wezel (2004). *From Widgets to Digits: Employment Regulation for the Changing Workplace.* Cambridge University Press, Cambridge, UK.

Storrs, Landon R.Y. (2000). *Civilizing Capitalism: The National Consumers' League, Women's Activism, and Labor Standards in the New Deal Era.* University of North Carolina Press, Chapel Hill.

Tomlins, Christopher L. (1985). *The State and the Unions: Labor Relations, Law, and the Organized Labor Movement in America, 1880–1960.* Cambridge University Press, Cambridge, UK.

Tomlins, Christopher L. (1992). "AFL Unions in the 1930s: Their Performance in Historical Perspective." *Journal of American History* 65(4): 1021–1042.

Tomlins, Christopher L. (1993). *Law, Labor, and Ideology in the Early American Republic.* Cambridge University Press, Cambridge, UK.

Tomlins, Christopher L. (2010). *Freedom Bound: Law, Labor, and Civic Identity in Colonizing English America, 1580–1865.* Cambridge University Press, Cambridge, UK.

Trachtenberg, Alan (1982). *The Incorporation of America: Culture and Society in the Gilded Age.* Hill and Wang, New York.

Turk, Katherine (2010). "Out of the Revolution, into the Mainstream: Employment Activism in the NOW Sears Campaign and the Growing Pains of Liberal Feminism." *Journal of American History* 97(2): 399–423.

VanderVelde, Lea S. (1989). "The Labor Vision of the Thirteenth Amendment." *University of Pennsylvania Law Review* 138(2): 437–504.

Weinrib, Laura M. (2012). "The Sex Side of Civil Liberties: *United States v. Dennett* and the Changing Face of Free Speech." *Law and History Review* 30(2): 325–386.

Witt, John Fabian (2000). "Rethinking the Nineteenth-Century Employment Contract, Again." *Law and History Review* 18(3): 627–658.

Witt, John Fabian (2001). "Toward a New History of American Accident Law: Classical Tort Law and the Cooperative First-Party Insurance Movement." *Harvard Law Review* 114(3): 690–841.

Witt, John Fabian (2004). *The Accidental Republic: Crippled Workingmen, Destitute Widows, and the Remaking of American Law*. Harvard University Press, Cambridge, MA.

Woodman, Harold D. (1995). *New South–New Law: The Legal Foundations of Credit and Labor Relations in the Postbellum Agricultural South*. Louisiana State University Press, Baton Rouge.

Zelizer, Viviana A. (1985). *Pricing the Priceless Child: The Changing Social Value of Children*. Basic Books, New York.

Zimmerman, Joan G. (1991). "The Jurisprudence of Equality: The Women's Minimum Wage, the First Equal Rights Amendment, and Adkins V. Children's Hospital, 1905–1923." *Journal of American History* 78(1): 188–225.

Chapter Seventeen

SITING THE LEGAL HISTORY OF POVERTY: BELOW, ABOVE, AND AMIDST

Felicia Kornbluh and Karen Tani

Where does "the legal history of poverty" begin and end? Virtually all law may be seen as the law of poverty. Property law is, in its unstated obverse, the law of poverty; the law of marriage is, among other things, the law of property distribution and mutual obligation between husband and wife; tax laws may impoverish the taxpayer or, by collecting paltry revenues, may prevent the state from remediating others' distress. Even when poor and working-class people have enjoyed access to lawyers and legal processes, law has helped generate, preserve, and legitimize inequalities of wealth. Some colleagues faced with this challenge have focused on public benefits law (Nice and Trubek, 1997). While we place much law outside of our framework, we widen our frame beyond public benefits or poverty law as traditionally understood.

We organize this chapter around sites where poor people encountered law: towns, institutions, courts, agencies, neighborhoods. Working from the classic statement, "Legal History from Below," by William Forbath, Hendrik Hartog, and Martha Minow, we argue that law's meaning in those sites – its force, significance, and promise – has come from "below," "above," and "amidst." The "below" perspective has become familiar. According to Forbath, Hartog, and Minow, formal law has been like a banner held aloft in a crowd; its operative meaning derives from its movement through the grasping hands of the people (1985: 765). We are profoundly shaped by this understanding of American law. However, we also emphasize the role of law from above in the historical experiences of poor people. And we argue that the law of poverty resulted equally from the actions

A Companion to American Legal History, First Edition.
Edited by Sally E. Hadden and Alfred L. Brophy.
© 2013 John Wiley & Sons Ltd. Published 2021 by John Wiley & Sons Ltd.

of people who were neither "above" nor "below": lower-level bureaucrats, social caseworkers, and neighborhood attorneys who made law amidst their daily interpretations of statutes and judicial decisions.

This perspective captures the field's complexity and encourages its most exciting new developments. Whereas "legal history from below" was once a vital critique of legal historical scholarship, social history has reigned for decades, and socio-legal history actively attracts practitioners (Welke and Hartog, 2009). Political history has likewise been reborn, in forms encompassing many of the concerns of social and cultural history (Jacobs, Novak, and Zelizer, 2003). Constitutional history, which once appeared moribund (Scheiber, 1981), has been similarly revivified (Kalman, 2005; Goluboff, 2007). By looking "above," "below," and "amidst" we seek to foster a richer, more consistent dialogue among scholars hailing from diverse traditions.

To highlight areas of common ground, and de-emphasize methodological and disciplinary differences, we focus on sites of legal encounter. To take one example: the welfare rights litigant Mrs. Sylvester Smith did not first encounter law when the Supreme Court adjudicated *King v. Smith* (1968), which overturned a regulation denying Aid to Dependent Children payments to mothers who "cohabited" with able-bodied men. Smith encountered law years earlier, following her husband's death in 1956, when a county agency deemed her eligible for public assistance, and in 1966, when the agency terminated her family's benefits on the basis of the "suitability" of her home. Smith's engagement with law continued when she approached the Lawyers' Constitutional Defense Committee, a private organization created to support the civil rights movement. Only then did she enter federal district court. Smith found law in a panoply of places and a range of forms: constitutional, statutory, administrative, informal, movement-centered, and "aspirational" (Hartog, 1987; 1988). We strive to capture this diversity. Moving roughly chronologically, we explore the legal history of poverty as it appeared in towns, institutions, local courts, state and federal agencies, urban neighborhoods, and appellate courtrooms to highlight how law was made from "below," "above," and "amidst."

Towns

Anglo-American towns are paradigmatic in the historiography of poverty. In British colonial America, where Elizabethan Poor Law prevailed, each town had a moral responsibility and a legal obligation to aid its needy members (Trattner, 1999: 11–12, 15–26). Towns raised the funds necessary to support their residents. Town officials made decisions about who would receive relief and on what terms. This structure survived the American Revolution, keeping decisions about relief at the level of the town, or, in some jurisdictions, just one step removed, at the county level (Friedman, 1985: 213). And as a practical and ideological matter, this intensely local form of relief shaped public responses to poverty through the early twenty-first century.

Local relief operations were embroiled in law and legal decision-making. Local overseers of the poor made complicated assessments of "settlement," the key determinant of local citizenship and therefore of public responsibility. They also sued other towns when confronted with a stranger's need, "warned out" those who lacked settlement, and policed potential paupers so that they would not gain rights to relief (Friedman, 1985: 150–53, 213; Trattner, 1999: 19–21, 24–25). When faced with a settled person in need, officials made more particularized determinations, deciding what form and amount of aid to give and what behavior to demand in return (Abramovitz, 1988: 85–86).

Early scholars explored local poor law as part of their argument for replacing this localistic paradigm with "modern" national- and state-level poverty policies. The most important were Edith Abbott, Grace Abbott, and Sophonisba Breckenridge, faculty at the University of Chicago School of Social Service Administration (SSA) and Progressive reformers. In the 1930s and 1940s, they and their students complained that the localistic approach had become outmoded: it ignored the mobility of America's poor and conflicted with the nation's liberal ethos and evolving sense of decency (Abbott, 1940; 1941; Kennedy and Breckenridge, 1934). These monographs remain important for excavating cases, statutes, and regulations that constituted poor law before the twentieth century.

The War on Poverty, and the 1960s movements for social and economic justice of the 1960s, inspired a new generation of historical scholarship on local poor law. A few major works, such as *From Poor Law to Welfare State*, aimed for generality and political or analytical agnosticism (Trattner, [1974] 1999: xxxiii, xxxv–xxxvi). Most scholarship of this generation, however, was preoccupied with power. One of the most influential interpretations was that of Frances Fox Piven and Richard Cloward. In *Regulating the Poor* (1971), they portrayed the principles of settlement from the Elizabethan era and England's New Poor Law of 1834 (any poor relief must be less generous than the lowest-paying forms of employment) as timeless touchstones of U.S. poverty policies (1971: 170). Through such principles, they argued, the government accommodated the most exploitative and impoverishing dimensions of the private labor market while allowing people to survive and maintain faith in the system. Localized poor laws lasted, Piven and Cloward claimed, because they served these purposes well; they declined in the 1930s when dominant producers required a more mobile labor force. Piven and Cloward viewed the New Deal's reforms and the War on Poverty as tools to tamp down dissent and maintain reserve armies of the unemployed (1971: xv). Their argument about the "regulatory" purpose of apparently generous policies was enormously influential and helped found the "social control" interpretation of social welfare law.

Piven and Cloward relied on historical evidence, but argued by means of case studies. Michael B. Katz, by contrast, attempted to be comprehensive and produced a more nuanced interpretation, both of local poor law and of social welfare law generally. In *In the Shadow of the Poorhouse*, a social history of welfare that relied on much legal-historical evidence, Katz concluded that welfare laws almost always distinguished the "impotent" and deserving poor from the "able" and therefore undeserving (Katz, 1986; 1989). While multiple purposes animated these laws, the separation of deserving from undeserving characterized policies and practices from the colonial period forward (Katz, 1986).

Social welfare professor Mimi Abramovitz added gender to Piven and Cloward's concerns about labor and Katz's about the deserving and undeserving. *Regulating the Lives of Women* (1988) posited that social welfare laws reinforced a "work ethic" and a patriarchal "family ethic" by encouraging male wage-earning and female economic dependency. Town-based poor relief fit her model because it was particularly harsh for women. When men absconded or died, a woman's home town and her husband's often wrangled over who should pay her relief; sometimes neither paid. If a deserted, widowed, or never-married woman sought a new settlement, that town might refuse her on the basis of moral or economic criteria or due to her purported membership in another community. In this way, local poor laws and their enforcers drove women to their households of origin or to legitimate unions with men (1988: 80–82).

After the 1980s, scholars demoted early American local poor law from its place as the (disturbing) model from which later policies were fashioned, but continued to link locality, law, and poverty. For example, from eighteenth-century "warning out" records of Rhode Island towns, historian Ruth Wallis Herndon produced fragmentary biographies and empirical analyses of the transient poor. While embracing legal history "from the bottom up," Herndon also revealed elements of law-creation from "amidst." "Warning out" was in some communities simply an annual ritual; town officials only enforced it strictly when economic disaster struck or neighbors complained (2001). Other scholars, such as Barbara Bellows, used local poor law records to complicate a field that generally ignores the South and the effects of race. Her study of Charleston, South Carolina, demonstrates an increasing preoccupation among white elites with "the political and economic implications of rising numbers of white paupers." New laws forced the able-bodied white poor to work, as poor relief administrators devised ways to elevate whites above poor blacks (1993: 55, 70, 109). Other scholarship on the South revealed unexpected local variation (Watkinson, 2001) and emphasized the long shadow cast upon local poor laws by the Civil War and Reconstruction (Green, 2003).

Thirty years after Piven and Cloward, town-based poor relief remained a revealing meeting point among non-elite people, their social betters, and state authorities. Kunal Parker derived lessons about citizenship from the history of those who fell through the system's cracks. In Massachusetts, indigent persons who lacked settlement were the state's responsibility. Sometimes immigrants fell into this category, but sometimes not. Slowly, Massachusetts made the pauper and the immigrant synonymous, starting with a 1794 law making settlement unavailable to those who could not own real property. Since immigrants belonged in this category, the state all but ensured that they would never be citizens and would struggle for economic security (Parker, 2001). Parker's study reminds scholars to think about poverty and immigration as inseparable. Moreover, he argued that citizenship is not only an affirmative category, creating rights, but also an exclusionary category, drawing lines between insiders and outsiders, those who will not be allowed to starve and those who will.

Institutions

A second important stream of law has placed poor people into custodial, correctional, and reformatory institutions. Known for generations as "indoor" relief, such institutions have deep roots in American soil but experienced their heyday in the nineteenth century (Rothman, 1971: 3–56). Government officials (aided by voluntary associations) created and maintained workhouses, orphanages, mental hospitals, reform schools, and other such facilities. Law was crucial: statutes enabled the construction of new facilities and vested them with state power; legislators and judges created legal categories ("insane," "unfit," "depraved") that defined occupants of the institutions; and legal processes legitimized decisions regarding commitment, treatment, and release (Willrich, 2003; Hartog, 1988).

Of the scholarship on institutions, David Rothman's *The Discovery of the Asylum* (1971) remains a landmark. Rothman argued that America's Jacksonian-era turn toward asylums, mental hospitals, and other institutions did not, as reformers claimed, indicate evolving standards of decency or the march of progress (1971: xiv–xvi). Though noting the nexus between poverty and institutionalization, Rothman also rejected economic determinism, for asylums spread with little regard for local needs or regional labor demands (1971: xvi). Rothman instead portrayed asylums as idealistic responses to destabilizing social forces: mass immigration, urbanization, industrial expansion. Legislators, philanthropists, public officials, and scholars saw in them a way to reform society's threatening elements while modeling social organization in a democratic society (1971: xix).

Scholars of Rothman's generation debated the nature of social reform and reformers' motivations (Platt, 1969; Mohl, 1971; Mennel, 1973; Grob, 1973; Boyer, 1978). Those who followed in the 1980s were more interested in the view from "below," and specifically whether the poor were objects of "social control." Barbara Brenzel's *Daughters of the State* (1983) was among the earliest and most careful efforts to imagine asylum development from the perspectives of working-class inmates and their families. Her study of the Lancaster, Massachusetts, State Industrial School for Girls illustrated how girls' families used the institution for their own ends. Parents sometimes sought institutionalization, knowing it would provide their daughters with food and shelter, and perhaps even the traits expected of decent, respectable women (1983: 5–7). Brenzel thus rejected "a gloomy revisionist parable of a wicked elite imposing its will on passive masses" in favor of a more nuanced story of "mixed feelings, mixed intentions, and mixed results" (1983: 167).

Writing at the same time as Brenzel, Gary Nash studied institutions and urban politics to help Americanize E.P Thompson's vision of lower-status people "making" history (Thompson, 1963). In an important 1976 article and later in *The Urban Crucible*, Nash used tax records, wills, and other residua of municipal governance to show how immigrants and transients who flooded Philadelphia after the Seven Years' War triggered a change in poverty policy: as they confronted city leaders with their destitution, an ad hoc system of small-scale almshouse care and outdoor relief evolved into a privately managed operation centered on a large new almshouse-workhouse. Nash's examination of the relationship between poor law and socio-economic hierarchy did not emphasize "regulation" of the poor. Instead, it highlighted poor people's rejection, via evasion and non-cooperation, of the assumption behind the policies, namely that industriousness led inevitably to economic success (Nash, 1976; 1986).

Michael Katz employed a similar approach. *In the Shadow of the Poorhouse* (1986) explored the many reasons why elites constructed and reconstructed institutions for the poor. Labor demands and fear of disorder mattered, he found, but so too did political patronage and custom. Katz also highlighted the role that poor people played in shaping policy. Most poorhouse inmates came and went as they pleased, often using the institution solely for short-term periods of crisis; they "virtually ran the larger poorhouses"; and they fought to keep their families together (Katz, 1983; 1986). Like Brenzel and Nash, Katz evidenced respect for the "social control" thesis but also a historian's nuanced appreciation of the intermingling of politics from above, below, and amidst.

Such research laid the groundwork for the next major trend in social welfare historiography. Drawing upon the theory of poor people's agency formulated by anthropologist James Scott (1985), Linda Gordon upended models of social control. She examined child protection agencies, which, although not carceral institutions, were vested with public powers. In addressing domestic abuse, they became immediately engaged in the homes and economic lives of poor and working-class people. In direct confrontation with Piven and Cloward, Gordon concluded that welfare laws and their agents did not "regulate" much. They certainly did not determine the behavior or attitudes of poor people (Gordon, 1988a; 1988b). Following Gordon, other historians in the late 1980s and 1990s searched for, and found, evidence of poor people's agency, even in the most apparently controlling institutional settings (Schneider, 1992; Kunzel, 1993).

Historians have continued to wrestle with questions about power, poverty, and incarceration. Michael Rembis' study of institutions for "feeble-minded" girls in Illinois found both "social control" and "agency," and refused to choose either model. But he pushed scholarship forward by analyzing poverty law not only in relation to class and sex or gender, but also ability and disability, terms he understood as historically and socially generated. In the institutionalization of the "feeble-minded," Rembis argued, these variables were mutually constitutive and reinforcing: young women's imbecility was defined by their poverty, and by their inability or unwillingness to maintain Victorian standards of sexual propriety (2011).

Local Courts

Another site where poor Americans have consistently encountered law is in local courts. Scholarship by Willard Hurst, his colleagues, and his students turned the study of legal history in this direction. Their investigations of sites outside the centers of elite legal practice revealed much about how regular people experienced, interpreted, and transformed law (Hurst, 1956; 1964; Nelson, 1975; Reid, 1980; Friedman and Percival, 1981). The general turn toward social history in the late 1970s and 1980s, along with the law and society movement, further encouraged scholars to study non-elite legal venues, while pushing Hurstian legal history to expand beyond its foundational concern with the relationship between law and political-economic development (Welke, 2000: 201).

Scholars entering local court archives in the 1980s recovered the legal and local dimensions of gender, labor, and economic need. Later scholarship focused more closely on race and region. Laura Edwards, for example, utilized a single county in North Carolina to reveal how former slaves, among other poor people, used local courts in the aftermath of the Civil War. Exploiting (and subverting) the postwar imperative to reconstruct the gendered southern household, women claimed protection against physical abuse; black and white laborers sought a bulwark against employers' power; and parents contested white planters' exploitation of African-American children (1997). In later work, Edwards noted that a legal system designed to buttress the power of propertied white men relied, at the local level, on the participation of the lowest-status members of southern communities, thereby giving them opportunities to shape law (2009: 58, 65). Edwards' work, like that of Ariela Gross (1998), Terri Snyder (2003), and Kelly Kennington (2009), has pushed historians to consider how poor southerners not only used the legal system but also leant it power and legitimacy.

Other important work on poor people and local courts has emerged from scholars interested in northern Progressivism. Michael Willrich studied the special municipal courts that Chicago created to deal with absent breadwinners, promiscuous women, and young men who had aged out of juvenile institutions. Located at "the ground floor of the American legal system," these courts touched the populations that reformers most hoped to reach, and covered the terrain that caused them the greatest anxiety, the realm "between public and private, the state and the market" (2003: xxxiv–xxxv). Judges referred hundreds of men and women annually to the Psychopathic Laboratory, a public clinic that tested for signs of mental defect and supported legal orders of sterilization and institutionalization (2003: 244–245). With the assistance of private agencies, judges attempted to "regulate" delinquent breadwinners, ordering them to "stay home at night" (2003: 163). Willrich's evaluation of Chicago's courts was damning. Some poor and working-class families used the courts for their own ends. But as between them and the legal and scientific authorities, "[i]t was never a fair fight" (2003: 268–269).

Later scholarship brought these research questions to other times and places (Hicks, 2003; Igra, 2000; Odem, 1995; Robertson, 2005), while still emphasizing local dimensions and plumbing questions of power and agency. In her exploration of specialized courts in post-World War II Philadelphia, Lisa Levenstein found that low-income African-American women used such courts to win financial support and protection against abuse from men in their lives. However, women's gains were often short-lived and required painful trade-offs: an abusive husband released on bond was free to earn wages for the family but also to commit violence (2009: 63–87). Unlike Willrich, Levenstein emphasized the agency implicit in these "hard choices." When women went to court, they chose the material benefits of judicial relief over the stigma and surveillance of welfare (2009: 67). Judicial actions also involved intrusive investigations, but many women resisted them by refusing to give accurate personal information (2009: 82–83).

Local to National: Federal Agencies

As significant as local poor laws have been, state and national governments also shaped important components of poverty law. To gain a full appreciation of this dimension of the past demands a willingness not only to consider law "from above," "below," and "amidst," but also to cross barriers between legal and political history and between history and the social sciences. Some of the most important historical work on state and national law has come from social scientists interested in the development of the U.S. state. These scholars have been particularly interested in social welfare programs, which they have viewed as measures of the state's development and indicators of its character (Skowronek, 1982; Weir, Orloff, and Skocpol, 1988; Skocpol, 1992; Lieberman, 1998). Naturally, they studied the New Deal, which triggered the expansion of federal welfare functions, but they also recovered the history of pre-New Deal state allowances for single mothers and old people, and federal pensions for veterans of the Revolutionary and Civil Wars (Skocpol, 1992; Quadagno, 1988; Jensen, 2003).

In the early and middle 1980s, while historically minded social scientists started "bringing the state back in" (Evans, Rueschemeyer, and Skocpol, 1985), social historians largely focused on localities and institutions. In the late 1980s, however, left feminist historians, sociologists, and political scientists began working together to rethink the origins and trajectory of the modern welfare state. They argued that European and American domestic politics were fundamentally gendered, both in the sense that statutes and public administration treated women and men differently, and in that women reformers created many of the most important domestic social policies (Gordon, 1994; Skocpol, 1992; Koven and Michel, 1993; Mettler, 1998). None of the scholars who did this work considered themselves a legal historian, but their gender analysis refreshed the historical study of public law and ground-level administrative law. And although this work has been critiqued for being too celebratory of elite women reformers and insufficiently interested in issues of race and empire (Mink, 1995; Kornbluh, 1996), it remains a model of inter- and sub-disciplinary collaboration.

Building on the first generation of feminist welfare scholarship, later work has turned the lens toward administrators, those who carried out state and national policies. They were the legal authorities many poor Americans most regularly encountered. Jennifer Mittelstadt studied post-World War II policymakers in the federal welfare bureaucracy. As New Dealers saw their hopes for a comprehensive welfare state fade, and as public assistance populations became less deserving in the public's eyes, Mittelstadt argued, federal administrators embraced the sympathetic notion of rehabilitation. Resulting policies grounded welfare recipients' deservingness in their potential for reform rather than their citizenship or need (2005). Examining the same decades, Karen Tani has studied interactions between federal bureaucrats and their state and local counterparts. She argues that the Social Security Act and its federal interpreters produced a more bureaucratized, professionalized, and, eventually, legalized system of welfare administration, but along the way incurred the wrath of state and local officials, leading ultimately to standoffs in federal court (2011).

Other scholarship with an eye toward this rising conflict is Felicia Kornbluh's *The Battle for Welfare Rights* (2007). In the late 1940s and 1950s, at the behest of state and local officials, welfare agencies weeded their rolls of never-married black women, of whom critics believed there were too many (Bell, 1965; Reese, 2005). In the 1960s, these practices became the target of agency- and court-centered reform efforts. Using administrative "fair hearings," welfare recipients, public welfare professionals, liberal legal scholars, and even some welfare administrators attacked agency practices and the statutes behind them. They contended that these laws violated poor people's legal and constitutional rights, and disrespected their privacy and dignity (Kornbluh, 2007; Reich, 1964).

Centralization Decentralized: Poor People and Lawyers in the Neighborhoods

A new socio-geographic politics of poverty emerged after World War II. The rhetoric of the time rendered poor people "invisible" (Harrington, 1962), but they were in fact more visible than they had been since the 1930s – and demanded a new accommodation. As African Americans, Latino/as and whites moved from South to North, farms to cities, and Mexico and Puerto Rico to the U.S. mainland, they encountered variations in localized legal measures that had long anchored responses to poverty: vagrancy prosecutions, restrictions on public aid, and attempts at "warning out." But their energy overwhelmed these older forms of legal and locational control.

There was no field of practice or scholarship called "poverty law" before the 1960s. Attorneys had long worked with poor clients (Davis, 1993), from African Americans claiming Civil War pensions (Collins, 2009), to migrants pursuing immigration appeals (Salyer, 1995), to working women with wage claims (Batlan, 2010). However, the modern practice of poverty law owes its existence to the African American civil rights movement, the great migrations and economic transformations of the post-World War II period, and the emergence of the problem of "poverty amidst plenty." These made poor people's need for counsel a staple of popular social-reform writing in the 1960s. In the view of liberals, equal access to representation became a vital test of the legal profession's – and the nation's–core values (tenBroek, *et al.*, 1966).

Since the 1960s, scholars have produced analytically and empirically rich work on the era's statutory reforms, known collectively as the War on Poverty. Although not especially diverse in method and research agenda– with the exception of recent work on "the grassroots" (Orleck and Hazirjian, 2011)–this scholarship is analytically diverse. Interpretations of the War on Poverty have ranged from neoconservative (Moynihan, 1969) to neo-Marxist (Piven and Cloward, 1971), from Panglossian (Patterson,

1981) to despondent (Matusow, 1984), from critical and outraged (Murray, 1984) to critical and sympathetic (Katz, 1989; Katznelson, 1989; O'Connor, 2001). Other interpretations have focused on gender (Abramovitz, 1988; Naples, 1998) and race (Quadagno, 1996; Brown, 1999). In contrast, the poverty law that lawyers, judges, legal intellectuals, and poor people self-consciously practiced in the 1960s has received less attention. Critical Legal Studies (CLS) scholars are perhaps the only ones who have criticized the effort to ameliorate or end poverty with law: without singling out poverty law, CLS challenged the very idea of using law, legalism, rights, and appellate litigation to pursue social change (Unger, 1983; Rosenberg, 1991).

Martha Davis' *Brutal Need* (1993) exemplified the restrained tone of the historical literature. Positioning herself as neither advocate nor critic, she revealed the local, urban roots of the modern practice of poverty law. She argued that attorneys and funders were drawn to law-centered strategies because of *Brown v. Board*, and the embarrassing gap between the Cold War promise of the "rule of law" and the lawlessness – both in violence and injustice – of America's cities. Against this backdrop, Davis explained, the Ford Foundation and the federal government in the early 1960s began providing counsel in low-income neighborhoods. Their experiments became models for the federal Legal Services Program (now the Legal Services Corporation, LSC), which funded poverty law think tanks in prestigious universities and attorneys in "ghetto" storefronts (Davis, 1993; O'Connor, 2001).

Although Davis did not critique poverty law, she underlined a conflict that plagued it from the start. While political and media leaders trumpeted poverty law as a positive innovation, one that would bring justice to struggling neighborhoods, other powerful interests worked against it. Largely for financial reasons, the American Bar Association initially resisted creating a federally funded corps of lawyers. Employers, landlords, and politicians joined them, fearing that legal services for the poor would change the balance of power in urban neighborhoods. This opposition kept legal services out of the original draft of the Economic Opportunity Act of 1964, the key statute of the War on Poverty, and ensured that its subsequent career was fraught with tension (Davis, 1993).

Thomas Hilbink's dissertation on "cause lawyering" contextualized this controversy within the history of social movements. Rather than placing the federal government, elite foundations, or the private bar at the story's center, Hilbink emphasized the southern movement for civil rights, the New Left, and the anti-war movement. These bequeathed to the bar a new approach to professional practice which was client-centered and sensitive to the impact of economic deprivation on the exercise of basic rights. Hilbink also found that the projects funded by LSC were far from the most radical experiments of politically minded attorneys in the 1960s and 1970s (2006).

Like Hilbink, attorney Kris Shepard found complexity in LSC's history. His study of federally funded legal services in the south found that between 1965 and 1996, attorneys represented thousands of people whose requests for food stamps, disability benefits, public housing, and other forms of welfare had been denied, or whose benefits had been discontinued. These efforts provided clients with millions of dollars that they would otherwise not have had. LSC lawyers also assisted clients in attempts to desegregate schools and contest incarceration and institutionalization (2007). Shepard's ultimate evaluation of federally funded legal services–that in making law accessible, it served the conservative function of "assimilat[ing] ... clients into American legal culture" (2007: 243) – invited more questions than it provided answers. Nonetheless, his ground-level description of legal services provides a model for future research.

Poor Law from Above: Appellate Courts

The movements of people and ideas after World War II became sharply politicized in the 1960s, challenging the ways in which race, sex, and politics produced poverty. Lawyers in neighborhoods were a liberal answer to these challenges: if poor people insisted on moving from South to North, or from rural hierarchies to the seeming social fluidity of cities, then lawyers would be sent to their new urban communities. However, increasingly in the 1960s, poor people went to law with concerns about the distribution of resources within the modern United States that required adjudication beyond the local area. Many LSC attorneys and other "cause" lawyers, despite (or perhaps because of) their elite backgrounds, embraced these challenges. Even more surprising, from an historical perspective, was the temporary receptiveness to their claims by the appellate judiciary. In the 1960s and 1970s, elite judges granted the poor access to the most privileged "sites" in creating and shaping American law.

Scholarship about activism on behalf of poor people in the appellate courts is relatively well developed. Although scholars have tended to neglect the economic dimensions of civil rights and women's liberation politics, they have fiercely debated the welfare rights strategy used in high courts and the reasons why, by the 1980s, it appeared a decisive failure. Political scientist Elizabeth Bussiere offered a strictly doctrinal explanation: Constitutional welfare rights failed, she claimed, because New Deal-era jurisprudence built a wall between economic matters and those involving "discrete and insular" minorities. As a result, litigators privileged statutory rather than constitutional claims, and so failed to gain the kind of ringing statement on behalf of poor people that African Americans had gained in *Brown* (1997). In contrast, William Forbath argued that economic rights have a place in America's constitutional tradition, and that the New Deal was their great moment of vindication. But Forbath, though less of a doctrinal essentialist than Bussiere, was similarly pessimistic about poverty as a constitutional category after the New Deal: welfare rights, Forbath claimed, were never as legally or politically viable as were the rights promoted in the 1930s, such as (white men's) right to work for decent wages (Forbath 2009; 2001). Davis' and Kornbluh's approach, in contrast to these two, emphasized the trajectory of the social movement for welfare rights and the changing political climate. They believed welfare rights were defeated, but were not ultimately unobtainable (Davis, 1993; Kornbluh, 2007).

Not all scholarship concerned failures of the welfare rights campaign. Other work sought to understand the ideas behind it. Many lawyers litigated on the basis of the "due process" clause of the Fourteenth Amendment; *Goldberg v. Kelly* (1970), which held that welfare clients were entitled to robust procedural protections before losing benefits, was a major victory because the decision noted government's constitutional obligation not to abrogate poor people's "brutal need" for aid (Kornbluh, 2008; Davis, 1993). Where did such ideas originate? Tani has focused on the rapid expansion of the regulatory state into the most private and important areas of American life. This, combined with high-visibility loyalty-security purges in the Cold War era, showed liberal lawyers how easily questions of due process bled into questions about the substance of government largesse (2008).

Scholars also explored efforts to create or resuscitate a substantive interpretation of the Equal Protection Clause. Tani's research suggests that legal understandings of equality encompassing economic security were part of American politics consistently from the New Deal forward: between the 1930s and the 1960s, federal bureaucrats administering public assistance programs believed that access to public benefits was a matter of both rights and equality (2011). Similarly, Felicia Kornbluh and Julie Nice found that professor and activist Jacobus tenBroek attempted in the 1940s to launch the concept of "substantive equal protection" into the American lexicon, on the basis both of an originalist understanding of the abolitionist origins of the Fourteenth Amendment and a reading of the jurisprudence of the Stone and Vinson Courts (Nice, 2008: 656; Kornbluh, unpublished). "Substantive equal protection" never caught on during the Cold War, but, like the work of pro-welfare bureaucrats, was discovered anew in the 1960s.

Other historical scholarship focused on particular appellate cases, less for their doctrinal significance than their relevance to social, cultural, and political history. Feminist historian Rickie Solinger reexamined *King v. Smith* (1968), the case we considered at the beginning of this chapter, in the context of battles over African-American self-determination in the Deep South. Applying what she described as a "reproductive justice" lens,

Solinger emphasized the significance of economic wellbeing to women's and reproductive rights while noting the partiality of *King*'s victory: in her view, Chief Justice Warren's decision accepted Alabama's view of women's sexual morality, and thus paved the way for later welfare cuts based on race, gender, and sexual behavior (2010).

Conclusion

Urban historians and social geographers have taught us to think of power as expressed in space and place (Gilmore, 2007; Silbey, 1995; Self, 2003). Legal historian Christopher Tomlins has underlined control over "loco-motion," or the free movement of persons, as a component of the colonial episteme of English North America, a regime that long survived the American Revolution (Tomlins, 2010). We have found something similar in the case of poverty and law. Poor people have met law in specific locations, institutional sites at which power has been exercised, interpreted, occluded, generated, contested, and transformed. One foundational project of the law of poverty has been the constraint of free movement by the propertyless. This is apparent from the laws of settlement and "warning out," and from the longstanding debate, most impassioned in the nineteenth century, over whether to grant relief only "indoors," within more-or-less carceral institutions, or whether to dispense it also "outdoors," to people in their own homes. When poor people, including women, immigrants, African Americans, and Latinos/as, refused to stay in place, they altered the landscape of poverty and public policy. They helped inspire the War on Poverty, and the battles over law and policy that ensued in legislatures, courts, and agencies, and in the streets.

In writing a historiography around these sites, we have built upon the scholarship of many others to observe that law took its meaning and authority from "below," "above," and "amidst." This frame will, we hope, encourage readers to think broadly and creatively about the laws that have affected poor people and the myriad ways in which poor people have shaped or transformed law. By emphasizing various sites of encounter, we also invite readers to consider scholarship from several disciplines and sub-disciplines. Law and poverty has attracted study from political scientists, sociologists, and legal scholars, as well as social, political, legal, and constitutional historians. Most important, this framework fits our understanding of how and why the law of poverty has changed over time. Neither elites nor "the crowd" may claim exclusive credit or blame. Judges and legislators, welfare claimants and needy strangers, low-level bureaucrats and neighborhood lawyers together have written the law of poverty.

REFERENCES

Abbott, Edith ([1940] 1966). *Public Assistance, American Principles and Policies.* Russell & Russell, New York.

Abbott, Grace (1941). *From Relief to Social Security, the Development of the New Public Welfare Services and their Administration.* University of Chicago Press, Chicago.

Abramovitz, Mimi (1988). *Regulating the Lives of Women: Social Welfare Policy from Colonial Times to the Present.* South End Press, Boston, MA.

Batlan, Felice (2010). "The Birth of Legal Aid: Gender Ideologies, Women, and the Bar in New York City, 1863-1910." *Law and History Review* 28: 931-971.

Bell, Winifred (1965). *Aid to Dependent Children.* Columbia University Press, New York.

Bellows, Barbara L. (1993). *Benevolence Among Slaveholders: Assisting the Poor in Charlestown 1760-1860.* Louisiana State University Press, Baton Rouge.

Boyer, Paul (1978). *Urban Masses and Moral Order in America, 1810-1920.* Harvard University Press, Cambridge, MA.

Brenzel, Barbara M. (1983). *Daughters of the State: A Social Portrait of the First Reform School For Girls in North America, 1856-1905.* MIT Press, Cambridge, MA.

Brown, Michael (1999). *Race, Money and the American Welfare State.* Cornell University Press, Ithaca, NY.

Bussiere, Elizabeth (1997). *(Dis)entitling the Poor: The Warren Court, Welfare Rights, and the American Political Tradition.* Pennsylvania State University Press, University Park.

Collins, Kristin A. (2009). "Administering Marriage: Marriage-Based Entitlements, Bureaucracy, and the Legal Construction of the Family." *Vanderbilt Law Review* 62: 1085-1167.

Davis, Martha F. (1993). *Brutal Need: Lawyers and the Welfare Rights Movement, 1960-1973.* Yale University Press, New Haven.

Edwards, Laura F. (1997). *Gendered Strife and Confusion: The Political Culture of Reconstruction.* University of Illinois Press, Urbana.

Edwards, Laura F. (2009). *The People and Their Peace: Legal Culture and the Transformation of Inequality in the Post-Revolutionary South.* University of North Carolina Press, Chapel Hill.

Evans, Peter B., Rueschemeyer, Dietrich, and Skocpol Theda, eds, 1985. *Bringing the State Back In.* Cambridge University Press, Cambridge, UK.

Forbath, William (2001). "The New Deal Constitution in Exile." *Duke Law Journal* 51: 165-222.

Forbath, William (2009). "Social and Economic Rights in the American Grain: Reclaiming Constitutional Political Economy." In Balkin and Siegel, eds, *The Constitution in 2020,* 55-67. Oxford University Press, New York.

Forbath, William, Hartog, Hendrik, and Minow, Martha. (1985). "Introduction: Legal Histories from Below." *Wisconsin Law Review* 1985: 759-766.

Friedman, Lawrence M. (1985). *A History of American Law.* Second ed. Simon and Schuster, New York.

Friedman, Lawrence M. and Percival, Robert V. (1981). *The Roots of Justice: Crime and Punishment in Alameda County, California, 1870–1910*. University of North Carolina Press, Chapel Hill.

Gilmore, Ruth Wilson (2007). *Golden Gulag: Prisons, Surplus, Crisis, and Opposition in Globalizing California*. University of California Press, Berkeley.

Goluboff, Risa L. (2007). *The Lost Promise of Civil Rights*. Harvard University Press, Cambridge, MA.

Gordon, Linda (1988a). *Heroes of Their Own Lives: The Politics and History of Family Violence*. Viking, New York.

Gordon, Linda (1988b). "What Does Welfare Regulate?" *Social Research* 55 (1988): 609–630.

Gordon, Linda (1994). *Pitied but Not Entitled: Single Mothers and the History of Welfare, 1890–1935*. Free Press, New York.

Green, Elna C. (2003). *This Business of Relief: Confronting Poverty in a Southern City, 1740–1940*. University of Georgia Press, Athens.

Grob, Gerald (1973). *Mental Institutions in America: Social Policy to 1875*. The Free Press, New York.

Gross, Ariela J. (1998). "Litigating Whiteness: Trials of Racial Determination in the Nineteenth Century South." *Yale Law Journal* 108: 109–188.

Harrington, Michael (1962). *The Other America*. MacMillan, New York.

Hartog, Hendrik (1987). "The Constitution of Aspiration and 'The Rights That Belong to Us All.'" *The Journal of American History* 74: 1013–1034.

Hartog, Hendrik (1988). "Mrs. Packard on Dependency." *Yale Journal of Law and the Humanities* 1: 79–104.

Herndon, Ruth Wallis (2001). *Unwelcome Americans: Living on the Margin in Early New England*. University of Pennsylvania Press, Philadelphia.

Hicks, Cheryl D. (2003). "'In Danger of Becoming Morally Depraved': Single Black Women, Working-Class Black Families, and New York State's Wayward Minor Laws, 1917–1928." *University of Pennsylvania Law Review* 151: 2077–2121.

Hilbink, Thomas (2006). "Constructing Cause Lawyering: Professionalism, Politics, and Social Change in 1960s America." Ph.D. diss., New York University.

Hurst, J. Willard (1956). *Law and the Conditions of Freedom*. University of Wisconsin Press, Madison.

Hurst, J. Willard (1964). *Law and Economic Growth: The Legal History of the Wisconsin Lumber Industry*. Harvard University Press, Cambridge, MA.

Igra, Anna R. (2000). "Likely to Become a Public Charge: Deserted Women and the Family Law of the Poor in New York City, 1910–1936." *Journal of Women's History* 11(4): 59–81.

Jacobs, Meg, Novak, William J., and Zelizer, Julian E., eds (2003). *The Democratic Experiment: New Directions in American Political History*. Princeton University Press, Princeton, NJ.

Jensen, Laura (2003). *Patriots, Settlers, and the Origins of American Social Policy*. Cambridge University Press, Cambridge, UK.

Kalman, Laura (2005). "The Constitution, the Supreme Court, and the New Deal." *American Historical Review* 110: 1052–1080.

Katz, Michael B. (1983). *Poverty and Policy in American History*. Academic Press, New York.

Katz, Michael B. (1986). *In the Shadow of the Poorhouse: A Social History of Welfare in America*. Basic Books, New York.

Katz, Michael B. (1989). *The Undeserving Poor: From the War on Poverty to the War on Welfare*. Pantheon Books, New York.

Katznelson, Ira (1989). "Was the Great Society a Lost Opportunity?" In Fraser and Gerstle, eds, *The Rise and Fall of the New Deal Order 1930–1980*, 185–211. Princeton University Press, Princeton, NJ.

Kennedy, Aileen and Breckenridge, S.P. (1934). *The Ohio Poor Law and Its Administration*. University of Chicago Press, Chicago.

Kennington, Kelly (2009). "River of Injustice: St. Louis's Freedom Suits and the Changing Nature of Legal Slavery in Antebellum America." Ph.D. diss., Duke University, Durham, NC.

Kornbluh, Felicia (1996). "The New Literature on Gender and the Welfare State: The U.S. Case." *Feminist Studies* 22(1): 171–197.

Kornbluh, Felicia (2007). *The Battle for Welfare Rights: Politics and Poverty in Modern America*. University of Pennsylvania Press, Philadelphia.

Kornbluh, Felicia (2008). "Recognition, Redistribution and Good China: Administrative Justice for Women Welfare Recipients Before *Goldberg v. Kelly*." *Yale Journal of Law and Feminism* 20: 165–193.

Kornbluh, Felicia (2011). "The Untold Story of Equal Protection: Disability, Race, and Economy in the Twentieth-Century Rewriting of the Fourteenth Amendment." Lecture before the Department of Political Science, Brooklyn College, City University of New York, February 17, 2011.

Koven, Seth and Michel, Sonya, eds (1993). *Mothers of a New World*. Routledge Press, New York.

Kunzel, Regina G. (1993). *Fallen Women, Problem Girls: Unmarried Mothers and the Professionalization of Social Work, 1890–1945*. Yale University Press, New Haven.

Levenstein, Lisa (2009). *A Movement Without Marches: African American Women and the Politics of Poverty in Postwar Philadelphia*. University of North Carolina Press, Chapel Hill.

Lieberman, Robert C. (1998). *Shifting the Color Line: Race and the American Welfare State*. Harvard University Press, Cambridge, MA.

Matusow, Allen J. (1984). *The Unraveling of America: A History of Liberalism in the 1960s*. Harper & Row, New York.

Mennel, Robert M. (1973). *Thorns and Thistles: Juvenile Delinquents in the United States, 1825–1940*. University of New Hampshire Press, Hanover.

Mettler, Suzanne (1998). *Dividing Citizens: Gender and Federalism in New Deal Public Policy*. Cornell University Press, Ithaca, NY.

Mink, Gwendolyn (1995). *The Wages of Motherhood: Inequality in the Welfare State, 1917–1942*. Cornell University Press, Ithaca, NY.

Mittelstadt, Jennifer (2005). *From Welfare to Workfare: The Unintended Consequences of Liberal Reform, 1945–1965*. University of North Carolina Press, Chapel Hill.

Mohl, Raymond A. (1971). *Poverty in New York, 1783–1825*. Oxford University Press, New York.

Moynihan, Daniel P. (1969). *Maximum Feasible Misunderstanding: Community Action in the War on Poverty*. Free Press, New York.

Murray, Charles (1984). *Losing Ground: American Social Policy 1950–1980.* Basic Books, New York.

Naples, Nancy A. (1998). *Grassroots Warriors: Activist Mothering, Community Work, and the War on Poverty.* Routledge Press, New York.

Nash, Gary B. (1976). "Poverty and Poor Relief in Pre-Revolutionary Philadelphia." *William and Mary Quarterly* 33: 3–30.

Nash, Gary B. (1986). *The Urban Crucible: The Northern Seaports and the Origins of the American Revolution.* Harvard University Press, Cambridge, MA.

Nelson, William E. (1975). *Americanization of the Common Law: The Impact of Legal Change on Massachusetts Society.* Harvard University Press, Cambridge, MA.

Nice, Julie (2008). "No Scrutiny Whatsoever: Deconstitutionalization of Poverty Law, Dual Rules of Law, and Dialogic Default." *Fordham Urban Law Journal* 35: 629–671.

Nice, Julie and Trubek, Louise (1997). *Cases and Materials on Poverty Law: Theory and Practice.* West Publishing, St. Paul, MN.

O'Connor, Alice (2001). *Poverty Knowledge: Social Science, Social Policy, and the Poor in Twentieth-Century U.S. History.* Princeton University Press, Princeton, NJ.

Odem, Mary (1995). *Delinquent Daughters: Protecting and Policing Adolescent Female Sexuality in the United States, 1880–1920.* University of North Carolina Press, Chapel Hill.

Orleck, Annelise and Hazirjian, Lisa, eds (2011). *The War on Poverty: A New Grassroots History, 1964–1980.* University of Georgia Press, Athens.

Parker, Kunal M. (2001). "State, Citizenship, and Territory: The Legal Construction of Immigrants in Antebellum Massachusetts." *Law and History Review* 19: 583–644.

Patterson, James (1981). *America's Struggle Against Poverty 1900–1980.* Harvard University Press, Cambridge, MA.

Piven, Frances Fox and Cloward, Richard (1971). *Regulating the Poor: The Functions of Public Welfare.* Pantheon Press, New York.

Platt, Anthony (1969). *The Child Savers: The Invention of Delinquency.* University of Chicago Press, Chicago.

Quadagno, Jill S. (1988). *The Transformation of Old Age Security: Class and Politics in the American Welfare State.* University of Chicago Press, Chicago.

Quadagno, Jill S. (1996). *The Color of Welfare: How Racism Undermined the War on Poverty.* Oxford University Press, Oxford.

Reese, Ellen (2005). *Backlash Against Welfare Mothers: Past and Present.* University of California Press, Los Angeles and Berkeley.

Reich, Charles A. (1964). "The New Property." *Yale Law Journal* 73: 733–787.

Reid, John (1980). *Law for the Elephant: Property and Social Behavior on the Overland Trail.* Huntington Library Press, San Marino, CA.

Rembis, Michael (2011). *Defining Deviance: Sex, Science, and Delinquent Girls, 1890–1960.* University of Illinois Press, Urbana.

Robertson, Stephen (2005). *Crimes Against Children: Sexual Violence and Legal Culture in New York City, 1880–1960.* University of North Carolina Press, Chapel Hill.

Rosenberg, Gerald N. (1991). *The Hollow Hope: Can Courts Bring About Social Change?* University of Chicago Press, Chicago.

Rothman, David L. (1971). *The Discovery of the Asylum: Social Order and Disorder in the New Republic.* Little, Brown, Boston.

Salyer, Lucy (1995). *Laws Harsh as Tigers: Chinese Immigrants and the Shaping of Modern Immigration Law.* University of North Carolina Press, Chapel Hill.

Scheiber, Harry N. (1981). "American Constitutional History and the New Legal History: Complementary Themes in Two Modes." *Journal of American History* 68: 337–350.

Schneider, Eric C. (1992). *In the Web of Class: Delinquents and Reformers in Boston, 1810s–1930s.* New York University Press, New York.

Scott, James C. (1985). *Weapons of the Weak: Everyday Forms of Peasant Resistance.* Yale University Press, New Haven.

Self, Robert (2003). *American Babylon: Race and the Struggle for Postwar Oakland.* Princeton University Press, Princeton, NJ.

Shepard, Kris (2007). *Rationing Justice: Poverty Lawyers and Poor People in the Deep South.* Louisiana State University Press, Baton Rouge.

Silbey, David (1995). *Geographies of Exclusion: Society and Difference in the West.* Routledge Press, London.

Skocpol, Theda (1992). *Protecting Soldiers and Mothers: The Political Origins of Social Policy in the United States.* Belknap Press of Harvard University Press, Cambridge, MA.

Skowronek, Stephen (1982). *Building a New American State: The Expansion of National Administrative Capacities, 1877–1920.* Cambridge University Press, Cambridge, UK.

Snyder, Terri L. (2003). *Brabbling Women: Disorderly Speech and the Law in Early Virginia.* Cornell University Press, Ithaca, NY.

Solinger, Rickie (2010). "The First Welfare Case: Money, Sex, Marriage, and White Supremacy in Selma, 1966: A Reproductive Justice Analysis." *Journal of Women's History* 22(3): 13–38.

Tani, Karen M. (2008). "Flemming v. Nestor: Anticommunism, the Welfare State, and the Making of 'New Property.'" *Law and History Review* 26: 379–414.

Tani, Karen M. (2011). "Securing a Right to Welfare: Public Assistance Administration and the Rule of Law, 1935–1960." Ph.D. diss., University of Pennsylvania.

tenBroek, Jacobus and Tussman, Joseph (1949). "Equal Protection of the Laws." *California Law Review* 37: 341–381.

tenBroek, Jacobus and Editors of the California Law Review, eds (1966). *The Law of the Poor.* Chandler Publishing, San Francisco.

Thompson, E.P. (1963). *The Making of the English Working Class.* Pantheon Books, New York.

Tomlins, Christopher (2010). *Freedom Bound: Law, Labor, and Civic Identity in Colonizing English America, 1580–1865.* Cambridge University Press, Cambridge, UK.

Trattner, William I. ([1974] 1999). *From Poor Law to Welfare State: A History of Social Welfare in America.* 6th edition. The Free Press, New York.

Unger, Robert Mangeibera (1983). *The Critical Legal Studies Movement.* Harvard University Press, Cambridge, MA.

Watkinson, James D. (2001). "'Fit Objects of Charity': Community, Race, Faith, and Welfare in Antebellum Lancaster County, Virginia, 1817–1860." *Journal of the Early Republic* 21: 41–70.

Weir, Margaret, Orloff, Ann Shola and Skocpol, Theda, eds (1988). *The Politics of Social Policy in the United States.* Princeton University Press, Princeton, NJ.

Welke, Barbara (2000). "Willard Hurst and the Archipelago of American Legal Historiography." *Law and History Review* 18: 197–204.

Welke, Barbara Young, and Hartog, Hendrik (2009). "'Glimmers of Life': A Conversation with Hendrik Hartog." *Law and History Review* 27: 629–656.

Willrich, Michael (2003). *City of Courts: Socializing Justice in Progressive Era Chicago.* Cambridge University Press, Cambridge, UK.

Chapter Eighteen

TAXES

Robin L. Einhorn

One reason legal historians generally know very little about tax history is that most other historians know even less. But another reason is specific to the legal history field: the fact that lawyers and law schools define taxation narrowly. Introductory tax courses rarely notice that the American tax system so much as includes levies other than the federal income tax, though the estate tax sometimes makes an appearance. This single-minded focus is appropriate preparation for practitioners, but it fosters a misleading picture of American taxation by ignoring two crucial facts: that one-third of all taxes actually are state and local rather than federal taxes, and that the income tax accounts for less than half of the federal total. Federal income taxes on individuals and corporations, in other words, may account for an overwhelming majority of the tax business in American law, but they comprise less than forty percent of all of the taxes Americans pay (White House, 2010; U.S. Bureau of the Census, 2010).

Yet as serious as this gap may be for contemporary analysis, it is disabling for historical comprehension. The reason is clear: except for a brief experiment during the Civil War, there was no federal income tax until after the 1913 ratification of the Sixteenth Amendment. From 1913 until World War II, moreover, only very high incomes were taxed. The modern mass individual income tax, including withholding from wages and salaries, was established to finance World War II and inaugurated a dramatic change. Seven percent of Americans paid the individual income tax in 1940 but sixty-four percent paid it in 1944 (Witte, 1985: 125). By this point, the federal government was also collecting Social Security payroll taxes and the

---

A Companion to American Legal History, First Edition.
Edited by Sally E. Hadden and Alfred L. Brophy.
© 2013 John Wiley & Sons Ltd. Published 2021 by John Wiley & Sons Ltd.

modern state and local tax regime was in place: most states relying on income and sales taxes, most local governments relying on property (real estate) taxes.

The literature on the history of American taxation has developed in three waves, more or less directly reflecting the interests and crises of particular periods. In the first, from the 1880s into the 1910s, economists explored the development of the tax system with the goal of persuading politicians to modernize it, particularly by introducing income taxes at the state and federal levels. In the second, centered in the 1940s, economists and lawyers mobilized historical research to defend the tax regime established to finance World War II, and especially its sharply progressive federal income tax. They portrayed this regime as the culmination of a century of reform aspiration, in which inequality and incompetence gave way to "modern" progressivity and professionalism. The third wave, still ongoing, developed amid the tax revolts of the 1980s: the property tax revolt launched by California's Proposition 13 and the income tax revolt associated with Ronald Reagan's presidency. Although some scholars in this wave have supported the tax revolts, many have seen them as raising the problem of how voters come to support tax policies that (in the scholars' views) actually hurt them.

More recently, an international and interdisciplinary movement to take taxation seriously as a historical phenomenon has coalesced under the rubric of the New Fiscal Sociology (Martin, Mehrotra, and Prasad, 2009). Historians, sociologists, political scientists, and economists have taken up the challenge Joseph Schumpeter famously issued in 1918, when he located "the thunder of world history" in the history of taxation and, in the budget, "the skeleton of the state, stripped of all misleading ideologies" (Schumpeter, [1918] 1954). The sociologist, political scientist, and historian Charles Tilly has been a more proximate influence. While Tilly's brilliant 1985 salvo "War Making and State Making as Organized Crime" likened early modern state-building in Europe to criminal "protection rackets," with monarchs fomenting wars to extort taxes from subjects, his more recent work associated extractive capacity (the ability to tax) with democratic political institutions (Tilly, 1985; 2009). It is unlikely that anyone else will duplicate Tilly's extraordinary range in the near future – worldwide expertise over many centuries – but annual seminars in the New Fiscal Sociology are attracting younger scholars to investigate the relationships between public finance and some of the central social and political processes of world history.

Within U.S. history, there is much basic work to be done, so much that the major books of the first – late-nineteenth-century – wave of scholarship are still essential reference material. Frank W. Taussig's *The Tariff History of the United States* (1888), Richard T. Ely's *Taxation in American States and Cities* (1888), and Edwin R. A. Seligman's *Essays in Taxation* (1895) and *The Income Tax* (1911) are dated in their advocacy, mainly for the adoption of income taxes, but they contain material that is unavailable (or much less accessible) elsewhere. They can also be entertaining; the authors' palpable disgust for the existing tax system led to colorful depictions, only enhanced by efforts at understatement. Taussig, for example, minced no words on the "cumbrous and intricate" tariff on woolen goods, "a great sham" adopted "simply because it concealed the degree of protection" it granted manufacturers. More generally, he could offer "no explanation" for the period's high protective tariffs that did "not reflect in some degree on the good name and the good faith of the national legislature" (Taussig, 1888: 215, 229). The major state and local tax of the period, the "general property tax," also invited abuse. Seligman found it "as destitute of theoretical justification as it is defective in its practical application" and, if this were not enough, "beyond all doubt one of the worst taxes known in the civilized world" (Seligman, [1895] 1913: 19, 62).

Taussig's stories about tariff legislation are familiar enough in basic outline. The battles of Whigs versus Democrats, then Republicans versus Democrats; farmers versus artisans, then farmers versus industrialists; North versus South and then North versus South and West are staples of U.S. history textbooks. To read Ely and Seligman, however, requires context. First, we must fully appreciate a fact that runs counter to our own experience of "government": that state and local governments usually collected more taxes than the federal government before World War II (Wallis, 2000). Second, we must suspend our usual expectations about data availability. Nobody collected comprehensive financial figures from the nation's state and local governments until the twentieth century, when the census began to survey government activities (Wallis, 2006). The upshot, paradoxically, is that we know least about the taxes levied by local governments (counties, cities, townships, and so on) in the period when they were the major taxing entities in the United States.

Nor is it only a matter of numbers. General property taxes have disappeared from history almost as completely as from modern tax policy. Unlike modern property taxes, which are levied on real estate (mostly land and buildings), the general property tax was levied, ostensibly, on both real estate and "personal property" – a capacious category including "tangible" assets such as livestock, machinery, vehicles, and jewelry, and "intangible" (paper) assets such as cash, stocks, and bonds. By the late nineteenth century, most state constitutions required these taxes to be "uniform" (levied at the same rate on all forms of taxed property) and "universal" (levied on all forms of property). These mandates were impossible to fulfill, not least because local assessors usually depended on self-reporting by taxpayers – without the W2s and 1099s or the powerful threat of Internal Revenue Service (IRS) audit that check fraudulent self-reporting in the modern U.S. income tax. The inevitable administrative failures then made the tax vulnerable to legal challenges. The general property tax of the nineteenth century, in sum, was not only completely unworkable, but also, as commentators routinely lamented, an irresistible enticement to fraud. Ely thought it brought "the morality of the community down to the level of its most unscrupulous members" (Ely, 1888: 229, 233). Or, as one of the many state tax commissions that investigated this situation complained, the general property tax was "debauching to the conscience and subversive of the public morals – a school for perjury, promoted by law" (quoted in Yearley, 1970: 86). To read Ely and Seligman is to enter an unfamiliar world, but one that bulked large in nineteenth-century American law, as the main subject, for example, of Thomas M. Cooley's *Treatise on the Law of Taxation* (1876).

The major works of the second wave of tax history, from the 1940s, are more thoroughly superseded by modern scholarship. It is hard not to cringe when we encounter Sidney Ratner's *American Taxation: Its History as a Social Force in Democracy* (1942), whose title announces its argument. Economist by training and New Dealer by experience, Ratner began by explaining that taxes should be judged not "merely by the dollars and cents raised," but by their promotion of economic equality. Tax history was the story of clashes between "political democracy and the concentrated economic power of big business and high finance," or the "thrust for social justice" and "counterthrust for private gain" (Ratner, 1942: 13, 16). Traditionally, regressive taxation was the norm, increasing inequality by imposing heavier tax burdens on people with lower incomes than people with higher incomes, especially by taxing consumption through tariffs, excises, and sales taxes. But modern income and estate taxes could achieve the opposite result; levied heavily at progressive rates, they could redistribute income in an egalitarian direction. Democrats did this during World War I, Ratner argued, and should do it on a larger scale for World War II.

The truly misleading aspect of Ratner's book, however, has nothing to do with ideology. It is its focus on federal taxes, ignoring the state and local taxes that have been so important in American history. Other major works from this period also focus on federal taxes, particularly Roy and Gladys Blakey, *The Federal Income Tax* (1940) and Randolph E. Paul, *Taxation in the United States* (1954). While these books were the standard introductions to the history of federal taxation for decades, they are now of interest mainly as primary sources. Today, the starting point is W. Elliot Brownlee's thoughtful and accessible survey, *Federal Taxation in America: A Short History* (1996). For Brownlee, the story obviously could not end where it had for Ratner, Paul, and the Blakeys. Instead, he demarcates two periods, or tax regimes, that establish context for their writings: a "democratic-statist" regime from 1916 to 1941, and an "era of easy finance" from 1941 to 1986. The point being, of course, that both of these eras have ended.

Meanwhile, the third wave of scholarship had challenged the progressive histories of the second. By the mid-1980s, scholars were taking a skeptical view of the liberal politics of income taxation. Writing in the midst of the Reagan era, as Congress was slashing income tax rates, Mark Leff and

Robert Stanley challenged the idea that it had ever intended to use progressive taxes for large-scale redistribution. In *The Limits of Symbolic Reform* (1984), Leff examined federal taxation during the New Deal, concluding that FDR's attacks on "malefactors of great wealth" did not extend to taxing them seriously. The ballyhooed "wealth tax" of 1935 offered only "symbolic" reform of what remained a highly regressive federal tax system – and became more regressive with the Social Security payroll tax (Leff, 1983). Stanley, in *Dimensions of Law in the Service of Order* (1993), looked at the political origins of the earlier federal income taxes, joining Leff in dismissing the idea that the United States ever had tax policies intended to "soak the rich." These taxes (of 1861, 1895, and 1913) were tiny, Stanley argued, and mere sops to a taxpaying population that bore much larger regressive burdens from tariffs.

The question of whether a liberal ideology of "social taxation" – using progressive taxes to promote economic equality – ever triumphed in the United States is still alive among scholars of twentieth-century taxation. Either way, however, the conservative turn in the 1980s brought major changes to American taxes and, especially, tax politics. This change was the focus of an important essay collection that Brownlee edited. *Funding the Modern American State, 1941–1995: The Rise and Fall of the Era of Easy Finance* (1996) showcased recent research on the arc of policy change in the second half of the twentieth century. Pairing these essays with those in the internationally (and sociologically) focused *New Fiscal Sociology* (Martin, Mehrotra and Prasad, 2009) offers a fairly thorough introduction to the present state of the field. Economists, political scientists, and lawyers still make essential contributions, but scholars trained as historians are finally also taking taxation seriously.

It is not that historians ever thought taxes were unimportant. The United States, after all, is often portrayed as having been founded in a tax revolt, with tax resistance therefore somehow imprinted on the national DNA. The significance of the British tax measures after 1763 (Sugar, Stamp, Townsend, and Tea acts) has waxed and waned in the views of Revolutionary historians, but remained important in popular culture, not to mention for students cramming for exams. So what was the significance of these levies? The Stamp Act, especially, has always been a puzzle, too mild an imposition to provoke the massive protests that set the conflict between colonies and Parliament into motion. The explanation in Edmund and Helen Morgan's classic *The Stamp Act Crisis* (1953), has held up remarkably well. Colonists, the Morgans argued, were more worried about the constitutional power to tax than about this tax on legal and commercial documents. Believing that Parliament could only tax the colonies the way it usually had in the past – asking the colonial assemblies to levy their own taxes and deliver the proceeds – colonists could reasonably view the Stamp Act as a threat to their political liberties.

John Brewer's more recent study of British public finance, *The Sinews of Power* (1990), strengthens this argument with important context. In eighteenth-century Britain, he shows, taxes were very heavy and highly regressive. With a land tax that raised only negligible sums, Britain financed its many wars (or, more precisely, funded the debts accrued for those wars) by taxing consumption through excises and tariffs. The Customs Service was a bastion of the "old corruption," while the Excise Office was a model of bureaucratic modernity. Colonial merchants had intimate knowledge of the Customs Service, including how to manipulate its weaknesses to their advantage. The Excise Office, however, was different from any public agency in the colonial experience. Either way, colonists had good reason to resist expansions of the authority of these agencies on their side of the Atlantic. Taxation within the colonies varied from colony to colony. In some, it was patently corrupt and oppressive – North Carolina stands out here. In others, such as Massachusetts and Pennsylvania, it functioned well (Einhorn, 2006). But nowhere in colonial America were taxes levied as regressively and heavy-handedly as in Britain. Since, in the British system, "constitutional" was basically a synonym for "customary," colonists had what they considered a constitutional right to insist on their traditional control over taxes. They conceded Crown power over the customs, but refused to yield on the new measures of the 1760s. George III and Parliament, needless to say, rejected the American constitutional analysis.

The implication of all this is that the American Revolution was not a "tax revolt" in the sense that often attracts modern commentators. It was about which governments should wield the tax power, rather than whether governments should tax or how much they could legitimately levy. But even if we were to treat 1776 as a tax revolt, the issue of an anti-tax DNA requires an analysis of 1789. There was a time when most historians treated the adoption of the Constitution as a conservative backlash against the liberty and equality of the Revolution, an elitist attempt to silence "the people," who had found their political voices in the revolutionary struggle (Jensen, 1940). In this analysis, Shays' Rebellion, expressing the democratic and libertarian yearnings of 1776, frightened elites into framing a Constitution that would centralize power and thereby allow them to oppress the people – including by taxing them. While most modern studies reject this formulation (but see Holton, 2007), there remains disagreement over what the Constitution was intended to do with regard to taxation.

The problem is that the Constitution's tax clauses are at once highly technical and overly vague. Article 1, section 8, grants Congress the power to levy taxes, duties, imposts, and excises as long as they are "uniform throughout the United States." In Article 1, section 2, however, and again in Article 1, section 9, the Constitution requires "direct taxes" to be apportioned among the states by population. Neither clause defines "direct taxes," though there may be a hint in the language "capitation, or other direct tax" in the second version.

But it is with some relief that we then come upon the unambiguous ban on export taxes and permission to levy a tax of up to $10 on each imported slave (this tax was never levied). The big question raised by all this verbiage is whether it was intended to facilitate or restrain the federal tax power.

Lawyers addressing this question through textual analysis, studying the texts generated in the debates over the Constitution's framing and ratification, disagree about the framers' intentions (Jensen, 1997; Ackerman, 1999; Johnson, 2005). Historians addressing it in the larger context of the 1780s, however, have been fairly unanimous that one of the main reasons for replacing the Articles of Confederation with the Constitution was to establish a viable federal tax power (Rakove, 1979; 1996; Einhorn, 2006; Edling, 2003). The problem was less that elites disliked democracy than that the Articles contained an unworkable tax system. Having borrowed large sums to finance the Revolutionary War, Congress depended on the state legislatures in exactly the way Parliament had depended on the colonial assemblies: it could tax only by asking the states to tax and deliver the proceeds (Brown, 1993). The states could not meet these requests ("requisitions"), but even if they could have raised the money, the Articles also required Congress to apportion their shares by the value of land and buildings in each state. The members of the Second Continental Congress, who drafted the Articles in 1777, understood that this was an absurd formula – many colonies had never assessed real estate value and could hardly start from scratch during the war – but they adopted it anyway after realizing that simpler formulas, based on population, generated impossibly divisive debates over how to count enslaved African Americans (Einhorn, 2006). Congress tried to adopt an impost, a national tax on imported goods, to replace the requisitions. It failed twice, since the most absurd aspect of the Articles of Confederation was that they could be amended only with the unanimous consent of the state legislatures. Shays' Rebellion erupted largely in response to the oppressive manner in which one state, Massachusetts, tried to solve the problem of the war debt on its own (Richards, 2002). Most American political leaders agreed that the only solution was to junk the Articles altogether.

No matter what else the framers of the Constitution were doing in Philadelphia, they were establishing a government that would be able to tax imported goods at the national level. In this sense, the Constitution was unquestionably "pro-tax" (Johnson, 2005). The federal government would also levy other taxes, such as excises, though these caused problems in the early republic, most famously when the 1791 excise on liquor production provoked the Whiskey Rebellion in Pennsylvania (Slaughter, 1986; Bouton, 2007). Edling (2003) exaggerates in arguing that the framers aspired to create a "fiscal-military state" to rival the major European powers, but they clearly did intend to create, and actually did create, a federal system in which Congress usually relied on import taxes while most state and local governments relied on property taxes.

On the issue of what kind of limit on the federal tax power the framers intended to set by requiring that "direct taxes" be apportioned to the states by population, the evidence suggests that, to the extent that they thought about this issue, the point was to distinguish consumption taxes on trade (imposts) and production (excises) from poll taxes (capitations) and property taxes (mainly on land and slaves). More specifically, the point was to ensure that Congress, now empowered to tax without state intervention, never levied slave taxes at rates high enough to threaten the institution of slavery (Einhorn, 2006). The Supreme Court agreed that "direct taxes" were poll and property taxes in *Hylton v. U.S.* (1796), ruling that a tax on pleasure carriages was not a "direct tax" that had to be apportioned by population. Alexander Hamilton had concocted *Hylton* as a test case (the parties agreed to fictitious facts), and three more of the original framers sat on the bench (Marcus, 1986–2007, 7: 358–369). In the end, though, the ruling rested less on memory or history than on practicality. The carriage tax could not be a "direct tax" under the Constitution because an apportionment would be nonsense, imposing the same number of dollars per person in every state regardless of whether it had relatively many or few carriages.

The Supreme Court addressed the "direct tax" issue again a century later, this time ruling that an income tax was a "direct tax" and therefore unconstitutional. The tax at issue in *Pollock v. Farmers' Loan and Trust Company* (1895) had been appended onto the Wilson-Gorman Tariff Act in 1894 in order to draw revenue from the industrial Northeast, which was both the nation's richest region and the major beneficiary of high protective tariffs. Southerners and westerners, certain that they bore disproportionate burdens, had resented the tariff for decades and demanded relief. Pegged at two percent and levied only on incomes over $4,000 (equivalent to over $100,000 today), this tax was very modest; hence the skeptical view of Stanley (1993) that it was a fig leaf over the much larger tariff. The issue, however, was whether it was constitutional. If an income tax was "direct," it could be levied only after being apportioned to the states by population. As with the carriages in *Hylton*, an apportioned income tax would levy the same number of dollars per person in the higher-income states of the Northeast and lower-income states of the South and West, defeating the purpose of income taxation. Nevertheless, the Court rejected the precedent from *Hylton* of construing the term "direct" narrowly. On the basis of a very strained historical argument about tax policy in the colonial era (that there had been income taxes much like the one being challenged), the *Pollock* majority claimed that the framers had indeed been thinking about income taxes as "direct taxes." Seligman (1911) demolished this argument with his own (better) historical research, but these dueling histories were not decisive in the end. The constitutionality of federal income taxes was settled by the Sixteenth Amendment, which exempted income taxes from the apportionment rule – though without resolving the issue of what might still count as an unconstitutional "direct tax" (Buenker, 1985; Ackerman, 1999; Weisman, 2002).

Nor was the tariff altogether free of constitutional challenge. The "impost" of the 1780s was framed as a flat five percent tax on all imported goods except war materiel, and in one version with higher rates on "luxury" imports (hard liquor and tropical produce). Tariffs, however, were designed with varying rates, sometimes as flat sums per pound, barrel, or other amount of goods and sometimes as percentages of the value of the goods ("ad valorem"). Overall rates could vary over time in response to revenue needs, but the heart of the usually byzantine tariff schedule was its system of "protection," mainly for domestic manufacturing. The tariff, in other words, was a national industrial policy. While the Constitution plainly authorized Congress to raise money by taxing imported goods, it said nothing about allowing Congress to use tariffs to plan the nation's economic development. This was the basis for the famous antebellum critiques by John C. Calhoun and other southerners, and the Democratic Party's insistence on a "tariff for revenue only" in the late nineteenth century.

Most literature about the tariff has always – rightly – emphasized this industrial policy aspect of its history, even though it was the major federal tax throughout the nineteenth century. While economists have been most interested in the degree to which tariff protection stimulated economic growth, political scientists have used tariff-making to illuminate larger themes about politics. E.E. Schattschneider's *Politics, Pressures, and the Tariff* (1935) is a classic of this genre. Analyzing the committee hearings for the infamous Smoot-Hawley Tariff of 1930, Schattschneider showed that there was little "policy" in tariff-making, which really was driven by elaborate log-rolling. Richard Bensel's *The Political Economy of American Industrialization* (2000) shows that the point of late nineteenth-century tariffs was less to protect industry than to build political capital that the Republican party spent on other major economic policies. Several historians have written useful books on the tariff recently (Wolman, 1992; Reitano, 1994), yet what Tom Terrill wrote about this literature decades ago remains true: most historians treat the tariff "as one treats an unwanted member of the family," discouraged by the "sheer volume of tariff rhetoric spewed forth by politicians and editors" (Terrill, 1973: 3). In fact, historians have sided with the Populists, whose 1892 Omaha Platform condemned "the uproar of a sham battle over the tariff," through which the major parties tried "to drown the outcries of a plundered people."

The tariff was one prong of the fiscal system the Constitution created. The other was the state and local taxes. These taxes varied tremendously from state to state in the early republic, though patterns gradually emerged. Regressive poll taxes on free male adults were abolished or levied at much lower rates after the Revolution (these poll taxes, levied for revenue purposes, must not be confused with later versions intended for voter disfranchisement). Property taxes, meanwhile, had converged by the 1830s into one of two patterns. In the North, states built on colonial legacies of general property taxation, assessing the value of many forms of property and levying ad valorem rates on the results. In the South, colonies had taxed land, slaves, and some other items, usually without assessing value. They taxed land at flat rates per acre, sometimes in "quality" categories, and slaves at flat rates per "head," sometimes in age and sex categories. By the 1830s, however, most southern states assessed the value of land and other forms of property including, in some states, the "value" of enslaved African Americans. Robin Einhorn's *American Taxation, American Slavery* (2006), a synthesis of this history, can be supplemented by Alvin Rabushka's encyclopedic *Taxation in Colonial America* (2008) and the review of tax debates in Robert A. Becker's *Revolution, Reform, and the Politics of American Taxation, 1763–1783* (1980). For the antebellum era, there are important studies of special topics, of which the essay by Richard Sylla, John B. Legler, and John J. Wallis, "Banks and State Public Finance in the New Republic" (1987) is especially significant.

Civil War taxation has attracted some interest (e.g., Thorndike, 2001), though mainly within general political histories of the war. Richard Bensel's *Yankee Leviathan* (1990) is the best example, particularly in its gloss on the much greater success of the Union than the Confederacy in raising tax revenue. Part of the Confederate problem was ideological, since southerners had long attacked federal taxation (that is, the tariff), but in this as in other policy areas, they overcame antebellum qualms. The decisive difference was economic: a relative absence of liquid capital in the South and the success of the Union naval blockade. State and local taxes for war-related purposes, from civil defense to bounty funds for military recruiting, are discussed mainly in studies focused on other issues (e.g., Einhorn, 1991). The one exception is critical: J. Mills Thornton's "Fiscal Policy and the Failure of Radical Reconstruction in the Lower South" (1982). Because Deep South states depended heavily on slave taxes paid by wealthy planters in the antebellum era, the abolition of slavery insured that postwar taxes fell much more heavily on the land of yeoman farmers. Along with hefty new government spending during Reconstruction to rebuild infrastructure, establish school systems, invest in railroads, and so on, the result was massive tax hikes for small farmers compared to what they paid in the late antebellum years. These tax increases, Thornton argues, must supplement "unvarnished racism" in explaining why white farmers supported the overthrow of Reconstruction (Thornton, 1982: 391). No matter how far we want to follow Thornton in downplaying the impact of racism, the tax problem he describes undoubtedly helped to alienate white farmers from Republican rule.

More generally, the southern states emerged from Reconstruction with tax systems that resembled their northern counterparts. Each state's property tax still had distinctive features, but by the late nineteenth century it finally made sense to talk about an American system of state and local taxation – featuring a general property tax that was already showing signs of obsolescence. Among the problems that Ely, Seligman, fellow economists, tax administrators, and taxpayers all criticized, the crucial one was the inability of local assessors to locate and value "intangible" personal property in ways comparable to their treatment of other property. Farmers could strike personal deals about the value of machinery or drive livestock across county lines at assessment time, but the urban wealth of an industrialized economy, held largely as paper, was beyond the reach of even very tenacious local assessors. Clifton K. Yearley's *The Money Machines* (1970) is a solid modern introduction to this problem, usefully supplemented by Glenn Fisher, *The Worst Tax?* (1996), and John Joseph Wallis, "A History of the Property Tax in America" (2001). The reform movement, led by the economists, has also drawn significant recent attention. Ajay Mehrotra (2008; 2009) provides the state and local back story for the early-twentieth-century "democratic-statist" regime Brownlee (1996) identifies for federal taxation. Mehrotra's work is especially useful on the intellectual foundations of the movement to replace general property taxes with income taxes and the importance of building new administrative capacity at the state level – a necessary step if the income taxes were to be levied with more success than the locally-administered general property taxes.

The big story of the twentieth century is the rise of federal taxation, especially the federal income tax. Total federal tax revenue increased from three percent of GDP in 1902 to twenty percent in 1992. Put another way, federal taxes raised only 0.8 cents per capita in 1902 but $4.90 in 1992. State and local taxes also rose dramatically, from 4.7 to sixteen percent of GDP and 1.3 cents to $3.94 per capita, but the federal story remains the critical one (Carter *et al.*, 2006: series Ca10, Ca14, Ea11, Ea12, Ea13). The reason is not only the larger federal numbers, but also the progressivity of the federal taxes, especially the income tax. Sven Steinmo's *Taxation and Democracy* (1993) explains that the heavy reliance on income taxation and absence of a VAT (value added tax) are unique features of the U.S. system, and may help explain the powerful American resistance to social welfare spending. In the United States, such spending is more redistributive than it is, for example, in Sweden, where more regressive taxation has accompanied more generous benefits. Nor can income taxes raise as much money as VATs except at impossibly high rates (Swedish taxes are double those of the United States). The federal income tax was made less progressive in the 1980s and again in the 2000s, but it remains the largest American tax. The puzzle is how the United States got such a relatively progressive federal tax structure in the first place, or, in Brownlee's phrase (1996), how the "democratic-statist" regime emerged in a nation ostensibly dedicated to individualism and minimalist government.

The answer is that "democratic-statism" was a response to the late-nineteenth-century "consumption tax regime," dominated by the tariff plus excises on liquor and tobacco. Because that system was so regressive, a progressive income tax that reallocated the federal burden could be portrayed as restoring the market-based distribution of income, not least by the westerners and southerners who resented the tariff (Brownlee, 1996: 29–38). It was no coincidence that the first permanent federal income tax was levied in a tariff law in 1913, as was its ill-fated 1894 predecessor. The outbreak of World War I, with Democrats controlling the federal government, guaranteed increased reliance on the new tax and sharply progressive ("soak-the-rich") rates. Congress also added the federal estate tax and an excess profits tax on corporations. When Republicans returned to power in 1921, they abolished the excess profits tax, slashed income tax rates, and added tax deductions to reward particular constituents, though Congress rejected the demand of some Republicans to replace the income tax with a national sales tax. The federal government still collected high tariffs, though excise revenues plummeted with Prohibition. The income tax reached only the wealthiest households by the late 1920s, mainly those with significant investment income. As a result, it was highly vulnerable to economic shocks such as a stock market crash. Because capital losses could be deducted from total income rather than only from capital gains and because, in some cases, "losses" could be manufactured by selling securities to friends temporarily, such corporate and financial titans as J.P. Morgan ended up owing no income tax for 1931 and 1932 (Leff, 1984: 59).

The Great Depression led to tax reforms at all levels of government. On the regressive side, the repeal of Prohibition produced a flood of federal and state excise revenue. Many states had begun to raise significant revenue by taxing gasoline sales in the 1920s; the demands of the 1930s led many to add the general retail-sales taxes that have been vital to state and local finance ever since. The sales taxes await their historian, but Robert Murray Haig and Carl Shoup (1934) compiled a great deal of useful detail. On the gas taxes, Paul Sabin's *Crude Politics* (2005) is especially interesting. By dedicating these taxes to road construction, states such as California assembled powerful constituencies in their favor. During the Depression, with states desperate for revenue, these constituencies, including the American Automobile Association, fought to prevent "diversion" of gas tax revenue to other purposes. In many states, meanwhile, property taxes were reeling from falling property values, their crises sometimes exacerbated by flagrant corruption in the 1920s. This was the situation in Chicago, where real estate interests organized a huge tax strike in the early 1930s. David T. Beito's *Taxpayers in Revolt* (1989) tells this story and that of a colorful response to the crisis: a national "pay your taxes" propaganda campaign featuring didactic radio programs with titles like "You and Your Government."

At the federal level, however, the major changes came with World War II. This is hardly surprising; wars usually produce major tax changes because they are expensive. Two recent books explore this issue in U.S. history: Sheldon D. Pollack's *War, Revenue, and State Building* (2009) and *War and Taxes* by Steven A. Bank, Kirk J. Stark, and Joseph J. Thorndike (2008). The big change during World War II was the transformation of the individual income tax from a "class tax" levied only on the very rich into a "mass tax" that reached deeply into middle-class salaries and wages of industrial workers, meanwhile maintaining progressivity with a steep schedule of marginal rates. Mass taxation of wages and salaries raised more predictable revenue than reliance on investment income and, with the addition of withholding, produced it steadily rather than in lump sums at the filing deadlines. And it produced huge quantities: the federal income tax raised $2.2 billion in 1939 and $35.1 billion in 1945 (Brownlee, 1996: 96). Persisting after the war, into a period of booming prosperity, this income tax underwrote Brownlee's "era of easy finance." Two scholars have glossed the social and political implications. Carolyn C. Jones (1996) describes the establishment of a "taxpaying culture." James T. Sparrow (2008) examines the idea of mass-based "fiscal citizenship." It is remarkable how easily Americans adapted to the mass income tax. Propaganda helped, with a sense of shared wartime sacrifice, but the dramatic change was the relationship of ordinary Americans to the federal government. We often credit the New Deal with building "liberal" political attitudes, but it was during World War II that ordinary Americans got used to making claims on – and trusting – "their" government.

It could not last forever. By the 1970s, with the waning of the long postwar economic boom, the "era of easy finance" ended. But the income tax system created during World War II is still, at least in outline, the dominant revenue producer in the United States. It has survived in part because Americans have enjoyed the public services it has financed and in part because its complex system of deductions and credits makes it resemble the late-nineteenth-century tariff, offering congressmen regular opportunities to grant favors to constituents and contributors. As the tariff combined this favor-granting with more or less coherent economic policies, the income tax has been the site for critical decisions about twentieth-century social policy. Several scholars have studied the "tax expenditures" that enact these policies, such as the mortgage interest deduction for home owners. Christopher Howard's *The Hidden Welfare State* (1997) and Jacob Hacker's *The Divided Welfare State* (2002) explore how tax expenditures came to subsidize a "private" system of social provision for the middle class. Unlike the less generous "public" system for the poor, this one has been relatively immune from cuts to "government spending." Edward J. McCaffery's *Taxing Women* (1997) explores the family policy implications of this tax regime, while Julian Zelizer's *Taxing America* (1998) traces how Wilbur Mills, as chairman of the House Ways and Means Committee, piloted the federal tax code through the 1960s and 1970s by building staff expertise and deploying a "closed rule" blocking floor amendments to the legislation crafted in his committee.

In the end, though, the "era of easy finance" could not survive the inflation of the 1970s, which had two devastating effects on tax policy. First, as housing prices soared, property taxes rose to crushing levels, especially when local governments modernized their assessment systems to capture price data effectively. Second, as nominal incomes soared, income tax "bracket creep" pushed middle-class families into brackets intended for millionaires. The property tax crisis broke in California, where voters enacted Proposition 13 in 1978, amending the state constitution to cut tax rates, limit assessment hikes, and require supermajority votes for taxes. Proposition 13 inspired the adoption of similar "tax-expenditure limitations" across the country, though most were less draconian (and patently inequitable) than California's. Peter Schrag's *Paradise Lost* (1998) charts the causes and especially the legacies of Proposition 13, while Isaac William Martin's *The Permanent Tax Revolt* (2008) offers a provocative analysis of the political connection between Proposition 13 and conservative tax politics.

Nationally, the result was the Reagan Revolution. The Economic Recovery Tax Act of 1981 slashed income tax rates and indexed rates for inflation to prevent future "bracket creep." The Tax Reform Act of 1986 then closed an array of income tax "loopholes" by abolishing many income tax deductions. Together, these measures helped to guarantee a future of chronic federal budget deficits. Brownlee (1996) offers a quick survey of this story, which journalists and economists treat in more detail (e.g., Birnbaum and Murray, 1987; Stein, 1996). The 1986 tax reform did not close all of the major "loopholes." Nor did it prevent further growth of the complex and particularistic tax expenditures that swell the federal income tax code. At this point, however, the historians yield to the tax lawyers, who navigate this system professionally.

References

Ackerman, Bruce (1999). "Taxation and the Constitution." *Columbia Law Review* 99(1): 1–58.

Bank, Steven A., Stark, Kirk J., and Thorndike, Joseph J. (2008). *War and Taxes*. Urban Institute Press, Washington.

Becker, Robert A. (1980). *Revolution, Reform and the Politics of American Taxation 1763–1783*. Louisiana State University Press, Baton Rouge.

Beito, David T. (1989). *Taxpayers in Revolt: Tax Resistance During the Great Depression*. University of North Carolina Press, Chapel Hill.

Bensel, Richard Franklin (2000). *The Political Economy of American Industrialization 1877–1900*. Cambridge University Press, New York.

Bensel, Richard Franklin (1990). *Yankee Leviathan: The Origins of Central State Authority in America, 1859–1877*. Cambridge University Press, New York.

Birnbaum, Jeffrey H. and Murray, Alan S. (1987). *Showdown at Gucci Gulch: Lawmakers, Lobbyists, and the Unlikely Triumph of Tax Reform*. Vintage Books, New York.

Blakey, Roy G. and Blakey, Gladys C. (1940). *The Federal Income Tax*. Longmans, Green, London.

Bouton, Terry (2007). *Taming Democracy: "The People," the Founders, and the Troubled Ending of the American Revolution*. Oxford University Press, New York.

Brewer, John (1990). *The Sinews of Power: War, Money, and the English State, 1688–1783*. Harvard University Press, Cambridge, MA.

Brown, Roger H. (1993). *Redeeming the Republic: Federalists, Taxation, and the Origins of the Constitution*. Johns Hopkins University Press, Baltimore.

Brownlee, W. Elliot (1996). *Federal Taxation in America: A Short History*. Cambridge University Press, Cambridge, UK.

Buenker, John D. (1985). *The Income Tax and the Progressive Era*. Garland, New York.

Carter, Susan B. et al., eds (2006). *Historical Statistics of the United States, Millennial Edition On Line*. Cambridge University Press, http://hsus.cambridge.org/HSUSWeb/ (last accessed October 12, 2012).

Cooley, Thomas M. (1876). *A Treatise on the Law of Taxation: Including the Law of Local Assessments*. Callaghan, Chicago.

Edling, Max M. (2003). *A Revolution in Favor of Government: Origins of the U.S. Constitution and the Making of the American State*. Oxford University Press, New York.

Einhorn, Robin L. (1991). *Property Rules: Political Economy in Chicago, 1833–1872*. University of Chicago Press, Chicago.

Einhorn, Robin L. (2006). *American Taxation, American Slavery*. University of Chicago Press, Chicago.

Ely, Richard T. (1888). *Taxation in American States and Cities*. Crowell, New York.

Fisher, Glenn W. (1996). *The Worst Tax?: A History of the Property Tax in America*. University Press of Kansas, Lawrence.

Hacker, Jacob S. (2002). *The Divided Welfare State: The Battle Over Public and Private Social Benefits in the United States*. Cambridge University Press, Cambridge.

Haig, Robert Murray and Shoup, Carl (1934). *The Sales Tax in the American States*. Columbia University Press, New York.

Holton, Woody (2007). *Unruly Americans and the Origins of the Constitution*. Hill and Wang, New York.

Howard, Christopher (1997). *The Hidden Welfare State: Tax Expenditures and Social Policy in the United States*. Princeton University Press, Princeton.

Jensen, Erik M. (1997). "The Apportionment of 'Direct Taxes': Are Consumption Taxes Constitutional?" *Columbia Law Review* 97(8): 2334–2419.

Jensen, Merrill (1940). *The Articles of Confederation: An Interpretation of the Social-Constitutional History of the American Revolution 1774–1781*. University of Wisconsin Press, Madison.

Johnson, Calvin H. (2005). *Righteous Anger at the Wicked States: The Meaning of the Founders' Constitution*. Cambridge University Press, New York.

Jones, Carolyn C. (1996). "Mass-Based Income Taxation: Creating a Taxpaying Culture, 1940–1952." In Brownlee, ed., *Funding the Modern American State, 1941–1995: The Rise and Fall of the Era of Easy Finance*, 107–147. Cambridge University Press, Cambridge, UK.

Leff, Mark H. (1983). "Taxing the 'Forgotten Man': The Politics of Social Security Finance in the New Deal." *Journal of American History* 70(2): 359–381.

Leff, Mark H. (1984). *The Limits of Symbolic Reform: The New Deal and Taxation, 1933–1939*. Cambridge University Press, Cambridge, UK.

Marcus, Maeva, ed. (1986–2007). *The Documentary History of the Supreme Court of the United States, 1789–1800*. 8 volumes. Columbia University Press, New York.

Martin, Isaac William (2008). *The Permanent Tax Revolt: How the Property Tax Transformed American Politics*. Stanford University Press, Stanford, CA.

Martin, Isaac William, Mehrotra, Ajay K., and Prasad, Monica, eds (2009). *The New Fiscal Sociology: Taxation in Comparative and Historical Perspective*. Cambridge University Press, Cambridge, UK.

McCaffery, Edward J. (1997). *Taxing Women*. University of Chicago Press, Chicago.

Mehrotra, Ajay K. (2008). "Forging Fiscal Reform: Constitutional Change, Public Policy, and the Creation of Administrative Capacity in Wisconsin, 1880–1920." *Journal of Policy History* 20(1): 94–112.

Mehrotra, Ajay K. (2009). "The Intellectual Foundations of the Modern American Fiscal State." *Daedalus* 1(2): 53–62.

Morgan, Edmund S. and Morgan, Helen M. (1953). *The Stamp Act Crisis; Prologue to Revolution*. University of North Carolina Press, Chapel Hill.

Paul, Randolph (1954). *Taxation in the United States*. Little Brown, Boston.

Pollack, Sheldon D. (2009). *War, Revenue, and State Building: Financing the Development of the American State*. Cornell University Press, Ithaca.

Rabushka, Alvin (2008). *Taxation in Colonial America*. Princeton University Press, Princeton.

Rakove, Jack N. (1979). *The Beginnings of National Politics: An Interpretive History of the Continental Congress*. Knopf, New York.

Rakove, Jack N. (1996). *Original Meanings: Politics and Ideas in the Making of the Constitution*. Knopf, New York.

Ratner, Sidney (1942). *American Taxation: Its History as a Social Force in Democracy*. W.W. Norton, New York.

Reitano, Joanne (1994). *The Tariff Question in the Gilded Age: The Great Debate of 1888*. Pennsylvania State University Press, University Park.

Richards, Leonard L. (2002). *Shays's Rebellion: The American Revolution's Final Battle*. University of Pennsylvania Press, Philadelphia.

Sabin, Paul (2005). *Crude Politics: The California Oil Market, 1900–1940*. University of California Press, Berkeley.

Schattschneider, E.E. (1935). *Politics, Pressures, and the Tariff*. Prentice-Hall, New York.

Schrag, Peter (1998). *Paradise Lost: California's Experience, America's Future*. University of California Press, Berkeley.

Schumpeter, Joseph A. (1954). "The Crisis of the Tax State." trans. W.F. Stolper and R.A. Musgrave, *International Economic Papers* 4: 5–38.

Seligman, E.R.A. ([1895] 1913). *Essays in Taxation*. Macmillan, New York.

Seligman, E.R.A. (1911). *The Income Tax: a Study of the History, Theory and Practice of Income Taxation at Home and Abroad*. Macmillan, New York.

Slaughter, Thomas P. (1986). *The Whiskey Rebellion: Frontier Epilogue to the American Revolution*. Oxford University Press, New York.

Sparrow, James T. (2008). "Buying Our Boys Back': The Mass Foundations of Fiscal Citizenship in World War II." *Journal of Policy History* 20(2): 263–286.

Stanley, Robert (1993). *Dimensions of Law in the Service of Order: Origins of the Federal Income Tax, 1861–1913.* Oxford University Press, New York.

Stein, Herbert (1996). "The Fiscal Revolution in America, part II: 1964–1994." In Brownlee, ed., *Funding the Modern American State, 1941–1995: The Rise and Fall of the Era of Easy Finance*, 194–286. Cambridge University Press, Cambridge, UK.

Steinmo, Sven (1993). *Taxation and Democracy: Swedish, British, and American Approaches to Financing the Modern State.* Yale University Press, New Haven.

Sylla, Richard, Legler, John B., and Wallis, John J. (1987). "Banks and State Public Finance in the New Republic: The United States, 1790–1860." *Journal of Economic History* 47(2): 391–403.

Taussig, F.W. (1888). *The Tariff History of the United States: A Series of Essays.* G.P. Putnam's Sons, New York.

Terrill, Tom E. (1973). *The Tariff, Politics, and American Foreign Policy, 1874–1901.* Greenwood Press, Westport.

Thorndike, Joe (2001). "An Army of Officials: The Civil War Bureau of Internal Revenue." *Tax Notes* 93: 1739–1760.

Thornton III, J. Mills (1982). "Fiscal Policy and the Failure of Radical Reconstruction in the Lower South." In Kousser and McPherson, eds, *Region, Race, and Reconstruction: Essays in Honor of C. Vann Woodward*, 349–394. Oxford University Press, New York.

Tilly, Charles (1985). "War Making and State Making as Organized Crime." In Evans, Rueschemeyer, and Skocpol, eds, *Bringing the State Back In*, chapter 5. Cambridge University Press, Cambridge, UK.

Tilly, Charles (2009). "Extraction and Democracy." In Martin, Mehrotra, and Prasad, eds, *The New Fiscal Sociology: Taxation in Comparative and Historical Perspective*, chapter 10. Cambridge University Press, Cambridge, UK.

U.S. Bureau of the Census (2010). *Statistical Abstract of the United States*, State and Local Government Finances and Employment, table 418, http://www.census.gov/compendia/statab/cats/state_local_govt_finances_employment.html (last accessed October 12, 2012).

Wallis, John Joseph (2000). "American Government Finance in the Long Run, 1790–1940," *Journal of Economic Perspectives* 14: 61–82.

Wallis, John Joseph (2001). "A History of the Property Tax in America." In Oates, ed., *Property Taxation and Local Government Finance*, 123–147. Lincoln Institute of Land Policy, Cambridge, MA.

Wallis, John Joseph (2006). "Government Finance and Employment." In Carter, et al., eds, *Historical Statistics of the United States, Millennial Edition On Line*, Cambridge University Press. http://hsus.cambridge.org/HSUSWeb/ (last accessed October 12, 2012).

Weisman, Steven R. (2002). *The Great Tax Wars: Lincoln to Wilson – The Fierce Battles over Money and Power That Transformed the Nation.* Simon and Schuster, New York.

White House (2010). *The President's Budget for Fiscal Year 2011*, Historical Tables, table 2.1, http://www.whitehouse.gov/omb/budget/Historicals (last accessed October 12, 2012).

Witte, John F. (1985). *The Politics and Development of the Federal Income Tax.* University of Wisconsin Press, Madison.

Wolman, Paul (1992). *Most Favored Nation: The Republican Revisionists and U.S. Tariff Policy, 1897–1912.* University of North Carolina Press, Chapel Hill.

Yearley, C.K. (1970). *The Money Machines: The Breakdown and Reform of Governmental and Party Finance in the North, 1860–1920.* State University of New York Press, Albany.

Zelizer, Julian E. (1998). *Taxing America: Wilbur D. Mills, Congress, and the State, 1945–1975.* Cambridge University Press, Cambridge, UK.

Further Reading

Ball, Douglas B. (1991). *Financial Failure and Confederate Defeat.* University of Illinois Press, Urbana.

Brownlee, W. Elliot, ed. (1996). *Funding the Modern American State, 1941–1995: The Rise and Fall of the Era of Easy Finance.* Cambridge University Press, Cambridge, UK.

Hanchett, Thomas W. (1996). "U.S. Tax Policy and the Shopping-Center Boom of the 1950s and 1860s." *American Historical Review* 101(4): 1082–1110.

Jones, Carolyn C. (1994). "Dollars and Selves: Women's Tax Criticism and Resistance in the 1870s." *University of Illinois Law Review* 265–309.

Sparrow, James T. (2011). *Warfare State: World War II Americans and the Age of Big Government.* Oxford University Press, New York.

Chapter Nineteen

LAW AND THE ADMINISTRATIVE STATE

Joanna L. Grisinger

Historians and political scientists writing about regulatory authority and the agencies that administer it often begin with the dichotomy sketched out by Thomas McCraw in his well-known article "Regulation in America" (McCraw, 1975). McCraw contrasts two groups of scholars: those who argued that agencies and commissions served the public by placing restrictions on powerful economic interests over their objections (the "public interest" thesis), and those who suggested that administrative officials were actually more sympathetic to business than to the public (the "capture" thesis). While others joined McCraw in criticizing this distinction between "public interest" and "capture" scholarship as overly facile, it nonetheless continues to operate as a starting point for authors offering their own, more nuanced analyses. As an introduction to the historical literature, however, these categories convey neither the depth nor the breadth of scholars' recent inquiries.

First, both narratives assume that agencies and commissions properly stand outside politics, as administrative theorists in the late nineteenth and early twentieth centuries envisioned. However, the most valuable scholarship takes for granted that agencies are subject to the same democratic and interest group pressures as Congress, the White House, and the courts – as well as novel pressures emerging from their independence, organizational design, and statutory authority. From this starting point, scholars have assessed agencies as legal institutions and policy makers in historical context, and asked broader questions about policy development, interest groups, and legal authority.

A Companion to American Legal History, First Edition.
Edited by Sally E. Hadden and Alfred L. Brophy.
© 2013 John Wiley & Sons Ltd. Published 2021 by John Wiley & Sons Ltd.

Second, asking whether agency governance is good or bad for business is a peculiarly economic question. The bureaucratic impulse extends far beyond the economic arena, into areas that include state and federal efforts to regulate immigration, restrict or expand civil rights, and investigate loyalty. The categories McCraw describes apply poorly to areas where the wide variety of interests at play make it difficult to identify either a single "public interest" or a particular group seeking to "capture" regulators. They also obscure important similarities; the formal organization and bureaucratic discretion of local zoning boards, state boards of public health, and the Immigration and Naturalization Service have much in common with the Interstate Commerce Commission (ICC) and the National Labor Relations Board (NLRB).

In recent decades, historians interested in legal history outside the courts have joined other scholars in wide-ranging studies of the growth of the administrative state and the development of individual agencies, the rise of administrative policy making, the expansion of federal employment, the evolution of administrative procedures, and the spread of bureaucratization throughout American life. Indeed, few areas of American history can be fully understood without discussion of the role of administrative agencies and the use of bureaucratic methods. Overall, this rich scholarship on law and the administrative state is animated by several key questions: (1) How did this bureaucratic development occur? (2) What law governed these new entities? (3) Who works in these agencies and commissions? (4) How does institutional structure affect bureaucratic operations? Finally, (5) what does policy making look like in these agencies?

Origins of the Administrative State

Studies of the origins of the administrative state suggest that the definition of the "administrative state" includes governance through regulation, governance dominated by regulation, governance organized through bureaucratic institutions, or some combination thereof. Scholars looking for the roots of each have, not surprisingly, found them in a variety of contexts. Each of these studies makes clear, however, that Americans have long struggled to balance public power and private rights.

As William J. Novak (1996) has demonstrated, in the decades before the Civil War, an enormous amount of local safety, morality, health, and economic regulation under the police power placed Americans squarely within a "well-regulated society." This ethos extended to federal coercive authority, as Gautham Rao (2008) describes in his study of the federal *posse comitatus* doctrine. Indeed, the federal government's reach extended broadly in the nineteenth century (Balogh, 2009). The Progressive Era saw the expansion of regulatory authority into new areas of American life, as state and federal governments passed laws regarding railroads, trusts, immigration, alcohol, racial segregation, social welfare, criminal justice, and zoning, to list just a few (Brock, 1984; Keller, 1990; 1994; Lees, 1994; Sklar, 1988; Wolf, 2008). As Barbara Welke (2001) explains, Americans demanding state action were adopting a new, more dependent, conception of liberty – and, in the case of railroad safety regulation, one that exchanged the freedom to control one's own actions with the right to be protected from harm.

Additional scholarship has targeted the origins of the gradual transition from democratic to bureaucratic government, as an administrative apparatus developed to manage the expansion of regulatory authority. Shaping the discussion about how governments change as they embark on regulatory projects is the "organizational school" of scholars, which focuses on the transformation of the way in which American businesses, social groups, and governments organized themselves (Galambos, 1970; 1983). Looking at state and federal governments in turn, scholars have sought to identify the point at which democratically elected legislatures and politically appointed officials were replaced by experts and boards removed from political pressure, in an apparent departure from traditional American governance and constitutional conceptions of the separation of powers (Rohr, 1986). In a study of the Post Office and General Land Office during the Jacksonian era, Matthew Crenson (1975) finds increasingly formal government structures and official rules replacing traditional values and social and professional ties. More broadly, William E. Nelson (1982) demonstrates how, in the decades surrounding the Civil War, each branch of the federal government became more expert, more specialized, and less responsive to democratic politics. As debates over slavery raised questions about the dangers of democracy, majoritarianism gave way to pluralistic politics focused on protecting individuals and minority groups and implemented through bureaucratic power.

The bulk of this scholarship, however, focuses on the decades between the Civil War and World War I, when Americans attempted to manage the transformations resulting from industrialization, urbanization, and immigration by flooding local, state, and federal landscapes with regulatory agencies. These institutions shared a preference for formal organizational structures and clearly defined responsibilities, along with a faith in experts and an optimism that new social science methods could produce apolitical and impartial solutions. For many Americans, bureaucratization offered an alluring alternative to the inherent irrationality and apparent corruption of democratic politics. Robert Wiebe (1967) attributes these changes to the Progressives – educated, middle-class reformers who were proud of their expertise and who sought to remake government and society along the same specialized lines by which they organized themselves. Key to this goal was government authority dedicated to ongoing investigations of specific social and economic problems – a process that demanded experts who could adjust their solutions accordingly. Having envisioned a path to social progress, Progressives designed political mechanisms that put themselves in charge. Municipal reform offers one example of authority centralized in the hands of the reformers (Hays, 1980); education policy offers another (Tyack, James and Benavot, 1987; Steffes, 2008). As Jon Teaford (2002) has demonstrated, the same centralizing reform impulse that moved power from state to federal hands encouraged states to reform themselves into better stewards of government authority. Centralized authority did not just benefit those who wielded it; Kolko (1963; 1965) argues that business interests found administrative agencies removed from the democratic process and staffed with sympathetic officials a notable improvement on unfettered competition and on enthusiastic and uneven state regulation.

Other scholars have focused less on reformers than on impediments to reform. The implementation of administrative power was considerably messier in practice than in theory, and these studies offer at least a partial explanation why. Barry Karl (1983) has suggested that efforts to remake the federal government along bureaucratic lines consistently failed to overcome Americans' persistent faith in individual decision-making and local control. Structural impediments also shaped the growing administrative state, and attention to how new rules and new agencies fit into existing political contexts is crucial. As Keller (1990) demonstrates, Progressive reformers quickly encountered the difficulties of imposing uniform laws on a decidedly non-uniform society. Stephen Skowronek makes clear the struggle involved in building a modern bureaucracy to replace the "state of courts and parties" in light of post-Civil War industrialization and urbanization. Old institutions had to be destroyed, and new ones negotiated; the result was an uneven and untidy state (Skowronek, 1982). Similar difficulties arose elsewhere, as the creation of state-level tax administration demonstrates (Mehrotra, 2008).

Origins of Administrative Law

State legislatures and Congress, in delegating authority to administrative officials to "fill in the blanks" of broad legislative directives, gave them enormous discretion. Thus, the question many scholars have asked is "who regulates the regulators?" On the federal level, Congress and the White House have traditionally competed for control over administrative agencies (Karl, 1963; Polenberg, 1968; Milkis, 1993; Arnold, 1998). A crucial role is also played by courts, which directly police agencies' delegated authority. Historians of administrative law have examined courts' attempts to balance administrative discretion and efficiency with the rule of law and fairness as judges created administrative law doctrines defining what administrative officials may and may not do (Rabin, 1986; Stewart, 1975; Schiller, 2005).

While Ann Woolhandler (1991) and Jerry Mashaw (2006; 2007; 2008; 2010; Mashaw and Perry, 2009) have probed the development of administrative law in the eighteenth and nineteenth centuries, inquiries into federal administrative law usually begin with the creation of the ICC in 1887, an independent commission with legislative, executive, and judicial authority. One key question is where to draw the line between administrative and judicial decision-making – or, put another way, whether agencies or courts should have the final say. William Chase's study (1982) of law schools' role in the formation of administrative law focuses on this issue of administrative finality. As Chase argues, law professors espoused doctrines that discouraged courts from inquiring into the substance of administrative decisions as a way of avoiding politics and bolstering their own expertise. In his own research into doctrinal development, G. Edward White (2000) emphasizes the contribution of conservative lawyers in shaping an administrative law that also reflected constitutional values. There were many pressures on administrative law; Gabriel Chin (2002) has argued that the minimal due process rights offered in early immigration law had a profound effect on administrative law doctrines. Such doctrinal debates illustrate the efforts to ensure due process in the administrative state during a period when agency safeguards appeared lacking. Lucy Salyer's study (1995) of immigration law in this period examines jurisdictional battles involving federal courts, which stood for due process and the rule of law, and immigration officials, who could act with greater haste and discretion. Those seeking to limit immigration fought to locate final authority in the officials, while Chinese immigrants found that judges, even those holding strong nativist views, felt bound to provide due process to the parties before them.

The role of agency expertise in legitimating the regulatory expansion of the New Deal has also attracted much attention from legal historians. As Morton Horwitz (1992) argues, the Legal Realist critique of the theory of delegation pushed administrative supporters to justify administrative discretion in terms of expertise. Jessica Wang (2005) examines how Securities and Exchange Commission (SEC) chairmen drew on ideas of legal pragmatism, emphasizing the SEC's knowledge, the need for flexibility, and the presence of existing limits to legitimate the Commission's actions. More broadly, Reuel Schiller describes the New Dealers' success in carving out a sphere of independence for agencies across the federal government (Schiller, 2007). At the same time, the growth of the administrative state presented lawyers with new opportunities and new challenges. Lawyers who took their administrative expertise back to law firms and law schools changed the face of legal practice and legitimized administrative law as a prestigious area of practice and academic inquiry (Auerbach, 1976; Kalman, 1990; Ernst, 2002). The New Deal also fractured the legal community's claim to neutrality and expertise, as elite lawyers outside the agencies saw administrative governance as a threat to their own professional status (Shamir, 1995; Ernst, 2009).

Battles over the legitimacy of the administrative process reached a fever pitch in the late 1930s, as the New Deal state experienced significant conservative resistance. Administrative procedure took on new political significance once the Supreme Court validated the constitutional status of the New Deal agencies, and lawyers involved in the administrative process tried to separate fact from fiction as they refuted claims of administrative unfairness (Grisinger, 2008). Procedure became a particularly legalistic way of reconciling these partisan debates, to the benefit of the lawyers involved (Ernst, 2008). These battles culminated in the Administrative Procedure Act (APA) of 1946, which attracted broad political attention given its potential to help or hinder the New Deal state (Shepherd, 1996). Studies of the APA's history and its provisions question its legacy and debate the degree to which it "judicialized" the administrative process (Brazier, 1996; Shepherd, 1996; Zeppos, 1997; McCubbins, Noll and Weingast, 1999).

The post-World War II, post-APA era of administrative law would be characterized by a turn away from expertise and toward pluralism on the one hand and proceduralism on the other (Schiller, 2000; 2002; Horwitz, 1992). Courts revisited their habits of deference (Merrill, 1997), and agencies turned increasingly to rulemaking in response to critiques of agency torpor (Schiller, 2001). Theodore Lowi's critique (1979; 1987) of pluralism charges that massive delegations of power to agencies allowed them to drift too far from the rule of law.

Who Regulates?

As the administrative state grew, so too did the number of Americans employed by agencies and commissions. Significant racial and gender preferences were built into the staffing of these allegedly apolitical positions, however. Looking at the origins of public administration as a field in the late nineteenth century, Camilla Stivers (2000) has demonstrated how the field's roots in the female-dominated field of social welfare activism were subsumed to a more "scientific" origins story that also happened to be entirely masculine. Tying scientific neutrality to masculinity, she argues, male reformers emphasized their field's objective qualities to differentiate themselves from the women working alongside them. Similar concerns about professional image were present in federal hiring, where merit-based selection rules went hand in hand with discriminatory practices (King, 2007). Policies such as the Civil Service Commission's "rule of three" (allowing agencies to select from among the top three candidates) and the use of applicant photographs allowed employers to discriminate even as civil service rhetoric emphasized the neutrality of the hiring process. As Margaret Rung (2002) has described, these discriminatory practices did more than block the advancement of non-white men and women; they fostered an image of the civil servant that associated merit with white men. Nor was discrimination limited to race and sex. As David Johnson (2004) demonstrates in his study of the purge of suspected homosexuals from federal employment following World War II, sexuality was both a source of anxiety for government officials concerned about the image of their departments and a convenient target for members of Congress already hostile to the agencies.

Given the discretion that administrators wielded, understanding who these administrators were is crucial. Thomas McCraw's history (1984) of the administrative state is rooted in the biographies of four individuals responsible for shaping it: Charles Francis Adams, Louis D. Brandeis, James M. Landis, and Alfred E. Kahn. Their creative power was not unlimited, however; as McCraw illustrates, the administrative solutions they offered worked only when consistent with the economic and political context of the era. Other scholars have shown how upper-level officials in every agency played a significant role in policy making, and in doing so brought their own class and professional standing to bear. Officials with legal training often reached for court-like procedures over non-legal solutions, thus shaping agency operations along quasi-judicial lines. Peter Irons' study of the lawyers involved in drafting New Deal statutes and defending them in court – most of whom came from elite law schools and shared liberal political views – suggests that legal strategy was at least as important as external pressures in statutes' ultimate fate (Irons, 1982).

While bureaucrats often have considerable authority to design and implement policy on their own terms, this authority is a function of their political and institutional environments. As Daniel Carpenter suggests, agencies can attain significant autonomy if they can develop "political legitimacy" for themselves. Bureaucratic autonomy thus explains the relative success of the Post Office and the Department of Agriculture, and the comparative difficulties of the Department of the Interior in the late nineteenth and early twentieth centuries (Carpenter, 2001). Brian Balogh (1991a) describes a similar autonomy in the nuclear power context, as officials at the Atomic Energy Commission (AEC) joined with professionalized experts in an example of the Cold War-era "proministrative state." As expertise was consolidated in the AEC and Congress, the Commission could forge its own path. Conversely, by contrasting civil rights lawyers at the Justice Department with those at the National Association for the Advancement of Colored People's (NAACP) Legal Defense Fund, Risa Goluboff (2007) demonstrates the power of institutional restraints. Government lawyers deciding among civil rights litigation strategies were limited by their own sense of what was institutionally possible (given the activities of the NLRB and the Fair Employment Practices Committee) and politically possible (given the power of southern Democrats in Congress and the difficulties of confronting Jim Crow head-on).

The lack of accountability inherent in administrative autonomy became particularly apparent during moments of national security tensions. Justice Department efforts to police patriotism during World War I indicate the ease with which government officials impose their own definitions of propriety (Capozzola, 2008; Thomas, 2008). Similar problems arose during World War II, as multiple agencies with authority over Japanese internment had enormous latitude to define standards for assessing loyalty. As Eric Muller (2007) has described, determinations of loyalty had more to do with bureaucrats' own assumptions than with the individuals in question, which made such determinations extremely difficult to challenge. In a series of case studies of bureaucratic power during the second Red Scare, Stanley Kutler (1982) describes bureaucrats hoarding power, imposing their own rules, and compelling the cooperation of others. Kutler's research thus indicates both the harm that can come from administrative discretion and the practical difficulty of challenging bureaucrats who have strayed beyond their legal authority.

Structure and Operation

Numerous studies of individual agencies and commissions have examined how the legal authority, organizational design, and political context of an institution influence its policy making. The interplay between internal dynamics and external forces, especially insofar as they guide the actions of those working within the agencies, is key to these narratives, and scholars have made clear that even formally independent agencies are thoroughly enmeshed with the other branches of government and with powerful, well-organized private interests. Through this scholarship, much of it by political scientists, students of the administrative process can see both the characteristics common in agency operations and the significant diversity of the administrative state (Wilson, 1980).

The Federal Communications Commission (FCC), traditionally one of the most powerful and controversial agencies, has been the subject of significant inquiry, and studies of the FCC's role in communications policy demonstrate the complex landscape in which the commission operates. The FCC's authority to issue highly lucrative broadcast licenses has, from the beginning, attracted enormous interest from private parties and Congress. While the FCC has an explicit congressional mandate to regulate on behalf of the "public interest" (Moss and Fein, 2003), officials have found it almost impossible to do so. Vigorous attempts to regulate the broadcast industry beginning in the late 1930s were subverted when industry organizations and legislators deployed the politics of anticommunism to divert the commission's attention away from industry practices and toward the loyalty of its own staffers and licensees (Brinson, 2004). FCC efforts to improve television programming in the 1950s and 1960s were similarly thwarted when the commission found itself no match for powerful industry interests with members of Congress on their side (Baughman, 1985). Additional case studies of ineffective FCC policy making from the 1960s on have questioned both the FCC's independence and its efficacy (Krasnow and Longley, 1978). The lack of independence among independent commissions is not unique to the FCC, of course; Michael Parrish, examining how federal securities policy developed in the 1930s against the failure of state regulatory efforts and national associationalism, has similarly identified multiple interests in play (Parrish, 1970). What looks like "capture," then, is evidence of broader weakness; without support elsewhere, the FCC, for example, retreated to non-controversial policies that often mirrored industry preference. These studies also question Marver Bernstein's (1955) much-cited theory that agencies become less aggressive as they age; policy making is as much affected by outside factors as by any "natural" progression in agency politics. Such research raises additional questions about what the "public interest" means in context. As a case study of one television licensing battle indicates, once new parties (in this case, civil rights activists) brought their own definitions into the administrative arena, the FCC was forced to chart new waters (Mills, 2004; Classen, 2004).

The complicated nature of agency relations has attracted significant interest from scholars, and the proliferation of New Deal agencies has offered them fertile grounds for study. The NLRB has been a subject of particular attention; James A. Gross (1974; 1981; 1995), in a three-volume history of the NLRB and federal labor policy from the 1930s through the 1990s, emphasizes the NLRB's organizational design, its domination by lawyers, its generally weak White House support, and powerful political resistance from Congress, employers, and the American Federation of Labor to explain the Board's tendencies toward legalism and cautious action. Government intervention into labor-management relations was thus a dubious victory for labor, as Christopher Tomlins (1985) argues. Labor unions' ability to protect themselves, earned through so much effort beginning in the nineteenth century, was weakened once the NLRB took charge of labor-management relations and prioritized industrial stability above all else.

In a comparative study, Kenneth Finegold and Theda Skocpol looked to institutional factors to explain why the National Recovery Administration's (NRA) economic recovery program failed while the Agricultural Adjustment Administration's (AAA) quite similar program succeeded (Finegold and Skocpol, 1995). The AAA's location in the Department of Agriculture allowed AAA officials to draw on the department's existing reputation, its staff's considerable expertise, its field organization, its existing ties to farm groups and universities, and its own interest in the new agency's success. The independent NRA, by contrast, had less institutional autonomy and lacked the bureaucratic capacity to implement its programs. Marion

Clawson's study (1981) of the short-lived National Resources Planning Board (NRPB) identifies similar institutional factors that led to the Board's failure. Additional examinations of state capacity and institution building during the New Deal and World War II have clarified the roles of the NRPB and the Budget Bureau as they have examined the development of fiscal policy (Katznelson and Pietrykowski, 1991; Brown, 1995).

The explosion of safety, health, and environmental regulation in the 1960s and 1970s has also attracted the attention of scholars, many of whom are interested in the lessons these new agencies learned from earlier ones. Richard A. Harris and Sidney M. Milkis (1996), comparing the trajectories of an elderly agency (the Federal Trade Commission) with a new one (the Environmental Protection Agency, EPA) in the 1970s and 1980s, examine how pressures for citizen involvement forced institutions to adopt new priorities. Rather quickly, however, as the conservative push toward deregulation created new pressures for both agencies, the difficulties of changing directions became evident. A study of the National Highway Transportation Safety Administration (NHTSA), established in 1966, indicates the power of context. While the NHTSA was intentionally designed in contrast to earlier bureaucratic models, the agency's expansive legal authority proved no match for the legal culture in which it was placed – a culture that accepted quasi-judicial models but looked askance at more aggressive methods (Mashaw and Harfst, 1990). A separate study of the EPA in its first two decades blames the agency's failures on its own officials, who failed to leverage the EPA's expertise in the public debate over environmental risks and benefits and thus left policy making up to interest groups and Congress (Landy, Roberts and Thomas, 1994).

Policy History

The emergence of agencies as key sites of governance has been important in scholarship investigating the development of twentieth-century liberalism (Brinkley, 1995; Ciepley, 2006) and the rise of consumerism and the political power of consumers involved therein (Cohen, 2004; Jacobs, 2005). In addition, scholars seeking to understand the development of individual policies – ranging from federal transportation regulation to civil rights to immigration – neglect at their peril the agencies and commissions which came to dominate these policy areas (Critchlow and Hawley, 1988; Zelizer, 2000).

Understanding welfare policy, for example, requires scholars to take seriously the multiplicity of state and federal agencies that administer it. Here as elsewhere, Progressives embraced bureaucratic trends, created uniform state and federal policies, and located responsibility in specialized agencies. As Michael Katz (1986; 2001) demonstrates, persistent assumptions about welfare became embedded in these institutions. Linda Gordon's study (1994) of the Progressive Era Children's Bureau indicates how educated white female reformers used their authority to shape policy based on their professional aims and maternalist policy preferences. Suzanne Mettler (1998) focuses attention on organizational design, as the gendered nature of welfare policy resulted not just from intentional bias but also from the institutional choices of New Deal politicians. Bureaucratic choices also offered reformers an opportunity to challenge the assumptions of welfare policy. As Martha Davis (1993) and Felicia Kornbluh (2007) have discussed, welfare rights activists demanded "fair hearings" in welfare proceedings – a legal reform that extended the kinds of rights guaranteed to businesses at the ICC and the SEC, for example, to individuals receiving government benefits.

Here, too, however, the problematic nature of bureaucratic autonomy is evident (Ernst, 1998). As Karen Tani (2008) has demonstrated in her work on Social Security benefits and anticommunism, the expansion of welfare benefits opened new opportunities for unwelcome state involvement. Similar concerns about bureaucratic authority are offered by Michael Willrich (2003), who, in his study of Chicago's Progressive Era municipal court, describes how reformers used their faith in social science and administrative institutions to justify enormous invasions into the lives of working-class families. Andrew J. Polsky (1991) examines additional efforts to place in bureaucratic hands authority to "normalize" individuals – efforts he argues have done significant injury to personal autonomy. This disconnect between reformers' confidence in their own methods and the rights of those affected is perhaps best illustrated in the case of eugenic sterilization. Here the power of scientific language and expertise, joined to decision-making authority institutionalized in state boards, was used to justify intrusions into individuals' reproductive capacities (Lombardo, 2008).

Regulations can do far more than simply coerce; they can create enduring definitions of race, gender, and sexuality. As Nayan Shah (2001) explains, public health regulations in San Francisco in the late nineteenth and early twentieth centuries served to legitimize discrimination against Chinese immigrants. Public health officials seeking broad powers publicized the poor conditions in Chinatown to justify city-wide public health regulations. Their official, quasi-scientific reports defined public health standards by reference to white, middle-class standards of living, thus associating the Chinese population with disease and creating an official, racialized vision of cleanliness and health that justified further regulation. Pippa Holloway's study (2006) of sexual regulation in Virginia similarly examines how legal definitions of acceptable sexual practices served a clear political function. By defining appropriate and inappropriate behavior, and doing so along class, race, and gender lines, politicians determined who was worthy of participating in government.

Immigration is where citizenship is most clearly expressed, of course, and the persistent linkage of citizenship and race has had an enormous effect on each set of categories. Mae Ngai (2004), looking at the numerical limits on immigration imposed by the Johnson-Reed Immigration Act of 1924, describes how the very process of limiting legal immigration produced a category of "illegal immigrants" – a new problem for the state, and one it would solve by expanding the regulatory apparatus. More troublingly, she argues, the statutory preference for immigrants from certain countries essentially racialized how the public perceived who was "legal" and who was not, regardless of their actual citizenship status. In Margot Canaday's study of "the *bureaucratization* of homosexuality," immigration is included among those areas in which the federal government created a binary definition of sexuality (Canaday, 2009: 4). Looking at agencies including the Bureau of Immigration, the military, and the Veterans Administration, Canaday explores how growing administrative capacities gave officials the authority to create and enforce definitions of acceptable (and unacceptable) sexuality. Such definitions had concrete effects on individuals' ability to become citizens and receive benefits and, more broadly, came to define citizenship.

Conclusion

While the richly textured work described above goes far to integrate the administrative state into broader narratives of American history, huge areas of inquiry remain for scholars interested in policy making and state building (Schiller, 2008). The field of civil rights, for example, has begun to consider how activists' encounters with agencies and commissions shaped both civil rights policy and the administrative state. Historians and political scientists have examined agencies specifically focused on the rights of minorities, such as the Fair Employment Practices Committee, the Equal Employment Opportunity Commission, and the Department of Health, Education, and Welfare (Reed, 1991; Kersten, 2000; Graham, 1990; MacLean, 2006). Mary Dudziak (2000) has demonstrated the importance of broadening the inquiry beyond these agencies, given the State Department's role in shaping civil rights policy during the Cold War. Scholars have also considered how, as the federal government entered new areas of American life, it lent legitimacy to local racial, ethnic, and gender protocols and established robust new ones. Thomas Sugrue (2005), in a nuanced discussion of the interrelation of housing and employment discrimination in post-World War II Detroit, emphasizes both the decisions made by government agencies and those made by private actors. Further research is needed on agencies' decisions in the civil rights arena, and here Sophia Z. Lee's research into the NAACP's relationship with the NLRB (2008) and the FCC and Federal Power Commission's role in fair employment policy (2010) offers some guidance. Much remains to be done to understand how institutional bureaucratic pressures have shaped civil rights policy – how, for example, internal pressures and institutional limits affected bureaucratic autonomy in the civil rights realm. It would also be useful to study how regulations established in earlier decades shaped and limited administrators' decision-making capacities and the ability of minority-owned businesses to compete in the marketplace.

More broadly, while significant attention has been devoted to federal economic regulation, additional studies of state-level regulation, and the relationship between federal and state agencies, would help complete our understanding of political economy and the administrative state. So too would more attention to examples of government authority on the outskirts of the state (Radford, 2003). Private voluntary associations and bar associations with symbiotic relationships to various administrative agencies are also ripe for analysis; studies of "iron triangles" and interest networks have touched on experts operating in particular fields (Heclo, 1978), but more focus on these groups could offer insight both into agency politics and into what the "organizational synthesis" has to offer in the years following the Progressive Era (Balogh, 1991b). While some scholars have brought the story of regulation forward into the post-World War II era (Peterson, 1985; Galambos, 1987; Landy and Levin, 1995), and have taken seriously the national security state (Hogan, 1998), the story of political development since World War II remains incomplete. One might examine how the explosion of federal health, safety, and environmental regulation beginning in the late 1960s put new demands on older agencies. Similarly, more research into when agencies and commissions learn from one another and when they clash could turn readers' attention to questions of federalism, expertise, and "path dependence" across the administrative state. Enterprising scholars might also situate the deregulation movement (Derthick and Quirk, 1985) within the growing literature on the rise of the conservative movement, and might question, as Sidney Milkis (1998) has, the role that Americans' concern about a powerful administrative state played in that movement.

References

Arnold, Peri E. (1998). *Making the Managerial Presidency: Comprehensive Reorganization Planning, 1905–1996.* 2nd Revised Edition. University Press of Kansas, Lawrence.

Auerbach, Jerold S. (1976). *Unequal Justice: Lawyers and Social Change in Modern America.* Oxford University Press, New York.

Balogh, Brian (1991a). *Chain Reaction: Expert Debate and Public Participation in American Commercial Nuclear Power, 1945–1975.* Cambridge University Press, Cambridge, UK.

Balogh, Brian (1991b). "Reorganizing the Organizational Synthesis: Federal-Professional Relations in Modern America." *Studies in American Political Development* 5: 119–172.

Balogh, Brian (2009). *A Government Out of Sight: The Mystery of National Authority in Nineteenth-Century America*. Cambridge University Press, Cambridge, UK.

Baughman, James L. (1985). *Television's Guardians: The FCC and the Politics of Programming 1958–1967*. University of Tennessee Press, Knoxville.

Bernstein, Marver H. (1955). *Regulating Business by Independent Commission*. Princeton University Press, Princeton, NJ.

Brazier, James E. (1996). "An Anti-New Dealer Legacy: The Administrative Procedure Act." *Journal of Policy History* 8: 206–226.

Brinkley, Alan (1995). *The End of Reform: New Deal Liberalism in Recession and War*. Alfred A. Knopf, New York.

Brinson, Susan L. (2004). *The Red Scare, Politics, and the Federal Communications Commission, 1941–1960*. Praeger, Westport, CT.

Brock, William R. (1984). *Investigation and Responsibility: Public Responsibility in the United States, 1865–1900*. Cambridge University Press, Cambridge, UK.

Brown, Michael K. (1995). "State Capacity and Political Choice: Interpreting the Failure of the Third New Deal." *Studies in American Political Development* 9: 187–212.

Canaday, Margot (2009). *The Straight State: Sexuality and Citizenship in Twentieth-Century America*. Princeton University Press, Princeton, NJ.

Capozzola, Christopher (2008). *Uncle Sam Wants You: World War I and the Making of the Modern American Citizen*. Oxford University Press, New York.

Carpenter, Daniel P. (2001). *The Forging of Bureaucratic Autonomy: Reputations, Networks, and Policy Innovation in Executive Agencies, 1862–1928*. Princeton University Press, Princeton, NJ.

Chase, William C. (1982). *The American Law School and the Rise of Administrative Government*. University of Wisconsin Press, Madison.

Chin, Gabriel J. (2002). "Regulating Race: Asian Exclusion and the Administrative State." *Harvard Civil Rights-Civil Liberties Law Review* 37: 1–64.

Ciepley, David (2006). *Liberalism in the Shadow of Totalitarianism*. Harvard University Press, Cambridge, MA.

Classen, Steven D. (2004). *Watching Jim Crow: The Struggles over Mississippi TV, 1955–1969*. Duke University Press, Durham, NC.

Clawson, Marion (1981). *New Deal Planning: The National Resources Planning Board*. Resources for the Future, by Johns Hopkins University Press, Baltimore, MD.

Cohen, Lizabeth (2004). *A Consumers' Republic: The Politics of Mass Consumption in Postwar America*. Vintage, New York.

Crenson, Matthew A. (1975). *The Federal Machine: Beginnings of Bureaucracy in Jacksonian America*. Johns Hopkins University Press, Baltimore, MD.

Critchlow, Donald T. and Hawley, Ellis W., eds (1988). *Federal Social Policy: The Historical Dimension*. Pennsylvania State University Press, University Park.

Davis, Martha F. (1993). *Brutal Need: Lawyers and the Welfare Rights Movement, 1960–1973*. Yale University Press, New Haven.

Derthick, Martha, and Quirk, Paul J. (1985). *The Politics of Deregulation.* Brookings Institution, Washington, DC.
Dudziak, Mary L. (2000). *Cold War Civil Rights: Race and the Image of American Democracy.* Princeton University Press, Princeton, NJ.
Ernst, Daniel R. (1998). "Law and American Political Development, 1877–1938." *Reviews in American History* 26: 205–219.
Ernst, Daniel R. (2002). "The Ideal and the Actual in the State: Willard Hurst at the Board of Economic Welfare." In Ernst and Jew, eds, *Total War and the Law: The American Home Front in World War II,* 149–183. Praeger, Westport, CT.
Ernst, Daniel R. (2008). "*Morgan* and the New Dealers." *Journal of Policy History* 20: 447–481.
Ernst, Daniel R. (2009). "The Politics of Administrative Law: New York's Anti-Bureaucracy Clause and the O'Brian-Wagner Campaign of 1938." *Law and History Review* 27: 331–372.
Finegold, Kenneth, and Skocpol, Theda (1995). *State and Party in America's New Deal.* University of Wisconsin Press, Madison.
Galambos, Louis (1970). "The Emerging Organizational Synthesis in Modern American History." *Business History Review* 44: 279–290.
Galambos, Louis (1983). "Technology, Political Economy, and Professionalization: Central Themes of the Organizational Synthesis." *Business History Review* 57: 471–493.
Galambos, Louis, ed. (1987). *The New American State: Bureaucracies and Policies since World War II.* Johns Hopkins University Press, Baltimore, MD.
Goluboff, Risa L. (2007). *The Lost Promise of Civil Rights.* Harvard University Press, Cambridge, MA.
Gordon, Linda (1994). *Pitied But Not Entitled: Single Mothers and the History of Welfare 1890–1935.* Free Press, New York.
Graham, Hugh Davis (1990). *The Civil Rights Era: Origins and Development of National Policy, 1960–1972.* Oxford University Press, New York.
Grisinger, Joanna (2008). "Law in Action: The Attorney General's Committee on Administrative Procedure." *Journal of Policy History* 20: 379–418.
Gross, James A. (1974). *The Making of the National Labor Relations Board: A Study in Economics, Politics, and the Law, 1933–1937.* State University of New York Press, Albany.
Gross, James A. (1981). *The Reshaping of the National Labor Relations Board: National Labor Policy in Transition, 1937–1947.* State University of New York Press, Albany.
Gross, James A. (1995). *Broken Promise: The Subversion of U.S. Labor Relations Policy, 1947–1994.* Temple University Press, Philadelphia.
Harris, Richard A. and Milkis, Sidney M. (1996). *The Politics of Regulatory Change: A Tale of Two Agencies.* 2nd Edition. Oxford University Press, New York.
Hays, Samuel P. (1980). *American Political History as Social Analysis: Essays.* University of Tennessee Press, Knoxville.
Heclo, Hugh (1978). "Issue Networks and the Executive Establishment." In King, ed., *The New American Political System,* 87–124. The American Enterprise Institute for Public Policy Research, Washington, DC.

Hogan, Michael J. (1998). *A Cross of Iron: Harry S. Truman and the Origins of the National Security State, 1945–1954.* Cambridge University Press, Cambridge, UK.

Holloway, Pippa (2006). *Sexuality, Politics, and Social Control in Virginia, 1920–1945.* University of North Carolina Press, Chapel Hill.

Horwitz, Morton J. (1992). *The Transformation of American Law, 1870–1960: The Crisis of Legal Orthodoxy.* Oxford University Press, New York.

Irons, Peter H. (1982). *The New Deal Lawyers.* Princeton University Press, Princeton, NJ.

Jacobs, Meg (2005). *Pocketbook Politics: Economic Citizenship in Twentieth-Century America.* Princeton University Press, Princeton, NJ.

Johnson, David K. (2004). *The Lavender Scare: The Cold War Persecution of Gays and Lesbians in the Federal Government.* University of Chicago Press, Chicago.

Kalman, Laura (1990). *Abe Fortas: A Biography.* Yale University Press, New Haven, CT.

Karl, Barry D. (1963). *Executive Reorganization and Reform in the New Deal: The Genesis of Administrative Management, 1900–1939.* Harvard University Press, Cambridge, MA.

Karl, Barry D. (1983). *The Uneasy State: The United States from 1915 to 1945.* University of Chicago Press, Chicago.

Katz, Michael B. (1986). *In the Shadow of the Poorhouse: A Social History of Welfare in America.* Basic Books, New York.

Katz, Michael B. (2001). *The Price of Citizenship: Redefining the American Welfare State.* Metropolitan Books, New York.

Katznelson, Ira and Pietrykowski, Bruce (1991). "Rebuilding the American State: Evidence from the 1940s." *Studies in American Political Development* 5: 301–339.

Keller, Morton (1990). *Regulating a New Economy: Public Policy and Economic Change in America, 1900–1933.* Harvard University Press, Cambridge, MA.

Keller, Morton (1994). *Regulating a New Society: Public Policy and Social Change in America, 1900–1933.* Harvard University Press, Cambridge, MA.

Kersten, Andrew Edmund (2000). *Race, Jobs, and the War: The FEPC in the Midwest, 1941–46.* University of Illinois Press, Urbana.

King, Desmond S. (2007). *Separate and Unequal: African Americans and the US Federal Government.* Revised Edition. Oxford University Press, Oxford.

Kolko, Gabriel (1963). *The Triumph of Conservatism: A Reinterpretation of American History, 1900–1916.* Free Press of Glencoe, New York.

Kolko, Gabriel (1965). *Railroads and Regulation, 1877–1916.* Princeton University Press, Princeton, NJ.

Kornbluh, Felicia (2007). *The Battle for Welfare Rights: Politics and Poverty in Modern America.* University of Pennsylvania Press, Philadelphia.

Krasnow, Erwin G. and Longley, Lawrence D. (1978). *The Politics of Broadcast Regulation.* 2nd Edition. St. Martin's Press, New York.

Kutler, Stanley (1982). *The American Inquisition: Justice and Injustice in the Cold War.* Hill and Wang, New York.

Landy, Marc K., Roberts, Marc J., and Thomas, Stephen R. (1994). *The Environmental Protection Agency: Asking the Wrong Questions from Nixon to Clinton.* Exp. Edition. Oxford University Press, New York.

Landy, Marc K. and Levin, Martin A., eds (1995). *The New Politics of Public Policy.* Johns Hopkins University Press, Baltimore, MD.

Lee, Sophia Z. (2008). "Hotspots in a Cold War: The NAACP's Postwar Workplace Constitutionalism, 1948–1964." *Law and History Review* 26: 327–377.

Lee, Sophia Z. (2010). "Race, Sex, and Rulemaking: Administrative Constitutionalism and the Workplace, 1960 to the Present." *Virginia Law Review* 96: 799–886.

Lees, Martha A. (1994). "Preserving Property Values? Preserving Proper Homes? Preserving Privilege?: The Pre-*Euclid* Debate over Zoning for Exclusively Private Residential Areas, 1916–1926." *University of Pittsburgh Law Review* 56: 367–439.

Lombardo, Paul A. (2008). *Three Generations, No Imbeciles: Eugenics, the Supreme Court, and* Buck v. Bell. Johns Hopkins University Press, Baltimore, MD.

Lowi, Theodore J. (1979). *The End of Liberalism: The Second Republic of the United States.* 2nd Edition. W.W. Norton, New York.

Lowi, Theodore J. (1987). "Two Roads to Serfdom: Liberalism, Conservatism and Administrative Power." *American University Law Review* 36: 295–322.

MacLean, Nancy (2006). *Freedom Is Not Enough: The Opening of the American Workplace.* Harvard University Press, Cambridge, MA.

Mashaw, Jerry L. (2006). "Recovering American Administrative Law: Federalist Foundations, 1787–1801." *Yale Law Journal* 115: 1256–1344.

Mashaw, Jerry L. (2007). "Reluctant Nationalists: Federal Administration and Administrative Law in the Republican Era, 1801–1829." *Yale Law Journal* 116: 1636–1741.

Mashaw, Jerry L. (2008). "Administration and 'The Democracy': Administrative Law from Jackson to Lincoln, 1829–1861." *Yale Law Journal* 117: 1568–1693.

Mashaw, Jerry L. (2010). "Federal Administration and Administrative Law in the Gilded Age." *Yale Law Journal* 119: 1362–1473.

Mashaw, Jerry L. and Harfst, David L. (1990). *The Struggle for Auto Safety.* Harvard University Press, Cambridge, MA.

Mashaw, Jerry L. and Perry, Avi (2009). "Administrative Statutory Interpretation in the Antebellum Republic." *Michigan State Law Review* 2009: 7–50.

McCraw, Thomas K. (1975). "Regulation in America: A Review Article." *Business History Review* 49: 159–183.

McCraw, Thomas K. (1984). *Prophets of Regulation: Charles Francis Adams, Louis D. Brandeis, James M. Landis, Alfred E. Kahn.* Belknap Press of Harvard University Press, Cambridge, MA.

McCubbins, Mathew D., Noll, Roger G. and Weingast, Barry R. (1999). "The Political Origins of the Administrative Procedure Act." *Journal of Law, Economics, and Organization* 15: 180–217.

Mehrotra, Ajay K. (2008). "Forging Fiscal Reform: Constitutional Change, Public Policy, and the Creation of Administrative Capacity in Wisconsin, 1880–1920." *Journal of Policy History* 20: 94–112.

Merrill, Thomas W. (1997). "Capture Theory and the Courts: 1967–1983." *Chicago-Kent Law Review* 72: 1039–1117.

Mettler, Suzanne (1998). *Dividing Citizens: Gender and Federalism in New Deal Public Policy.* Cornell University Press, Ithaca, NY.

Milkis, Sidney M. (1998). "Remaking Government Institutions in the 1970s: Participatory Democracy and the Triumph of Administrative Politics." *Journal of Policy History* 10: 51–74.

Milkis, Sidney M. (1993). *The President and the Parties: The Transformation of the American Party System since the New Deal.* Oxford University Press, New York.

Mills, Kay (2004). *Changing Channels: The Civil Rights Case that Transformed Television.* University Press of Mississippi, Jackson, MS.

Moss, David A. and Fein, Michael R. (2003). "Radio Regulation Revisited: Coase, the FCC, and the Public Interest." *Journal of Policy History* 15: 389–416.

Muller, Eric L. (2007). *American Inquisition: The Hunt for Japanese American Disloyalty in World War II.* University of North Carolina Press, Chapel Hill.

Nelson, William E. (1982). *The Roots of American Bureaucracy, 1830–1900.* Harvard University Press, Cambridge, MA.

Ngai, Mae M. (2004). *Impossible Subjects: Illegal Aliens and the Making of Modern America.* Princeton University Press, Princeton, NJ.

Novak, William J. (1996). *The People's Welfare: Law and Regulation in Nineteenth-Century America.* University of North Carolina Press, Chapel Hill.

Parrish, Michael E. (1970). *Securities Regulation and the New Deal.* Yale University Press, New Haven, CT.

Peterson, Gale E. (1985). *President Harry S. Truman and the Independent Regulatory Commissions, 1945–1952.* Garland Publishing, Inc., New York.

Polenberg, Richard (1966). *Reorganizing Roosevelt's Government: The Controversy over Executive Reorganization 1936–1939.* Harvard University Press, Cambridge, MA.

Polsky, Andrew J. (1991). *The Rise of the Therapeutic State.* Princeton University Press, Princeton, NJ.

Rabin, Robert L. (1986). "Federal Regulation in Historical Perspective." *Stanford Law Review* 38: 1189–1326.

Radford, Gail (2003). "From Municipal Socialism to Public Authorities: Institutional Factors in the Shaping of American Public Enterprise." *Journal of American History* 90: 863–890.

Rao, Gautham (2008). "The Federal *Posse Comitatus* Doctrine: Slavery, Compulsion, and Statecraft in Mid-Nineteenth-Century America." *Law and History Review* 26: 1–56.

Reed, Merl Elwyn (1991). *Seedtime for the Modern Civil Rights Movement: The President's Committee on Fair Employment Practice, 1941–1946.* Louisiana State University Press, Baton Rouge.

Rohr, John A. (1986). *To Run a Constitution: The Legitimacy of the Administrative State.* University Press of Kansas, Lawrence.

Rung, Margaret C. (2002). *Servants of the State: Managing Diversity & Democracy in the Federal Workforce, 1933–1953.* University of Georgia Press, Athens.

Salyer, Lucy E. (1995). *Laws Harsh as Tigers: Chinese Immigrants and the Shaping of Modern Immigration Law.* University of North Carolina Press, Chapel Hill.

Schiller, Reuel E. (2000). "Enlarging the Administrative Polity: Administrative Law and the Changing Definition of Pluralism, 1945–1970." *Vanderbilt Law Review* 53: 1389–1453.

Schiller, Reuel E. (2001). "Rulemaking's Promise: Administrative Law and Legal Culture in the 1960s and 1970s." *Administrative Law Review* 53: 1139–1188.

Schiller, Reuel E. (2002). "Reining in the Administrative State: World War II and the Decline of Expert Administration." In Ernst and Jew, eds, *Total War and the Law: The American Home Front in World War II*. Praeger, Westport, CT.

Schiller, Reuel E. (2005). "'Saint George and the Dragon': Courts and the Development of the Administrative State in Twentieth-Century America." *Journal of Policy History* 17: 110–124.

Schiller, Reuel E. (2007). "The Era of Deference: Courts, Expertise, and the Emergence of New Deal Administrative Law." *Michigan Law Review* 106: 399–442.

Schiller, Reuel E. (2008). "The Administrative State, Front and Center: Studying Law and Administration in Postwar America." *Law and History Review* 26: 415–427.

Shah, Nayan (2001). *Contagious Divides: Epidemics and Race in San Francisco's Chinatown*. University of California Press, Berkeley.

Shamir, Ronen (1995). *Managing Legal Uncertainty: Elite Lawyers in the New Deal*. Duke University Press, Durham, NC.

Shepherd, George B. (1996). "Fierce Compromise: The Administrative Procedure Act Emerges from New Deal Politics." *Northwestern University Law Review* 90: 1557–1683.

Sklar, Martin J. (1988). *The Corporate Reconstruction of American Capitalism, 1890–1916: The Market, the Law, and Politics*. Cambridge University Press, Cambridge, UK.

Skowronek, Stephen (1982). *Building a New American State: The Expansion of National Administrative Capacities, 1877–1920*. Cambridge University Press, Cambridge, UK.

Steffes, Tracy L. (2008). "Solving the 'Rural School Problem': New State Aid, Standards, and Supervision of Local Schools, 1900–1933." *History of Education Quarterly* 48: 181–220.

Stivers, Camilla (2000). *Bureau Men, Settlement Women: Constructing Public Administration in the Progressive Era*. University Press of Kansas, Lawrence.

Stewart, Richard B. (1975). "The Reformation of American Administrative Law." *Harvard Law Review* 88: 1667–1813.

Sugrue, Thomas J. (2005). *The Origins of the Urban Crisis: Race and Inequality in Postwar Detroit*. Revised Edition. Princeton University Press, Princeton, NJ.

Tani, Karen M. (2008). "*Flemming v. Nestor*: Anticommunism, the Welfare State, and the Making of 'New Property.'" *Law and History Review* 26: 379–414.

Teaford, Jon C. (2002). *The Rise of the States: Evolution of American State Government*. Johns Hopkins University Press, Baltimore, MD.

Thomas, Jr., William H. (2008). *Unsafe for Democracy: World War I and the U.S. Justice Department's Covert Campaign to Suppress Dissent*. University of Wisconsin Press, Madison, WI.

Tomlins, Christopher L. (1985). *The State and the Unions: Labor Relations, Law, and the Organized Labor Movement in America, 1880–1960*. Cambridge University Press, Cambridge, UK.

Tyack, David B., James, Thomas, and Benavot, Aaron (1987). *Law and the Shaping of Public Education, 1785–1954*. University of Wisconsin Press, Madison.

Wang, Jessica (2005). "Imagining the Administrative State: Legal Pragmatism, Securities Regulation, and New Deal Liberalism." *Journal of Policy History* 17: 257–293.

Welke, Barbara Young (2001). *Recasting American Liberty: Gender, Race, Law, and the Railroad Revolution, 1865–1920*. Cambridge University Press, Cambridge, UK.

White, G. Edward (2000). "The Emergence of Agency Government and the Creation of Administrative Law." In *The Constitution and the New Deal*, 94–127. Harvard University Press, Cambridge, MA.

Wiebe, Robert H. (1967). *The Search for Order, 1877–1920*. Hill and Wang, New York.

Willrich, Michael (2003). *City of Courts: Socializing Justice in Progressive Era Chicago*. Cambridge University Press, Cambridge, UK.

Wilson, James Q. ed. (1980). *The Politics of Regulation*. Basic Books, New York.

Wolf, Michael Allan (2008). *The Zoning of America: Euclid v. Ambler*. University Press of Kansas, Lawrence.

Woolhandler, Ann (1991). "Judicial Deference to Administrative Action – A Revisionist History." *Administrative Law Review* 43: 197–245.

Zelizer, Julian E. (2000). "Clio's Lost Tribe: Public Policy History Since 1978." *Journal of Policy History* 12: 369–394.

Zeppos, Nicholas S. (1997). "The Legal Profession and the Development of Administrative Law." *Chicago-Kent Law Review* 72: 1119–1157.

Chapter Twenty

Law and Religion

Steven K. Green

Historians have been writing about church-state arrangements in America since Cotton Mather penned his apology for the New England Puritan commonwealths, *Magnalia Christi Americana*, in 1697. Like other areas of legal history, the scholarship regarding the interaction of law and religion has been broad and diverse. Because the topic attracts scholars from multiple disciplines – religious history, sociology of religion, church and state, early American history, political science, and the law – it is not the sole purview of legal historians. And because scholars commonly write in specific disciplines, it frequently is difficult to keep abreast of scholarship being produced in related fields. In addition, each discipline has its own approach to questions concerning law and religion in American history. Is it best approached through a study of religious movements and conflicts, of social and cultural interactions, as a subset of political development, or chiefly as a legal/constitutional question? Finally, the scholarship on law and religion has not been immune to ideological interpretations or polemical treatises. Questions regarding the interaction of law and religion have always had political and legal ramifications. As Justice Wiley Rutledge remarked in 1947, "No provision of the Constitution is more tied to or given content by its generating history than the religious clause of the First Amendment" (*Everson v. Board of Education*, 330 U.S. 1, 33 (1947)).

That said, the scholarly study of law and religion has generally fallen into four eras: the colonial period; the founding period; the nineteenth century; and the twentieth century. Situated at the core of each era are those issues that involve more conventional church-state questions: Did the New

---

A Companion to American Legal History, First Edition.
Edited by Sally E. Hadden and Alfred L. Brophy.
© 2013 John Wiley & Sons Ltd. Published 2021 by John Wiley & Sons Ltd.

England Puritans maintain a theocracy? What was the nature of the religious establishments in the remaining colonies? What did disestablishment mean to the members of the founding generation? How does one explain the informal "Protestant establishment" of the nineteenth century? Are the post-incorporation decisions of the Supreme Court on church and state consistent with the nation's legal and religious traditions? And what role should "originalism" play in Court adjudication? While scholarship on these and related questions could fill many bookshelves, the constitutional issues of church and state only touch the surface of this broad field. Scholars have recognized that the history of law and religion involves other questions, *viz*: How did notions of higher law influence developing attitudes about the mutability of the law? What role did the British common law's recognition of Christian tenets ("Christianity is part of the common law") play in the adaption of the common law in America? How did disestablishment impact the organization and polity of churches and religious charities? And how did religious customs and practices influence the development of legal areas such as probate and divorce law? Because the law and religion are both cultural and social constructs – and, to an extent, represent two of the more important institutions of any society – each entity has frequently influenced the development of the other in addition to impacting the culture as a whole.

General Studies and Approaches

Considered historiographically, the earlier studies about the interaction of law and religion in American history reflected a conventional church-state approach: tracing the evolution of religious liberty and disestablishment in the American colonies, the early states, and at the national level. These studies concentrated on the rise of colonial charters with their church-state regimes, the creation of the religious liberty provisions in the state and federal constitutions, and those laws that reinforced or modified formal church-state relationships. Overall, these earlier works were uncritical, describing the regime of American church-state relations in progressive and glowing terms (absent criticizing the religious intolerance of the Puritans). This was because the United States was the first nation to disestablish state religions, an event Americans proudly associated with democratic and liberal values. At the same time, nineteenth-century historians emphasized the religiosity of American citizens and institutions, in contradistinction to the emerging secularism of Europe. One such work was Philip Schaff's *Church and State in the United States* (1888), which set out to establish the superiority of the American church-state experience over all others. Schaff, a Swiss academic who had immigrated to the United States in mid-century, wrote as much for European audiences as for those in America. Schaff's work was followed by Isaac A. Cornelison's *The Relation of Religion to Civil*

Government (1895), Sanford H. Cobb's *The Rise of Religious Liberty in America: A History* (1902), and Carl Zollmann's *American Civil Church Law* (1917). Like Schaff's work, these later books had a hagiographic quality, and all sought to demonstrate that American notions of church-state separation did not preclude government support of religion (i.e., Christianity) or that separation implied that Americans were an irreligious people. The subtitle to Cornelison's book was revealing: American was "A State Without a Church, but not Without a Religion." These early histories reflected the then prevailing view that the law and Christianity were mutually reinforcing. That perspective was demonstrated in Zollmann's book:

> Christianity is not the legal religion of the state as established by law ... but this is not inconsistent with the idea that it is in fact and ever has been the religion of the people. ... A distinction must therefore be made between a religion preferred by law and a religion preferred by the people without the coercion of the law, between a legal establishment and a religious creed freely chosen by the people themselves. (Zollmann, 1917: 12–13)

These early works set the pattern for church-state histories into the twentieth century. Most focused on the colonial and founding periods with little attention being afforded the nineteenth century, other than to examine the church-state conflicts between the federal government and the Mormon Church. One exception to that pattern was Alvin W. Johnson's *The Legal Status of Church-State Relationships in the United States* (1934), which discussed legal developments of the nineteenth and early twentieth centuries thematically: Bible reading in the public schools; the teaching of evolution in the schools; state aid to religious schools; and Sunday law regulations. Still, like most histories written through mid-century, Johnson's book concentrated on legal doctrines and processes – constitutions, statutes, judicial decisions – at the expense of cultural considerations. The most comprehensive work on church-state interactions written in the mid-twentieth century is undoubtedly Anson Phelps Stokes' massive *Church and State in the United States* (1950). This three-volume work is the most detailed study of not only church-state relations but of religious influences on the law generally. Stokes' work remains an indispensable resource, despite a thematic organization that defies chronology. In 1964, historian and lawyer Leo Pfeffer produced a one-volume abridgement, giving the work a more separationist approach that reflected Pfeffer's ideological perspective (Stokes and Pfeffer, 1964).

The most significant development that occurred in church-state scholarship at mid-century was a shift in ideological perspective. Responding in part to the growing secularization of American culture and the Supreme Court's early church-state decisions reflecting a "separationist" approach, historical scholarship generally followed suit. Works remained hagiographic to a degree, but now they emphasized the heroic efforts of the Framers to disentangle religion from government. Scholarship of the middle-twentieth century also frequently affirmed the "secularization thesis" – that the regime of church-state separation instituted by the Founders led to the gradual secularization of the culture (Blau, 1949; Butts, 1950; Pfeffer, 1953).

The standard separationist interpretation to church-state history, with its secularization thesis, came under attack beginning in the 1970s. This critique was spurred in part by a conservative reaction to the high court's separationist holdings, in particular its school prayer decisions of 1962–1963 and its seminal holding of *Lemon v. Kurtzman* (1971) prohibiting public aid to religious schools. The revisionist scholarship also coincided with a rise in studies about the founding period that was inspired by the nation's bicentennial. An important revisionist critique that predated the 1970s was Mark deWolfe Howe's *The Garden and the Wilderness: Religion and Government in American Constitutional History* (1965), which challenged the standard interpretation that the Founders intended to adopt a Jeffersonian-Enlightenment model of strict church-state separation. Howe argued that the Court and many historians had "erred in disregarding the theological roots of the American principle of separation," which was more accurately reflected in Roger Williams' religious "philosophy than that of Jefferson's." Howe's influential book inspired a new generation of scholarship which, in examining early statutes, speeches, correspondence, and sermons, maintained that members of the founding generation intended religion and the law to be mutually reinforcing. Representative works include: Michael J. Malbin, *Religion and Politics: The Intentions of the Authors of the First Amendment* (1978); Robert L. Cord, *Separation of Church and State: Historical Fact and Current Fiction* (1982); and Gerard V. Bradley, *Church-State Relationships in America* (1987). This "accommodationist" interpretation of church-state history soon found a receptive audience among the more conservative justices of the Rehnquist and Roberts Courts. Since the 1980s, the ideological divisions in church-state history have tended to reflect either the separationist or accommodationist perspectives.

More recent general studies of church-state development include: John Witte, Jr. and Joel A. Nichols, *Religion and the American Constitutional Experiment* (2011) and Kent Greenawalt, *Religion and the Constitution* (2006, 2008). An additional resource is *Religion and American Law: An Encyclopedia* (2000), edited by Paul Finkelman. A dated, but still useful resource is *Church and State in America: A Bibliographical Guide* (1986), edited by John F. Wilson.

Although conventional church-state studies that emphasize constitutional issues continue to dominate scholarship about law and religion, an alternative approach emerged in the 1970s, inspired chiefly by Harold Berman, a professor at Harvard and Emory law schools. Termed the "Law and Religion" movement, this approach examines the way in which religion and law have interacted historically and how they have influenced each other's development, often on a practical level. These scholars seek to demonstrate that the levels of interaction between law and religion have been much deeper, and more lasting, than is acknowledged under the standard church-state approach with its constitutional emphasis. Explaining this alternative approach in 1974, Berman wrote that both historically and currently, "law and religion share certain elements, namely ritual, tradition, authority, and universality." The "main theme is that our basic legal concepts and institutions derive much of their meaning from a historical development in which religion had played a major part." The law and religion approach also contains a normative aspect:

> [L]aw and religion ... need each other – law to give religion its social dimension and religion to give law its spirit and direction as well as the sanctity it needs to command respect. Where they are divorced from each other, law tends to degenerate into legalism and religion into religiosity. (Berman, 1974: 13–14, 25)

This broader approach to the history of law and religion has encouraged scholarship on non-constitutional topics such as the religious influences on the development of domestic and probate law. Berman's work inspired a generation of scholars and led to the founding of the *Journal of Law and Religion* and the Center for the Study of Law and Religion at Emory University Law School (Berman, 1983; Witte and Alexander, 1988).

The remainder of this chapter considers developments and scholarship about law and religion under various historical periods.

Colonial Era

The religious aspect to the founding of the British-American colonies is a persistent and important theme in U.S. history. Religion was a significant motivating factor behind the settlement of many of the colonies, not solely the Puritan commonwealths of New England. Some settlers fled religious persecution in Europe, while others sought merely to enhance their opportunities for religious expression. Numerically, dissenters from the Church of England constituted the majority of colonial residents by the early eighteenth century. British Calvinists – Independents (Puritans) and Separatists (Pilgrims) – settled New England, Catholics organized Maryland, Dutch Reformed established New Amsterdam (New York), Quakers established Pennsylvania, and Baptists, Jews and heretics of various stripes sought refuge in Rhode Island. In the southern colonies, French Huguenots (Protestants) and Jews found sanctuary in Charleston, South Carolina, while Mennonites, Moravians and Quakers settled in the Piedmont of North Carolina. Despite this strong impulse for enhanced religious freedom, most colonial governments created religious establishments and afforded limited toleration to dissenting faiths – Pennsylvania and Rhode Island excepted. Officially recognized religion with financial support from and regulation by the state was the chief model that Europe offered, and the colonies responded accordingly. In addition to providing tax support for the established Church of England (southern colonies) or for sanctioned Protestant churches (elsewhere), colonial assemblies regularly intervened in church affairs, such as organizing parishes and mandating the teaching of certain church doctrines. One's ability to hold public office and participate in civic affairs often turned on religious affiliation, as well. The legal relationships with religion did not end with the establishments, however. All of the colonies, even those without official establishments, adopted laws regulating behavior, for example, Sabbath attendance, swearing and blasphemy, gambling, drunkenness, sexual promiscuity. As Perry Miller and David Flaherty have demonstrated, behavioral codes reflected the prevailing societal attitude toward morality and did not necessarily turn on the religious fervor of the local governments. Nonetheless, these laws retained a strong religious basis and reinforced Christian values in the society (Miller, 1956; Flaherty, 1978).

The Puritan commonwealths of New England have dominated study of the colonial period, even outside the field of legal history. To a degree, this attention is deserved, as the Puritans, believing themselves to be a "called" or "chosen" people, thought about matters of church and state more than any other group. As a result, the scholarship on the religious and legal relationships in New England is quite rich. The bulk of scholarship, particularly that written in the mid-twentieth century, frequently discussed church-state interactions as part of larger cultural, social or intellectual engagements, such as Perry Miller's two-volume *The New England Mind* (1939, 1953) and William McLoughlin's two-volume *New England Dissent* (1971). Other authors have examined these issues in works exploring the organization and structure of Puritan society, including Edmund S. Morgan's *The Puritan Dilemma* (1958). A popular area of scholarship for considering church-state conflicts in colonial New England has been Roger William's establishment of Rhode Island as a haven for religious freedom. Williams not only organized the first colony in America without a religious establishment; he also engaged John Cotton and other Puritan leaders in an ongoing debate over the appropriate relationship between the sacred and profane realms. Williams articulated the precursor to a "wall of separation between church and state" with his metaphor of a "hedge or wall of Separation between the Garden of the Church and the Wilderness of the World" (Gaustad, 1991: 43).

Discussions of legal-religious interactions also appear in general histories of New England. The Puritan commonwealths, particularly Massachusetts Bay, were the first colonies to adopt comprehensive legal codes. Because of their religious proclivities, the Puritans looked to the Bible – in particular the Pentateuch – as a chief source of legal authority. George Lee Haskins' *Law and Authority in Early Massachusetts* (1960) remains an indispensable source on the evolution of the law and legal institutions in seventeenth-century Massachusetts and contains an extensive discussion of the development of the early Mosaic-based legal codes. Haskins maintained that the Massachusetts codes influenced legal development in other colonies, not only those in New England, notwithstanding their strong religious content. More recent studies relying on local court records have confirmed the importance of Puritan thought on legal development generally, not solely on criminal and behavioral laws, but in areas of property rights, inheritance, and domestic relations.

A large body of scholarship has traced the legal-religious relationships in the remaining colonies. Again, most have been conventional church-state histories, emphasizing the rise and fall of the colonial establishments, plus related legal developments. One frequently cited work, including by members of the Supreme Court, is Thomas J. Curry's *The First Freedoms: Church and State in America to the Passage of the Frist Amendment* (1986). Curry's work discusses church-state developments in the colonies by periods and regions, and it has become a leading resource on the topic. Another important study, one that examines the ongoing controversy between the Church of England and dissenting churches in colonial America, is Carl Bridenbaugh's *Mitre and Sceptre* (1962). A recurring theme in the literature has been to explain the impetus for colonial disestablishment and the transition from religious toleration to religious liberty. Evolving notions of freedom of conscience and disestablishment – and the extent to which these developments reflected a transition from a religious to a secular worldview among the Founders – remains contested ground among scholars. Two recent works that discuss the evolution of these concepts in the colonies are Frank Lambert's *The Founding Fathers and the Place of Religion in America* (2003) and Chris Beneke's *Beyond Toleration: The Religious Origins of American Pluralism* (2006). Additional areas of scholarly debate involve the extent to which late-Puritan thought and the democratizing impulse of the spiritual Great Awakening (1740s) influenced the development of republican thought leading up to the American Revolution. Understandably, this question has frequently been the domain of religious and intellectual historians, notwithstanding its implications for constitutional and legal history.

Founding Period

Literature on the religious aspects of the founding is similarly immense. Scholarship has ranged from general studies on the religious influences on republican theory and constitutional development to specific works on disestablishment at the state and federal levels. Scholars have long been interested in identifying the ideological basis for the republican principles that informed the nation's constitutional and legal systems. Two indispensable studies are Bernard Bailyn's *The Ideological Origins of the American Revolution* (1967) and Gordon S. Wood's *The Creation of the American Republic* (1969). While both intellectual histories examine a broad range of philosophical and political impulses that informed republican thought – classical, Whig, Enlightenment, the common law – both contain extensive discussions of the religious influences on conceptions of law and government during the founding period. All subsequent histories examining the ideological bases of the founding have built on these works. The majority of scholars acknowledge that the Founders relied on a variety of philosophical and political traditions in crafting the nation's government; where they diverge is over which traditions to emphasize over others. Works that see a greater role of religion in the political and legal developments leading up to constitutional formation include Ellis Sandoz, *A Government of Laws* (1990) and Barry Alan Shain, *The Myth of American Individualism: The Protestant Origins of American Political Thought* (1994). Such works commonly emphasize the influence of religious covenants/compacts and higher law on members of the founding generation. At the same time, these works usually minimize the impact of secular Enlightenment thought during the founding period or see a larger religious aspect to the political theories upon which the Founders relied.

The impetus for constitutional disestablishment at the state and national levels has attracted much scholarly interest. Each of the thirteen colonies had its own existing church-state arrangement and went through its own process of disentangling its legal and religious regimes. Thomas Curry's *The First Freedoms* (1986) provides an overview of that process on a state-by-state basis. Disestablishment occurred relatively easily in those colonies that had maintained weak establishments and had greater religious diversity – for example, North Carolina and New York. Attempts to continue the public support of religion in a handful of other states – Maryland, South Carolina, Georgia – were quickly frustrated by apathy and popular resistance to taxation. These episodes have received some attention, but scholarship has focused on those states where establishments were more entrenched or dismantling them was more contentious. Virginia, more than any other state, has been the subject of much study. This is because Virginia was home to three leading reformers of church-state matters, Jefferson, Madison, and George Mason, and to other leading political figures of the day, such as George Washington and Patrick Henry. Also, Virginia's struggle over disestablishment took place in the years immediately preceding the drafting of the Constitution, which many have argued provides insight into contemporary understandings of the First Amendment. From 1785–1786, the Virginia assembly considered creating a system of non-preferential support of religion, an effort that was scuttled chiefly through the efforts of

Madison, who is also given credit for drafting the First Amendment. The beginning place for study of the Virginia struggle remains Thomas E. Buckley's *Church and State in Revolutionary Virginia, 1776–1787* (1977), although the episode is covered in many general histories as well. In contrast to the other states, New England states resisted dismantling their church-state arrangements, with Massachusetts and New Hampshire inserting provisions for the public support of religion (i.e., Protestant churches) in their revolutionary constitutions (Connecticut initially retained its Charter rather than drafting a constitution). Disestablishment did not occur in New England until the early nineteenth century, with Massachusetts finally succumbing in 1833. Formal disestablishment did not end the relationships between religion and the law, however. Even disestablished states such as Pennsylvania retained laws regulating Sabbath behavior and religious tests for public office holding and for forms of civic participation.

Scholarship on disestablishment at the national level is similarly extensive, with historians exploring several related questions: Upon what experiences and models did the Founders draw in drafting the religion clauses and prohibiting religious tests for federal office holding? What was the prevailing understanding of free exercise and religious conscience, particularly whether it exempted religious conduct from being subject to general laws? Did the Founders understand disestablishment to prohibit all support and favoritism of religion or only the preferential support of one denomination over others? Is the Establishment Clause a statement about federalism, in that the Founders intended to prohibit only a national church and not interfere with state religious arrangements? How did the Founders see religion as interacting with government institutions, and vice versa? Leading the more separationist accounts are works by Leo Pfeffer (1953) and Leonard Levy (1986). Arguments that the prevailing perspective among the Founders was more accommodating of religion are represented by the works of Robert Cord (1982), Gerard Bradley (1987), and Daniel Dreisbach (2002), among others. Works discussing the federalism interpretation of the Establishment Clause include Donald L. Drakeman, *Church, State, and Original Intent* (2010) and Steven Smith, *Foreordained Failure* (1995).

An important addition to the literature about the founding period is Derek Davis' *Religion and the Continental Congress, 1774–1789* (2000), which explores the events leading up to the drafting of the First Amendment at the national level. Davis argues that while the actions of the Continental Congresses concerning religious matters – appointing chaplains and declaring days of thanksgiving, for example – reflected prevailing attitudes in the newly emerging states (the majority of which maintained establishments at that time), one sees an evolution in attitudes toward church-state relations that laid the foundation for greater religious liberty and disestablishment at the state and national levels. Another important contribution to the founding literature is Mark Douglas McGarvie's *One Nation Under Law* (2004), which argues that the Contract Clause of the Constitution was instrumental in bringing about disestablishment, in that it helped transform churches from public institutions into private, voluntary associations. This change in legal status, according to McGarvie, influenced the way in which people perceived the public role of churches and of religion generally. A final significant addition to the scholarship on the founding is Frank Lambert's *The Founding Fathers and the Place of Religion in America* (2003), which argues that avoiding sectarian strife was a leading concern of the Founders. This in turn led them to embrace a free-market theory of religion, which then affected attitudes toward religious equality and church-state separation.

Nineteenth Century

Until recently, church-state historians have overlooked the nineteenth century, focusing instead on the colonial and founding periods. This is a shame, as it is a rich field that has been examined by legal, religious and cultural historians for some time. The issues raised by the interaction of law and religion during the nineteenth century are interesting and diverse, chiefly because American law was in its developmental stage while American religion was being transformed by evangelicalism, experimentalism, and immigration. How did disestablishment at the national and state levels impact the development of nineteenth-century culture? How is disestablishment reconciled with the de facto Protestant establishment that arose early in the century and dominated American culture into the 1920s? More particularly, how did disestablishment impact specific legal fields, such as the law governing religious and charitable institutions? What did the gradual professionalization and systemization of the law suggest about evolving legal attitudes toward the relationship between law and religion? In addition to these thematic questions, several important events occurred during the nineteenth century that not only impacted the culture but also introduced a jurisprudence upon which modern church-state doctrine would build: the conflict over Bible reading in the public schools; the controversy over the public funding of religious schools and charitable institutions; the involvement of civil courts in resolving internal church disputes; the legal and political conflict between the national government and the Mormon Church; and the federal policy of "civilizing" Native Americans through "Christianization," to name the more significant issues.

Standard legal histories have long acknowledged the important legal developments that took place during the nineteenth century. The common law – an amalgam of British and indigenous colonial laws – was "Americanized" or "transformed" by social, economic, and demographic forces. New legal fields arose (e.g., negligence and corporation law) while old fields (e.g., property and contract law) underwent major adjustments. Movements arose to standardize and codify the law, and to make it more "scientific." Legal historians have noted that this dramatic process of change also included a fundamental shift in lawyers' attitudes toward the nature and function of the law, leading many to reject notions that the law reinforced fixed, eternal principles of right and justice. In its place, according to Morton Horwitz, arose a view of the law as dynamic, instrumental, and democratic. The emergence of an instrumental conception of the law challenged earlier ideas of the law being grounded in "higher" or divine law (Horwitz, 1977). As Ohio lawyer John Milton Goodenow wrote in 1819, "laws, which man creates from himself, in his social state, are not emanations of Divine Will, nor yet the pure institutions of nature and reason, but changeable and arbitrary in their formation; they are necessarily of a positive, local existence" (1819: 3). This conceptual shift, as well as the law's increasingly practical applications, led to a secularization of the law. The law lost much of its morally reinforcing role; contract law, for example, became less concerned about assessing fault in a breach and more interested in identifying fair compensation.

Closely related to the overall transformation of the law was the decline of the maxim that Christianity formed part of the common law. The idea that the law recognized and enforced Christian principles had been popular since the middle ages. Based in part on higher law concepts, the maxim was reinforced by a handful of seventeenth- and eighteenth-century British legal decisions that had punished blasphemy on the ground that "whatever strikes at the very root of Christianity tends manifestly to a dissolution of civil government." William Blackstone popularized the maxim in his *Commentaries* – widely published in the American colonies – and early American jurists including James Kent and William Story endorsed the concept. For the first half of the century, American jurists applied the maxim, or at least endorsed the notion that the law should reinforce religious principles, in several dozen legal decisions upholding prosecutions for blasphemy and Sunday law violations. But as discussed in Steven K. Green's *The Second Disestablishment: Church and State in Nineteenth-Century America* (2010), judges and lawyers began to reject religious justifications for such laws in mid-century, replacing them with secular justifications such as nuisance and health-safety rationales. By the end of the century, the maxim, and religious justifications for behavioral laws, had all but disappeared from the legal landscape. Enforcement also declined. This "secularization" of the law, spurred by the law's standardization and a growing religious pluralism, impacted the development of other legal fields, as well, such as inheritance and domestic law. Morton Borden examines this episode from a Jewish perspective in *Jews, Turks, and Infidels* (1984), which has been cited in a handful of Supreme Court opinions. Another useful resource that examines efforts of conservative Protestants to stem the perceived tide of cultural and legal secularization is Gaines M. Foster, *Moral Reconstruction: Christian Lobbyists and the Federal Legislation of Morality, 1865–1920* (2002).

As mentioned, religious historians have long noted the significance of the century for religious development. Two important works are Robert T. Handy's *A Christian America: Protestant Hopes and Historical Realities* (1984), and *Undermined Establishment: Church-State Relations in America, 1880–1920* (1991), which discuss the evolution of church-state relations from a religious perspective. More recently, church-state scholars have begun to write about the nineteenth century. One influential work is Philip Hamburger's *Separation of Church and State* (2002), cited by members of the Supreme Court. Hamburger's comprehensive study argues that the idea of "separation" of church and state was alien to the majority of people during the founding period, including many who advocated disestablishment (absent core Jeffersonians). Instead, the concept arose during the nineteenth century, chiefly as Protestants and freethinkers reacted to the growing numerical and political strength of the Catholic Church. According to Hamburger, separation of church and state became the rallying cry for those who sought to preserve the Protestant character of public schooling and to prevent the public funding of Catholic schools. "[B]ecause of its history – both its lack of constitutional authority and its development in response to prejudice – the idea of separation should, at best, be viewed with suspicion," Hamburger writes (Hamburger, 2002: 483). Other legal scholars have challenged Hamburger's thesis that the notion of separation of church and state was not widely acknowledged before 1840. Steven Green's *The Second Disestablishment* offers an alternative analysis of the events of the nineteenth century, arguing that separation was an evolving impulse that arose through a series of conflicts, many of which were unrelated to the Protestant-Catholic conflict. A third approach to the idea of separation is found in David Sehat's *The Myth of American Religious Freedom* (2011), which argues that the prevailing motif of the century was one of a "coercive and exclusionary ... moral regime" that stifled religious pluralism. For Sehat, separationism was a myth.

The most significant church-state conflict of the nineteenth century was the School Question, which encompassed the interrelated issues of Protestant Bible reading and prayer in the public schools and the public funding of religious schools. Questions over the religious character of public education arose with its inception in the early 1800s, and despite the "Protestant settlement" of a nonsectarian curriculum that emphasized the teaching of universal Protestant values, Catholics, Jews and freethinkers attacked the system as being too Protestant, while conservative Protestants condemned nonsectarianism for being too secular. Early legal challenges to prayer and Bible reading failed, though the Ohio and Wisconsin supreme courts later found such practices to be unconstitutional in 1873 and 1890, respectively. The Protestant character of public schooling led Catholic officials to establish parochial schools, but Catholics were generally unsuccessful in securing a share of state school funds due to opposition by Protestants and educational officials. Both issues came to a head in the 1870s with a proposed amendment to the Constitution to prohibit the public funding of religious education (the "Blaine Amendment"). Although Congress failed to pass the Blaine Amendment, several states subsequently enacted similar provisions in their constitutions. Aspects of this controversy are considered in several legal histories, including Hamburger's *Separation of Church and State* (2002) and Green's *Second Disestablishment* (2010), which disagree about how much of the conflict was attributable to anti-Catholic sentiments. A more comprehensive examination of the nineteenth-century School Question is contained in Green's subsequent book, *The Bible, the School, and the Constitution* (2012). John T. McGreevy examines this controversy from the Catholic perspective in *Catholicism and American Freedom* (2003), though chiefly through a cultural approach. A history that places the funding controversy within the broader context of Reconstruction is Ward M. McAfee, *Religion, Race, and Reconstruction* (1998).

A second, highly contentious church-state controversy of the century was the "Mormon Problem" – the forty-year political and legal battle between the federal government and the Church of Jesus Christ of Latter-day Saints. Political and legal conflict embroiled the Mormon Church in Missouri and Illinois during the 1830s and 1840s, culminating in the assassination of Mormon founder Joseph Smith. The controversy escalated in the 1850s after the majority of Mormons fled to Utah and the church announced the tenet of plural marriage. Congress enacted a series of laws between 1863 and 1890 to outlaw polygamy and crush the power of the Mormon Church. Mormon leaders were prosecuted in federal courts, with several appeals reaching the Supreme Court. Many of the Court's earlier explorations into the meaning of church-state relations grew out of these cases. Discussions of the legal conflict are contained in general histories of the Mormon Church; a handful of works dedicated to examining the legal issues also exist. A fresh analysis is found in Sarah Barringer Gordon's *The Mormon Question: Polygamy and Constitutional Conflict in Nineteenth-Century America* (2002), which places the conflict within the larger context of Protestant attitudes toward gender and marriage and of a Protestant commitment to the image of America as a Christian nation. An important work in the literature is Edwin Brown Firmage and Richard Collin Mangrum's, *Zion in the Courts: A Legal History of the Church of Jesus Christ of Latter-day Saints, 1830–1900* (1988), which not only discusses the legal conflict between the U.S. government and the Mormon Church, but also examines how Mormons developed their own internal body of law for resolving legal disputes among the Saints.

Finally, a frequently overlooked church-state issue of the nineteenth century was the "civilization" policy of the U.S. government involving Native Americans. Beginning with George Washington's administration, the federal government viewed Christianity as a means to make Indians industrious and compliant. In 1819, Congress established the "Civilization Fund" to support Christian benevolent associations; in a short time, Moravian, Catholic, Baptist, Methodist and Presbyterian missionaries established mission schools among various tribes and began receiving federal funding. After years of mismanagement and corruption among Indian agents, President Ulysses Grant instituted the "Peace Policy" in 1869 to reform the system. The new initiative relied heavily on religious groups to formulate and administer federal Indian policy through a new Board of Indian Commissioners, popularly called the "Church Board." Religious missions were assigned reservations and received federal funding for their educational activities, which included converting Indians to Christianity. The Peace Policy continued until 1899 when it fell apart due to conflict between Protestants and Catholics over the latter's increasing share of funding. Nonetheless, a federal policy of discouraging Native American religious practices and encouraging conversion to Christianity persisted until the 1930s. This sad chapter in American history is discussed in several works, including R. Pierce Beaver, *Church, State, and the American Indians* (1966), Robert H. Keller, Jr., *American Protestantism and United States Indian Policy, 1869–82* (1983), and the histories by Francis Paul Prucha (1962; 1976).

The Twentieth Century

Perhaps because the twentieth century is the recent past, its history of the interaction of law and religion is still being written. Nonetheless, several studies examine the leading events and controversies of the twentieth century: the rise of Protestant Fundamentalism and its conflict with an increasingly secular culture (culminating in the infamous "Scopes Trial" over the teaching of evolution in the public schools); the modern Supreme Court's entry into adjudicating church-state controversies beginning in the 1940s; the Court's controversial decisions banning prayer and Bible reading in the public schools in the early 1960s; and the rise of the conservative Christian Right and its impact on public policy. The events of the first half of the century are discussed in Anson Phelps Stokes' *Church and State in the United States* (1950), including those controversies that led up to the Court's early decisions on the public funding of religious education and "released time" for religious education in the public schools. Philip Hamburger examines the religious school funding controversy that produced *Everson v. Board of Education* (1947) in *Separation of Church and State* (2002), arguing that Protestant and liberal opposition to the Catholic Church informed the Court's holding. John T. McGreevy discusses the same controversy in *Catholicism and American Freedom* (2003), though concluding that distrust and misunderstanding among both Protestants and Catholics fueled the controversy. The various religious and legal issues raised by the *Everson* decision are also examined in the compilation *Everson Revisited: Religion, Education, and Law at the Crossroads* (1997), edited by Jo Renee Formicola and Hubert Morken. The involvement of Jewish organizations in the modern Court's church-state cases is discussed in Gregg Ivers, *To Build a Wall: American Jews and the Separation of Church and State* (1995).

The controversy over religious exercises in the public schools, highly controversial throughout the nineteenth century, generally abated after the 1920s, only to resurface in 1948 with the case of *McCollum v. Board of Education*. There the Court struck down in-school released time for religious instruction, only to back away from that decision four years later by allowing the same practices to occur off school campuses (*Zorach v. Clauson*). More controversial were the Court's decisions in 1962 and 1963 banning school directed prayer and readings from the Bible (*Engel v. Vitale*; *Abington School District v. Schempp*). Ever since those latter cases, the legal and cultural issues raised by in-school religious exercises have been a popular area for scholars. An early work providing background information on the controversy and the fall-out in Congress is Donald E. Boles, *The Bible, Religion, and the Public Schools* (1965). More recent studies of the controversy include Bruce J. Dierenfield, *The Battle over School Prayer: How Engel v. Vitale Changed America* (2007); Joan DelFattore, *The Fourth R: Conflicts over Religion in America's Public Schools* (2004); Frank S. Ravitch, *School Prayer and Discrimination* (1999); Rodney K. Smith, *Public Prayer and the Constitution* (1987); and two works by Robert S. Alley, *Without a Prayer: Religious Expression in the Public Schools* (1996) and *School Prayer: The Court, the Congress, and the First Amendment* (1994). Closely related to the legal conflict over school prayer is the controversy over teaching evolution or creationism in the public schools. This dispute dates back to the Scopes Trial of 1925 but remains an ongoing legal issue. Representative works that consider the legal and policy implications of the controversy, most discussing its historical development, include: Frank S. Ravitch, *Marketing Intelligent Design: Law and the Creationist Agenda* (2011); Michael B. Berkman, *Evolution, Creation and the Battle to Control America's Classrooms* (2010); and Edward J. Lawson, *Trial and Error: The American Controversy over Creation and Evolution* (1985).

Finally, several histories examine the evolution of the modern Court's jurisprudence on church-state matters. Two books by Ronald B. Flowers examine the controversial church-state holdings of the Warren and Burger Courts from a cultural and legal perspective: *That Godless Court?* (2005) and *Religion in Strange Times: The 1960s and 1970s* (1984). Works critical of the jurisprudence of the Warren and Burger Courts include Robert Cord, *Separation of Church and State* (1982) and James Hitchcock, *The Supreme Court and Religion in American Life* (2004), while works that criticize the Burger and Rehnquist Courts for retreating from its separationist legacy include Gregg Ivers, *Lowering the Wall: Religion and the Supreme Court in the 1980s* (1991), and Derek Davis, *Original Intent: Chief Justice Rehnquist and the Course of American Church/State Relations* (1991).

All in all, the intersection of law and religion is an important part of the nation's legal history and is an area worthy of additional study. One underexplored subject is the degree to which religious perspectives influenced the legal strategies of the civil rights movement. An important study is David L. Chappell's *A Stone of Hope: Prophetic Religion and the Death of Jim Crow* (2004). Another promising area for future scholarship concerns the interactions between the dominant legal culture and the traditions and practices of non-Judeo-Christian religions (e.g., the law's recognition of Sharia law). And an issue that deserves more scholarly attention is the way in which discrete religious communities (e.g., Old Order Amish; Ultra-Orthodox Jews) have used the dominant legal structures (and developed their own legal alternatives) to reinforce their "otherness," instead of the law always being seen as a force of assimilation and secularization.

References

Alley, Robert S. (1994). *School Prayer: The Court, the Congress, and the First Amendment.* Prometheus Books, Buffalo, NY.

Alley, Robert S. (1996). *Without a Prayer: Religious Expression in the Public Schools.* Prometheus Books, Buffalo, NY.

Bailyn, Bernard (1967). *The Ideological Origins of the American Revolution.* Harvard University Press, Cambridge.

Beaver, R. Pierce (1966). *Church, State, and the American Indians.* Concordia Pub. House, St. Louis.

Beneke, Chris (2006). *Beyond Toleration: The Religious Origins of American Pluralism.* Oxford University Press, New York.

Berkman, Michael B. (2010). *Evolution, Creation and the Battle to Control America's Classrooms.* Cambridge University Press, New York.

Berman, Harold J. (1974). *The Interaction of Law and Religion.* Abington Press, Nashville.

Berman, Harold J. (1983). *Law and Revolution: The Formation of the Western Legal Tradition.* Harvard University Press, Cambridge.

Blau, Joseph L. (1949). *Cornerstones of Religious Freedom in America.* Beacon Press, Boston.

Boles, Donald E. (1965). *The Bible, Religion, and the Public Schools.* Iowa State University Press, Ames, IO.

Borden, Morton (1984). *Jews, Turks, and Infidels.* University of North Carolina Press, Chapel Hill.

Bradley, Gerard V. (1987). *Church-State Relationships in America.* Greenwood Press, Westport, CT.

Bridenbaugh, Carl (1962). *Mitre and Sceptre: Transatlantic Faiths, Ideas, Personalities, and Politics, 1689–1775.* Oxford University Press, New York.

Buckley, Thomas E. (1977). *Church and State in Revolutionary Virginia, 1776–1787.* University Press of Virginia, Charlottesville.

Butts, R. Feeman (1950). *The American Tradition in Religion and Education.* Beacon Press, Boston.

Chappell, David L. (2004). *A Stone of Hope: Prophetic Religion and the Death of Jim Crow.* University of North Carolina Press, Chapel Hill.

Cobb, Sanford H. (1902). *The Rise of Religious Liberty in America: A History.* Cooper Square Pub, New York.

Cord, Robert L. (1982). *Separation of Church and State: Historical Fact and Current Fiction.* Lambeth Press, New York.

Cornelison, Isaac A. (1895). *The Relation of Religion to Civil Government.* G.P. Putnam's Sons, New York.

Curry, Thomas J. (1986). *The First Freedoms: Church and State in America to the Passage of the Frist Amendment.* Oxford University Press, New York.

Davis, Derek H. (1991). *Original Intent: Chief Justice Rehnquist and the Course of American Church/State Relations.* Prometheus Books, Buffalo.

Davis, Derek H. (2000). *Religion and the Continental Congress, 1774–1789.* Oxford University Press, New York.

DelFattore, Joan (2004). *The Fourth R: Conflicts over Religion in America's Public Schools.* Yale University Press, New Haven.

Dierenfield, Bruce J. (2007). *The Battle over School Prayer: How Engel v. Vitale Changed America.* University of Kansas Press, Lawrence, KS.

Dreisbach, Daniel L. (2002). *Thomas Jefferson and the Wall of Separation Between Church and State.* New York University Press, New York.

Drakeman, Donald L. (2010). *Church, State, and Original Intent.* Cambridge University Press, New York.

Finkelman, Paul (2000). *Religion and American Law: An Encyclopedia.* Garland Pub, New York.

Firmage, Edwin Brown and Mangrum, Richard Collin (1988). *Zion in the Courts: A Legal History of the Church of Jesus Christ of Latter-day Saints, 1830–1900.* University of Illinois Press, Urbana.

Flaherty, David (1978). "Law and the Enforcement of Morals in Early America." In Friedman and Scheiber, eds, *American Law and the Constitutional Order: Historical Perspectives.* Harvard University Press, Cambridge.

Flowers, Ronald B. (1984). *Religion in Strange Times: The 1960s and 1970s.* Mercer University Press, Macon, GA.

Flowers, Ronald B. (2005). *That Godless Court? Supreme Court Decisions on Church-State Relations.* Westminster John Knox Press, Louisville, KY.

Formicola, Jo Renee and Morken, Hubert, eds (1997). *Everson Revisited: Religion, Education, and Law at the Crossroads.* Rowman & Littlefield, Lanham, MD.

Foster, Gaines M. (2002). *Moral Reconstruction: Christian Lobbyists and the Federal Legislation of Morality, 1865–1920.* University of North Carolina Press, Chapel Hill.

Gaustad, Edwin S. (1991). *Liberty of Conscience: Roger Williams in America.* William B. Eerdmans, Grand Rapids, MI.

Goodenow, John Milton (1819). *Historical Sketches of the Principles and Maxims of American Jurisprudence*. James Wilson, Steubenville, OH.

Gordon, Sarah Barringer (2002). *The Mormon Question: Polygamy and Constitutional Conflict in Nineteenth-Century America*. University of North Carolina Press, Chapel Hill.

Green, Steven K. (2010). *The Second Disestablishment: Church and State in Nineteenth Century America*. Oxford University Press, New York.

Green, Steven K. (2012). *The Bible, the School, and the Constitution: The Clash that Shaped Modern Church-State Doctrine*. Oxford University Press, New York.

Greenawalt, Kent (2006, 2008). *Religion and the Constitution*. Princeton University Press, Princeton.

Hamburger, Philip (2002). *Separation of Church and State*. Harvard University Press, Cambridge.

Handy, Robert T. (1984). *A Christian America: Protestant Hopes and Historical Realities*, 2nd Edition. Oxford University Press, New York.

Handy, Robert T. (1991). *Undermined Establishment: Church-State Relations in America, 1880–1920*. Princeton University Press, Princeton.

Haskins, George Lee (1960). *Law and Authority in Early Massachusetts*. The Macmillan Co., New York.

Hitchcock, James (2004). *The Supreme Court and Religion in American Life*. Princeton University Press, Princeton.

Horwitz, Morton J. (1977). *The Transformation of American Law, 1780–1860*. Harvard University Press, Cambridge.

Howe, Mark deWolfe (1965). *The Garden and the Wilderness: Religion and Government in American Constitutional History*. University of Chicago Press, Chicago.

Ivers, Gregg (1991). *Lowering the Wall: Religion and the Supreme Court in the 1980s*. Anti-Defamation League, New York.

Ivers, Gregg (1995). *To Build a Wall: American Jews and the Separation of Church and State*. University of Virginia Press, Charlottesville.

Johnson, Alvin W. (1934). *The Legal Status of Church-State Relationships in the United States*. University of Minnesota Press, Minneapolis.

Keller, Jr., Robert H. (1983). *American Protestantism and United States Indian Policy, 1869–82*. University of Nebraska Press, Lincoln.

Lambert, Frank (2003). *The Founding Fathers and the Place of Religion in America*. Princeton University Press, Princeton.

Lawson, Edward J. (1985). *Trial and Error: The American Controversy over Creation and Evolution*. Oxford University Press, New York.

Levy, Leonard W. (1986). *The Establishment Clause: Religion and the First Amendment*. Macmillan, New York.

Malbin, Michael J. (1978). *Religion and Politics: The Intentions of the Authors of the First Amendment*. American Enterprise Institute, Washington, DC.

McAfee, Ward M. (1998). *Religion, Race, and Reconstruction*. State University of New York Press, Albany.

McGarvie, Mark Douglas (2004). *One Nation Under Law: America's Early National Struggles to Separate Church and State*. Northern Illinois Press, DeKalb, IL.

McGreevy, John T. (2003). *Catholicism and American Freedom.* W.W. Norton & Co., New York.

McLoughlin, William G. (1971). *New England Dissent, 1630–1830.* Harvard University Press, Cambridge.

Miller, Perry (1939). *The New England Mind: The Seventeenth Century.* Harvard University Press, Cambridge.

Miller, Perry (1953). *The New England Mind: From Colony to Province.* Harvard University Press, Cambridge.

Miller, Perry (1956). *Errand into the Wilderness.* Belknap Press of Harvard University, Cambridge.

Morgan, Edmund S. (1958). *The Puritan Dilemma: The Story of John Winthrop.* Little, Brown & Co., Boston.

Pfeffer, Leo (1953). *Church, State and Freedom.* Beacon Press, Boston.

Prucha, Francis Paul (1962). *American Indian Policy in the Formative Years.* Harvard University Press, Cambridge.

Prucha, Francis Paul (1976). *American Indian Policy in Crisis: Christian Reformers and the Indian, 1865–1900.* University of Oklahoma Press, Norman.

Ravitch, Frank S. (1999). *School Prayer and Discrimination.* Northeastern University Press, Boston.

Ravitch, Frank S. (2011). *Marketing Intelligent Design: Law and the Creationist Agenda.* Cambridge University Press, New York.

Sandoz, Ellis (1990). *A Government of Laws: Political Theory, Religion, and the American Founding.* Louisiana State University Press, Baton Rouge.

Schaff, Philip (1888). *Church and State in the United States.* G.P. Putnam's Sons, New York.

Sehat, David (2011). *The Myth of American Religious Freedom.* Oxford University Press, New York.

Shain, Barry Alan (1994). *The Myth of American Individualism: The Protestant Origins of American Political Thought.* Princeton University Press, Princeton.

Smith, Rodney K. (1987). *Public Prayer and the Constitution: A Case Study in Constitutional Interpretation.* Scholarly Resources, Wilmington, DE.

Smith, Steven (1995). *Foreordained Failure.* Oxford University Press, New York.

Stokes, Anson Phelps (1950). *Church and State in the United States.* Harper & Row, New York.

Stokes, Anson Phelps and Leo Pfeffer (1964). *Church and State in the United States.* Harper & Row, New York.

Wilson, John F. (1986). *Church and State in America: A Bibliographical Guide.* Greenwood Press, Westport, CT.

Witte, Jr., John and Nichols, Joel A. (2011). *Religion and the American Constitutional Experiment*, 3rd Edition. Westview Press, Boulder, CO.

Witte, Jr., John and Alexander, Frank S. (1988). *The Weightier Matters of the Law: Essays on Law and Religion.* Scholars Press, Atlanta.

Wood, Gordon S. (1969). *The Creation of the American Republic.* W.W. Norton, New York.

Zollmann, Carl (1917). *American Civil Church Law.* Columbia University Press, New York.

Chapter Twenty-one

LEGAL HISTORY AND THE MILITARY

Elizabeth L. Hillman

War and military law have long captured the attention of legal historians. Yet since the terrorist attacks on the United States in 2001, interest in the history of armed conflict and military action has intensified among legal historians, including some of the field's most accomplished scholars. John Fabian Witt's study of the nineteenth-century origins of the laws of war weaves the history of Americans' moral engagement with war into a new synthesis of U.S. political, constitutional, and intellectual history (Witt, 2012). Mary Dudziak's *War Time* analyzes the period from World War II through the twenty-first-century wars against terrorism to recast the temporal limits of war as a constructed reality with profound implications for legal and political discourse (Dudziak, 2012). Military legal history has been transformed from a relatively narrow specialty into an essential part of the tapestry of American and international history.

It has also been thrust into the mainstream of legal thought through judicial opinions. Decisions of the U.S. Supreme Court and other federal courts, as well as opinions of military courts such as the United States Court of Military Commission Review, have relied on precise, factual analysis of past military tribunals to resolve legal issues in cases involving the post-9/11 prosecution of suspected terrorists. The question of whether "joint criminal enterprise" or "providing support to the enemy" constitute an offense chargeable under the twenty-first-century laws of war has been answered by recourse to prosecutions during the Civil War, the Philippine insurrection, World War II, and other conflicts. Like the efforts of scholars to place U.S. reactions to contemporary military and political threats into historical

A Companion to American Legal History, First Edition.
Edited by Sally E. Hadden and Alfred L. Brophy.
© 2013 John Wiley & Sons Ltd. Published 2021 by John Wiley & Sons Ltd.

context, the legal challenges crafted by attorneys defending those charged at military commissions has sparked renewed interest in military legal history.

This chapter explores the historiography of military legal history in four parts. The first sketches the historiography of military justice, focusing on the evolution of distinctive systems of criminal justice intended to maintain good order and discipline among U.S. military personnel. The second steps back to assess briefly how scholars have drawn out the interactions between military and civilian politics and law. The third outlines major topics in the history of military legal protections for human rights, including the history of the laws of war and the development of increasingly strong international norms of procedural and substantive human rights for both civilians and service members who face trial by military courts. The fourth suggests trends likely to influence the future study of these arenas of history and law. Military legal history is contested terrain, occupied by military historians who often seek to prove the fairness and legitimacy of special military rules and procedures yet under siege by others doubtful that rules of law can effectively either restrain or punish the violence of the state once unleashed.

Military Justice

Maintaining control over the persons armed on behalf of the state is the primary rationale for the existence of a separate military criminal justice system. The extent of military jurisdiction, the types of crimes prosecuted, and the quality of due process available to accused members of the military have changed over time, reflecting shifts in the social and political milieu both within the ranks and in civil society. Twenty-first-century treatises on military law reveal both persistent differences in military versus civilian courts – such as the authority of a commanding officer to investigate, prosecute, and influence a trial and punishment – and increasing convergence as military procedural rules have edged closer to civilian norms of criminal process (Schlueter *et al.*, 2008; Gilligan and Lederer, 2007). But it was not always so.

Two anthologies on key issues – one concerning GI rights during the Vietnam War era and its aftermath that remains incisive forty years after it first appeared (Finn, 1971), the other concerning globalization, evolving standards of due process, and the challenges of preserving civilian control over military justice (Fidell and Sullivan, 2002) – reveal the shifting contours of military justice and the distinctions from civilian criminal justice that have characterized the history of military courts. Notable differences that have been examined by historians and legal scholars include the crimes that can be charged (at court-martial, military offenses like unauthorized absence as well as civilian offenses like assault may be alleged), the triers of fact (at court-martial, military members rather than a jury of one's peers), evidentiary rules, and punishments (Hillman, 2005).

A growing historiography of military justice is recasting the history of military courts from the colonial era through the twenty-first-century military commissions. Early American military justice was rooted in British practice, making U.S. military "courts" as harsh, arbitrary, and feared as they were in the eighteenth-century British army and navy. In 1775, the Massachusetts assembly adopted articles of war based on the British rules, and soon after the Continental Congress did likewise for both the army and the navy (Lurie, 1992; Siegel, 1998). George Washington, John Adams, and Thomas Jefferson were among the key leaders who sought to ensure that commanders would have the power to enforce strict discipline, regardless of the restrictions that power placed on soldiers' rights. Enforcing discipline and preserving lines of rank and authority was a priority, and Caroline Cox's work traces the social distance between officers and enlistees that remained wide throughout the Revolution (Cox, 2004). The elite gentleman officers of the Revolutionary era often held posts of civil as well as military authority and were obliged to hold themselves apart from the common soldier, lest they risk court-martial for the crime of "conduct unbecoming an officer and a gentleman," an offense that remains a crime in the contemporary military (Hillman, 2008).

The soldiers in the Continental Army had few rights, but they were protected against being tried in military courts for non-military offenses if a civil authority requested that the suspect be turned over or if the alleged offense was a serious civilian crime (Wiener, 1958; Winthrop, 1920). Law favored civil over military jurisdiction, preferring to limit the military courts as much as possible. Because military courts are Article I courts under the Constitution's statement of executive authority rather than Article III courts under the federal judiciary, they do not trigger the same constitutional protections as civil courts. This has made courts-martial inherently suspect to many observers, despite the application of much of the Bill of Rights to courts-martial in post-World War II reform (Wiener, 1958). In early American military justice, the limited rights of service members accused of crimes were in large part a reflection of the limited rights of individuals accused before civilian criminal courts. *Billy Budd*, Herman Melville's short novel (based on a true story) about a sailor who is court-martialed for killing a malevolent superior officer became a literary touchstone for the difficult plight and limited rights of members of the military (Melville, 1992).

As it did to so many areas of law, the Civil War posed grave challenges to military justice, including the prior limits on military jurisdiction (Neff, 2010). Because of the unprecedented demands of the war, military authority grew along with executive power. Many historians and legal scholars have sought to identify the key military and political players and trace the changes over which they presided. Jonathan Turley trains a critical eye on Civil War general William Tecumseh Sherman, who considered civilianization a grave risk to military effectiveness and in particular sought to preserve a separate military justice system despite the risk that posed to U.S. democracy (Turley, 2002b). John Fabian Witt explores Colonel Francis Lieber's leadership in attempting to restrain the violence of war with an explicit code of conduct (Witt, 2012). Joshua E. Kastenberg's *The Blackstone of Military Law* is the first biography of Civil War veteran and colonel William Woolsey Winthrop. Winthrop, descended from one of the United States' first families, authored a brilliant treatise, *Military Law and Precedents*, that was definitive from the time it was first published in 1895 into the twenty-first century, when it was still being cited by the Supreme Court (Kastenberg, 2009). Kastenberg reveals many connections between Colonel Winthrop and civilian legal elites, pointing out how the modernization of the army involved legal as well as administrative, bureaucratic, and operational changes, tying military legal history into the history of the army itself. Two classic works help to reveal these changes in the officer corps and leadership of the armed forces after the Civil War: Edward Coffman's *The Old Army*, which covers the period from the early national era through the end of the nineteenth century, and Peter Karsten's *The Naval Aristocracy*, which focuses on the post-Civil War period (Coffman, 1988; Karsten, 2008).

World War I brought more civilian lawyers into military service, where the progressive impulse for reform soon took hold to address obvious deficiencies in fairness at court-martial, especially the influence of commanders on trials, high conviction rates, and inconsistent sentencing (Lurie, 1992; United States Army, 1993). Most historical accounts of this period study the famous Ansell-Crowder controversy, which pitted Major General Enoch Crowder against a reform-minded subordinate, Brigadier General Samuel Tilden Ansell. While the acting judge advocate general of the army, Ansell reacted to two highly publicized courts-martial by challenging the fairness and constitutionality of the existing system of military justice. The first involved the trial of dozens of African American soldiers after a deadly race riot in Houston on Aug 20, 1917. The second also took place in Texas, but at Fort Bliss, where a group of non-commissioned officers were charged with mutiny for refusing to obey an order to attend a drill formation after they were arrested, convicted, and harshly punished for playing craps, a minor violation of military rules. Together, these courts-martial highlighted the arbitrary and prejudicial nature of commanding officers' decisions about what criminal charges to file against soldiers accused of wrongdoing (Lurie, 1992; Lindley, 1990).

The Crowder-Ansell dispute became a much-cited turning point in the history of U.S. military justice. It revealed how personalized substantive disputes over military law could become, as well as how deep the tension is between reformers and those who, like Crowder did, believe military justice is best viewed as an instrument of command and ought to be governed by rules separate from the civilian rules (Lindley, 1990). The first volume of Jonathan Lurie's definitive history of the United States Court of Military

Appeals analyzes this tension between military and civil justice, and between reformers and defenders of the unique military system (Lurie, 1992).

Not until after World War II, however, did the military adopt Ansell's model of a military justice system of judicial tribunals subject to civilian supervision (Lindley, 1990). Because the war brought so many into contact with military justice, Ansell's proposals to codify crimes, specify maximum punishments, limit the authority of commanders, provide counsel for the accused, and create independent judicial review finally attracted widespread support (Lurie, 1992). When the Department of Defense convened a committee to draft a uniform code to apply across the services, Edmund Morgan, a Harvard Law professor who had served as judge advocate under Ansell, was appointed chair and succeeded in enacting many of Ansell's proposals into law. William T. Generous' study of the adoption of the Uniform Code of Military Justice, the greatest reform in the history of American military law, examines both the process of revising military justice and the resistance that reform triggered (Generous, 1973).

Although the historiography of the Korean War has deepened greatly, there remain few close studies of military justice during that period, despite a massive court-martial docket from the war that in many ways anticipated the disciplinary challenges of the Vietnam War era. An essential study of the evolution of the armed forces before the Vietnam War argues that the period after the Korea War until the start of the Vietnam conflict is a critical moment in U.S. military history (Bacevich, 1986). An exception to the limited scholarship available regarding this period is my own study of general courts, the most serious type of court-martial, akin to a civilian felony trial, during the Cold War, arguing that the political concerns of military leaders influenced the nature of crimes charged and the sentences meted out at courts-martial (Hillman, 2005).

The Vietnam War era has received considerable attention from scholars of military legal history. They have focused on prosecutions for wartime atrocities (Barnett, 2010; Solis, 1997; Bilton and Sims, 1993) as well as the changes the war brought to the military legal corps and the practice of military justice in the field (Borch, 2004; Allison, 2007; Lurie, 1998). Gary Solis' study of Marine Corps lawyers during Vietnam is an indispensable account of the challenges that face judge advocates who try high-stakes cases in the midst of a complex political climate and resource-limited, dangerous environments (Solis, 1989). An in-depth study of the prosecution of Howard Levy, a military doctor court-martialed for dissent and disobedience, by legal scholar Robert N. Strassfeld reveals the ways in which the debate over the wisdom and efficacy of the war effort influenced the prosecution of crime and subsequent appeals of courts-martial (Strassfeld, 1994). A carefully researched history of "fragging," or the murder of officers by their troops, among U.S. forces during the Vietnam War, attempts a comprehensive portrait of not only this military crime, but also the political landscape and individual, often idiosyncratic, intent that motivates this sort of violent crime (Lepre, 2011). Racism in military justice was a concern of military and civilian leaders as well as service members throughout this period. Its grim dimensions are examined critically in studies of both courts-martial and soldier dissent (Hillman, 2005; Moser, 1996). Literary scholar Alice Kaplan's trenchant study of two U.S. army courts-martial during World War II unravels the complexity of racialized military justice (Kaplan, 2005).

Rape has long been associated with war, but the prosecution of sexual violence within the military became more prominent in both public discourse and military justice with a series of sexual assault scandals in the late twentieth century. Although the court-martial rate remained low throughout this period, courts-martial for sexual harassment, assault, and misbehavior embarrassed military leaders and challenged the skill and professionalism of judge advocates (Hillman, 2005; 2008). Both the extent and origin of these crimes has been the subject of much dispute among military historians and policymakers. The Tailhook debacle in 1991, at which naval aviators took part in a drunken bacchanal that included extensive sexual misconduct, was the first of a series of scandals involving sex crimes by military personnel (Zimmerman, 1995; Benedict, 2009).

Before leaving the history of military justice, a few of the page-turning historical narratives of notorious military criminal investigations and prosecutions deserve mention. Jack Hamann, a Seattle journalist, wrote an award-winning and deeply researched study of the 1944 Fort Lawton riots between African-American soldiers assigned to segregated port companies and Italian prisoners of war (Hamann, 2005). The suspicious death of a POW during the riot led to the court-martial of forty-three African-American soldiers; three were charged with murder, the rest for rioting. Twenty-eight were convicted and sentenced to confinement despite serious procedural shortcomings throughout the investigation and prosecution. Several compelling accounts of the horrifying My Lai massacre during the Vietnam War expose failures of leadership prior to the massacre and in the cover-up that followed (Belknap, 2002; Bilton and Sims, 1993). Many of these accounts stress the professionalism of the judge advocates involved in the investigation and trials that resulted from the massacre (Belknap, 2002; Eckhardt, 2000). The Abu Ghraib prisoner abuse scandal in 2003 has received similarly extensive and probing treatment, both in a book by military prosecutors whose reconstructions of events include elaborate detail (Graveline and Clemens, 2010) and in the official report of the army general assigned to investigate the incidents (Taguba, 2004). Twelve soldiers were eventually court-martialed for maltreatment of prisoners, dereliction of duty, and other charges related to prisoner abuse at Abu Ghraib. The highest-ranking among those prosecuted was Lieutenant Colonel Steven L. Jordan, who received a reprimand after being found guilty of disobeying an order not to discuss statements made during the investigation (Graveline and Clemens, 2010). The military's involvement in the use of torture during the interrogation of suspected terrorists in the post-9/11 legal regime has also attracted the attention of scholars and critics, some of whom have compiled extensive documentary records of civil and military records (Greenberg and Dratel, 2005).

Military Influence on Civilian Law and Politics

Military justice, even when due process is strictly observed and the alleged offense is a minor infraction, involves crime and indiscipline that are likely to give civilian observers cause to doubt the state of morale and discipline within the ranks. The relationship between civilian society and the military, and between the branches of government and the military, is an essential, but less spectacular, aspect of military law than the court-martial. The balance of power between the branches of government and the armed forces is a topic of frequent study by political scientists as well as constitutional and political historians. George Q. Flynn's volume on conscription in the U.S. from World War II through the Vietnam War is an excellent example of placing a distinctive military issue – in this case, how to meet the personnel demands of a modern armed force at war – into its larger social, legal, and political context (Flynn, 1993).

The ways in which the framers of the Constitution opted to "provide for the national defense" is a key starting point for the essential historical study of civil-military relations, Richard H. Kohn's collection of essays on the Constitution (Kohn, 1991). Kohn delineates the reasons that a democracy must assert control over its military, describes the processes by which that principle has been pursued, and articulates the structure and practice of civil governance of military forces. The framers of the Constitution wanted neither a standing army nor a separate military society (Turley, 2002b).

The demands of the Civil War, however, altered not only the balance of federal and state power but also the authority of the military, not least in the ways that the demand for troops led to new legal and political regimes (Geary, 1986). President Lincoln exercised executive authority on many military matters, including a sweeping use of the pardon power in cases of convicted deserters. Harold Holzer's collection of Lincoln's writings on war conveys the depth of thought with which Lincoln weighed issues of war, law, and the military (Holzer, 2011). And Jonathan Turley argues that after the Civil War, a "military pocket republic" emerged that gave the military extensive autonomy and authority despite the U.S.'s historic reluctance to tolerate such military power (Turley, 2002a).

Andrew J. Bacevich's *Washington Rules* assails the dysfunctional civil-military relationships that permitted the post-WWII U.S. to become warlike in its actions and grandiose in its aspirations even as both politicians and public discourse left the military, and the sacrifices of its members, behind (Bacevich, 2010). Brian McAllister Linn, perhaps the most accomplished contemporary historian of the U.S. military, characterizes the intellectual dimensions of internal military debates over the use of force and relations with civil authorities, noting significant differences among the branches of service and the ways in which self-proclaimed "revolutions" in military thought and strategy more often choose to recycle past dogma and provoke resistance to reform rather than embrace hard-won insight and encourage change (Linn, 2011).

The battle for control of the military has flared at many points among the executive, legislative, and judicial branches of government. A notable early twenty-first-century example of the struggle for control of military policy was the dust-up over the end of discrimination against gay and lesbian service members in 2010–2011 (Belkin, 2011; Mazur, 2010). After a district court found the "don't ask/don't tell" policy violated the due process and free speech clauses of the Constitution in 2010, both the President and Congress asserted their authority to establish military policy and prevent judicial intervention.

Legal scholars have also argued that the rise of judicial deference to the military in the late twentieth century undermined the principle of civilian control and contributed to the isolation of service members from civil society (Mazur, 2010; Fidell, 2009–2010). Robert L. Goldich casts the army as the paradigmatic service for understanding civil-military relations and military culture, arguing that the shift to an all-volunteer force after the Vietnam War effectively created an army of legionnaires who fight on the nation's behalf rather than a citizen-soldier militia that operates under the control of civilian authority (Goldich, 2011). Goldich's vision of the historically deviant nature of the all-volunteer army is echoed in Bacevich's work, which sees the isolation of civil society from the military as especially troubling given the extensive use of military force by civil government (Bacevich, 2010). Philippa Strum's compelling account of the Virginia Military Institute's resistance to gender integration provides further evidence of the gap between self-styled military culture and the norms of civil society as it relates the legal struggle of young women to gain admission to an elite, state-funded educational institution (Strum, 2002).

Civil-military relations figure in the history of the administrative state as well, a reality that has brought the regulation and governance of the armed forces into the growing historiography of administrative law and regulation. Mark Wilson argues that the military was a powerful source of economic regulation from World War II through the 1970s, when the renegotiation of war profits was a much-debated statutory requirement (Wilson, 2010). Douglas

Stuart casts the erosion of legal restrictions on military operations and the use of the force as essential to understanding the rise of national security as the dominant paradigm for understanding U.S. objectives (Stuart, 2008).

Military Law and Human Rights

The law of war has been at the core of the evolution and elevation of human rights law. As a result, its history has long attracted the attention of military legal historians (Karsten, 1978). The history of the Geneva Conventions, the history touchstone of international humanitarian law, has been analyzed by military legal scholars interested in understanding the constraints that law places on the violence and destruction of armed conflict. Scholars and former military officers Gary Solis and Fred Borch authored an annotated guide that reveals the historic foundations and analyzes contemporary interpretations of the Geneva Conventions (Solis and Borch, 2010).

Whether law has effectively constrained the violence of U.S. military forces is a frequent topic of scholarly debate. Historian John Grenier's important study of the early American ways of war argues that excessive brutality and violence was a central aspect of U.S. war-making from the origins of the nation (Grenier, 2008). Fine-grained analyses of military operations and human rights violations during the Civil War have further expanded our understanding of how law influenced, and sometimes limited, military operations. During the war, federal authorities and commanding officers applied military law to limit civilian casualties, manage reprisals, and deal with the challenges of hostage-taking (Neff, 2010; Weitz, 2005). Mark Weitz's study places human rights deprivations into the center of the narrative of military operations, reconstructing the civilian impact as well as military significance of specific actions. For example, in 1863 the Union army ordered the evacuation of three Missouri counties and part of a fourth in an effort to halt the guerrilla warfare of irregulars in that area. The result was a human rights disaster in which loyalists and rebel sympathizers alike lost property and freedom as they were forced into either military stations within the district or out of the area altogether (Weitz, 2005). Daniel T. Sutherland's comprehensive analysis of guerilla warfare during the Civil War reveals the legal, social, and political complexities of irregular warfare (Sutherland, 2009). The savage tactics he recounts, however, must be tempered by Mark Neely's assessment that the Civil War violence was less brutal or unrestrained than many historians portray (Neely, 2007).

Most significantly for the development of human rights law, the Union adopted the Lieber Code in 1863, a restatement of the laws of war that became a key template for all subsequent efforts to articulate principles to restrain the brutality of war (Neff, 2010; Witt, 2012). Francis Lieber, a remarkable lawyer and scholar, was far from the only talented attorney in the Department of War. Edwin Stanton, Secretary of War for most of the Civil War, was a protégé of Samuel Chase and would have joined Chase on the Supreme Court had Stanton not died after being nominated and confirmed by the Senate (Neff, 2010). Mark Neely's work makes clear, however, that civil liberties during the Civil War were severely compromised by military arrests and trials of civilians, notwithstanding the 1866 opinion of the Supreme Court in *Ex parte Milligan* that rejected the authority of a military tribunal (Neely, 1991).

Debates over law and war beyond *Milligan* reached the U.S. Supreme Court during the Civil War as well, leaving fertile ground for historians interested in judicial review of military decision-making (Neely, 2011). Historian Stephen C. Neff points out that neither side considered the conflict a civil war – for the North, it was a law enforcement exercise, for the South, a war between nations (Neff, 2010). In the *Prize Cases*, the Supreme Court decided that a state of war existed in April 1861, when President Lincoln proclaimed a blockade of the southern states. The Court held that the state of rebellion was sufficient to constitute a state of war if the courts could not stay open (Neff, 2010; McGinty, 2008). The Court was sharply divided in the *Prize Cases* as it applied international law and decided that the Confederacy was in fact a belligerent (Neely, 2011). In *Ex parte Vallandigham*, the Supreme Court declined to review the decision of the military commission that had convicted Ohio politician Clement L. Vallandigham (Neely, 1991).

Not until World War II did so many issues of military law and high politics return to the civilian judiciary and attention of the public. Historians and journalists have been drawn to the dramatic narrative of the Nazi saboteurs who landed on American shores only to be undone by their own mistakes and prosecuted at a secret military commission (Fisher, 2003; Dobbs, 2004). The postwar prosecutions of war criminals made a tremendous impact on the evolution of human rights. Studies of the Nuremberg tribunal and the prosecution of Japanese leaders before a military tribunal, both of which were dramatic affairs that generated tremendous public interest, abound (Taylor, 1992; Marrus, 1997). The 1961 film, *Judgment at Nuremberg*, directed and produced by Stanley Kramer, brought the use of military tribunals to try war criminals into popular culture. The history of the Nuremberg trials has been complemented by close examination of less-publicized incidents such as the 1947 Mauthausen trial and executions near Munich, which resulted in forty-eight hangings of men convicted in a hasty seven-week trial for abuse and killing of prisoners in a concentration camp (Jardim, 2011).

Studies of the evolution of the role of U.S. military lawyers have illuminated the extent to which judge advocates' duties and impact have expanded to meet the demand for compliance with international human rights law in particular. "Operational law" advisors have a broad range of responsibilities in each phase of combat operations and must possess a working knowledge of treaty-based and customary law of war as well as U.S. policy (Solis, 2010). The military commissions at Guantanamo Bay and other government actions taken to advance the war against international terrorists, Iraq, and Afghanistan after September 11, 2001 have attracted extensive criticism from human rights attorneys and journalists (Danner, 2004; Olshansky, 2007; Smith, 2007). Historians and constitutional law scholars have plunged into the fray with close studies of the use of military commissions in the past (Fisher, 2005; Glazier, 2005). These works of history have influenced judicial decisions regarding the constitutionality and legitimacy of U.S. military commissions in the armed conflicts of the early twenty-first century. Legal scholar Eugene R. Fidell has argued that twenty-first-century U.S. military justice is out of step with contemporary international norms because it relies on military courts to try civilian and retired military personnel as well as to prosecute civilian offenses, both of which violate internationally accepted human rights principles (Fidell, 2011).

Trends

Military legal history continues to evolve as new sources are discovered and more connections drawn between this area of study and other aspects of constitutional, social, and political history. Mark E. Neely Jr.'s study of nationalism during the Civil War suggests many issues of military law and practice that have yet to be fully reckoned with by historians, including the use of underage soldiers and the torture of suspected deserters (Neely, 2011). Neely counsels greater attention to judicial records in habeas corpus cases in order to uncover this history (2011: 198).

Military cases have become staples of constitutional law casebooks since the revival of military commission after the 9/11/2001 attacks on the U.S., demonstrating the centrality of military legal issues to core questions of the status and history of executive power, congressional authority, and judicial competence. Issues of military law that arise in courtrooms are a rich source of material for historians seeking to refine U.S. constitutional and political history. Judicial opinions and other legal documents created through prosecutions at both courts-martial and military commissions have left a record yet to be fully examined but rife with insight into war crimes, military culture, and military discipline, each of which has implications for larger civil questions of how to manage interpersonal violence, understand shifting cultural norms, and create appropriate behavioral incentives. Most issues of military law and policy echo comparable civil issues, making the history of military law essential to a complete history of U.S. federal and state criminal law and procedure. Consider, for example, sexual assault within the U.S. armed forces, which has left behind unmistakable trauma as well as an utter lack of consensus as to whether military rape has been adequately addressed by the military justice system. The sustained attention of scholars is likely to uncover more historical data about the extent, legal responses, and social consequences of sexual assault in the military, resulting in more accurate visions of the problem that could enhance our understanding of sexual violence outside the armed forces as well as within the ranks. Some of this data will come from legal sources other than criminal trials and appeals. Suits for civil damages and veterans' benefits related to sexual assault have led attorneys and advocates to collect and analyze information about service members' experiences that will be of great value to historians as well.

Because so much legal reform takes place outside the courts, especially in a realm of law and practice deemed as distinctive and deserving of judicial deference as military operations are, new information about legislative reform will likely shape future scholarship as well. Available through both the Library of Congress and the Harvard Law School Library is a new digital collection of reports, correspondence, notes, draft, agendas, and hearing material based on the materials that Edmund Morgan compiled as chairman of a committee convened by Secretary of Defense James Forrestal in 1948 to produce a single code to replace the separate codes that existed for the various services. Its work led to the greatest reform in the history of the U.S. court-martial: the adoption of the Uniform Code of Military Justice (UCMJ) in 1950. The records of Professor Morgan's committee are a key resource for those in search of the history of the UCMJ drafters' intentions and challenges. Like this collection, other primary source materials are being digitized and made available through collaborations of the Library of Congress with government entities like the U.S. Army Judge Advocate General's Legal Center and School Library in Charlottesville, Virginia.

Contested changes in laws and regulations regarding the integration of the armed forces across lines of race, gender, and sexual orientation will likely attract renewed scholarly interest as more records, official and otherwise, become available regarding the late-twentieth-century military. With the end of the ban on open service by gays and lesbians in 2011, greater openness about the past and present of service members' lives and military experiences could give scholars a deeper understanding of military society and culture. Tracing the means by which various out-groups have opened the doors to military service recasts broader narratives of civil rights history as well.

The history of military prisons is another aspect of military legal history that will likely be influenced by greater disclosure of post-9/11 detention facilities and practices as well as discovery of details about past military prisons. For example, Camp Lawton in Georgia was the site of a Confederate prison that replaced Andersonville in the fall of 1864, but only in 2010 was the exact location of its stockade identified. The material culture of prisoners of war has been fertile ground for many recent museum exhibits and analyses.

It seems likely that the Camp Lawton discovery will bring new artifacts and perspectives into the public and scholarly discourse of the Civil War.

Despite the aspirations of international human rights law, historians are likely to undermine any single narrative that sees war as progressively cleaner, less brutal, and more humane, or military law as steadily more respectful of procedural justice and human rights. The history of bombing, for instance, is full of technological advances that promise greater accuracy, yet the destruction caused by aerial bombing of even the most carefully scrutinized list of targets has continued to generate outrage and anguish. The laws of war will remain an essential starting point for historical assessments of the legality of tactics during war, but historians who dig deeper will uncover a reality impossible to categorize through concepts like "proportionality," which bars destruction that would not result in a commensurate military gain, and "discrimination," which requires a military to distinguish between civilian and military targets. Debates over how military strategies, tactics, laws, and cultural norms have operated in the past will continue to shape the law in and around the twenty-first-century armed forces.

References

Allison, William Thomas (2007). *Military Justice in Vietnam: The Rule of Law in an American War*. University of Kansas Press, Lawrence.

Bacevich, Andrew J. (2010). *Washington Rules: America's Path to Permanent War*. Henry Holt, New York.

Bacevich, Andrew J. (1986). *The Pentomic Era: The U.S. Army Between Korea and Vietnam*. National Defense University Press, Washington, D.C.

Barnett, Louise (2010). *Atrocity and American Military Justice in Southeast Asia*. Routledge, New York.

Belkin, Aaron (2011). *How We Won, Progressive Lessons From the Repeal of Don't Ask, Don't Tell*. Huffington Post Media Group, New York.

Belknap, Michal R. (2002). *The Vietnam War on Trial: The My Lai Massacre and the Court-Martial of Lieutenant Calley*. University Press of Kansas, Lawrence.

Benedict, Helen (2009). *The Lonely Soldier: The Private War of Women Serving in Iraq*. Beacon Press, New York.

Bilton, Michael and Sims, Kevin (1993). *Four Hours in My Lai*. Penguin, New York.

Borch, III, Frederic L. (2004). *Judge Advocates in Vietnam: Army Lawyers in Southeast Asia, 1959–1975*. University Press of the Pacific, Honolulu.

Coffman, Edward M. (1988). *The Old Army: A Portrait of the American Army in Peacetime, 1784–1898*. Oxford University Press, New York.

Cox, Caroline (2004). *A Proper Sense of Honor: Service and Sacrifice in George Washington's Army*. University of North Carolina Press, Chapel Hill.

Danner, Mark (2004). *Torture and Truth: America, Abu Ghraib, and the War on Terror*. New York Review of Books, New York.

Dobbs, Michael (2004). *Saboteurs: The Nazi Raid on America*. Alfred A. Knopf, New York.

Dudziak, Mary (2012). *War Time: An Idea, Its History, Its Consequences.* Oxford University Press, New York.

Eckhardt, William G. (2000). "My Lai: An American Tragedy." *University of Missouri at Kansas City Law Review* 68 (Summer): 671–703.

Fidell, Eugene R. (2009–2010). "Justice John Paul Stevens and Judicial Deference in Military Matters." *University of California Davis Law Review* 43: 999–1020.

Fidell, Eugene R. (2011). "Military Law." *Daedalus: The Journal of the American Academy of Arts and Sciences* 140(3): 165–178.

Fidell, Eugene R. and Sullivan, Dwight H., eds (2002). *Evolving Military Justice.* Naval Institute Press, Annapolis.

Finn, James, ed. (1971). *Conscience and Command: Justice and Discipline in the Military.* Random House, New York.

Fisher, Louis (2003). *Nazi Saboteurs on Trial.* University Press of Kansas, Lawrence.

Fisher, Louis (2005). *Military Tribunals and Presidential Power: American Revolution to the War on Terrorism.* University Press of Kansas, Lawrence.

Flynn, George Q. (1993). *The Draft, 1940–1973.* University Press of Kansas, Lawrence.

Geary, James W. (1986). "Civil War Conscription in the North: A Historiographical Review," *Civil War History* 32: 208–228.

Generous, Jr., William T. (1973). *Swords and Scales: The Development of the Uniform Code of Military Justice.* Kennikat Press, Port Washington, New York.

Gilligan, Francis A. and Lederer, Fredric I. (2007). *Court-Martial Procedure.* 3rd Edition. LexisNexis, New York.

Glazier, David (2005). "Precedents Lost: The Neglected History of the Military Commission," *Virginia Journal of International Law* 46: 5–81.

Goldich, Robert L. (2011). "American Military Culture from Colony to Empire." *Daedalus: The Journal of the American Academy of Arts and Sciences,* 140(3): 58–74.

Graveline, Christopher and Clemens, Michael (2010). *The Secrets of Abu Ghraib Revealed: American Soldiers on Trial.* Potomac Books, Washington D.C.

Greenberg, Karen J. and Dratel, Joshua L., eds (2005). *The Torture Papers: The Road to Abu Ghraib.* Cambridge University Press, New York.

Grenier, John (2008). *The First Way of War: American War Making on the Frontier, 1607–1814.* Cambridge University Press, New York.

Hamann, Jack (2005). *On American Soil: How Justice Became a Casualty of World War II.* University of Washington, Seattle.

Hillman, Elizabeth Lutes (2005). *Defending America: Military Culture and the Cold War Court-Martial.* Princeton University Press, Princeton, NJ.

Hillman, Elizabeth L. (2008). "Gentlemen under Fire: The U.S. Military and 'Conduct Unbecoming.'" *Law & Inequality* 26: 1–57.

Holzer, Harold, ed. (2011). *Lincoln on War.* Algonquin Books, Chapel Hill, NC.

Kaplan, Alice (2005). *The Interpreter.* The Free Press, New York.

Karsten, Peter (1978). Law, Soldiers, and Combat. Greenwood Press, Westport, CT.

Karsten, Peter (2008). *The Naval Aristocracy: The Golden Age of Annapolis and the Emergence of Modern American Navalism.* The Naval Institute Press, Annapolis.

Kastenberg, Joshua E. (2009). *The Blackstone of Military Law: Colonel William Winthrop.* The Scarecrow Press, Inc., Lanham, MD.

Kohn, Richard H., ed. (1991). *The United States Military Under the Constitution of the United States, 1789–1989.* New York University Press, New York.

Jardim, Tomaz (2011). *The Mauthausen Trial: American Military Justice in Germany.* Harvard University Press, Cambridge, MA.

Lepre, George (2011). *Fragging: Why U.S. Soldiers Assaulted Their Officers in Vietnam.* Texas Tech University Press, Lubbock, Texas.

Lindley, John M. (1990). *"A Soldier is Also a Citizen": The Controversy over Military Justice, 1917–1920.* Garland Publishing, Inc., New York.

Linn, Brian McAllister (2011). "The U.S. Armed Forces' View of War." *Daedalus: The Journal of the American Academy of Arts and Sciences* 140(3): 33–44.

Lurie, Jonathan (1992). *Arming Military Justice: The Origins of the United States Court of Appeals for the Armed Forces, 1775–1950.* Princeton University Press, Princeton, NJ.

Lurie, Jonathan (1998). *Pursuing Military Justice: The History of the United States Court of Appeals for the Armed Forces, 1951–1980.* Princeton University Press, Princeton, NJ.

Marrus, Michael R. (1997). *The Nuremberg War Crimes Trial 1945–46: A Documentary History.* Bedford/St. Martin's Press, New York.

Mazur, Diane H. (2010). *A More Perfect Military: How the Constitution Can Make Our Military Stronger.* Oxford University Press, New York.

McGinty, Brian (2008). *Lincoln and the Court.* Harvard University Press, Cambridge.

Melville, Herman (1992 [1924]). *Billy Budd.* TOR Books, New York.

Moser, Richard (1996). *The New Winter Soldiers: GI and Veteran Dissent during the Vietnam Era.* Rutgers University Press, New Brunswick, NJ.

Neely, Jr., Mark E. (1991). *The Fate of Liberty: Abraham Lincoln and Civil Liberties.* Oxford University Press, New York.

Neely, Jr., Mark E. (2007). *The Civil War and the Limits of Destruction.* Harvard University Press, Cambridge, MA.

Neely, Jr., Mark E. (2011). *Lincoln and the Triumph of the Nation: Constitutional Conflict in the American Civil War.* University of North Carolina Press, Chapel Hill.

Neff, Stephen C. (2010). *Justice in Blue and Gray: A Legal History of the Civil War.* Harvard University Press, Cambridge.

Olshansky, Barbara J. (2007). *Democracy Detained: Secret, Unconstitutional Practices in the U.S. War on Terror.* Seven Stories Press, New York.

Schlueter, David A., Rose, Charles H., Hansen, Victor, and Behan, Christopher (2008). *Military Crimes and Defenses.* LexisNexis, New York.

Siegel, Jay (1998). *Origins of the United States Navy Judge Advocate General's Corps: A History of Legal Administration in the United States Navy, 1775 to 1967.* Government Printing Office, Washington, D.C.

Smith, Clive Stafford (2007). *Eight O'Clock Ferry to the Windward Side: Seeking Justice in Guantanamo Bay.* Nation Books, New York.

Solis, Gary D. (1989). *Trial by Fire: Marines and Military in Vietnam.* Marine Corps History and Museums Division, Washington, D.C.

Solis, Gary D. (1997). *Son Thang: An American War Crime.* Naval Institute Press, Annapolis, MD.

Solis, Gary D. (2010). *The Law of Armed Conflict: International Humanitarian Law in War*. Cambridge University Press, New York.

Solis, Gary D. and Borch, Fred L. (2010). *Geneva Conventions*. Kaplan Publishing, New York.

Strassfeld, Robert N. (1994). "The Vietnam War on Trial: The Court-Martial of Dr. Howard B. Levy." *Wisconsin Law Review* 1994: 839–963.

Strum, Philippa (2002). *Women in the Barracks: The VMI Case and Equal Rights*. University Press of Kansas, Lawrence.

Stuart, Douglas T. (2008). *Creating the National Security State: A History of the Law that Transformed America*. Princeton University Press, Princeton, NJ.

Sutherland, Daniel T. (2009). *A Savage Conflict: The Decisive Role of Guerrillas in the American Civil War*. University of North Carolina Press, Chapel Hill.

Taguba, Antonio M. (2004). *Article 15-6 Investigation of the 800th Military Police Brigade (the Taguba Report)*. U.S. Army, Washington, D.C.

Taylor, Telford (1992). *The Anatomy of the Nuremberg Trials*. Alfred E. Knopf, New York.

Turley, Jonathan (2002a). "The Military Pocket Republic." *Northwestern University Law Review* 97: 1–133.

Turley, Jonathan (2002b). "Tribunals and Tribulations: The Antithetical Elements of Military Governance in a Madisonian Democracy." *George Washington Law Review* 70: 649–768.

United States Army, Judge Advocate General's Corps (1993). *The Army Lawyer: A History of the Judge Advocate General's Corps, 1775–1975*. William S. Hein, Buffalo, NY.

Wiener, Frederick Bernays (1958). "Courts-Martial and the Bill of Rights: The Original Practice I." *Harvard Law Review* 72: 1–49.

Weitz, Mark W. (2005). *The Confederacy on Trial: The Piracy and Sequestration Cases of 1861*. University Press of Kansas, Lawrence.

Wilson, Mark R. (2010). "Taking a Nickel out of the Cash Register: Statutory Renegotiation of Military Contracts and the Politics of Profit Control in the United States during World War II." *Law and History Review*, 28(2): 343–384.

Winthrop, William (1920). *Military Law and Precedents*. 2nd Edition. Government Printing Office, Washington, D.C.

Witt, John Fabian (2012). *Lincoln's Code: The Laws of War in American History*. The Free Press, New York.

Zimmerman, Jean (1995). *Tailspin: Women at War in the Wake of Tailhook*. Doubleday, New York.

Chapter Twenty-two

CRIMINAL LAW AND JUSTICE IN AMERICA

Elizabeth Dale

Criminal justice is a comparatively new subject for historians of American law. If the birth of modern legal history dates to the work of J. Willard Hurst and the Wisconsin school in the 1950s and 1960s, legal historians did not begin to devote sustained attention to criminal justice until Lawrence M. Friedman's *Crime and Punishment in American History* was published in 1994. The youth of the field means that Friedman's work remains one of the few general histories of crime and punishment in the United States (see also Walker, 1998), but the passage of more than twenty years since his book was published means there are works enough to constitute a recognizable field of study. That is particularly true if we expand our scope to include the treatment of criminal law issues in works that focus on other types of legal history, or look at the historical analysis of criminal justice that often is embedded in studies of criminology or policy history. In the first two sections below, I pull studies from these different genres together to sketch a general introduction to the history of criminal law in the United States. In the third and final section, I then trace some developing trends in the field.

Overview

Although there are few general studies of the history of criminal law in America, a number of histories canvas criminal law in particular periods. These works generally break the field into three familiar eras: the colonial

---

A Companion to American Legal History, First Edition.
Edited by Sally E. Hadden and Alfred L. Brophy.
© 2013 John Wiley & Sons Ltd. Published 2021 by John Wiley & Sons Ltd.

era (Chapin, 1983), the nineteenth (Dale, 2011) and the twentieth centuries (Willrich, 2008). Within each period certain issues are the focus of most of the investigations. Thus studies of the earliest period explore how theories of right and wrong derived from a mix of transplanted legal rules and customs in the early seventeenth century were transformed into a system of justice that increasingly was based on Enlightenment principles at the start of the nineteenth century (Friedman, 1994; Meranze, 2008). While no study has called that narrative into question, several recent works have positioned that story of borrowed and transplanted law in the larger history of the Atlantic World (Pagan, 2003), complicating our understanding of the spaces encompassed by histories of criminal law in the early Americas and reminding us that legal traditions and customs were transplanted not only by Europeans, but by Africans as well (Scott, 2011). Other studies consider how different colonies translated English law to fit their own particular needs, and the extent to which they created distinctive legal systems in the process (Chapin, 1983). Most often these histories explore the distinction between criminal justice systems based on the "godly discipline" typically associated with Puritan Massachusetts and the social control model found in colonies like Virginia (Chapin, 1983; Norton, 1996). However, a number of works have called elements of that division into question: In his study of the legal order in Pennsylvania, William Offutt explored the influence of Quaker principles on criminal justice in the Delaware Valley (Offutt, 1995), adding another dynamic to the mix. In a later study of "the sexual revolution" in early America Richard Godbeer raised questions about the extent to which the laws New England actually imposed a moral order (Godbeer, 2004). And in a recent essay, Richard Ross challenged that division in another way, suggesting that the division between godly discipline and social control models might best be understood in a transnational (as opposed to colonial) perspective (Ross, 2008).

If histories of the first, colonial era of criminal justice looked at questions of transplant and translation of law, studies that look at criminal law in the nineteenth century often focus on the creation of a distinctive American system of criminal law. Some look at turn-of-the-century efforts to reform criminal justice (Nelson, 1967; Preyer, 1983), tracing the ways in which those reform efforts were influenced by Enlightenment principles, an interest in Americanizing the law to reflect the break with England, and the desires of state governments to carve out a space of power (Wilf, 2010). Recent work has demonstrated that while reform efforts began at the end of the eighteenth century, the process took much of the first half of the nineteenth century and often was contested by popular forces eager to retain their customary authority (Edwards, 2009). A number of early studies of criminal law and justice in the nineteenth century explored whether, and to what extent, systems of criminal law reflected regional differences, particularly the differences created by slavery (Hindus, 1980) and the notions of race and class that arose after Emancipation (Ayers, 1984). While much of the work on criminal justice in the nineteenth century has continued that focus on the impact of the division between the slave holding South and the North, that is not the only regional distinction studied in the literature. Several legal histories explore the influence of westward expansion, considering ways in which people in frontier societies created systems of criminal justice (Reid, 1997) and sometimes resisted those forces (Courtwright, 1996). Other studies have looked more narrowly at criminal justice in the nation's cities. Many of these explore the creation and implementation of what Lawrence Friedman called the "Victorian Compromise," the idea that public order became more important than policing morality with the result that many bad acts, though nominally crimes, were tolerated if they happened out of sight (Friedman, 1994: 127). Friedman associated that compromise with the first half of the nineteenth century, and a number of studies have elaborated on that insight, exploring how this compromise worked, and failed, in antebellum cities (see, e.g., Gilfoyle, 1992; Cohen, 1998). But other studies have uncovered similar compromises in the late nineteenth century (Best, 1998). These studies suggest that in the later period, the compromise was complicated by racial attitudes that often set limits on those informal arrangements (Blair, 2010).

Regardless of their precise perspective, many of the studies of criminal law in the nineteenth century reveal a tension between state efforts to create a rule of law in a formal system of criminal justice and popular attempts to resist or ignore those forces (Dale, 2011). In contrast, histories of criminal justice in the twentieth century typically are accounts of how the forces of the state triumphed (Pfeifer, 2004; Willrich, 2008). That triumph was complicated by a shift away from local control of criminal justice (Keire, 2001; Foster, 2002) and a number of studies describe a process increasing federal influence that evolved in three stages: In its earliest manifestation, which began in the last decades of the nineteenth century, the process involved the passage of a number of statutes creating federal crimes (Hamm, 1995; Keire, 2001) and the creation of federal agencies to police those laws (McWilliams, 1990). Then, in the years after World War I, efforts to decrease local control over criminal justice moved into the courts as the Supreme Court gradually began to use the Bill of Rights to review criminal justice in state courts (Goodman, 1995). This court-centered undertaking picked up steam during the New Deal and continued through the Warren Court (Stuntz, 2011). Then in its most recent iteration, the decline of local control over criminal law in the twentieth century rested on national "tough on crime" policies and victim's rights movements. Those efforts in the last decades in the twentieth century made punishments more severe and the criminal justice state more pervasive (Simon, 2007; Willrich, 2008).

For all that periodization dominates the field of criminal justice, several narratives cut across the centuries. One is the story of changes in imprisonment that led to the creation of what Robert Perkinson has called "America's Prison Empire" (Perkinson, 2010). Studies trace the American embrace of imprisonment to the rise (Meranze, 1996) and spread of the penitentiary in the nineteenth century (McLennan, 2008), and then show how the penitentiary system expanded dramatically with the rise of the war on crime in the middle of the twentieth century (Thompson, 2010; Perkinson, 2010). A related story, which also cuts across the divisions of the centuries, examines the relationship between criminal justice and social hierarchy, particularly hierarchies of race, class, and gender. Studies reveal a trajectory that began with the use of criminal justice to control Native Americans (Kawashima, 2001), women, and slaves (Brown, 1996) in early America, then continued into the nineteenth century where criminal law was used to control unruly women (Branson, 2008), slaves (Campbell, 2007), and workers (Avrich, 1984) or members of other dangerous classes (Shelden, 2007). Finally, in the twentieth and early twenty-first centuries, laws associated with the wars on drugs and terror were used to subordinate and disenfranchise minority communities (Thompson, 2010; Alexander, 2010; Stuntz, 2011). A third narrative that cuts across most of the history of criminal law in the United States traces the relationship between changes in criminal law and the constitutional order. That relationship is most obvious in studies of the rise and evolution of rights-based jurisprudence in the twentieth century (Willrich, 2008). But the constitutional aspect of criminal justice also was revealed in the changing dynamics of power between local communities and the state government (Edwards, 2009), between state and federal governments (Burns, 2010), and between the people and the institutions of the state (Pfeifer, 2004; Dale, 2011).

Building a History From Fragments

Those narratives of criminal justice are complicated by the fact that the history of criminal justice in the United States is a fragmented one. Often this fragmentation is geographic: the history of criminal justice has been intensely local, told in terms of cities (Steinberg, 1989), counties (Friedman and Percival, 1981), states (Williams, 1959; Waldrep, 1998), or regions (Ayers, 1984). That segmentation reflects a fundamental reality: Even today there is not one criminal justice system in the United States, there are more than fifty (in addition to the criminal justice system in each state, the District of Columbia, Puerto Rico, and the federal government, there are systems of criminal law for Indian Tribal Lands, the military, and American territories). At the same time, the geographic fragmentation of the field is exacerbated by the fact that many historians focus on specific aspects of the criminal justice system. There are, for example, a number of studies that look at the history of particular crimes. Most popular are histories of homicide (Lane, 1997; Monkonnen, 2001; Adler, 2006; Roth, 2009), an emphasis that is driven by the reality that homicide rates in the United States have long outstripped those of other, comparable Western nations (Monkkonen, 2006). Once again, many of these studies are local (Monkkonen, 2001; Adler, 2006), though several recent works have tried to trace national trends (Lane, 1997; Roth, 2009). While many of these studies look at all types of killings (Lane, 1997; Adler, 2006), some look at particular types of homicide, such as infanticide (Hoffer and Hull, 1981), lynching (Pfeifer, 2004), and the criminalization of abortion (Reagan, 1997).

While homicide is the focus of many studies, there is a growing body of historical work that looks at other particular crimes and their punishments. A number of histories examine morals offenses, particularly sex crimes: Sharon Block has studied rape in early American law (Block, 2006), while Mary Odem has looked at the creation of statutory rape laws in the twentieth century (Odem, 1995). There are also studies of domestic crimes from incest (Sacco, 2009) to spouse abuse (McCormick, 2007). A number of recent works have considered the criminalization of sexuality (Richards, 2009), prostitution (Romesburg, 2009), and obscenity (Friedman, 2000; Dennis, 2009). Another group of studies have looked at the history of laws criminalizing alcohol (Foster, 2002; Stewart, 2011), and drugs (Spillane, 1998; Kohler-Hausmann, 2010). There are also works that look at economic crimes, including crimes of fraud (Mihm, 2007) and smuggling (Griffith, 2004; Cohen, 2010). Studies in the latter category cover a range of subjects, from efforts to control the smuggling of items (Cohen, 2010) to attempts to halt the traffic in people (Griffith, 2004; Obadele-Starks, 2007). Those studies of particular crimes are complemented by a number of works that examine the histories of specific defenses, such as the insanity defense (Rosenberg, 1968), or other legal protections like habeas corpus (Wert, 2011) and the requirement of proof beyond a reasonable doubt (Shapiro, 1991). Yet another group of specialized histories look at the rise and fall of the so-called "unwritten law," a practice (which sometimes attained the level of doctrine) that excused those who murdered men who raped or seduced women (Hartog, 1997) and women who seduced other women's lovers (Bakken, 1998).

Just as many studies look at the histories of specific crimes, so too a significant number of studies focus on the various institutions of the system of criminal justice, from the police (Monkkonen, 1981; Miller, 1999) to prisons (Meranze, 1996; McLennan, 2008). In addition to several general works (Monkkonen, 1981; Miller, 1999), the work on policing has looked at the development of police departments in various northern (Lane, 1971; Ethington, 1987; Lindberg, 1998) and southern cities (Rousey, 1996). This literature includes a number of works that look at specific types of policing, from the creation of slave patrols (Hadden, 2001) to the role of the police in juvenile justice at the turn of the twentieth century (Wolcott, 2005). Still another group of historical works look at policing at the federal level, exploring the federal posse comitatus (Rao, 2008) and various federal law enforcement agencies (Johnson, 1981; McWilliams, 1990). Recently several works have looked at a number of abuses in policing: the "rise of the surveillance state" (McCoy, 2009), the use and misuse of the lie detector (Alder, 2007), some departments' use of torture to induce confessions (Conroy, 2000), and the problem of homicides by police officers (Adler, 2012).

If we move from the police to the courts, we find the history of criminal process is equally fragmentary. Several areas, particularly criminal trials, have received considerable attention from historians. Much of this work has been done in the form of case studies. Read individually, these works provide a variety of perspectives on criminal justice: Some explore how formal law intersected with popular ideas of justice (Dale, 2003), or consider how outcomes are influenced by social and cultural forces such as gender (MacLean, 1991; Cohen, 1998) or racial norms (Goodman, 1995; Trotti, 2008). In one classic study, Charles Rosenberg used the trial of the assassin Guiteau for the murder of President Garfield to explore popular attitudes toward the insanity defense (Rosenberg, 1968). Other histories, like a recent history of the John Brown trial (McGinty, 2009) and an older, but classic work on prosecutions under the Espionage Acts after World War I (Polenberg, 1987), demonstrate how the political anxieties of the times help to determine verdicts. Read as a whole, these studies offer a glimpse at how procedures in felony trials changed over time, and that image is elaborated by studies of crime and justice in particular places (Friedman and Perceival, 1981; Waldrep, 1998) that describe how and why trial practice changed. Other works add to our understanding of the criminal justice system by looking at the procedures and jurisdictions of other criminal and quasi-criminal courts. There are several studies that look at juvenile courts (Tanenhaus, 2004; Bush, 2010) and petty criminal courts (Steinberg, 1989; Willrich, 2003) in particular jurisdictions. Biographies and autobiographies of trial lawyers also provide glimpses at the workings of the criminal justice system at particular moments in time (Farrell, 2011).

But we could do more to understand the historic role of the other major actor in criminal trials: the criminal jury. Some early empirical works studied jury verdicts in particular places (Bodenhamer, 1983), and there are also works that look at shifts in the theory of jury power in criminal cases (Harrington, 1999). The struggle for the right to participate in juries, by women (Kerber, 1999) and African Americans (Waldrep, 2010), has also been the subject of some study. But more could be done to unpack the jurors' role in the criminal justice system and the impact of social or economic status on verdicts (Dale, 2006). Given work that has been done on juries by other social scientists (Vidmar and Hans, 2007) this seems to be a particularly fruitful area for more complicated, perhaps empirical history.

But for all this, the picture we have of the workings of the criminal courts in history is still incomplete and episodic; Michael Millender's unpublished dissertation is the only study that tries to provide a national account of changes in the criminal trial (Millender, 1996). Another problem is that these studies of criminal trials, fascinating as they are, provide a somewhat distorted picture of the history of criminal justice, since trials, especially jury trials, have not been the norm in the criminal courts for many years. Some recent studies have tried to correct this imbalance, considering the rise and spread of the plea bargain (McCanville and Mirsky, 1995; Vogel, 1999; Fisher, 2004). But given the significant effect of plea bargains on conviction rates and the workings of the criminal courts (Lane, 1997), more could be done in this area.

So, too, there is room for more work on post-trial procedures and protections. While Carolyn Strange has done some work in the area of the pardon power (Strange, 2010), there are few other studies that consider the significance of that point where criminal law and politics met and the role of pardons in relation to criminal appeals. Nor is there much work on the area of criminal appeals. Although countless studies trace the path of famous cases to the United States Supreme Court (Lewis, 1964; Polenburg, 1987; Goodman, 1995), and a few histories of state appellate courts (Meyer, Agata and Agata, 2006; Manley and Brown, 2006) discuss criminal appeals briefly, there is very little work that specifically explores when or how the appellate process began to play a role in the criminal justice system.

The situation with respect to punishment is somewhat different. There are any number of studies that look at the rise of prisons and penitentiaries (Hindus, 1980; Meranze, 1996). These studies are often regional: works about the North focus on the rise and development of the penitentiary (Meranze, 1996; McLennan, 2008), while studies of the South look at the creation of convict labor practice and their ultimate demise in the years after the Civil War (Mancini, 1996). But some offer a comparative approach (Hindus, 1980). There is also an extensive literature on capital punishment (Banner, 2002), anti-capital punishment efforts (Masur, 1989), and the extent to which social factors like race and class influenced capital punishment across the history of the United States (Allen and Chubb, 2008). But while a recent book by Anne-Marie Cusac looks at the history of punishment in the United States (Cusac, 2010), there are few other studies that consider the range of other punishments that were imposed by criminal courts in the United States (see, e.g., Williams, 1959). Likewise, more could be done to consider the relationship between torture and punishment (Garland, 2005).

Law, especially criminal law, does not exist in a vacuum. Because histories of criminal law are strongly influenced by both criminology and the law and society movement, there are a number of histories of criminal justice that explore the relationship between society and the institutions and practices of criminal justice. That dynamic can run in multiple directions: law may be constituted by society, society may be constituted by law. Thus, studies of the history of criminal law consider how and why legal practices and processes influenced crime rates (Monkkonen, 2001; Dale, 2006) or explore how social attitudes shaped the way the criminal justice system treated particular offenses (Roth, 2009). Because criminal law is often a site in which power is revealed, a number of studies look at how understandings of gender (Carlson, 2009) and race (McGuire, 2010) helped determine how different people experienced the criminal justice system as victims (McGuire, 2010) or defendants (Gross, 2006; Carlson, 2009) or both (McNair, 2009). A related body of work traces the various social mechanisms that people used when they enacted extralegal justice. While much of the work in this area looks at the most violent forms of popular justice, the lynch mob and the vigilante (Brown, 1975; Pfeifer, 2004), those were not the only means by which local communities took the law into their own hands. Sometimes, this is done through shame or shunning (Dale, 2006), other times extralegal processes of judgment and punishment were expressed through community-based mobs (Brown, 1975), quasi-official law and order leagues (Gilfoyle, 1992), and other forms of non-lethal violence (Dale, 2011).

Criminal justice is also shaped by, and constitutive of, culture and several histories look at the role of criminal justice in popular culture. In addition to general overviews of the field (Papke, 1987), there are studies that look at the treatment of criminal trials in particular genres, exploring how crime and punishment have been treated in the press (Tucker, 1994; Cohen, 1998), literature (Borowitz, 1977), or film (Rafter, 2000). In her study of the trial reports published as popular works in the nineteenth century, Karen Halttunen explained the ways that those reports tracked changing views of women, as murders and victims (Halttunen, 1998). In other books, Patricia Cline Cohen and Michael Trotti considered how newspaper coverage, and its absence, influenced the outcomes of murder trials at the beginning and end of the nineteenth century (Cohen, 1998; Trotti, 2008), while I have considered how newspapers and other forms of popular pressure influenced the investigation and prosecution of trials (Dale, 2001). Another recent work by Cheree Carlson extended that analysis of popular opinion in a different direction, considering how popular theories of womanhood and femininity played out in arguments of counsel into the early decades of the twentieth century (Carlson, 2009). Some studies of popular justice look to the cultural basis of those practices. Following Bertram Wyatt-Brown (Wyatt-Brown, 1982), many of these studies have traced out the role that honor culture played in justifying these popular forms of justice (Rothman, 2008). But while Wyatt-Brown asserted that honor culture was a distinctly southern phenomenon, recent works have found notions of honor influenced popular justice in the North, as well (Lane, 1997). Other studies have tied popular efforts to judge and punish to traditional theories of popular justice (Waldrep, 2002; Pfeifer, 2004; Hill, 2010), or have considered the ways in which religious ideas enabled acts of popular justice (Ayers, 1987; Waldrep, 1990).

Newer Trends

As all this suggests, in the field of legal history criminal justice, although relatively young, is a rich area of study that connects with a range of social, political and economic issues. The sizable body of work that already has been written engages a number of aspects of the history of crime and its punishment. But a number of more recent works have begun to push the study of criminal justice in several new directions.

Quite a few recent histories, particularly those that look at criminal law in the twentieth century, focus on the failures of the system (Willrich, 2008; Stuntz, 2011). This emphasis is partly a consequence of the reform cycles that dominate discussions of criminal justice in the twentieth century: movements for reform of law or punishment invariably ground their claims for change on arguments about the failure of the status quo. But the emphasis also reflects the sense that at the start of the twenty-first century criminal justice in the United States bears very little resemblance to that in other developed nations. Incarceration rates are higher, homicide rates, though declining, remain high, and an extraordinary percentage of the population are convicted and punished for a crime at some point in their lives. Given employment practices that often permit, and sometimes encourage, employers not to hire people with criminal records, the high rate of punishment and conviction have long-term economic consequences, particularly for African-American men, who are disproportionately arrested, charged, convicted, and incarcerated for crimes (Stuntz, 2011). Several of the recent works that have grappled with this issue have offered a variety of historical explanations for its cause (Simon, 2007; Alexander, 2010). But while these studies use history to explain the problems they detect, their historical analysis is often subordinated to their discussion of policy. As a result, further historical study might be useful to help test these arguments.

So too, early studies that celebrated the ways in which provisions of the Bill of Rights were applied to protect criminal defendants in state court trials (Lewis, 1964), have given way to works that note the limits of the rights-based prohibitions (Rejali, 2007) or argue that our rights-based system has become an inflexible and unjust process (Stuntz, 2011). But more work could be done to ground these revisionist arguments in history. In addition, the work on defendant's rights needs to be complemented by more studies that explore the rise and influence of the victim's rights movement (Willrich, 2008). But while more work could be done to uncover the impact of the turn towards rights, rights are not the only means by which the criminal justice systems in the United States engage the constitutional order. Recent works on popular sovereignty (Frank, 2010) and citizenship (Kirkpatrick, 2008) have suggested close ties between criminal justice and citizenship by exploring how and why "the people" take the law into their own hands to judge and punish others. Most obviously, these studies do so by exploring the relationship between formal law and popular justice, and tracing how and why formal law ultimately succeeded in suppressing lynch mobs and vigilante justice (Ethington, 1987; Brundage, 1993; Pfeifer, 2004).

A number of other studies have begun to consider the relationship between criminal justice and the state. Following Weber, we have long assumed that criminal justice was the prerogative of the state, and many histories of criminal justice are studies of state power as well (Cohen, 2010). But studies of extralegal justice suggest an alternative vision of crime and punishment in American history by exploring how private parties often laid claim to the powers to judge and punish wrongdoing and were frequently successful in doing so. As Phillip Ethington's study of the relationship between the vigilante movement and police in San Francisco suggests (Ethington, 1987), the relationship between police and less formal processes of law enforcement is an interesting area of study. There has been some work in this field: Several studies look at the roles that the Committee of Fourteen and the Society for the Suppression of Vice played in vice prosecutions in New York City in the early twentieth century (Friedman, 2000). In a recent article Jessica Wang explored the public role of private groups in animal control in New York City (Wang, 2012). And studies of vigilante movements also consider whether and to what extent those efforts engaged with formal systems of policing (Brown, 1975; Kirkpatrick, 2009). Another variation on this theme is suggested by works that consider the fuzzy boundaries between racketeering and private policing (Cohen, 2004) or street gangs as agents of social control (Cooley, 2011). In another study, Heather Ann Thompson has taken the connection between criminal justice and citizenship in another direction, considering how punishment regimes and the carceral state have helped deny some people (mostly African Americans) the rights of citizenship (Thompson, 2010). In effect, these works suggest that the history of criminal law tracks the long-standing struggle over where sovereign power was located in the United States constitutional order and how it should be expressed (Dale, 2011). But more could be done to explore that dynamic.

While those works reflect changes within the history of criminal law in the United States, a number of recent works have begun to push the boundaries of criminal legal history. Some remind us that borrowed ideas of criminal justice were transported across borders (Wilf, 2010), consider how police practices like torture and surveillance crossed and then recrossed national borders (Rejali, 2007; McCoy, 2009), or place the rise of the prison into global history (Gibson, 2011). While these works are a beginning, far more could be done to explore the extent to which criminal law and justice in the United States has partaken in transnational, and global elements across history (see *AHR Forum*, 2012).

A number of other studies have begun to embed the history of criminal law in the United States in the world by looking at the history of criminal law comparatively. This approach builds on a number of the earliest works in criminal law, which compared criminal justice across regions in the United States (Hindus, 1980), or across the Anglo-American world (Hoffer and Hull, 1981; Miller, 1999). These earlier works covered the scope of criminal justice, from policing (Miller, 1999), through particular crimes (Hoffer and Hull, 1981), to criminal process (Smith, 1996) and punishment (Hindus, 1980). Recently, scholars have returned to this approach: In his study of the criminal jury in France, James Donovan compared French practices to those in the United States (Donovan, 2010); in another study, John Conroy compared the use of torture by military and police forces in Ireland, Israel and the United States (Conroy, 2000). There are also studies that have compared approaches to punishment: one recent essay considered the birth of prisons in both comparative and global perspective (Gibson, 2011), while a recent book compared notions of punishment in Europe and the United States (Whitman, 2005). As more and more work is being done on the history of criminal justice in other countries, there are more possibilities for more comparative work of this sort. Likewise, work on the relation between the state and crime and systems of justice in other countries (Bridenthal, 2012) invites even more complicated transnational comparisons.

Comparative study need not, of course, cross national boundaries. Don Romesburg's recent work on male youth sex work, for example, compares the way adolescent girls and boys understood their lives as sex workers and how they were treated by the police and courts when they were suspected of sex work in turn-of-the-century Chicago (Romesburg, 2009). His work also hints at the differences between adult sex workers and youth. Similarly, William Bush's study of juvenile justice in twentieth-century Texas considered the role that race played in determining how youth were treated by the state's juvenile courts (Bush, 2010). These studies suggest that internal comparisons, based on very focused studies of how different people have experienced criminal justice across the history of the United States also may be a fruitful area of investigation.

References

Adler, Jeffrey (2006). *First in Crime, Deepest in Dirt: Homicide in Chicago, 1875–1920*. Harvard University Press, Cambridge.

Adler, Jeffrey (2012). "'The Killer Behind the Badge': Race and Police Homicide in New Orleans, 1925–1945." *Law & History Review* 30: 495.

AHR Forum (2012). "AHR Forum: Liberal Empire and International Law." *American Historical Review* 117: 1–148.

Alder, Ken (2007). *The Lie Detectors: The History of An American Obsession.* Free Press, New York.

Alexander, Michelle (2010). *The New Jim Crow: Mass Incarceration in the Age of Colorblindness.* The New Press, New York.

Allen, Howard W. and Clubb, Jerome M. (2008). *Race, Class and Death Penalty: Capital Punishment in American History.* SUNY Press, Albany.

Avrich, Paul (1984). *The Haymarket Tragedy.* Princeton University Press, Princeton.

Ayers, Edward L. (1984). *Vengeance and Justice: Crime and Punishment in the 19th Century American South.* Oxford University Press, New York.

Bakken, Gordon Morris (1988). "The Limits of Patriarchy: Women's Rights and 'Unwritten Law' in the West." *Historian* 60: 702–717.

Banner, Stuart (2002). *The Death Penalty: An American History.* Harvard University Press, Cambridge.

Bauerlein, Mark (2001). *Negrophobia: A Race Riot in Atlanta, 1908.* Encounter Books, San Francisco.

Best, Joel (1998). *Controlling Vice: Regulating Brothel Prostitution in St. Paul.* Ohio State University Press, Columbus.

Blair, Cynthia M. (2010). *I've Got to Make My Livin': Black Women's Sex Work in Turn-of-the-Century Chicago.* University of Chicago Press, Chicago.

Block, Sharon (2006). *Rape and Sexual Power in Early America.* University of North Carolina Press, Chapel Hill.

Bodenhamer, David J. (1983). "The Democratic Impulse and Legal Change in the Age of Jackson: The Example of Criminal Juries in Antebellum Indiana." *The Historian* 45: 206–219.

Borowitz, Albert (1977). *Innocence and Arsenic: Studies in Crime and Literature.* Harper and Row, New York.

Branson, Susan (2008). *Dangerous to Know: Women, Crime and Notoriety in the Early Republic.* University of Pennsylvania Press, Philadelphia.

Bridenthal, Renate (2012). "Forum: The Hidden History of Crime, Corruption, and States." *Journal of Social History* 45: 575–581.

Brown, Kathleen (1996). *Good Wives, Nasty Wenches, and Anxious Patriarchs: Gender, Race and Power in Colonial Virginia.* University of North Carolina Press, Chapel Hill.

Brown, Richard Maxwell (1975). *Strains of Violence: Historical Studies of American Violence and Vigilantism.* Oxford University Press, New York.

Brundage, William Fitzhugh (1993). *Lynching in the New South: Georgia and Virginia, 1880–1930.* University of Illinois Press, Urbana.

Burns, Adam (2010). "Without Due Process: Albert E. Pillsbury and the Hoar Anti-Lynching Bill." *American Nineteenth Century* 11: 233–252.

Bush, William S. (2010). *Who Gets a Childhood? Race and Juvenile Justice in Twentieth-Century Texas.* University of Georgia Press, Athens.

Campbell, James W. (2007). *Slavery on Trial: Race, Class and Criminal Justice in Antebellum Richmond Virginia.* University Press of Florida, Gainesville.

Carlson, A. Cheree (2009). *The Crimes of Womanhood: Defining Femininity in a Court of Law.* University of Illinois Press, Urbana.

Chapin, Bradley (1983). *Criminal Justice in Colonial America, 1606–1660.* University of Georgia Press, Athens.

Chauncey, George (1994). *Gay New York: Gender, Urban Culture, and the Making of the Gay Male World, 1890–1940*. Basic Books, New York.

Cohen, Andrew Wender (2004). *The Racketeer's Progress: Chicago and the Struggle for the Modern American Economy, 1900–1940*. Cambridge University Press, New York.

Cohen, Andrew Wender (2010). "Smuggling, Globalization and America's Outward State, 1870–1909." *Journal of American History* 97: 371–398.

Cohen, Patricia Cline (1998). *The Murder of Helen Jewett: The Life and Death of a Prostitute in Nineteenth-Century New York*. Alfred A. Knopf, New York.

Cooley, Will (2011). "'Stones Run It:' Taking back Control of Organized Crime in Chicago, 1940–1975." *Journal of Urban History* 37: 911–932.

Courtwright, David T. (1996). *Violent Land: Single Men and Social Disorder from the Frontier to the Inner City*. Harvard University Press, Cambridge.

Cusac, Anne-Marie (2010). *Cruel and Unusual: The Culture of Punishment in America*. Yale University Press, New Haven.

Dale, Elizabeth (2001). *The Rule of Justice: The People of Chicago versus Zephyr Davis*. Ohio State University Press, Columbus, OH.

Dale, Elizabeth (2003). "A Different Sort of Justice: The Informal Courts of Public Opinion in Antebellum South Carolina." *South Carolina Law Review* 54: 627–649.

Dale, Elizabeth (2006). "Getting Away with Murder." *American Historical Review* 111: 95–103.

Dale, Elizabeth (2011). *Criminal Justice in the United States, 1789–1939*. Cambridge University Press, New York.

Dennis, Donna (2009). *Licentious Gotham: Erotic Publishing and its Prosecution in Nineteenth-Century New York*. Harvard University Press, Cambridge.

Donovan, James M. (2010). *Juries and the Transformation of Criminal Justice in France in the Nineteenth and Twentieth Centuries*. University of North Carolina Press, Chapel Hill.

Edwards, Laura (2009). *The People and the Peace: Legal Culture and the Transformation of Inequality in the Post-Revolutionary South*. University of North Carolina Press, Chapel Hill.

Ethington, Philip J. (1987) "Vigilantes and the Police: The Creation of a Professional Police Bureaucracy in San Francisco, 1847–1900." *Journal of Social History* 21: 197–227.

Farrell, John A. (2011). *Clarence Darrow: Attorney for the Damned*. Random House, New York.

Fisher, George (2004). *Plea Bargaining's Triumph: A History of Plea Bargaining in America*. Stanford University Press, Stanford.

Foster, Gaines (2002). *Moral Reconstruction: Christian Lobbyists and the Federal Legislation of Morality, 1865–1920*. University of North Carolina Press, Chapel Hill.

Frank, Jason (2010). *Constituent Moments: Enacting the People in Postrevolutionary America*. Duke University Press, Durham.

Friedman, Andrea (2000). *Prurient Interests: Gender, Democracy and Obscenity in New York City, 1909–1945*. Columbia University Press, New York.

Friedman, Lawrence M. and Perceival, Robert V. (1981). *The Roots of Justice: Crime and Punishment in Alameda County, California, 1870–1910*. University of North Carolina Press, Chapel Hill.

Friedman, Lawrence M. (1994). *Crime and Punishment in American History*. Basic Books, New York.

Fritz, Christian G. (2008). *American Sovereigns: The People and America's Constitutional Tradition Before the Civil War*. Cambridge University Press, New York.

Garland, David (2005). "Penal Excess and Surplus Meaning: Public Torture Lynchings in Twentieth Century America." *Law and Society Review* 39: 793–833.

Gibson, Mary (2011). "Review Essay: Global Perspectives on the Birth of the Prison." *American Historical Review* 116: 1040–1063.

Gilfoyle, Timothy J. (1992). *City of Eros: New York City, Prostitution, and the Commercialization of Sex, 1790–1920*. W.W. Norton, New York.

Godbeer, Richard (2004). *Sexual Revolution in Early America*. Johns Hopkins University Press, Baltimore.

Goodman, James (1995). *Stories of Scottsboro*. Vintage Books, New York.

Griffith, Sarah M. (2004). "Border Crossings: Race, Class and Smuggling in Pacific Coast Chinese Immigrant Society." *Western Historical Quarterly* 35: 473–492.

Gross, Kali N. (2006). *Colored Amazons: Crime, Violence and Black Women in the City of Brotherly Love, 1880–1910*. Duke University Press, Durham.

Hadden, Sally E. (2001). *Slave Patrols: Law and Violence in Virginia and the Carolinas*. Harvard University Press, Cambridge.

Halttunen, Karen (1998). *Murder Most Foul: The Killer and the American Gothic Imagination*. Harvard University Press, Cambridge.

Hamm, Richard F. (1995). *Shaping the Eighteenth Amendment: Temperance Reform, Legal Culture, and Politics, 1880–1920*. University of North Carolina Press, Chapel Hill.

Harrington, Matthew (1999). "The Law-finding Function of the American Jury." *Wisconsin Law Journal*: 337–440.

Hartog, Hendrik (1997). "Lawyering, Husbands' Rights, and the 'Unwritten Law' in Nineteenth-Century America." *Journal of American History* 84: 67–96.

Hill, Karlos K. (2010). "Black Vigilantism: The Rise and Decline of African American Lynch Mob Activity in the Mississippi and Arkansas Deltas, 1883–1923." *Journal of African American History* 95: 26–43.

Hindus, Michael (1980). *Prison and Plantation: Crime, Justice and Authority in Massachusetts and South Carolina, 1767–1878*. University of North Carolina Press, Chapel Hill.

Hoffer, Peter and Hull, N.E.H. (1981). *Murdering Mothers: Infanticide in England and New England, 1558–1803*. New York University Press, New York.

Johnson, David R. (1981). *American Law Enforcement: A History*. Forum Press, Santa Ana.

Kawashima, Yasuhide (2001). *Igniting King Philip's War: The John Sassamon Murder Trial*. University Press of Kansas, Lawrence.

Keire, Mara L. (2001). "The Vice Trust: A Reinterpretation of the White Slavery Scare in the United States, 1907–1917." *Journal of Social History* 35: 5–41.

Kerber, Linda (1999). *No Constitutional Right to Be Ladies: Women and the Obligations of Citizenship*. Hill and Wang, New York.

Kirkpatrick, Jennet (2008). *Uncivil Disobedience: Studies in Violence and Democratic Politics*. Princeton University Press, Princeton.

Kohler-Hausmann, Juilly (2010). "'The Attila the Hun Law': New York's Rockefeller Drug Laws and the Making of a Punitive State." *Journal of Social History* 44: 71–95.

Lane, Roger (1971). *Policing the City: Boston, 1882–1885*. Harvard University Press, Cambridge.

Lane, Roger (1997). *Murder in America: A History*. Ohio State University Press, Columbus.

Lewis, Anthony (1964). *Gideon's Trumpet*. Random House, New York.

Lindberg, Richard (1998). *To Serve and Collect: Chicago Politics and Police Corruption from the Lager Beer Riot to the Summerdale Scandal*. Southern Illinois University Press, Carbondale.

MacLean, Nancy (1991). "The Leo Frank Case Reconsidered: Gender and Sexual Politics in the Making of Reactionary Populism." *Journal of American History* 78: 917–948.

Mancini, Matthew J. (1996). *One Dies, Get Another: Convict Leasing in the American South, 1866–1928*. University of South Carolina Press, Columbia.

Manley, Walter W. and Brown, Canter (2006). *The Supreme Court of Florida, 1917–1972*. University of Florida Press, Gainesville.

Masur, Louis P. (1989). *Rites of Execution: Capital Punishment and the Transformation of American Culture, 1776–1865*. Oxford University Press, New York.

McCanville, Mike and Mirsky, Chester (1995). "The Rise of the Guilty Pleas: New York, 1800–1865." *Journal of Law and Society* 22: 443–474.

McCormick, Brian T. (2007). "Conjugal Violence, Sex, Sin and Murder in the Mission Communities of Alta California." *Journal of the History of Sexuality* 16: 391–415.

McCoy, Alfred W. (2009). *Policing America's Empire: The United States, the Philippines, and the Rise of the Surveillance State*. University of Wisconsin Press, Madison.

McGinty, Brian (2009). *John Brown's Trial*. Harvard University Press, Cambridge.

McGuire, Danielle (2010). *At the Dark End of the Street: Black Women, Rape and Resistance–A New History of the Civil Rights Movement from Rosa Parks to the Rise of Black Power*. Random House, New York.

McLennan, Rebecca (2008). *The Crisis of Imprisonment: Protest, Politics, and the Making of the American Penal State*. Cambridge University Press, New York.

McNair, Glenn (2009). *Criminal Injustice: Slaves and Free Blacks in Georgia's Criminal Justice System*. University of Virginia Press, Charlottesville.

McWilliams, John C. (1990). *The Protectors: Harry J. Anslinger and the Federal Bureau of Narcotics, 1930–1962*. University of Delaware Press, Newark.

Meranze, Michael (1996). *Laboratories of Virtue: Punishment, Revolution, and Authority in Philadelphia, 1760–1835*. University of North Carolina Press, Chapel Hill.

Meranze, Michael (2008). "Penalty and the Colonial Project: Crime, Punishment, and the Regulation of Morals in Early America." In Grossberg and Tomlins, eds, *The Cambridge History of Criminal Law in America: Volume I: Early America (1580–1815)*. Cambridge University Press, New York.

Meyer, Bernard S., Agata, Burton C. and Agata, Seth H. (2006). *The History of the New York Court of Appeals, 1932–2003*. Columbia University Press, New York.

Mihm, Stephen (2007). *A Nation of Counterfeiters: Capitalists, Con Men and the Making of the United States*. Harvard University Press, Cambridge.

Millender, Michael (1996). "The Transformation of the American Criminal Trial, 1790–1875." Ph.D. diss., Princeton University.

Miller, Wilbur (1999). *Cops and Bobbies: Police Authority in New York and London, 1830–1870*. 2nd Edition. Ohio State University Press, Columbus.

Monkkonen, Eric H. (1981). *Police in Urban America, 1860–1920*. Cambridge University Press, New York.

Monkkonen, Eric (2001). *Murder in New York City*. University of California Press, Berkeley.

Monkkonen, Eric (2006). "AHR Forum: Homicide: Explaining America's Exceptionalism." *American Historical Review* 111: 76–94.

Myers, Tamara (2006). *Caught: Montreal's Modern Girls and the Law, 1869–1945*. University of Toronto Press, Toronto.

Nelson, William E. (1967). "Emerging Notions of Modern Criminal Law in the Revolutionary Era: An Historical Perspective." *N.Y.U. Law Review* 42: 450–482.

Norton, Mary Beth (1996). *Founding Mothers and Fathers: Gendered Power and the Forming of American Society*. Alfred Knopf, New York.

Obadele-Starks, Ernest (2007). *Freebooters and Smugglers: The Foreign Slave Trade in the United States after 1808*. University of Arkansas Press, Fayetteville.

Odem, Mary E. (1995). *Delinquent Daughters: Protecting and Policing Adolescent Female Sexuality in the United States, 1995–1920*. University of North Carolina Press, Chapel Hill.

Offutt, William M. (1995). *Of "Good Laws" and "Good Men": Law and Society in the Delaware Valley, 1680–1710*. University of Illinois Press, Urbana.

Pagan, John Ruston (2003). *Anne Orthwood's Bastard: Sex and Law in Early Virginia*. Oxford University Press, New York.

Papke, David Ray (1987). *Framing the Criminal: Crime, Cultural Work and the Loss of Critical Perspective, 1830–1900*. Archon Books, Hamden, CT.

Perkinson, Robert (2010). *Texas Tough: The Rise of America's Prison Empire*. Metropolitan Books, New York.

Pfeifer, Michael (2004). *Rough Justice: Lynching and American Society, 1874–1947*. University of Illinois Press, Urbana.

Polenberg, Richard (1987). *Fighting Faiths: The Abrams Case, the Supreme Court and Free Speech*. Penguin Books, New York.

Preyer, Kathryn (1983). "Crime, the Criminal Law and Reform in Post-Revolutionary Virginia." *Law and History Review* 1: 53–85.

Rafter, Nicole (2000). *Shots in the Mirror: Crime Films and Society*. Oxford University Press, New York.

Rao, Gautham (2008). "The Federal Posse Comitatus Doctrine: Slavery, Compulsion, and Statecraft in Mid-Nineteenth-Century America." *Law & History Review* 26: 1–56.

Reagan, Leslie J. (1997). *When Abortion Was a Crime: Women, Medicine, and Law in the United States, 1867–1973*. University of California Press, Berkeley.

Reid, John Phillip (1997). *Law for the Elephant: Property and Social Behavior on the Oregon Trail*. Huntington Library, San Marino.

Rejali, Darius (2007). *Torture and Democracy.* Princeton University Press, Princeton.
Richards, David A.J. (2009). *The Sodomy Cases: Bowers v. Hardwick and Lawrence v. Texas.* University Press of Kansas, Lawrence.
Romesburg, Don (2009). "'Wouldn't a Boy Do?' Placing Early-Twentieth-Century Male Youth Sex Work into Histories of Sexuality." *Journal of the History of Sexuality* 18: 367–392.
Rosenberg, Charles E. (1968). *The Trial of the Assassin Guiteau: Psychiatry and the Law in the Gilded Age.* University of Chicago Press, Chicago.
Ross, Richard (2008). "Puritan Godly Discipline in Comparative Perspective: Legal Pluralism and the Sources of 'Intensity.'" *American Historical Review* 113: 975–1002.
Roth, Randolph (2009). *American Homicide.* Belknap Press, Cambridge.
Rothman, Joshua (2008). "The Hazards of the Flush Times: Gambling, Mob Violence and the Anxieties of America's Market Revolution." *Journal of American History* 95: 651–677.
Rousey, Dennis C. (1996). *Policing the Southern City: New Orleans, 1805–1889.* Louisiana State University Press, Baton Rouge.
Sacco, Lynn (2009). *Unspeakable: Father-Daughter Incest in American History.* Johns Hopkins University Press, Baltimore.
Scott, Rebecca J. (2011). "Slavery and Law in Atlantic Perspective: Jurisdiction, Jurisprudence, and Justice." *Law & History Review* 29: 915–924.
Shapiro, Barbara J. (1991). *Beyond Reasonable Doubt and Probable Cause: Historical Perspectives on the Anglo-American Law of Evidence.* University of California Press, Berkeley.
Shelden, Randall G. (2007). *Controlling the Dangerous Classes: A History of Criminal Justice in America.* 2nd Edition. Allyn and Bacon, Boston.
Simon, Jonathan (2007). *Governing through Crime: How the War on Crime Transformed American Democracy and Created a Culture of Fear.* Oxford University Press, New York.
Smith, Bruce Philip (1996). "*Circumventing the Jury: Petty Crime and Summary Jurisdiction in London and New York City, 1790–1855.*" Ph.D. diss., Yale University, New Haven.
Spillane, Joseph F. (1998). "The Making of an Underground Market: Drug Selling in Chicago, 1900–1940." *Journal of Social History* 32: 27–47.
Steinberg, Allen (1989). *The Transformation of Criminal Justice: Philadelphia, 1800–1880.* University of North Carolina Press, Chapel Hill.
Stewart, Bruce E. (2011). *Moonshiners and Prohibitionists: The Battle over Alcohol in Southern Appalachia.* University Press of Kentucky, Lexington.
Strange, Carolyn (2010). "The Unwritten Law of Executive Justice: Pardoning Patricide in Reconstruction-era New York." *Law & History Review* 22: 894–930.
Stuntz, William J. (2011). *The Collapse of American Criminal Justice.* Harvard University Press, Cambridge.
Tanenhaus, David (2004). *Juvenile Justice in the Making.* Oxford University Press, New York.
Thompson, Heather Ann (2010). "Why Mass Incarceration Matters: Rethinking Crisis, Decline, and Transformation in Postwar American History." *Journal of American History* 97: 703–734.

Tucker, Andie (1994). *Forth & Scum: Truth, Beauty, Goodness, and the Ax Murder in America's First Mass Medium*. University of North Carolina Press, Chapel Hill.

Trotti, Michael Ayers (2008). *The Body in the Reservoir: Murder & Sensationalism in the South*. University of North Carolina Press, Chapel Hill.

Vidmar, Neil and Hans, Valerie, eds (2007). *American Juries: The Verdict*. Prometheus Books, Amherst, NY.

Vogel, Mary (1999). "The Social Origins of Plea Bargaining: Conflict and Law in the Process of State Formation, 1830–1860." *Law and Society Review* 33: 161–246.

Waldrep, Christopher (1990). "'So Much Sin': The Decline of Religious Discipline and the 'Tidal Wave' of Crime." *Journal of Social History* 25: 535–552.

Waldrep, Christopher (1998). *Roots of Disorder: Race and Criminal Justice in the American South, 1817–1880*. University of Illinois Press, Urbana.

Waldrep, Christopher (2002). *The Many Faces of Judge Lynch: Extralegal Violence and Punishment in America*. Palgrave McMillan, New York.

Waldrep, Christopher (2010). *Jury Discrimination: The Supreme Court, Public Opinion, and a Grassroots Fight for Racial Equality in Mississippi*. University of Georgia Press, Athens.

Walker, Samuel (1998). *Popular Justice: A History of American Criminal Justice*. 2nd Edition. Oxford University Press, New York.

Wang, Jessica (2012). "Dogs and the Making of the American State: Voluntary Association, State Power, and the Politics of Animal Control in New York City, 1850–1920." *Journal of American History* 98: 998–1024.

Wert, Justin J. (2011). *Habeas Corpus in America: The Politics of Individual Rights*. University Press of Kansas, Lawrence.

Whitman, James (2005). *Harsh Justice: Criminal Punishment and the Widening Divide Between America and Europe*. Oxford University Press, New York.

Wilf, Steven (2010). *Law's Imagined Republic: Popular Politics and Criminal Justice in Revolutionary America*. Cambridge University Press, New York.

Williams, Jack Kenny (1959). *Vogues in Villainy: Crime and Retribution in Antebellum South Carolina*. University of South Carolina Press, Columbia, SC.

Willrich, Michael (2003). *City of Courts: Socializing Justice in Progressive Era Chicago*. Cambridge University Press, New York.

Willrich, Michael (2008). "Criminal Justice in the United States." In Grossberg and Tomlins, eds, *The Cambridge History of Criminal Law in America: Volume III: The Twentieth Century and After (1920–)*. Cambridge University Press, New York.

Wolcott, David B. (2005). *Cops and Kids: Policing Juvenile Delinquency in Urban America, 1890–1940*. Ohio State University Press, Columbus, OH.

Wyatt-Brown, Bertram (1982). *Southern Honor: Ethics and Behavior in the Old South*. Oxford University Press, New York.

Further Reading

Heap, Chad (2009). *Slumming: Sexual and Racial Encounters in American Nightlife, 1885–1940*. University of Chicago Press, Chicago.

Himmelstein, Jerome L. (1983). *The Strange Career of Marihuana: Politics and Ideology of Drug Control in America*. Greenwood Press, Westport.

Holloway, Philippa Elizabeth (1999). "Tending to Deviance: Sexuality and Public Policy in Urban Virginia, Richmond and Norfolk, 1920–1950." Ph.D. diss., Ohio State University, Columbus.

Lebsock, Susanne (2003). *A Murder in Virginia: Southern Justice on Trial.* W.W. Norton, New York.

Melossi, Dario (2008). *Controlling Crime, Controlling Society: Thinking about Crime in Europe and the United States.* Polity Press, Malden.

O'Reilly, Kenneth (1983). *Hoover and the Un-Americans: The FBI, HUAC, and the Red Menace.* Temple University Press, Philadelphia.

Saunt, Claudio (2010). "'My Medicine is Punishment': A Case of Torture in Early California, 1775–1776." *Ethnohistory* 57: 679–708.

Spillane, Joseph F. (2000). *Cocaine: From Medical Marvel to Modern Menace in the United States, 1884–1920.* Johns Hopkins University Press, Baltimore.

Tuttle, William M. (1970). *Race Riot: Chicago in the Red Summer of 1919.* University of Illinois Press, Urbana.

Von Drehle, David (2003). *Triangle: The Fire that Changed America.* Grove Press, New York.

Chapter Twenty-three

INTELLECTUAL PROPERTY

Steven Wilf

The big story often told about intellectual property law is that it has grown big. According to this historical commonplace, unprecedented protection has been afforded to intangible property over time through intellectual property regimes such as copyright, trademark, and patent. Legislatures and courts have been remarkably solicitous of claims to ownership made as either a common law property right or through legislation. This growth has become even more notable in recent years with the enlargement of the scope of the subject matter covered by intellectual property rights, the lengthening duration or terms, and the availability of a wide array of civil and criminal sanctions. As a result, the public domain has shrunk. While in earlier times there may have been little protections afforded knowledge, in the past few years we have witnessed an unprecedented use of legal power as rent-seeking owners of intellectual property assert their enlarged proprietary rights (Fisher, 1999; Lessig, 2006). Robert Merges has called intellectual property's last century a "hundred years of solicitude" (Merges, 2000). Some scholars warn of a new or second enclosure of the commons (Boyle, 2010; Hyde, 2010).

There is no doubt that intellectual property law is currently more pervasive than it was in earlier periods. In many ways, intellectual property seems to be a modern invention. Although traditional societies may have imposed control over esoteric knowledge, no regular procedural method existed for obtaining property rights in ideas or expression (Hesse, 2002). A number of scholars have discussed the process of how the first modern patent statute, England's Statute of Monopolies (1624), shifted patents

---

A Companion to American Legal History, First Edition.
Edited by Sally E. Hadden and Alfred L. Brophy.
© 2013 John Wiley & Sons Ltd. Published 2021 by John Wiley & Sons Ltd.

from discretionary monarchical letters of monopoly for certain industries to protection afforded novel inventions when defined procedural and substantive requirements are met (Bracha, 2004; Biagioli, 2011). Similarly, Britain's Statute of Anne (1710) has been touted as the first modern copyright statute, replacing privileges awarded guilds with a grant to authors (Bracha, 2010; Van Houweling, 2010). America's patent and copyright systems emerged in the shadow of these comprehensive British statutes, and their progeny, contemporary intellectual property laws, have proved sufficiently elastic to apply to a remarkable range of technologies.

Expansion and Indeterminacy

Various scholars have contested this simple model of expansion. Increasingly, they have pointed to the enormous gap between rights granted on the books and the weak policing of infringement. During the nineteenth century, for example, criminal copyright sanctions were introduced to halt the spread of illegal copying of theatrical productions (Litman, 2010). Mass produced recorded music in the early twentieth century and the collection of royalties for its performance was met with frequent attempts to elude payment (Wilf, 2008). With the birth of Hollywood, the new technology of film created new challenges for enforcement (Decherney, 2012).

As Eduardo Moisés Peñalver and Sonia Katyal have shown, not all past infringement was due simply to the difficulty of enforcement. Violations also occurred because ordinary citizens viewed intellectual property rights as less robust than real property rights. Partly this is because intellectual property is non-rivalrous, which means that its consumption does not prevent – as with so many tangible goods – its further utilization by other consumers. Partly, this is because the legal rights granted do not always match the intuitions of citizens. And, partly, this is because the ease of appropriation, which is increasingly true with digital media, does not create the same sense of trespass. Often infringers, especially in copyright, have intentionally adopted the pose of "outlaw" (Peñalver and Katyal, 2010). In short, the curse – or blessing – of intellectual property's bigness might be that proprietary rights have grown more extensive as the sheer quantity of piracy has been on the march as well.

The Metaphysical Club

During the past few decades, the history of American intellectual property law has become increasingly important. The United States Supreme Court has made frequent references to historical copyright and patent cases (Dallon, 2006). A sense of urgency animates research into the history of intellectual property. Intellectual property's economic significance and the surrounding contentious policy debates underscore the vital importance of the legal regulation of knowledge. The preoccupation with the escalating claims of intellectual property reflects scholarly identification with progressive elements in society who have raised alarms over the shrinking of the public sphere. Jessica Litman, for example, has convincingly demonstrated the decisive role of interest groups in shaping such legislation as the 1976 Copyright Act and the Digital Millennium Copyright Act (Litman, 2001). Similarly, there has been a growing recognition of the need to reexamine the essential categories of intellectual property law in historical terms. What is the subject matter – or, in other words, what is a text, an invention, or an identifying commercial symbol? Who is an author or a true inventor? And how do changes in media and inventive production lead to different sorts of regulation?

Quite recently there has been a turn towards history. Intriguingly, this trend emerged first within other, non-legal disciplines. Cultural studies sparked an interest in the social construction of everyday life. New disciplinary forms such as literature's new historicism, the history of the book, the social history of consumption and material life, the economic history of innovation, and the social construction of technology addressed the development of the knowledge regulation when the subject was still largely overlooked by mainstream history departments and legal historians (McGill, 1997; Khan, 2008; Wilf, 2012).

Why has it taken so long for a sophisticated legal historical literature on intellectual property to materialize? How do we account for the previously missing voice of history? Those in the law academy have founded justification for extensive property rights in intangibles largely upon philosophical arguments. Intangible, inchoate, and faced with the claim that information is a public good, intellectual property seems harder to justify than real property. Indeed, while real property's logic of actual possession establishes the right to exclude, intellectual property is grounded upon abstract claims of rights in ideas or expression for intangibles whose physical copies might remain within the possession of another. The absence of any immediate loss through the use of another, the ease of copying through new technologies, and fuzzy borders between what may be rightfully taken – such as the idea/expression dichotomy in copyright – and misappropriation places a significant burden upon those who seek to restrict the unfettered use of the products of the mind.

Rather than seeing intellectual property as a historically constructed category, almost every discussion of intellectual property law begins with the classic three just justifications for their protection: labor theory, personality theory, and a utilitarian assessment. Labor theory grounds these rights upon the labor invested in the work of intellectual property. According to John Locke, a person should reap where he or she has sown.

The contribution of labor might be the actual effort to produce a written work or invent a new device, it might be the capital contributed to such projects, or it could even be a flash of genius with real intellectual worth, but requiring very little investment over time. The second major theory, often identified with Hegel, suggests that the proper development of personhood requires control over certain property. An artist, for example, has a special relationship to their works of art, and this deep, often complex emotional connection should be recognized by law. Utilitarian, or law and economics justifications, thirdly, have also been frequently cited to suggest the importance in providing a system of incentives for the production and dissemination of intellectual property. Creators will hoard their creations if they are not given rewards for disclosing them. The utilitarian justification, of course, has given rise to a sizeable law and economics scholarly literature intended to analyze the optimal levels of incentive necessary to promote the production of intellectual property (Hughes, 1988; Fisher, 2001; Merges, 2011; Alexander and Peñalver, 2012).

These justifications have come under increasing critical scrutiny. The sense of fixed, timeless justifications legitimizing a property right has been replaced by a deeply skeptical understanding of the cultural and historical contingency of intellectual property. Influenced by new historicism, which sought to understand the text within its historical context, literary scholars turned toward the history of copyright in order to understand the authorial control over the means of production. Mark Rose interrogated the shift in the eighteenth century from the medieval notion of vesting rights of replication in the owner of a manuscript to the author. He traces the invention of authorship as a concept and shows how it was inextricably linked to property (Rose, 1993). Rose's work was the point of departure for a number of different threads in the history of copyright. The invention of authorship, a number of historians of early modern and nineteenth–century British copyright have contended, has been matched by a series of other invented legal traditions. Ronan Deazley argues that the idea of perpetual copyright under the common law was largely a nineteenth-century invention (Deazley, 2008), Isabella Alexander shows how uncertain the concept of the public interest has always been since the "encouragement of learning" was identified as an important purpose of copyright in the Statute of Anne (1710), (Alexander, 2010), while Simon Stern underscored the creative ways that the property metaphor was applied to early British copyright (Stern, 2012).

Mark Rose, Martha Woodmansee, and Peter Jaszi have argued that the creativity-based view of originality is related to the ideology of the romantic author, the notion that the writer is not merely a craftsman, but a unique individual uniquely responsible for a unique product (Rose, 1993; Jaszi, 1991; Woodmansee, 1984; Woodmansee and Jaszi, 1994; Wilf, 1999). Although all authorship is a matter of influences, copyright law embraced the idea of authorship as a privileged and persistent concept. Throughout the nineteenth century, romantic authorship displaced the rival claims of the centrality of the work and served as the underpinnings of such legal doctrines as the originality requirement and work-for-hire (Zemer, 2007).

The unsettling of the concept of authorship influenced other disciplines as well. While the history of the book has been largely concerned with the technology of textualism – modes of production, trade networks for disseminating text, the transition from orality to literacy, emerging public spheres, and questions of readership – the very nature of a fixed text remains as a kind of bedrock for the field. Adrian Johns, in *The Nature of the Book: Print and Knowledge in the Making* shows how early modern texts were unfixed, and, in fact, often constantly kept in flux by the tinkering of compositors, correctors and printers. Piracy, abridgment, unauthorized editions, and unabashed forgery left texts at the mercy of a much larger circle willing to remake texts (Johns, 2000; Sherman, 2011).

Plasticity, chimerical reinvention, and indeterminacy were the watchwords of this strand of British copyright history. It not only influenced scholarship in the makings of British literary property (Temple, 2002; Saint-Amour, 2003), but also a wave of research by American academics specializing in American literature. Meredith McGill's *American Literature and the Culture of Reprinting* 1834–1853 describes the practice of reprinting British works in the United States without either the permission of the author or the payment of royalties due to the absence of international copyright protection. Such a culture of reprinting, which indeed comprised the majority of publication in the antebellum America, undermined the stable form of texts – often collected and reassembled unmoored from their original source – as well as reliable attribution to authors (McGill, 2003).

Copyright, in other words, is critical for a host of transformations towards the commodification of expression and the creation of a broad readership. Martin Buinicki has identified the way nineteenth-century American writers became embroiled in debates over the protection of literary property. He sees authors as the epicenter of a series of negotiations to establish a firm legal footing for copyright (Buinicki, 2006). Stephen Best identifies intellectual property as "fugitive properties," intangible and elusive, which are constantly slipping beyond set boundaries. Sound recordings, for example, allow the disembodied voice to be reproduced and disseminated in ways never before imagined. The human image – so inextricably connected to personality and identity – now becomes a commodity which can be easily transferred from one person to another (Best, 2004).

Similarly, the new social history of technology recognizes the importance of examining the ownership of scientific knowledge, not simply the act of discovery (Biagioli, 2006). Indeed, just as the concept of the romantic author has been deconstructed so has the idea of a true inventor (Bracha, 2009). How do we credit an individual with discovery when scientific knowledge is cumulative? What happens to the inventor with the emergence of widespread corporate laboratories in the 1920s (Noble, 1979)? And what function does the myth of the true inventor serve in the construction of legal doctrine (Swanson, 2011a)?

Alain Pottage and Brad Sherman have probed the very notion of the invention as an intangible. As they point out, all forms of intellectual property take some form of expression. Patents must be represented through patented models (which were required in the United States from 1790 to 1880), embodiment and disclosure requirements in words, or through diagrams (Pottage and Sherman, 2010). Accordingly, even the idea of intellectual property as the property law of intangibles is a cultural fabrication.

Justice Joseph Story famously remarked in 1841 that copyright and patents approach nearer than any other sort of legal subject area "to what might be called the metaphysics of the law, where the distinctions are, or at least may be, very subtle and refined, and sometimes almost evanescent" (Story, 1841: 344). It is not surprising that the protection of intangibles should be described in transcendental terms since the troublesome questions at the core of defining intellectual property have led to an understanding of the field as a sort of metaphysical club. If the narrative of relentless growth seems to march forward without limitations, the story of intellectual property's indeterminacy often lacks an appreciation of the quite tangible social and political factors that shape intellectual property's development over time. Not surprisingly, then, the turn towards history has prompted an increasingly contingent, complex story.

Towards Other Narratives

Neither of the two core historiographic narratives described – expansion or indeterminacy – has adequately captured the sedimentary layering of legal norms with the contextual push and pull of various forces, including new technologies, economic imperatives, political debates, and shifting cultural ideas about the nature of knowledge. William Fisher has called intellectual property "several, partially overlapping doctrines," and the history of these doctrines is "involuted and idiosyncratic" (Fisher, 1999: 2). For this reason, it is difficult to adapt a single master narrative. Indeed, there is a question of whether there is even a distinct legal concept called intellectual property. The many regimes of intellectual property create a plethora of different histories.

The story of intellectual property law may be told in various ways. First, it might be a narrative about how these various different regimes came to be regarded as intellectual property, a term that for the United States appeared first in a federal court case in 1845 (Hughes, 2006). This would describe the similarities, the boundary tending between regimes, and, inevitably, the ways copyright, trademark, patent, and other regimes came to be conceptually intertwined. Such a narrative might be called the family romance story of intellectual property law.

A second narrative thread would be to show how intellectual property responded to technological innovation. The steamboat, railroad, telegraph, telephone, synthetic chemicals, cinema, and internet transformed intellectual property law. While identifying legal reactions to new technologies is a classic law and society approach, it is important to resist the lure of technological determinism. Technology's influence is often less a matter of simply extending protection to novel subject matter, than a question of how new technologies challenge or even disturb existing legal categories. The rise of the player piano industry, for example, led to a rethinking of copyright's commonplace that a form of expression must have a human reader (Ginsburg, 2001). Similarly, the notion of patenting life forms, even if the technology is relatively straightforward, presses against the traditional boundaries of patent law (Kevles, 2011). In a sophisticated essay, Robert Merges describes the ways that intellectual property encounters new technologies by experiencing disequilibrium until doctrinal innovations are incorporated, sifted, and used to create new normative structures. Drawing upon Thomas Kuhn's *The Structure of Scientific Revolutions*, Merges argues for a model of breakdown and reconstruction for intellectual property law (Merges, 2000).

A third approach is to deeply situate intellectual property in a particular past set of internal practices within different economic arenas. The work of Steven Usselman (2002) on railroads, Christopher Beauchamp (2008) on telephone technology, Adam Mossoff (2011) on sewing machines, Catherine Fisk (2010) on Madison Avenue advertising firms, and Kara Swanson (2011b) on food and drug production are examples of this approach. Within particular industries, such as those listed above, the battle over ownership of intellectual property was particularly fierce. Beauchamp describes the importance of litigation as a crucible for making patent law, and how patterns of legal disputes with repeat players might be established (Beauchamp, 2009).

In her book on the development of trade secret law, *Working Knowledge: Employee Innovation and the Rise of Corporate Intellectual Property 1800–1930*, Catherine Fisk shows how not simply the extent of the scope of intellectual property protection, but the question of who owns the property right has shifted over time. Prior to the Civil War, workplace knowledge was vested in the employee who came up with the idea. Employers were permitted what was called a shop right, which recognized employer reliance upon an employee invention. In the early twentieth century, the legal rules concerning workplace knowledge began to change (Fisk, 2001; 2009). The 1909 Copyright Act included a work made for hire doctrine which granted employers copyright in employee creations (Fisk, 2003). Patent law identified a duty for employees to assign patents for inventions developed within the employment relationship. Trade secret recognized a broad range of duties owed by employees to employers, including confidentiality, and became the basis for establishing a default rule making employers the owners of workplace knowledge and limiting employee mobility (Fisk, 2009). In a story that seemed to echo Marxist notions of the expropriation of labor capital, control over workplace knowledge shifted from the employee to corporations.

Identifying the Ages of American Intellectual Property Law

These three approaches – the construction of regimes, intellectual property legal rules as a response to technological innovation, and the identification of different intellectual property legal cultures in different industries – might be woven into the broader narrative of intellectual property as shifting to reflect changing ideas about political economy over time. Wilf has recently suggested that the history of intellectual property is as full of chronological discontinuities as it is a story of continuities (Wilf, 2012). One of the most notable ruptures takes place in the eighteenth century. The United States was the first country in the world to constitutionalize intellectual property (Walterscheid, 2002; Ochoa and Rose, 2002). Some of the Framers were amateur scientists and tinkerers. Others, like Alexander Hamilton and Tench Coxe, saw new technologies as a means to achieve economic independence (Ben-Atar, 2004). Almost all of those at the Constitutional Convention were veterans of the pamphlet wars of the Revolution period who appreciated the importance of print culture as a republican forum. Others saw technology as a means of allowing artisans to forge a new aristocracy founded upon the products of the mind.

American intellectual property law was born around the same time as modern intellectual property proprietary rights were granted to authors and inventors and in the midst of the founding of a new republic. The tension between two elements – one focused on private gain and the other upon public good – has animated much of the history of United States regulation of knowledge. We have no recorded debates surrounding the adoption of the Constitution's Intellectual Property Clause (Article I, Section 8). It is the sole clause in the original Constitution which states a given purpose, "promoting the progress of science and useful arts." Scholars have debated the meaning of this clause – whether it includes the public welfare. But more importantly, from its very beginnings, the United States was a literary republic where books and journals formed the sinews of a public sphere necessary to construct an informed citizenry (Wilf, 2010). Similarly, America was a patent republic where a patent was construed as the expression of a freely-made bargain between the inventor and the public (Biagioli, 2006).

Throughout the 1780s and 1790s, Jeffersonian and Hamiltonian approaches to patent differed. Hamilton believed that bounties should be bestowed on those bringing new inventions to America from abroad. Jefferson argued that federal bounties were not within the enumerated powers of Congress. Doron Ben-Atar has unpacked this important debate about how to design an intellectual property system that facilitates, rather than limits, the transfer of knowledge across borders. The New Republic encouraged artisans to share their craft knowledge – what we might call trade secrets – in contrast to the British policy of imposing limitations on artisan emigration (Ben-Atar, 2004).

Historians have been excavating other debates about the grounding of intellectual property that suggests the fluidity of justifications. Jane Ginsburg, in a path-breaking article, discussed the differences between the natural law underpinnings of the French Copyright Act of 1791 and the utilitarian basis for late-eighteenth-century American copyright (Ginsburg, 1990). Much of early patent law, Adam Mossoff has argued, was dominated by the idea that the standard for patenting should be liberal because it was grounded upon natural law (Mossoff, 2007).

A second major disjuncture for intellectual property law's watershed moment, scholars have noted, emerges from the controversies of the Early Republic. At the beginning of the early nineteenth century intellectual property law sought to sharpen the distinction between monopoly and intellectual property. Jacksonian democrats abhorred monopolies. But why was intellectual property not a traditional monopoly? In the landmark Supreme Court case, *Wheaton v. Peters* (1834), which rejected common law copyright and established copyright solely as a statutory regime, historians have identified the underpinnings of pro-public domain values (Joyce, 2005). This case has been seen as shaping core pro-public domain features of United States copyright: the establishment of limited terms over perpetual property rights and the creation of formalities that would place all non-compliant works in the public domain.

Scholars identify patent law's watershed moment as the 1836 Patent Act. This legislation, which established the Patent Office, marked the beginning of what seems to us a familiar patent system: a professional corps of examiners, an administrative appeal process, the numerical filing of patents (Walterscheid, 1998; Mossoff, 2009). Unlike traditional cartels, patent was achieved on merit without discrimination. But, ironically, the debate over how welcoming the United States should be towards patent continued through the 1840s and early 1850s, when courts were divided between strict and liberal understandings of the construction of claims (Post, 1976). While inventors were originally the major constituency for the Patent Office, the mid-nineteenth-century growing use of equity courts to decide patent cases tended to favor emerging industrial interests (Lubar, 1991).

Zorina Khan argues that the institutionalized gate-keeping of the United States nineteenth-century patent system proved to be democratic – though this is easier to claim when looking at patents issued rather than patterns of litigation – in contrast to those of Britain and France. In America, the examination process was based upon merit and the fees were kept low. As a result, there were many applications for just one or two patents, and women as well as free blacks obtained patents. This relatively open patent system explains America's increasingly important role as a center for technological and economic innovation (Khan, 2005). Moreover, the Patent Office fostered networks of innovation. Partly due to the barriers of filing for a patent in a central location, partly due to the need for specialists with a hybrid of technical and legal expertise, patent practitioners emerged with a particular professional identity in the nineteenth century (Swanson, 2009). The development of various patent cultures – mechanic, scientific, industrial, and market centered – has been a centerpiece of the nineteenth-century history of patent.

What constitutes an intellectual property system? Scholars have noted that different regimes have different historical trajectories in different periods (Wilf, 2012). Must it be rooted in the Intellectual Property Clause in the Constitution? If so, this would pertain only to copyright and patent. Must it have at its core creative or inventive activities? If so, this would seem to disfavor largely commercial protections. By the middle of the nineteenth century, these questions were raised in the course of controversies over the nature of trademark law. In 1871, Congress passed a statute against foreign copyright of the trade dress of watches, and provided for the registration of timepieces by the Treasury Department. But with the Constitutional transformation wrought by the Civil War amendments – and the notion of a robust federal role for the enforcement of rights – the move was afoot for shifting trademark from commercial regulation under state police power to a full-fledged form of intellectual property governance within a national regime. In 1870, Congress passed a statute providing for federal registration and, in 1876, a second bill imposed federal criminal sanctions for those infringing upon trademarks. The very title of the 1870 law, which claims to revise "statutes relating to patents and copyright," clearly envisioned trademarks as a kind of appendage to other forms of federally regulated intellectual property. In the *Trade-Mark Cases* (1877), however, the United States Supreme Court found that an exclusive use of trademarks was founded upon common law and state statutes. According to the Court, the Congressional power to regulate trademarks had no basis in either the Intellectual Property Clause, which specifically referred to those two regimes, or the Commerce Clause. Trademarks lacked the essential quality of intellectual property – originality. It was not until the 1946 passage of the Lanham Act, under the New Deal conception of an expanded Commerce Clause, that trademark became a national form of protection and fully joined the cluster of intellectual property regimes (Wilf, 2008).

If the primary story for patent law might be the creation of administrative capacity – and the challenges it faced from various constituencies and litigation – and the story for trademark might be the elusive search for a federal law that might embrace an increasingly national market, then copyright's narrative might be told as a tale of how a limited protection for a small number of literary works became an instrument for the legal regulation of knowledge in an industrial society (Goldstein, 2003).

Copyright, literary scholars such as Meredith McGill have shown, enables the absorption of a once private text into a market culture (McGill, 1997). The interaction of text and commerce – with a plethora of influences from ideologies of national culture, technologies of manufacture, and a constantly shifting reading public – varied from one historical period to another (Zboray, 1993). In the 1830s, Henry Clay promoted copyright as part of his American System – a way to establish sinews of culture that would link together different regions of the country in much the same way as canals or railroads create infrastructure that might traverse physical distance (Wilf, 2011). However, as Trish Loughran has pointed out, reading publics were often local, and – as was the case with abolitionist literature – print culture often exacerbated regional conflict (Loughran, 2007).

Nearly a half century ago, Lyman Patterson argued that copyright can most usefully be viewed as a series of ideas formulated and directed towards a common end (Patterson, 1968). Oren Bracha has argued that the doctrinal categories of copyright law are incoherent because they were created by contending ideologies and economic interests in the nineteenth century (Bracha, 2008). Each of these, including fair use, the idea/expression dichotomy, the making of a right of adaptation which provides for rights over derivative works such as abridgments and translations, and originality were largely created as a result of court decisions. If patent law was fabricated in the shadow of an administrative agency with a gate-keeping responsibility to provide protection only for worthy inventions, copyright law was often constructed by courts in the course of litigation, and minimal attention was paid to limiting subject matter.

In general, the second half of the nineteenth century was marked by the expansion of copyright. The very definition of literary property was enlarged in 1856 to include dramatic works. In 1865, photography, which had come into its own during the Civil War, was afforded copyright protection (Hughes, 2011). The Copyright Act of 1870 broadened copyright's scope to include paintings, drawings, chromo-lithographs, statues, and fine art models. Courts were increasingly reluctant to make aesthetic distinctions. In *Bleistein v. Donaldson Lithographing Company* (1899), Oliver Wendell Holmes' first decision since joining the United States Supreme Court, a series of advertising posters for a travelling circus were deemed to fall under copyright. *Bleistein* reflected the fact that no national trademark system could prevent the posters from being readily copied – but this only placed a greater burden upon copyright to serve as a mechanism for protection.

Changes in the technology of book manufacturing – the rise of the industrial book as a mass produced object – had widespread consequences for copyright. To regulate the intense competition among publishers operating outside of the official copyright system, an informal framework, courtesy of the trade, was developed. Courtesy of the trade protected an unofficial, customary right to reprint British works in the United States that were not copyright protected under American law without other publishers rushing to produce similar editions. As Meredith McGill has shown, readers, authors, and publishers often had different approaches to copyright's new-found print capitalism (McGill, 2003).

The protection of derivative works extended far beyond the original confines of copyright. Reflecting an older approach, the court in *Stowe v. Thomas*, 23 F. Cas. 201 (C.C.E.D. Pa. 1853), which stated that an unauthorized German translation of *Uncle Tom's* Cabin did not constitute a copy, decided that "the creations of the imagination of the author have become as much public property as those of Homer or Cervantes." But the backlash among authors and publishers was notable. The 1870 Copyright Act reserved to authors the right to dramatize or translate their own works. A core argument throughout the late nineteenth and early twentieth century proffered by promoters of copyright was that United States literary property provided grounding for American civic culture. Yet, as scholars have noted, the growth of derivative works, the decline of a defense of innocent infringement, and – with the passage of the 1976 Copyright Act – the end of a formalities requirement that left most works in the public domain meant that copyright protected many more works than it had in the past (Reese, 2007; Sprigman, 2004).

Until 1891, when the United States recognized international copyright, most works published in America were English reprints published without the original publisher's permission and without the payment of a royalty to the original author. However, after the 1886 founding of the Berne Convention with its international copyright standards, America became increasingly seen as an outlier. A movement of copyright reformers pressed for the protection of the rights of foreign authors. This political mobilization ultimately resulted in the Chace Act of 1891 (Barnes, 1974; Seville, 2006; Wilf, 2011). By the time of the New Deal, copyright was stretched to include aspects of industrial design (Wilf, 2008). In our times, of course, copyright has been required to serve as the legal regulatory mechanism for digital information, internet communication, and electronic commerce.

New Directions

The development of intellectual property law is a fairly recent addition to the field of legal history. However, the increasing significance of intellectual property in economic and cultural terms, the intensity of public debates on its scope, and the complex, often difficult to unpack stories of its past have led to the emergence of a particularly sophisticated historical literature within a remarkably short amount of time. The master narrative of intellectual property's relentless growth has broken down. Discontent with the explanatory purchase of philosophical and economic justifications of intellectual property recently has led to a turn to history. In a remarkably brief amount of time, research of exceptional quality has investigated the doctrinal and conceptual architecture of intellectual property, its metaphors, and the way its legal rules operate when situated in particular industries. Nevertheless, a great deal of work remains to be done.

We still need to know more about how intellectual property functioned in fact as well as in law. Beyond legal rules embodied in statutes and cases, there is a dearth of information about the effect of intellectual property upon the lives of both ordinary citizens and within various workplaces. What debates are taking place about the regulation of knowledge? What cadres of lawyers, patent agents, and corporate legal representatives are intimately concerned with intellectual property law, and how are their professional concerns articulated? Do various social groups – such as women – experience the contours of intellectual property law in a different way (Merritt, 1991; Khan, 2000; Homestead, 2005)? And how is the delicate balance between enforcement and overlooked infringement maintained?

Adrian Johns has argued that intellectual property is a shadow, a doppelgänger of piracy. The appropriation of expressive or technical knowledge is countered by the construction of legal frameworks (Johns, 2009). Of course, there is some truth to this argument. But intellectual property has its own internal logic. It has proponents, interested parties – from tinkering mechanics to aspiring writers, critics, pirates and outlaws – and those, such as judges and legislators, who must grapple with the intricacies of this particular area of the law. Their stories remain to be uncovered. The relationship between protection and infringement is incredibly complex.

The focus on official intellectual property law has largely ignored unofficial forms of protection. In the early nineteenth century, newspaper editors engaged in an informal system of exchange, mid-nineteenth century courtesy of the trade provided order to the lawless area of American reprints of British works, and garment manufacturers invented their own system of design protection when Congress and the courts failed to provide a solution to unbridled copying. What extra-legal mechanisms existed beyond the boundaries of intellectual property law?

Finally, we need to consider intellectual property outside of the straightjacket of national legal histories. Jane Ginsburg pioneered comparative analysis of United States intellectual property law by examining the different strands of the late-eighteenth-century genesis of copyright. While the French found a natural right grounded upon the notion of the author as creator, Anglo-American copyright has often been seen as a utilitarian incentive.

Ginsburg showed how these strands often worked their way into both American and Continental European copyright systems (Ginsburg, 1990). The lens should be comparative. But we must also recognize the ever present effect of international forces – international treaties and conventions, pressure for protection from abroad, and alternative models of knowledge regulation – on the making of United States intellectual property.

This area of research is especially timely as we experience a shift towards harmonization and internationalization in the protection of copyright, trademark, and patents. Intellectual property has been called a territorial system of law – one developing within a specific jurisdiction. Although scholars recognize that the Agreement on Trade-Related Aspects of Intellectual Property Rights (TRIPs) and a variety of international agreements have altered this conception, it is less well-known that United States intellectual property has always grappled with its place in the world. As Christopher May and Susan Sell have shown, intellectual property rights did not emerge as a functional set of optimal legal improvements, but as a series of policy decisions which maximize particular economic interests and often benefit one country over another (May and Sell, 2006).

Intellectual property has often been considered an exceptional area of law. Its intangible subject matter, its fluid boundaries, its unusual growth in the modern period, its reliance upon metaphors and analogies to real property, its ever so reified justifications for legal rights in place of ordinary intuitions about ownership, the incoherence of assembling various regimes – copyright, trademark, and patent – into a single, unified, overarching field of intellectual property law, and, finally, its gestures in the direction of metaphysics have fostered this impression. But the fundamental problems of intellectual property's past – identifying legal boundaries and policing – are common to all forms of law even if the nature of its subject matter creates particular difficulties. There is no intellectual property exceptionalism, no legal *Sonderweg*. In the end, intellectual property's history might be like all other legal histories – only more so.

References

Alexander, Gregory S. and Eduardo, Peñalver, M. (2012). *An Introduction to Property Theory*. Cambridge University Press, Cambridge, UK.

Alexander, Isabella (2010). *Copyright Law and the Public Interest in the Nineteenth Century*. Hart, Oxford.

Barnes, James J. (1974). *Authors, Publishers, and Politicians: The Quest for an Anglo-American Copyright Agreement 1815–1854*. Routledge & Kegan Paul, London.

Beauchamp, Christopher (2008). "The Telephone Patents: Intellectual Property, Business, and the Law in the United States and Britain 1876–1900." http://papers.ssrn.com/sol3/papers.cfm?abstract_id=1311730 (last accessed October 12, 2012).

Beauchamp, Christopher (2009). "Technology's Trials: Patent Litigation in United States Courts 1860–1910." http://lapa.princeton.edu/uploads/BeauchampPaper.pdf (last accessed October 12, 2012).

Ben-Atar, Doron (2004). *Trade Secrets: Intellectual Piracy and the Origins of American Industrial Power.* Yale University Press, New Haven.

Best, Stephen M. (2004). *The Fugitive Properties: Law and the Poetics of Possession.* University of Chicago Press, Chicago.

Biagioli, Mario (2006). Patent Republic: Representing Inventions, Constructing Rights and Authors. *Social Science Research* 73: 1129–1172.

Biagioli, Mario (2011). "Patent Specification and Political Representation: How Patents Became Rights." In Biagioli, Jaszi, and Woodmansee, eds, *Making and Unmaking Intellectual Property: Creative Production in Legal and Cultural Perspective.* University of Chicago Press, Chicago.

Bleistein v. Donaldson Lithographing Company, 188 U.S. 239. http://en.wikipedia.org/wiki/Bleistein_v._Donaldson_Lithographing_Company (last accessed October 12, 2012).

Boyle, James (2010). *The Public Domain: Enclosing the Commons of the Mind.* Yale University Press, New Haven.

Bracha, Oren (2004). "The Commodification of Patents 1600–1836: How Patents Became Rights and Why We Should Care." *Loyola LA Law Review* 38: 177–244.

Bracha, Oren (2008). "The Ideology of Authorship Revisited: Authors, Markets, and Liberal Values in Early American Copyright." *Yale Law Journal* 118: 186–271.

Bracha, Oren (2009). "Geniuses and Owners: The Construction of Inventors and the Emergence of American Intellectual Property." In Hamilton and Brophy, eds, *Transformations in American Legal History: Law, Ideology, and Methods – Essays in Honor of Professor Morton J. Horwitz.* Harvard University Press, Cambridge.

Bracha, Oren (2010). "The Statute of Anne: An American Mythology." *Houston Law Review* 47: 877–918.

Buinicki, Martin (2006). *Negotiating Copyright: Authorship and the Discourse of Literary Property in Nineteenth Century America.* Routledge, London.

Dallon, Craig (2006). "Original Intent and the Copyright Clause: Eldred v. Ashcroft Gets it Right." *Saint Louis Law Journal* 50: 307–359.

Deazley, Ronan (2008). *Rethinking Copyright: History, Theory, Language.* Edward Elgar, London.

Decherney, Peter (2012). *Hollywood's Copyright Wars: From Edison to the Internet.* Columbia University Press, New York.

Fisk, Catherine (2001). "Working Knowledge: Trade Secrets: Restrictive Covenants in Employment and the Rise of Corporate Intellectual Property 1800–1920." *Hastings Law Journal* 52: 441–535.

Fisk, Catherine (2003). "Authors at Work: The Origins of the Work-for-Hire Doctrine." *Yale Journal of Law & the Humanities* 15: 1–70.

Fisk, Catherine (2009). *Working Knowledge: Employee Innovation and the Rise of Corporate Intellectual Property 1800–1930.* University of North Carolina Press, Chapel Hill.

Fisk, Catherine (2010). "The Modern Author at Work on Madison Avenue." In Saint-Amour, ed., *Modernism and Copyright.* Oxford University Press, Oxford, UK.

Fisher, III, William W. (1999). "The Growth of Intellectual Property Law: A History of the Ownership of Ideas in the United States." cyber.law.harvard.edu/people/t/iphistory.pdf (last accessed October 12, 2012).

Fisher, III, William W. (2001). "Theories of Intellectual Property." In Munzer, ed., *New Essays in the Legal and Political Theory of Property*. Harvard University Press, Cambridge.

Ginsburg, Jane (1990). "A Tale of Two Copyrights: Literary Property in Revolutionary France and America." *Tulane Law Review.* 64: 991–1023.

Ginsburg, Jane (2001). "Copyright and the Control Over New Technologies of Dissemination." *Columbia Law Review.* 101: 1613–1647.

Goldstein, Paul (2003). *Copyright's Highway: From Gutenberg to the Celestial Jukebox*. Stanford University Press, Stanford.

Hesse, Carla (2002). "The Rise of Intellectual Property, 700 B.C.–A.D. 2000." *Daedalus* 131: 26–45.

Homestead, Melissa J. (2005). *American Women Authors and Literary Property, 1822–1869*. Cambridge University Press, Cambridge, UK.

Hughes, Justin (1988). "The Philosophy of Intellectual Property." *Georgetown Law Journal* 77: 287–366.

Hughes, Justin (2006). "Copyright and Incomplete Historiographies: Of Piracy, Propertization, and Thomas Jefferson." *Southern California Law Review* 79: 993–1084.

Hughes, Justin (2011). "The Photographer's Copyright – Photography as Art, Photography as Database." *Cardozo Legal Studies Research Paper No. 347*. http://papers.ssrn.com/sol3/papers.cfm?abstract_id=1931220 (last accessed October 12, 2012).

Hyde, Lewis (2010). *Common as Air: Revolution, Art, and Ownership*. Farrar, Straus and Giroux, New York.

Jaszi, Peter (1991). "Toward a Theory of Copyright: The Metamorphoses of 'Authorship.'" *Duke Law Journal* 1991: 455–502.

Johns, Adrian (2000). *The Nature of the Book: Print and Knowledge in the Making*. University of Chicago Press, Chicago.

Johns, Adrian (2009). *Piracy: The Intellectual Property Wars from Gutenberg to Gates*. University of Chicago Press, Chicago.

Joyce, Craig (2005). "A Curious Chapter in the History of Judicature: *Wheaton v. Peters* and the Rest of the Story of Copyright in the New Republic." *Houston Law Review* 42: 325–391.

Kevles, Daniel J. (2011). "New Blood, New Fruits: Protection for Breeders and Originators, 1789–1930." In Biagioli, Jaszi, and Woodmansee, eds, *Making and Unmaking Intellectual Property: Creative Production in Legal and Cultural Perspective*. University of Chicago Press, Chicago.

Khan, B. Zorina (2000). "'Not for Ornament': Patenting Activity by Women Inventors." *Journal of Interdisciplinary History* 33: 159–195.

Khan. B. Zorina (2005). *The Democratization of Invention: Patents and Copyrights in American Economic Development, 1790–1920*. Cambridge University Press, Cambridge, UK.

Khan, B. Zorina (2008). "Innovations in Law and Technology 1790–1920." In Grossberg and Tomlins, eds, *The Cambridge History of Law in America*. Cambridge University Press, Cambridge, UK.

Lessig, Lawrence (2006). *Code and Other Laws of Cyberspace, Version 2.0.* Basic Books, New York.

Litman, Jessica (2001). *Digital Copyright.* Prometheus Books, Amherst.

Litman, Jessica (2010). "The Invention of Common Law Play Right." *Berkeley Technology Law Journal* 25: 1381–1425.

Loughran, Trish (2007). *The Republic in Print: Print Culture in the Age of U.S. Nation Building, 1770–1870.* Columbia University Press, New York.

Lubar, Steven (1991). "The Transformation of Antebellum Patent Law." *Technology and Culture* 32: 932–959.

McGill, Meredith (1997). "The Matter of the Text: Commerce, Print Culture, and Authority of the State in American Copyright Law." *American Literary History* 9: 21–59.

McGill, Meredith (2003). *American Literature and the Culture of Reprinting 1834–1853.* University of Pennsylvania Press, Philadelphia.

May, Christopher and Sell, Susan K. (2006). *Intellectual Property Rights: A Critical History.* Lynne Rienners, London.

Merges, Robert (2000). "One Hundred Years of Solicitude: Intellectual Property Law 1900–2000." *California Law Review* 88: 2187–2240.

Merges, Robert (2011). *Justifying Intellectual Property.* Harvard University Press, Cambridge.

Merritt, Deborah J. (1991). "Hypatia in the Patent Office: Women Inventors and the Law, 1865–1900." *American Journal of Legal History* 35: 235–306.

Mossoff, Adam (2007). "Who Cares What Thomas Jefferson Thought about Patents? Reevaluating the Patent 'Privilege' in Historical Context." *Cornell Law Review* 92: 953–1012.

Mossoff, Adam (2009). "The Use and Abuse of IP at the Birth of the Administrative State." *University of Pennsylvania Law Review* 157: 2001–2050.

Mossoff, Adam (2011). "The Rise and Fall of the First American Patent Thicket: The Sewing Machine War of the 1850s." *Arizona Law Review* 53: 165–212.

Noble, David (1979). *America By Design: Science, Technology, and the Rise of Corporate Capitalism.* Alfred A. Knopf, New York.

Ochoa, Tyler and Rose, Mark (2002). "The Anti-Monopoly Origins of the Patent and Copyright Clause." *Journal of the Copyright Society of the U.S.A.* 49: 675–706.

Patterson, Lyman Ray (1968). *Copyright in Historical Perspective.* Vanderbilt University Press, Nashville.

Peñalver, Eduardo Moisés and Katyal, Sonia (2010): *Property Outlaws: How Squatters, Pirates, and Protesters Improve the Law of Ownership.* Yale University Press, New Haven.

Post, Robert C. (1976). "'Liberalizers' v 'Scientific Men' in the Antebellum Patent Office." *Technology and Culture* 17: 24–54.

Pottage, Alain and Sherman, Brad (2010). *Figures of Invention: A History of Modern Patent Law.* Oxford University Press, Oxford, UK.

Reese, R. Anthony (2007). "Innocent Infringement in U.S. Copyright Law: A History." *Columbia Journal of Law & the Arts* 30: 133–184.

Rose, Mark (1993). *Authors and Owners: The Invention of Copyright.* Harvard University Press, Cambridge.

Saint-Amour, Paul K. (2003). *The Copywrights: Intellectual Property and the Literary Imagination*. Cornell University Press, Ithaca.

Seville, Catherine (2006). *The Internationalisation of Copyright Law: Books, Buccaneers and the Black Flag in the Nineteenth Century*. Cambridge University Press, Cambridge, UK.

Sherman, Brad (2011). "What is a Copyright Work?" *Theoretical Inquiries in Law* 12: 99–122.

Sprigman, Christopher (2004) "Reform(aliz)ing Copyright." *Stanford Law Review* 57: 485–568.

Stern, Simon (2012). "'Room for One More': The Metaphorics of Physical Space in the Eighteenth-Century Copyright Debate." *Law & Literature* 24: 113–150.

Story, Joseph (1841). Folsom v. Marsh, 9 F. Cas. 342 (C.C.D. Mass. 1841).

Swanson, Kara W. (2009). "The Emergence of the Professional Patent Practitioner." *Technology and Culture* 50: 519–548.

Swanson, Kara W. (2011a). "Authoring an Invention: Patent Production in the Nineteenth-Century United States." In Biagioli, Jaszi, and Woodmansee, eds, *Making and Unmaking Intellectual Property: Creative Production in Legal and Cultural Perspective*. University of Chicago Press, Chicago.

Swanson, Kara W. (2011b). "Food and Drug Law as Intellectual Property Law: Historical Reflections." *Wisconsin Law Review* 2: 331–397.

Temple, Kathryn (2002). *Scandal Nation: Law and Authorship in Britain 1750–1832*. Cornell University Press, Ithaca.

Usselman, Steven W. (2002). *Regulating Railroad Innovation: Business, Technology, and Politics in America 1840–1920*. Cambridge University Press, Cambridge, UK.

Van Houweling, Molly S. (2010). "Author, Autonomy, and Atomism in Copyright Law." *Virginia Law Review* 96: 549–640.

Walterscheid, Edward C. (1998). *To Promote the Progress of Useful Arts: American Patent Law and Administration 1798–1838*. F.B. Rothman & Co., Littleton, Colorado.

Walterscheid, Edward C. (2002): *The Nature of the Intellectual Property Clause: A Study in Historical Perspective*. William S. Hein & Co., Buffalo.

Wilf, Steven (1999). "Who Authors Trademarks?" *Cardozo Arts & Entertainment Law Journal* 7: 1–46.

Wilf, Steven (2008). "The Making of the Post-War Paradigm in American Intellectual Property Law." *Columbia Journal of Law & the Arts* 31: 139–207.

Wilf, Steven (2010). "The Moral Lives of Intellectual Properties." In Hamilton and Brophy, eds, *Transformations in American Legal History: Law, Ideology, and Methods–Essays in Honor of Professor Morton J. Horwitz*. Harvard University Press, Cambridge.

Wilf, Steven (2011). "Copyright and Social Movements in Late Nineteenth-Century America." *Theoretical Inquiries in Law* 12: 123–160.

Wilf, Steven (2012). "Introduction." In Wilf, ed., *Intellectual Property Law and History*. Ashgate, London.

Woodmansee, Martha (1984). "The Genius and the Copyright: Economic and Legal Conditions of the Emergence of the 'Author'." *Eighteenth-Century Studies* 17: 425–448.

Woodmansee, Martha and Jaszi, Peter (1994). *The Construction of Authorship: Textual Appropriation in Law and Literature*. Duke University Press, Durham.

Zboray, Ronald J. (1993). *A Fictive People: Antebellum Economic Development and the American Reading Public*. Oxford University Press, Oxford, UK.

Zemer, Lior (2007). *The Idea of Authorship in Copyright*. Ashgate, London.

Part IV

Legal Thought

Chapter Twenty-four

Law and Literature

Jeannine Marie DeLombard

The origins of the critical enterprise known as "Law and Literature" – which in recent years has broadened out into the field of "Law, Culture, and the Humanities" (LCH) – are often traced to James Boyd White's *The Legal Imagination: Studies in the Nature of Legal Thought and Expression* (1973). Examining legal themes and topics in belletristic works, White and subsequent scholars of "Law *in* Literature" such as Ronald Dworkin, Owen Fiss, Robert Weisberg, Richard K. Weisberg, and Thomas C. Grey have explored the humanistic value of literary study for legal criticism and practice. An overlapping inquiry into "Law *as* Literature" emerged in the 1980s and 1990s, as Stanley Fish, Peter Brooks, Paul Gewirtz, Guyora Binder, and others began to employ literary critical methodologies to analyze narrative, form, rhetoric, intertextuality, genre, and interpretation in legal discourse. Arising out of ideological debates within the legal academy, both approaches can be seen as part of the contemporaneous Critical Legal Studies (CLS) movement's effort to challenge law's purported ideological neutrality. In particular, CLS opposed the concurrent trend toward rationalist utilitarianism represented by the Law and Economics movement – which in turn offered the most influential criticism of the Law and Literature endeavor in Richard Posner's 1988 book of that name, pointedly subtitled "A Misunderstood Relation."

In the meantime, literary study in the U.S. was abandoning the formalism of mid-century New Criticism, opening itself up to the theoretical perspectives of linguistics and philosophy in the 1970s and 1980s, and then to history and political science with the move toward Cultural Studies and New Historicism in the 1980s and 1990s. When, in 1984, Robert Ferguson

A Companion to American Legal History, First Edition.
Edited by Sally E. Hadden and Alfred L. Brophy.
© 2013 John Wiley & Sons Ltd. Published 2021 by John Wiley & Sons Ltd.

averred, "the study of law in American literature is ... long overdue," he was not ignoring the work of his fellow legal scholars so much as placing a new stress on the latter area of study. Building on the work of historian Perry Miller, Ferguson and his immediate successor Brook Thomas introduced an important strain of Americanist scholarship by demonstrating law's significance to the national literary canon (1984: 8).

As its title suggests, Thomas' *Cross-Examinations of Law and Literature* (1987) sought "to compare a culture's law with its literature" on the premise that "literature, in a much more obvious way than law, reveals the stories that a culture tells about itself" and can thus "demystify the narratives that serve to legitimate the legal order" (1987: 5). Taken up by influential works like Wai Chee Dimock's *Residues of Justice* (1996), this comparatist approach itself came under scrutiny as scholars in law schools joined those from a range of humanities disciplines in seeking a methodology that could address law's integral place in everyday life. Rather than separate entities to be compared and contrasted, law and literature could now be seen as mutually constitutive components of an encompassing culture.

As attuned as Posner to institutional differences between law and literature, the late Robert Cover remains one of the most influential theorists and practitioners of this more holistic approach. "To live in a legal world," Cover observed, leaving no doubt that each of us inhabits such a universe, "requires that one know not only the precepts, but also their connections to possible and plausible states of affairs. It requires that one integrate not only the 'is' and the 'ought,' but the 'is,' the 'ought,' and the 'what might be.' Narrative so integrates these domains" (1983: 10). Central to history, politics, and cinema, as well as law and literature, narrative is just one means by which legal policies and practices acquire their quotidian meanings and the cultural endeavors of non-official actors shape law.

Rosemary J. Coombe offered a manifesto for the nascent Law, Culture, and the Humanities movement when she proclaimed, "the relationship between law and culture should not be defined." Historicizing the emergence of these discursive fields "as autonomous realms in Enlightenment and Romantic imaginaries" and noting their "parallel trajectory in ideologies that legitimate and naturalize bourgeois class power and global European hegemonies," Coombe called instead for the outright "rejection of reified concepts of law and culture" (2000: 21). Many of the works in the recent explosion of scholarship on American law and literature have done just that. Recounting U.S. history from the vantage of recent LCH scholarship, this chapter shares most of its sources' assumption that "to recognize that law has meaning-making power ... is to see that social practices," including the production and reception of cultural texts, "are not logically separable from the laws that shape them and that social practices are unintelligible apart from the legal norms that give rise to them" (Sarat and Kearns, 2000: 10).

Yet even as this survey confirms that the American legal system in general and "courtrooms" in particular "are compulsive generators of texts," it cannot fully reconstruct the full "continuum of publication" that stretches between official legal documents and belles-lettres (Ferguson, 2007: 25). More than merely connecting law to literature, interstitial cultural texts such as popular press coverage of adultery trials (Hartog, 1997; Korobkin, 1998), or the lawyerly oratory that imbued stump speeches and commencement addresses alike (Ferguson, 1984: 305–317; Brophy, 2001) profoundly shaped the way Americans read and understood more conventional legal events and literary works. Here, brevity and comprehensiveness require us to limit the very expansiveness that has entered into recent critical discussions by focusing on these latter – as when Ferguson pairs the 1887 Haymarket trials with William Dean Howells' *A Hazard of New Fortunes* (2001 [1890]), or the 1953 execution of Julius and Ethel Rosenberg with E.L. Doctorow's *Book of Daniel* (1971).

Moving chronologically, this overview of the United States' commingled legal and literary histories begins by drawing on a resource untapped by all but a few LCH scholars (Hoeflich, 2010; Brophy, 1995–1996). The field of Book History attends to the materiality of written texts, which is inseparable from the politics, economics, and science of their production and circulation. Book History methodologies push LCH scholars to deepen their analysis beyond abstracted discussions of texts and practices by examining their objects of study *as* objects. If such an inquiry seems particularly urgent in the current epoch of rapid textual dematerialization, it can also tell us a great deal about the coeval development of law and literature in early America – as we can see if we turn to *Typographia. An Ode, on Printing. Inscribed to the Honourable William Gooch, Esq; His Majesty's Lieutenant-Governor, and Commander in Chief of the Colony of Virginia* (1730).

Part of a larger colonial genre of state odes and elegies, John Markland's poem lauds its dedicatee for bringing to the tobacco-growing colony the printing that will resuscitate art and law on the far side of the Atlantic:

> Great Representative!
> What Thanks shall we return? What Honours shew?
> ...
> By whom our Hopes revive:
> By whom all *Arts* recovr'ing live
> That erst like drooping Plants had dropt their Head.
> And once again, with native Vigour thrive:
> From whom Virginia's Laws, that lay
> In blotted *Manuscripts* obscur'd,
> By vulgar Eyes unread,
> Which whilome scarce the Light endur'd,
> Begin to view again the Day,
> As rising from the Dead. (Markland, 1730: 10)

Sixty years earlier, Governor William Berkeley had written to the Lords Commissioners of Foreign Plantations, "I thank God, there are no free schools nor printing ... for learning has brought disobedience, and heresy, and sects into the world, and printing has divulged them, and libels against the best government. God keep us from both" (quoted in Hall, 2007: 56). Although scribal and printed forms of writing and publishing would continue to thrive alongside each other in early America (Hall, 2008), the Protestant Reformation and the more recent English Civil War had alerted political authorities like Berkeley to the threat posed by cheap, vernacular, print productions.

Ironically, it was the effort to rescue *laws* from "blotted ... Manuscripts" that would soon lead to the establishment of print shops in Virginia and her sister colonies. Four years before setting *Typographia*'s type, William Parks had been invited to neighboring Maryland by lawyer and oppositionist assemblyman Thomas Bordley, who wanted the colony's laws and other government business printed locally. The same year that Parks published the magisterial folio, *A Compleat Collection of the Laws of Maryland* (1727), he commenced the *Maryland Gazette*, the first colonial newspaper to appear on the North American mainland south of Philadelphia. Before long, he was publishing political pamphlets – thereby justifying Beverley's fears – as well as almanacs and the occasional literary work by a local writer (notably, Maryland poet "laureate" Ebenezer Cooke), and selling imported English books (Shields, 2007: 442; Winton, 2007: 227). As his apprentice James Davis would do in North Carolina, Parks repeated this business model in Virginia (Winton, 2007: 224–230, 243). Having come to Williamsburg expressly to print the colony's laws, he published not only the *Virginia Gazette* but the colony's first printed poem, *Typographia*. Documenting the historical inextricability of American law and literature, the poem affirms in its very material existence Markland's figurative association of the resurrection of legal texts with the revitalization of arts, from printing to versifying.

Throughout early America, as in Maryland, Virginia, and North Carolina, legal and government publishing occasioned, underwrote, or, in some cases, vied with more literary endeavors, even as literature, especially in its published form, was subject to a range of commercial and official controls. Among the many "good Effects of my having learnt a little to scribble," Benjamin Franklin recalled in his *Autobiography* (1791–1818), was "that the leading men, seeing a News Paper now in the hands of one who could also handle a Pen, thought it convenient to oblige & encourage me," through patronage positions like his 1736 appointment to the clerkship of the General Assembly, which in turn "secur'd to me the Business of Printing the Votes, Laws, Paper Money, and other occasional Jobbs for the Public, that, on the whole were very profitable" (2008: 64, 67). Well after political independence, trade policies and regulations would help to produce a distinctly American notion of literature and authorship. *Wheaton v. Peters* (1834), a copyright case between rival Supreme Court reporters, established the republican understanding of print publications as the property of the public rather than the author (McGill, 2003). The American reluctance to treat authors as owners dovetailed with the legal doctrine of couverture to authorize women's entry into the public sphere of print (Homestead, 2005). For, instead of competing against their male protectors as proprietary authors in the literary marketplace, popular nineteenth-century women writers like Catharine Sedgwick, Harriet Beecher Stowe, Fanny Fern, E.D.E.N. Southworth, and Augusta Jane Evans could be seen as selflessly making generous contributions to the commonweal.

Before they could do so, however, American letters had to be liberated from the colonial system of "patronage" and "protection" that Markland found so indispensible to the arts (1730: iii). If "the pen and the press had merit equal to the sword" during the Revolution, it was thanks to the pointed polemics and slashing rhetoric of the era's pamphleteers, many of whom were members of "the colonial legal fraternity" (David Ramsay, 1789, quoted in Ferguson, 1994: 426, 441). In the gradual transfer of authority from the ministry to a cadre of professionalizing lawyers, the published sermons of Cotton Mather and Jonathan Edwards gave way to the legal argumentation of John Adams, Richard Bland, James Otis, and Martin Howard (Miller, 1965; Ferguson, 1994: 426–469). Like printed sermons and statute books, a work such as lawyer John Dickinson's *Letters from a Farmer in Pennsylvania* (1768) also sought "vulgar Eyes." But, seeking to disrupt rather than maintain the established political order, the Revolutionary pamphlet credited a newly united American public itself with "a truly legal authority," as corset-maker-turned-journalist Thomas Paine put it in *Common Sense* ([1776] 1987: 91).

It would not be long, however, before legally trained elites Thomas Jefferson, John Jay, Alexander Hamilton, and James Madison once again turned to pen and press – not to consolidate and activate the power of the people through pamphleteering, but to organize and constrain it through "the literature of public documents" (Ferguson, 1994: 470). In the hands of men who understood legal and literary skills to be coextensive, the forms and instruments of the English common law, from the adversarial pleading to the contract, could be made to yield a powerful narrative of national origins in documents like the Declaration of Independence and the Constitution (Ferguson, 1984; 1994: 470–495).

With its rational, textual intervention "in the course of human events," the Declaration of Independence seeks to realize the era's progressive faith in the perfectability of human beings and the societies in which they order themselves. The dark side of the Age of Reason's emphasis on human agency emerged in the 1780s and 1790s, as incapacity for such self-control appeared to produce the gory excesses of the French and the Haitian revolutions abroad, and violent outbursts like Shays' Rebellion and the Whiskey Rebellion at home. As these contradictory impulses played themselves out on the international stage, literary lawyers exploited a range of genres in works that, from John Trumbull's poetic mock epic, *M'Fingal* (1775–1782); to Royall Tyler's play, *The Contrast* (1787); to Hugh Henry Brackenridge's colossal novel, *Modern Chivalry* (1792–1815), presented legal forms and logic as a corrective to an increasingly disorderly, and often anti-legalist, democratic populism (Ferguson, 1984: 96–128). It was left to novelist Charles Brockden Brown, who had abandoned his legal career in hopes of founding a national literature, to demonstrate how the very verbal acts by which Americans sought to declare their independence and constitute their identity were compromised by the susceptibility of *all* texts to conflicting interpretations (Williams, 2003).

When in *Wieland* (1798), Brown dramatized the prevailing crisis of textual authority by fictionalizing ephemeral accounts of William Beadle's and James Yates' divinely inspired massacres of their own families, he shared in his culture's tendency to make "criminal law the lingua franca of popular politics" (Wilf, 2010: 10). For over a century, the gallows had been the site where law and literature most frequently and visibly met in early American culture. Well before Romantics, abolitionists, and other reform-minded writers began to incorporate the voices of slaves, Indians, and the poor into their poetry and prose, gallows literature introduced the purportedly first-person perspectives of such subordinates into the public sphere of print (DeLombard, 2012). During the revolutionary period, cheap crime literature joined a broader "ideological insurgency" as subordinates like Massachusetts apprentice Esther Rodgers, Christian Mohegan Moses Paul, and manumitted Delaware slave Abraham Johnstone gained public presence and textual authority through ever more critical contributions to the proceedings (Cohen, 1993: 143).

A cohort of legal professionals responded to this popular anti-legalism by following up earlier, haphazard, efforts to collect and print colonial statutes with a far more comprehensive editorial and publishing endeavor (Hoeflich, 2010). Along with initial forays into printed court reports and professional periodicals, this undertaking generated treatises like St. George Tucker's heavily annotated *Blackstone's Commentaries* (1803), James Kent's *Commentaries on American Law* (1826–1830), and Joseph Story's *Commentaries on the Constitution of the United States* (1833). By "forc[ing] existing laws into a unitary body" and "creating the impression of orderly progress over time," these works yielded a kind of legal meta-fiction, an historical narrative of progressive legal development on a grand scale (Edwards, 2009: 39). Perversely emphasizing the scientific rationality of a hallowed common law tradition, this mystical legal formalism cast judges from Blackstone and James Wilson to Kent and Lemuel Shaw as "living oracles" of a higher law whose rulings summoned a sovereign people into being (Blackstone quoted in Smith [2013]). And, while the sublime eloquence of these expositors was demonstrating that "legal commentaries can be rendered interesting to the general scholar and the man of literary taste" (as a review of Story's *Law of Bailments* (1832) marveled), lawyers like William Wirt and Daniel Webster were transforming even the most mundane proceedings into legal spectacles in packed antebellum courtrooms (Miller, 1965: 139, 151; Ferguson, 2007: 79–116). These trends coalesced in the widely printed oratory of Abraham Lincoln, through whom the reforming Christian visionary and the practical Blackstone lawyer spoke with one voice (Ferguson, 1984: 305–317).

Rather than diverging as a result of the professionalization of lawyers and authors, law and literature converged in new ways in the nineteenth-century United States (Thomas, 1987). Writers as diverse as James Fenimore Cooper, Susan Warner, Herman Melville, Rebecca Harding Davis, and (later) Kate Chopin exposed the "operative conditions and ... limits of justice" through literary displays of that which "remains unredressed, unrecovered, noncorresponding" in the legal process (Dimock, 1996: 6). At the same time, antebellum literature also – and not entirely naively – sought to authorize the court of public opinion as an alternative to what was increasingly seen as a corrupt or unresponsive legal system (Grossberg, 1996). Well before Congress had passed the Indian Removal Act of 1830, the Supreme Court had designated the Cherokees a "domestic, dependent nation" in *Cherokee Nation v. Georgia* (1831), or President Andrew Jackson had refused to uphold the Court's subsequent recognition of Cherokee sovereignty in *Worcester v. Georgia* (1832), activists laid the groundwork for other antebellum reform movements by using print to gain a hearing before an adjudicative public. Cherokee Elias Boudinot adopted not just a Founder's name but the revolutionary generation's print tactics when he followed his pamphlet *Address to the Whites* (1826) with publication of his nation's 1827 Constitution in the bilingual *Cherokee Phoenix* (1828; Perdue, 1996). Anticipating later abolitionist propaganda campaigns, American periodicals covered the anti-removal petition drive led by the coming generation of white women writers. Catherine Beecher and her younger sister Harriet, along with Lydia Sigourney and Angelina Grimké, modeled how respectable women could use print media to extend their influence beyond the private sphere of the home, to which they were confined by gender and class ideology, into the traditionally masculine public sphere of politics and law (Hershberger, 1999).

Exerting moral suasion in print to effect legal and political change in movements for everything from temperance to women's rights, a diverse group of antebellum reformers, many of whom were evangelical Christians, reclaimed the religious authority eschewed by a secularizing legal profession to criticize state and federal law (Clark, 1995). The new genre of the fugitive slave narrative drew on both the criminal confession and the tradition of religious witnessing to challenge the slave's civil death by eliciting the literary fugitive's "'testimony 'to' what Slavery really is'" to try "the perpetrators of slaveholding villainy" and their "slaveholding abettors" in the North before "the bar of public opinion" (Harriet Jacobs and Frederick Douglass quoted in DeLombard, 2007: 2, 12, 133). Stowe's *Uncle Tom's Cabin* (1852), which the author claimed had been inspired by both a divine vision and the Fugitive Slave Law of 1850, became America's first international bestseller. Developing and popularizing an alternative, evangelical "jurisprudence of love and sentiment," the novel invoked higher law to reject both the property claims of slaveholders and the conservative legal thinking that placed law and order above moral considerations of humanity – a tactic that lay and professional interlocutors from both sections immediately challenged in published reviews, book-length rebuttals, and apologist fiction (Brophy, 1995–1996: 479). Stowe's example proved an enduring one. Spurred by the 1871 Indian Appropriations Act, which denied Indian sovereignty and made individual Indians wards of the state, activist journalist Helen Hunt Jackson followed *A Century of Dishonor* (1881), which recounted the long history of broken U.S.-Indian treaties, with her hugely popular sentimental novel, *Ramona* (1884). Extending into the twentieth century, print debates over indigenous and African-American rights highlight how the agonistic process of recounting alternative histories, both individual and collective, within and against the conventions of "official stories" of the nation and its origins, contributed to the ongoing development of an increasingly cosmopolitan American constitutionalism (Wald, 1995: 2; Suggs, 2000; Crane, 2002).

That some, such as Ralph Waldo Emerson, Douglass, and Charles Sumner, derived their "higher law constitutionalism" from the dynamic interplay of "conscience (moral inspiration) and consent (political dialogue)" indicates the continued importance of contract to literary and legal conceptions of citizenship (Crane, 2002: 6). Nowhere, perhaps, was the nineteenth-century faith in contract's transformative effects more evident than in the "poetics of punishment" that emerged when the efforts of an ideologically diverse group of early national and antebellum penal reformers – including anti-gallows writers John O'Sullivan, William Gilmore Simms, Lydia Maria Child, Walt Whitman, and Southworth – resulted in both offenders and their punishments being relocated behind the walls of the nation's new asylums (Smith, 2009: 6; Barton, 2006; Jones, 2011). This withdrawal from public view completed the criminal's metamorphosis "from common sinner into mental alien" (Halttunen, 1998: 35). Removed from the civic landscape, prisoners entered more deeply into the national consciousness, where they were imagined individually to recapitulate the abandonment of the state of nature for civil society through their own, exemplary civic dissolution and reconstitution (Smith, 2009). Tirelessly subjecting fictional madmen, racial subordinates, drunkards, simians, and prisoners alike to cognate rituals of civil death and often grotesque resurrections, Edgar Allan Poe's gothic "meditations on incapacitation" highlighted "the evident whimsy of the law's exercise of its personifying powers" at a time when the corporation, like the slave, stood as a highly visible "creature of law" (Dayan, 2001: 107; *Dartmouth v. Woodward* (1819) quoted in Best, 2004: 12).

Together, antebellum law and literature accustomed the American public to think with a lawyer's discernment about the differences among humanness, personhood, and citizenship, particularly as delineated by boundaries of social inclusion, civic belonging, and political membership. Far from denying slaves' humanity, slaveholders and legislators found that what the formerly enslaved Reverend James W.C. Pennington deplored in *The Fugitive Blacksmith* (1849) as "the chattel principle, the property principle, the bill of sale principle" worked best when slaveholders' exploitation of blacks' humanity was coordinated with legal authorities' occasional recognition of slaves' culpability as persons (1849: iv; Hartman, 1997; Wong, 2009). To assign slaves what James Madison in *Federalist* 54 (1788) called "the mixed character of persons and of property" may have been inhuman, as abolitionists protested, but the designation had no bearing on blacks' status *as* humans (Madison, Hamilton, and Jay, 1988: 332). Just as Poe's fiction registered how the slave's "retractable personhood" might trouble the line between humans and brutes or between persons and property, highly publicized legal crises involving fugitive slaves, African-American mariners, and globe-trotting black authors revealed "the hermeneutic limit of an emergent liberal discourse of contract premised on universalized notions of will and free choice in a partially free world" (Dayan, 2002: 80; Wong, 2009: 100).

The Emancipation Proclamation (1861) and the Thirteenth Amendment (1863) appeared to affirm the United States' eligibility to be counted among the "progressive societies" that Victorian treatise writer Sir Henry Maine saw moving "*from Status to Contract*" (quoted in Thomas, 1997: 2). Writing in the era of the Chinese Exclusion Act (1882), the *Civil Rights Cases* (1883), and *Plessy v. Ferguson* (1896), realists such as Howells, Henry James, and Mark Twain would craft novels that interrogate contract's epochal promise to replace a "transcendent" ordering of society based on hereditary status, as well as the coercion, sentimentalism, and paternalism that maintained it, with more democratic transitory exchange relationships characterized by volition, consent, and, above all, self-ownership (Thomas, 1997: 12).

Their predecessors were not indifferent to the tantalizing promise of contract. In the decades before the Civil War, when Married Women's Property Acts and sensational divorce, custody, and adoption proceedings were reshaping family law, sentimental female novelists such as Stowe, Warner, and Maria Susanna Cummins deployed the genre's melodramatic separations and deaths imaginatively to reconstruct the family by eliminating "the paternalism of consanguinity" and resorting to "a paradigm of contract" wherein "individual family members ... have rights that must be guaranteed and protected," rights which are "increasingly ... understood in affective terms" (Weinstein, 2004: 9; Grossberg, 1988; Hartog, 1997). Concurrently, writers like Child and Stowe were idealizing the legally unrecognized marriages of slaves as a purer alternative to the often harsh reality of the legal bond between man and wife (Chakkalakal, 2011). Looking westward, those positioned on either side of the protracted debate over polygamy in the Mormon territory of Utah placed consensual conjugal unions at the heart of the constitutionally protected federal union (Gordon, 2002). Moving from the domestic spaces of women's novels into predominantly male courtrooms, this sentimental rhetoric helped to authorize women plaintiffs in adultery cases while recasting marriage as a matter of reciprocal affective exchange instead of a husband's property rights (Korobkin, 1998).

For sailors, as for women, contracts inaugurated rather than terminated unequal status relations. Because this state of affairs did not end with the Civil War, slavery remained an important touchstone for authors seeking to reconcile the contractarian thinking derived from Enlightenment social contract theory with the new contractualism of nineteenth-century liberal market capitalism. "Who ain't a slave?" asks Ishmael in *Moby-Dick* (1851) before signing on to an exploitative whaling contract under tyrannous Captain Ahab (Melville, [1851] 1988: 6). Explicitly identifying normatively white sailors with slaves in scenes of flogging, escape, and capture, future lawyer and treatise writer Richard Henry Dana, Jr.'s *Two Years Before the Mast* (1840) and up-and-coming novelist Herman Melville's *Typee* (1846), *Omoo* (1847), *Redburn* (1849), and *White-Jacket* (1850) raised consciousness about sailors' rights at a moment when anti-abolitionists and reformers alike protested the "wage slavery" of a white, northern, urban laborer like Melville's eponymous "Bartleby, the Scrivener" (Levine, 1989; Wallace, 2008). Whether or not these maritime novels led to the 1850 act prohibiting flogging on naval and merchant ships, it is telling that Melville wrote *Billy Budd, Sailor*, his posthumously published reflection on maritime despotism, in the same decade that the U.S. Supreme Court held in *Robertson v. Baldwin* (1897) that because "seamen are treated by Congress ... as deficient in that full and intelligent responsibility for their acts which is accredited to ordinary adults," the Thirteenth Amendment's "provision against involuntary servitude was never intended to apply to their contracts" (*Robertson*; Gutoff, 2006).

Melville may have intended irony when, in *Battle-Pieces* (1866), he depicted the Confederacy's bloody defeat as a "victory of LAW," but many of his generation did see in the Fourteenth Amendment "a victory of legal process in general and American constitutional law ... in particular" (Nabers, 2006: vi). As the Enforcement Acts of 1870–1871 and the Civil Rights Act of 1875 were weakened by the rulings in *United States v. Cruikshank* (1876), the *Civil Rights Cases*, and *Plessy*, and with decisions like *Robertson*, the *Slaughterhouse Cases* (1873), and *Lochner v. New York* (1905) putting the Reconstruction Amendments in service of capitalism, however, many came to suspect that the true victor was not justice but the judiciary. The vernacular echo of Chief Justice Roger B. Taney's notorious dictum (blacks have "no rights which the white man [is] bound to respect") preserves *Scott v. Sandford* (1857) as the lower-water mark in judicial authority. Similarly, the idiomatic survival of phrases like "separate but equal" (*Plessy*), "the marketplace of ideas" (*Abrams v. United States* [1919]), "clear and present danger" (*Schenck v. United States* [1919]), and "shouting fire in a crowded theatre" (*Schenck*) gauge the Court's resurgence at century's end. Not coincidentally, the latter three phrases have their origins in decisions written by Oliver Wendell Holmes, Jr. Named after his poet and essayist father, the venerable "Autocrat of the Breakfast Table," the younger Holmes joined fellow Boston Brahmin Henry James in ushering in a subtle new alignment of law and literature. Rejecting the still-powerful antebellum notion of the novelist's moral duty, James' *Art of Fiction* (1884) eschewed the idealism of the romance as developed by Nathaniel Hawthorne and Stowe in favor of the realist doctrine that "the novel is history" (James quoted in Moddelmog, 2000: 6–11). Holmes shared James' historicist emphasis on narrative's importance in assigning meaning to lived cultural experiences. "The life of the law has not been logic: it has been experience," he proclaimed in *The Common-Law* (1881), rejecting nineteenth-century Legal Formalism for a Realism that would situate law in the midst of contending social, economic, and political forces (2009: 31).

A principled critic of what he saw as realism's political and moral irresponsibility, Albion Tourgée stands as the apotheosis of a nineteenth-century higher law constitutionalism that looked to the wider culture to ensure that law be guided by conscience and validated by consent. He also represents the havoc such convictions could wreak under the reunified nation's new legal regime. As North Carolina's Superior Court Justice (1868–1874), Tourgée's participant-observation of painful efforts first to reconstruct the South along more equitable race and class lines and then to "redeem" state governments for white propertied interests inspired *A Fool's Errand, By One of the Fools* (1879). A "run-away bestseller," the novel prompted comparisons to *Uncle Tom's Cabin*, the corresponding print rebuttals, and Tourgée's own bestselling sequel, *Bricks without Straw* (1880; Elliott, 2006: 170). Tourgée's literary fame introduced him to a new generation of black activists who, from anti-lynching pamphleteer and journalist Ida B. Wells to the American Citizens Equal Rights Association of Louisiana (ACERA), were determined to see the rule of law upheld in the face of rampant racial terrorism. Recruited by ACERA to serve as *Plessy*'s lead attorney, Tourgée cannily adapted antebellum print strategies to a Gilded Age public but could not overcome an unsympathetic bench. The result was over a half century of *de jure* segregation – and, critic Kenneth W. Warren contends, the birth of African-American literature as a self-consciously separate but emphatically equal cultural phenomenon that would terminate, with the Jim Crow era itself, in *Brown v. Board of Education* (1954; Warren, 2011: 88). On the other side of the color line, novelist William Faulkner probed law's role in creating and maintaining what Tourgée had identified – and Cheryl I. Harris has theorized – as a "property" interest in whiteness, most notably in *Go Down, Moses* (1942) (quoted in Harris, 1993: 1748; Davis, 2003).

If "responsibility talk was at least as common as rights talk" during the Long Nineteenth Century, literature helps us to hear the changes in vernacular legal discourse that occurred between the Civil War and the Cold War (Blumenthal, 2008: 185). As we have seen, early national and antebellum writers had conceived questions of political and social accountability largely in terms derived from criminal and constitutional law. Over the course of the nineteenth century, however, Americans were finding in the emergent field of torts an alternative idiom of liability and damages as they sought to reconcile the new contractualism with lingering status relations and struggled to balance individual human agency against corporate power (Goodman, 1998). Indeed, even constitutional rights talk could be translated into the language of civil wrongs, as Judge Joseph P. Bradley maintained in the *Civil Rights Cases* and as increasing numbers of African-American and other poor or disenfranchised plaintiffs were demonstrating in lawsuits against railroad and streetcar companies (Welke, 2001). As this popularized legal jargon followed more common speech forms into the realist novels of Howells, James, Stephen Crane, and Edith Wharton, however, it seemed primarily to voice the needs of middle-class men suddenly threatened by a "perilously alienable" male personhood in the Age of Contract (Travis, 2005: 14).

These shifts in legal register only intensified as matters of privacy and publicity, usually framed today as issues of human sexuality or state security, gained prominence in the new century. Samuel L. Warren and Louis D. Brandeis' "The Right to Privacy" (1890) holds a special place in American law and letters as the rare instance when published legal scholarship, rather than legislative or judicial action, created a new area of law: the tort right to privacy. But it was during the Cold War that, in the mingled shadows cast by the First, Third, Fourth, Fifth, and Ninth Amendments, privacy was found to be a constitutional right for first married couples (*Griswold v. Connecticut* [1965]) and then for the non-normative pregnant female person (*Roe v. Wade* [1973]) – albeit not initially for gay men

(*Bowers v. Hardwick* [1986]; *Lawrence v. Texas* [2003]) . Overlooking the legal historical significance of the denial of privacy to enslaved African Americans (Davis, 1997; Shamir, 2006: 97–146), we tend to attribute the privacy right's ascendency to a late-twentieth-century consternation over the apparent shift from commercial to governmental forms of intrusion. With movements for women's and gay rights insisting that "the personal is political" and "Silence = Death," privacy itself has gone public with confessional discourse's migration into a range of cultural forms, from mass-mediated celebrity tell-alls to the autobiographical poetry of James Russell Lowell, Anne Sexton, Sylvia Plath, W.D. Snodgrass, and Paul Monette (Nelson, 2002). This was, after all, the century that saw literary obscenity's transformation from crime into First Amendment right. Conducted on three continents and focusing on now-classic works such as James Joyce's *Ulysses* (1990 [1922]), Theodore Dreiser's *American Tragedy* (2010 [1925]), D.H. Lawrence's *Lady Chatterley's Lover* (2006 [1928]), Henry Miller's *Tropic of Cancer* (1994 [1934]), and Vladimir Nabokov's *Lolita* (1989 [1955]), obscenity trials involving U.S. courts or American literature ultimately seem less notable for pitting legal repression against literary freedom than for prompting international dialogue on what constitutes "literature" during the rise and fall of a modernist opposition of elite art forms to mass culture (Ladenson, 2007).

Centering on Euro-American texts and courts, the transnational marketing and policing of books, authors, and publishers offers a particularly striking instance of how the global flow of commodities and labor was once again reconfiguring law and literature in the twentieth-century U.S. Occurring against the backdrop of U.S. wars in the Philippines, Japan, Korea, and Vietnam and the emergence of a "Pac Rim" economic zone, "the incorporation of Asian migrant labor into the United States requires us to grapple with the fully industrial modernity of race" at the moment of the nation's ambivalent expansion into the new frontier of imperialist global capitalism (Lye, 2005: 9). From an Asian-American Studies perspective, literary works from this period distribute themselves along a legal historical timeline that commences with the era of exclusion, restriction, and regulation under the Chinese Exclusion Act of 1882, the Asiatic Barred Zone Act of 1917, the National Origins Act of 1924, and the Tydings-McDuffie Act of 1834; proceeds through the contradictory mid-century period wherein legislative repeal was accompanied by the legally sanctioned mass internment of Japanese American citizens under Executive Order 9066 (1942) and *Korematsu v. United States* (1944); and terminates in the era following the elimination of the national origins quota system by the Immigration and Nationality Act (1965). Crucially, the aggregate of governmental legislation and individual human endeavors that Lisa Lowe refers to as "immigrant acts" reveals the transnational, materialist origins of American racial formation, personhood, and citizenship not only in texts like John Luther Long's

"Madame Butterfly" (1898), Carlos Bulosan's *America is in the Heart* (2000 [1946]), and Maxine Hong Kingston's *China Men* (1989 [1980]), but in works which, like Frank Norris' *The Octopus* (1994 [1901]) and John Steinbeck's *The Grapes of Wrath* (2006 [1939]), lack explicitly Asian themes or characters (Lowe, 1996). Whether through federal exclusion acts, state alien land laws, or statutory restrictions on sexuality and marriage such as the Page Law (1875), the Expatriation Act (1917), the Cable Act (1922), the War Brides Act (1945), and the Immigration Act (1946), American literature illustrates how immigration law has shaped the contours of the nation and its inhabitants (Lye, 2005; Koshy, 2004; Thomas, 2007: 177–214).

The combustive interaction of law and literature on the nation's borders has shaken the conceptual foundations of the former. Liberal legal thought's constitutive opposition of force to consent is powerfully undermined in the poetry and prose of Ana Castillo, Cherríe Moraga, and Maria Helena Viramontes, whose works display a feminist awareness for how, since the Treaty of Guadalupe Hildalgo (1848), "the history of Anglo and Mexicano/Chicano interaction" has been "one of territorial occupation through legal manipulation working in concert with violence" (Gutiérrez-Jones, 1995: 44). Little surprise, then, that Chicano playwright Luis Valdez should join Communist propagandist-turned-Book-of-the-Month Club author Richard Wright and a host of black, Latino/a, and Native American literary convicts – notably, Chester Himes, Iceberg Slim, Raúl Salinas, Ricardo Sánchez, Jimmy Santiago Baca, Miguel Piñero, and Judy Lucero – in probing the relationship between racialized criminality and political protest (Franklin, 1989; Harlow, 1992; Suggs, 2000; Brown, 2002; Hames-García, 2004). In a twenty-first-century United States where a figure like reputed Latin Kings gang member-turned-accused al Qaeda "enemy combatant" José Padilla/Abdullah al-Muhajir embodies the commissure of the ongoing "War on Crime" with the more recent "War on Terror," prison literature promises to gain a new relevance as it poses difficult questions about the growing identification of public safety with a globalizing racial hegemony (Olguín, 2010).

The discursive isolation imposed on today's inmates at Guantánamo Bay and supermax prisons under perversely formalist interpretations of the Eighth Amendment contrasts sharply with the innovative carceral cultural initiatives that led to the burst of public expression by prisoners in the 1970s (Dayan, 2011: 71–112; Bernstein, 2010). As the epistolary and memoiristic modes of Martin Luther King, George Jackson, Malcolm X, Angela Y. Davis, and Leonard Peltier were politicizing the prisoner's conventionally confessional voice, a first-person subjectivity was seeping into professionally "objective" forms of writing, from journalism to legal scholarship. New Journalism's treatment of legal crises ranged from documentary accounts of government attempts to repress anti-Vietnam

War protests in Norman Mailer's *Armies of the Night* (1994 [1968]) and Oscar Zeta Acosta's *The Revolt of the Cockroach People* (1989 [1973]), to meditative reworkings of the True Crime genre in "nonfiction novels" like Truman Capote's *In Cold Blood* (2002 [1966]) and Mailer's *Executioner's Song* (2000 [1979]).

Chicano lawyer, activist, and (temporary) prisoner Acosta's *Autobiography of a Brown Buffalo* (1989 [1972]) offers a bridge from the New Journalism and prison arts movements to later novelistic and first-person prose experiments by legal colleagues Derrick Bell (*And We Are Not Saved: The Elusive Quest for Racial Justice*, 1989), Patricia J. Williams (*The Alchemy of Race and Rights: Diary of a Law Professor*, 1991), Gerald P. Lopez (*Rebellious Lawyering: One Chicano's Vision of Progressive Law Practice*, 1992), and Richard Delgado (*The Rodrigo Chronicles: Conversations About America and Race*, 1995). The latter works exemplify the "storytelling" methodology advocated by the academic Critical Race Theory (CRT) movement, which sought to radicalize CLS' liberal rhetorical analysis of law as ideology by taking an activist, vernacular approach to law's more material, coercive effects at intersections of race, class, gender, and imperialism (Gutiérrez-Jones, 2001).

Ironically, the very celebration of CRT storytelling and Law-and-Literature scholarship as self-consciously *interdisciplinary* endeavors may well be the strongest indication that, after two centuries, the legal and literary professions have finally severed from each other. Outside the academy, the popularity of John Grisham confirms the extent to which law and literature have become separate, autonomous fields. The author of one Innocence Project-inspired work of nonfiction (*The Innocent Man: Murder and Injustice in a Small Town*, 2006), as well as books on baseball and the South, the former lawyer and Mississippi state representative (1983–1990) has made the legal thriller his lucrative "brand," as indicated by the titular labels affixed to bestselling novels like *The Litigators* (2011), *The Associate* (2009), *The Appeal* (2008), *The King of Torts* (2003), and *The Chamber* (1994). Just as novels by legal professionals Erle Stanley Gardner and John D. Voelker launched, respectively, the *Perry Mason* TV series (1957–1966) and the Otto Preminger film *Anatomy of a Murder* (1958), Grisham's works have become the basis for feature films like *The Firm* (1993) and *The Pelican Brief* (1993), as well as spinoff TV series, including *The Client* (1995–1996) and *The Firm* (2012). Typically centering on the problem-solving lawyer, the genre has been taken up by lawyer-novelists Lisa Scottline (a.k.a. "the female John Grisham") and Michael Nava (creator of the Lambda Literary Award-winning mystery series featuring gay Latino criminal defense lawyer Henry Rios).

Meticulously attentive to the technical niceties that preoccupy a tightly knit professional community, Grisham's works resemble the police and medical procedural dramas that attracted large television audiences at the turn of the twentieth-first century. Thus, even as they frequently controvert the stereotype of lawyers as slick, well-educated, heartless elites through populist portrayals of street lawyers and second-rate law students living hand-to-mouth existences, the legal thriller's realist claim to reveal the law's inner workings ultimately reinforces the notion that lawyers, judges, and legislators inhabit a separate realm. Law does not impose order on the messiness of American life; quite the contrary, it often disrupts individual lives. But because law is portrayed as an insular profession rather than a political or social force, Grisham's works, in contrast to nineteenth-century fiction and nonfiction, do not call upon their audiences to transform what is often portrayed as a corrupt, inefficient legal system, much less the larger society in which it operates. The procedural emphasis on logic does not prevent the genre from portraying the life of the law as experience, but it is an experience far removed from that of the lay reader – an object for narrative contemplation, not activist intervention. As Grisham's mass cultural ubiquity attests, this phenomenon is not contained within the covers of the printed book, but extends across a range of media and information technologies. It is to these venues that we must look for new dispositions of law in American culture.

References

Acosta, O.Z. (1989 [1972]). *Autobiography of a Brown Buffalo*. Vintage, New York.

Acosta, O.Z. (1989 [1973]). *The Revolt of the Cockroach People*. Vintage, New York.

Amory, H. and Hall, D.D., eds (2007). *A History of the Book in America. Volume 1: The Colonial Book in the Atlantic World*. American Antiquarian Society-University of North Carolina Press, Chapel Hill.

Barton, J.C. (2006). "The Anti-Gallows Movement in Antebellum America." *REAL: Yearbook of Research in English and American Literature* 22: 145–178.

Bernstein, L. (2010). *America Is the Prison: Arts and Politics in Prison in the 1970s*. University of North Carolina Press, Chapel Hill.

Best, S.M. (2004). *The Fugitive's Properties: Law and the Poetics of Possession*. University of Chicago Press, Chicago.

Blumenthal, S.L. (2008). "Metaphysics, Moral Sense, and the Pragmatism of the Law." *Law and History Review* 26(1): 177–185.

Brophy, A.L. (1995-1996). "'over and above ... there broods a portentous shadow, – the shadow of *law*': Harriet Beecher Stowe's Critique of Slave Law in *Uncle Tom's Cabin*." *Journal of Law and Religion* 12(2): 457–506.

Brophy, A.L. (2001). "The Rule of Law in Antebellum College Literary Addresses: The Case of William Greene." *Cumberland Law Review* 31(2): 231.

Brown, M. (2002). *Gang Nation: Delinquent Citizens in Puerto Rican, Chicano, and Chicana Narratives*. University of Minnesota Press, Minneapolis.

Bulosan, C. (2000 [1946]). *America is in the Heart*. University of Washington Press, Seattle.

Capote, T. (2002 [1966]). *In Cold Blood*. Random House, New York.

Chakkalakal, T. (2011). *Novel Bondage: Slavery, Marriage, and Freedom in Nineteenth-Century America*. University of Illinois Press, Champaign.

Cohen, D.A. (1993). *Pillars of Salt, Monuments of Grace: New England Crime Literature and the Origins of American Popular Culture, 1674–1860*. Oxford University Press, New York.

Clark, E.B. (1995). "'The Sacred Rights of the Weak': Pain, Sympathy, and the Culture of Individual Rights in Antebellum America." *Journal of American History* 82(2): 463–493.

Coombe, R.J. (2000). "Contingent Articulations: A Critical Cultural Studies of Law." In Sarat and Kearns, eds, *Law in the Domains of Culture*, 21–64. University of Michigan Press, Ann Arbor.

Cover, R. (1983). "The Supreme Court, 1982 Term – Foreword: Nomos and Narrative." *Harvard Law Review* 97(4): 4–68.

Crane, G.D. (2002). *Race, Citizenship, and Law in American Literature*. Cambridge University Press, Cambridge, UK.

Davis, P.C. (1997). *Neglected Stories: The Constitution and Family Values*. Hill and Wang-Farrar, Straus, and Giroux, New York.

Davis, T.M. (2003). *Games of Property: Law, Race, Gender, and Faulkner's Go Down, Moses*. Duke University Press, Durham.

Dayan, C. (2011). *The Law Is a White Dog: How Legal Rituals Make and Unmake Persons*. Princeton University Press, Princeton.

Dayan, J. (2001). "Poe, Persons, and Property." In Kennedy and Weissberg, eds, *Romancing the Shadow: Poe and Race*, 106–126. Oxford University Press, Oxford, UK.

Dayan, J. (2002). "Legal Slaves and Civil Bodies." In Castronovo and Nelson, eds, *Materializing Democracy: Toward a Revitalized Cultural Politics*, 53–94. Duke University Press, Durham.

DeLombard, J.M. (2007). *Slavery on Trial: Law, Print, and Abolitionism*. University of North Carolina Press, Chapel Hill.

DeLombard, J.M. (2012). *In the Shadow of the Gallows: Race, Crime, and American Civic Identity*. University of Pennsylvania Press, Philadelphia.

Dimock, W.C. (1996). *Residues of Justice: Literature, Law, Philosophy*. University of California Press, Berkeley.

Doctorow, E.L. (1971). *The Book of Daniel: A Novel*. Random House, New York.

Dreiser, T. (2010 [1925]). *An American Tragedy*. Signet Classics, New York.

Edwards, L.F. (2009). *The People and Their Peace: Legal Culture and the Transformation of Inequality in the Post-Revolutionary South*. University of North Carolina Press, Chapel Hill.

Elliott, M. (2006). *Color-Blind Justice: Albion Tourgée and the Quest for Racial Equality from the Civil War to* Plessy v. Ferguson. Oxford University Press, Oxford, UK.

Ferguson, R.A. (1984). *Law and Letters in American Culture*. Harvard University Press, Cambridge.

Ferguson, R.A. (1994). "The American Enlightenment, 1750–1820." In Bercovitch and Patell, eds, *The Cambridge History of American Literature, Volume I, 1590–1820*. Cambridge University Press, Cambridge.

Ferguson, R.A. (2007). *The Trial in American Life*. University of Chicago Press, Chicago.

Franklin, B. (2008 [1791–1818]). *Autobiography and Other Writings.* Oxford University Press, Oxford.

Franklin, H.B. (1989). *Prison Literature in America: The Victim as Criminal and Artist.* Oxford University Press, New York.

Goodman, N. (1998). *Shifting the Blame: Literature, Law, and the Theory of Accidents in Nineteenth-Century America.* Princeton University Press, Princeton.

Gordon, S.B. (2002). *The Mormon Question: Polygamy and Constitutional Conflict in Nineteenth-Century America.* University of North Carolina Press, Chapel Hill.

Grossberg, M. (1988). *Governing the Hearth: Law and the Family in Nineteenth-Century America.* University of North Carolina Press, Chapel Hill.

Grossberg, M. (1996). *A Judgment for Solomon: The d'Hauteville Case and Legal Experience in Antebellum America.* Cambridge University Press, New York.

Gutoff, J.M. (2006). "Fugitive Slaves and Ship-Jumping Sailors: The Enforcement and Survival of Coerced Labor." *University of Pennsylvania Journal of Labor and Employment Law* 9(1): 87–116.

Gutiérrez-Jones, C. (1995). *Rethinking the Borderlands: Between Chicano Culture and Legal Discourse.* University of California Press, Berkeley.

Gutiérrez-Jones, C. (2001). *Critical Race Narratives: A Study of Race, Rhetoric, and Injury.* New York University Press, New York.

Hall, D.D. (2007). "The Chesapeake in the Seventeenth Century." In Amory and Hall, eds, *A History of the Book in America. Volume 1: The Colonial Book in the Atlantic World,* 55–82. American Antiquarian Society-University of North Carolina Press, Chapel Hill.

Hall, D.D. (2008). *Ways of Writing: The Practice and Politics of Text-Making in Seventeenth-Century New England.* University of Pennsylvania Press, Philadelphia.

Halttunen, K. (1998). *Murder Most Foul: The Killer and the American Gothic Imagination.* Harvard University Press, Cambridge.

Hames-García, M.R. (2004). *Fugitive Thought: Prison Movements, Race, and the Meaning of Justice.* University of Minnesota Press, Minneapolis.

Harlow, B. (1992). *Barred: Women, Writing, and Political Detention.* University Press of New England, Hanover, NH.

Harris, C.I. (1993). "Whiteness As Property." *Harvard Law Review* 106(8): 1707–1791.

Hartman, S.V. (1997). *Scenes of Subjection: Terror, Slavery, and Self-Making in Nineteenth-Century America.* Oxford University Press, New York.

Hartog, H. (1997). "Lawyering, Husbands' Rights, and 'the Unwritten Law' in Nineteenth- Century America." *Journal of American History* 84(1): 67–96.

Hershberger, M. (1999). "Mobilizing Women, Anticipating Abolition: The Struggle against Indian Removal in the 1830s." *Journal of American History* 86(1): 15–40.

Hoeflich, M.H. (2010). *Legal Publishing in Antebellum America.* Cambridge University Press, New York.

Holmes, Jr., O.W. (2009). *The Path of the Law and the Common Law.* Kaplan, New York.

Homestead, M.J. (2005). *American Women Authors and Literary Property, 1822–1869.* Cambridge University Press, New York.

Howells, W.D. (2001 [1890]). *A Hazard of New Fortunes*. Penguin, New York.
Jones, P.C. (2011). *Against the Gallows: Antebellum American Writers and the Movement to Abolish Capital Punishment*. University of Iowa Press, Iowa City.
Joyce, J. (1990 [1922]). *Ulysses*. Vintage.
Kingston, M.H. (1989 [1980]). *China Men*. Vintage, New York.
Koshy, S. (2004). *Sexual Naturalization: Asian Americans and Miscegenation*. Stanford University Press, Stanford.
Korobkin, L.H. (1998). *Criminal Conversations: Sentimentality and Nineteenth-Century Legal Stories of Adultery*. Columbia University Press, New York.
Ladenson, E. (2007). *Dirt for Art's Sake: Books on Trial from Madame Bovary to Lolita*. Cornell University Press, Ithaca.
Lawrence, D.H. (2006 [1928]). *Lady Chatterley's Lover*. Penguin, New York.
Levine, R.S. (1989). *Conspiracy and Romance: Studies in Brockden Brown, Cooper, Hawthorne, and Melville*. Cambridge University Press, Cambridge, UK.
Long, J.L. (1898). "Madame Butterfly." *Century Illustrated Magazine* 55(3): 374–393.
Lowe, L. (1996). *Immigrant Acts: On Asian American Cultural Politics*. Duke University Press, Durham.
Lye, C. (2005). *America's Asia: Racial Form and American Literature, 1893–1945*. Princeton University Press, Princeton.
Madison, J., Hamilton, A., and Jay, J. (1988). *The Federalist Papers*. Penguin, New York.
Mailer, N. (1994 [1968]). *The Armies of the Night: History as a Novel, the Novel as History*. Penguin, New York.
Mailer, N. (2000 [1979]). *The Executioner's Song*. Signet, New York.
Markland, J. (1730). *Typographia. An Ode, on Printing*. Williamsburg.
McGill, M.M. (2003). *American Literature and the Culture of Reprinting 1834–1853*. University of Pennsylvania Press, Philadelphia.
Melville, H. (1988 [1851]). *Moby-Dick*. Northwestern University Press and Newberry Library, Evanston.
Miller, H. (1994 [1934]). *Tropic of Cancer*. Grove Press, New York.
Moddelmog, W.E. (2000). *Reconstituting Authority: American Fiction in the Province of the Law, 1880–1920*. University of Iowa Press, Iowa City.
Nabers, D. (2006). *Victory of Law: The Fourteenth Amendment, the Civil War, and American Literature, 1852–1867*. Johns Hopkins University Press, Baltimore.
Nabokov, V. (1989 [1955]). *Lolita*. Vintage, New York.
Nelson, D. (2002). *Pursuing Privacy in Cold War America*. Columbia University Press, New York.
Norris, F. (1994 [1901]). *The Octopus: A Story of California*. Penguin, New York.
Olguín, B.V. (2010). *La Pinta: Chicana/o Prison Literature, Culture, and Politics*. University of Texas Press, Austin.
Perdue, T., ed. (1996). *Cherokee Editor: The Writings of Elias Boudinot*. University of Georgia Press, Athens.
Paine, T. (1987). *The Thomas Paine Reader*, eds Michael Foot and Isaac Kramnick. Penguin, London.
Pennington, J.W.C. (1849). *The Fugitive Blacksmith ; or, Events in the History of James W. C. Pennington, Pastor of a Presbyterian Church, New York, Formerly a Slave in the State of Maryland, United States*. Charles Gilpin, London.

Documenting the American South http://docsouth.unc.edu/neh/penning49/penning49.html (last accessed October 12, 2012).

Posner, R.A. (1988). *Law and Literature: A Misunderstood Relation*. Harvard University Press, Cambridge.

Robertson v. Baldwin 165 U.S. 275 (1897).

Robinson, M. (1998). "Collins to Grisham: A Brief History of the Legal Thriller." *Legal Studies Forum* 22: 21–35.

Sarat, A. and Kearns, T.R., eds (2000). *Law in the Domains of Culture*. University of Michigan Press, Ann Arbor.

Shamir, M. (2006). *Inexpressible Privacy: The Interior Life of Antebellum American Literature*. University of Pennsylvania Press, Philadelphia.

Shields, D.S. (2007). "Eighteenth-Century Literary Culture." In Amory and Hall, eds, *A History of the Book in America. Volume 1: The Colonial Book in the Atlantic World*, 434–476. American Antiquarian Society-University of North Carolina Press, Chapel Hill.

Smith, C. (2009). *The Prison and the American Imagination*. Yale University Press, New Haven.

Smith, C. (2013). *The Oracle and the Curse: A Poetics of Justice, from the Revolution to the Civil War*. Yale University Press, New Haven.

Steinbeck, J. (2006 [1939]). *The Grapes of Wrath*. Vintage, New York.

Suggs, J. (2000). *Whispered Consolations: Law and Narrative in African American Life*. University of Michigan Press, Ann Arbor.

Thomas, B. (1987). *Cross-Examinations of Law and Literature: Cooper, Hawthorne, Stowe, and Melville*. Cambridge University Press, Cambridge, UK.

Thomas, B. (1997). *American Literary Realism and the Failed Promise of Contract*. University of California Press, Berkeley.

Thomas, B. (2007). *Civic Myths: A Law-and-Literature Approach to Citizenship*. University of North Carolina Press, Chapel Hill.

Travis, J. (2005). *Wounded Hearts: Masculinity, Law, and Literature in American Culture*. University of North Carolina Press, Chapel Hill.

Wald, P. (1995). *Constituting Americans: Cultural Anxiety and Narrative Form*. Duke University Press, Durham.

Wallace, R.K. (2008). "Fugitive Justice: Douglass, Shaw, Melville." In Levine and Otter, eds, *Frederick Douglass and Herman Melville: Essays in Relation*, 39–68. University of North Carolina Press, Chapel Hill.

Warren, K.W. (2011). *What Was African American Literature?* Harvard University Press, Cambridge.

Weinstein, C. (2004). *Family, Kinship, and Sympathy in Nineteenth-Century American Literature*. Cambridge University Press, Cambridge, UK.

Welke, B.Y. (2001). *Recasting American Liberty: Gender, Race, Law, and the Railroad Revolution, 1865–1920*. Cambridge University Press, Cambridge, UK.

White, J.D. (1973). *The Legal Imagination: Studies in the Nature of Legal Thought and Expression*. Little, Brown, Boston.

Wilf, S. (2010). *Law's Imagined Republic: Popular Politics and Criminal Justice in Revolutionary America*. Cambridge University Press, New York.

Williams, D.E. (2003). "Writing under the Influence: An Examination of *Wieland*'s 'Well Authenticated Facts' and the Depiction of Murderous Fathers in Post-Revolutionary Print Culture." *Eighteenth-Century Fiction* 15(3): 643–668.

Winton, C. (2007). "The Southern Book Trade in the Eighteenth Century." In Amory and Hall, eds, *A History of the Book in America. Volume 1: The Colonial Book in the Atlantic World*, 224–246. American Antiquarian Society-University of North Carolina Press, Chapel Hill.

Wong, E.L. (2009). *Neither Fugitive nor Free: Atlantic Slavery, Freedom Suits, and the Legal Culture of Travel*. New York University Press, New York.

Chapter Twenty-five

LEGAL THOUGHT FROM BLACKSTONE TO KENT AND STORY

Steven J. Macias

Early in his career, Lawrence Friedman – the "greatest of American social-legal historians," according to Robert Gordon (2009) – critiqued Perry Miller's classic work on the "Legal Mentality" in antebellum America, claiming that Miller's search for systematic legal thought was in vain because of the "lack of a great jurisprudential school in the early days of the republic." Friedman backed up his assertion by noting that, unlike civil law systems, common law systems were not dependent upon "scholars" to serve as authoritative guides; rather, "cases and enactments" made the law in early America. "Therefore there was no *need* for a system of jurisprudence, and none sprang up. The common law countries were weak in philosophy of law" (Friedman, 1968: 1254). Nearly forty years later, Friedman reiterated his belief that Miller's work was "not very enlightening"; however he now acknowledges that "the literature on legal literature and legal thought is not entirely satisfactory" (Friedman, 2005: 589). Although one cannot help but agree with Friedman that the historiographical output on early American legal thought over the past half-century is far from ideal, one also cannot but wonder to what extent the early critiques of socio-legal historians stunted the growth of this field of history writing. Happily the tide is turning as working historians are now returning to the intellectual and jurisprudential work-product of early American legal scholars. This chapter examines the historiography of legal thought in America from the publication of William Blackstone's *Commentaries* in the 1760s to the deaths of

A Companion to American Legal History, First Edition.
Edited by Sally E. Hadden and Alfred L. Brophy.
© 2013 John Wiley & Sons Ltd. Published 2021 by John Wiley & Sons Ltd.

James Kent and Joseph Story, the last of the early republic's intellectuals to compose major works of jurisprudence.

*****

The principal investigative questions of the historiography here concern legal frameworks rather than particular legal doctrines or discrete fields of substantive law. Thus, questions about sources of law, legal epistemology, and methods of legal reasoning take center stage. One might wonder whether an historical inquiry into such topics is necessarily at odds with the more dominant socio-legal history practiced by Friedman and others. Some historians of jurisprudence seem to suggest just that. Michael Lobban writes, in the introduction to his examination of early nineteenth-century English jurisprudence, that he "will focus almost wholly on internal legal debates and considerations of legal doctrines without looking closely at social influences and political considerations outside the courts which influenced the development of law" (Lobban, 1991: 15). In arguing for the "relative autonomy" of the law, Lobban emphasizes the artificiality of the forum in which legal thought is developed, articulated, and sanctioned. Duncan Kennedy, who early in his career examined Blackstone's work, also attempted "a history of American legal thought." In explaining why he provided no causal narrative in his consideration of the sources, he said, "The goal was to provide a description of transformations that had been ignored, along with a mechanics of transformations. I thought that recognition of what changed would be an interesting and important event, even if I had nothing to contribute to the quest for larger causes" (Kennedy, 2006: ix, xvi). Kennedy explicitly criticized "social history" or "history from the bottom up" as "a form of self-marginalization." He explained, "if you were interested in attacking the way people at the top used law to support the status quo," then you had to have a detailed knowledge of what counts as a good legal argument (2006: xxvii–xxviii).

As we will see, more recent works have employed new methods of cultural history that mediate the tension between an older form of intellectual history and the critiques of social historians. By examining the law's relationship to other forms of high culture, such as literature, history, and philosophy – all of which necessarily interact with society writ large – we learn how legal ideas interact with larger cultural concerns while being able to consider law as a semi-autonomous cultural form.

Blackstone and English Influences on America

Recent works on British legal thinkers, Blackstone, Lord Mansfield, and Jeremy Bentham, all give short shrift to their respective contemporaneous influences on American legal thought. Wilfred Prest's recent biography of

Blackstone is a highly personal portrayal of the Great Commentator, focusing to a lesser extent on his own jurisprudence (Prest, 2008). James Oldham's work on Mansfield and Philip Schofield's work on Bentham focus much more on the content and consequences of their subjects' ideas (Oldham, 2004; Schofield, 2006). Combined with other studies on English legal thought, these studies paint a picture of the English common law in the age of revolutionary and early republican America.

Historians were once squarely interested in the influence of Blackstone on American legal thought. In 1938, David Lockmiller published *Sir William Blackstone*, and included a final chapter on "Blackstone in America," in which he famously concluded, "Blackstone's influence has been far greater in the United States than in England" (1938: 182). Lockmiller explained the influential imbalance by noting that Blackstone was but one of several noteworthy lawyers writing in late-eighteenth century England, whereas for Americans, he was "almost without peer" (1938: 183). Daniel Boorstin published the still-in-print *The Mysterious Science of the Law* in 1941, which was a work of high intellectual history, attempting to contextualize Blackstone's *Commentaries* within existing European thought, particularly the fields of religion, natural science, aesthetics, and history (Boorstin, [1941] 1996).

The few recent works about Blackstone's impact on American jurisprudence emphasize his influence, or lack thereof, on a discrete group of legal intellectuals. Thus, Craig Klafter discusses the early American Blackstone annotator, St. George Tucker, as influenced more by a desire to show where Blackstone went wrong than to promote Blackstone's ideas themselves. Far more important to Tucker and other turn-of-the-century republican legal theorists was Montesquieu, whose republican principles tempered Blackstone's aristocratic ones (Klafter, 2006). Michael Hoeflich understands the Americanizing endeavors of Tucker and others to be less political. According to Hoeflich, these Blackstone revisers were "doing very much the same sort of thing that medieval glossators on Roman, canon and Talmudic law did with their marginal annotations or glosses" (Hoeflich, 2009: 172).

Other historians emphasize that Blackstone's endeavor was more radical than previously thought. Where Boorstin portrayed Blackstone as a conservative systematizer and justifier of the present, Lobban tells us that Blackstone's goal was to apply Roman methods of organization and analysis to the English common law. In other words, Blackstone "sought to use the Roman law on its own terms" (Lobban, 1991: 26). This proved problematic for Blackstone because the principal source of Roman law was natural law, while the sources of common law were highly varied and relied much more on judges and precedent than did the Roman law. Because Blackstone attempted to put the common law into an institutional structure that employed a fundamentally different sort of analytical construct, legal writers after Blackstone faced problems, specifically with the roles of history, sovereignty, and the common law forms of action, which natural law did not address (Lobban, 1991: 41).

David Lieberman agrees that natural law proved problematic for Blackstone with particular regard to sovereignty and legislation in the English constitutional order. Lieberman's focus is on the role of legislation in legal theory, and he concludes that the *Commentaries* "offered no direct, programmatic guidance on the question of the validity of an act of parliament which violated the laws of nature" (Lieberman, 1989: 55). One of Blackstone's explicit objectives was to enable English legislators – especially the future ones sitting in his Oxford lectures – "to better inform themselves of the common law" (1989: 63). But Blackstone's failure to distinguish "between an historical explanation and a moral justification" for English law would cause problems, not only for Bentham, but for American colonists as well (Lieberman, 1989: 49). This issue points to the *Commentaries*' role in the constitutional debates preceding the American Revolution. Although a significant literature exists on this topic, its constitutional implications far exceed the scope of the present chapter.

What American legal historians gain from the history of this English legal thought is an appreciation of Blackstone's concern with innovation. In the histories of early republican jurisprudence, American concerns with the role of precedent and history take on new significance if we adopt Lobban's and Lieberman's analysis of Blackstone. American jurisprudence can be better seen as a conversation with English legal innovators, rather than as a reaction to colonial stasis.

In considering American colonial law's final decades, historians have generally regarded it as less than theoretically sophisticated. One of the realities facing colonial lawyers was that they had to wear multiple hats, unlike their more specialized English counterparts. Thus John Adams noted in 1758 that the American lawyer "must do the duty of a counsellor, a lawyer, an attorney, a solicitor, and even of a scrivener" (Boorstin, 1958: 195). Combined with the fact that many colonial judges were laymen untrained in the law, American lawyers had neither the time nor incentive to develop a learned jurisprudence. "Needless to say," explains Daniel Boorstin, "colonial America produced no great legal systems or encyclopaedias. What it did produce were the varied, dispersed, and miscellaneous efforts of hundreds of laymen, semi-lawyers, pseudo-lawyers, and of a few men of solid legal training" (1958: 201). William Nelson, in emphasizing the overarching importance of precedent, explains the low level of intellectual effort: "Americans of the prerevolutionary period expected their judges to be automatons who mechanically applied immutable rules of law to the facts of each case" (1975: 19).

Nevertheless, the political struggles that the colonists experienced with Parliament forced the revolutionary leaders to think systematically about the nature of law. Whether colonial legal thinkers ever adhered to a true natural law paradigm, as Nelson suggests, by the time the pre-revolutionary struggles began, there existed "a basic ambiguity in the American mind about the nature of law that was carried into the Revolution" (Wood, 1969: 295). Gordon Wood explains that the Americans "were firmly committed to the modern notion of statute law based on legislative enactment – a commitment implicit in their resort to fundamental law and written charters" (1969: 295). Contrary to the Boorstin notion, "colonial adjudication was not simply a matter of applying some kind of crude, untechnical law to achieve common-sense 'frontier' justice." For Wood, "by the middle of the eighteenth century, in Massachusetts and New York at least, colonial jurisprudence approached very closely that of the English" (1969: 297).

Wood's thesis is supported by a number of shorter studies on pre-revolutionary lawyers. Daniel Coquillette discusses John Adams' self-conscious attempt to distinguish himself at the bar by studying Roman law. Adams, along with other practicing lawyers, would meet in a formal reading group in 1765 to discuss the civilian natural law writers (1984: 82). Likewise, John Jay, while a practitioner in New York's colonial courts, would gather with fellow lawyers to moot points of law (Johnson, 1976: 1282). Interestingly, both Adams' and Jay's groups contained individuals who would later take up the loyalist cause, perhaps indicating that legal and constitutional thought could remain distinct only for so long.

The Legal Mind in the Early Republic

One key starting point for post-revolutionary jurisprudence is Perry Miller's Pulitzer Prize-winning *The Life of the Mind in America: From the Revolution to the Civil War*. "The great issue of the nineteenth century," according to Miller, was "the never-ending case of Heart versus Head" (Miller, 1965: 100). He offered this as an alternative to what he believed to be the reigning error in then-current historiography, namely that partisan politics best explained differences of opinion in the legal realm.

Nearly twenty years after Miller's *Life of the Mind* appeared in print, Robert Ferguson noted, "little has been added to Miller's insistence that lawyers and legal thought were crucial to literary development in the antebellum period." In *Law and Letters*, Ferguson chose to emphasize how "the struggle for a collective identity imposed aesthetic and intellectual boundaries" that were particularly legal in character and uniquely understood through the medium of the lawyer-writer's literary output (Ferguson, 1984: 5–9). Ferguson's main insight was that in the antebellum era, "the bond between knowledge, general literature, and law remained paramount, and the epistemological implications involved would shape the meanings Americans attached to all three concepts" (1984: 28).

In explaining the sources of legal knowledge, Ferguson latched on to American legal scholars' frequent praises of Blackstone as revelatory of "the lawyer's epistemological self-confidence." What the Americans were really praising was Blackstone's organization and eloquence – his true accomplishment. Because there was a dearth of native statutory and case law, early American lawyers looked to mastery of "more generic proficiencies," such as philosophy, history and rhetoric, in determining professional competence. What Blackstone did was to "convert general knowledge into design and then into power in places where others found only confusion" (Ferguson, 1984: 31).

Few historians who studied Blackstone's own thought or early American legal thought would disagree with Ferguson. Daniel Boorstin viewed the *Commentaries* as the product of Enlightenment views of history, science, religion, and moral philosophy. He concluded that Blackstone's work was a product of its time, exhibiting then-existing tensions in English culture between logic and mystery (Boorstin, 1996). Michael Lobban, although agreeing that eighteenth-century lawyers found law in more general bodies of knowledge, concluded that Blackstone's effort was actually a challenge to this epistemological eclecticism. English lawyers challenged the *Commentaries* as too superficial (Lobban, 1991).

It makes sense that American and English lawyers would view Blackstone's efforts differently. If Blackstone was indeed a challenge to legal orthodoxy, as Lobban believes, then it is understandable why the English bar would view Blackstone's apparent simplification of their profession as an affront. However, for that very reason, Americans found Blackstone's endeavors to be a blessing. The simpler it imposed order on a new nation's laws, the better.

The search for order, of course, is not a theme unique to the historiography of the early republic, but it nevertheless is an enduring one. Central to that search for order is the role of law. Historians explaining the common law's resilience in the United States (despite overt attacks upon it) have turned to the stability it provides in an otherwise volatile culture. This very question motivated Miller in the first place.

Miller began "The Legal Mentality" by retelling James Fenimore Cooper's story of frontiersman Natty Bumppo. In Cooper's Leatherstocking Tales, Miller found explanatory binaries that illuminated the cultural struggles in the new nation. On Bumppo's side was the heart and its associated elements: nature, wilderness, common justice, instinct, and feelings. The Jeffersonians advocated this side, preferring cultural, if uncultivated, independence through native means to dependence on more sophisticated English ways. These democratic republicans also had a Protestant preference for popularizing specialized knowledge, which, for law, meant putting law books into people's hands. Bumppo was interesting to Miller because Cooper's character is eventually subdued and civilized by none other than one Judge Temple, the law incarnate.

The other side – and, in the early republic, the victorious one – was dominated not by the heart, but by the head. The head was associated with society, the intellect, formal law, and artificial restraints on conduct. Politically, Federalists (also identified as aristocrats and monarchists by their enemies) dominated this side of the spectrum. Rather than natural, instinctual justice, these conservatives relied on the common law for the rules of society. The head side had a preference for Blackstone and, it seemed, other English standards of excellence.

Recent cultural historians basically confirm Miller's thesis that support for the idea of the common law had more to do with abstractions than with concrete economics or political affiliation. Marshall Foletta's story of second-generation "young Federalists" in *Coming to Terms with Democracy* focuses much more on their patriotic hopes and visions than on their partisan intrigues. Foletta explains their support of the common law, not as a means of maintaining a Federalist stronghold on the judiciary, but as a means of maintaining a cultural aristocracy impervious to the uncouth designs of the Democrats. "Young Federalists" created institutions such as common schools, universities, civic and philanthropic organizations, and literary journals, all designed to reinforce an idealized cultural hegemony (Foletta, 2001: 136). The common law, especially as taught at the emerging university law schools of the 1820s and 1830s, kept at bay those less qualified to practice this "real science." It was not that the young Federalists naively resisted the rising democratic tide sweeping across the country – they wanted to find ways to channel it into an orderly framework. As Foletta explains, "Holding this framework together was a web of law that required scientific and professional execution," one that could provide society "a more unified and authoritative set of moral, religious, and legal truths" (Foletta, 2001: 172).

American intellectuals' cultural interaction with the law was not limited to Foletta's New England-based young Federalists. Michael Hoeflich presents a history of the "high culture" of law in his work explaining the legacy of Roman and civil law upon American jurisprudence. One of the most interesting and unique features of Hoeflich's analysis is his focus on southern thinkers. "In the first half of the nineteenth century," Hoeflich tells us, "there flourished a brilliant and distinctive legal culture in the southern United States." He contrasts northern lawyers, with their focus on "the more technical aspects of law," with southern lawyers, who were "also men of broad culture." Hoeflich raises an historiographical challenge that has yet to be dealt with by legal historians: "it is particularly unfortunate that as the antebellum southern tradition died out and the historiography of the period became obsessed with analyzing the influence of slavery, the full vitality and breadth of this tradition have been utterly forgotten" (Hoeflich, 1997: 50–51).

Michael O'Brien's recent, multi-volume, work on antebellum southern thought is a welcome addition to intellectual history, doing in essence for the South what Perry Miller had done for the New England Puritans

(2004). He shows that sincere thinkers existed, even among social groups popularly presumed to be reactionary, who grappled with the persistent questions of social ordering. Even though O'Brien divides his second volume into sections on discrete disciplines such as history, literature, government, economics, philosophy, and theology, one notices the omission of law. Law's absence is especially noticeable because O'Brien's previous work included a biography of native South Carolinian Hugh S. Legaré, United States Attorney General under President John Tyler and widely recognized to be the most intellectual of practicing lawyers (O'Brien, 1985). No less than Progressive historian Vernon Parrington included a chapter on Legaré in his monumental *Main Currents in American Thought* as a representative of the conservative legal mind (1927).

The only other intellectual historian of the South who attempted to capture law as a field of thought interdependent on the more general intellectual milieu was Richard Beale Davis. For Davis, O'Brien, and Michael Hoeflich, Legaré played a prominent role in explaining what jurisprudence meant for southern thinkers. What Davis wanted to explain was why southerners of Legaré's generation, who, in another age might have been poets, novelists, or critics, clung steadfastly if conflictedly to the legal profession (Davis, 1949). Even though Davis wrote before Ferguson, another way to consider Davis' concern is to ask why all of Ferguson's lawyers-turned-writers were northern. Davis explained how law and oratory went hand-in-hand in Jeffersonian Virginia and how subsequent generations learned that Jefferson, Marshall, and Madison were the figures one should strive to emulate (Davis, 1964). In other words, the social pressures (and opportunities) were stronger in the South for channeling one's creativity into the legal profession.

Hoeflich includes Legaré among three South Carolinians, the other two being Francis Lieber and James Walker, who employed continental legal scholarship in their work on the American common law. Lieber, the German émigré who eventually made his way to New York and Columbia University, was a close friend of Joseph Story and published many of the Justice's writings on legal topics in his *Encyclopedia Americana*. Moreover, Lieber's 1838 *Legal and Political Hermeneutics*, dedicated to Chancellor Kent, demonstrated not only his "extensive knowledge of Roman and civilian sources but also his ability to employ principles contained in these systems to analyze Anglo-American law" (Hoeflich, 1997: 58). It was Legaré, however, whose library contained more works on the civil law than the Library of Congress. And it was Legaré who began a literary journal, the *Southern Review*, designed to rival the young Federalists' *North American Review*, especially with its inclusion of legal articles. Hoeflich points to the wide circulation of Lieber's books and Legaré's journal articles, as well as Legaré's performance as Attorney General, to conclude that civil law made some headway into antebellum American jurisprudence.

More than southern jurists helped spread civilian notions of law to American lawyers (Stein, 1966). Hoeflich counts Joseph Story as the most prominent American jurist to actively rely on Roman and civil law concepts. In order to appreciate Hoeflich's claims about Story, we need a better picture of the historiographical narrative of the leading lights of American jurisprudence, namely reflexive admirers Story and New York's James Kent. Both Kent and Story, as part of their legacies, left American law libraries with volumes to rival Blackstone. Even before Kent and Story wrote their *Commentaries*, however, several other leading jurists made an impact on American jurisprudence either through lectures, published works, or both. Most notable among those earlier jurisprudents was James Wilson.

A native of Scotland, James Wilson came to America in 1766 and settled in the Philadelphia region. Reared on doctrines of the Scottish Enlightenment, Wilson read law soon after his arrival in Pennsylvania. He became the first professor of law at the College of Philadelphia in 1790 and there delivered a widely regarded series of law lectures that many contemporaries considered to have rivaled Blackstone's lectures. Such an occasion was Wilson's first lecture at which none other than President Washington was in attendance. However, Wilson's lectures were not published until after his death in 1804 by his son. Given that Wilson was one of the first appointees to the new Supreme Court in 1789, one might expect to find an incisive exposition of early American jurisprudence in the lectures. The only recent work devoted exclusively to Wilson's ideas is Mark Hall's *The Political and Legal Philosophy of James Wilson* (1997). Hall criticizes previous scholars for not recognizing Wilson's "traditional Christian conception of natural law" (1997: 37). He further contends that Wilson's moral aims posed a stark contrast to the materialism of many British thinkers.

English historian Michael Lobban concluded that Wilson, along with Kent and Story, presented a "more scholarly view" of the early American vision of law (2007). However, Lobban found little coherence when he examined their writings in depth. Lobban makes much of the anti-lawyer and anti-British hostility against which these legal scholars were writing in order to explain their defense of law as a customary system. On the whole, the Americans appeared to be more in keeping with Lockean consent theorists than Blackstonian command theorists. This is because their sources of law so often appear to be metaphysical, such as God's will for Wilson in particular, and otherwise natural law based. Lobban describes what he calls Wilson's Baconianism, also shared by Story. This legal philosophy held that natural law was universal, but that its application was subject to local and historical variations, and that its principles could be inductively sought. These tenets amounted to what contemporary jurisprudents would call *legal science* (Hoeflich, 1986; Schweber, 1999).

James Kent's lesser popularity as compared to Joseph Story is probably linked to the fact that Kent never sat on the United States Supreme

Court. As a result, Kent has had no sustained book-length treatment in over seventy years. Daniel Hulsebosch has begun to turn the tide, publishing several recent articles on Kent (2009a; 2009b). Of all early American legal scholars, only Kent matched Blackstone in publishing a four-volume original work that purported to be a comprehensive analysis of American law. Although no major recent biography exists, Kent has drawn the attention of several prominent legal historians (Langbein, 1993; Watson, 1993; White, 1998).

One dominant feature of this historiography is a general concurrence that Kent and Story triumphed in their jurisprudential endeavors. Perry Miller was one of the few who thought Kent and Story's greater reputations among historians were responsible for the slighting of University of Maryland's first law professor, David Hoffman (Miller, 1965: 118). A more common judgment is that of G. Edward White, who thought, "The most influential legal historians of the late eighteenth and early nineteenth centuries, when American jurisprudence took its distinctive character, were James Kent and Joseph Story" (White, 1976: 1250). Although it is sometimes difficult to glean any differences between the two in the histories of early American law, Kent's uniqueness comes through most clearly, not in his political attitudes, but in his jurisprudential outlook.

David Raack set out to prove that "Kent's legal thought does in fact merit serious attention." Overlooked by historians White, Friedman, and Horwitz, and overshadowed by contemporaries Marshall, Story, and Shaw, the New York Chancellor was a worthy legal thinker whose ideas, when they have been considered, have been frequently mischaracterized. "Kent was neither closed-minded nor reactionary: he was an intellectual, interested in new ideas and opinions. He was not the inveterate conservative that he is often portrayed" (Raack, 1989: 325). Kent's image as a conservative was cemented with a 1939 biography, *James Kent: A Study in Conservatism* (Horton, 1939). Likewise, Kent's counterpart, Joseph Story, was similarly stuck with a conservative label by his biographer, Kent Newmyer, who subtitled the work, "Statesman of the Old Republic," suggesting that the Justice was somehow passed by in time, and frequently spoke of his "New England conservatism" (1985: 173, 182, 226, 238).

There are several reasons Kent loomed large among his contemporaries. First, as a member of the state supreme court then as Chancellor of New York, he wrote many opinions at a time when few published law reporters existed anywhere in the nation. As a result, the New York reports had the ability to influence more than just the development of New York law. After the state's mandatory retirement age forced him off the bench at age sixty, Kent then reassumed the post of law professor at Columbia University, which he had previously held prior to his judicial appointments, and proceeded to write and publish his *Commentaries on American Law* between 1826 and 1830.

Kent's *Commentaries* have not fared as well under historical evaluation as Blackstone's. According to Lobban, "Kent's theoretical discussions of the foundations of the common law were not profound, and in some areas, seemed inconsistent" (Lobban, 2007: 147). Perhaps that sort of frank judgment can only come from a working English historian, but it was certainly not unheard of in Kent's own time. One hopes that some work in the near future will capture a fuller contemporaneous evaluation of Kent.

John Langbein has examined Kent's *Commentaries* in the context of the history of legal literature, concluding that "it is instructive to see Kent's *Commentaries* not so much as an early treatise, but as a late institutionalist" (Langbein, 1993: 586). Coming from the European civil law tradition, legal institutes attempted a comprehensive description of an entire legal system and were primarily didactic in nature, oriented towards the neophyte in training. While European institutes were intended to reconcile the national law with the Roman law, Kent was interested in reconciling American law with the English common law.

Substantively, Kent's endeavors have been labeled "nationalistic" by numerous historians. Most recently, Hulsebosch has applied the metaphor of "empire" to Kent's efforts, explaining that Federalist jurists like Kent applied a "transjurisdictional conception of law" to promote "an empire of law in which law was conceived as a set of legal principles that should operate everywhere in the union" (Hulsebosch, 2009b: 378). Hulsebosch wants to go even further, however, in arguing that English legal culture exerted an imperial reign in America well after the Revolution. Judging by the works that Kent read and used in his writings, "American law became more Anglicized than ever" (2009b: 379). In a sense, the imperialism of English law was mediated by Kent and likeminded jurists who were transmitting this Anglo legal culture through their treatises and judicial opinions.

Historians of Kent's thought have highlighted his original and frequent use of foreign authority (White, 1998: 247). However, in considering Kent's use of the civil law, he apparently fared worse than the jurists examined by Hoeflich. According to Alan Watson's study of Kent's Roman and civil law citations in both his judicial opinions and his *Commentaries*, they served largely as "mere window dressing" (Watson, 1993: 49, 61–62). In fact, Watson found that Kent continued to cite post-Revolutionary English law, seemingly reinforcing Hulsebosch's claim that English law continued, perhaps even increased, its authority in America. Thus, whenever Kent actually employed a foreign citation, there was almost always ample Anglo-American authority to back up the underlying proposition. What was Kent's purpose, then, citing works like Pothier, Emerigon, and Valin? Was it to infer a large body of knowledge because, as Ferguson argued, the contemporary culture measured a lawyer's worth by his mastery of breadth?

Kent himself offered an explanation for his foreign citations within his personal correspondence. Recalling his time riding circuit with Jeffersonian judges, Kent observed, "The judges were Republican and very kindly disposed to everything that was French, and this enabled me, without exciting any alarm or jealousy, to make free use of such authorities and thereby enrich our commercial law" (Watson, 1993: 48). The explicit focus of Kent, Story and others on commercial law has created a legal history industry dedicated to explaining this so-called "transformation in American law" – a shift from personalized justice toward the impersonal, commercial focus it retains in our capitalist world. Jurisprudentially speaking, however – focusing on the intellectual motivation behind the commercial emphasis – historians have found mixed motives.

For Miller, the evolution of American common law represented a shift from "a philosophy of law which was primarily contractual in character to one that was conscious of history" (Miller, 1965: 127). Thus, the explicit renunciation of static English common law principles was symbolic of more than a desire to foster commerce; it recognized that an ideal national law could never be considered ahistorically. Calls for a native American jurisprudence, therefore, were not a rejection of commerce, but of England's commercial laws. Instead, American jurists urged lawyers and legislators to recognize that the United States represented something new in history and therefore required a new jurisprudence to meet its needs. According to Miller, what Kent, Story *et al.* were attempting was getting the lawyers' minds "out of the eighteenth century and into the nineteenth" (Miller, 1965: 127).

The Supreme Court

The historiography surrounding the United States Supreme Court is quite plentiful. However, works that primarily examine the legal philosophy of the Court, as opposed to its political and constitutional significance, are fewer in number. One reason might be, as Perry Miller somewhat wryly noted of the Court: "what it has to say about the activity of mind, we are bound to confess that it is a sorry spectacle" (Miller, 1965: 218). Other than James Wilson and Joseph Story, few members of the Court contributed to the intellectual development of the legal profession. Nevertheless, some historians have read the Marshall Court opinions within the context of the larger jurisprudential background.

As G. Edward White recognized in his study of the Marshall Court, "The most fundamental, and at the same time the most unsettled, issue of early-nineteenth-century American jurisprudence involved the nature and sources of law in the American republic" (1988: 112). White claims that "the term 'common law' underwent a change in meaning" in the early nineteenth century in response to tensions that arose in the federal judiciary. Initially, the term signified specific areas of law, "the body of doctrines associated with the nonconstitutional and nonstatutory decision of English and early American courts." Eventually, "common law" came to stand for a methodology that enhanced "both judicial discretion and judicial power" (White, 1988: 119). This interpretation, however, runs counter to David Lieberman's suggestion that the common law and the English constitution were inextricably intertwined in the late eighteenth century (2006: 347). Lieberman's interpretation seems to find support on American shores in an 1824 volume by Peter Du Ponceau on federal court jurisdiction, but no scholarly treatment of Du Ponceau's work on jurisdictions has yet been published.

As to the Court's docket, White contends, "Natural law was ... pertinent to constitutional cases but not dispositive of them." Contrary to the late nineteenth century's "stark separation of moral and legal principles," during the Marshall Court, "no such jurisprudential separation existed." The period, White tells us, was characterized "by a fusion ... of doctrines drawn from moral philosophy and doctrines extracted from the common law and other legal sources" (White, 1988: 675). However, one might contrast that conclusion with findings that discuss contemporary critics of the Marshall Court as too legalistic and not attentive enough to morality (Klafter, 1993: 60–62). Likewise, the legal positivism that was emerging during the Marshall Court, especially at the hands of Jeremy Bentham, was motivated entirely by moral philosophy; it was not devoid of it. Instead, for Bentham and his American codification champions, it was natural law that was immoral (Schofield, 2006). As early as the late Marshall Court era, "Bentham was helping to lay the foundations for the rise of pragmatism" (King, 1986: 141).

White tests his theory that natural law performed real work at the Supreme Court by contrasting contracts clause cases and those involving racial minorities. (It must be noted, however, that White leaves "natural law" largely undefined except to emphasize that it was the opposite of written law). He concludes that the contracts clause cases "can be treated as an example of the blending of natural law concepts and constitutional language, [while] the Court's slave trade cases represented a separation of natural rights principles from the slavery context" (1988: 703). This is largely unsatisfying as an intellectual investigation, however, because as White himself writes, the Court's primary motivation seemed to be benefitting "propertied white males" in one set of cases, and "the achievement of a politic disposition [of] sensitive issues" in the other set of cases (1988: 698, 703). White's most recent work reinforces the notion that "it was a political Court," "[sensitive] to public opinion" (2012: 227–228).

We could again contrast the Justices with Bentham, a legal intellectual motivated primarily by jurisprudential thought. The same utilitarian philosophy that led Bentham to call for codification and a whole host of other law reform efforts also led him to pronounce slavery as immoral (Schofield, 2006: 214). Indeed, Story himself, the Court's sole intellectual, who had "strong antislavery feelings," nevertheless had to temper his moral convictions with political considerations (Newmyer, 1985: 347, 353).

In another work focused on the Marshall Court, Kent Newmyer states "the central axiom of Marshall's judicial philosophy: that judges had a special place in the republican scheme of government because scientific law guaranteed 'disinterested' judging" (2001: 212–213). Newmyer devotes a chapter of his Marshall biography to describing the Chief Justice as a "Lockean Liberal." By this, Newmyer seems to mean nothing more than Marshall enforced the sanctity of property and contract rights as against claims based on the public good. Newmyer recognizes that the preference for contract was shared by "intellectuals of the age such as Blackstone, William Paley, Story, Kent, and Gulian Verplanck" (2001: 261). But those five legal theorists had such divergent views as to how contract was supposed to work, especially Paley and Verplanck, that the foray into Locke and liberalism feels unproductive. One is left with the suspicion that Marshall and the Marshall Court were far more interested in politics and "capitalism" than with jurisprudence.

Works on broader themes such as religion and custom find ways to weave Supreme Court case law into their narratives, thus providing the richness missing from Court-centered histories. But even then, the Supreme Court bench appears to be a passive cast of characters in the midst of a more general intellectual trend or jurisprudential movement.

Religion and Custom in Early America

Early American legal thinkers, drawn from the ranks of the social elite, shared the upper class' suspicion of evangelicalism, although most adhered to the notion that Christianity was part of the common law. Part of the emerging scientific outlook of the educated strata included the application of reason to fields of knowledge where mystery once reigned supreme, including both law and religion. Although the cross-pollination between and among early republican theology and jurisprudence has not nearly received the attention it merits, we can at least glean some of the intellectual impulses of those who were concerned with both fields from the existing historiography.

As Alfred Brophy tells us, "Law was similar to religion, but the passionate thinking of religion was different from the process of legal thought" (Brophy, 1999: 1189). This is certainly the case if we are talking about evangelical religion. However, it is also important to consider that legal intellectuals were not simply battling evangelicalism as lawyers. Many were also considering the theological implications of rationality on religion, which certainly affected their views of natural justice that underlay their legal opinions. Although some scholars have explored the relationship between theological and legal thought in late-eighteenth century New England, this aspect remains underexplored in the latter decades of the early republic (Gerardi, 1994; Valeri, 1994). As we will see with Ferguson's explanation of Story's anti-evangelicalism, legal professionals gravitated toward a rational Christianity. But even within this group of rationalists, theological ideas varied widely.

In a recent essay, Ferguson adds to his previous *Law and Letters* thesis that the confluence of law and letters exemplified in the early republic by the lawyer-writers eventually yielded to a narrower professionalism devoid of intellectual eclecticism. In 1844 the Supreme Court overruled an 1819 Marshall Court decision, liberalizing rules on testamentary charity giving. Arguing for the old rule was Daniel Webster, whose three-day theatrical courtroom performance resembled the appeals to the emotions of decades-earlier revivalism. By contrast, the prevailing Horace Binney authored a brief and delivered an argument that resembled the professionalism of the modern-day lawyer. As Ferguson concludes, "Webster's mere eloquence missed the point now that decisions required detailed case law instead of general social principles and the best expression of opinion" (Ferguson, 2004: 245).

This supposed change identified by Ferguson has yet to be explored in much detail for major jurisprudential figures of the antebellum era. Thus, one of the most prolific legal writers, David Hoffman, was also one of the most insistent that Christianity inform the new American jurisprudence. However, very little has been written on Hoffman's ideas (Shaffer, 1981; 1982). Likewise, John Neal, a self-proclaimed follower of Jeremy Bentham's utilitarianism and editor of the first American edition of Bentham's *Principles of Legislation* in 1830, could never give up Christianity (King, 1966). Both Hoffman and Neal took to writing fiction later in life, with Neal becoming quite well known in his time. According to David Carlson, Neal's novels fit well within the substantive framework described by Ferguson, even if we have to extend his timeline a bit to allow Neal into the lawyer-writer set (Carlson, 2007). But one still wonders how the religious influences manifested themselves, if at all.

Like religion, the important role of custom in the early American republic has captured the attention of numerous legal historians. Although some legal historians discuss the decline of precedent as a result of the new Enlightenment-influenced legal science, others contextualize the diminishing importance of precedent within the overall diminution of the role of custom in American culture.

Ellen Pearson's new monograph, *Remaking Custom: Law and Identity in the Early American Republic*, is ostensibly about how the "first generation of legal scholars used their lectures and writings to explain American law and its history and character" (2011: 1). But most insightfully, she shows how legal scholars were the best articulators of a sort of American exceptionalism. Pearson finds that the Americanization of "custom" helped the new nation emerge from England's shadow. Americans "reframed custom in a common-law culture by adding elements of consent and choice" (Pearson, 2011: 12). These lawyer-scholars historicized the law for their students "so that they could articulate ... the origins and evolution of the common law within their states and their nation" (Pearson, 2011: 16). These changes in the idea of the common law created a "more fluid system," which, in turn, allowed more democratic changes in state constitutions and less restrictive understandings of property law, slavery, and treatment of Native Americans, at least at the elite level.

Of course, stories about the decline of custom help other historians explain something as momentous as the American Revolution itself. Because colonists placed less importance on customary forms of both governance and social hierarchies, they were able to rebel against British misrule. If true, one might expect to see custom, or the lack thereof, playing a role in colonial legal systems before and during the Revolution. However, that study is still to be written.

Another recent work argues that an accurate historical discussion of custom must squarely differentiate law from politics. While the decline of custom might be relevant in the political realm, it was not well recognized in the legal realm. Kunal Parker examines "the historical relationship among American democracy, law, and history" in his new work on "legal thought before modernism" (Parker, 2011). Parker wants readers to appreciate the real philosophical constraints under which early-nineteenth-century legal thinkers operated, in particular, the constraint of non-historical time. The notions of "immemoriality" and "insensibility" were central to the common law so, "even as [its] defenders agreed that the law should be subjected to historical critique and demystified, they would argue that the common law embodied the logic of history itself" (2011: 78). For Parker, attempts to historicize law in the legal realist vein were unknown in the early nineteenth century.

Codification

The final piece of the jurisprudential puzzle in the early republic is codification. Perry Miller closed "The Legal Mentality" with a section on codification, explaining how awkwardly it fit into legal thought of the time. There was something odd about the rejection of codification during the overlapping periods of Enlightenment rationality and suspicion of English forms of governance. One might have thought that scientific reformers would have seized upon the opportunity to create a legal system from scratch, the way the Framers created a constitution from first principles. One might further think that in breaking away from England, the American legal profession would have welcomed the chance to leave the old system behind in favor of a native code of laws. Instead, what Miller found was a "perverse glorification of the Common Law" as the perfection of reason that had only failed in its clarity because of the ignorance of the pettifoggers who peddled it (Miller, 1965: 242).

In the 1820s, codes were discussed in a civil, if less than enthusiastic, manner. Or, as Miller explains, "For a short, happy period codification was a professional problem" (Miller, 1965: 249). To the extent codification gained traction at this time, it was on the heels of England's law reform efforts in 1828 and part of the more general trend of simplifying, ordering, and arranging branches of human knowledge. It appears, however, as if some of the friends of codification proved to be its worst enemies. Vocal codification proponents like Robert Rantoul and William Sampson had close ties to the immigrant and labor underclasses and, thus, their efforts became associated with the pettifoggers against whom legal elites were working (Miller, 1965: 251–252; Bloomfield, 1976).

Justice Story's role in the codification movement is unique, mostly because he was the principal author of the 1836 report on the codification of Massachusetts law. Most historians who have studied Story in this context have labeled him a moderate. Even Newmyer, the historian most committed to the view of Story as a conservative, explains how the Justice had to balance "between radical perfectionism and entrenched conservatism" in refuting the claims of the staunchest codifiers while acknowledging the benefits of numerous legal codes for his own state of Massachusetts (Newmyer, 1985: 272–274).

Charles Cook, who has written the sole monograph on the codification movement, likewise viewed Story as the earliest articulator of the moderate position. Story "was among the first to modify the Benthamite codification formula to make it compatible with the common law system" (Cook, 1981: 105). Cook believed Story combined the American preference for legal development through trial-and-error, over and above philosophical abstraction, with Bentham's desire to clarify an otherwise jumbled mess. Story even went so far as to promote moderate codification in Francis Lieber's *Encyclopedia Americana*. But, as Newmyer explains, these writings were primarily directed at "stubborn common lawyers who resisted any reform at all" (Newmyer, 1985: 275).

Scholars of codification agree that something happened in the 1830s to turn the issue from a mere professional disagreement into something more consequential. Cook argues that the codification debate became ideological with conservative forces stronger than their competitors (1981: 158). More insightfully, Miller suggests that the real issue was "a division between two opposing ideas of America ... a dispute over the identity of the nation" (1965: 254). Amid "the noisy debate," Miller concludes, "was basically a contest between nationalism and cosmopolitanism" (1965: 255). More curiously, disagreement reigns over what to make of David Dudley Field's endeavors in the 1840s, resulting in New York's adoption of the Field

Code of Civil Procedure in 1846. Were they the successful culmination of a movement that had begun a generation earlier, or were they the final death throes of a basically failed movement?

Craig Klafter nicely sets out the varying explanations in his work on American legal thought. Whereas Cook saw the decline of the codification movement in the strength of its opponents, Klafter argues that "the movement's decline was a product of its own limited success ... once it had been accomplished with regard to key subject areas there was little need to continue it" (Klafter, 1993: 118–119). But it is only Miller and Edward Widmer who convincingly place Field's efforts into a larger cultural context.

Field was part of the Young America movement, a group of literary and political figures who were critical of Americans' continued emulation of English writers. While the more famous Young Americans included Melville, Hawthorne, and Holmes, Field shared their "national particularism" (Miller, 1965: 256). For Field and his allies, the essential point was "the establishment of an identity for the nation" (Miller, 1965: 263). Widmer picks up where Miller left off, suggesting an even stronger connection between the legal and literary movements of the time.

In *Young America*, Widmer tells us that the legal debate over codification "resembled nothing so much as an exegetical quarrel among literary critics" (1999: 158). Field and other Young Americans rejected looking abroad for standards of excellence in all things legal and literary. Inspired by New York State Senator Gulian Verplanck's speech on law reform in 1839, Field wrote to Verplanck, thus beginning his career as codification champion. Widmer concludes, "the call for codification was a cry for a curb on the romantic imagination, and for a heightened realism related to an improved understanding of modern America" (1999: 176).

Recall that Kent and Story were also nationalists. They, however, remained "within the context of an international culture" where standards of civilization were fundamentally European (Miller, 1965: 264). By contrast, Field and the Young Americans, although learned in European literature and law, sought to set standards of international culture for America. Widmer brings the generations together even more clearly: "worshipping the Revolution, as the codifiers did, allowed them to express generational disaffection and worship their elitist grandparents at the same time, to be both radical and conservative" (1999: 183).

Conclusion

In an essay on new directions in the legal history of colonial New England, Richard Ross praised Barbara Shapiro's work on early modern England and suggested that we needed to adopt the same approach for American legal history. That is, we need to investigate how the legal system responded to developments in epistemology, as well as "changing ideas of human nature" and "the notion of balance in the natural, intellectual, and political worlds" (Ross, 1993: 40). I suggest the same holds for the legal history of America in the early republic and antebellum eras. New works by Kunal Parker and Ellen Holmes Pearson are exciting contributions in this direction. We are still awaiting, however, works that place religion at the center of their analysis and those that focus on intellectual biography, as opposed to political biography. In this latter vein, Philip Schofield's intellectual biography of Bentham is representative (2006).

Too many historical personalities in works discussed above maintained interests not only in law, literature, philosophical history, and natural science, but also in religion. For many, philosophizing about religion took precedence over and above all other intellectual endeavors. The theological publications of Gulian Verplanck, David Hoffman, Simon Greenleaf, Thomas Cooper, and John Neal have yet to be explored in any detail, much less for their impact on these figures' legal ideas.

Finally, we need stories of intellectual interactions. The voluminous textual output in the form of treatises, lectures, law journals, and other periodical publications has yet to be examined as a national conversation among legal elites, which we have every reason to believe it was. We know Kent and Story were mutual admirers, but how did they respond to each other through their *Commentaries*? One suspects that many speeches and journal articles were responses to conversations that have yet to be recovered.

References

Bloomfield, Maxwell H. (1976). *American Lawyers in a Changing Society, 1776–1876.* Harvard University Press, Cambridge, MA.

Boorstin, Daniel J. ([1941] 1996). *The Mysterious Science of the Law: An Essay on Blackstone's Commentaries.* Harvard University Press, Cambridge, MA. Reprint, University of Chicago Press, Chicago, IL.

Boorstin, Daniel J. (1958). *The Americans: The Colonial Experience.* Vintage Books, New York.

Brophy, Alfred L. (1999). "Reason and Sentiment: The Moral Worlds and Modes of Reasoning of Antebellum Jurists." *Boston University Law Review* 79: 1161–1213.

Carlson, David J. (2007). "'Another Declaration of Independence': John Neal's *Rachel Dyer* and the Assault on Precedent." *Early American Literature* 42(3): 405–434.

Cook, Charles M. (1981). *The American Codification Movement: A Study of Antebellum Legal Reform.* Greenwood Press, Westport, CT.

Coquillette, Daniel R. (1984). "Justinian in Braintree: John Adams, Civilian Learning, and Legal Elitism, 1758–1775." In Sheppard, ed., *The History of Legal Education in the United States: Commentaries and Primary Sources, Volume 1*, 75–92. Salem Press, Inc., Pasadena, CA.

Davis, Richard Beale (1949). "The Early American Lawyer and the Profession of Letters." *Huntington Library Quarterly* 12(2): 191–205.

Davis, Richard Beale (1964). *Intellectual Life in Jefferson's Virginia, 1790–1830*. University of Tennessee Press, Knoxville.

Ferguson, Robert A. (1984). *Law and Letters in American Culture*. Harvard University Press, Cambridge, MA.

Ferguson, Robert A. (2004). *Reading the Early Republic*. Harvard University Press, Cambridge, MA.

Foletta, Marshall (2001). *Coming to Terms with Democracy: Federalist Intellectuals and the Shaping of an American Culture*. University Press of Virginia, Charlottesville.

Friedman, Lawrence M. (1968). "Heart against Head: Perry Miller and the Legal Mind." *Yale Law Journal* 77: 1244–1259.

Friedman, Lawrence M. (2005). *A History of American Law*. 3rd Edition. Simon & Schuster, New York.

Gerardi, Donald F. (1994). "Zephaniah Swift and Connecticut's Standing Order: Skepticism, Conservatism, and Religious Liberty in the Early Republic." *New England Quarterly* 67(2): 234–256.

Gordon, Robert W. (2009). "Friedman, Lawrence M." In Newman, ed., *The Yale Biographical Dictionary of American Law*, 207–208. Yale University Press, New Haven, CT.

Hall, Mark David (1997). *The Political and Legal Philosophy of James Wilson, 1742–1798*. University of Missouri Press, Columbia.

Hoeflich, Michael (1986). "Law & Geometry: Legal Science from Leibniz to Langdell." *American Journal of Legal History* 30: 95–121.

Hoeflich, Michael (1997). *Roman and Civil Law and the Development of Anglo-American Jurisprudence in the Nineteenth Century*. University of Georgia Press, Athens, GA.

Hoeflich, Michael (2009). "American Blackstones." In Prest, ed., *Blackstone and His Commentaries: Biography, Law, and History*, 171–184. Hart Publishing, Oxford.

Horton, John Theodore (1939). *James Kent: A Study in Conservatism, 1763–1847*. D. Appleton-Century Co., New York.

Hulsebosch, Daniel J. (2005) *Constituting Empire: New York and the Transformation of Constitutionalism in the Atlantic World, 1664–1830*. University of North Carolina Press, Chapel Hill.

Hulsebosch, Daniel J. (2009a). "Debating the Transformation of American Law: James Kent, Joseph Story, and the Legacy of the Revolution." In Hamilton and Brophy, eds, *Transformations in American Legal History: Essays in Honor of Professor Morton J. Horwitz*, 1–27. Harvard Law School, Cambridge, MA.

Hulsebosch, Daniel J. (2009b). "An Empire of Law: Chancellor Kent and the Revolution in Books in the Early Republic." *Alabama Law Review* 60(2): 377–424.

Johnson, Herbert Alan (1976). "John Jay: Lawyer in a Time of Transition, 1764–1775." *University of Pennsylvania Law Review* 124(5): 1260–1292.

Kennedy, Duncan (2006). *The Rise and Fall of Classical Legal Thought*. Beard Books, Washington, DC.

King, Peter J. (1966). "John Neal as a Benthamite." *New England Quarterly* 39(1): 47–65.

King, Peter J. (1986). *Utilitarian Jurisprudence in America: The Influence of Bentham and Austin on American Legal Thought in the Nineteenth Century.* Garland Publishing, New York.

Klafter, Craig Evan (1993). *Reason over Precedents: Origins of American Legal Thought.* Greenwood Press, Westport, CT.

Klafter, Craig Evan (2006). "St. George Tucker: The First Modern American Law Professor." *Journal of the Historical Society* 6(1): 133–150.

Langbein, John H. (1993). "Chancellor Kent and the History of Legal Literature." *Columbia Law Review* 93(3): 547–594.

Lieberman, David (1989). *The Province of Legislation Determined: Legal Theory in Eighteenth-Century Britain.* Cambridge University Press, New York.

Lieberman, David (2006). "The Mixed Constitution and the Common Law." In Goldie and Wokler, eds, *The Cambridge History of Eighteenth-Century Political Thought*, 317–346. Cambridge University Press, New York.

Lobban, Michael (1991). *The Common Law and English Jurisprudence, 1760–1850.* Oxford University Press, New York.

Lobban, Michael (2007). "The Age of the Federalists." In *A History of the Philosophy of Law in the Common Law World, 1600–1900.* Volume 8, *A Treatise of Legal Philosophy and General Jurisprudence.* Springer, Dordrecht.

Lockmiller, David A. (1938). *Sir William Blackstone.* University of North Carolina Press, Chapel Hill.

Miller, Perry (1965). *The Life of the Mind in America from the Revolution to the Civil War.* Harcourt, Brace & World, Inc., New York.

Nelson, William E. (1975). *Americanization of the Common Law: The Impact of Legal Change on Massachusetts Society, 1760–1830.* Harvard University Press, Cambridge, MA.

Newmyer, R. Kent (1985). *Supreme Court Justice Joseph Story: Statesman of the Old Republic.* University of North Carolina Press, Chapel Hill.

Newmyer, R. Kent (2001). *John Marshall and the Heroic Age of the Supreme Court.* Louisiana State University Press, Baton Rouge.

O'Brien, Michael (1985). *A Character of Hugh Legaré.* University of Tennessee Press, Knoxville.

O'Brien, Michael (2004). *Conjectures of Order: Intellectual Life and the American South, 1810–1860.* 2 volumes. University of North Carolina Press, Chapel Hill.

Oldham, James (2004). *English Common Law in the Age of Mansfield.* University of North Carolina Press, Chapel Hill.

Parker, Kunal M. (2011). *Common Law, History, and Democracy in America, 1790–1900.* Cambridge University Press, New York.

Parrington, Vernon L. (1927). *Main Currents in American Thought: An Interpretation of American Literature from the Beginning to 1920.* Harcourt, Brace & Co., New York.

Pearson, Ellen Holmes (2011). *Remaking Custom: Law and Identity in the Early American Republic.* University of Virginia Press, Charlottesville.

Prest, Wilfrid (2008). *William Blackstone: Law and Letters in the Eighteenth Century.* Oxford University Press, New York.

Raack, David W. (1989). "'To Preserve the Best Fruits': The Legal Thought of Chancellor James Kent." *American Journal of Legal History* 33(4): 320–366.

Ross, Richard J. (1993). "The Legal Past of Early New England: Notes for the Study of Law, Legal Culture, and Intellectual History." *William and Mary Quarterly* 50(1): 28–41.

Schofield, Philip (2006). *Utility and Democracy: The Political Thought of Jeremy Bentham*. Oxford University Press, New York.

Schweber, Howard (1999). "The 'Science' of Legal Science: The Model of the Natural Sciences in Nineteenth-Century American Legal Education." *Law and History Review* 17(3): 421–466.

Shaffer, Thomas L. (1981). "David Hoffman on the Bible as a Law Book." *Christian Legal Society Quarterly*, Fall 1981.

Shaffer, Thomas L. (1982). "David Hoffman's Law School Lectures, 1822–1833." *Journal of Legal Education* 32: 127–138.

Stein, Peter (1966). "The Attraction of the Civil Law in Post-Revolutionary America." *Virginia Law Review* 52: 403–434.

Valeri, Mark (1994). *Law and Providence in Joseph Bellamy's New England: The Origins of the New Divinity in Revolutionary America*. Oxford University Press, New York.

Watson, Alan (1993). "Chancellor Kent's Use of Foreign Law." In Reimann, ed., *The Reception of Continental Ideas in the Common Law World, 1820–1920*, 45–62. Duncker & Humblot, Berlin.

White, G. Edward (1976). "The Path of American Jurisprudence." *University of Pennsylvania Law Review* 124(5): 1212–1259.

White, G. Edward (1988). *The Marshall Court and Cultural Change, 1815–35*. Volumes 3–4, *The Oliver Wendell Holmes Devise: History of the Supreme Court of the United States*. Macmillan Publishing Company, New York.

White, G. Edward (1998). "The Chancellor's Ghost." *Chicago-Kent Law Review* 74(1): 229–262.

White, G. Edward (2012). *Law in American History, Volume 1: From the Colonial Years Through the Civil War*. Oxford University Press, New York.

Widmer, Edward L. (1999). *Young America: The Flowering of Democracy in New York City*. Oxford University Press, New York.

Wood, Gordon S. (1969). *The Creation of the American Republic, 1776–1787*. University of North Carolina Press, Chapel Hill.

Chapter Twenty-six

AMERICAN JURISPRUDENCE IN THE NINETEENTH AND EARLY TWENTIETH CENTURIES

James D. Schmidt

Perhaps it is because the United States Supreme Court has been the bailiwick of white men of European descent throughout most of its history, but surveying the scholarship about American jurisprudence from the early republic to the New Deal era reveals a trajectory somewhat at odds with other areas of the wider profession, and indeed, with many corners of law and society studies. While many areas of the profession have been infused with the insights of social and cultural history since the 1960s and 1970s, most of the scholars who study legal thought and modes of judicial decision-making did not begin to adopt these methods until after the turn of the twenty-first century. In part, this has occurred because early scholarship on American jurisprudence was heavily influenced by the Progressive historians, and indeed, Progressive jurists and legal scholars themselves. Hence, it often advanced a crude class analysis of the judiciary, especially of the federal courts in the Gilded Age and Progressive Eras. In response, many scholars in the field have stressed instead the importance of ideology (or sometimes "principle") as a guiding force in the development of an American jurisprudence.

Work on American judging and legal thought in the Long Nineteenth Century can be divided into the three obvious areas: the antebellum period; the postbellum era; and the Progressive period and after. This is not to suggest that there are identifiable "traditions" or "ages" of American law as some scholars have done (White, 1976; Gilmore, 1977; Herget, 1990). Indeed, there has been much continuity and overlap of the central issues concerning judges and legal writers, which is not surprising given the staying power of capitalism. Rather, these historical periods also align (more

A Companion to American Legal History, First Edition.
Edited by Sally E. Hadden and Alfred L. Brophy.
© 2013 John Wiley & Sons Ltd. Published 2021 by John Wiley & Sons Ltd.

or less) with how historians have approached the past. Historians who have looked at the antebellum era naturally have focused on how judicial thinkers responded to the market revolution, the growth of slavery, and the crisis of the Union. Many scholars have seen this era as one driven by instrumentalism in judicial reasoning; that is, decisions were driven by a desire to reach a particular social or economic end. Those who look at the later nineteenth and early twentieth centuries have focused on how courts and legal writers dealt with the rapid urbanization and industrialization of the nation. Here the stress has often been on a perceived shift away from instrumentalism to an emphasis on formalism: the alignment of decisions with previous precedent or with a set of first principles. Finally, those who look directly at the Progressive Era through the New Deal have mainly examined the main current of legal thought in those reforming eras: Legal Realism. Realism and related movements challenged formalism and sought to align law with the new social sciences and new social forces they studied. In crudest terms, the main area of disagreement has been about why these shifts occurred and has centered on the simple question of whether ideas inside the legal field or forces outside of it have driven changes in legal thought.

The Instrumentalist Era

Disentangling jurisprudential principles from general legal history or the history of law and the economy in the antebellum period would be a difficult and likely fruitless task. Much of the scholarship in earlier eras of law and society studies focused almost exclusively on those issues. While much debate ensued about the causes, legal and constitutional historians in the post-World War II period envisioned the years before the Civil War as a time in which jurists cleared out the restraints of the British legal system to "release" a period of expansion, both legal and economic. The founding father of this outlook was, of course, J. Willard Hurst, whose own work and that of his disciples fills the pages of this volume. In the diminutive *Law and the Conditions of Freedom* (1956), Hurst envisioned jurists in nineteenth-century America as hewing to an essentially liberal, middle-class faith in democracy that "released" the energies of an emerging entrepreneurial capitalism. Even though economic growth was the outcome, legal minds were driven more by ideas than interest. While certainly more critical and grounded in daily reality than the technical histories being proffered by law scholars, Hurst's view aligned with the reigning consensus school in the discipline of history.

Writing at about the same time, Leonard Levy (1957) studied these processes via the life of influential Supreme Judicial Court of Massachusetts Chief Justice Lemuel Shaw. Levy's work broke new ground by turning attention to the state courts, the location of much of the action in the nineteenth century, but his biography also contributed to a growing understanding of jurists' efforts to modernize the law by making it scientific, in the sense of being systematic. The monumental intellectual historian Perry Miller had advanced this notion late in his career (1965). For Miller, however, jurists and law writers such as Joseph Story and James Kent represented a conservative elite whose scientific endeavors made law into an instrument that limited changed rather than promoting it.

Such notions slowly crept into common understandings of jurisprudential thinking in the antebellum era. Hence by 1973, when Lawrence Friedman first published his magisterial *History of American Law*, a paradigm for understanding judicial reasoning and law in general had been established. Later dubbed "functionalism" by critical scholars, this outlook assumed the law followed society, that social and economic change altered judicial reasoning and decision-making. So, for instance, *caveat emptor* arose as a response to burden of litigation prompted by implied warranty. New forms of land conveyance eased the process of property transfer.

By the 1970s, scholars had begun to develop much more nuanced understandings of Hurst's original notions of law and economic growth. Enter Morton Horwitz and his detractors. In *The Transformation of American Law, 1780–1860* (1977), Horwitz almost single-handedly altered the field of American legal history by arguing that antebellum jurists consciously promoted a pro-capitalist agenda. Like other law and society scholars, Horwitz reviewed the substantive developments of the era: the shift to contract; the rise of tort; *caveat emptor* and other pro-business doctrines. Like his predecessors, he stressed the instrumentalist leanings of antebellum jurists. But what made the book controversial is that Horwitz saw such instrumentalism as a concerted effort by jurists to aid capitalists by what he called the "subsidization of economic growth." At the end of the book, Horwitz pointed to the idea he would develop later: that after this period of pro-business creation, the judiciary rested in a period of formalism that protected what they had wrought.

Love it or hate it, *Transformation I* became the touchstone for a generation of scholars thinking about law and judicial reasoning in antebellum America. Longer responses appeared, some directly arguing Horwitz, others laying out alternative paradigms. On the specific matter of commercial law, for example, Tony Freyer (1981) examined *Swift v. Tyson* (1842) and concluded that it laid the foundation for a national commercial law by drawing on a much broader range of sources than Horwitz had contended. Freyer stressed the persistence of local concerns, as did William Novak in *The People's Welfare* (1996), a book that suggested not so much a different understanding for jurisprudence but a general diminution of the higher circles of law in favor of a persistent localism until Reconstruction. Christopher Tomlins (1993) moved his work back into the antebellum era and found that while jurists did promote the interests of capitalists, they did so by drawing on republican ideals. In the main, Tomlins' examination of how law became the "modality of rule" in the post-Revolutionary era advanced Horwitz's assertion about the devaluing of alternative forms of decision-making, but Tomlins' approach jettisoned the more crass elements of consciousness present in *Transformation I*. Another scholar who stressed the importance of "little r" republicanism was R. Kent Newmyer (1985), whose biography of Joseph Story demonstrated how a commitment to this organizing cultural principle guided Story's efforts to align the law with economic growth in the antebellum era. The most thoroughgoing refutation came from Peter Karsten, whose numerous articles and book-length *Heart Versus Head* (1997) offered a nineteenth-century judiciary influenced by emerging notions of "sentimentalism," a judiciary who protected the weak against rapacious capitalism, a judiciary who looked out for the little guy. Given that eminent jurists such as Story or Shaw often said directly that they were helping "enterprise," it is hard to see how Karsten's sentimental judges really could have won the day. Still, in looking beyond the burned-over district of American legal history in the northeastern corridor, Karsten provided a valuable service. For older generations of scholars, "the economy" was about capitalism, but another area of economic activity had just as much influence on the tone of judicial thinking in the first half of the nineteenth century: slavery. Much has been written on the actual workings of slave law. From Thomas Morris' encyclopedic *Southern Slavery and the Law, 1619–1860* (1999) to Ariela Gross' subtle *Double Character* (2006), scholars delved into how the legal results of human bondage played out, but less attention has been paid to the ways in which a slave society influenced American jurisprudence in general. Legal scholar Robert M. Cover's *Justice Accused* (1975), however, did confront directly the nature of judicial decision-making in slave cases. Cover argued that while jurists experienced internal moral turmoil when deciding cases involving slaves, they largely applied the devices of legal formalism. In a brilliant and complex interpretation, Mark Tushnet (1981) also explored the ideological conflicts of slavery and the law. Tushnet stressed a core dichotomy at the heart of slave law and judicial reasoning: the inherent split between humanity and interest contained in human bondage.

The place where slave law has entered the historiography of jurisprudence is where it intersects with the Constitution. Many years ago, William Wiecek (1977) demonstrated how a "federal consensus" that only states could abolish slavery dramatically influenced the nature of the antislavery movement. In particular, Wiecek stressed the importance of the great English case of *Somersett v. Stewart* (1772) which established the principle that freedom was a natural condition and slavery had to be supported by positive, local law. This notion began to break down in the 1840s, he argued, as proslavery jurists gained influence on the U.S. Supreme Court and the radical abolitionist movement took shape in the North, a breakdown of regional and legal comity also traced by Paul Finkelman (1981). The culmination was *Dred Scott*, thoroughly examined by many scholars, but given unsurpassed treatment by Don Fehrenbacher (1978). Published posthumously, Fehrenbacher's book on the case stood Roger B. Taney in the dock for his rabidly pro-southern bias, but in terms of jurisprudential development, saw the case as the application of a thoroughly developed sense of judicial review.

Roger Taney is not one of the more popular chief justices of the U.S. Supreme Court, and with good reason. Taney's promotion of the slaveholder's interests has been one source of a persistent question in the history of American jurisprudence. Was there or has there been as distinctly "southern judicial tradition"? This question was explored in some depth in the 1980s in a pair of volumes with expressive and paradoxical titles: *Ambivalent Legacy* (1984) and *Uncertain Tradition* (1989). Collections of essays edited by James Ely and David Bodenhamer (in the former) and Ely and Kermit Hall (in the latter), the books more or less concluded that the South possessed a distinct legal and constitutional heritage that nonetheless remained tied to larger movements elsewhere in the Union. In the following decade after these volumes appeared, the question of southern distinctiveness in American jurisprudence was taken up with much greater depth by Timothy Huebner in *The Southern Judicial Tradition* (1999). A collective biography of six southern jurists, the book located the center of the southern judicial tradition in the tension between an emergent national legal culture and the demands of growing southern sectionalism. Southern judges, Huebner argued, did not see themselves as outside of social, economic, or political change. Examining substantive matters of murder, economy, federalism, and slavery and race, the volume envisioned social context as vital for southern judging. As might be expected, race took center stage in southern jurisprudence and in Huebner's account. In fact, race represented the only area in which southern judges "differed substantially" from their northern counterparts.

Perhaps no southerner exemplified the drive to regional distinctiveness more than John C. Calhoun. As author of the doctrine of "state interposition" during the 1832 Nullification Crisis, Calhoun is often seen as a founding father of states' rights. More recent assessments, however, connect the South Carolinian to broader currents in American thought. H. Lee Cheek (2001), for instance, understood Calhoun's thought as springing from a particular stripe of republicanism, a southern Atlantic branch that leaned heavily on notions of community. Michael Bernath (2010) expanded on this notion in *Confederate Minds*, an examination of how southern intellectuals sought to forge the basis for an independent southern culture during the Civil War. Such treatments pointed towards a resolution of the paradoxes posited by earlier work on southern legal history and led to the notion that there was indeed a southern jurisprudence that fit into a broader national context.

That national context had an international dimension in the wider currents of western thought in the post-Enlightenment era. The utilitarianism of Bentham and Mill suggested a new way of understanding moral goods, with obvious implications for the meaning of law, while the rise of modern math and science suggested that certainty could be found in the ordering of things. Scholars ranging from Perry Miller (1965) to G. Edward White (1980) to Michael Hoeflich (1986) have noticed how European philosophical traditions informed American legal thought. White stressed the ways in which nineteenth century intellectuals focused on "'conceptualization' – the transformation of data into comprehensive theories of potentially universal applicability" (White, 1980: 6). A central notion was the shift from a view stressing natural (or even divine) law to a positivistic, scientific paradigm. Though these changes are usually located in the postbellum era, Hoeflich in particular argued that the roots of this shift lay in the antebellum importation of European notions of science, particularly those of Gottfried Wilhelm Leibniz. American jurists and law writers developed "the idea that law can be reduced to a set of first principles, on the order of mathematical axioms, and that by the use of deductive method, these principles can yield all necessary consequences" (Hoeflich, 1986: 96).

Modern jurisprudential development depended heavily on the transmission of case law and the other ephemera of the legal field. For a long time scholars took the means of that communication process for granted, but Michael Hoeflich's 2010 book on *Legal Publishing in Antebellum America* revealed the inner workings of law's knowledge base by looking carefully at the obscure men who edited and published law books. Legal education itself evolved tremendously in this era, from the ancient practice of reading law in the office of an accomplished lawyer to formal training in modern university. Central to this story was C.C. Langdell and the inception of the sequenced courses, examinations, and the famous case book method at Harvard Law School. As a father of formalism Langdell has had many detractors, but in more recent times, he has found his champions. Bruce Kimball's (2009) biography envisions Langdell's methods as a form of "academic meritocracy," that, while adopted almost universally, nonetheless discriminated against those outside the elite. William LaPiana (1994) provided another revisionist account of Langdell, arguing that much of the impetus for the case method came as a result of a crisis in legal practice. The introduction of code pleading after 1848 eviscerated the old common law forms and led to a search on the part of Langdell and others for a new science of law that would provide order in the ensuing chaos. "The construct Langdell and his contemporaries worked to create was a melding of logic and experience: the use of science to better understand and practice," LaPiana noted (LaPiana, 1994: viii). The end goal was better practicing lawyers as much as any commitment to a particular mindset.

Instrumentalism Becomes Formalism

In the wake of the Civil War and the constitutional revolution of Reconstruction, the legal and constitutional order of the United States changed irrevocably. Indeed, as William Novak argued in *The People's Welfare* (1996) only then did the pervasive localism of early American law come to an end. As industrialization and urban growth destroyed the relatively isolated communities of the preindustrial era, the nation's legal community faced the daunting challenge of adjusting the legal underpinnings of an agrarian society to a mechanized one. A new jurisprudence emerged, but exactly what it was and why it evolved as it did has been one of the liveliest areas of debate among scholars for many decades. In fact, the question of when and why the shift to formalism occurred has not always been located in the postbellum era. William Nelson (1974), for example, argued that the shift began in the antebellum era as instrumentalism proved detrimental to the antislavery cause. Still, the Gilded Age has often been seen as an era of "formalism," both inside the law and in a broader, cultural sense. It has been envisioned as an era where titans of industry sought economic and political power and used the law to defend their interests. Scholars inside of legal history have begged to differ with this general picture for many years. The prevailing interpretation, with its critics, suggests that the story is not as simple as all of that. Doctrines such as "liberty of contract" or "substantive due process" which undergirded the laissez-faire constitutionalism of the era turn out to have roots in the well-intentioned movements of jurists to protect something other than corporate giants such as the sugar trust.

Much of the debate centered on what is usually dubbed "classical legal thought." This worldview was amply sketched by William M. Wiecek in *The Lost World of Classical Legal Thought* (1998). Classical thought, he argued, should be seen as "a way of thinking about law [that] was abstract, formal, conceptualistic, categorical, and (sometimes) deductive" (Wiecek, 1998: 4). More than simply class bias, this mindset, nonetheless, legitimated power of all kinds, economic, social, and political. As a mode of jurisprudence, it stressed the individual, conceiving of litigants as "juristic equals," and it held that law was found, not made. Its roots were antebellum, and its pinnacle came in 1905 in *Lochner v. New York*. Eventually, classical legal thought failed, for it could no longer account for the social and economic realities of modern life. The death knell came in 1937's momentous departure, but classicism had been much in decline before that time.

By the time *Lost World* appeared, Wiecek could draw on decades of scholarship about Gilded Age jurisprudence. Scholars had been "reconsidering" laissez-faire constitutionalism and generally finding that it did not reflect the views of economic and political elites. Rather, the postbellum bench looked back to Jacksonian ideas of republicanism and free labor (Benedict,

1985). Stephen Siegel outlined the contours of this interpretation as part of a 2002 *Law and History Review* forum on Gilded Age revisionism, identifying four main elements. First, ideology, not class, is the prime causative motor of history. Second, laissez-faire constitutionalism arose from the application of principles that held legislation should not favor one class or another. Third, "in private law, Gilded Age jurists also developed a free-enterprise- friendly body of legal doctrine, but advanced it as the natural outcome of their scientific approach to legal decision making." Finally, public and private law were not in conflict; rather both sought to advance elementally "liberal, Lockean values" (Siegel, 2002: 632).

If the revisionists agreed that late-nineteenth- and early-twentieth-century jurisprudence was not guided by class interests, they did not align about what did actually influence juridical thought. Reaching back to the antebellum era and forward to the New Deal, Herbert Hovenkamp (1991) carefully delineated the relationship between classical economic theory and legal thought. Looking at the contracts and commerce clauses, rate regulation, substantive due process, labor law, and antitrust, Hovenkamp affirmed the influence of laissez-faire economics but rejected the notion that such applications served the business community in a direct, class-based manner. While such accounts treated Gilded Age jurisprudence as essentially secular, Mark Warren Bailey (2004) stressed religion and especially "academic moral philosophy," an influence missed by historians following in Progressive critique of laissez-faire constitutionalism. This outlook had been central to the college training of many postbellum jurists and it gave them "an unshakeable belief in an individualistic, voluntaristic, and moral social order resting on eternal metaphysical truth" (Bailey, 2004: 23). Backwards-looking in nature, this mode of jurisprudence was truly conservative, for it aimed to preserve an essentially eighteenth-century view of human nature and its relation to law and society.

The influence of the revisionist view appeared clearly in the Fuller Court volume of the *Oliver Wendell Holmes Devise History of the Supreme Court of the United States*. As the body who oversaw the heyday of laissez-faire constitutionalism, the Fuller Court provided the perfect place for Owen Fiss (1993) to apply revisionism to the classic decisions that exemplified Gilded Age jurisprudence. In keeping with the dominant outlook, Fiss downplayed the social and economic causes and consequences of the Court's pro-business and white supremacist decisions and instead argued that the justices were committed on principle to limited government and order liberty. Fiss looked to Justices Brewer and Peckham as guiding lights, as "the source of the ideas that gave the Court its sweep and direction" (Fiss, 1993: 33). That direction consisted in "the social contract tradition," a view that understood politics and society as distinct spheres and held government legitimate only to the extent that it promoted individual liberty. Given such an outlook, both *Plessy* and *Lochner* become debates about the police power. While acknowledging the shortcomings of this view, Fiss averred that if the Fuller Court can be seen as a failure, it was because of an "attachment to a conception of liberty that consisted almost entirely of a demand for limited government" (Fiss, 1993: 21).

Much of the older historiography against which the revisionists crusaded took its impetus from one particular egregious decision, the infamous *Lochner v. New York* (1905). In striking down a New York law regulating the working hours of bakers, the Court seemed to verify its critics, then and since, that it had turned into nothing more than a shill for a capitalist elite. Not so, said the revisionists. This view of *Lochner* found its most vivid expression in Howard Gillman's 1993 book, *The Constitution Besieged*. The assault that Gillman envisioned was not one undertaken by the captains of industry, but rather by those who sought to rein them in. Or at least, that's how the Court at the time saw regulatory activity, he argued. Following hard on the heels of the revisionists, Gillman dubbed *Lochner* a "serious, principled effort" to apply Jacksonian understandings of the police power as legitimate only to the extent it did not promote "class legislation," that is, legislation that did not explicitly and exclusively benefit one social group. In this jurisprudential view, developed in the federal and especially in the state courts in the antebellum era, the state acted as a neutral arbiter over a society in which economic independence served as the basis for political participation and a good society came from steady commerce and limited government.

Many scholars accepted the general outlines of the revisionist camp, but nonetheless offered divergent or more critical readings of its main currents. A good example of such a position appeared in the work of Paul Kens, whose books on Justice Stephen Field (1997) and on *Lochner* (1990; 1998) supplied a different reading of the antebellum, republican heritage. Kens did not go so far as to revive the class-based interpretation of the Progressives, but he did stress the influence of laissez-faire thinking and Social Darwinism, a view that was increasingly out of sync with mainstream reformers then and since, a fact that explains the controversy, then and since.

On the other end of the spectrum, David Bernstein stressed the libertarian aspects of *Lochner* and Progressive Era jurisprudence in general. In *Only One Place of Redress* (2001), Bernstein surveyed how laissez-faire decisions curtailing the power of unions actually turned out to help African-American workers who "benefited greatly from decisions preserving free labor markets" (2001: 7). A decade later, Bernstein (2011) mounted a direct defense of *Lochner* itself, outlining how the decision lay grounded in precedent and how its libertarian dimensions lay the basis for a great deal of jurisprudential development thereafter.

If Kens and Bernstein pointed toward something of a revision of the revision, works in the 2000s took matters in novel directions that not so much rejected the older debates as much as sidestepped them. For instance, Kunal

Parker (2006) explored the law of custom in the late nineteenth century, illuminating an often forgotten but nonetheless critical area of law. Turning a critical eye on the entire conception of "police power" and the conundrum of control in an egalitarian, self-regulating republic, Markus Dirk Dubber (2005) located the origins of the police power in patriarchal household governance. In this view, decisions such as *Lochner* represented but a bump along the road to the nearly unquestioned acceptance of policing. Roy Kreitner (2006) took on the notion of contract, central to Progressive-era expressions about the liberty of that construct, and found that the modern conception was not as ancient as scholars had always assumed. Rather, modern contract thinking came about in the later nineteenth century as a result of "a revolution in private law undertaken by classical legal scholars" (2006: 1). This epistemological upheaval formed part of a larger "cultural negotiation over the nature of the individual subject and his role in a society undergoing transformation" (2006: 2). By contract, Kreitner meant *enforceable* agreements. To get to that point, legal theorists outlined "the autonomous calculating subject" and case law provided a place for "a more complex cultural negotiation of subjectivities" (2006: 3). Kreitner examined this process by exploring three seemingly "marginal" areas of law: gifts, wagers, and incomplete contracts. An examination of these "borders of contract" revealed the "calculating subject," Kreitner argued, for "calculation is based on singularity, on eliminating competing impulses and undefined responsibilities to others" (2006: 12).

Realism and its Legacies

By the turn of the twentieth century, the orthodoxies of Gilded Age jurisprudence were under siege from reformers both inside and outside of the legal field. Progressive reformers railed against decisions such as *Lochner* and sought, unsuccessfully, to rein in the power of the judiciary. Inside the bench and bar, new voices began to question the law as a set of abstract universals that were discovered, not made. Led by Roscoe Pound, one set of legal reformers forged a new way of understanding the law that is usually dubbed "sociological jurisprudence." These legal minds hoped to make law more responsive to the social, economic, and political problems of urban-industrial America. Indeed, they believed that data derived from the emerging social sciences could form just as sound a basis of decision-making as could precedent. Picking up where sociological jurisprudence left off, a group of scholars known as Legal Realists mounted a much more extensive critique of the law and legal process itself. Leading lights such as Karl Llewellyn and Jerome Frank turned the methods of social science on the legal field itself, seeking to understand how and why the legal process produced the outcomes it did. As always, when one poses the central epistemological question ("how do we know what we know?") about a field of knowledge, the Realist project threatened (or promised, given one's point of view) to destroy the law itself. Hence, in some fashion, the Legal Realists predicted the later twentieth-century rise of the critical legal studies movement. What Morton White (1947) once called the "revolt against formalism" swept through the legal system, but to what extent it changed anything is a matter of some debate.

The historiography of Progressive Era jurisprudence is interwoven with law writers from the time, particularly such towering figures as Oliver Wendell Holmes, Jr. and Benjamin Cardozo. From his masterpiece, *The Common Law* (1881), to the more accessible essay, "The Path of the Law" (1897), Holmes articulated a vision of law that lodged it in the realities of modern society, abandoning the idea of a set of universal moral abstracts previous to legal rules. Deeply disillusioned by the Civil War, Holmes and other pragmatists in the Metaphysical Club sought to "bring ideas and principles and beliefs down to a human level because they wished to avoid the violence they saw hidden in abstractions" (Menand, 2000: 440). As applied to legal reasoning, as G. Edward White (1995) has pointed out, this desire left Holmes trying to balance logic and experience, the personal and the professional. If Holmes pointed toward this path, Cardozo (along with many other Progressives) opened the way. In a series of lectures at Yale, later published as *The Nature of the Judicial Process* (1921), Cardozo interrogated the nature of judicial decision-making, acknowledging the philosophical dimension but pointing towards history, tradition, sociology, and "the sub-conscious" as influential on judicial thought. Law then was not cut off from society. Indeed, Cardozo pointed out a judge must obtain "knowledge just as the legislator gets it, from experience and study and reflection; in brief, from life itself" (1921: 113). As one of Cardozo's biographers, Richard Polenberg (1997) has noted, these beliefs also sprang from his own deeply-seated personal values about such matters as criminality and sexuality.

Early scholarly treatments of this Progressive revolt tended to focus on the leading lights and internal history of the Realist movement, and indeed, much more ink has been spilled on Llewellyn and his associates than on Pound. Wilfred Rumble's 1968 book on the Realist movement laid out its basic contours. While other scholars would later disagree, Rumble saw the self-proclaimed leaders of the movement as its heart. Frank and Llewellyn, as well as Herman Oliphant, Underhill Moore, and Felix Cohen, he argued, did not constitute a school of jurisprudence, but they did share a common set of roots and goals. Grounded in pragmatism, sociological jurisprudence, and the social sciences in general, these men rejected the notion of hewing faithfully to established rules. They desired a self-conscious approach to decision-making, an approach where law would serve the cause of social justice.

While Rumble acknowledged divergences between the Realists, other scholars went further. William Twining (1973), who had worked with Llewellyn and edited his papers, argued in a biography that Llewellyn had never made the firm commitment to scientific reasoning as had Jerome Frank. Rather, Llewellyn's achievement was to demonstrate how sociological jurisprudence could work in practice, how the law could actually be studied empirically. Edward Purcell (1973) also included the Realists in his more general work on how social science produced a "crisis of democratic theory." Later, Purcell would show how such leading Progressive jurists as Louis Brandeis would carry out the long battle to reduce the power of the courts, a Realist goal (2000).

Attempts to curtail the effects or alter the nature of judicial power in the Progressive Era also came from outside the courts during the early twentieth century, and scholars of various stripes have examined these labors. William Ross (1994a) traced the efforts of Progressive Era labor activists to place actual legislative restrictions on the power of the federal bench. On the other side of the coin, however, Ross (1994b) also showed how the federal bench used substantive due process to pursue essentially libertarian ends in the 1920s, curtailing legislative restrictions on parochial education. Other accounts of sociological jurisprudence in practice also stressed the ways it altered both legal practice and daily life. Daniel Ernst (1995) looked at Progressive lawyers and the law of industrial disputes. Felice Batlan (2006) investigated how the settlement house movement led to the "gendering of urban legal culture." In an award-winning study of the Municipal Court of Chicago, Michael Willrich (2003) demonstrated how reformers went about "socializing justice" by incorporating Pound's principles into the daily practice of the law.

Although numerous historians traced the effects of the Progressive jurisprudential reform, much of the scholarly attention has remained focused on the movement itself, and debate has remained centered on its meanings and its effects. A central problematic in the study of Legal Realism is the matter of definition. Practitioners at the time rarely agreed, a fact evinced by the short life of the Institute of Law at Johns Hopkins University, which could be said to have died from a lack of definition (Schlegel 1995; White, 1997). One scholarly attempt to pin down the Realists was undertaken by Laura Kalman (1986) in her careful study of the Realist movement at Yale. Centered on New Haven, the book also attended to the Harvard Law School, which early on rejected the movement, and on Columbia, where Llewellyn and Oliphant held sway until administrative changes resulted in the departure of several Realist faculty members. After 1928, Kalman argued, Yale became the center of the movement, but there, too, institutional factors limited its impact. By the postwar period, the movement had waned. Still, Realism contained an important message, one that even daunted the Realists themselves: "that all law is politics" (1986: 230–231).

That notion, or rather its denial, took center stage in the second installment in Morton Horwitz's *Transformation of American Law*, which appeared in 1992. *Transformation II* represented a departure for Horwitz. Whereas the first volume had studied change in the courts, the second volume concentrated more on jurisprudential theorists, especially the Realists and their struggle with classicists. The latter created and maintained the fictional line between politics and society, in short, the neutral state. It was this line that the Realists sought to undermine, a move that created a "crisis of legal orthodoxy." Agreeing with the Realists that "the development of law cannot be understood independently of social context" (1992: vii), Horwitz traced legal change to the social and economic changes of urban-industrial America. Reacting to these changes but also to the intellectual currents of the day, Oliver Wendell Holmes Jr. emerged as "the most important and influential legal thinker America has had" (1992: 109), and his famous "Path of Law" essay marked the birth of modern legal thinking in its reaction of the separation of law and politics. Among full bore Realists, Horwitz downplayed Llewellyn and Frank and instead highlighted the work of Robert Lee Hale and Morris Cohen, who mounted a thoroughgoing critique of property. Like many other scholars, Horwitz concluded that the movement faded after World War II as the rise of the administrative state and the belief in proceduralism reinforced the line between state and society.

The wide range of Realist thought has led scholars to something of a gambit: pick a Realist and end up at a different spot. Such was the case with John Henry Schlegel's 1995 account of the movement. Rather than shining the light on the assault on formalism, Schlegel located the heart of the movement in the adoption of social science methods and the general stance of empiricism. Hence, he also lowered the status of Llewellyn and Frank, replacing them with Underhill Moore, Walter Wheeler Cook, Herman Oliphant, and others of a more scientific stripe. Doing so revealed critical fissures in Realism, especially between the demands of the profession of law and the disciplines of social science. For instance, Cook could incorporate insights from John Dewey and use social science as a tool to organize the law but not in a way that deployed empiricism to critique the legal system as a whole. The career of Underhill Moore exemplified the conflict between the critical stance of the social sciences and law as a mechanism for the creations of societal norms. Additionally, Schlegel noted, as did Realism's critics at the time, the use of actual social science methods was often shallow. All of these factors contributed to Realism's failure.

The eclecticism of Realism, then, produced both its failure and divergent scholarly treatments of that failure. N.E.H. Hull (1997) embraced this fact and made it central to her interpretation of Realism and Progressive Era jurisprudence in general. Accepting the notion of the assault on formalism and the search for an alternative, Hull looked carefully at Roscoe Pound and Karl Llewellyn and at the famous 1930–1931 spat between the two that is often used to symbolize the departures between sociological jurisprudence and Legal Realism. Both were influenced by the new social science, Hull maintained, but Pound retained much more faith in the common law and the legal profession, while Llewellyn hoped to undermine the system's complacency with the application of behavioral social science. In general, however, Hull concluded the Progressive jurisprudence and American legal thinking in general should be seen as a *bricolage*, a "process of assembling the bits and pieces" (1997: 340).

By the early twenty-first century, the longstanding belief in a strict formalist-Realist divide had begun to erode. Neil Duxbury pointed the way toward this reformulation of the period in *Patterns of American Jurisprudence* (1995). Rather than seeing strict periods of time, one following on the other, Duxbury envisioned complex and overlapping patterns of thought. Formalism had various strains, primarily Langdellian science and Social Darwinist laissez-faire constitutionalism. As for Realism, it was not a movement, but an "intellectual mood" (1995: 3). Brian Tamanaha (2009) went beyond Duxbury to declare that both formalism and Realism were "myths" that needed to be shattered. Instead, he argued for a "balanced realism" that included both "a skeptical aspect and a rule-bound aspect" (6). That is, Tamanaha noted, judges should be seen as both influenced by social and political location *and* by the inner logic of the law.

While scholars such as Duxbury and Tamanaha looked to undermine the traditional formalist-Realist divide, others looked forwards to the critical legal studies movement. Numerous scholars of Realism noted that its adherents frequently backed up from the epistemological abyss, yet at the same time, they suggested that Realism contained the seeds of the critical standpoint. Indeed, the two approaches would seem to have much in common, with the crits simply embracing the notion that discovery of the indeterminacy of law *should* undermine the legal system. Such is not the case, argued Wouter De Been in the cleverly titled *Legal Realism Regained: Saving Realism from Critical Acclaim* (2008). De Been agreed with previous scholars that Realism represented part of the revolt against formalism and that it did not constitute a systematized, coherent body, but he hoped to reclaim it from the crits, who he thought had sullied its practical legacy. To set off one approach from the other, De Been examined how each one approached history, the social sciences, and the power of language. In his view, the Realists understood history as shaping law; the crits vice versa. Social science, for the critical thinkers, obscured the political nature of the law and helped legitimate power structures, while for the Realists it was a tool for better policy making. Finally, while both movements accepted that language shaped social concepts and influenced choices, the critical legal studies movement was much less sanguine about the ability to overcome these constraints. The best elements of Legal Realism offered a way out of postmodern paralysis, for it "shows us that we can do without a firm ground, that we can do without such tattered foundational concepts as rationality, objectivity, and human nature and still keep faith in the project of understanding and improving law" (2008: 180).

*****

The question of whether the Realists can be or should be reclaimed is a fitting question with which to end this survey. Over the last several decades there has been a turn away from the more radical elements of critical legal studies, if those ever held much sway in the first place. Nonetheless, the central dilemmas raised by scholars of the Realist movement can be applied to the history and historiography of American jurisprudence in general. If it is to be more than interior intellectual history, it will have to come to terms with critical theory in a variety of fields, but doing so risks (promises) to undermine the norm-setting power of law and the legal profession. This, of course, was precisely the goal of the more radical Realists and many of the crits. As the Realist themselves discovered, the ability of the legal profession (indeed, of all professions including history) to insulate itself is strong, but so are the tools at the disposal of modern scholars. New worlds in the history of American jurisprudence await discovery.

References

Bailey, Mark Warren (2004). *Guardians of the Moral Order: The Legal Philosophy of the Supreme Court, 1860–1910*. Northern Illinois University Press, DeKalb.

Batlan, Felice (2006). "Law and the Fabric of the Everyday: Settlement Houses, Sociological Jurisprudence, and the Gendering of Urban Legal Culture." *Southern California Interdisciplinary Law Journal* 15: 235–284.

Benedict, Michael Les (1985). "Laissez-faire and Liberty: A Re-evaluation of the Meaning and Origins of Laissez-faire Constitutionalism" *Law and History Review* 3: 293–331.

Bernath, Michael T. (2010). *Confederate Minds: The Struggle for Intellectual Independence in the Civil War South*. University of North Carolina Press, Chapel Hill.

Bernstein, David E. (2001). *Only One Place of Redress: African Americans, Labor Regulations, and the Courts from Reconstruction to the New Deal*. Duke University Press, Durham, NC.

Bernstein, David E. (2011). *Rehabilitating Lochner: Defending Individual Rights against Progressive Reform*. University of Chicago Press, Chicago.

Cardozo, Benjamin N. (1921). *The Nature of the Judicial Process*. Yale University Press, New Haven.

Cheek, H. Lee (2001). *Calhoun and Popular Rule: The Political Theory of the Disquisition and Discourse*. University of Missouri Press, Columbia.

Cover, Robert (1975). *Justice Accused: Anti-Slavery and the Judicial Process*. Yale University Press, New Haven.

De Been, Wouter (2008). *Legal Realism Regained: Saving Realism from Critical Acclaim*. Stanford Law Books, Stanford.

Dubber, Markus Dirk (2005). *The Police Power: Patriarchy and the Foundations of American Government*. Columbia University Press, New York.

Duxbury, Neil (1995). *Patterns of American Jurisprudence*. Oxford University Press, New York.

Ely, Jr., James W. and Bodenhamer, David J. (1984). *Ambivalent Legacy: A Legal History of the South*. University of Mississippi Press, Jackson.

Ernst, Daniel R. (1995). *Lawyers Against Labor: From Individual Rights to Corporate Liberalism*. University of Chicago Press, Chicago.

Fehrenbacher, Don (1978). *The Dred Scott Case: Its Significance in American Law and Politics*. Oxford University Press, New York.

Finkelman, Paul (1981). *An Imperfect Union: Slavery, Freedom, and Comity*. University of North Carolina Press, Chapel Hill.

Fiss, Owen M. (1993). *The Troubled Beginnings of the Modern State, 1888–1910*. Macmillan, New York.

Freyer, Tony (1981). *Harmony and Dissonance: The Swift and Erie Cases in American Federalism*. New York University Press, New York.

Friedman, Lawrence (1973). *A History of American Law*. Simon and Schuster, New York.

Gillman, Howard (1993). *The Constitution Besieged: The Rise and Demise of Lochner Era Police Powers Jurisprudence*. Duke University Press, Durham.

Gilmore, Grant (1977). *The Ages of American Law*. Yale University Press, 1977, New Haven.

Gross, Ariela (2006). *Double Character: Slavery and Mastery in the Antebellum Southern Courtroom*. University of Georgia Press, Athens.

Hall, Kermit and Ely, Jr., James W. (1989). *An Uncertain Tradition: Constitutionalism and the History of the South*. University of Georgia Press, Athens.

Herget, James (1990). *American Jurisprudence 1870–1970*. Rice University Press, Houston.

Hoeflich, Michael H. (2010). *Legal Publishing in Antebellum America*. Cambridge University Press, New York.

Holmes, Jr., Oliver Wendell (1881). *The Common Law*. Little Brown, Boston.

Holmes, Jr., Oliver Wendell (1897). "The Path of the Law." *Harvard Law Review* 10: 457–478.

Horwitz, Morton J. (1977). *The Transformation of American Law, 1780–1860*. Harvard University Press, Cambridge.

Horwitz, Morton J. (1992). *The Transformation of American Law, 1870–1960: The Crisis of Legal Orthodoxy*. Oxford University Press, New York.

Hovenkamp, Herbert (1991). *Enterprise and American Law, 1836–1937*. Harvard University Press, Cambridge, Massachusetts.

Huebner, Timothy S. (1999). *The Southern Judicial Tradition: State Judges and Sectional Distinctiveness, 1790–1890*. University of Georgia Press, Athens.

Hull, N.E.H. (1997). *Roscoe Pound and Karl Llewellyn: Searching for an American Jurisprudence*. University of Chicago Press, Chicago.

Hurst, J. Willard (1956). *Law and the Conditions of Freedom*. University of Wisconsin Press, Madison.

Kalman, Laura (1986). *Legal Realism at Yale 1927–1960*. University of North Carolina Press, Chapel Hill.

Karsten, Peter (1997). *Heart Versus Head: Judge-Made Law in Nineteenth-Century America*. University of North Carolina Press, Chapel Hill.

Kens, Paul (1990). *Judicial Power and Reform Politics: The Anatomy of Lochner v. New York*. University Press of Kansas, Lawrence.

Kens, Paul (1997). *Justice Stephen Field: Shaping Liberty from the Gold Rush to the Gilded Age*. University Press of Kansas, Lawrence.

Kens, Paul (1998). *Lochner v. New York: Economic Regulation on Trial*. University Press of Kansas, Lawrence.

Kimball, Bruce (2009). *The Inception of Modern Professional Education: C.C. Langdell, 1826–1906*. University of North Carolina Press, Chapel Hill.

Kreitner, Roy (2006). *Calculating Promises: The Emergence of Modern American Contract Doctrine*. Cambridge University Press, New York.

LaPiana, William P. (1994). *Logic and Experience: The Origin of Modern American Legal Education*. Oxford University Press, New York.

Levy, Leonard (1957). *Law and the Commonwealth of Chief Justice Shaw*. Harvard University Press, Cambridge.

Menand, Louis (2000). *The Metaphysical Club*. Farrar, Straus, and Giroux, New York.

Miller, Perry (1965). *The Life of the Mind in America*. Harcourt, Brace, New York.

Morris, Thomas D. (1999). *Southern Slavery and the Law*. University of North Carolina Press, Chapel Hill.

Nelson, William E. (1974). "The Impact of the Antislavery Movement upon Styles of Judicial Reasoning in Nineteenth Century America." *Harvard Law Review* 87: 513–566.

Newmyer, R. Kent (1985). *Supreme Court Justice Joseph Story: Statesman of the Old Republic*. University of North Carolina Press, Chapel Hill.

Novak, William (1996). *The People's Welfare: Law and Regulation in Nineteenth-Century America*. University of North Carolina Press, Chapel Hill.

Parker, Kunal M. (2006). "Context in History and Law: A Study of the Late Nineteenth-Century American Jurisprudence of Custom." *Law and History Review* 24: 473–518.

Polenberg, Richard (1997). *The World of Benjamin Cardozo: Personal Values and the Judicial Process*. Harvard University Press, Cambridge.

Purcell, Jr., Edward A. (1973). *The Crisis of Democratic Theory: Scientific Naturalism & the Problem of Value*. University Press of Kentucky, Lexington.

Purcell, Jr., Edward A. (2000). *Brandeis and the Progressive Constitution: Erie, the Judicial Power, and the Politics of the Federal Courts in Twentieth-Century America*. Yale University Press, New Haven.

Ross, William G. (1994a). *A Muted Fury: Populists, Progressives and Labor Unions Confront the Courts, 1890–1937*. Princeton University Press, Princeton, NJ.

Ross, William G. (1994b). *Forging New Freedoms: Nativism, Education, and the Constitution, 1917–1927*. University of Nebraska Press, Lincoln.

Rumble, Wilfred E. (1968). *American Legal Realism: Skepticism, Reform, and the Judicial Process*. Cornell University Press, Ithaca.

Schlegel, John Henry (1995). *American Legal Realism and Empirical Social Science*. University of North Carolina Press, Chapel Hill.

Siegel, Stephen A. (2002). "The Revision Thickens." *Law and History Review* 20: 631–637.

Tamanaha, Brian Z. (2009). *Beyond the Formalist-Realist Divide: The Role of Politics in Judging*. Princeton University Press, Princeton, NJ.

Tomlins, Christopher (1993). *Law, Labor and Ideology in the Early American Republic*. Cambridge University Press, New York.

Tushnet, Mark (1981). *The American Law of Slavery, 1810–1860: Considerations of Humanity and Interest*. Princeton University Press, Princeton, NJ.

Twining, William (1973). *Karl Llewellyn and the Realist Movement*. Wiedenfeld and Nicolson, London.

White, G. Edward (1976). *The American Judicial Tradition: Profiles of Leading American Judges*. Oxford University Press, New York.

White, G. Edward (1980) *Tort Law in America: An Intellectual History*. Oxford University Press, New York.

White, G. Edward (1995). *Justice Oliver Wendell Holmes: Law and the Inner Self*. Oxford University Press, New York.

White, G. Edward (1997). "The American Law Institute and the Triumph of Modernist Jurisprudence." *Law and History Review* 15: 1–47.

White, Morton (1947). *Social Thought in America: The Revolt against Formalism*. Oxford University Press, Oxford.

Wiecek, William M. (1977). *The Sources of Antislavery Constitutionalism in America, 1760–1848*. Cornell University Press, Ithaca.

Wiecek, William M. (1998). *The Lost World of Classical Legal Thought: Law and Ideology in America, 1886–1937*. Oxford University Press, New York.

Willrich, Michael (2003). *City of Courts: Socializing Justice in Progressive Era Chicago*. Cambridge University Press, New York.

Chapter Twenty-seven

CRITICAL LEGAL STUDIES

John Henry Schlegel

Critical Legal Studies (CLS) is best seen as both a short-lived movement in American legal thought and a group of American law teachers who were associated with the Conference on Critical Legal Studies. The movement first gained notice with the publication of Roberto Unger's book *Knowledge and Politics* in 1975. The Conference, the tangible embodiment of the group, had its first meeting in 1977. Yet, by 1990 the movement had lost what intellectual cohesiveness it once had and the Conference on Critical Legal Studies had stopped meeting regularly. CLS survives, however, as one of many "perspectives" that academic law recognizes as an appropriate basis for analyzing law.

As very few people today know the theory generally shared by the CLS movement and group, theory that inflected the distinctive historical studies that are the subject of this chapter, and understanding this work is quite difficult without understanding that theory, what follows next is a brief summary of the three major propositions that CLS historians more or less accepted.

The first proposition, known as the indeterminacy thesis, asserted that since law was structured as a system of binary oppositions it allowed two opposed conclusions in any significantly litigated case. The second, known as the critique of rights, asserted that because of the indeterminacy at the heart of law, rights could and would be manipulated in the interest of the dominant forces in a given society and so provided limited protection from the actions of others or the state for individuals and groups outside those dominant forces. These two assertions were drawn together in the phrase "law is politics," which conveyed the idea that the results in individual cases

A Companion to American Legal History, First Edition.
Edited by Sally E. Hadden and Alfred L. Brophy.
© 2013 John Wiley & Sons Ltd. Published 2021 by John Wiley & Sons Ltd.

were less likely to reflect the neutral application of legal rules, than the range of considerations regularly brought to bear in partisan political dispute. The third proposition followed from the conclusion that law is politics. It asserted that, since legal rules had no determinate force in legal decision-making, they often served to legitimate choices made in support of dominant social interests, choices that were neither inevitable nor disinterested.

Together these three propositions suggested that historical study might be useful for explicating the way that what might appear to be solid legal doctrine hid choices made that were seen as obvious, even necessary, but were anything of the kind. But the type of historical study implied was anything but specified. Given that most CLS scholars were law professors, it is not wholly surprising that a significant portion of the most prominent historical work centered on the history of legal doctrine seen as a species of intellectual history modestly related to the history of ideas. Such was not an uncontested choice. Some CLS scholars preferred historical study less directly tied to legal doctrine and more steeped in the context in which law was done and experienced. The resulting dispute produced more than a few articles, though one captured the majority position particularly effectively – Robert Gordon's "Critical Legal Histories" (1984a).

Theory and a Good Set of Examples

This piece began with a long, elegant criticism of what Gordon rightly claimed to be the standard evolutionary functionalist understanding of the place of law in society, the notion that law *necessarily* responds and adapts to the needs of the society in which it is found. He found such understandings, as well as contemporary attempts to shore them up, to be insufficient to capture the way that the distinctions between law and society, law and economy, law and the family obscured the constitutive part that law played in social life, the way that law "has been imbricated in and has helped to structure the most routine practices of social life" (1984a: 125). He then praised, though not uncritically, the effort of CLS scholars to contribute to the history of legal consciousness and on pragmatic grounds defended their use of appellate case law and treatises as sources for understanding such consciousness.

The dissenting scholars' position was seldom put into print in the CLS years, though Gordon knew it well. They conceded the implausibility of the proposition that law was necessarily functional, but believed that nevertheless law often was functional and so that the pursuit of functional understandings of law ought to be central to critical historical scholarship. And for them, the fact that law played a constitutive role in social life implied that social life played a constitutive role in law and so that the study of social life was just as likely to expose the structure of the joint construct – law/life – as was the study of legal consciousness. These scholars thus focused on the history of social/economic/family life.

The impact of propositions such as Gordon and others offered about the writing of history in a critical vein can be seen by examining in sequence three works by individuals who shared a wall between their offices at the Harvard Law School. Morton Horwitz's *The Transformation of American Law, 1780–1860* (1977); Duncan Kennedy's "Toward an Historical Understanding of Legal Consciousness" (1980); and Horwitz's *The Transformation of American Law, 1870–1960* (1992). All three scholarly presentations directly addressed legal consciousness, though not in the same way.

Horwitz's (1977) argument is simple to state. In the years between 1780 and 1860 changes in the common law (and, to a lesser extent, statutes) altered the substance of the law from a set of rules that reflected an agrarian world where the protection of existing uses and social relationships was paramount to a set of rules that undermined existing uses and social relationships in the name of being more amenable to economic development. In addition, the book asserted that these changes were in fact supportive of the economic development that they were said to facilitate and also had the effect of altering the distribution of wealth away from those who relied on traditional modes of agricultural and craft employment for their place in the society and towards those engaged in entrepreneurial and commercial activity.

Horwitz received much criticism for not recognizing that this particular change in the common law started earlier (and inferentially for the assertion that the change caused the redistribution of wealth from one social class to another). However, the more interesting thing for present purposes was that he had made a functional argument – changes in the law were intended to, and did, assist economic growth led by entrepreneurial and commercial interests – but not a necessitarian one, an intellectual position that Gordon (1984a: 61, n.11) had considered, but explicitly rejected.

The final chapter of Horwitz (1977) previewed the coming of what was called formalism, the shift from a substantive (economic development) to a formal (internal logic) justification for the content of law. This shift was said to be a strategy for preserving the gains that the entrepreneurial and commercial classes had made against the expected push back from economic interests that had been disfavored by the change. Kennedy (1980) distanced itself from Horwitz (1977) by speaking of classical, not formalist legal thought, and emphasizing a more structuralist understanding of law.

Kennedy (1980) presented what it called "classical legal thought" through an examination of *Lochner v. New York* and *In re Debs* to make an important historical point: At least during the years dominated by classical legal thought, judges did not think of law functionally, but as a closed deductive system of logical entailment, founded on the notion of the judiciary as the umpire of a system of law based on entities – individuals, corporations and governments – whose powers were "absolute within their spheres" (1980: 5).

The piece made it clear that it denied "the importance neither of ideologies like laissez-faire, nor of concrete economic interests, nor the underlying structure of political power," but insisted that legal consciousness, "an entity with a measure of autonomy," was "a set of concepts and intellectual operations that evolves according to a pattern of its own, and exercises an influence on results distinguishable from those of political power and economic interest." Thus, legal consciousness, which included "larger structures of social thought and action," and "which has its own structure," "mediates" the influence of power and interest "on particular legal results." It thus constituted a "third tier between interest or power and outcomes" that "greatly complicates the task of historical exposition" (1980: 4).

Somewhat inconsistently, the piece mostly expounded the classical underpinnings of the two classic cases and paid but modest attention to the other two tiers – power and interest, the centerpieces of Horwitz's understanding of antebellum law. Still, in response, Horwitz (1992) chose to give "cultural factors somewhat more explanatory weight," though continuing "to insist that the development of law cannot be understood independently of social context" (1992, vii).

While in Horwitz (1977) cases were buttressed with the discussion of the early treatise literature, in Horwitz (1992) the form of argument was reversed. Simultaneously, the structuring force to the narrative shifted from a struggle between agrarian interests and commercial and manufacturing interests, fought out primarily in the courts, to a struggle between Classical Legal Thought and Progressive Legal Thought, primarily fought out in the bookstores and academic journals. In this latter struggle, academic writers, and sometimes judges in their opinions, were, if Classical partisans, resisting or, if Progressive partisans, attempting to master, "the massive centralization of economic power" and "the dislocating forces of urbanization, massive immigration and industrialization" (1992: 4). Power and interest had been moved from the center of discussion to the periphery; formal legal thought, from the periphery to the center.

This is not to say that the book was less than forthright when asserting the importance of social context for understanding law, but only that the choice to focus on the mandarin literature of law, a literature that strove for ever more generality of principle and so abstraction from context, a choice that Kennedy recommended and Gordon defended, meant that it would be difficult to tie context to power and interest. What sufficed were explanatory statements such as "Economic specialization and organizational complexity moved agency law to center stage" (1992: 39); or "In general, there appears to be a strong correlation between the rise of the corporation and the emergence of an anti-individualistic objective theory in all fields of law" (1992: 45); or "[T]he doctrine of apparent authority had grown by leaps and bounds during the last two decades of the nineteenth century in response to the growing prominence of the corporate form in business relations" (1992: 46).

Now, none of these statements was in any way unsound. However, the explanation offered for their causal chasteness, that the demise of "objective causation" and the concomitant rise in multi-causal modes of explanation made it impossible to offer stronger statements – "As one sees both theories and causes as more contingent, one's belief in one's own objectivity is also drawn into question" (1992: viii) – demonstrated a continuing tie to notions of deterministic scientific method that might have led readers to question its author's asserted rejection of notions of objective causation.

Narrower Fields of Historical Inquiry

Most of the historical work by scholars indentified with Critical Legal Studies was not of the broad sweep exemplified by the work of Horwitz and Kennedy. And only sometimes was it of the kind envisioned by Gordon and Kennedy. It ranged from detailed studies of rather narrow, usually doctrinally delimited, areas of law to suggestive rather than detailed pieces of various kinds. Nor was this work uniformly distributed over doctrinal categories or even possible non-doctrinal categories. Work in four areas, two doctrinal (constitutional and labor law), and two non-doctrinal (legal profession and theory), provide a sound overview of CLS scholarship and so I have concentrated on them. Examples of scholarship in other areas are noted below under Further Reading.

Constitutional Law

Four pieces on constitutional law provide a good introduction to the real range of CLS historical practice. James Kainen (1982) is a classic example of CLS doctrinal history. The piece demonstrated how the limits on, and changes in, federal jurisdiction first created Contracts Clause law and then destroyed its ability to protect property rights as the legal understanding of property expanded from land and other physical things to include the rights of persons in an increasingly intangible world of commerce. It also showed how the substantive rights of property created by the Supreme Court in decisions under the diversity jurisdiction made accessible an understanding of the judicial function that allowed the Court to shift its protection of property from the Contracts Clause's limited range to the potentially broader substantive due process clause of the Fourteenth Amendment.

Treanor (1985) similarly showed how the English idea that property is protected from executive, but not legislative takings, was transformed in America to a right that protected property from both, then traveled from federal to state Constitutional law. It then explained the problems for taxation and regulation that accompanied the expansion of the dephysicalization of property discussed by Kainen (1982).

Both pieces were grounded in the nineteenth-century shift from republican to liberal ideas about the nature of political authority. Others explored this topic. Horwitz (1987) used the generally accepted understanding of republican and liberal political theory – the former grounded in a vision of an active political community of shared values and the latter with no grounding other than the absolute differences of human interests one from another – to explore the process by which liberalism undermined republican ideas about the substantive content of law and so brought with it the idea of the neutral, non-redistributionist state. It then tried to show that any legal version of liberal law contained within it a vision of the substantive content of law that liberalism denied.

Konefsky (1981) picked up this story in the early part of the twentieth century. It contrasted the biographies of four political scientists, all rural boys who came to the big city and worried about the survival of democracy in urban life, but were stymied in their pursuit of a grounding for that life, with biographies of three law professors, immigrants all, who also had faith in American democracy born of the choices it offered them, but who, in the aftermath of Legal Realism, could find support for democratic life only in orderly process. The piece then suggested that, while all these men of great faith in democracy were surely more worthy of attention than contemporary scholars with little faith, the failure of their attempts to justify democracy could be traced to an unwillingness, part of the liberal political theory that they shared, to embrace a substantive understanding of democracy that directly addressed capitalism.

Any more than cursory examination of these four pieces should suggest that the primary question addressed by CLS historians was the change in legal thought/theory during the "Long Nineteenth Century (1789–1920)".[1] Though such would be too narrow an understanding, it would not be a mistake. While CLS scholars offered up various specifications of the thought that made up both parts of that change and various specifications of when that transition took place, most contrasted some variety of pre-liberal political theory and liberal political theory. This shift is implicit in Kainen (1982) and Treanor (1985), and more explicit with Horwitz (1987) and Konefsky (1981).

Labor Law

The major area of concern to CLS historians was labor law. Atleson (1983), someone who regularly denied the identification of his work with CLS because of his interest in social scientific research and the group's antipathy to such, provides the basic critical understanding of labor law. This book proceeded from a perceived disjuncture between the text of the National Labor Relations Act and the decisions rendered under this Act. It examined many of these decisions in an attempt to determine what values and so assumptions about labor informed them. It identified a large set – production must be maintained; capital must be allowed mobility; unless controlled, employees will act irresponsibly; and labor is clearly the very junior partner in the common enterprise that management and labor are engaged, and, as such, is expected to treat management with deference and respect and not interfere with managerial prerogatives – and tied these values and assumptions to the nineteenth-century common law of master and servant as reshaped by the notion of free contract, a set of ideas that presumably were to be superseded by the National Labor Relations Act.

Most CLS work in labor law was concerned with understanding how the state of affairs identified by Atleson came to be. Steinfeld (1991) attempted to understand how indentured servitude came to disappear in the early nineteenth century, how what is known of as free labor today – employees able to leave a job at will and employers able to fire workers at will as well – came to be the dominant way of understanding labor during that century.

The book began in the fourteenth century, a time when almost no workers could be called free in the sense of not being subject to a regime of legal compulsion that established the term of the labor agreement and often the rate of pay, as well as provided legal process for securing a worker's faithful completion of that term. It then traced several variations on this general set of obligations and charted the subtle and interconnected changes to them in both England and the American Colonies over the succeeding five hundred years. Over these years the understanding that the labor relationship was somehow a mixture of both jurisdiction over the laborer and property in him changed first to one where jurisdiction over the laborer disappeared, but property in the worker's labor could be transferred by agreement, then finally to one that emphasized contract, freely entered into. Simultaneously, legal compulsion was replaced by compulsion based on economic need. In America, as part of this change, indentured servitude came to be seen not as labor freely contracted for, but as unfree labor, suspiciously close to slave labor, and so came first to be disfavored, and then disappeared.

Becker (1983) detailed a piece of Steinfeld's story by focusing on the British woolen and worsted industry in the eighteenth century. As that industry changed from being an interrelated network of individual producers plying narrow trades to production of goods by a small manufacturers, owners of raw materials acted to create a product by serially entrusting the materials to tradesmen, each of whom would perform a small part of the production process. This "putting out" system conflicted with an older, customary practice that allowed apprentices and journeymen to use the master's tools and to take as their own the leftovers from any process. The new class of manufacturers objected to these customary practices and used the criminal law in an attempt to suppress them.

Two scholars looked carefully at the early nineteenth-century American cases in which labor unionists were prosecuted for conspiring against their employers or others. Holt (1986) examined these cases, not for the legal doctrine, but for the arguments made on behalf of the workers and for the judicial response to them. The workers' arguments focused on the destruction of the life of the independent journeyman, rooted in a community of masters and journeymen exercising traditional skills and practices, as that life was transformed into the wageworker, a transformation that both Steinfeld (1991) and Becker (1983) chronicled, though in different ways. Judicial opinions showed a pattern of judicial indifference to the workers' arguments, hostility to their objectives and support for the developing entrepreneurial capitalism represented by the masters, even when, as was the case with Justice Shaw's opinion in *Commonwealth v. Hunt*, the result reached supported the Journeymen's position.

Konefsky (1989) also focused on *Commonwealth v. Hunt*, but instead of being compared to other labor injunction cases, it was compared to *Farwell v. Boston & Worchester Railroad*, Shaw's case that contributed to establishing the fellow-servant rule in tort. Though not rejecting Holt's analysis of *Hunt* in terms of class bias, the piece examined the role of the freedom of contract analysis that Shaw used to bridge the republican political ideology of virtue in a community and the liberal political ideology that accompanied the expansion of commercial capitalism. Here, the "free" in freedom of contract drew on the notion of freedom inherent in republican ideology, as well as on the notion that freely contracting individuals would bring prosperity to the state. It thus allowed economic individualism to don the mantle of republican virtue.

Forbath (1985) noted that republican thought allowed for two readings of free labor. One was an understanding that rooted freedom in the possession of property as the prerequisite for participation in citizenship; the other took freedom in a more literal sense – as the freedom to sell one's labor. Both notions were part of the many strands of thought that led to northern abolitionism in the years before the Civil War and that coalesced in the adoption of the Fourteenth Amendment. Forbath saw Justice Field's dissent in the *Slaughterhouse Cases* as the basis for the diffusion of the second, liberal notion of freedom that infused substantive due process decisions protecting the formal freedom of both labor and management to contract. He contrasted this notion with that of many labor organizations, particularly the Knights of Labor, that fought for the alternative, republican understanding of free labor and so for cooperative ownership of production process in order to secure labor's participation in civic life.

Feinman (1976) addressed the topic of employment at will, a doctrine that crystallized in the late nineteenth century. After presenting a brief summary of the changing structure of employment relations in the years after the Revolution, it emphasized the logical incompatibility of the English rule that presumed employment for a year with the prevailing contract doctrine that emphasized the will of the parties. However, Fineman rejected the notion that the employment at will rule reflected the idea of freedom of contract, for the presumption underlying that rule was equally incompatible with will theory. Instead, he suggested that, given that most of the crucial cases in New York State involved middle management of large corporate entities, the rule was developed as part of a dispute between owners of the new corporations and middle management about its role and status, especially security of such employment during periods of economic stress.

Two pieces examined labor in the Gilded Age. Stone (1974) looked at steel, an industry where old craft structures had not turned into either factory work or the "putting out" of sweated labor. As production increased, the traditional system where operatives were paid by the ton and hired their own crews out of that per ton payment, thus exercising control over both the amount of work and its pace, was maintained until the great steel strike of 1892. When the workers lost that strike, steel manufacturers introduced a system of work that through mechanization decreased the need for unskilled, as well as for skilled, workers as it transferred knowledge of production processes from workers to management. Thereafter, the steel companies introduced various practices that cemented management's control of production – individualized pay rates, hierarchical job ladders, changed ways of training skilled workers, a repositioned foreman's job, and recruitment of new managers from the college educated – as well as instituted various welfare benefits that better tied workers to their employer. This new order of production increased production and decreased costs, benefits that flowed to employees only very marginally.

Avery (1988) drew a picture of the judicial understanding of labor violence from an examination of major cases about strikes and secondary boycotts in these years. These judges saw workers as irrationally prone to violence targeting property, as intimating a willingness to engage in violence when establishing picket lines or engaging in other forms of concerted activity, and as always attempting moral coercion of others. The judges concluded that workers needed to be restrained from acting other than in the pursuit of a narrowly construed self-interest, and even then, allowed workers to engage only in the most gentlemanly of conduct.

Two pieces brought this long story of American labor down into the late twentieth century. Klare (1978) looked carefully at the period after the adoption of the Wagner Act for the roots of the contemporary understanding of labor management relations. The piece began with a brief overview of labor-management disputes before and after the passage of the Wagner Act, as well as a similar overview of the various attitudes toward the Act on the part of labor and management groups. After establishing that the text of the Act did not foreordain any particular reading of the Act's quite general provisions, it then looked at several important Supreme Court opinions that directed the development of the Act away from a possible reading that would have empowered rank and file employees to exercise even partial control of the labor relationship and toward one that emphasized contractualism, a public interest that might over-ride worker interests, union control of workers that might similarly override self-directed worker action, and a style of judicial reasoning in labor cases that would work to hide the import of these choices that might have been made otherwise.

Tomlins (1985) began with an examination of the workings of the American Federation of Labor, a federation of craft unions with a strong aversion to government intervention in labor markets that extended well beyond fighting to eliminate the availability of labor injunctions for employers opposed to recognizing and bargaining with unions. It conceived itself not as an agent for a given set of workers, but as a principal, contracting directly with an employer on behalf of a trade, in effect protecting the already organized employers and their employees from competition by an employer paying less than "union scale."

Having thus set the scene, Tomlin's book recounted in detail the push for labor legislation in the Depression years that led to the adoption of the Wagner Act and the growth of the new National Labor Relations Board's bureaucracy that attempted to develop a set of rules under the new legislation. Administrative battles raged within and without the Agency between those who championed the Act's emphasis on employee self-determination and those who emphasized its other goal of creating economic stability and increasing production of goods by ensuring labor peace. The former group saw unions as occupying the role of agent, not principal; the later group, as occupying the role of principal in disciplining and stabilizing workforce participation in continuous production, a role that came to be seen as the price of policies that both provided for the continuity of representation and financed the concomitant growth of union bureaucracies. This later view, dubbed "industrial pluralism," adopted first by the War Labor Board during World War II, and then modestly re-enforced by the Taft-Hartley Act, was ultimately dominant, affirming the old AFL's view of the role of unions as principal, but at the cost of completely undercutting its accompanying desire to escape from pervasive government control.

The number of pieces written about labor makes it easy to see the actual range of CLS historical practice. While there were no strong functionalist claims of the kind that Gordon (1984a) inveighed against, there was little of the pure explication of doctrinal structure that Kennedy (1980) practiced and advocated. The closest to Kennedy (1980) was Steinfeld (1991), which looked at doctrinal change in the light of changes in political thought, but engaged in anything but a structuralist analysis. Atleson (1983) looked at doctrine to disclose judicial assumptions about the world of workers; Avery

(1988) did the same using judicial argument; and Holt (1986) partly completed the circle by using argument as evidence of a more generalized anti-worker bias. Konefsky (1989) looked at doctrine as a way of bridging holes in political theory; Klare (1978) used political theory to understand doctrinal choice. Becker (1983) examined change in economy to understand employer invocation of law; Feinman (1976), to explain changes in doctrine. Tomlins (1985) focused on bureaucratic conflict for the shaping of doctrinal choice. Forbath (1985) focused almost exclusively on political theory; Stone (1974), almost exclusively on economic change. There is little to hold together this set of historiographic choices except a willingness to examine whatever seemed interesting in order to understand the shape of an intertwined law/capitalism in England and America over something like five hundred years; a preference to focus on the nineteenth century, hardly surprising in legal history during these years; and an underlying sense that the shift from republican to liberal political theory is relevant to certain changes in law.

Legal Profession

Two scholars did significant work on the American legal profession. Konefsky (1982) interrogated two points in Daniel Webster's career. The first was his work as a country lawyer in a small up-river town, and later down-river in Portsmouth, New Hampshire, mostly doing debt collection, a practice where litigation was largely for the purpose of securing a creditor's claim as a prelude to the attempt to force the debtor's performance of the obligation. This practice recognized the high degree of interdependence between merchants and between merchants and their customers, and so the sense that the failure of one might bring the failure of all. It also allowed for a certain degree of independence as an advocate – now and again representing creditors as well as debtors. The second, Konefsky (1983), was Webster's later work in Boston and Washington, where his practice centered in representation of the mercantile and industrial elite, a world of property and its defense, of the more impersonal marketplace. Here, both as an advocate and a political officeholder, Webster was more specialized in his role and more dependent on the fortunes of his clients. Simultaneously, his style of advocacy shifted from the more emotional to the more technical.

Konefsky (1989) looked at the same, early-nineteenth-century period, but this time attempted to buttress the argument made in Horwitz (1977) about the relationship between legal and economic elites in these years. Here Konfesky (1989) focused on Boston lawyers and contrasted two social organizations, the Anthology Society of Boston, circa 1805, a literary society dominated by ministers, but that included nearly a majority of lawyers, and The Friday Evening Club of fifty years later, with its admixture of lawyers, mercantilists and industrialists. The earlier group was concerned with the need to create order in post-revolutionary society – the more literary types, by establishing guidelines for conduct, style and taste; the lawyers, by creating a stable set of norms that could pull communities together, particularly in commercial relations. Merchants, though not members, shared this understanding of their task, emphasizing the duty of fiscal responsibility. Over time the ministers ceded their place at the center of elite Boston culture. Thereafter, the lawyers and merchants who made up elite society solidified their alliance by joint participation in economic activity, as well as in local and national politics. Just as importantly, they also built their new alliance through intermarriage. Thus, values were shared by the newer legal and economic elites because they shared political and social relationships and not just because law and economy practiced some form of action at a distance.

Robert Gordon (1983) made a first stab at answering the question that Gordon (1984a) treated more generally: What is the relationship between the abstract legal thought of lawyers and their day-to-day practice activities? Gordon (1983) began by examining, and then rejecting as "instrumental," two answers to this question – a functional response to social needs or a product of interest group politics. It similarly rejected arguments offered in support of the proposition that the Langdellian reforms of legal education were designed to serve the needs of the emerging corporate bar. Then, it posited that the writings of elite practitioners and academics shared a common ideological consciousness that ran across practice areas, as well as academic writing, law reform and public service work.

In support of this proposition, the piece first examined three versions of the notion of legal science that both academics and practitioners recognized – the antebellum Whig-Federalist and Jefferson-Jackson versions, both of which saw lawyers as engaging in the job of defining rights so as to mediate between faction; the postbellum liberal version, that saw the lawyer's job as that of establishing and policing the limits to the rights of individuals, so as to isolate those spaces where the free play of will was not limited by law; and the twentieth-century Progressive version, that saw the job of the lawyers as balancing the conflicting claims of individuals and groups within the society. Finally, focusing on liberal legal science, the piece examined two regular activities of corporate lawyers – the drafting of state incorporation statutes and individual corporate charters and the practice of corporate reorganization in bankruptcy – both of which the piece asserted were better made sense of by ideological, than instrumental, explanations.

A much briefer companion piece, Gordon (1984b), attempted to explain the way that corporate lawyers made sense of their law reform activities aimed at making the law into a more integrated, more certain whole, at a time when their practice activities were destroying certainty and so wholeness. After surveying the ways in which wholeness was destroyed and noting the three responses that lawyers did not make – withdrawing into traditional practice, officially segmenting the bar on the English model into elite barristers and ordinary corporate technicians, and reinvigorating the notion of law as a public calling – the piece examined three strategies taken – raising legal science into rarified abstractions completely divorced from practice, following the Progressive program of instituting more effective local institutions of law, and promoting corporatist positions. When none of these ideologies received general acceptance, the bar took three divergent paths – the reactionary embrace of liberal legal science, the schizophrenic idea that lawyers needed to take time off from practice to engage in public service, and the withdrawal into the role of apolitical technician.

Legal Theory

Kennedy (1979) presented a profoundly structural analysis of Blackstone's *Commentaries* by focusing on what to contemporary sensibilities seemed to be anomalies in that work's organizational categories. This analysis was designed to illuminate the apologetic, and so legitimating, strategies behind Blackstone's defense of English law from liberal criticism. It began with what Kennedy asserted is the "fundamental contradiction" with which liberalism must deal: The free individual's wish to connect with others and that individual's fear that others will not connect, but rather dominate or oppress the self, as well as the possibility that if the State came to the aid of the individual so as to prevent domination, in doing so it too might dominate or oppress the self.

The piece then sequentially looked at Blackstone's distinction between rights and wrongs, which was designed to demonstrate that the writ system was not irrational; its distinction between the absolute and relative rights of persons, which was designed to demonstrate that the status hierarchies still embedded in the common law were not contrary to the rights of Englishmen because they were both convenient for securing rights and implicitly consented to by free men; and its distinction between things real and things personal, which was designed to demonstrate that the state of English property law protected freedom by having overthrown feudal property law. Together these propositions served to legitimate the status quo and, together with the notion of rights itself, worked to show that the rule of law mediated the fundamental contradiction.

Mensch (1982) told the story of legal thought in America for the two hundred years after the American Revolution. It argued that the pre-classical world that Kennedy (1979) explicated and which was refined during the classical era that Kennedy (1980) explicated were intellectually destroyed by American Legal Realism. However, as a practical matter Realism was an incomplete project in that it allowed scholars to construct many new versions of liberal legal thought, all subject to the Realist critique, but not defeated by it.

Schlegel (1989) also addressed the fate of American Legal Realism, though from inside the legal academy. The piece noted that though the law professors said that they were teaching their students to "think like a lawyer," they were primarily teaching their students the rules of law, and that the intellectual challenge of reordering law begun in the 1870s that formed a part of the law professors' professional identity was over before World War I. Realism suggested that, with this task completed, law professors should look outside of the law reports to understand law and that the resulting understanding should be brought back into the law schools. After Realism had died as an active force in the legal academy, the law professors were still faced with teaching students the rules of law. With all sorts of academic professionals better able to examine law outside of the reports, it was simply easier for post-World War II legal academics to reenact their existing professional identity than to pick up where Realism had left off. So, the law professors repeatedly chose to play with varieties of theory that fit with their day-to-day teaching activities.

CLS writing on legal profession and legal theory are best treated together, as these topics are largely separable from doctrinal considerations. Here Schlegel (1989) explains behavior with explicit causal, and sometimes instrumental, arguments, seen as sufficient, but not necessary. Konefsky (1982) and Konefsky (1983) are more suggestive than explicitly causal, leaving the reader to infer causation, while Konefsky (1989) provides evidence to support the causal argument made in Horwitz (1977). Filling out the range of CLS approaches to history is Gordon (1983, 1984a) who worked hard to supply causal, but ideological, rather than instrumental, explanations for lawyer behavior, while Kennedy (1979) embraced ideology, but eschewed causation, and Mensch (1982) eschewed ideology for clean description.

Some Modest Observations

As shown by examining the work on constitutional law or labor or legal profession and theory, whatever Gordon (1984a) or Kennedy (1980) might have said, CLS historical practice was not based on a distinctive understanding of method in legal history. What then holds that practice together such as to justify inclusion in this book? Surely CLS scholars were not the first to recognize the there was a significant change in law and legal theory during the Long Nineteenth Century or that in the years after 1865 there was a significant change in the institutions of legal practice. And those others tried to explain these changes too.

Here I think that it is important to return to where I began – the three propositions that CLS scholars more or less accepted. If the structure of law rendered its content logically indeterminate to the extent that rights could and would be manipulated in the interest of dominant forces in a given society, and decisions undertaking such manipulation could and would be articulated in terms that hopefully legitimated the choices made, then for a group of scholars as deeply disaffected from law as taught and understood in the 1960s and 1970s, as were those who identified with CLS, the question of how American society came to its present state might well, and did, loom large. If method did not hold the group together, critique from a particular political perspective thus could.

Although the personal politics of members of the group ranged from Holt's Marxism all the way to Schlegel's Midwestern populism, as well as off in several vectors from various points on that wobbly line, all these positions were somewhere to the left of the liberal wing of the Democratic Party. Despite all of the possible political arguments that might have been developed from their differing positions, CLS historians suppressed these possible disputes and instead affirmed a critique of common understandings of law as taught and thought. For a time, their affirmation served as a common bond and their history grew out of that bond.

This is most clear among the labor historians, but also reasonably obvious in Konefsky (1981) and Horwitz (1987) on constitutional law, Konefsky (1982, 1983, 1988) and Gordon (1983, 1984b) on legal profession, as well as Mensch (1982) and Schlegel (1989) on legal theory. In each of these pieces there is a sense of devolution … from what? Not a decline from some golden age. There is no golden age thought among the CLS historians. But, perhaps from the promise of republican thought in the years of the early republic, or of the postbellum constitutional amendments, or of the New Deal. Often this sense of decline seems to be a result of the growth of industrial capitalism.

The major exceptions to this feeling of devolution are the doctrinal work of Kennedy (1980) and students from Harvard in these years, of which Kainen (1982) and Treanor (1985) provide good examples. Filio-piety is hardly a bad thing when the work produced is so good, and, as for Kennedy, whose politics is often supposed, if not known, it is important to remember that the point of his patient work on classical legal thought was to highlight the extent to which choices that were made way back then were still possible now and so to undermine the sense that current choices were far more limited than the current version of neo-Blackstonian apologetics seemed to admit.

Even when evaluating doctrinal scholarship from CLS, it should be remembered that most CLS historians were or soon would be faculty teaching in law schools. Doctrinal work was, or soon would be, of use both daily in the classroom and also when trying to engage other law teachers in discussion. Less useful, it seems to me, would be to tie CLS doctrinal work to the fight over instrumentalism/functionalism, a fight that was treated as presenting an either/or alternative to the history of legal doctrine/political theory, for it is a mistake to see this question as one of either/or, rather than of both/and.

While it was fun to engage in these arguments, they were not significantly reflected in the scholarship produced, and so in the end were not as important as the participants, myself included, might clearly have thought.

From time to time people ask me to explain what happened to the CLS movement, as have your editors. The shortest answer, perhaps the truest, is that like American Legal Realism, CLS disappeared as does water poured into sand. Lives changed, families grew, people aged. New movements appeared – feminist theory and critical race theory – that shared the politics that kept CLS together, but not the commitment to ungroundedness. But, what did not appear were any new CLS ideas with the power of either the indeterminacy thesis or the critique of rights. The movement's fifteen minutes of Warholian fame was over.

Which is not to say that the scholars, including especially the historians, who were part of the movement did not keep producing work with an identifiable CLS voice. Many did, though some moved on to other activities and a few came to reject their earlier work. Likewise, new scholars have arisen whose work bears a similar voice. It is not that the water was wasted, but rather that the Sahara of legal scholarship that the CLS movement sought to challenge slowly covered over the place into which the water was poured. CLS became just another perspective on law, recognized in the act of being marginalized.

A Note on Histories and Bibliographies

Two works speak directly to the history of Critical Legal Studies: Schlegel (1984) and Tushnet (1991). Two bibliographies attempt to cover the field for somewhat different perspectives even than my own: Kennedy and Klare (1984), as supplemented by Newman (1986), and Bauman (1996).

Notes

1 Grossberg, M and Tomlins, C., eds (2008) *The Cambridge History of Law in America* 3: xv.

References

Atleson, J.B. (1983). *Values and Assumptions in American Labor Law*. University of Massachusetts Press, Amherst.

Avery, D. (1988). "Images of Violence in Labor Jurisprudence: The Regulation of Picketing and Boycotts, 1894–1921." *Buffalo Law Review* 37: 1–117.

Bauman, R.W. (1996). *Critical Legal Studies: A Guide to the Literature*. Westview, New York.

Becker, C. (1983). "Property in the Workplace: Labor, Capital, and Crime in the Eighteenth-Century British Woolen and Worsted Industry." *Virginia Law Review* 69: 1487–1515.

Feinman, J.M. (1976). "The Development of the Employment at Will Rule." *American Journal of Legal History* 20: 118–135.

Forbath, W. (1985). "The Ambiguities of Free Labor: Labor and the Law in the Gilded Age." *Wisconsin Law Review* 1985: 767–817.

Gawalt, G.W. (1984). *The New High Priests: Lawyers in Post-Civil War America*. Greenwood Press, Westport, CT,.

Geison, G.L. (1983). *Professions and Professional Ideologies in America*. University of North Carolina Press, Chapel Hill.

Gordon, R.W. (1983). "Legal Thought and Legal Practice in the Age of American Enterprise, 1870–1920." In Geison, ed., *Professions and Professional Ideologies in America*, 70–139. University of North Carolina Press, Chapel Hill.

Gordon, R.W. (1984a). "Critical Legal Histories." *Stanford Law Review* 36: 57–125.

Gordon, R.W. (1984b). "'The Ideal and the Actual in Law': Fantasies and Practices of New York City Lawyers, 1870–1910." In Gawalt, ed., *The New High Priests: Lawyers in Post-Civil War America*, 51–74. Westport, Boston.

Holt, W. (1986). "Labor Conspiracy Cases in the United States, 1805–1842: Bias and Legitimation in Common Law Adjudication." *Osgoode Hall Law Journal* 22: 591–663.

Horwitz, M.J. (1977). *The Transformation of American Law, 1780–1860*. Oxford University Press, New York.

Horwitz, M.J. (1987). "Republicanism and Liberalism in American Constitutional History." *William and Mary Law Review* 29: 57–74.

Horwitz, M.J. (1992). *The Transformation of American Law, 1870–1960*. Oxford University Press, New York.

Joerges, C. and Trubek, D., eds (1989). *Critical Legal Thought: An American-German Debate*. Nomos, Berlin.

Kainen, J. (1982). "Nineteenth Century Interpretations of the Federal Contract Clause: The Transformation From Vested to Substantive Rights Against the State." *Buffalo Law Review* 31: 381–480.

Kairys, D. (1982). *The Politics of Law: A Progressive Critique*. Basic Books, New York.

Kennedy, D. (1979). "The Structure of Blackstone's Commentaries." *Buffalo Law Review* 28: 205–382.

Kennedy, D. (1980). "Toward an Historical Understanding of Legal Consciousness: The Case of Classical Legal Thought in America, 1850–1940." In Spitzer, ed., *Research in Law and Sociology*, 3–24. Jai Press, Greenwich, CT.

Kennedy, D. and Klare, K. (1984). "A Bibliography of Critical Legal Studies." *Yale Law Journal* 94: 461–490.

Klare, K. (1978). "Judicial Deradicalization of the Wagner Act and the Origins of Modern Legal Consciousness, 1937–1941." *Minnesota Law Review* 62: 265–339.

Konefsky, A.S. (1981). "Men of Great and Little Faith: Generations of Constitutional Scholarship." *Buffalo Law Review* 30: 365–384.

Konefsky, A.S. (1982). "Introduction." In Konefsky and King, eds. *The Papers of Daniel Webster (Vol. 1): Legal Papers, The New Hampshire Practice*, xxxi–ix. The University Press of New England, Hanover.

Konefsky, A.S. (1988) "Law and Culture in Antebellum Boston." *Stanford Law Review* 40: 1119–1159.
Konefsky, A.S. (1989). "'As Best Subserve Their Own Interests': Lemuel Shaw, Labor Conspiracy and Fellow Servants." *Law and History Review* 7: 219–239.
Konefsky, A.S. and King, A.J., eds (1982). *The Papers of Daniel Webster (Vol. 1): Legal Papers, The New Hampshire Practice.* The University Press of New England, Hanover.
Konefsky, A.S. and King, A.J., eds (1983). *The Papers of Daniel Webster (Vol. 2): Legal Papers, The New Hampshire Practice.* The University Press of New England, Hanover.
Mensch, E. (1982). "The History of Mainstream Legal Thought." In Kairys, ed., *The Politics of Law: A Progressive Critique*, 18–39. Basic Books, New York.
Newman, M.S. (1986). "A Bibliography of the Critical Legal Studies Movement, 1984–1986." New York Law School, New York.
Schlegel, J.H. (1984). "Notes Toward an Intimate, Opinionated, and Affectionate History of the Conference on Critical Legal Studies." *Stanford Law Review* 36: 391–411.
Schlegel, J.H. (1989). "American Legal Theory and American Legal Education: A Snake Swallowing its Tail?" In Joerges and Trubek, eds. *Critical Legal Thought: An American-German Debate*, 49–84. Nomos, Berlin.
Spitzer, S., ed. (1980). *Research in Law and Sociology* [vol.3]. Jai Press, Greenwich, CT.
Steinfeld, R. (1991). *The Invention of Free Labor: The Employment Relation in English and American Law and Culture, 1350–1870.* University of North Carolina Press, Chapel Hill.
Stone, K.v.W. (1974). "The Origins of Job Structures in the Steel Industry." *Review of Radical Political Economics* 6: 113–173.
Tomlins, C. (1985). *The State and the Unions: Law, Labor Relations and the Organized Labor Movement in the United States, 1880–1960.* Cambridge University Press, New York.
Treanor, W.M. (1985). "The Origins and Significance of the Just Compensation Clause of the Fifth Amendment." *Yale Law Journal* 94: 694–716.
Tushnet, M. (1991). "Critical Legal Studies: A Political History." *Yale Law Journal* 100: 1515–1544.
Unger, R.M. (1975). *Knowledge and Politics.* Simon and Schuster, New York.

Further Reading

Alexander, G.S. (1987). "The Transformation of Trusts as a Legal Category, 1800–1914", *Law and History Review* 5: 303–350.
Auerbach, J.S. (1976). *Unequal Justice: Lawyers and Social Change in America.* Oxford University Press, New York.
Binder, G. (1986). "Angels and Infidels: Hierarchy and Historicism in Medieval Legal History." *Buffalo Law Review* 35: 527–99.
Chase, A. (1979). "The Birth of the Modern Law School." *American Journal of Legal History* 23: 329–348.

Chase, A. (1981). "Origins of Modern Professional Education: The Harvard Case method Conceived as Clinical Instruction in Law." *Nova Law Review* 5: 323–363.

Frug, G. (1980). "The City as a Legal Concept." *Harvard Law Review* 93: 1057–1154.

Harring, S.L. (1983).*Policing a Class Society: The Experience of American Cities, 1865–1915*. Rutgers University Press, New Brunswick.

Hay, D., Linebaugh, P., Rule, J.G., Thompson, E.P., and Winslow, C. (1975). *Albion's Fatal Tree: Crime and Society in Eighteenth Century England*. Pantheon Books, New York.

Horwitz, M.J. (1982). *"The Doctrine of Objective Causation."* In Kairys, ed., *The Politics of Law: A Progressive Critique*, 201–213. Basic Books, New York.

Horwitz, M.J. (1985). "*Santa Clara* Revisited: The Development of Corporate Theory." *West Virginia Law Review* 88: 173–224.

Mensch, E. (1981). "Freedom of Contract as Ideology." *Stanford Law Review* 33: 753–772.

Mensch, E. (1982). "The Colonial Origins of Liberal Property Rights." *Buffalo Law Review* 31: 635–735.

Nockleby, J.T. (1980). "Tortious Interference with Contractual Relations in the Nineteenth Century: The Transformation of Contract, Property and Tort." *Harvard Law Review* 93: 1510–1539.

Papke, D.R. (1987). *Framing the Criminal: Crime, Cultural Work, and the Loss of Perspective: 1830–1900*. Archon Books, Hamden.

Peller, G. (1988). "'Neutral Principles' in the 1950s." *Michigan Journal of Law Reform* 21: 561–622.

Peritz, M. (1990). "A Counter-History of Antitrust Law." *Duke Law Journal* 1990: 263–320.

Schlegel, J.H. (1985). "Between the Harvard Founders and the American Legal Realists: The Professionalization of the American Law Professor." *Journal of Legal Education* 35: 311–325.

Singer, J. (1982). "The Legal Rights Debate in Analytical Jurisprudence from Bentham to Hohfeld." *Wisconsin Law Review* 1982: 975–1059.

Soifer, A. (1987). "Status, Contract and Promises Unkept." *Yale Law Journal* 96: 1916–1959.

Thompson, E.P. (1975). *Whigs and Hunters: The Origin of the Black Act*. Pantheon Books, London.

Tushnet, M. (1981). *The American Law of Slavery, 1810–1860*. Princeton University Press, Princeton.

Vandevelde, K. (1980). "The New Property of the Nineteenth Century: The Development of the Modern Concept of Property." *Buffalo Law Review* 29: 325–367.

Chapter Twenty-eight

THE INTERNATIONAL CONTEXT: AN IMPERIAL PERSPECTIVE ON AMERICAN LEGAL HISTORY

Clara Altman

The history of U.S. global power is a history of empire-building, including the assumption of U.S. sovereignty over foreign lands and peoples, as well as less direct influence in foreign countries, such as through the promotion of global capitalism and free trade. Law has been at the center of this history since the nation's founding. Law constituted American empire.

This chapter places the historiography of American law in an imperial perspective. An imperial legal historiography centrally concerns the relationship between law and the expanding power and reach of the state. This approach to American legal history takes as its subject the new territories, peoples, cultures, and legal systems brought within the state's reach, and the legal and political mechanisms for managing the cultural, social, and legal difference engendered by expansion. In doing so, it considers the ways that law facilitated the creation and maintenance of structures of political, economic, and cultural inequality based on territorial divisions.

Until recently, the "exceptionalism" of American legal and political traditions significantly circumscribed studies about the history of U.S. global power. American law emerged from a rejection of empire. It could not itself be imperial, so the story went. To the extent that legal historians addressed U.S. global power, they hewed closely to this exceptionalist narrative by treating American empire as a contained – even "accidental" – early twentieth-century misstep and American imperialism as more benign than European forms. Within these parameters, historians treated U.S. territorial growth and colonization across the North American continent as a history of expanded republicanism, not empire-building. They viewed U.S. colonialism

A Companion to American Legal History, First Edition.
Edited by Sally E. Hadden and Alfred L. Brophy.
© 2013 John Wiley & Sons Ltd. Published 2021 by John Wiley & Sons Ltd.

at the turn of the twentieth century as a constitutional blunder and not a central part of the main lines of legal development. And they understood U.S. global power in the twentieth century in terms of the nation's influence or hegemony, but not in terms of imperialism. These intellectual contortions masked that the U.S. did what empires do: expanded the jurisdiction of the state to draw different territories, peoples, and cultures within its reach and then developed legal and political mechanisms for managing difference within its sovereign borders.

American legal histories written over the past two decades have developed a new image of U.S. global power, reflecting both the tremendous influence of the U.S. state abroad and its history as an empire. These new approaches emerged from internal developments in the study of American history as well as the agenda-setting influence of U.S. foreign affairs. Within American history, the "international" turn, combined with calls for a "return to the state" (after state power receded from view in the outpouring of cultural and social history of the 1980s and 1990s), pointed legal scholars toward questions of U.S. state power abroad. The call for understanding the relationship between law and U.S. global power gained new urgency in the wake of 9/11 and the Global War on Terrorism. Issues of executive power in foreign affairs, the rights of non-citizens at home and abroad, legality and illegality in war, and respect for international law took center stage in public discourse. Debates about American cultural hegemony in the modern world shifted toward talk of hard power and the U.S.'s formal empire. Joining the widespread reevaluation of U.S. global power taking place across various disciplines and subfields, historians of American law produced innovative studies of the reach of American law beyond U.S. borders, law and U.S. global power, and law and empire.

To trace these developments I divide the chapter into three sections: the constitutional order, the international order, and legal borderlands. These categories reflect emerging scholarship in the field and point to three broad agendas for an imperial history of American law. First, an imperial history of American law integrates the mechanisms of state power and global expansion into the history of American constitutional development. Second, it examines the ways that international law has structured American empire-building. Finally, an imperial history of American law explores the cultural and social dimensions of local encounters between distinct legal systems and their relationship to the growth of the American state. All three track the reach of the state and American law as they expand across the globe. This approach makes territories, borders, and jurisdictional boundaries on the North American continent and overseas sites of inquiry that capture the power and scale of the American empire, the legal orders that structure it, and the different legal systems within it. I conclude by suggesting that future research across these three categories take up the links between the legal history of American imperialism and the development of global capitalism, and continue to integrate the experiences of colonial subjects with imperial legal processes, discourses, and institutions in to the main lines of American legal history.

The Constitutional Order

An imperial perspective on American constitutionalism challenges many central assumptions that have shaped constitutional history. It requires understanding how structures and mechanisms of government accord tremendous power to the state to facilitate its participation in an international order of states, to enable territorial expansion and the extension of its sovereignty, and to support interventionist foreign policy. An imperial perspective recognizes the various ways American constitutionalism produces and constitutes U.S. state power.

This new imperial approach to American constitutionalism challenged core assumptions about constitutional history. Seminal texts, such as Gordon Wood's *The Creation of the American Republic* (1969), Bernard Bailyn's *The Ideological Origins of the American Revolution* (1967), and Jack P. Greene's *Peripheries and Center* (1986), described the central innovation of American constitutionalism as the development of mechanisms to restrain government power. Historians' core ideas about American constitutional development proceeded from this perspective: American constitutionalism was inward-looking from the founding, concerned primarily with the internal structure of federalism and restraints on government power. Within these parameters, the key agendas for constitutional history were to examine the historical processes through which American law, particularly Supreme Court jurisprudence, perfected the balance of power and liberty promised by the U.S. Constitution.

The traditional parameters of American constitutional history sat uncomfortably alongside the history of U.S. territorial aggrandizement, wars of conquest, and the emergence of U.S. global power. Arthur Schlesinger, Jr. (1973), Walter LaFeber (1987) and other historians pointed to the failure of American constitutional history to confront U.S. global power. At a time when criticism of postwar U.S. foreign policy grew with popular discontent over the ongoing Vietnam War, Louis Fisher (1985), among others, began to reconsider how American constitutionalism balanced foreign affairs concerns against constitutional restraints on government power. Their explanations of the apparent drift of the American state from the original promise of balanced power and liberty toward global power centered on the notion of an "imperial presidency." According to LaFeber, the history of U.S. foreign affairs showed that at times of war and foreign policy crises, "imperial presidencies, weak congresses, and cautious courts" upset the constitutional balance of power and liberty (1987: 695–696).

The imperial presidency narrative emphasized the increasing aggrandizement of executive power in foreign affairs from Presidents Jefferson, Polk, Lincoln, and McKinley in the nineteenth century to Theodore Roosevelt, Woodrow Wilson, FDR, Nixon, and Reagan in the twentieth century. It highlighted the Supreme Court's gradual concession to a powerful foreign affairs president, and a Congress that was weak in the face of war and foreign policy crises. According to LaFeber, when the U.S. emerged as a global power at the turn of the twentieth century "a strong doubt about the ability of the traditional constitutional system to deal with global issues [acted] as an acid to eat away the system's checks and balances" (1987: 708).

The imperial presidency narrative re-emerged in popular discourse as well as in historical scholarship with the onset of the Global War on Terrorism and the unilateralism of the Bush Administration (Teitel, 2003). New authors stressed that excessive executive power in the international sphere threatened liberties and the erosion of democracy at home. Several books including Geoffrey Stone's *Perilous Times* (2004) and Mark Tushnet's edited collection *The Constitution in Wartime* (2005) showed how U.S. foreign affairs shaped American constitutional law at home, and often threatened rights and liberties (Fisher, 2005). Although the imperial presidency narrative helped to redress the gap between U.S. foreign policy and prevailing narratives of American constitutionalism, it had limitations. It focused on foreign affairs crises, and emphasized bad political actors and the failure of the U.S. Supreme court to restrain them. In this narrative, American law did not create an imperial state, nor was empire foundational to American political development. Although it had failed in practice, by design American constitutionalism still ought to restrain the state from empire-building and global power. Thus, U.S. global power was less an issue of law, and more an issue of politics and foreign policy.

In recent years historians have challenged the paradigm of "imperial presidencies, weak congresses, and cautious courts" as a sufficient explanation of the relationship between American constitutionalism and the rise of U.S. global power. As John Witt (2012) and Mary Dudziak (2012) have argued, our prevailing frameworks in American legal history isolate war from American legal development by perpetuating an image of war as a temporally bounded state of exception. According to Witt, the "rupture narrative of law and war" in which law restrains power and war is lawless, is "most certainly wrong" (2010: 768). And William Novak has argued that despite the rising global power of the U.S. state throughout its history, the traditional parameters of American constitutional thought perpetuate an image of a "weak" state. As Novak writes, "the history that America most frequently tells itself highlights a story of relative powerlessness" (2008: 752).

In recent years, historians have looked beneath politics and beyond times of war to understand how American law provided the foundation for an imperial state. David Armitage (2008), and Daniel Hulsebosch and David

Golove (2010) have shown that the nation's Founders were not only concerned with the structure of federalism and the balance of powers at the founding, they also looked outward to assess the nascent nation's place in the global order. By the time of the American Revolution the Westphalian nation-state system dominated the international politics of the Western world. The Westphalian system made statehood, evidenced by ultimate political authority resting in a single legitimate sovereign, the defining characteristic of membership in the community of "civilized states." Recognition as a "civilized state" carried with it the ability to engage in international negotiations, to engage in war, and the power to demand that foreign governments keep out of domestic affairs (Golove and Hulsebosch, 2010: 946–970).

Golove and Hulsebosch argue that American constitutional design helped ensure U.S. admission to the European state system by institutionalizing respect for international law. Foreign nations needed assurance that the United States would be a reliable participant in the world political order, and that meant enforcing, and respecting, the law of nations. By developing a set of constitutional mechanisms that would ensure respect for the law of nations and adherence to treaties with foreign governments, the Founders demonstrated that the young nation was entitled to act as an equal sovereign in the nation-state system. Thus they insulated enforcement of the law of nations from political processes by assigning it to an independent judiciary, gave the executive authority over the conduct of foreign affairs, and required that the executive faithfully execute federal laws as well as the law of nations (Golove and Hulsebosch, 2010).

Early American law also integrated English mechanisms of imperial authority and reformulated them for the American state. Paul Halliday and G. Edward White have argued that the language of the Suspension Clause was not part of the history of Anglo-American liberties as it came to be understood in America, but rather the language of imperial justice and royal prerogative (2008: 679). Further, the Founders constructed a legal system that broke with British conceptions of legal jurisdiction, but only to reformulate core concepts into a powerful imperial system of jurisprudence. In *Constituting Empire* (2005), Hulsebosch "recover[s] the nexus between empires and constitutions" by tracing the history of New York constitutional culture from the British Empire to the American Empire. He shows that a range of actors including colonial agents worked with the constitutional arguments circulating in the British Empire and reformulated them into a conception of law that emphasized a rational system of rules. This interpretation shifted away from British notions of constitutionalism that emphasized determining the appropriate institution to resolve a dispute and moved toward a conception of law that emphasized jurisprudence. The shift from common law constitutionalism to jurisprudence emerged from the experience of colonists within the British Empire who confronted increasing mobility in the new world. Rights claims require enforcement and the state carried the promise of legal institutions with the expansion of sovereignty. Seen in this light, American constitutionalism was not only born out of empire, but is fundamentally imperial.

Over the course of the nineteenth century, American constitutionalism facilitated formal territorial empire-building. But as Sanford Levinson and Bartholomew Sparrow explain, *Marbury v. Madison* and the advent of judicial review consistently overshadows the Louisiana Purchase in the annals of American constitutional development. As the contributors to Levinson and Sparrow's edited collection *The Louisiana Purchase and American Expansion* (2005) show, President Jefferson's decision to set aside his doubts about the constitutionality of acquiring new territory by treaty in 1803 to complete the purchase of France's Louisiana Territory not only doubled the size of the nation, but laid the groundwork for the construction of America's continental empire. Jefferson may not have had visions of a European-style empire, but he harnessed the empire-building capacity of the treaty power, a move that facilitated American expansion into the twentieth century.

As the imperial state expanded its reach across the North American continent, the federal courts provided post-hoc legal justifications and developed a substantial body of jurisprudence outlining the legal parameters for colonial governance in the territories (Burnett, 2005; Sparrow, 2006). These cases provided the legal foundation for state power in U.S. overseas colonialism at the turn of the twentieth century (Burnett, 2005: 814–834). In the early twentieth century, in a series of Supreme Court cases collectively referred to as the *Insular Cases*, the U.S. Supreme Court affirmed the legality of U.S. colonialism in the new overseas territories acquired at the end of the Spanish-American War. In *Downes v. Bidwell* (182 U.S. 244) the Court created a new category in constitutional law for "unincorporated territories." The decisions marked a significant shift in American law away from a system of transcontinental expansion in which the U.S. government organized territories for subsequent admission as states, toward a doctrine that permitted indefinite unequal political status for certain territories (Lawson and Seidman, 2004; Sparrow, 2006).

The federal courts have also been central institutions defining the boundaries of American citizenship and belonging within the empire. Constructions of the status of Indians as "domestic dependent nations," and Puerto Ricans, Filipinos and other colonial subjects as "foreign in a domestic sense" created new categories of belonging to resolve the tensions of geography and sovereignty produced by expansion (Cleveland, 2002: 31–37; Burnett and Marshall, 2001). The *Insular Cases* engendered political, social, and civic inequality within the American empire by categorizing Puerto Ricans as not quite citizens but not quite subjects either (Burnett and Marshall, 2001). These inequalities persist for residents of the island territories, where inhabitants lack equal representation and are unable to vote in federal elections. The *Insular Cases* have not been overturned and continue to shape

Supreme Court decisions about the reach of American law across borders. They received renewed attention when the Supreme Court took up the constitutional questions surrounding President Bush's use of America's Guantanamo Bay Detention Facility (a vestige of early twentieth-century imperialism) to hold suspected terrorists in the Global War on Terrorism. In 2008, the U.S. Supreme Court relied upon the *Insular Cases* in *Boumediene v. Bush* (553 U.S. 771), to hold that prisoners were entitled to fundamental rights, which included the writ of habeas corpus, in territories under American sovereign authority.

The *Insular Cases*, and more recently *Boumediene*, are essential parts of the relationship between ideas about territoriality and the reach of American law in constitutional jurisprudence. In the late nineteenth century, the government resolved the uncertainties about the reach of American law in the U.S.-Mexico borderlands by resorting to rigid definitions of territoriality and pursuing unilateral legal solutions, such as the practice of extradition, to deal with the lawlessness in the region (Margolies, 2011). The U.S. government has also proven willing to intrude upon the sovereignty of other nations in the interest of extending U.S. influence abroad. In the early twentieth century, motivated by the demands of U.S. citizens in the treaty ports and by ideas of the inadequacy of Chinese law, the U.S. government established a U.S. District Court in Shanghai to administer American law (Scully, 2001; Ruskola, 2005). Over the course of the twentieth century, the Supreme Court justified other incursions on the sovereignty of foreign nations to extend the reach of American law with the growing U.S. presence across the globe. In *Does the Constitution Follow the Flag?* (2009) Kal Raustiala argues that during the twentieth century the U.S. became ever more willing to break established rules of territoriality. The U.S. government increasingly applied "its laws to some actors in some places while denying it to other actors in other places." (2009: 215) According to Raustiala, extraterritoriality, that is, the exercise of domestic laws beyond the nation's sovereign borders, has existed alongside intraterritoriality, the existence of distinct legal regimes within the nation's sovereign borders. The U.S. has used extraterritoriality to diminish or control legal difference in the global community, and simultaneously used intraterritoriality for expansion and global political power.

The International Order

An imperial approach to American law integrates the U.S. into the global history of modern imperial powers. As it did for the European empires, international law provided the structures, rationales, and discourses of empire-building from its emergence in the seventeenth century. Historians trace the origins of modern international law to Hugo Grotius whose writings initiated the European public law tradition, and they trace its concrete legal structures to the Peace of Westphalia in 1648 which ended Europe's bloody Thirty Years' War and gave rise to the modern system of territorially bounded nation states (van Ittersum, 2006). International law (then known as the Law of Nations), comprised of natural law principles, accepted state practices, and treaties, governed relations between sovereign European states. Beginning in the late eighteenth century Europe's system of sovereign states expanded with the emergence of new states and with colonization. By the twentieth century international law was said to have become "universal."

Until recently, the history of modern international law was largely the province of historians of Europe who generally took an epochal approach that traced major shifts in the global political order. Wilhem Grewe's book, translated as *The Epochs of International Law*, is a good example of this approach (Grewe, 2000). The construction and expansion of international law was seen as largely a European process. The U.S. occupied a unique place in the global order as a young nation that emerged from the British Empire and rejected the politics of the "Old World." At a broad structural level, the U.S. contributed to the expansion of the norms of modern international law, but the nation did not constitute its power through international law or seek to actively reshape the laws of the global order until the end of World War II (Grewe, 2000). Indeed, in the prevailing narrative the U.S. appeared largely isolationist until the twentieth century when President Wilson, influenced by lawyers in the U.S. foreign policy establishment, embraced visions of resolving global conflict through international institutions at the end of World War I (Zasloff, 2003; Boyle, 1999). Then when the U.S. emerged as a major global power after World War II, it projected values of liberalism and free market capitalism alongside ideas about human rights onto a new international legal order (Borgwardt, 2007).

American legal historians and scholars of international law have posed substantial challenges to this traditional narrative of the relationship of the U.S. to international law. This work moves in two overlapping directions. International law scholars have moved away from the epochal approach to provincialize and localize international law and consider its "social" dimensions alongside broader structural ones (Anghie, 2005; Koskenniemi, 2002; Witt, 2011). They have taken a closer look at the processes of expansion, the role of colonialism, and the multiple actors shaping international law. At the same time, American legal historians have examined what David Golove and Daniel Hulsebosch have called the "cosmopolitan context" of American legal history and considered anew the place of the U.S. in the global political order and the structural transformations precipitated by the arrival of the U.S. on the geopolitical scene (Golove and Hulsebosch, 2010: 933).

Rethinking the global context of the founding raises questions about how historians conceive of the significance of American constitutionalism for the development of the modern international order. David Armitage has argued that the American Revolution initiated the transition from a world of empires to a world of states (2008: 141). According to Armitage, the Declaration solidified an association between independence and external sovereignty in the global order. Its capacious language provided a model for revolutionaries in Haiti and Spanish America in the late eighteenth and early nineteenth centuries, in the Balkans and Korea after World War I, and in former British, French and Portuguese territories in the major wave of decolonization after World War II. The Declaration of Independence became a model for emerging states and solidified the connection between a formal declaration of independence and external sovereignty that became the defining feature of international politics. But declarations of independence did not assure the protection of rights for the citizens of emerging states. Indeed, the compatibility of notions of self-determination and human rights with state sovereignty "remains one of the unresolved questions of the contemporary global order" (2008: 141).

The law of nations shaped the nation's foundational legal structures and provided the intellectual tradition for U.S. nation-building and diplomacy. The Declaration of Independence and the U.S. Constitution announced the nation's participation in the global order on the terms of the Westphalian system, and indicated that the U.S. would abide by the law of nations in its foreign affairs (Armitage, 2008; Golove and Hulsebosch, 2010). The U.S. integration in the global system of states called upon American legal thinkers to articulate the place of the law of nations in American law. For that, they drew from the public international law tradition of English philosophers (Janis, 2004). According to Mark Janis, American jurists such as Henry Wheaton and James Kent initiated an "American tradition of international law," which sought to use international law to "affirm the recently-won independence and sovereignty of the United States" (Janis, 2004: 25). And the Supreme Court looked to international law to articulate and define the power of the young nation in foreign affairs (Janis; 2004, 2010).

International law also had a central place in the American legal order as a venue and ideological framework for the nation's illiberal policies. It was a primary legal terrain in the struggle over the institution of slavery. International law provided U.S. courts with "conflict of laws" principles, which structured the institution of slavery (Finkelman, 1981; Janis, 2010: 92–115). Slaveholders found justification for slavery in the notion that the modern political order demanded competent legal actors and only provided recognition to those capable of self-government. Yet international law also provided a means of transcending U.S. courts and law. Abolitionists turned to international courts established to end the slave trade to promote individual rights and the end of slavery in the U.S. (Martinez, 2007).

The concept of sovereignty in international law furnished the American imperial state with a legal framework for structuring colonial difference and rationalizing inequality. U.S. policies towards tribal Indians, immigrants, and people in the island territories at the turn of the twentieth century, called upon the Supreme Court to provide a framework for ordering and naming the social and cultural pluralism produced by territorial and population growth (Sparrow, 2006; Burnett and Marshall, 2001; Welke, 2010). Concepts of sovereignty, which emphasized capacity for self-government, provided the logics for inequality under the law (Aleinikoff, 2002; Cleveland, 2002). As T. Alexander Aleinikoff has argued, the construction of the Plenary Power doctrine giving the government nearly unchecked power over various groups came from a vision of "a state endowed with the power to control its territoriality and take its place as an equal among other foreign states and a nation that defined itself in ethno-racial terms as Anglo-Saxon" (2002: 6). In 1857 in the infamous *Dred Scott* decision, Chief Justice Taney relied on international law to hold that people of African descent were not U.S. citizens (Janis, 2010: 99–113).

During the late nineteenth and early twentieth century, in the "Age of High Imperialism," public international law moved away from the Grotian natural law tradition toward more scientific positivist framings that made the state the ultimate source of legal authority. As the law of nations gave way to the modern practice of international law, European and American international lawyers linked sovereignty to the organization of a "civilized" state and provided central logics for the increasing colonization of the globe by Western powers (Coates, 2010; Koskenniemi, 2002). In *The Gentle Civilizer of Nations: The Rise and Fall of International Law, 1870–1960* Martti Koskenniemi shows how European international lawyers increasingly came to see international law as "the juridical conscience of the civilized world" (2002: 511). They touted European public administration as the answer to the perceived threat of non-Western societies descending into anarchy (2002: 176), and sought to use international law to shape international progress. As in Europe, international law in the late nineteenth and early twentieth century United States changed from its origins in political theory toward the practice of a group of lawyers who sought to expand U.S. power through international law (Coates, 2010).

By the early twentieth century, U.S. empire-building had substantially contributed to the expansion of Western legal norms. The advance of the American system of jurisprudence and assertions of U.S. sovereignty facilitated what scholars describe as the "universalization" of international law (Becker Lorca, 2010). Postcolonial scholars have long argued that the narrative of the universality of international law is a tool of Western imperialism. Imperial powers justified colonial rule by taking Western traditions and the experience of European states and universalizing them as markers of civilization. According to Antony Anghie (2005), international law scholars have also presumed universality by ignoring the production of international law in colonial settings and instead assuming that international law came to the colonies fully formed. As Anghie has argued, the persistence of the idea of a universal international law has obscured the ways that colonialism produced the central doctrines of international law, namely sovereignty. Further, Arnulf Becker Lorca has shown that "semi-peripheral" jurists "appropriated" Western ideas of international law and adapted them to local contexts to put them to use toward nationalist ambitions (Becker Lorca, 2010). The constitutive relationship between international law and colonization undermines narratives that frame the global legal order as a construct of idealistic internationalists. Indeed, the history of the relationship between formal colonization and international law is a central part of a longer history of liberal internationalism framed by a belief among Western lawyers that international law shapes the progress of the world (Koskenniemi, 2002).

During the twentieth century, as the U.S. gained increasing global power, it took a leading role in reshaping the international legal and political order. At the end of the two world wars, the U.S. exercised its power to promote international solutions to conflict between states. International lawyers in the U.S. foreign policy establishment played a substantial role in the development of internationalist ideas in diplomacy leading to the League of Nations after World War I (Boyle, 1999; Coates, 2010; Zasloff, 2003). Realist framings of international law reaching back to George Kennan's postwar critiques had posited a stark opposition between national and international law and cast internationalist visions as the projection of "legal-moralism" into U.S. foreign policy (Boyle, 1999: 8–10). Positing international law as either a detriment to national interests or a positive good in global politics, scholars have often traced twentieth-century legalist visions in foreign affairs to utopianism and idealism (Janis, 2010: 143). But recent work by Benjamin Coates (2010) and Yves Dezalay and Bryant Garth (2008) transcends the divisions between domestic and foreign in Realist conceptions of international legal history to show how American lawyers facilitated U.S. imperialism in the twentieth century.

International institutions and the emerging human rights regime in international law after World War II provided the foundations for what is often described as an American-led "liberal international order" characterized by the promotion of human rights, national self-determination, and free trade. After World War II, U.S leaders promoted international mechanisms of conflict resolution and contributed to the development of ideas about universal human rights (Borgwardt, 2007; Glendon, 2002). In *A New Deal for the World* (2007), Elizabeth Borgwardt argues that the 1941 Atlantic Charter represented President Roosevelt's attempt to internationalize the New Deal. FDR and Winston Churchill yoked anti-fascism to the language of human rights. In doing so, they articulated an international set of "fundamental freedoms" that would be used by contemporaries and postwar movements for self-determination. According to Borgwardt, U.S. support for human rights grew out of the experience of the Great Depression and originated with FDR and a political boost from the new cosmopolitanism of the American people. In Borgwardt's account the IMF, the World Bank, the UN Charter, and the Nuremberg Trials established an international human rights regime. However, this "multilateral moment" was lost to unilateralism, globalization, and neo-liberalism (Borgwardt, 2007). Indeed, the U.S. has proven reluctant to give up sovereignty to international justice and human rights institutions. Kevin Jon Heller (2011) argues that the Nuremberg Military Tribunals contributed substantially to the form and substance of modern international criminal law. But despite early contributions to the development of international criminal law, the U.S. government has been unwilling to submit to the jurisdiction of an international criminal tribunal. Mark Mazower has argued that historians have reacted to the perceived failures of the United Nations and postwar international institutions with a historical picture that is "astonishingly jejune" (2009: 5). Historians have ascribed idealistic intentions to political figures whose intentions and true commitment to human rights are at the very least questionable, and who often doubted the promise of the institutions that they crafted.

While the state proved reluctant to be bound by the international legal regime, postwar human rights discourse provided civil rights groups with new ways of challenging inequality in American law. In *Eyes off the Prize* (2003), Carol Anderson shows how African American rights activists, emboldened by the Universal Declaration of Human Rights, initially embraced an expansive vision of human rights. However, confronted by the narrower visions of Presidents Roosevelt and Truman, they narrowed theirs as well, and followed a more circumscribed civil rights agenda. In *Cold War Civil Rights* (2000), Dudziak argues that the distance between the rhetoric of American foreign policy during the Cold War and the realization of rights for African Americans at home propelled developments in civil rights. The Civil Rights Movement exposed the hypocrisy in U.S. government Cold War rhetoric of global moral authority. As race discrimination within the U.S. undermined the government's claims to moral authority abroad, U.S. political leaders including Presidents Truman, Eisenhower, and Kennedy became increasingly supportive of civil rights reform (Dudziak, 2000).

Narratives of the postwar transformations in the global legal order that emphasize a deep commitment on the part of the U.S. government to decolonization obscure the tremendous continuities in the history of U.S. empire-building and support for imperialism. This included the maintenance of America's colonial empire in the Caribbean, as well as U.S. military and monetary support to maintain the status quo in the French, British, and Dutch empires. Further, legal historians are only beginning to come to terms with the history of the ongoing struggle with decolonization in the American empire (Burnett and Marshall, 2001). Christina Duffy Burnett has argued the central contribution of the *Insular Cases* to constitutional doctrine was the construction of an idea of territorial "deannexation" in American law (Burnett: 2005). But while the cases created the legal framework for decolonization, the independence of the Philippines at the close of World War II remains the outlier case, in a formal U.S. empire that has endured to the present.

Legal Borderlands

Empire-building rests on the construction and expansion of systems of legal authority. But beneath the structures – the ways that jurists, politicians, and lawyers imagine and articulate the power of the state – are social and cultural struggles over law and systems of legality. At the legal borderlands of the American empire the state's power is not a foregone conclusion, but a process with social and cultural dimensions. As Mary Dudziak and Leti Volpp have described the term, legal borderlands are "contact zones between distinct physical spaces," and ideas, as well as spaces of ambiguous legal status (Dudziak and Volpp, 2005: 595). I use the idea of legal borderlands here primarily to connote encounters at the edges of U.S. sovereign power on the North American continent and overseas. The form of these encounters varied over time and across geographic spaces. They include colonization, exercises of extraterritorial jurisdiction, and overseas nation-building. These are the spaces where the American state is weakest, where its sovereignty is most in question, and where local actors support and undermine processes of constructing imperial rule.

Studies of America's legal borderlands are beginning to illuminate the diverse agents of legal change in the American empire, its plural legal regimes, the social and cultural dimensions of imperial rule, and the various ways that legal change facilitates the spread of American power. This work emerges from converging traditions: the law and society tradition in American legal history as well as the interdisciplinary fields of colonialism studies and socio-legal studies. Lauren Benton's *Law and Colonial Cultures* (2002) is a seminal work at the intersection of those fields. Benton explains how colonial states from the fifteenth through the nineteenth century sought to control plural legal regimes. She traces a global shift from multiple and diverse legal regimes to state-centered law, which produced cultural conflict and struggle. As she explains, "[j]urisdictional lines dividing legal authorities were the focus of struggle precisely because they signified other boundaries of cultural struggle" (2002: 2).

In U.S. territorial expansion, the spread of the Anglo-American common law reshaped local legal and social orders. Stuart Banner, Allison Brownell Tirres, and Lisa Ford have shown how the expansion of American sovereignty on the North American continent during the eighteenth and nineteenth centuries was entwined with the transformation of local legal cultures and the expansion of the Anglo-American common law. In *Settler Sovereignty* (2010) Ford examines how common law legal doctrines and state-centered criminal law regimes replaced local mechanisms of conflict resolution in Georgia. According to Banner (2005), the expansion of Anglo-American property law accompanied the erosion of respect for native land claims. Similarly, Tirres (2011) has shown that the arrival of the state not only transformed legal forms in El Paso during the second half of the twentieth century, but social structures as well. But, she argues, the advance of American law was not driven by the metropole. Rather, Anglo-American, Mexican, and Native American residents of El Paso demanded legal protections for property rights and border enforcement, pulling the power of the federal government to the region.

American law supported the "civilizing" missions of various actors who helped advance the power of the U.S. imperial state. Sally Merry has shown the various ways that New England lawyers and missionaries used the law to discipline the everyday life and labor of Hawaiians from the early nineteenth to the twentieth century. In *Colonizing Hawaii* (1999) she suggests that the Hawaiian upper class embraced courts and judges to ensure recognition as civilized sovereigns. Both processes, the cultural transformations initiated in law by the arrival of missionaries and lawyers, and the transition to Western secular law, ultimately facilitated further colonization. As Merry describes it, law was both a mechanism for the expansion of state power, but also for resistance to empire. Hawaiians also deployed modes of legality to structure the colonial order and discipline foreigners. Noelani Arista (2009) argues that Hawaii's legal transformation may have been precipitated by the arrival of Anglo-American missionaries in the late eighteenth and early nineteenth centuries, but it was not necessarily driven by them. Using native Hawaiian texts and methods of analysis, Arista argues that local chiefs recognized that they could use written law to discipline foreigners and maintain their legal authority.

During the twentieth century, the U.S. government deployed American constitutional doctrines and ideas abroad in U.S.-led attempts to construct new legal and political orders. As Anna Leah Fidelis T. Castaneda (2009) has argued, American constitutional law shaped the political structure of U.S. colonialism in the Philippines. According to Castaneda, the political order constructed under U.S. authority blended American constitutional law with the authoritarianism inherent in colonial rule. The result was a constitutional framework for major social interventions by the U.S. government that incorporated authoritarianism into the political structure inherited by the Philippine state. Castaneda challenges long-standing narratives that linked failures of democratic state-building in the islands to Filipino culture rather than to American design. As she shows, liberal constitutionalism under colonial conditions created a political order that produced only halting democracy in post-colonial Philippines.

The tension between authoritarianism and democracy runs through U.S. twentieth-century efforts to deploy American constitutionalism in nation-building abroad. After World War II, U.S. occupation governments reconstituted the German and Japanese legal orders along an American model (Gaab, 1999; Kostal, 2011). Castaneda argues that these nation-building projects had roots in U.S. colonial state-building from the turn of the century, an approach that still serves as a model for reconstruction projects in Iraq and Afghanistan.

Legal encounters at the borderlands of American empire not only transformed local cultures, but also reshaped the U.S. imperial state. In some cases, U.S. officials honed techniques of social control in colonial settings that shaped the legal landscape back home (Buenger, 2009; McCoy, 2009; McCoy and Scarano, 2009: 329–389; Willrich, 2011). American lawyers, judges, lawyer-diplomats, missionaries and ordinary citizens facilitated the movement of American legal ideas, doctrines, and institutions abroad (Dudziak, 2008; Billias, 2009). They also built intellectual and institutional connections with foreign legal cultures, contributing to what John Witt has called the "bounded contingency," of American law and legal culture, which has been at times resistant to foreign influences and at other times substantially shaped by them (Witt, 2007: 6).

An Agenda for an Imperial History of American Law

This chapter suggests three broad research agendas for an imperial history of American law. An imperial history accounts for the ways that the internal legal order of the American state constituted U.S. territorial expansion and global power. It incorporates American legal history into the international legal history of modern imperial powers and examines how international law shaped the U.S. imperial state. And it examines the local cultural and social dimensions of the legal change produced by empire-building.

Greater attention to two particular issues that cut across these three agendas will significantly add to our understanding of the legal history of American empire. First, we need a better understanding of the relationship between the legal history of American empire and the global economy. How has U.S. empire-building shaped development of global capitalism? Where have economic rationales intersected with legal modes of intervention abroad? Second, studies have shown that law has been a mechanism of colonial rule and foreign intervention. Yet we know much less about foreign perspectives on American law and what colonial scholars refer to as law's "counter-hegemonic potential," especially during the twentieth century. What has it meant for foreign peoples to encounter American law, legal modes of intervention, and legal experts and discourses? This involves shifting our lens from the metropole to the colonies, territories, and sites of foreign intervention, and looking back at the empire from the various perspectives of local actors interacting with the American state.

References

Aleinikoff, T. Alexander (2002). *Semblances of Sovereignty: The Constitution, The State, and American Citizenship*. Harvard University Press, Cambridge.

Anderson, Carol (2003). *Eyes off the Prize: The United Nations and the African American Struggle for Human Rights, 1944–1955*. Cambridge University Press, New York.

Anghie, Antony (2005). *Imperialism, Sovereignty, and the Making of International Law*. Cambridge University Press, New York.

Arista, Noelani (2009). "Histories of Unequal Measure: Euro-American Encounters with Hawaiian Governance and Law, 1793–1827." Ph.D. diss., Brandeis University.

Armitage, David (2008). *The Declaration of Independence: A Global History*. Harvard University Press, Cambridge.

Bailyn, Bernard (1967). *The Ideological Origins of the American Revolution*. Harvard University Press, Cambridge.

Banner, Stuart (2005). *How the Indians Lost Their Land: Law and Power on the Frontier*. Harvard University Press, Cambridge.

Becker Lorca, Arnulf (2010). "Universal International Law: Nineteenth-Century Histories of Imposition and Appropriation." *Harvard International Law Journal* 51(2): 475–552.

Benton, Lauren (2002). *Law and Colonial Cultures in World History, 1400–1900*. Cambridge University Press, New York.

Billias, George Athan (2009). *American Constitutionalism Heard Round the World, 1776–1989: A Global Perspective*. New York University Press, New York.

Borgwardt, Elizabeth (2007). *A New Deal for the World: America's Vision for Human Rights*. Belknap Press, Cambridge.

Boyle, Francis Anthony (1999). *Foundations of World Order: The Legalist Approach to International Relations (1898–1922)*. Duke University Press, Durham.

Buenger, Nancy (2009). "Extraordinary Remedies: The Court of Chancery and Equitable Justice in Chicago." Ph.D. diss., University of Chicago.

Burnett, Christina Duffy (2005). "Untied States: American Expansion and Territorial Deannexation." *The University of Chicago Law Review* 72(3): 797–879.

Burnett, Christina Duffy and Marshall, Burke, eds (2001). *Foreign in a Domestic Sense: Puerto Rico, American Expansion, and the Constitution*. Duke University Press, Durham.

Castaneda, Ann Leah Fidelis T. (2009). "Spanish Structure, American Theory." In McCoy and Scarano, eds, *Colonial Crucible: Empire and the Making of the Modern American State*, 365–374. The University of Wisconsin Press, Madison.

Cleveland, Sarah H. (2002). "Powers Inherent in Sovereignty: Indians, Aliens, Territories, and the Nineteenth Century." *Texas Law Review* 81 (November): 1–284.

Coates, Benjamin (2010). "Transatlantic Advocates: American International Law and U.S. Foreign Relations, 1898–1919." Ph.D. diss., Columbia University.

Dezalay, Yves and Garth, Bryant G. (2008). "Law, Lawyers, and Empire." In Grossberg and Tomlins, eds, *The Cambridge History of Law in America, Vol III*, 718–757. Cambridge University Press, New York.

Dudziak, Mary L. (2000). *Cold War Civil Rights: Race and the Image of American Democracy*. Princeton University Press, Princeton.

Dudziak, Mary L. (2008). *Exporting American Dreams: Thurgood Marshall's African Journey*. Oxford University Press, New York.

Dudziak, Mary L. (2012). *War Time: An Idea, Its History, Its Consequences*. Oxford University Press, New York.

Dudziak, Mary L. and Volpp, Leti (2005). "Introduction: Legal Borderlands: Law and the Construction of American Borders." *American Quarterly* 57 (September): 593–610.

Finkelman, Paul (1981). *An Imperfect Union: Slavery, Federalism, and Comity*. University of North Carolina Press, Chapel Hill.

Fisher, Louis (1985). *Constitutional Conflicts Between Congress and the President*. Princeton University Press, Princeton.

Fisher, Louis (2005). *Military Tribunals and Presidential Power: American Revolution to the War on Terrorism*. University of Kansas Press, Lawrence.

Ford, Lisa (2010). *Settler Sovereignty: Jurisdiction and Indigenous People in America and Australia, 1788–1836*. Harvard University Press, Cambridge.

Gaab, Jeffrey S. (1999). *Justice Delayed: The Restoration of Bavaria Under American Occupation, 1945–1949*. Peter Lang, New York.

Glendon, Mary Ann (2002). *A World Made New: Eleanor Roosevelt and the Universal Declaration of Human Rights*. Random House, New York.

Golove, David and Hulsebosch, Daniel (2010). "A Civilized Nation: The Early American Constitution, the Law of Nations, and the Pursuit of International Recognition." *New York University Law Review* 85 (October): 932–1066.

Greene, Jack P. (1986). *Peripheries and Center: Constitutional Development in the Extended Politics of the British Empire and the United States, 1607–1788*. University of Georgia Press, Athens.

Grewe, Wilhelm (2000). *The Epochs of International Law*. Translated and revised by Michael Byers. Walter de Gruyter, Berlin.

Halliday, Paul D. and White, G. Edward (2008). "The Suspension Clause: English Text, Imperial Contexts, and American Implications." *Virginia Law Review* 94(3): 515–714.

Heller, Kevin Jon (2011). *The Nuremberg Military Tribunals and the Origins of International Criminal Law*. Oxford University Press, New York.

Hulsebosch, Daniel (2005). *Constituting Empire: New York and the Transformation of Constitutionalism in the Atlantic World, 1664–1830*. The University of North Carolina Press, Chapel Hill.

Janis, Mark Weston (2004). *The American Tradition of International Law: Great Expectations, 1789–1914*. Oxford University Press, New York.

Janis, Mark Weston (2010). *America and the Law of Nations 1776–1939*. Oxford University Press, New York.

Koskenniemi, Martii (2002). *The Gentle Civilizer of Nations: The Rise and Fall of International Law, 1870–1960*. Cambridge University Press, Cambridge.

Kostal, R.W. (2011). "The Alchemy of the Occupation: Karl Lowenstein and the Legal Reconstruction of Nazi Germany, 1945–1946." *Law and History Review* 29(1): 1–52.

LaFeber, Walter (1987). "The Constitution and United States Foreign Policy: An Interpretation." *The Journal of American History* 74(3): 695–717.

Lawson, Gary and Seidman, Guy (2004). *The Constitution of Empire: Territorial Expansion and American Legal History*. Yale University Press, New Haven.

Margolies, Daniel S. (2011). *Spaces of Law in American Foreign Relations: Extradition and Extraterritoriality in the Borderlands and Beyond, 1877–1898*. University of Georgia Press, Athens.

Martinez, Jenny S. (2007). "Anti-Slavery Courts and the Dawn of International Human Rights Law." *Yale Law Journal* 117 (Fall): 550–641.

Mazower, Mark (2009). *No Enchanted Palace: The End of Empire and the Ideological Origins of the United Nations*. Princeton University Press, Princeton.

Merry, Sally (1999). *Colonizing Hawaii: The Cultural Power of Law*. Princeton University Press, Princeton.

McCoy, Alfred W. (2009). *Policing America's Empire: The United States, the Philippines, and the Rise of the Surveillance State*. The University of Wisconsin Press, Madison.

McCoy, Alfred W. and Scarano, Francisco A., eds (2009). *Colonial Crucible: Empire and the Making of the Modern American State*. The University of Wisconsin Press, Madison.

Novak, William (2008). "The Myth of the Weak American State." *The American Historical Review* 113(3): 752–772.

Raustiala, Kal (2009). *Does the Constitution Follow the Flag? The Evolution of Territoriality in American Law*. Oxford University Press, New York.

Ruskola, Teemu (2005). "Canton is Not Boston: The Invention of American Imperial Sovereignty," *American Quarterly* 57(3): 859–884.

Schlesinger, Jr., Arthur M. (1973). *The Imperial Presidency*. Houghton Mifflin, Boston.

Scully, Eileen P. (2001). *Bargaining with the State From Afar: American Citizenship in Treaty Port China, 1844–1942*. Columbia University Press, New York.

Sparrow, Bartholomew (2006). *The Insular Cases and the Emergence of American Empire*. University of Kansas Press, Lawrence.

Sparrow, Bartholomew and Levinson, Sanford, eds (2005). *The Louisiana Purchase and American Expansion, 1803–1898*. Rowman & Littlefield, New York.

Stone, Geoffrey (2004). *Perilous Times: Free Speech in Wartime from the Sedition Act of 1798 to the War on Terrorism*. W.W. Norton, New York.

Teitel, Ruti G. (2003). "Empire's Law: Foreign Relations by Presidential Fiat." In Dudziak, ed., *September 11 in History: A Watershed Moment?* 194–212. Duke University Press, Durham.

Tirres, Allison Brownell (2011). "The View from the Border: Law and Community in the Nineteenth Century." In Brophy and Hamilton, eds, *Transformations in American Legal History II: Essays in Honor of Morton J. Horwitz*, 218–236. Harvard University Press for Harvard Law School, Cambridge.

Tushnet, Mark, ed. (2005). *The Constitution in Wartime: Beyond Alarmism and Complacency*. Duke University Press, Durham.

Van Ittersum, Martine Julia (2006). *Profit and Principle: Hugo Grotius, Natural Rights Theories and the Rise of Dutch Power in the East Indies, 1595–1615*. Brill Academic Publishers, Leiden.
Welke, Barbara Young (2010). *Law and the Borders of Belonging in the Long Nineteenth Century United States*. Cambridge University Press, New York.
Willrich, Michael (2011). *Pox: An American History*. Penguin Press, New York.
Witt, John Fabian (2007). *Patriots and Cosmopolitans: Hidden Histories of American Law*. Harvard University Press, Cambridge.
Witt, John Fabian (2011). "A Social History of International Law: Historical Commentary." In Sloss, Ramsey, and Dodge, eds, *International Law in the U.S. Supreme Court: Continuity and Change*, 164–191. Cambridge University Press, New York.
Witt, John Fabian (2012). *Lincoln's Code: The Laws of War in American History*. Free Press, New York.
Wood, Gordon (1969). *The Creation of the American Republic, 1776–1787*. University of North Carolina Press, Chapel Hill.
Zasloff, Jonathan (2003). "Law and the Shaping of American Foreign Policy: From the Gilded Age to the New Era." *New York University Law Review* 78 (April): 239–273.

Index

Abington School District v. Schempp 401
abolition of slavery 159–160, 171
abolitionists 152, 159–160
aboriginal title 128–129
abortion *see* reproductive rights
Abrams v. United States 473
Adkins v. Children's Hospital 110
administrative agencies 87, 93, 113–114, 116, 213, 309, 320, 338, 367–379, 450, 533
   see also specific agency or commission names
administrative law 367–379
administrative state 116, 236, 295, 308, 315, 367–379, 413, 518
Administrative Procedure Act 372
adoption 212, 471–472
affirmative action 321
Africa 155–156, 165, 193, 231, 422
African Americans 105, 152–189, 216–217, 231, 309, 311, 319–321, 336, 340–341, 355, 411, 422, 427, 430, 474–475, 554
   Freedmen's Bureau, and 172, 217, 312
   freedom, and 117, 171–185, 311
   labor coercion after the Civil War 312
   labor movement, and 320
   lawyers 173, 179, 182–183, 196–197, 258
   Title VII, and 320
   women 193, 197–198, 201, 203–204, 336
   see also slaves; slavery
African Americans, Gilded Age law and 514
Age of Revolution 161
   see also American Revolution
Agricultural Adjustment Administration 375
Agriculture, Department of 373
Aid to Dependent Children 200, 220, 318
   see also children
Alabama 179, 182
Alper, Jonathan L. 154
American Anti-Boycott Association 314
American Civil Liberties Union 108, 202, 319
American exceptionalism 313
American Federation of Labor 313, 318, 375, 533
   see also labor
American negro slavery 152–153, 164
   economics of 156–158, 161–162
   extralegal legacy 153–154, 158, 161
   gender and slavery 164–165

A Companion to American Legal History, First Edition.
Edited by Sally E. Hadden and Alfred L. Brophy.
© 2013 John Wiley & Sons Ltd. Published 2021 by John Wiley & Sons Ltd.

inheritance 162
institutionalist perspectives on 154–156, 158–160, 162–163, 165
legal culture 156–158, 162–163, 165, 335
origins debate 154–156
race 154–156, 162, 165
servant-or-slave debate 154–155
Western culture, in 155
see also slave community; slave patrols; slaveholders; slaves; slavery
American Revolution 133, 160–161, 163, 193–194, 211, 213, 251, 278, 330, 337, 342, 353–355, 393, 407–408, 448, 468, 485–489, 499, 547
Ansell, Samuel T. 409–410
antebellum Period 67–85, 96, 130–136, 141, 152, 162–163, 176–177, 219, 252, 277–279, 290–293, 296–297, 299, 308, 333–334, 357, 368, 445, 447, 449, 453, 468–472, 484–502, 525–527, 531, 536
anti-Catholic sentiment 233, 399
anti-enticement rules 310
anti-lynching movement 178, 473
anti-miscegenation laws 175
Anti-Peonage Statute of 1867 311
anti-slavery 73–74, 152–153, 159, 496, 509, 512
antitrust 294–298, 313, 513
appeals 13, 338, 410, 428
apprenticeship 58–60, 310, 466, 468, 530
see also indentured servitude
Aptheker, Herbert 159
Articles of Confederation 355
Asian Americans 118, 220, 234–237, 475–476
assimilation 127, 138, 141, 230, 233, 235, 239, 402
assumpsit 90–91
Atlantic slave trade 18, 157–158, 161, 229, 233, 496, 551
Atlantic system 157
Atlantic world 11, 13–14, 16, 35, 275, 423
Atleson, James B. 529–530
Atomic Energy Commission 373
Avery, Dianne 532

Bailyn, Bernard 47–48, 354, 515
Ballagh, James C. 152
bankruptcy 71, 79, 299–300

bastards *see* non-marital children
Beard, Charles 48, 271, 277
Becker, Craig 530–531
Behrendt, Stephen D. 157
Bentham, Jeremy 485–487, 496, 498, 500, 502, 511,
Berlin, Ira 161–162, 166
best interests of the child doctrine 213
see also child custody; family law
Bible, the 152, 389, 392, 396, 398–401
Bilder, Mary S. 48, 252, 254, 260
Billy Budd 73
birth rate 210, 220
Black freedom struggle 171
Black Power 159
Blackburn, Robin 157
Blackstone, William 37, 50, 55, 58, 94, 397, 468–469, 484–87, 489–90, 492–94, 497, 536
Blackstone's Commentaries see William Blackstone
Blassingame, John W. 159–161
Bleistein v. Donaldson Lithographing Company 451
borderlands 12–13, 240, 544, 549, 555–557
borrowing 280, 423, 431
constitutional 8, 10, 12
law 8, 18
Boumediene v. Bush 549
Bowers v. Hardwick 475
Brandeis, Louis 199, 373, 474, 517
see also sociological jurisprudence
Brazil 156
British Empire 48–49, 142, 547, 550
see also colonialism; empire; imperialism
British North America *see* colonial America
see also specific colony
Brown v. Board of Education 101, 114–116, 118, 181–183, 201, 339, 474
Buchanan v. Warley 109
Bureau of Indian Affairs 127, 142, 144
see also Native Americans
Bureau of the Budget 376
bureaucracy 113, 116, 203, 210, 233, 236, 294, 317, 330, 337, 341, 354, 367–379, 533–534

Canada 11, 198, 142, 147
canals 70, 451
capital punishment 179, 185, 428

capitalism 16, 71–72, 96, 157–158, 182, 210, 212, 253, 255, 270, 272–273, 276, 278, 281, 294, 298, 308, 311, 314, 320, 452, 472–473, 475, 497, 506–509, 529, 531, 534, 538, 543, 545, 551, 557
  see also liberalism; market
Cardozo, Benjamin N. 516
Caribbean 11, 17
Carroll, Joseph C. 159
case method 511
casebooks 145, 211, 416
Catterall, Helen Tunnicliff 152
Chace Act 452
Chae Chan Ping v. U.S. 236
Cherokee Nation v. Georgia 134, 469
Chesapeake Bay 10–12, 162, 218, 310
Chew, Benjamin 31
Chicago 98–99, 258, 336, 377, 432, 517
Chicano/as 476–477
child custody 58–59, 212–213, 471
childcare 221
children 10, 17, 58–60, 77, 95, 108, 200, 219, 280, 303, 317, 333–335, 426–427, 432
  see also Aid to Dependent Children; family law; orphanages
Children's Bureau 200, 220, 317, 377
children's rights 58–59, 213, 317
Chinese Exclusion Case 230, 235, 475
Chinese Exclusion laws 235, 237, 239, 471, 475
Christian(ity) 388–389, 397, 399–400, 492, 497–498
  see also Puritans; Quakers; religion; religion and law
citizenship 75, 105, 109, 135, 173, 176, 190, 195–196, 200, 204–205, 212, 218, 229–248, 309, 316, 318–322, 331, 333, 361, 378, 431, 470–471, 475, 531, 548
citizenship, birthright 218, 232
civil liberties 79, 107–108, 114–118, 319, 415
  see also American Civil Liberties Union
civil-military relations 412–413
civil rights 114–118, 171–172, 181–184, 201–204, 241–243, 319–321, 330, 338–340, 368, 378–379, 402, 471, 475, 554
  Department of Justice, Civil Rights Section 319
  labor movement, and 320
  NAACP Legal Defense and Educational Fund 320
  religion 402
Civil Rights Act of 1875 473
Civil Rights Act of 1964 181, 183, 319
civil rights activists 117, 180, 182, 218, 375
Civil Rights Cases 471, 473–474
Civil Service Commission 372
Civil War 79, 86, 93, 152, 156, 160, 164, 251, 310, 312, 317, 332, 338, 349, 358, 369, 408–409, 412, 414, 416–418, 450, 472, 510, 512, 516
  industrialization, after 310
  pensions 317, 337–338
class 424–425, 429
classical legal thought see legal theory
Classical Liberalism 72, 214, 256, 301
Clayton Act 313
Cleveland v. Board of Education 203
codification 80, 397, 417, 499–501
Coke, Lord 55, 58
Cold War 105, 116, 214, 242, 341, 373, 378, 410, 474, 554
College of Philadelphia 492
colonial America 7–45, 27, 72, 131–133, 138–140, 142, 153–155, 163–165, 191–193, 210, 213, 218, 230–232, 239, 250–251, 270–271, 274, 278, 291, 309–310, 330–332, 342, 353–355, 358, 371, 387–393, 408, 422–424, 466–467, 484–489, 501, 530
colonial legal systems 9, 12, 231, 252, 423, 487–488, 500, 556
colonialism 7, 9, 11, 132, 134–135, 211, 237, 548, 550, 552, 556
color-blind jurisprudence 172, 185, 321
Columbia Law School 491, 493, 517
Comaroff, John 9
comity 164, 510
Commentaries on American Law see also Kent, James
Commentaries on the Laws of England see Blackstone, William
commerce clause 136, 229, 271, 295, 319
common law 19, 55, 61, 95, 133, 191–192, 217, 272, 291, 310, 321, 388, 394, 396–397, 484–490, 495–496, 500, 526, 555–556
  of crimes 52

recognition of Christianity 388–389, 397
common law marriage 212
Commonwealth studies 290
  see also Handlin Mary; Handlin Oscar
Commonwealth v. Alger 94
Commonwealth v. Hunt 531
communist groups 179, 182, 240, 374, 377
Communist Party 240, 315
comparative law 13–16, 18, 35, 428, 432
Confederate States of America 510
Congress of Industrial Organizations 318
  see also labor
Connecticut 14, 28–30, 35, 58, 191
conscription 412
consensus historians 271, 291, 507
conspiracy doctrines 313
Constitutional Convention 46, 50, 448
constitutional order 10, 12, 424–425, 430–431, 545, 549
consumption studies 281
contraceptives 214
contract law 18, 59–60, 68–69, 72, 78, 90–92, 96, 114, 289, 300–301, 311, 319, 321, 393, 397, 472, 497, 508, 513, 519, 531–532
convict leasing 179, 312
Cooper, James Fenimore 73, 469, 489
copyright 442–454, 467
  courtesy of the trade 452–453
  culture of reprinting 445
  fair use 451
  innocent infringement 451
  photography 451
  right of adaptation (derivative work) 451
  romantic authorship 444–445
  sound recordings 445
corporate liberalism 293–294
corporations 68, 70, 79–80, 270, 279, 290, 294–296, 298, 303, 349, 532
court-packing plan 111–112, 314
courts
  admiralty 33
  appellate 69, 78, 180, 212–213, 235, 340–342
  county 33, 55
  federal 52, 235–236, 277, 295, 408, 494–496 see also United States Supreme Court
  juvenile 200, 427
  local 55, 69, 98, 119, 162–163, 176, 212, 236, 272, 335–336, 377, 425, 473
  military 407–418
  women's use of 58
Cover, Robert 73, 153–154, 464, 509
coverture 176, 191–195, 219, 274, 467
credit 270, 273, 275–279, 281
crime literature 468
criminal conspiracy 280, 310
criminal law 15–17, 28, 31–35, 37, 69, 77, 107, 110–111, 114–115, 132, 136, 162–163, 172, 177–180, 184–185, 233, 242, 369, 407, 416, 422–432, 442, 468, 554
critical legal history 308–309, 312, 314–315
critical legal studies 184, 211, 273, 308–309, 312, 314–315, 339, 464, 477–478, 516, 519–520, 524–542
  constitutive role of law 525
  critique of rights 524, 538
  decline of 539
  devolution of law 538
  disputes within 525–526, 538
  evolutionary functionalism in history 525, 526
  indeterminacy thesis 524, 538
  law is politics 524
  legitimation 525, 538
  personal politics 538
critical race theory 477, 539
Crowder, Enoch 409
cultural history 54, 127, 272, 330, 485, 506
culture war 211
Cumberland Law School 76
custom, law of 8, 36, 56, 60, 88, 136, 177, 422, 426, 492, 498–499, 515

Dartmouth College v. Woodward 471
Davis, David Brion 155
Davis, Thomas J. 163
death penalty *see* capital punishment
Declaration of Independence 467, 551
Defense of Marriage Act 211, 221
Degler, Carl N. 154–156
Delaware 13, 30–31, 468
democracy 72, 76, 112, 155, 276, 280, 290, 310, 313, 352, 355, 369, 409, 412, 499, 507, 529, 546, 556–557

Democrats 52, 71–72, 76, 80, 351, 357, 360, 373, 449, 490, 538
Department of Justice archives 130
Dickinson, John 31, 467
Digital Millennium Copyright Act 443
disestablishment 388, 393–396
divine law 152
divorce 194, 210–211, 213, 215, 219, 260, 388, 471–472
Dixon, Thomas 172
doctrine of discovery 132–133
domestic dependent nations 548
domestic relations law *see* family law
domestic violence 215
Donnan, Elizabeth 157
Dos Passos, John 173
Douglass, Frederick 74, 164, 470
Downes v. Bidwell 548
Dred: A Tale of the Great Dismal Swamp 74
Dred Scott v. Sandford 79, 165, 218, 473, 510, 552
Du Bois, W.E.B. 157, 173
Dudziak, Mary 378, 406, 546, 554–555
Dutch, the 30, 156, 391

early America *see* colonial America
  see also specific colony
economic development 60, 68–71, 114, 162, 212, 269–303, 450, 509, 526
economic-regulation 14, 16–18, 87, 110, 182, 269–288, 289–307, 368, 379, 413
  see also administrative state; *Lochner* era
economic thought 60, 69–72, 75, 274–278, 290
education 108, 136, 173, 182, 203, 358, 389–390, 396, 398–402
  see also legal education
Edwards, Laura F. 55–56, 62–63, 69, 80, 162–163, 176, 335–336
Eighteenth Amendment 110
Elkins, Stanley 157–160
Eltis, David 157
emancipation 62, 74, 91, 153, 160, 174, 179, 217, 301, 309, 311, 424, 471
Emerson, Ralph Waldo 67, 470
eminent domain 70, 94–95, 528
  see also property rights; regulatory takings; takings

empire 10, 13, 17–18, 31, 33, 48–49, 142, 215, 276, 322, 337, 494, 543–544, 546–552, 554–558
  see also colonialism; imperialism
employment at will rule 311
Engel v. Vitale 401
Engerman, Stanley L. 158
England 10, 16, 28, 47, 95, 133, 142, 191–192, 198, 213, 217–218, 276, 353–354, 422, 441–442, 444, 450, 452–453, 485–489, 496, 530, 534, 536
English North America *see* colonial America or specific colony
Enlightenment 47–48, 58, 73–74, 275, 390, 394, 423, 464, 472, 489, 492, 498–499
  see also Scottish Enlightenment
entirety doctrine 310
Environmental Protection Agency 376
epistemology 488–489, 502
Equal Employment Opportunity Commission 202, 378
Equal Rights Amendment 203–204, 218, 317
  see also women's rights
Establishment Clause *see* First Amendment
Everson v. Board of Education 387, 400–401
Ex Parte Crow Dog 129, 135, 137–138
Ex Parte Milligan 415
Ex Parte Vallandigham 415
ex-slave autobiographies 159, 164
  see also slave testimony
extralegal 8, 18, 424, 427, 429, 431

Fair Employment Practices Commission 373, 378
Fair Labor Standards Act 318, 322
family law 58–59, 194, 199, 204, 209–221, 242, 277–278, 302–303, 311, 316–317, 320, 334, 426–430, 471–472
  see also children; Defense of Marriage Act; divorce; non-marital children; orphanages; polygamy; women
Farwell v. Boston & Worcester Railroad Corporation 293, 310, 531
federal agencies 336–338
  see also administrative agencies

federal common law 52
  see also common law
Federal Communications
  Commission 374–375, 378
federal courts see courts, federal
Federal Power Commission 378
Federal Trade Commission 376
federalism 50, 110, 136, 164, 215, 314, 379, 395, 510, 545, 547
Federalists (political party) 52, 72, 276, 490–491
Feinman, Jay M. 531–532
feminism 127, 195–196, 201–204, 218, 318, 320–321, 340, 476
feminist jurisprudence 211
fictional literature 73–75, 470–472, 475, 478
Fifth Amendment 70, 195, 236, 474
  see also eminent domain; takings
finances, 278–279, 361
  see also bankruptcy; market
Finkelman, Paul 61, 164, 390, 510
Finley, Moses I. 155
First Amendment 107–108, 114, 387, 394–402, 413, 474–475
Flanigan, Daniel 153
Fletcher v. Peck 134
Fogel, Robert William 158
Fong Yue Ting v. U.S. 236
Forbath, William E. 112–113, 329, 341, 531
Ford, Lacy K. 162
forfeiture of wages 280, 310
formalism 86–87, 89–90, 100, 109, 154, 198, 314, 463, 468, 473, 507–509, 512–516, 518–519, 526
  see also legal theory
founding, political theories of 47–48
Fourteenth Amendment, due process clause of 96, 214, 341, 407, 413, 528, 531
Fourteenth Amendment, equal protection clause 172, 191, 195–197, 199, 201–204, 218, 232, 236, 341, 473, 528, 531
Fourteenth Amendment, liberty clause 108
Fourth Amendment 474
fragging 410
France 10, 213, 432, 449–450, 468
free labor ideology 96, 311, 314, 317, 530–531
free markets 289

free persons of color 62
Freedmen's Bureau 172, 217, 312
freedom of contract 69, 108, 289, 301, 393, 531–532
freedom suits 217
Freehling, William W. 162
Freund, Ernst 99
Frey, Sylvia R. 161
Freyre, Gilberto 156
Friedman, Lawrence M. 91–92, 184, 250–254, 300, 302, 422–424, 484, 493, 508
Fugitive Slave Law of 1850 470
fugitive slaves 164, 470–471
functionalism 508

Gabriel's Conspiracy (1800) 62
Gaspar, David Barry 164
gay marriage 221
gender 108, 175, 190–205, 211, 274, 302, 311, 316, 332, 335, 337, 373, 377–378, 413, 417, 422, 424–425, 427, 429, 432, 474
gender roles 77, 210
General Land Office 369, 375
Genovese, Eugene D. 158, 216–217
Georgia 32, 130–136
Germans 10, 12, 30–32
Gibbons v. Ogden 295
Gilded Age 230, 293–295, 313–314, 474, 506, 512–515, 532
  see also Progressive Era
global slave trade 158
globalization 320–322
  see also transnational
Goldberg v. Kelly 341
Goodell, William 152
goods 274–276, 280
Gordon, Linda 199–201, 204, 213, 220, 317, 334–335, 337, 377
Gordon, Robert W. 249–250, 254–256, 484, 525–528, 533, 535–538
Gordon-Reed, Annette 164–165
Gray, John Chipman 89
Great Depression 105, 113–114, 182, 220, 240, 314, 360
Great Negro Plot of 1741 163
Greenleaf, Simon 502
Griswold v. Connecticut 214, 474
Gross, Ariela J. 78, 80, 162, 165, 237, 509

Grossberg, Michael 36, 58–60, 211–218, 259–260
Guam 237

Hadden, Sally E. 163–164, 426
Hall, Kermit 251, 510
Handlin, Mary 70, 154–155, 271, 290
Handlin, Oscar 70, 154–155, 230, 234, 271, 290
Harisiades v. Shaughnessy 240
Hartog, Hendrik 38, 55, 63, 70, 75, 215, 219, 255, 260, 329
Harvard Law School 76, 89, 410, 417, 511, 517, 526
Harvard University 67
Hawaii 556
Health, Education, and Welfare, Department of 378
Hemings, Sally 164–165
Henry, Patrick 394
Hermes, Katherine 11, 36, 131–132
Higginbotham, A. Leon Jr. 153, 184
higher law 388, 394, 397, 469–740, 473
   see also divine law; natural law
Hine, Darlene Clark 164
historiography 171–172, 485
history of consumption 443
history of the book 3, 254, 443, 445, 465–466
Hoeflich, Michael 72, 486, 490–492, 494, 511
Hofstadter, Richard 106, 158–159, 293, 298
Hohfeld, Wesley 94, 271
Holmes, Oliver Wendell 1, 89, 300, 451, 478, 501, 516, 518
Holt, Wythe 531, 534, 538
Holton, Woody 161
homestead cases 212
honor 59, 75, 78, 162, 172, 429,
Horwitz, Morton 53–54, 68–69, 71–72, 76–77, 80, 109, 113, 212, 216, 247–248, 252–253, 272–273, 291–293, 297, 300, 302–303, 310, 371, 397, 508–509, 518–519, 526–529, 534, 537–538
household, composition of 210, 213, 219–220
Houston, Charles H. 180
Hualapai 128, 130
   see also U.S. v. Santa Fe

Hulsebosch, Daniel 31, 49, 61, 493–494, 546–547, 550
human rights law 183, 322, 407, 414–416, 418, 550–555
Hurd, John C. 152
Hurst, J. Willard 3, 46, 53, 68–69, 212, 248–250, 271, 290–291, 296, 301, 303, 335, 422, 507–508
Hylton v. U.S. 356

immigrants 12–13, 27–32, 36, 61, 98–99, 107, 114, 118, 221, 228–246, 257, 280, 320–322, 333–334, 342, 368–371, 376–378, 471, 475, 500, 527, 529, 552
Immigration Act of 1924 (Johnson–Reed Act) 233, 322, 378
Immigration Act of 1965 220, 241
Immigration and Naturalization Service 239, 368
immigration law 107, 215, 220–221, 228–243, 321–322, 333, 368–369, 371, 376, 378, 471, 475–476
   see also assimilation
imperialism 7–8, 10, 238–239, 494, 544–557
   see also colonialism; empire
incarceration, *see* mass incarceration; prisons
In re Debs 526
income tax 349–352, 359–362
   direct tax, as a 356
indentured servitude 17, 32, 59–60, 155, 231, 280, 309–310, 530
Indian New Deal 145–146
Indian Removal 72, 76, 143, 469
Indian title 132, 134
Indian tribes 134–135, 138, 145–147, 218
   see also Hualapai; Native Americans
industrial pluralism 312–315
industrial unionism 313
   see also American Federation of Labor; Congress of Industrial Organizations; labor
Industrial Workers of the World 313
   see also Knights of Labor
industrialization 92–93, 95, 99, 162, 257, 293, 296, 302, 357, 359, 369–370, 518, 527, 535, 538

infancy 214
infant mortality rate 220
infanticide 16, 28, 426
infantilization 160
inheritance 12, 27, 33, 136–137, 162, 192, 209, 211, 214, 218, 388
Innis, Harold 272
insanity 426–427
instrumentalism 53–58, 212, 273, 290–291, 397, 507–511.
  see also judges as instrumentalists; legal theory
Insular Cases 237, 548–549, 554
insurance 91, 93, 279, 297, 302–303, 313, 317
intellectual property 441–459 *see also* copyright; patent law; trademark
  Constitution's intellectual property clause 448
  infringement 442, 451–453
  justifications 443–444, 449, 453–454
  outlaw 442, 455
  Patent Office 449
  sanctions 441–442, 450
  Trade Mark Cases 450
international copyright 445, 452
international institutions 553–554
International Labor Defense 179
international law 10–11, 407, 416, 452, 550, 552–553, 555–557
  see also transnational
Interstate Commerce Commission 368, 371, 377
Ireland 13, 35, 233

Jacobs, Harriet 164, 165
Jacobson v. Massachusetts 100
Japan 210, 233–235, 240, 475, 557
Japanese internment 374, 475
Jefferson, Thomas 164, 390, 394, 408, 448–449, 467, 548
Jeffersonians 276, 390, 398, 448, 489, 494–495
Jim Crow 156, 172, 174, 177, 183, 320, 373, 402, 474
Johnson v. M'Intosh 71, 131–134, 138
Jones, Bernie D. 162
Jordan, Winthrop D. 77, 156
judges 73–76, 78, 80, 87–88, 115, 153, 175
  see also individual names of judges

judges, as instrumentalists 68, 212–213, 273, 336, 507–512, 537
  see also instrumentalism; legal theory
judicial branch *see* courts
judicial patriarchy 213, 336
Judiciary
  Act of 1789 52
  Act of 1801 52
jurisprudence 37, 69, 72–75, 80, 86, 88–90, 96, 98, 108–110, 113, 131, 133, 172, 185, 198–199, 272, 293, 295, 308, 314, 317, 321, 340–341, 401, 425, 484–523, 547–549, 552
  see also critical legal studies; formalism; laissez-faire constitutionalism; legal theory; liberalism; republicanism
jurisprudence of sentiment 74, 470
jury 185, 427
Justice, Department of 117, 130, 144, 146–147, 178, 241, 319, 373, 374
juveniles *see* children
juvenile courts, *see* courts, juvenile

Kainen, James L. 528
Karsten, Peter 68, 72, 292–293, 300, 302, 409, 509
Katz, Stanley 252
Kaye, Anthony E. 161
Kelley, Florence 97, 198–199
Kennedy, Duncan M. 485, 526–528, 533, 536–537
Kennedy, John F. 201, 554
Kennedy, Randall 184
Kent, James 252, 397, 468, 485, 491–495, 497, 501–502, 508, 551
Kent's *Commentaries* 468, 493–494
Kentucky 52–53
Kerber, Linda 193–194, 201–202, 204–205, 243, 521
Kimball, Bruce 89, 511
King v. Smith 330, 341
Klare, Karl E. 532–533
Klein, Herbert S. 157
Knights of Labor 313, 531
  see also industrial unionism; labor
Konefsky, Alfred S. 529, 531, 534–535
Korean War 410
Korematsu v. U.S. 475
Ku Klux Klan 164

labor 59–61, 106, 112–113, 117, 152–166, 176, 198–199, 201, 203, 240, 270, 273, 280, 294, 302–303, 308–309, 311–314, 317–318, 375, 425, 443, 447–448, 500, 513, 529–534, 538
   see also American Federation of Labor; Congress of Industrial Organizations; employment at will; indentured servitude; industrial unionism; Industrial Workers of the World, Knights of Labor; National Labor Relations Act; National Labor Relations Board; slavery; slaves; strikes; Taft-Hartley Act
labor injunctions 313, 319
laissez-faire constitutionalism 88, 96, 109, 312, 317, 512–513, 519
   see also formalism; legal theory
land claims 130, 138, 146–147
land use 95, 146
Langdell, Christopher Columbus 89, 300, 511, 519, 535
Latin America 242, 322
Latinos 118, 322, 338, 342, 476–477
law and literature 54, 73–75, 408, 429, 443–445, 463–493, 488–489, 498, 501
law of nations 547, 550–552
Lawrence v. Texas 211, 475
legal categories 17–18
legal education 75–76, 196, 247–260, 371, 490, 511, 516–517, 529, 535–538
   see also names of individual law schools
legal language 32, 47, 355, 519
legal literacy 252
legal orthodoxy 86, 109, 489, 518
legal pluralism 27, 36–38, 310, 555–556
legal profession 54–55, 70, 73, 75–76, 80, 93, 113, 179, 196, 247–260, 338–340, 397, 409–411, 414–415, 427, 453, 495, 534–536
   see also individual names of lawyers
   African-American lawyers 117, 182–183, 196–198, 201, 258
   American aristocracy, as 248–249
   capitalism and 253, 257
   cause lawyers 235, 260, 339–340
   colonial America, in 13, 29–31, 33, 46–47, 54, 58, 250, 252, 467

   corporate lawyers 250–251
   Cravath model 251, 257
   day-to-day practice of 253–254, 256
   debt collection and 251, 254–255
   divorce lawyers 260
   economics of practice and 250
   elite lawyers 235, 249, 253, 256, 258
   female lawyers 196–198, 201–203, 258–259
   hemispheres of 259
   hired guns, as 249, 477–478
   immigrants and 257–259
   Jewish lawyers 257–258
   large law firms 256, 258
   law reform, and 128, 535–536
   legal-aid lawyers 117, 259, 339
   nineteenth century 54, 70, 175, 255–256, 371, 534–535
   non-elite lawyers 256–257
   personal injury lawyers 258–259
   politics and 250
   professionalization of 250, 252
   railroad lawyers 258–259
   rural lawyers 257–258, 260
   sole practitioners 260
   stratification of 256–257
   urban lawyers 260
   Wall Street and 250
legal positivism 55, 88, 90, 496
   see also legal theory
legal publishing 35, 54–55, 248, 251–255, 352, 484, 494, 511
   biographies 254–255
   conservative tradition 248
   intellectual history and 252–253
   legal papers, publication of 253–255
   periodization 251–252
   prosopography 251
   see also law and literature; treatises
Legal Realism 86, 109–110, 273, 371, 499, 507–520, 529, 536–537, 539
   see also legal theory
legal science 86, 256, 492, 498, 535–536
legal theory
   classical 80, 86–88, 92, 94, 109, 506, 526–527
   liberal 529, 538
   Marxist 157
   Progressive 86–87, 527
   republican 529, 538

see also Blackstone, William; critical legal studies; feminist jurisprudence; formalism; higher law; instrumentalism; jurisprudence; laissez-faire constitutionalism; Legal Realism; liberalism; natural law; republicanism; sociological jurisprudence
legal treatises *see* treatises
legalism 111, 113, 183, 339, 375, 391, 553
Lemon v. Kurtzman 390
lesbian and gay rights 203, 221, 234, 413, 417
   see also Defense of Marriage Act; family law; gender; gender roles
Levy v. Louisiana 218
liability rule 68, 92
liberal internationalism 553
liberalism 48, 69, 72, 97, 105–106, 111–119, 214, 275–276, 278, 293–294, 301, 376, 497, 529, 536, 550
Lieber Code 409, 414
Lieber, Francis 409, 414, 491, 500
Lincoln, Abraham 72, 75–76, 79, 247, 253, 255, 412, 415, 469
Litchfield Law School 76
literary movements
  modernism 499
  realism 473
  sentimentalism 68, 471, 509
  see also jurisprudence; Legal Realism; legal theory
living wage 311
Llewellyn, Karl 68, 131, 515–519
local government 52, 56, 59, 62, 87, 98–100, 231, 272, 335, 350–351, 355, 362, 392,
local law 55–57, 62, 137, 163, 230, 233, 334, 424, 555–556
  see also courts, local; regionalism
localism 59, 111, 119, 162–163, 215, 258, 278, 332, 335, 338, 425, 466, 508, 512
Lochner v. New York 86, 98, 101, 108, 473, 512–515, 526
Lochner era 85–88, 97–98, 101, 108–114, 295, 314, 317
Lochnerism (see *Lochner* era)
Locke, John 48, 50, 443, 492, 497, 513

Lone Wolf v. Hitchcock 142
Long Nineteenth Century 194, 317, 474, 506, 529, 537
Lost Cause 172
Louisiana 55, 157
Louisiana Purchase 548
Loving v. Virginia 218
lynching 164, 172, 177–180, 426, 429, 431
  see also anti-lynching movement

Mack, Kenneth 117, 182–183, 197, 251, 253, 258–260
Madison, James 394–395, 467, 471, 491
Maine, Henry 471
Mallon, Mary 100
Manning, William 272
manumission 153, 160, 162
Marbury v. Madison 548
market 91, 176, 179, 269–303, 396, 459, 507, 509
market revolution 69–72, 507
market studies 270, 276, 278
marriage 12, 136–137, 173, 175–176, 191–195, 213, 215–217, 329, 361
marriage, customs 209
marriage, right to 193, 176, 193, 212, 214
Married Women's Independent Nationality Act 218
married women's property acts 77, 79, 194–195, 212, 316, 471–472
Marshall, John 71, 75, 131–134, 136, 295, 496–498
Marshall, Thurgood 180
Marshall trilogy 131–134
Martin, Bonnie 157
Marxism 157, 272, 448, 538
Maryland 33, 280, 391, 394, 466
Mason, George 394
Mason-Dixon line 160–161, 217
mass incarceration 184
Massachusetts 10, 13, 27–30, 35, 51, 53, 70, 73, 75, 94, 131, 231, 252–254, 273, 279, 290, 333, 354, 391–395, 408, 422–423, 468, 488, 500, 507–508, 534
master-servant relationship 60, 91, 153, 310
  see also indentured servitude
maternal justice 213
matriarchy 216

matrimony *see* marriage; marriage, customs; marriage, right to
McBratney v. U.S. 129
McCollum v. Board of Education 401
McKitrick, Eric 157
Melville, Herman 73, 408, 469, 472, 501
Mensch, Elizabeth 536–537
mercantilism 276
merchants 270, 275–276, 281
Merry, Sally 7, 556
Metaphysical Club 442, 516
Mexico 237–238, 241, 338, 549
Meyer v. Nebraska 108–109, 214
Mid-Atlantic legal history 30–32
migration *see* immigration
military 182, 239, 317, 337, 352–353, 360–361, 406–418
  human rights 414–416
  September 11, 2011 242, 406, 412, 416, 544
  see also American Revolution; Civil War; Vietnam War; World War I; World War II
military commissions 406–408, 416
military justice 407–412, 416–417
Miller, Perry 73–74, 252, 392, 464, 484, 488–490, 493, 495, 499–501, 508, 511
Minor v. Happersett 195, 201
Minow, Martha 118, 211, 329
miscegenation laws 164–165, 217, 218
Mississippi 173, 177, 179, 312
Moby Dick 472
modernization process 210
money 162, 270, 277–282, 357, 466
  see also capitalism; economic development; market
monopoly 442, 449
  see also trusts
moral economy 272
Mormon Church (Church of Jesus Christ of Latter-day Saints) 215, 218, 389, 396, 399, 472
Morris, Thomas D. 34, 61, 153, 509
mortgages 80, 153, 361
Mosaic Code 393
mothers' pensions 219, 317
Moynihan Report 216
Muller v. Oregon 199
Murray, Pauli 201–202

narrative 464, 470
Nash, Gary B. 160–161, 251, 334
National Association for the Advancement of Colored People (NAACP) 114, 117, 174, 178–183, 202, 260, 320, 373, 378
  anti-lynching work 178
  Black freedom struggle 174, 182–183
  Scottsboro case 179
  segregation 180–181
National Consumers League 199
National Highway Transportation Safety Administration 376
National Industrial Recovery Act 315
National Labor Relations Act (Wagner Act) 315, 318–320, 530, 532–533
National Labor Relations Board 315, 368, 373, 375, 378
National Organization for Women (NOW) 202–205, 321
  see also women's rights
National Parks 142–143
National Recovery Administration 315, 375
National Resources Planning Board 376
Native Americans 7–12, 19, 36–49, 63, 70–71, 98, 118, 127–151, 232, 278, 396, 399–400, 425, 468, 470, 476, 495, 499, 552, 556
natural law 8, 73–74, 88, 90, 152, 197, 394, 397, 449, 470, 486–487, 492, 496, 550, 552
  see also higher law
natural resources 142–144
naturalization law 228–230, 232, 235, 237
Nelson, William 53–55, 79, 273, 369, 487–488, 512
neo-liberalism 554
  see also liberalism
New Deal 69, 88, 106, 110–113, 118, 136, 182, 191, 198, 200–201, 220, 257, 289–290, 297–298, 314–315, 317–320, 331, 337, 340–341, 352–353, 361, 371–372, 375–377, 424, 450, 513, 538
  Indian New Deal 145
  Second New Deal 314
new economic history 272, 274

New England 11, 15–16, 28–30, 34, 36–37, 54–57, 62, 193, 255, 275, 310, 387, 391–395, 490, 493, 497, 501, 556
New England legal history 28–30
New France 7–8, 11–12, 15–16, 33
New Hampshire 36, 55, 395, 534
new historicism 443–444, 463
New Jersey 30–31
New Left historians 112, 293–294
New Netherlands 10–11
New Right 321
New Spain 7–9, 11–18, 33, 156–157
New York 11, 30–32, 49, 55, 79, 136, 163, 191, 228, 231, 254, 258, 301, 394, 488, 491–492, 500–501, 532, 547
New York City 30–31, 70, 163, 228, 235, 256–258, 302, 431, 491
New World 26, 155, 157, 547
nineteenth century 46–104, 110, 129–141, 171–185, 191–200, 210, 228–240, 249–251, 255–256, 273, 293–295, 297, 313, 316–317, 322–341, 367–370, 387–399, 423–424, 429–431, 441–452, 467–478, 506–520
  see also antebellum period; Gilded Age; Reconstruction; Progressive Era
Ninth Amendment 474
no-fault divorce 219
non-marital children 218
non-rivalrous goods 442
North American Review 491
North Carolina 32–33, 35, 56, 159, 162–163, 335, 354, 391, 394, 466, 473
Northwest Ordinance (1787) 49, 61
Novak, William 55–56, 70, 97–99, 107, 109, 292–293, 368, 508, 512, 546
Novel 73–74, 160, 172, 217, 408, 468–474, 477, 491, 498
  see also fictional literature; law and literature
nuclear family 210–212
nuisance law 95, 291, 397
Nullification Crisis 510
Nuremberg military tribunals 415, 554

Obama, Barack 185
objective causation 528
obscenity 426, 475

originalism 388
orphanages 59, 220, 333

Page, Thomas Nelson 178
Paine, Thomas 467
pardons 412, 428
parental rights 213
parenthood 213
Pares, Richard 157
Patent Act of 1836 449
Patent Law 441–442, 446–451, 453–454
  true inventor 443, 445–446
  see also intellectual property
patriarchy 59, 211, 213, 216–217
Pennsylvania 11, 13, 31–32, 51, 275, 277, 354, 391–392, 395, 422–423, 492
pensions 200, 219, 282, 316–317, 337–338
  see also mothers' pensions
Personal Responsibility and Economic Opportunity Act 221
personhood 77, 444, 471, 474–475
  corporate 297
peyote 131
Phi Beta Kappa 67
Philadelphia, Pennsylvania 30–31, 34, 71, 164, 251, 258, 275, 334, 336, 355, 466, 492
philanthrophy 72
Philippines 237–238, 406, 555–556
Phillips, Ulrich B. 158–160
Pierce v. Society of Sisters 108–109
plantation economy 157–158
plantation system 157, 159–163, 276
Plato 153
plea bargains 428
Plessy v. Ferguson 181, 471, 473–474, 513
Poe, Edgar Allan 471
poetry 54, 468, 475–476
police 69, 80, 164, 179–180, 259, 426–427, 431–432
police power 86, 94, 96–98, 199, 292, 314, 368, 450, 514–515
poll taxes (capitations) 356–357
Pollock v. Farmers' Loan and Trust Company 356
polygamy 215, 217–218, 399, 472
  see also family law
Pomeroy, John Norton 90
popular constitutionalism 319

popular culture 429
popular sovereignty 51, 431
  see also sovereignty
Post Office 369, 373
Pound, Roscoe 198, 247–248, 515–519
poverty 68, 117, 162, 176, 183, 192, 194, 219–220, 231, 241, 292, 329–348, 361, 474
  see also warning out
pragmatism 371, 498, 516
pregnancy 57, 93, 203, 214, 474
  see also reproductive rights
printing 72, 445, 465–469, 473–474, 478
prisons 69, 184, 198, 240, 312, 411, 424–425, 431–432, 470–471
  literature 476–477
  military 411, 417–418
privacy 3, 114, 194, 214–215, 338, 474–475
Prize Cases 196
probate records 33, 56–57, 80, 209
  see also inheritance
Progressive Era 113, 142, 175, 198–200, 218–220, 233–240, 293–297, 313–314, 330–335, 368–370, 377, 379, 507, 513–514, 516–518, 532–533, 535–537
  see also Gilded age
Progressive historians 48, 274–277, 293, 350–352, 491, 506, 513
progressive taxation 350, 359
  challenges 353
Progressivism, 97, 100, 106–109, 113, 336, 367–379, 409
  see also Progressive Era
Prohibition 107, 110–111, 360, 425
property 12, 16, 30, 32, 169–170, 276, 278, 280–281
property justifications 443–444, 449, 453
property rights 54, 63, 68–71, 77, 79, 94–96, 128, 133, 146–147, 176, 192, 231, 272, 278, 301–302, 351, 441–454, 528–529, 536
Property taxes 351–352, 358–359, 362
Proposition 13 (California, 1978) 350, 360, 362
proslavery 73–75, 78–79, 154, 509
protective labor legislation for women 199, 202–203
public domain 441, 449, 452
public health 98–100, 234, 314, 368, 377

public interest 99, 117, 249, 367–368, 374, 444, 533
public schools and religion 389–390, 398–399, 400–401
  see also education
Puerto Rico 237–239, 338, 425, 548
punishment 428, 431
  see also capital punishment
Puritan legal codes 392–393
Puritans 10, 15–16, 131, 191, 387–388, 391–393, 422–423

Quakers 10, 32, 391, 423
quantum meruit 310
Quarles, Benjamin 159, 160

race riots 172, 409
racial identity 165, 175
racial passing 217
racial stereotypes 160
railroads 68, 70, 76, 93, 175, 232, 255, 258–259, 291, 293–294, 296–297, 299, 302, 315, 331–333, 358, 369, 447, 451, 474
rape 164, 178, 180, 192, 215, 411, 416–417, 426
Reagan, Ronald 321, 350, 352, 362, 546
Reconstruction 86–101, 110, 156, 171–176, 178, 196, 232, 293, 295–296, 308, 310, 312, 319, 332, 349, 358, 369, 399, 409, 450, 473–474, 512
Redfield, Isaac 94
Rediker, Marcus 158
reform 98, 105–106, 111, 113, 198–199, 219–220, 309, 330, 369–370, 372, 409, 422–423, 430, 470–471, 500–501, 535
refugee law 239, 242
regionalism 7, 11, 18, 26–38, 54, 57–59, 63, 119, 136, 164–165, 179, 192, 215, 230, 233, 250, 272, 310–311, 422–424, 425–426, 429–430, 510
  see also courts, local; local law
regressive taxation 352–353, 359–360
  colonial Britain, in 354
regulatory takings 94–95
  see also eminent domain; takings
religion 8, 14–16, 18, 36, 63, 114, 118, 152, 191, 204, 275, 292, 387–402, 430, 466, 469, 488–489, 497–498, 557
  see also Christianity; Puritans; Quakers

religion and law 8, 10, 12–16, 118, 128–130, 134, 387–402, 422–423, 492, 497–498, 513, 534–535, 556
  see also First Amendment
reproductive rights 204, 211, 214–215, 342, 426
republican literary culture 467
Republican Party 55, 96, 172–173, 176, 179, 182, 184, 193, 314–315, 321, 351, 357–358, 360
republicanism 47–48, 50, 54, 57–59, 76, 213, 249, 270, 301, 486, 495, 497, 509–510, 512, 529, 531, 534
resistance to slavery 158–159, 161, 163
  see also anti-slavery; proslavery
Revolutionary era *see* Age of Revolution; American Revolution
Rhode Island 28, 30, 36, 48, 52–53, 252, 332, 391–392
Richardson, David 18, 167
Robertson v. Baldwin 472–473
Roe v. Wade 204, 214, 474
Roman law 486, 488, 490–492, 494
Roosevelt, Franklin D. 111–112, 182, 314–315, 545
Roosevelt, Theodore 546
Rothman, David 333–334
Rothman, Joshua D. 162

same-sex marriage *see* gay marriage
Schenck v. U.S. 473
Schlegel, John Henry 253, 518, 537
schools *see* education; legal education
Schwarz, Philip J. 34, 153
Scott, Dred 165
  see also Dred Scott v. Sandford
Scott, Harriet ("Mrs. Dred Scott") 165, 217
  see also Dred Scott v. Sandford
Scottish Enlightenment 48, 492
Scottsboro "boys" 179
  see also National Association for the Advancement of Colored People (NAACP)
Securities and Exchange Commission 371, 377
securities law 279, 295–299
segregation 109, 114–115, 155–156, 159, 171–177, 180–184, 320, 369, 474
  gender 175–176
  northern states, in 177

  origins of 174–175
  see also Jim Crow
Seneca Falls Convention 194
sentimental literature 72–75, 470–72
sentimentalism 68, 72, 80, 471, 509
separation of ownership and control 296–297
servants 155
  see also indentured servitude
sex discrimination, 201–202, 204
  see also Equal Employment Opportunity Commission; feminism; gender roles
sexual assault 193, 411, 416–18
  see also rape
sexual harassment 203, 411
sexuality 15, 193, 204, 211, 217, 234, 373, 377–78, 426, 474, 476, 516
Shaw, Lemuel 73, 75, 94, 310, 469, 507, 531
Shays' Rebellion (1786) 51, 354–355, 468
Sheppard-Towner Act 317
Sherman Act 298, 313
Sherman, William T. 408
Sixteenth Amendment 349, 356
Sixth Amendment 236
slander 18, 192
Slaughterhouse Cases 473, 531
slave communities 158, 160
slave narratives 470
slave patrols 163–164, 426
slave testimony 159–160
slave trade cases 496, 551
slaveholders 153, 158–162
slavery 14, 16, 18, 33–34, 59, 61–62, 67, 70–79, 91, 152–153, 155–157, 159–160, 171, 174, 176, 216–218, 231, 278, 280, 309, 355, 358, 423–425, 470, 490, 496, 499, 507, 509–510, 551
  in the Northwest Ordinance (1787) 61
slaves 17, 57, 62, 136, 152–167
  commodities, as 70, 155, 157, 471
  communities among 158
  families among 158, 193
  literacy 62
  mortgaging of 153, 157
  rebellion 62, 468
  status of 153–156
  taxes on 355–356, 358
  see also African Americans; American negro slavery; labor
social construction of technology 443

social control 8, 12, 18, 98, 111, 127–28, 190, 200, 332, 334, 423, 431, 557
social history 2, 47, 51, 61–62, 77–78, 161, 181, 190, 197, 209, 215, 255, 259, 309, 330, 332, 335, 443, 445, 485, 544
social insurance 313, 317–318
Social Security Act 200, 220, 337, 349, 377
social workers 98, 213, 335–337
socialization functions 93, 213
socio-legal studies 47, 242, 330, 484–502, 555
sociological jurisprudence 90, 97, 198–199, 515, 517–519
Somersett v. Stewart 509–510
South 32–34, 61–62, 135–136, 152, 154, 161–165, 176, 191–192, 216–217, 259, 275, 319, 351, 356, 373, 424, 426, 428, 490–492, 510
South Carolina 27, 32–33, 56, 162–163, 175, 178, 254, 332, 391, 394, 491
Southern Christian Leadership Conference 181
Southern Review 491
sovereignty 7, 10–12, 128–131, 135–138, 146, 431, 470, 543, 549, 551–553, 555
Stampp, Kenneth M. 158–159
staples thesis 272
State, Department of 378
State v. Tassels 135
Statute of Anne 442
Statute of Monopolies 441, 444
Steinfeld, Robert J. 530–531
Stone, Katherine van Wezel 532
Stono Rebellion 163
Story, Joseph 75, 252, 397, 446, 468, 485, 491–493, 495–497, 500, 508–509
Stowe, Harriet Beecher 74, 217, 452, 467, 470, 472–473
   See also *Uncle Tom's Cabin*
Stowe v. Thomas 452
strikes
   Professional Air Traffic Controllers Organizations 321
   of 1877 313
   of 1892 532
   of 1934 315
   tax strike 360
Styron, William 160
suffrage *see* voting rights
sugar 157, 512

Supreme Court of the United States *see* United States Supreme Court
suspension clause 547
Swift v. Tyson (1842) 295, 508

Taft-Hartley Act 315–316, 533
takings 70, 94, 528
   see also eminent domain; property rights; regulatory takings
Talton v. Mayes 129
Taney, Roger 473, 510, 552
   see also Dred Scott v. Sandford
Tannenbaum, Frank 156
tariffs 351–354, 356, 359–360
   as industrial policy 357
taxes 51, 95, 107, 129, 277, 316, 329, 349–366, 529
technological determinism 447
technology 447
television 375, 477
tender years rule 213
territoriality 549
territories 136–137, 237, 424, 555
   see also Guam; Puerto Rico; unincorporated territories
Third Amendment 474
Thirteenth Amendment 311, 319–320, 471–472
Thorpe v. Rutland and Burlington R.R. Co. 94
Title VII of Civil Rights Act of 1964 183, 201–203, 319–321
   see also Civil Rights Act of 1964
tobacco 157, 275, 359, 465
Tocqueville, Alexis de 155, 216–217, 248–249
Tomlins, Christopher 11, 26, 36, 61, 97–98, 113, 153, 279–280, 310, 342, 375, 508, 533
tort law 68, 72, 90, 92–93, 302–303, 474
trade related aspects of intellectual property rights 454
trade secret 447–449
trademark 441–447, 450–451, 454
   see also intellectual property
Trademark Act of 1870 450
Trade-Mark Cases 450
trans-Atlantic slave trade, *see* Atlantic slave trade
transnational 11, 16, 18, 106, 198, 221, 321, 423, 431–432, 475, 494, 543–558

Treanor, William Michael 528–529, 538
treaties 8, 12, 128, 130–132, 138–142, 144–146, 454, 470, 547, 550
treatises 96, 128, 138–140, 213, 254–255, 352, 445, 449, 451, 467–468, 485–502, 511, 527
treaty rights 130, 137–138, 141–142, 145–146
tribal recognition 147
Truman, Harry S. 178
trusts 192, 198, 296, 298, 369
Turner, Nat 77, 160
Tushnet, Mark 181, 253, 509, 546
twentieth century 105–124, 145–146, 159, 171–185, 200–205, 210, 228–250, 255–260, 295–297, 335–342, 387–390, 400–402, 423–424, 426, 441–452, 506–520, 524–540, 543–557
Typhoid Mary 100

Uncle Tom's Cabin 217, 452, 470, 473
Unger, Roberto M. 524
Uniform Code of Military Justice 417
unincorporated territories 548
United Nations 554
U.S. Civil War *see* Civil War
U.S. v. Carolene Products 114
U.S. v. Cruikshank 473
U.S. v. Kagama 129
U.S. v. Santa Fe 129, 146
U.S. v. Winans 142
United States Supreme Court 96–98, 105, 115, 129–131, 138, 142, 144, 173–174, 179, 181–182, 185, 195, 211, 214, 218, 229, 236–237, 240, 255, 313, 341, 372, 388–402, 415, 442, 492–503, 506–520, 528–530
  Burger Court 401–402
  Rehnquist Court 390, 402
  religion, and the 390, 400–402
  Roberts Court 390
  Warren Court 401
Universal Declaration of Human Rights 554
University of Maryland 158–159, 493
University of North Carolina at Chapel Hill 159
urban centers and urbanization 88, 95, 98–99, 176, 182, 192, 257, 280, 293, 330–334, 359, 369–370, 424–425, 507, 518, 527

Urofsky, Melvin 97
utilitarianism 75, 443–444, 453, 463, 496, 498, 511

vaccination 100
VanderVelde, Lea 165, 217, 319
Vaughan, Alden T. 156
Verplanck, Gulian 497, 501–502
Veterans Administration 378
victim's rights 424, 430
Victorian compromise 424
Vietnam War 407, 410–413, 545
violence against women 215
Virginia 11, 13–14, 16, 18–19, 27, 32–34, 37, 55, 57, 62, 77, 136, 152, 154, 160, 163, 177, 180, 192–193, 254, 309, 377, 394–395, 423, 465–466, 491
voting rights 136, 172–174, 181, 184, 196, 230
Voting Rights Act 181

wage labor 270, 280–281
Wagner Act 315, 318–320, 530, 532–533
  see also National Labor Relations Act; National Labor Relations Board
Waldstreicher, David 161
Walker, Timothy 67
War for U.S. Independence (1775–1783)
  see American Revolution
war on drugs 185
War on Poverty 220, 331, 338–339, 342
warning out 330–332, 342
warranty 78
Warren, Charles 30, 96–97, 247
Washington, George 51, 62, 394, 399, 408, 492
water rights 141–145
Watson, Alan 155, 494
Webster, Daniel 75–76, 247, 249, 255–256, 469, 498, 534
Weld, Theodore Dwight 152
welfare 112–113, 200, 204, 213, 217, 220, 331–332, 334–335, 337–341, 369, 372, 376–377
welfare state
  citizenship 316
  gender 113, 203–204, 316–318
  race 318
Welke, Barbara Y. 93, 165, 175, 193–195, 205, 302, 369
Wesley, Charles H. 159
West Coast Hotel Co. v. Parrish 199

western expansion 49, 61, 63
Westphalia, Treaty of 547, 550
Wharton, Francis 89
Wheaton v. Peters 449, 467
Whigs 71–72, 75–76, 80, 351, 394, 535
Whiskey Rebellion (1794) 51, 355, 468
White, G. Edward 2, 108, 112, 302, 371, 493, 495–496, 511, 515, 547
white supremacy 172, 177–178, 180
widows 191–192, 206, 218–219, 318
Wiecek, William M. 152, 509, 512
Wilkinson, Charles 129
Williams, Eric 157
Williams, Roger 19, 390, 392
Williams v. Lee 129
Willrich, Michael 98, 100, 336, 432, 517
wills 57–58, 192, 209, 334
Wilson, James 469, 492, 495
Wilson, Woodrow 196, 546, 550
Winters v. U.S. 144
Winthrop, William W. 409
Wirt, William 75, 469
Wisconsin 91, 291
witchcraft 16–17, 19, 26, 35
women 10, 17–19, 28, 33–34, 56–58, 77, 93, 97, 164–165, 176, 178, 190–205, 217, 232, 258, 302, 309, 311–312, 314, 316, 319–321, 332, 336–338, 424–425, 427, 453, 469
  see also family law
women's rights 56–58, 80, 97, 105, 110, 112–113, 117–118, 127, 190–208, 316, 474–475
  see also Equal Rights Amendment; gender; gender roles; married women's property acts; National Organization for Women; sexual assault; sex discrimination; sexual harassment
  home-care and homework 321–322
  property rights 56–58
  unions, and 318
  unpaid labor in the home, and 316
  women attorneys 196–198
Wong Wing v. U.S. 236
Wood, Betty 156
Wood, Gordon 47–48, 275, 394, 488, 545
Wood, Peter 163
Woodson, Carter G. 159
Woodward, C. Vann 156, 174
Worcester v. Georgia 129, 131, 134–137, 146, 469
workplace discrimination 117, 320
World War I 107, 146, 182, 313, 352–353, 360, 369, 374, 409, 424, 427, 551
World War II 105, 116, 179, 182, 272, 349–353, 360–361, 374–376, 406, 408, 410–413, 415, 518, 533
Wright, Cleo 178

Yale Law School 517
Yellin, Jean Fagan 164
Yick Wo v. Hopkins 236
Young America movement 501

Zilversmit, Arthur 160
Zorach v. Clauson 401